W9-BAI-066

SECOND EDITION

# *Daytrips*
# IRELAND

Atlantic Ocean

Inishowen

Ballycastle

Derry

Letterkenny

Carrickfergus

Donegal

NORTHERN
IRELAND

BELFAST

Lough Erne

Enniskillen

SLIGO

Armagh

Westport

Knock

Roscommon

Boyne Valley

Clifden

Lough Corrib

GALWAY

IRELAND

DUBLIN

Aran Islands

Kildare

Killaloe

Lough Derg

Wicklow

Ennis

Shannon

LIMERICK

Adare

Kilkenny

Tipperary

Cashel

Dingle

Tralee

Cahir

Wexford

KILLARNEY

WATERFORD

Blarney

CORK

Bantry

Kinsale

100 Miles
100 Km

SECOND EDITION

# *Daytrips*

# IRELAND

## 55 *one day adventures by car, rail or bus including 59 maps*

### PATRICIA TUNISON PRESTON

**HASTINGS HOUSE**
*Book Publishers*
**Norwalk, Connecticut**

# Acknowledgments

*Daytrips Ireland* is dedicated to John J. Preston, my husband and travel partner who has made this book possible by his patience, curiosity, enthusiasm, and good humor.

Special recognition is also extended to Fr. Charlie Coen, Ireland's "musical priest" and my Irish mentor and inspiration.

A sincere "thank you" goes to many friends in Ireland and the US who have provided encouragement and help over the years. In particular:

Irish Tourist Board: Joe Byrne, Marie Fullington, Orla Carey, and Ruth Moran in New York; Paddy Derivan, Bill Morrison, and Joe Lynam in Dublin; and Margaret Cahill in London.

Aer Lingus: Jack Foley and Rosemarie Curran.

CIE Tours: Brian Stack, Dennis Savage, Susan Cloyd, Jim Kelly, and Joe Fallon.

Shannon Airport Marketing: Lorraine Grainger.

Northern Ireland Tourist Board: David Boyce, Annette Cunningham, Maebeth Fenton, and Mo Durkan.

... and our many friends throughout the island of Ireland.

While every effort has been made to insure accuracy, neither the author nor the publisher assume legal responsibility for any consequences arising from the use of this book or the information it contains.

Edited by Earl Steinbicker, creator of the DAYTRIPS series.

ISBN: 0-8038-2003-8
Cover design and book layout by Mark Salore.
*Printed in the United States of America.*
10 9 8 7 6 5 4 3 2 1

# Contents

# Introduction

An island just over 300 miles long and 170 miles wide, Ireland is made-to-measure for daytrips. It is about the same size as Maine or South Carolina, with a 1,790-mile coastline, compact and easily walkable cities, and a well sign-posted network of roads. No part of Ireland is more than 70 miles from the sea, and no city is more than 50 to 100 miles from a neighboring city.

It is literally possible to drive cross-country between east to west in a few hours, or to travel from the southern edge of the country to the northern rim in a day, but why rush? Why pack and unpack and change hotels every day? More and more people are discovering the beauty and flexibility of daytrip travel in Ireland. Just base yourself in a few key areas of your choice and tour via daytrips. There is so much to see and to do, and all within close range of the major cities. Best of all, Ireland is a friendly, English-speaking country, and provides a warm welcome for overseas travelers. Visitors are encouraged to reach out and to be a part of the Irish lifestyle.

This book describes 55 of the most historic and enjoyable destinations (including five routes designed just for shoppers), giving a step-by-step itinerary, whether it is a walking tour or a driving route. It's a simple and enriching way to go around on your own, taking in all the major sites, yet allowing plenty of time for options and individual choices.

*Daytrips Ireland* is not intended to be a comprehensive guide to every segment of the country, listing every single town, suburb, attraction, or activity. It focuses, instead, on eight broad areas of maximum tourist interest—Dublin, the Southeast, Cork, Kerry, the Shannon Area, the West, Sligo and Donegal, and the North. Each of these has one major city or town, that, for reasons of transportation and accommodations, usually makes the most logical base for daytrips in its region. These are Dublin, Waterford, Cork City, Killarney, Limerick, Galway, Sligo or Donegal, and Belfast or Derry. Other towns or resorts, of course, can be substituted as bases; and these possibilities are suggested in the text whenever practical.

Daytrips have many advantages over the usual point-to-point itineraries, especially for short-term visitors. You can target your sightseeing to places that really interest you, instead of "doing" the entire region town by town. If you prefer to sightsee on foot, you can pick cities and towns that offer the best walking itineraries, or if you enjoy driving in the countryside, you can select the itineraries that appeal to you most. You can pick-and-choose and mix-and-match—a couple of days for walking and then a day of driving, or vice versa. Daytrips are also ideal for business travelers with a free day or so available between meetings.

The benefits of staying in one hotel or guesthouse for a while are obvious. No packing and unpacking every day! Three-night or weekly-rates are often more economical, especially in conjunction with airline or tour operator package plans. There is no pressure to keep moving on, to reach a new destination early each night. Best of all, you can really settle in to one hotel or guesthouse—get to know the shops, the pubs, and the local scene. Your suitcase remains in one place while you go out on care-free daytrips.

Flexibility is the keynote of the daytrip style of touring. There is no need to pre-plan every moment of your vacation since daytrips give you the freedom to venture wherever you please. Feel like going to County Wicklow today? Ah, but this is Sunday, when the roads are loaded with local Dubliners out for an afternoon drive. Better try a walk around Temple Bar today. Or, is rain predicted for an entire day in Galway? You certainly don't want to be on rough waters going out to the Aran Islands. A better choice would be the indoor museums and mansions of Roscommon. Similarly, if the skies are socked in around the Ring of Kerry, head to the indoor attractions of Tralee. Daytrips give you the freedom to adjust to local conditions.

About half of the daytrips in this book are designed as walking tours around base cities and other nearby cities and towns. The remaining tours cover the countryside and usually require a car, although some of the trips can be followed using public transportation. In most cases, options are outlined with every daytrip.

All of the suggested do-it-yourself tours in this book are delineated in both the text and on a map. Practical considerations such as time and weather are included, along with price-keyed restaurant recommendations and background information.

The trips have been arranged in a geographic sequence following convenient transportation routes. In some cases, trips require a half-day of walking followed by a half-day of driving or public transport, to take in the far-flung sites. This is noted when relevant.

Destinations were chosen to appeal to a wide variety of interests, and include off-the-beaten path discoveries as well as proven favorites. In addition to the usual cathedrals, castles, monuments, monasteries, museums, gardens, national parks, and heritage centers, there are Viking alleys, medieval lanes, working farms, craft centers, outdoor markets, fishing ports, boat rides, distilleries, breweries, horse-drawn cart trips, offshore islands, dolphin expeditions, narrow gauge railway rides, cave explorations, walled cities, beehive huts, crannogs, boglands, thatched cottages, and even a windmill. Some sites reflect history going back thousands of years, while other places are high-tech and state-of-the-art. A dozen of the daytrips are designed for the sheer pleasure of driving beside awesome scenery, with just a few attractions that you might want to see along the way. After all, who could improve on the Lakes of Killarney, Bantry Bay, Ring of Kerry, Dingle Peninsula, the Lough Derg

Drive, West Clare, Galway Bay and Connemara, Donegal Bay, the Atlantic Highlands, Inishowen Peninsula, Antrim coast, or Lough Erne?

To help you pick the sights and sites that you most want to see, we have listed the times of opening and admission fees wherever possible. Many attractions are free or others, like churches and cathedrals, welcome donations, to help with their upkeep.

Finally, a gentle disclaimer. Places have a way of changing without warning, and errors do creep into print. If your heart is absolutely set on a particular sight, you should check first to make sure that the opening times are still valid. Phone numbers for the local tourist information offices are included for this purpose. In recent years, phone numbers in Ireland have also been changing at a rapid rate, adding one or more digits to area codes or local numbers. Every effort has been made to incorporate the latest numbers in our text, but if you have trouble making a call, check with the local operator or tourist office.

One last thought—it really isn't necessary to see everything at any given destination. Be selective. Choose what appeals to you. Some buildings can be enjoyed from the outside; you don't have to plod through every corridor. Conversely, if one attraction really wins your fancy, you might find yourself spending a half-day or more in one spot. That's OK, too. Your one-way adventures in Ireland should be fun, not an endurance test. If time starts to run out, just amble into the nearest café or pub, sit down, and sample a little Irish hospitality. There will always be another day. In Ireland, the adage is: *"He who made time made plenty of it."*

Happy Daytripping!

## Comments?    Ideas?

We'd love to hear from you. Ideas from our readers have resulted in many improvements in the past, and will continue to do so. And, if your suggestions are used, we'll gladly send you a complimentary copy of any book in the series. Please send your thoughts to Hastings House, Book Publishers, 9 Mott St., Norwalk CT 06850, or fax us at (203) 838-4084, or e-mail to Hhousebks@aol.com. Web Site: www.DaytripsBooks.com

# Section I

# DAYTRIP STRATEGIES

## GETTING AROUND

From the moment of arrival, you'll feel at home in Ireland. And that applies to both the Republic of Ireland and Northern Ireland. Although the six counties in the North are technically different (see Section IX), they are very similar to the other 26 when it comes to tourism and hospitality.

Getting around is easy. It's an English-speaking land and all signage and announcements are in English. In the Republic, the Irish language (Gaelic) is often used as well, particularly on government buildings or in public transportation. Directional signs specify miles as well as kilometers.

As for noticeable differences from your own home environment, there are two things about the island of Ireland that stand out. Firstly, traffic travels on the left, so you have to look left to orient yourself to the oncoming traffic when crossing a street, and, when driving, always keep left. Secondly, street signs in cities and towns are usually not on poles or freestanding posts, but instead are fastened to the sides or corners of buildings or along walls. So, remember the secret to success in getting around is twofold—look left and look up.

For cities and towns, the best way to get around is invariably on foot, although some far-flung sights will require public transport or a self-drive car. For scenic tours in the countryside, the best plan usually is to rent a car. If you'd rather not drive, then Ireland's network of buses and trains will come to the rescue in most cases, although you'll have to pass on some of the remote areas.

This first section of the book discusses transportation, holidays, food and drink, some hints on the suggested tours, and sources of additional information. The book then goes on to describe 55 of the most exciting daytrips in Ireland.

About half of these excursions are walking tours; the rest are designed to be made by car, rail, or bus. In choosing a mode of public transportation, remember that a round-trip is called a return journey or a return trip, and a one-way fare is called a single journey.

## BY RAIL:

**Irish Rail** *(Iarnrod Éireann)*, a division of **CIE—Ireland's Transport Company** *(Coras Iompair Éireann)*, operates a network of swift and clean train services throughout Ireland. Mainline routes run between Dublin and major cities and towns throughout Ireland as far as Sligo in the northwest and to Killarney in the southwest.

**Northern Ireland Railways** links up with Irish Rail for service between Dublin and Belfast and beyond. Rail services are strongest on the east and southeast coasts. Journeys between Dublin and other major cities average two to three hours. Unlike much of Europe, there are no super high-speed trains in service although there are express trains between Dublin and Cork, Dublin and Belfast, and other high-density business corridors. Trains offer first class and coach seating, with dining cars on board most runs. Irish Rail is a member of the **Eurail** system, so travelers who buy a Eurail pass for travel in other European countries can use the pass in the Republic of Ireland.

Most rail services do not require advance reservations, except for first class cars or special trains. You can buy a ticket at the station on the day of travel, or a few days ahead, to be sure of a seat.

## BY BUS:

**Irish Bus** *(Bus Éireann)*, also a division of **CIE—Ireland's Transport Company** *(Coras Iompair Éireann)*, operates an extensive network of express and local bus services throughout the Republic of Ireland. The six counties of Northern Ireland are covered by **Ulsterbus**, and some services are operated jointly by both companies. There are very few towns and hamlets in Ireland or Northern Ireland that are not covered by bus. Both Irish Bus and Ulsterbus also operate sightseeing tours in the summer months. Advance reservations are not required for most bus journeys, although it is wise to make specific arrangements a day or two ahead during the summer months. Buy tickets at local stations or depots or on the bus on the day of travel.

## RAIL/BUS PASSES & TIMETABLES:

If you intend to use public transport often, there are several good-value passes that you should consider. All are available in advance of a visit from a travel agent or from the North American office of **CIE Tours International**, 100 Hanover Ave., Cedar Knolls, NJ 07927-0501, ☎ 1-800-CIE-TOUR (1-800-243- 8687), Internet: www.cietours.com. If you wish to wait until you get to Ireland, you can also purchase these passes at the Irish Rail or Bus Eireann offices in Dublin or Limerick, but not at smaller depots throughout the country. Here are the options:

**Irish Explorer Rail & Bus Pass**, providing unlimited travel on Irish Rail and Irish Bus services for $158. Valid for 8 days out of 15 consecutive days, it also covers local rail services in Dublin and city bus services in Cork, Limerick, Galway, and Waterford.

**Irish Explorer Rail Pass**, valid for unlimited train travel throughout the Republic of Ireland and on Dublin rapid transit and suburban rail services, priced at $106 for 5 days out of 15 consecutive days.

**Irish Rover Pass**, valid for unlimited rides on Irish Rail and Northern Ireland Rail as well as suburban and rapid transit services around Dublin and suburban services in the North, is priced at $132, and is valid for five days of travel out of 15 consecutive days. .

**Emerald Card**, a rail/bus combination pass that gives the option to use both rail and bus services interchangeably throughout Ireland and Northern Ireland. This pass, which is valid for 8 days of travel out of 15 consecutive days and includes bus/train networks within major cities such as Dublin, Belfast, Cork, Galway, Limerick, and Waterford, is priced at $182. A longer pass, good for 15 days out of 30, costs $316.

All prices quoted are for adults; children under 12 pay half-price.

In addition, information on train and bus timetables can be obtained in advance on the Internet by logging on to the following web sites: **Irish Rail**—www.irishrail.ie; **Irish Bus**—www.buseireann.ie; **Dublin Bus**—www.dublinbus.ie; **Northern Ireland Railways**—www.nirailways.co.uk; **Ulsterbus**—www.ulsterbus.co.uk.

## BY CAR:

Meandering along the open roads is one of the best ways to get to know Ireland. Get out into the countryside and meet the people. Distances are short, roads are uncrowded, and road signs are easy to understand. In the rural parts of the country, the only "traffic" you'll meet is of the four-legged variety—sheep or cows crossing the road. Ireland has the lowest traffic density of any EU country and less than one-third of the density of US roads.

It's true that the Irish drive on the left side of the road, but after a few hours of re-programming your inner directionals to "think left," it's not hard to adjust. Try not to drive after getting off a transatlantic flight. Take time to recover from jet lag, get accustomed to seeing traffic on the left, and then get behind a wheel.

Other than the M50, which curves around Dublin City, Ireland has very few large divided highways, called motorways or dual carriageways; although Northern Ireland has two extensive motorways, M1 and M2. In general, roads are superior in Northern Ireland, although the Republic's roads have improved greatly in the past five years, thanks to EU funding.

In the Republic, most signs give place names in English and Irish (Gaelic). In the *Gaeltacht* (Irish-speaking) districts of Cork, Kerry, Galway, Mayo, and Donegal, signs may only appear in Irish, or with Irish in the predominant position. Major routes are designated with an "M" (for Motorway, such as the M50), an "N" (for national road) and regional routes with an "R" (regional or local) in the Republic; and by an "A" (for main road) and "B" (for secondary road) in Northern Ireland.

Speed limits for the Republic of Ireland and Northern Ireland are the same—30 mph in cities and towns, 60 mph on the open road, and 70 mph on divided highways and motorways. Distances are posted in miles and kilometers. Seat belts are required for the driver and all passengers. Pedestrians have right of way, especially at marked crossings. Ireland has strict rules against mixing driving with alcohol; do not drink and drive.

Compared to other aspects of an Irish vacation, the cost of renting a car is high, averaging $250 or more per week for a standard shift and $500 or more for an automatic car, depending on size of vehicle and season. Car rental rates quoted by most companies do not include CDW (collision damage waiver) or VAT (Value Added Tax), a form of local sales tax that amounts to 12.5% of the rental cost. The cost of petrol (gasoline) is also high. An imperial gallon of gas costs approximately $4. The only consolations are that distances are short and cars are relatively small so a tank of gas goes a long way. For comfort and stress-free driving, aim to cover no more than 100 to 150 miles a day. If two or more people are sharing costs, a car can be good value, but if one person is using a car alone, it is expensive. Gas stations honor major US credit cards such as American Express, Mastercard (known as Access or Eurocard) and Visa.

Cars can be rented at airports and in major cities from a large number of international firms such as **Alamo**, **Avis**, **Budget**, **Europcar**, **EuroDollar**, **Hertz**, and **Thrifty**. In addition, several local Irish-based agencies provide full-service operations at very competitive costs. A reliable Irish-based firm with a US reservation office is **Dan Dooley Rent-a-Car**, ☎ 1-800-331-9301, Internet: www.dan-dooley.ie. As for documentation, all you need is a valid US driver's license to rent a car in Ireland and Northern Ireland. Certain age requirements, usually ranging from 21 or 23 to 70 or 75, also apply but vary from company to company; be sure to check in advance if you are "old enough" or "young enough" to rent.

## A DRIVER'S GLOSSARY:

| | |
|---|---|
| **bonnet** (of a car) | hood |
| **boot** (of a car) | trunk |
| **car park** | parking lot |
| **cul de sac** | dead end |
| **diversion** | detour |
| **dual carriageway** | divided highway |
| **gear lever** | gearshift |
| **give way** | yield |
| **lay-by** | scenic look-out |
| **loose chippings** | rocks/pebbles on the road |
| **lorry** | large truck |
| **multi-story carpark** | enclosed parking garage |
| **no overtaking** | no passing |
| **petrol** | gasoline |
| **road up** | road surface being worked on |
| **roundabout** | traffic circle |

**silencer**            muffler

**Approximate Conversions**
**1 mile** = 1.6 km      **1 US gallon** = 3.78 liters
**1 KM** = 0.6 miles     **4.5 liters** = 1 imperial gallon

## BY AIR:

Ireland has five international airports (Shannon, Dublin, Cork, Knock, and Belfast) and at least six regional airports (Waterford, Kerry, Galway, Aran Islands, Derry, and Carrick Finn). **Aer Lingus**, Ireland's national airline, operates a network of services throughout Ireland and on to Britain and the rest of Europe. Visitors on a tight schedule might consider flying from one part of Ireland to another, but that can be quite costly. Since distances in Ireland are so small, the average visitor rarely uses airplanes as touring vehicles. Flying is a practical alternative if you are visiting only two or three "bases," such as Dublin and Shannon, Kerry, Cork, or Galway, and have limited time, and are not planning to hire a car.

As to transatlantic service, **Aer Lingus** is the leader to Ireland, with over 60 years of experience. The words *Aer Lingus*, from the Irish language, literally mean air fleet. And what a fleet it is—new Airbus A-300 equipment with a distinctive green shamrock logo on the tail of each jet and an interior that reflects Ireland's great literary traditions. The cabin crew provides a friendly and attentive service that can best be described as "Ireland in the air."

Aer Lingus operates daily year-round service between the US and Ireland, offering far more flights than any other carrier from New York, Newark, Boston, Chicago, and Los Angeles. Nonstop flights are operated to Shannon and Dublin, with one-stop service to Belfast. Connections are available from over 100 US cities via partner carriers. For complete information, consult a travel agent or call Aer Lingus, ☎ 1-800-IRISH AIR (1-800-474-7424), Internet: www.aerlingus.ie.

American carriers offering services to Ireland include **Continental Airlines,** ☎ 1-800-231-0856 or www.continental.com from Newark to Shannon and Dublin; and **Delta Airlines,** ☎ 1-800-241-4141 or www.delta-air.com from New York and Atlanta to Shannon and Dublin.

## BY BICYCLE:

Although you could travel from place to place around Ireland by bicycle, only the most experienced cyclists would find it desirable day after day. Biking can be fun, however, once you reach a destination. Many of the walking tours in this book can easily be followed by bicycle.

Bikes can be rented all over Ireland in large cities and small towns. Ask at the tourist information offices for a list of companies that rent locally.

# FOOD AND DRINK

Eating well is an important part of the Irish vacation experience. Irish cuisine is often featured in good food publications and broadcasts. In 1996 alone, the NBC-TV morning program, The Today Show, broadcast for a full week from Ireland, spotlighting the hot spots of Irish cuisine, while the American magazine Bon Appetit devoted a full issue to the renaissance of Irish food.

Don't expect Irish stew and corned beef and cabbage whenever you go, although you may still be able to find it occasionally, usually with a creative new twist. Look instead for fresh ingredients from the sea, the farm, or the garden, all cooked to perfection. For lunch, enjoy homemade soups and seafood chowders, platters of smoked salmon, prawns, mussels or oysters, an assortment of farmhouse cheeses, or freshly made salads and sandwiches, not to mention home-baked brown bread, scones, and pastries. For dinner, fresh wild salmon and trout enhances most menus, as does local free-range beef, lamb, and poultry. Regional dishes such as boxty (potato pancakes with fillings), colcannon (mashed potatoes and cabbage), carrigin moss (seaweed pudding), and potato bread are also tasty treats. Snacks are available at many places throughout the day, and don't overlook the local supermarket or deli for innovative picnic ingredients.

To wash it down, remember that fine whiskey and beer are synonymous with the Emerald Isle—from *Old Bushmills, John Power, Tullamore Dew, Paddy,* and *John Jameson* whiskies to *Bailey's Irish Cream* and *Irish Mist. Guinness,* the black frothy stout, is undoubtedly the national drink in Ireland's pubs, but close behind is *Harp lager, Smithwicks ale,* and locally-brewed *Budweiser.* Irish coffee, a blend of coffee, whiskey, cream, and sugar, is a favorite drink, especially on a chilly day. But equally popular are strong cups of *Barry's Tea* or freshly brewed *Bewley's Coffee,* not to overlook natural sparkling and still spring waters, from *Ballygowan* and *Tipperary* to *Glenpatrick, Kerry,* and other local brands. Tap water, pure and plentiful, is also safe to drink.

To help you in making choices during your travels, several restaurants are listed for each destination in this book. Most of these are long-time "don't miss" favorites of experienced travelers, and some are new and trendy. We have also tried to include a good selection of cafés and self-service restaurants that serve fresh and inexpensive items for a quick snack throughout the day. There is also the occasional pub, the centerpiece of Irish social life, and a good place for a quick meal, with or without a drink. The approximate average price range per person is as follows:

| £ | — | Inexpensive. Lunch costs under $5; dinner about $10 or less. |
| ££ | — | Moderate. Lunch costs $5 to $10; dinner about $15 to $30. |

£££    —    Expensive. Lunch costs $15 to $30; dinner costs $35 and up.

X    —    Days closed

To help you make your selections, the Irish Tourist Board publishes an annual *Dining in Ireland* booklet and the Northern Ireland Tourist Board publishes *The Where to Eat* guide and *A Taste of Ulster* booklet. You may also wish to purchase one or more of the commercial publications specializing in Irish dining, such as the *Bridgestone Top 100 Restaurants* by John and Sally McKenna or the *Tipperary Water Travelers & Diners Guide* by Georgina Campbell, both published in Ireland.

Many restaurants in Ireland offer a "tourist menu," usually a three-course meal at a set price, representing very good value. Tourist menus, often confined to certain early dining hours, are usually displayed in the front window of a restaurant. Look for "early bird" specials, too—many Irish restaurants are catching on to this marketing idea, to fill their tables with an early seating of tourists since locals like to eat late. In the cities, you'll also find "pre-" and "post-theatre" menus at reduced rates.

Irish restaurants usually offer two types of main menus. The first is fixed price, for full lunches or dinners, normally a three- or four- or five-course meal, for one set price. Choices are offered for each course—from appetizers (often called "starters"), to soups or salads, main courses or entrées, and desserts or cheese plates. These meals are sold for one inclusive price, whether you eat every course or not.

Alternatively, if your appetite or budget is smaller, you can choose from an à la carte menu, a list of various items in all categories. You can choose just a salad and a main course, or simply a main course.

The à la carte style of pick-and-choosing individual items also prevails at Irish bistros, cafés, pubs, wine bars, coffee shops, and other informal types of restaurants.

Service charge, usually between 10% and 15%, is automatically added to bills at many restaurants, particularly hotel restaurants and those establishments serving fixed price meals. In recent years, however, the à la carte eateries have dropped the service charge concept in favor of tipping at the customer's discretion. In either case, the restaurant's policy is normally printed on the menus or posted. There is no universal rule, so if you are not sure, ask. You want to avoid tipping twice just as much as you want to avoid not tipping at all. There is no service charge added in pubs, but it is customary to leave a small gratuity for table service.

One useful tip: Ireland's new network of heritage centers offers a great variety of inexpensive and freshly prepared food, usually on a self-service basis. It is convenient to combine sightseeing with a snack, especially knowing that standards are reliable, and prices are comparable or better than local cafés.

# PRACTICALITIES

**HOLIDAYS:**

Public holidays are as follows:

**Republic of Ireland**

January 1—New Year's Day
March 17—St. Patrick's Day
Date varies—Good Friday
Date Varies—Easter Monday
1st Mon. in May—May Bank Holiday
1st Mon. in June—June Bank Holiday
1st Mon. in Aug.—August Bank Holiday
4th Mon. in Oct.—October Bank Holiday
December 25—Christmas
December 26—St. Stephen's Day

**Northern Ireland**

January 1—New Year's Day
March 17—St. Patrick's Day
Date varies—Easter Monday
1st Mon. in May—May Day Bank Holiday
Last Mon. in May—Spring Bank Holiday
July 12—Orangeman's Day
Last Mon. in Aug.—Summer Bank Holiday
December 25—Christmas
December 26—Boxing Day

**RAINY-DAY TRIPS:**

Yes, it does rain in Ireland, although not nearly as much as many people think. The average annual rainfall is 30 inches in the east and 50 inches in the western mountainous areas. Chances are you will experience some rain in Ireland, but usually only a passing shower or two. If the forecast is ominous for a whole day, remember that it might be sunny just a few miles away, so check weather reports for areas around your base. It might be raining in Galway City, but sunny in Connemara or off the coast on the Aran Islands, or vice versa. Cities are a good place to be on rainy days, thanks to their profusion of museums, covered markets, and shopping centers. Indoor attractions abound in Dublin, Waterford, Kilkenny, Cork, Tralee, Limerick, Galway, Sligo, Belfast, Derry, and Armagh.

Ireland's many heritage centers, a fairly recent development, are a boon to rainy day travelers. Not only do they present comfortable shelter, food service, and rest rooms in out-of-the-way places, but heritage centers provide a chance to learn a little history and experience the best of an area, via exhibits and audiovisuals, in case it is too inclement to walk the territory outside. Another good alternative for rainy days is Ireland's great array of craft and product centers—such as the Guinness Brewery, Avoca Woollen Mills, Waterford Crystal, the Old Jameson Distillery, Galway

Crystal, Foxford Woollen Mills, Donegal Parian China, Belleek Pottery, Old Bushmills Distillery, and the many craft villages and shops.

**ADMISSION PRICES:**

The prices shown in this book for admissions to attractions are given in Irish pounds *(punts)* for places in the Republic of Ireland *(Sections II through VIII)* and in British pounds sterling for places in Northern Ireland *(Section IX).* Both currencies use a £ symbol. At the time of writing, the Irish pound or punt is worth approximately £1 = $1.30 US. The British (Northern Ireland) pound is worth approximately £1 = $1.60 US.

**MONEY-SAVING TIPS:**

Save money on sightseeing by buying discount admission cards and booklets of coupons. Once purchased, these cards and coupons provide free access to certain sites, or discounts, two-for-one entry admissions, and other reduced rate deals. There are two major programs:

**Heritage Card**—provides unlimited admission to all sites operated by Duchas—The Heritage Service of Ireland, a unit of the government's Department of Arts, Culture, Gaeltacht and the Islands. There are over 70 sites including castles, historic buildings, monasteries, monuments, abbeys, museums, galleries, heritage centers, great houses, forts, prehistoric sites, islands, parks, and wildlife areas.

Among the famous attractions included are: the Rock of Cashel, Clonmacnois, Muckross House & Gardens, Newegrange and the Bru na Boinne Visitor Centre, Ceide Fields, Charles Forty, Blasket Centre, Hill of Tara, Kilkenny Castle, and the National Parks at Connemara, Derryname, Glenveagh, Killarney and Wicklow.

The Heritage Card costs £15 ($21) for adults and £6 ($9) for children, so if you plan on visiting at least four or five sites during the course of your stay, you'll save money, and if you visit two or three sites a day for a week or two (which is normal in the course of sightseeing), you'll easily save two or three times the cost of the card!

Purchase the card at any member site, or in advance by contacting Anne Grady, Education & Visitor Service, 51 St. Stephen's Green, Dublin 2, Ireland, ☎ 01-661-3111, fax 01-661- 6764, e-mail: info@heritage.ie, Internet: www.heritageireland.ie.

**Ireland at a Glimpse**—is a pocket-size book of 2-for-1 admission coupons valid at over 100 attractions throughout the Republic of Ireland and Northern Ireland. The attractions are listed by region, with handy maps as well, to help you plan your sightseeing in an organized way.

The choice of sites, which ranges from castles and caves to heritage parks and folk parks, historic houses, gardens, abbeys, museums, heritage centers and distilleries, to zoos, includes many of Ireland's most popular attractions such as Malahide Castle, Ceol, and the Writers' Museum in Dublin, plus Blarney Castle, Bunratty Castle & Folk Park, "Jeanie Johnston" Visitor Shipyard, Tralee & Dingle Steam Railway, Glin Castle, Irish National

Heritage Park, Powerscourt House & gardens, Irish National Stud, Aillwee Cave, Galway Crystal, Kylemore Abbey, National Famine Museum, James Joyce Museum, Belleek Pottery, Old Bushmills Distillery, and many more!

The Ireland at a Glimpse Book is the most extensive of Ireland's discount programs—if every coupon is suded, the potential savings amount to over $450, For example, admission to Ceol in Dublin is normally £3.95 per person, but with this book, two people get in for £3.95 or less than £2 per person. Multiply that by two or three site visits a day, and the savings really add up.

It costs $14.95 to purchase the book in the US by mail-order from a selection of bookshops or you can buy it at many shops in Ireland for £8.99 or 7.99 stg. in the UK. For full information about how to order, e-mail peter@peterlittlepublications.co.uk or visit the web site: www.peterlittle publications.co.uk.

# SMART SHOPPING

In this edition of *Daytrips Ireland*, we have added five special shopping tours—for the cities and towns of Dublin, Belfast, Cork, Killarney and Galway. But you don't have to take a shopping tour to find great gifts—and great values—all over Ireland. One of the best things about shopping in Ireland for American citizens and other non-EU visitors is that purchases *can be* tax free. We stress *can be* because it is not automatic—it takes a little effort on your part. Here's how it works.

In Ireland, almost all consumer products are subject to Value Added Tax—VAT, for short. VAT is a "hidden tax"—already added into the purchase price of any souvenirs bought on a visit (there are two notable exceptions in Ireland: no VAT on books and no VAT on children's clothing and footwear).

However, as visitors to the EU, Americans are *entitled* to get a refund of VAT paid. And as it happens, Ireland is one of the best places in Europe to shop and get VAT refunds. Unlike all other EU countries, *Ireland requires no minimum purchase*. The VAT rate in Ireland varies, but it is usually around 21% on the net price of the goods which equates to 17.36% of the selling price. So, you can get back around 17% of the selling price, after service fees are subtracted.

Of course, you can avoid VAT altogether by mailing gifts home, making purchases at Shannon and Dublin's Duty Free Airport shops, or by buying goods at Ireland's churches, abbeys, and other non-profit organizations that operate as charitable trusts.

Assuming that you shop in a variety of commercial shops and are carrying your purchases back with you directly to the U.S., there are three major refund systems. All of these systems involve some paperwork. *The prime rule is that you have to get a VAT-refund form at the time of purchase from each store in which you shop.* This is very important!

**Global Refund** (formerly known as European Tax Free Shopping and also as Cashback)—This is by far the largest and most reliable VAT-refund system. Simply make purchases either by cash or credit card, and then request a European Tax Free Shopping form from the store clerk. He/she fills in the necessary store details; you fill in your name and home address, etc. Save all the forms till departure day. At Shannon or Dublin Airport, hand in your forms to the Global Refund desk. After a service fee for each store is deducted (between 2% and 3% of the invoice totals), you will get a refund of cash (in US dollars, Irish pounds, or any other currency of your choice) into your hand before you leave Ireland. Real money on the spot! *Note:* a fee of 60p (about 85¢) is charged on all cash refunds in currencies other than Irish. You also get a printed receipt with complete details of your total purchases, service charges, and VAT refund. If you prefer to have a credit applied to your credit card, that is another option. If you don't have time or forget to submit your VAT forms at the airport before departure, you have 90 days to mail them back.

**TaxBack**—Make purchases by credit card or cash and receive a TaxBack form. Fill out the forms and keep till the end of your trip. When you get to the airport, go to the TaxBack desk and they take your receipts (they do not automatically give you copies for your records). This company promises to send you a refund by check or credit card (Visa or Mastercard only), after deducting a service charge of 2% to 3% on the gross price of total goods purchased. They do not give cash into your hand.

**Dutifree**—This system is almost as easy as mailing your goods back home, but without the cost of postage. With this system, you must pay by credit card. Stores take off the VAT at the time of purchase (less a service fee of 2% to 3%), and give you a form. However, you must remember to hand in (or mail postage-free) your forms at departure from Ireland. If you don't submit your forms, then your credit card will be charged the VAT plus a fee of £2.50 (about $3.50). This is a new system and so far only a few stores participate. More stores will sign on, no doubt, in time. If you don't have a credit card, but still want to make a purchase, you pay the full price including VAT and the company sends you a check (less the 2% to 3% service charge) within six weeks.

*Above all, always remember to get a VAT refund form each time you make a purchase. You can't get any refund (cash, check or credit card rebate) without a form. It's always worth the effort - and, as they say on TV, it's your money.*

(Note: The above information is an excerpt from my pocket-sized brochure "Guide to the ABCs of VAT." For a free copy in the U.S., send a self-addressed business size envelope with a first-class stamp on it, to Patricia Tunison Preston, 471 Route 199, Red Hook, NY 12571 USA. For orders going outside the U.S., send a self-addressed business size envelope along with US $1 for airmail postage.

# SUGGESTED TOURS

The do-it-yourself walking tours in this book are relatively short and easy to follow. They usually begin at a local train or bus depot or a central location such as a tourist information office. The driving tours are likewise compact, usually no more than 100 miles per day, with various options. These tours also depart from a central transport or tourist information point. Suggested routes are shown in heavy broken lines on the maps, while the circled numbers refer to major attractions or points of reference along the way, with corresponding numbers in the text.

Trying to see everything in any given town could easily become an exhausting marathon. You will certainly enjoy yourself more by being selective and passing up anything that does not catch your fancy. Absolution will be granted if you fail to visit every church or ruined monastery.

Practical information, such as the opening times and admission charges of various attractions, is as accurate as possible at the time of writing. Everything is, of course, subject to change. Always check with the local tourist office if an attraction is unexpectedly closed.

### OUTSTANDING ATTRACTIONS:

An * asterisk before any item, be it an entire daytrip, a single attraction, or just one painting in a museum, denotes a special treat that in the author's opinion, should not be missed. Asterisks are used very sparingly in this book; even so, you may disagree with some of the choices, but on balance these *-items should appeal to most travelers most of the time.

# TOURIST INFORMATION

Everywhere you go in the friendly Emerald Isle, someone is there to help you. Throughout the cities and countryside, there are more than 100 branches of the **Irish Tourist Board/Bord Fáilte** (The Board of Welcomes) and 25 branches of the **Northern Ireland Tourist Board**. Just look for a sign with a big "**i**" for information. The "**i**" symbol in the Republic is white, set into a green rectangle; in Northern Ireland, the "*i*" symbol is white, slanted, and set into a red hexagon. And if you don't see an "**i**" sign, ask a local person for help. The Irish will happily go out of their way to set a visitor in the right direction.

Many offices are open year-round and some are seasonal. The locations of these offices are shown on the daytrip maps by the "**i**" symbol, and repeated along with address and phone number under the "Practicalities" section for each trip.

To phone ahead from one part of Ireland to another with a different area code, you must first dial the area code as shown, using the "0." To phone from the US or other country, dial the international code, the country code (353 for Ireland and 44 for Northern Ireland), the area code (without the "0") and then the local number.

Most public phones are equipped to accept a local "callcard," a prepaid telephone calling card sold in various denominations in post offices, shops, other outlets, and from telephone company offices in major cities (Éirecom in the Republic and British Telecom in Northern Ireland). Just insert the card, dial a number, and the cost of the call is subtracted electronically from the card. No need to figure out exact change for coin boxes.

**ADVANCE PLANNING:**

For up-to-the-minute travel news on Ireland, visit my web site—www.irelandexpert.com. It takes up where this book leaves off—presenting the latest information on new hotels and attractions, money-saving tips, itinerary advice, our specially designed tours, and lots more. Click "Ask Pat" and post a question about travel in Ireland—and I'll provide you with an answer online within 24 hours. It's the only Irish web site that provides such a personalized and accurate information service. And it's free. Put the two words "Ireland" and "expert" together—and you are on your way to my web site—www.irelandexpert.com.

The Irish Tourist Board and Northern Ireland Tourist Board have branches all over the world that will help in planning a trip. In North America, these are located as follows:

### Irish Tourist Board
345 Park Ave., 17th floor, **New York**, NY 10154
☎ 800-223-6470 or 212-418-0800, Fax 212-371-9052 or 371-9059
Internet: http:/www.Irelandvacations.com

160 Bloor Street East, Suite 1150, **Toronto**, Ontario M4W 1B9, Canada
☎ 416-929-2777, Fax 416-929-6783

### Northern Irish Tourist Board
551 Fifth Ave., Suite 701, **New York**, NY 10176
☎ 800-326-0036 or 212-922-0101, Fax 212-922-0099
Internet: http://www.ni-tourism.com

2 Bloor Street West, Ste. 1501, **Toronto**, Ontario M4W 3E2, Canada
☎ 800-576-8174 or 416-925-6368, Fax 416-925-6033

If you would like to read up on Ireland regularly before and after a trip, two publications, both produced in Dublin, are well worth a subscription:

*Ireland of the Welcomes* is a full-color bi-monthly magazine published by the Irish Tourist Board. It is a well-written and well-researched magazine with a literary flair that covers Irish lifestyle of the past and present, with special emphasis on traditions, history, poetry, and music, as well as informative profiles of Irish people and beautiful scenic photographs. For subscription information, contact Ireland of the Welcomes, PO Box 54161, Boulder, CO 80322, ☎ 800-876-6336 or 303-678-0439.

*Inside Ireland* is a quarterly 30+-page newsletter and an information service all in one. It presents a chatty selection of what's new and interesting in Ireland, plus trends, restaurant reviews, shopping tidbits, and more. Subscribers, who are considered "members" of the Inside Ireland, also receive discount coupons on accommodations and restaurants in Ireland and special services such as genealogy information, real estate news, and briefings on buying property or retiring in Ireland. Readers' questions are answered in print and individually. It's more than a publication—it's like having a special friend or correspondent on the scene in Ireland. For subscription information, write to Brenda Weir, Editor, Inside Ireland, PO Box 1886, Dublin 16, Ireland.

## TRAVEL TO IRELAND WITH THE AUTHOR:

Each year, the author of this book, Patricia Tunison Preston, and her husband John Preston, organize and accompany at least one group tour to Ireland—tours of scenic areas and cities, music/literary trails, Christian sites, and shopping/craft tours, too.

If you've enjoyed reading this book, do consider joining Pat on one of here future trips to Ireland. For a brochure with full information on upcoming tours, contact Patricia Tunison Preston, 471 Route 199, Red Hook, NY 12571 USA; or send an e-mail request to: ppreston@ulster.net.

# Section II

# DAYTRIPS IN AND AROUND
# DUBLIN

Over the years, a walk around Dublin's Fair City has always been highly recommended. The Vikings braved fierce seas in long wooden ships to reach Dublin's shores and settle in. The Normans came as conquerors but made themselves at home sauntering along the cobbled streets. The English invaded and stayed 800 years. Molly Malone made a career out of walking the streets with her wheelbarrow. James Joyce chronicled almost every nook and cranny of the city. The list goes on, right up until today as Dublin continues to delight residents and visitors alike.

And why not? Rimmed by the Irish Sea and sheltered on three sides by mountains, Dublin is one of Europe's most picturesque capitals. It is bisected from west to east by the River Liffey, which has no less than 14 bridges spanning its wide embrace.

Rich in history and steeped in progress, Dublin's streetscapes are a harmonious blend of narrow laneways and wide avenues, medieval castles and multi-story shopping centers, 18th-century Georgian landmarks and glassy skyscrapers, horse-drawn carriages and double-decker buses, dozens of chic sidewalk cafés and over a thousand friendly pubs.

Dublin is the nation's heart and soul—a political, social, economic, and educational hub. It is home to over one million people, a quarter of the Irish population, about half of whom are under 25. And with residents like U2, Sinead O'Connor, the Chieftains, Maeve Binchy, and Hugh Leonard, Dublin is a musical and literary tour de force.

Above all, Dublin is comfortably immersed in the 21st century, with new hotels, restaurants, theaters, attractions, transportation systems, shopping centers, pedestrianized streets and squares, and indeed whole new neighborhoods like Customs House Quay and Temple Bar. If you haven't been to Dublin in a few years, you'll hardly recognize it. And if you have never been here before, you have a real treat ahead. Get out your best walking shoes and enjoy.

# GETTING AROUND

A compact capital with many pedestrianized streets, Dublin is a very walkable city. In fact, during rush hours and other peak traffic times, sightseeing on foot is often the easiest, fastest, and most practical way to get around.

In finding an address, be advised that there are no street signs on poles, as we know them in many American cities and towns. Street names (usually in English, but sometimes in the Irish language and in English) are not on signposts but are affixed to the corner of buildings, usually on the second story. So look up on the buildings to see the name of a street!

Our five tours of downtown Dublin are all designed as walking tours. If you prefer to use some public transport, then Dublin offers some very visitor-friendly options, such as:

## BUSES:

From early morning till late at night, **Dublin Bus** operates a network of colorful double-decker and single-deck buses throughout the city and suburbs. Hop on board a double-decker bus to get from one end of the city to the other, or to the far-flung sites such as Phoenix Park, the Irish Museum of Modern Art, and suburban settings.

Most buses originate at or near O'Connell Street, Abbey Street, and Eden Quay on the north side, and from Aston Quay, College Street, and Fleet Street on the south side. Bus stops are located every two or three blocks and destinations and schedules are posted on revolving notice boards at each stop.

Each bus displays a number and its destination over the front window; buses destined for the city center are marked with the Gaelic words *An Lar* which means "Centre." Fares are calculated on the distance traveled, and the bus driver collects fares as you enter the front of the bus; exact change is not required. If you have questions or would like a system map, stop into Dublin Bus, 59 Upr. O'Connell Street, ☎ 01-873-4222. If you know you'll be doing a lot of travel by public transport, ask for information about special reduced rate one-day, four-day, and weekly passes.

## RAIL TRANSIT:

Dublin has no subway, but it does have the next best thing—an electrified above-ground rail service, known as the **DART** *(Dublin Area Rapid Transit)*. It runs along the Dublin Bay coast, connecting the downtown area to the northern suburbs as far north as Howth, and to the popular residential southern suburbs such as Ballsbridge, Dun Laoghaire, and Dalkey, as far south as Bray. The DART is also a time-saving way to travel downtown between the north side and south side of the River Liffey.

Board the DART from any of three downtown stations: Connolly Station on the north side, and Tara Street Station or Pearse Station, both on the south side. Full information is available from **Irish Rail**, 35 Lr. Abbey

St., ☎ 01-836-6222, or at any DART station. Reduced rate one-day, four-day, and one week passes are also sold for use on the DART or for use on a combination of bus and DART services.

For trips to the more distant inland northern or southern suburbs, Irish Rail also provides regularly scheduled train services from Dublin's Connolly and Pearse Stations.

## TOURS:

For sightseeing in an independent style, **Dublin Bus** operates the **Dublin City Hop on—Hop off Tour**, a continuous all-day bus service that stops at 13 different historical and cultural attractions with on/off bus privileges, from May to September. This service can be used in conjunction with some of our walking tours, to conserve your energy in going between major attractions.

For an overview of the city, Dublin Bus also offers a three-hour "Grand Tour" of Dublin, departing daily all year at 10:15 a.m. and 2:15 p.m. Similar tours are conducted on a seasonal basis by **Gray Line**, **Guide Friday**, and other local companies. Get a complete list at the Dublin Tourism Centre.

## TAXIS:

Hiring a taxi can be an expensive way to see the city, but if your time is limited, it might be the most practical option. Some taxi drivers will quote a flat one-day rate, if contacted and agreed in advance.

Taxis do not cruise the streets searching for fares, so you must look for a taxi or ask your hotel concierge to telephone for one. The custom in Dublin is for taxis to line up and wait for customers at a taxi rank, indicated by a sign Taxi. Ranks are located outside almost all of the larger hotels, bus and train stations, and on prime thoroughfares, such as Upr. O'Connell Street and the north side of St. Stephen's Green. Taxis are metered; rates are fixed by law and are posted in each taxi. There are extra charges for additional passengers, luggage, and for hiring before 8 a.m. and after 8 p.m., all day Sunday, at the airport, or by phone. Drivers appreciate a tip of at least 10%.

## BY CAR:

Unless you enjoy sitting in traffic jams, finding your way along unmarked one-way streets, and jockeying for space between double-decker buses, don't drive in Dublin. As difficult as driving is, finding a parking space is even more of a challenge. Walking is the safest and fastest way to go in downtown Dublin, with a little help from local public transport.

For trips into the Dublin suburbs and surrounding counties, the opposite is true. It is usually best to rent a car, whether it is self-drive or chauffeur-driven. All major international car rental firms are represented in Dublin, as are many local services. Get the latest information from the Dublin Tourism Office.

# PRACTICALITIES

**WHEN TO GO:**

Dublin is always in season. Because of Ireland's relatively mild climate, sightseeing in January can be just as enjoyable as June. Downtown attractions are open throughout the year, although winter hours are usually shorter than peak season times. Most sightseeing bus tours don't operate in the November–February period, which can be considered an advantage or disadvantage, depending on how you look at it. Theaters and concert halls are in full swing throughout the year, although some cabaret shows, such as Jurys or Doyles, operate only from May through October.

The streets of Dublin can be very crowded with tourists from all over the world in summer, particularly hoards of European students who come to learn English, so spring and fall have distinct advantages if you want to avoid long lines at attractions or check-out counters of shops. Major events, such as *St. Patrick's Week* in March, the *Horse Show* in August, and the *Theatre Festival* in October, also draw large crowds.

**TOURIST INFORMATION:**

The **Dublin Tourism Centre**, Suffolk St., Dublin, ☎ 01-605- 7700, is a great one-stop source of visitor information. It is ideally located near many hotels and within two blocks of Grafton Street or Trinity College, the hub of the city.

Housed in the former St. Andrews Church, this office is an attraction in itself. It includes a row of information desks and a lodging reservations service in the original nave of the church, and an audiovisual presentation on Dublin in the former cloister. On the choir level is *The Belfry*, a coffee shop surrounded by stained-glass windows and overlooking the main floor. In addition, the facilities include a gift shop, book store, bureau de change (money exchange), and booking desks for bus tours, transport and ferry services. It is open every day of the year except for a few days during the Christmas-New Year's period, with extended evening hours in the summer. Just in case you stop by after hours, Dublin Tourism provides an automated 24-hour information and reservations service outside the front door. For online information before you arrive in Dublin, visit the following web site: www.visitdublin.com

**TELEPHONE AREA CODE:**

The telephone area code for all numbers in Dublin is 01.

**MONEY SAVERS:**

In addition to the country-wide money-savers listed in our introductory chapter, Dublin's **Super Saver Card** provides admission to seven of Dublin's leading attractions for one flat rate of £16 for adults, £12.50 for seniors and students; and £8.50 for children. If all sites are visited, this represents a 25% reduction off normal admission charges. The card is valid for entrance to: Dublin Writers Museum, Shaw Birthplace, the Joyce Tower, Dublin's Viking Adventure, Malahide Castle, Newbridge House, and the Fry Model Railway Museum. Purchase the card at the Ticket Desk, Dublin Tourism, Suffolk St., or by credit card call to ☎ 01-605-7754.

"**Dublin's Magical Trail of Culture**," an attractive full-color booklet published by Duchas—the Irish Heritage Service, points visitors to six Duchas-run cultural sites in Dublin that do not charge admission to tour their premises—Chester Beatty Library, Irish Museum of Modern Art, National Gallery of Ireland, National Library of Ireland, National Museum of Ireland, and the National Concert Hall. (Note: although the latter building can be toured for free, it does charge admission for concerts, from £3).

This pocket-sized booklet describes each attraction in detail, with opening hours, and incorporates a fold-out map of Dublin city centre, showing the location of these six sites as well as other Duchas-run attractions in the city. For the sites that do charge admission, you can save money by purchasing a Heritage Card, which is valid for sites in Dublin and all over Ireland (see page 18). The booklet is available free of charge at Irish Tourist Board offices and at the six properties featured.

**FOOD AND DRINK:**

A selection of restaurants, cafés, and pubs in different price categories has been included for each of the Dublin tours. All of these are on or near the suggested routes.

# The Old City

Where and when did Dublin begin? This tour traces the path of Dublin's earliest recorded history, a walking route to places of early Christian, Viking, Norman, and Medieval heritage. One of the most exciting things about this part of Dublin is that it is slowly re-inventing itself as a section of importance to Dubliners and to visitors. In recent years, many old buildings have been rejuvenated and restored, new housing and businesses have been encouraged, and new architecturally-attuned hotels, restaurants, and pubs are being added to the old cobbled streetscape.

## GETTING THERE:

The Old City area is slightly west of today's city center. You can walk to St. Patrick's Cathedral, the starting point of this tour, in about 15–20 minutes from the Dublin Tourism Office or Grafton Street, or you can take a taxi, or a bus (#49, 49A, 50, 50A, 56A, 65, 65B, 77, or 77A from Eden Quay). The best way to get to the cathedral and other points along the way without too much walking is to take a *Dublin City Hop on—Hop off Tour* offered by Dublin Bus. It provides a continuous service between 13 major sights, with on/off boarding and re-boarding privileges for a full day. You can board at the Dublin Tourism Office, the Dublin Bus office on O'Connell Street, Trinity College, or other major mid-city stops. The route includes five major points in the Old City—St. Patrick's Cathedral, Dublin Castle, Dvblinia, Dublin's Viking Adventure, and the Guinness Hop Store. After a day's touring, you can take the bus back to any other center city location.

## GETTING AROUND:

Aside from the *Dublin City Hop On—Hop off Tour* described above, the only other practical way to get around the Old City is to walk or to engage a taxi for a half-day or day.

## PRACTICALITIES:

The Old City is one of the hilliest parts of Dublin, with some very steep inclines and occasional cobbled streets. Wear comfortable and supportive shoes! If you are not used to walking, take the *Dublin City Hop on—Hop off Tour*, described above, to get from place to place. The vehicular traffic at the intersections of wide and busy streets such as High, Francis, Patrick, and Lord Edward, moves at a very swift pace, so be sure to look carefully for oncoming traffic, and cross only at designated pedestrian areas.

Up until a few years ago, this part of Dublin was fairly neglected, and some buildings are still in disrepair or ruin. There were few hotels in the area until about five years ago when Jurys Christchurch Inn opened and suddenly tourists were roaming the streets at regular intervals. Now hotels are springing up like wildflowers on streets such as Francis, Fishamble, and Parliament, formerly commercial zones. Thanks to government grants, a lot of rejuvenation has taken place including the building of residential apartments. However, parts of the Old City are still lonely at night, so walking tours should be confined to daylight hours.

## FOOD AND DRINK:

As might be expected, some of Dublin's oldest restaurants and pubs are in the Old City area. The Guinness Brewery, which has produced Ireland's distinctive dark stout since 1759, is located about three long blocks west of the Old City, and is worth a detour or a separate trip if time is short. Here are some places that should not be missed:

**The Brazen Head** (20 Lr. Bridge St., at Merchant's Quay, two blocks north of The Cornmarket) With a history that goes back to 1198, this spot claims to be Dublin's oldest pub. Walk through the cobbled courtyard and into the lantern-lit rooms to enjoy a drink, snack or light lunch in a memorabilia-filled atmosphere. Buffet at lunch. ☎ 679-5186. £

**Leo Burdock's** (2 Werburgh St., just off Christ Church Place) Established in 1913, this is Dublin's oldest take-out "fish-and-chip shop." ☎ 454-0306. £

**Castle Vaults Bistro** (Palace St., off Dame St.) Housed in the vaults of Dublin Castle, this self-service eatery offers indoor and outdoor seating for snacks, pastries, and light lunches. ☎ 677-0678. X: Sun. £

**Lord Edward** (23 Christ Church Place) Dating back to 1890, this upstairs dining room is Dublin's oldest seafood restaurant. At lunchtime, light snacks and pub grub are available in the downstairs bar. ☎ 454-2420. X: Sun. £££

**Old Dublin** (90/91 Francis St.) Located amid a row of antique shops, this restaurant features the Scandinavian recipes of Viking Dublin. ☎ 454-2028. X: Sun. £££

**The Refectory** (2–4 Lord Edward St., one block east of Christ Church) Open for breakfast and lunch only, this informal self-service eatery is a favorite with students for hefty portions of salads, omelets, and burgers at low prices. ☎ 679-9643. £

## SUGGESTED TOUR:

Although evidence of human life in Ireland can be traced back at least 10,000 years, published accounts of Dublin go back only to AD 130–180, when the geographer Ptolemy pinpointed it on the map as a place of note, but he used the word *Eblana* as the place name. Like most great European cities, Dublin sprang up beside a body of water, the **River Liffey**. The settlement began as a ford at the junction of two important

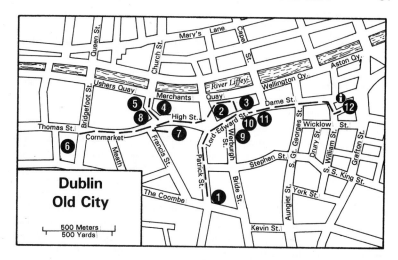

Dublin
Old City

500 Meters
500 Yards

trading routes, the Liffey and its tributary, the Poddle. It became known as
*Baile Atha Cliath*, a name that means *Town of the Hurdle Ford*. Eventually,
it was referred to as *Dubhlinn*, an Irish or Gaelic word meaning *Dark Pool*.
From those days, all that remains visible today is the River Liffey.

In the 5th century Dublin became a focal point when St. Patrick visited and converted the inhabitants to Christianity. Start your tour at:

**\*ST. PATRICK'S CATHEDRAL** (1), Patrick's Close, ☎ 475-4817. *Open
Mon.–Sat. April–Oct. 9–5; Nov.–Feb 9–4; Sun. year-round varied according
to worship services. Adults £2, seniors and students £1.50. Tours.*
This is Dublin's oldest Christian site, built on land that was known as
Cross Poddle, because the River Poddle flowed beside it. It was here, on
the grounds now known as St. Patrick's Park that Patrick baptized converts
at a small spring. Just inside the entrance gate of the Park, a small stone
marks the site of the spring, known today as St. Patrick's Well. A church of
some sort and size has stood on this site since Patrick's days, but it was not
elevated to the status of cathedral until 1213. Today St. Patrick's is the
longest church in Ireland, with a 300-foot interior, and walls filled with
memorials of the past. The massive west tower, dating from 1370, houses
the largest ringing peal of bells in Ireland. Although the cathedral has had
many deans, by far the most celebrated was Jonathan Swift, author of
*Gulliver's Travels,* who presided here from 1713 to 1744. Swift is buried
here, as is his beloved "Stella" (Esther Johnson). His pulpit and chair and
other belongings are on display in the north transept.

The focus of the city shifted to the banks of the River Liffey in the 9th
century when the Vikings sailed into Dublin Bay. The Norse built a sea fort

beside the River Liffey in 841 and the Danes took possession of the town 12 years later. These Viking raiders called the settlement *Dyflin*, to suit their language. Follow Patrick Street northward, the pathway of the original River Poddle, to:

**\*CHRIST CHURCH CATHEDRAL** (2), Christ Church Place, ☎ 677-8099. *Open daily 10–5. Donation: Adults £2, children £1. Tours.*
Here is Dublin's other great cathedral and the centerpiece of the city's Viking heritage. Officially named the Cathedral of the Holy Trinity, it was built as a wooden church in cruciform style in 1038 for Sitric Silkenbeard, the Norse king of Dublin, and has been enlarged and rebuilt over the years. Highlights include magnificent stonework and graceful pointed arches, with delicately chiseled supporting columns; the tomb of Strongbow, the Norman Earl of Pembroke; and a crypt considered Dublin's oldest surviving building which includes the official Stocks of the Liberty of Christchurch, made in 1670, where criminals were fastened for public ridicule. Today the Cathedral is the mother church for the Diocese of Dublin and Glendalough of the Church of Ireland (Protestant).

From Christ Church, walk down **Winetavern Street**, which, as its name suggests, was originally a medieval drinking center. Once lined with taverns and alehouses, it was the hub of trades related to drinking, such as cask-making. In a different vein, Pickett's Tower, a square stone building, once stood at the bottom of the street. A publishing house, it produced the first book printed in Ireland in 1551—an edition of *The Book of Common Prayer.* Beside the Liffey is Wood Quay. Although today you will see a modern office complex, the home of the Dublin Corporation Civic Offices, this was the site of the original Viking city of Dublin. During recent excavations, before the offices were built, archaeological digs revealed the layout, houses, walls, and quays of Dublin as they existed in the 9th to 11th centuries. To see a display of artifacts found during the Wood Quay digs, and a re-creation of Dublin as it existed in Viking times, take a slight detour one block east along Essex Quay to Essex Street and visit:

**DUBLIN'S VIKING ADVENTURE** (3), Lower Exchange Street, off Essex Street, ☎ 679-6040. *Open Tues.–Sat. 10–4:30. Adults £4.95, seniors, students and children 12–17 £3.95, children 3–11 £2.95. Tours. Shop.*
Step inside this indoor theme park—and you are suddenly in Viking Dublin! The hour-long "adventure" starts with a simulated sea voyage via "longboat" back in time to *Dyflin* of a thousand years ago, followed by a walk-through tour of a typical Dublin street in Viking times and visits to prototypes of homes and workplaces, all enhanced by the commentary of live actors who bring history to life by their interactive chat, costumes, and hands-on props. Enjoy the sights, sounds, and aromas of early Dublin. Afterward, there are exhibits from Wood Quay including a walk-around

graded wall that depicts the various layers of Dublin history.

The Viking Adventure is housed in the former Franciscan church of SS. Michael and John, built in 1815. Prior to that, the building was one of Dublin's most notable playhouses, the Smock Alley Theatre (1661–1790).

Before you get to Essex Quay, you will see **Fishamble Street** on the right; this narrow passage was once a Viking fish market. In subsequent years it was a fashionable street and home to a music hall that opened in 1741. Although the music hall is long gone, a plaque on a remaining building indicates that the first performance of Handel's *Messiah* was given here on April 13, 1742.

Return to Christchurch Place and continue walking west to **High Street**, one of Dublin's principal streets in the Middle Ages. On the right hand side are the two churches named St. Audeon, in honor of St. Ouen of Rouen, patron saint of the Normans who came to conquer the Irish after the Vikings. The first church, with a dark stone exterior and Corinthian portico, is relatively modern, dating back to the 19th century. The second smaller church is the original **St. Audeon's Church** (4), built by the Normans c. 1190 and said to be the only surviving medieval parish church in Dublin. It was recently restored and is open to the public. *Adults £1.50, seniors and students £1, children 60p. Hours vary, see posting outside.* The churchyard has been turned into a park to showcase the old city walls, dating back to 1214. A set of steps leads down to **St. Audeon's Arch**, the only gateway of the old city that is still standing. The gate and surrounding walls were restored in the 1880s. Although the church is partly in ruins, significant sections have survived, including the west doorway, which dates from 1190, and the nave from the 13th century. In addition, the 17th-century bell tower houses three bells that were cast in 1423, making them the oldest in Ireland. The grounds also include an early Christian gravestone, dating to the 8th century.

The avenue in front of St. Audeon's is known as **The Cornmarket** because in the 13th century it was an important trade and street market site. Nothing remains of the original cornmarket except the name.

As a slight detour, turn right from The Cornmarket and follow Bridge Street down toward the Liffey. On the left hand side, you will come to **The Brazen Head** (5), dating back to 1198 and reputed to be the city's oldest pub. Step inside and explore the various rooms filled with Dublin City memorabilia.

For a more extended detour, follow The Cornmarket to Thomas Street West, for three long blocks, to Crane Street and suddenly the rich aroma of roasting hops will tell you that you have reached the entrance to:

**\*THE GUINNESS HOPSTORE** (6), James's Gate, Crane Street, ☎ 408-4800. *Open Apr.–Sept., Mon.–Sat. 9:30–5, Sun. 10:30–4:30; Oct.–Mar., Mon.–Sat. 9:30–4, Sun. noon–4. Adults £5, seniors and students £4, children £1. Shop.*

It's difficult to come to Ireland and not encounter Guinness Stout (simply called "Guinness" by the natives), the distinctive dark beer famous for its thick creamy head. Recognized as Ireland's national drink, Guinness has been a focal point of the Irish beverage industry since 1759. This brewery, one of the largest in the world, produces more than 10 million glasses of Guinness a day. Although tours are not allowed in the actual brewing areas, visitors are welcome to tour the Hop Store, a four-story 19th-century building that has been converted into "The World of Guinness Exhibition." It tells the whole story of Guinness through hands-on exhibits, an audiovisual presentation, and a sampling.

Return to The Cornmarket and then cross over to **Francis Street**, known as Dublin's "antiques row" because of its abundance of fine antique shops and indoor markets including the **Iveagh Market**, a Victorian building of great character. The exterior includes arches with carved heads of Moors and other Oriental traders. Another notable building, about mid-way along the street, is the church of **St. Nicholas and Myra**, a handsome neoclassical structure of fairly recent vintage, dating back to the 1830s.

From Francis Street, return to The Cornmarket and make a right onto High Street. Take the cut-off to the right for **Back Lane**, a narrow thoroughfare dating from 1610 and once the location of a Jesuit university and chapel. Now it is home to **Mother Redcaps Market** (7), a former shoe factory and now a weekend indoor market, offering everything from antiques and used books and coins, to silver, handcrafts, leather products, knitwear, music tapes, furniture, and even a fortune teller. Farm-made cheeses, baked goods, marmalades, and jams are also sold by the people who make them. *Open Fri.–Sun. 10–5:30. No admission charge.*

Back Lane is also the address of **Tailors Hall**, c. 1418 and 1706, Dublin's last surviving guild hall, set up in the Middle Ages to represent the interests of craftsmen and traders. Built for the guild of tailors, it was also used by other guilds—hosiers, tanners, saddlers, and barber-surgeons. Since 1983 it has been the headquarters of An Taisce (the National Trust for Ireland) and not open to the public for tours.

Return to High Street, and at the corner of High and Winetavern Streets, you will see a picturesque bridge linking Christchurch Cathedral with its Synod Hall. In recent years, the hall has been converted into:

**DVBLINIA** (8), St. Michael's Hill, Christ Church Place, ☎ 679-4611. *Open April–Sept., daily 10–5; Oct.–March, Mon.–Sat. 11–4, Sun. 10–4:30. Adults £3.95, seniors, students, and children £2.90. Tours. Shop. Café.*

Dublin as a medieval city—from the coming of the Anglo-Normans in 1170 to the Reformation and the closure of the monasteries in the 1530s—is the theme of this attraction. A tour starts with a scale model of the old city and an illuminated Medieval Maze, complete with visual effects, background sounds, and aromas. The next segment depicts everyday life in medieval Dublin, with a diorama, as well as a prototype of a 13th-century quay along the banks of the Liffey. You can roam among craftsmen and guildsmen at work, learn what they were paid, visit a typical merchant's house of the 15th century, and enter a medieval parish church. The final segment takes you into the Great Hall for a 360-degree wrap-around portrait of medieval Dublin via a 12-minute cyclorama-style audiovisual. Afterward, you can also climb the 17th-century St. Michael's Tower for a panoramic view of modern Dublin. Allow one to two hours to complete a visit.

From Christchurch Place, continue one block east to Castle Street and **St. Werburgh's Church** (9), a 17th- to 18th-century structure of Anglo-Norman origin on the site of an earlier Viking foundation. *Open by appointment (☎ 478-3710) or at services each Sunday at 10:30; no admission charge.*

St. Werburgh's was once the parish church of:

**\*DUBLIN CASTLE** (10), Castle Street, off Dame Street, ☎ 677-7129. *Open Mon.–Fri. 10–5, Sat.–Sun. 2–5. Adults £3, seniors, students, and children over 12 £2, under 12 £1. Tours. Shop. Café.*

Built between 1208 and 1220, Dublin Castle is the historic center of Dublin. It sits on ground that was part of an original 9th-century Viking fortress and moat, and it is believed that a defensive rath or earthenwork stood here before that. Representing some of the oldest surviving architecture in the city, this building was the focal point of British power in Ireland for seven centuries until it was taken over by the Irish in 1922. It is now the centerpiece of the Irish government. The circular keep known as the Record Tower, built in 1204, and the Bermingham Tower which was added in the 14th century, are the only remaining features of the original castle. The most important section is the State Apartments, once the residence of English viceroys and now the setting for government ceremonial functions, such as the inauguration of Ireland's presidents, state receptions, and meetings for the heads of the European Union. The castle complex also includes the Chapel Royal, built between 1807 and 1814; an undercroft showcasing recent archaeological excavations; and the Treasury, built in 1712-15 and believed to be the oldest surviving purpose-built office building in Ireland.

The castle is also home to two other notable museums, both offering free admission—the **Chester Beatty Library and Gallery of Oriental Art**, now housed in the Clock Tower Building (formerly located in Ballsbridge). The Beatty collection is a priceless assortment of decorated manuscripts, paintings, and some of the earliest known Biblical papyri. *Open Tues.–Sat. 10–5 and Sun. 2–5.* In addition, the castle's 13th-century Norman Record Tower is the home of the **Irish Police Museum**. The only one of its kind in Ireland, the Police Museum displays uniforms and memorabilia from the Irish forces of law and order throughout the centuries—from the present Garda Siochana, to the earlier Dublin Metropolitan Police (1836-1925), the Irish Constabulary (1836–67), and the Royal Irish Constabulary (1867-1922).

To the east of Dublin Castle, as Dame Street meets Parliament Street, is **City Hall** (11), a square building in Corinthian style erected between 1769 and 1779. Formerly Dublin's Royal Exchange, this building contains many items of historical interest including 102 royal charters and the mace and sword of the city. The building itself is designed as a circle within a square, with fluted columns supporting a dome-shaped roof over the central hall. *Open during normal business hours, Mon.–Fri. 10–1 and 2:15–5. No admission charge.*

From City Hall, continue eastward along Dame Street until you reach Trinity Street; turn right and at the corner of Trinity and Andrew Streets is the former **St. Andrews's Church** (12)—a Gothic-style building dating back to 1866 and reputed to have Viking and medieval roots—recently given new life as the **Dublin Tourism Office**. It's no wonder that the city's main visitor center/tourist information office is housed in such an historic site—just look at what was once across the street.

Continuing past the tourist office to Suffolk Street, cross over to **Church Lane**. Use your imagination to picture what stood here 1,000 years ago—*Thingmote*, a 40-foot high earthen mound built by the Vikings as the location of their parliaments and assemblies. A temporary palace was built on the site in 1172 for meetings between the Norman King Henry II and Irish chieftains. In medieval times, it served as a place for public entertainment and executions until it was leveled in 1681. Excavations along Suffolk Street have unearthed weapons from the Norse period which are now in the National Museum. End your tour here or by returning the tourist office, which has an excellent book shop offering booklets and brochures about Dublin's early years.

# *The South Side – Georgian & Cultural Center

I n recent years, the heart of Dublin has shifted from O'Connell Street, on the north side of the River Liffey, to Grafton Street on the south side of the river. The focal point is the sector stretching just south of the O'Connell Bridge, from Trinity College to St. Stephen's Green, with Grafton Street as the connection. A busy shopping thoroughfare, Grafton Street is a buzz of activity, from buskers and sidewalk artists to a constant stream of shoppers and browsers. Restricted to pedestrians during prime business hours, Grafton Street has had a ripple effect—fanning out to a ring of surrounding streets where still more shops are situated, plus a variety of museums, government buildings, cultural centers, 18th-century architectural landmarks and squares, restaurants, and hotels. This area is "the place" to be in Dublin, for locals and visitors alike.

## GETTING THERE:

On Dublin's south side, it seems that almost all streets lead to Trinity College. All cross-city buses stop at or near Trinity College, and the **Dublin City Hop on—Hop off Tour** stops right outside the college's front gate; or you can take the DART from any station on the line to Tara Street Station.

## GETTING AROUND:

Because of Dublin's many one-way streets and narrow lanes, the best way to do this tour is to walk.

## PRACTICALITIES:

Anytime is a good time for this tour, although it is best to avoid weekday rush hours as downtown streets can get very congested. The best starting time is around 10 a.m. on weekdays, 9 a.m. on Saturdays, with finishing time around 4 p.m. On Sundays, many attractions and some shops do not open until 11 a.m. or later, so head to the churches and cathedrals first and save other sites till afternoon.

## FOOD AND DRINK:

**Bewley's Café** (78/79 Grafton St.) A Dublin tradition, this three-story café is the city's favorite spot for coffee, tea, a snack or a hearty meal. Relax amid a decor of high ceilings, stained glass, and dark woods, or take in a lunchtime play. ☎ 677-6761. £

**Blazing Salads** (South William St., on the top floor of the Powerscourt Townhouse Centre) Open only during shopping hours, this place is a favorite for vegetarians and health-food fans, with a wide array of salads and other meatless dishes, free from wheat, yeast, and dairy products. X: Sun. ☎ 671-9552. £

**Café Bell** (Clarendon St., in the courtyard of St. Teresa's Church) Ensconced in a serene ecclesiastical setting yet just a block from the bustle of Grafton Street, this Old World dining room offers homemade soups, salads, casseroles, and baked goods. ☎ 671-8466 or 671-8127. X: Sun. £

**The Commons** (85–86 St. Stephen's Green) Nestled in the basement of a Georgian landmark building, this elegant restaurant overlooks a "secret garden" and is bedecked with contemporary Irish art. The menu offers French cuisine so good that it has merited a Michelin star. ☎ 478-0551. X: Sun. £££

**Cooke's Café** (14 South William St., behind the Powerscourt Townhouse) A trendy blend of Californian and Mediterranean cuisine is served at this popular shopfront eatery, with indoor and outdoor seating. All breads are baked by Cooke's own bakery. ☎ 679-0536. ££

**Davy Byrnes** (21 Duke St., off Grafton St.) Dating back to 1873, this pub is a favorite with poets, writers, and yuppies who come for the turn-of-the-century atmosphere and the pub grub. James Joyce mentioned it in Ulysses as "a moral pub." ☎ 677-5217. £

**Fitzers** (51 Dawson St.) This Irish-style bistro offers indoor and outdoor seating, with an eclectic menu of steaks, burgers, pastas, chilis, and curries. There are four other branches throughout the city including one at the National Gallery. ☎ 677-1155. £

**The Olde Stand** (37 Exchequer St., around the corner from the Dublin Tourism Office) This old pub is known for its hearty stews and steaks, served amid a sports-bar atmosphere. ☎ 677-7220. £

**Pasta Fresca** (2–4 Chatham St., one block from Grafton St.) If you crave a pizza or pasta, this trattoria is a good choice, but it's very popular, so get there early or be prepared to wait. ☎ 679-2402. £

**Patrick Guilbaud** (21 Upr. Merrion St.) For a big splurge, reserve a table (well in advance) at this modern and "in" spot, housed in a Georgian house that is part of the posh Merrion Hotel. Named for its French-born owner, it has earned two Michelin stars and countless other awards. ☎ 676-4192. X: Sun., Mon. £££

**Tosca** (20 S. Suffolk St.) offers stylish southern European cuisine at competitive prices, especially during the early evening hours when "Beat the clock" prices prevail (Mon.–Fri. 5:30–7). Choices range from braised lamb shank and smoked salmon pizza, to roast breast of chicken with field mushrooms or vegetable lasagne. Top off a meal with just-brewed cappuccino. Owner is Norman Hewson, brother of U2's Bono. ☎ 679-6744. £ and ££

**Trocadero** (3 St. Andrew St., around the corner from the Dublin Tourism office) A theatrical atmosphere, clientele, and decor prevail at this long-established restaurant, considered as "the Sardi's of Dublin." It is known for its steaks and pre-theater and post-theater menus. ☎ 677-5545. ££

## SUGGESTED TOUR:

Start this tour from the bus stop at College Green or from **Tara Street Station** (1). Turn left at the front exit of the station and walk along Tara Street for one block to Pearse Street. Take a right on Pearse and walk one block to College Street and College Green which faces the front entrance to Dublin's #1 visitor attraction:

**\*TRINITY COLLEGE** (2), College Green, ☎ 608-2320 or 608-2308. *The Old Library: Mon.–Sat. 9:30–5:30; Sun. Oct.–May noon–4:30 and June–Sept. 9:30–4:30. Adults £4.50, seniors and students £4, children under 12 free. "The Dublin Experience": May–Sept. 10–5. Adults £3, seniors and students £2.50, children under 12 £1.50. Combined ticket to both: Adults £6, seniors and students £5.50, children under 12 £1.50. Tours. Bookshop. Cafeteria.*

With an impressive 300-foot-wide Palladian facade, Trinity College stands out on the Dublin streetscape. Founded in 1592 by Queen Elizabeth I, Trinity is the oldest university in Ireland, and the sole constituent college of the University of Dublin, although most of the buildings in the current layout were erected over the period 1752-59. Over the centuries, Trinity has turned out some very impressive alumni—from Jonathan Swift and Oscar Wilde to Nobel Prize winner Samuel Beckett, and Bram Stoker (author of *Dracula*) as well as Ireland's first president, Douglas Hyde, and first woman (1990-97) president, Mary Robinson.

On either side of the main gate are statues of two other famous graduates, the orator Edmund Burke (left, as you enter), and the playwright and poet, Oliver Goldsmith. Passing under the archway, you will enter the wide cobbled quadrangle called **Parliament Square**. Directly ahead is the **Campanile**, donated in 1853 by the Archbishop of Armagh, Lord Beresford. Behind the Campanile, at the far end of the square, is a row of red brick buildings, the **Rubrics**, dating from 1700—the oldest surviving buildings of the College. To the right is the **Examination Hall**, designed by Sir William Chambers and built between 1779 and the mid-1780s, and to the left is the **Chapel**, also designed by Chambers, added in 1798. The only chapel in Ireland that is shared by all Christian denominations, it also has a small adjacent cemetery, known as **Challoner's Corner**, reserved for burials of Provosts of the College. Beside the Chapel is the **Dining Hall**, designed in 1743 by Richard Cassels.

To the right is the **Old Library**, designed by Thomas Burgh and built between 1712-32. The centerpiece of this building is the Colonnades Gallery on the ground floor. This exhibition space contains some of the college's greatest treasures including the world-famous **\*Book of Kells**, a

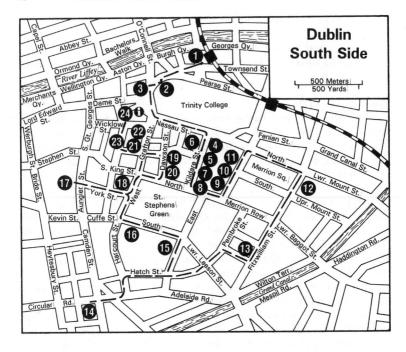

hand-scripted and illuminated edition of the Four Gospels dating back to the 9th century or earlier. Each day a new page is turned for visitor viewing. Other ancient items on permanent exhibit include the *Books of Armagh* and *Durrow*, a copy of the 1916 *Proclamation of the Irish Republic*, and an elaborately carved harp, dating to the 15th/16th century and considered to be Ireland's oldest harp, made of willow with 29 strings. After passing through the exhibit area, visitors are directed upstairs for a walk-through tour of the library's most celebrated room, the 210-foot-long and 40-foot-high **Long Room**. Recognized as the largest single chamber library in Europe, the Long Room contains over 200,000 of the library's oldest books. The total Trinity library collection, spread over eight buildings, consists of more than 3 million volumes published from the 16th to the 20th centuries, a figure that is always growing, thanks to the copyright law of 1801 specifying that a copy of every book printed in Britain or Ireland must be sent here.

Beyond the Rubrics is **New Square**, built in 1838-44, containing a printing house and a museum. A multimedia audiovisual exhibition, "The Dublin Experience," which tells the story of Dublin from its origins to the present day, is on view from May through September in the Davis Theater.

Return to the front gate of Trinity and cross over College Green to see the:

**BANK OF IRELAND** (3), 2 College Green, ☎ 677-6801. *Open Mon.–Wed. and Fri. 10–4, Thurs. 10–5. Tours of House of Lords, Tues. at 10:30, 11:30, and 1:45. "The Story of Banking," Tues.–Fri. 10–4. Adults £1.50, seniors and students £1.*

Built originally to house the Irish Parliament, this unique windowless structure is regarded as one of the finest specimens of Dublin's 18th-century architecture. Begun in 1729 from the design of Sir Edward Lovett Pearce, the surveyor-general of Ireland, the building was enhanced in 1765 by the work of James Gandon. Initially, this grand Georgian-era symbol enjoyed a short-lived glory as the seat of government, but when the Irish Parliament voted itself out of existence in 1800 (the only recorded Parliament in history to do so), power then shifted back to London. It became the headquarters of The Bank of Ireland in 1801. Even though it has served as a working bank ever since, you can still tour the original House of Lords room, with its elaborate coffered ceilings, heirloom tapestries, and a Waterford Crystal chandelier dating back to 1765. The adjacent Bank of Ireland Arts Centre, in the old bank armory, is the setting for "The Story of Banking" museum. Spread over three floors, the exhibition reflects the role played by banking in the economic and social development of Ireland in the past 200 years.

From the Bank, cross back over College Green to the front of Trinity and then make a left turn onto Nassau Street, which rims the south border of the college grounds. Continue on Nassau, a busy shopping strip, to Kildare Street and then make a right. The building on the left-hand side is the:

**IRISH GENEALOGICAL OFFICE & HERALDIC MUSEUM** (4), 2 Kildare St., ☎ 661-8811. *Open Mon.–Fri. 10–2:30. Free.*

Do you have Irish roots? Look no further. This is the home of Ireland's chief herald and the only museum of its kind in the world that focuses exclusively on the uses of heraldry. Exhibits include shields, banners, coins, paintings, porcelain, and stamps depicting coats-of-arms. If you are interested in tracing your Irish family name or ancestral roots, this is the place to start. The building itself, originally used as the Kildare Street Club for the Dublin elite, was erected in 1861 in a Venetian style. The intricate and witty carvings of animals around the window ledges have been well preserved.

Next door is the:

**NATIONAL LIBRARY OF IRELAND** (5), Kildare St., ☎ 661-8811. *Open Jan.–Nov., Mon. 10–9, Tues.–Wed. 2–9, Thurs.–Fri. 9–5, Sat. 10–1. Closed Dec. for stock taking. Free.*

Founded in 1877, this is the largest public library in the country, the repository for a half-million books, prints, and manuscripts. It has an unrivaled collection of maps of Ireland and an extensive accumulation of Irish newspapers, as well as first editions of many Irish authors such as Swift,

Yeats, Shaw, Joyce, and Goldsmith. Like its next-door neighbor, it also has an extensive collection of ancestral information and records, to help in family searches.

As you exit the National Library, you will be facing Molesworth Street. You may wish to make a slight detour here to see the:

**MASONIC HALL** (6), 17 Molesworth St., ☎ 676-1337. *Open May–Sept., Mon.–Fri. for tours at 11:30 a.m. and 2:30 p.m. Admission is £1 per person.*

Recently open to the public and officially known as the Freemasons Hall, this pillar-fronted building dates back to 1865. Highlights include an audiovisual presentation on the history of Irish Freemasonry, plus a walk-through tour of the four main rooms including the Grand Lodge Room, with a unique checker-board carpet representing the good and evil in the world and an ornate 19th-century organ; and the Royal Arch Room, decorated in Egyptian style with sphinxes and seven-branch candelabras.

Returning to Kildare Street, cross over to the:

**NATIONAL MUSEUM OF IRELAND** (7), Kildare St. ☎ 677-7444. *Open Tues.–Sat. 10–5, Sun. 2–5. Free. Shop, Café.*

Home of many great historic treasures, this museum is worth several hours of your time to learn about Ireland's heritage. Opened in 1890, it displays many archaeological treasures, dating from 2000 BC to the 20th century. The collections consist of six distinct areas: "The Treasury," a suite of rooms housing a collection of Celtic antiquities including such one-of-a-kind pieces as the Tara Brooch, Ardagh Chalice, and Cross of Cong; "Ór—Ireland's Gold," the finest collection of prehistoric gold artifacts in Europe; "Prehistoric Ireland," an exhibition spotlighting the everyday material culture of the time; "Viking Ireland," focusing on Irish archaeology from 800-1200 AD; "The Road to Independence," dealing with Irish history from 1916-21; and "Ancient Egypt," a collection of Egyptian archaeology. A sister location of this museum, featuring decorative arts and the economic, social, political, and military history of Ireland, is at Collins Barracks on the North Side of the city (see page 72).

At the foot of Kildare Street, make a left to see the fanciful brick and white-trimmed facade of the **Shelbourne Hotel** (8), 27 St. Stephen's Green. One of Dublin's landmark hotels, the Shelbourne dates back to 1824 and played an important role in Irish history (the Irish constitution was signed in room #112 in 1921), and it has often been host to world leaders, literary giants, and stars of stage and screen. Just past the hotel, on Merrion Row, you'll see a set of wrought-iron gates of a small 17th- and 18th-century cemetery, known as the **Huguenot Graveyard**, last used in 1901 and usually locked.

Continue along Merrion Row and make a left at Upr. Merrion Street. On the left, you will pass a series of government buildings, followed by the entrance to the **Natural History Museum** (9), a division of the National

Museum of Ireland. This branch focuses on the zoological aspect of Ireland's history, with collections on wildlife, ranging from mammals and birds to butterflies and insects. *Open Tues.–Sat. 10–5, Sun. 2–5; admission is free.*

Merrion Street now merges into Merrion Square West, a segment of the rectangular park known as **Merrion Square**. Laid out in 1762, it is considered to be the core of the best preserved section of Georgian Dublin. The leafy park is rimmed by four streets of impressive Georgian townhouses. It has always been a distinguished address for Dubliners, from Daniel O'Connell (#50), William Butler Yeats (#82), and George Russell, otherwise known as AE (#84), to Oscar Wilde and his parents, Sir William and Lady Speranza Wilde (#1). The park contains flowers, shrubs, trees, and benches, as well as the Rutland Fountain of 1791, one of the few Georgian drinking fountains left in the city.

The prime building overlooking this section of Merrion Square is:

**LEINSTER HOUSE** (10), Kildare St. and Merrion Square, ☎ 678-9911. *Open May–Sept., Tues.–Thurs., hours vary. Free.*

Set back from the street and surrounded by a wrought-iron fence and entrance gates, this impressive building is the meeting place of Ireland's government, Dáil Eireann (House of Representatives) and Séanad (Senate). Dating back to 1745 and designed with a 140-foot facade, this building once ranked as the largest Georgian building in Dublin. With an impressive central pediment and Corinthian columns, it is said to have been the model from which James Hoban, the Irish-born architect, later designed the White House in Washington DC. It is usually open for tours when the Dáil is not in session, but phoning in advance is strongly recommended.

Adjacent is the:

**\*NATIONAL GALLERY OF IRELAND** (11), Merrion Square West, ☎ 661-5133. *Open Mon.–Wed. and Fri.–Sat. 10–5:30, Thurs. 10–8:30, Sun. 2–5. Free. Shop. Café.*

Dublin's cultural hub, this expansive building has recently had the greatest overhaul of its history—an extensive £9 million ($15 million) refurbishment program. The gallery, which welcomes over one million visitors a year, is home to an outstanding collection of European works, from Rembrandt and Caravaggio to Goya, with particular emphasis on Dutch, French, German and Italian paintings.

As might be expected, the gallery also houses an extensive collection of works by Irish artists including a Yeats Museum, showing paintings by Jack B. Yeats, foremost Irish painter of the 20th century, and his father John Yeats.

Recent enhancements have included the addition of several new rooms and exhibit spaces, ranging from a striking ground-floor Atrium, to a new print room and icon collection area. In addition, there was a total remodeling of the north wing, as well as new hydraulic elevators, lighting, decor, signage, and benches specially designed by a furniture school in the west of Ireland.

Among the gallery's staunchest supporters over the years was Dublin writer and Nobel Prize-winner, George Bernard Shaw, author of *Pygmalion* (on which the musical *My Fair Lady* was based), who spent many of his early days studying informally here instead of at school. As a result, Shaw bequeathed one-third of his royalties to the gallery and hence it is often referred to as "The My Fair Lady Gallery."

Walk along Merrion Square to see the splendid array of brick-fronted Georgian houses, each with its own colorful door, or a distinctive knocker, fanlight, ornamental balcony, or iron footscraper. Turn right onto Merrion Square East which then leads into Lr. Fitzwilliam Street, another thoroughfare distinguished by its Georgian buildings. For a chance to see what the interior of a Georgian townhouse looks like, step into:

**NUMBER TWENTY-NINE** (12), 29 Lr. Fitzwilliam St., ☎ 702-6165. *Open Tues.–Sat. 10–5, Sun. 2–5. Adults £2.50; seniors, students, and children over 16, £1; free for children under 16.*

This restored four-story townhouse has been turned into a walk-through museum depicting the lifestyle of a Dublin middle-class family during the period 1790-1820—from the basement to the attic including prototypes of a family living room, bedrooms, playroom, nursery, and kitchen. The displays include works of art of the time, carpets, curtains, floor coverings, decorations, paintwork, plasterwork, and bellpulls. This museum is the joint effort of Ireland's National Museum and the Electricity Supply Board (ESB). The board's offices are next door, built recently but retaining a Georgian brick-fronted theme.

Cross from Lr. Fitzwilliam to Upr. Fitzwilliam, via Baggot Street, to see **Fitzwilliam Square** (13), dating back to 1820, and the last and smallest of the great Georgian squares to be developed. It is also the only city center park of its kind to remain private, for use of the residents of the square only. The Georgian buildings that surround this square are today primarily offices for doctors, dentists, and professionals. Walk around Fitzwilliam Square and make a left onto Pembroke Street, also lined with impressive Georgian townhouses, which leads into Lr. Leeson Street.

Make a right and follow this street for one block to the southeast corner of **St. Stephen's Green**.

Alternatively, literary enthusiasts may want to take a left at the corner of Pembroke and Lr. Leeson Streets, and make a four-block detour to check out the home of one of Ireland's most celebrated scribes. Walk in a westerly direction from Leeson via Lr. and Upr. Hatch Streets, crossing over Camden and Grantham Streets, to Synge Street, to visit:

**THE SHAW BIRTHPLACE** (14), 33 Synge St., ☎ 475-0854. *Open May–Oct. Mon.–Sat. 10–5, Sun. 11–5. Adults £2.70; seniors, students, and children aged 12–18 £2.20, children 3–11 £1.40.*

Nestled on a quiet residential street, this simple two-story terraced house dates back to 1838, and was the birthplace nearly 20 years later of George Bernard Shaw (1856-1950), one of Ireland's four Nobel Prize winning writers. It is said that Shaw drew much of his early inspiration from the house and its neighborhood. A plaque at the front of the house identifies Shaw simply as "Author of many plays." Furnished in Victorian style to re-create the atmosphere of Shaw's youth, the rooms on view are the kitchen, maid's room, nursery, drawing room, and a couple of bedrooms including young Bernard's. The adjacent "town garden" is planted with flowers and bushes that are reminiscent of the fragrances, aromas, and colors of a mid-19th-century garden.

If you take the Shaw Birthplace detour, it will now be a 15-minute walk back to the southeast corner of St. Stephen's Green. You can save a few steps, after walking Upr. Hatch Steet, by making a left at Earlsfort Terrace, instead of returning to Lr. Leeson Street.

Once you have arrived at **St. Stephen's Green**, enter via the nearest gate and then take a stroll or sit back and relax on a bench, to enjoy this magnificent 22-acre park. Usually referred to simply as "Stephen's Green" or "The Green" by the locals, this leafy oasis is the oldest of Dublin's park-like squares. Dating back to medieval times, it was first enclosed in 1670 and formally laid out as a public park in 1880. It contains flowers, trees, and shrubs of all types, as well as statuary, gazebos, an ornamental lake, and a scented garden for the blind, with plants identified on braille tags. In the summer months, a Victorian bandshell is the setting for free lunchtime concerts or Shakespearean plays. Return to the outer walkway outside of the railings to complete your walking tour.

For a slight detour, make a left onto Earlsfort Terrace and visit the **National Concert Hall** (15), a turn-of-the-century building that was originally part of the National University of Ireland. Today it is a prime venue for orchestral performances, concerts, and recitals. Reservations for all performances are recommended, ☎ 671-1533.

Follow St. Stephen's Green along its south and west sides, passing a series of interesting buildings, such as **Iveagh House**, 80 St. Stephen's Green, built for a bishop in 1736 but currently used as the offices for Ireland's Department of Foreign Affairs, and is not open to the public.

Several doors down is **Newman House** (16), 85/86 St. Stephen's Green, ☎ 706-7422. Dating back to 1740 and the historic seat of the University of Ireland, this building is named after John Henry Newman, first rector of the university and celebrated cardinal who wrote the influential Discourses on the Scope and Nature of University Education. The structure is a blend of two restored townhouses, distinguished for their elaborate plasterwork and interior design. In addition to suitable memorabilia and furnishings, the basement houses a Michelin-starred restaurant, The Commons. A visit to Newman House includes a guided tour and exhibition on recent restoration work. *Open June–Aug., Tues.–Fri. noon–5, Sat. 2–5, and Sun. 11–2. Adults £2, seniors and students £1.*

From St. Stephen's Green West, you can make a short detour one block west at York Street to Aungier Street, to visit **Whitefriar Street Carmelite Church** (17), 57 Aungier St., ☎ 475-8821. One of the largest churches in the city, it was built in 1825–27 on the site of a pre-Reformation Carmelite priory (c. 1539) and an earlier Carmelite abbey (13th century). Extended over the years, it contains the 15th-century black oak Madonna, known as "Our Lady of Dublin." This church is also a popular place to visit in mid-February because the body of St. Valentine is enshrined here, a gift to the people of Dublin from Pope Gregory XVI in 1836. *Open Mon. and Wed.–Fri. 8–6:30, Tues. 8 a.m.–9:30 p.m., Sat. 8–7, Sun. 8–7:30. Admission is free.*

Returning to St. Stephen's Green West, one of the most eye-catching buildings along this route is the **St. Stephen's Green Shopping Centre** (18) on the northwest corner of the Green. It is a modern multi-story indoor shopping mall with a fanciful domed Victorian facade. At this juncture begins the southern end of Grafton Street, Dublin's fashionable shopping corridor. Stroll up Grafton Street, making a few stops en route.

At Anne Street, take a slight detour to the right for one block to Dawson Street. Straight ahead is **St. Anne's Church** (19), dating back to 1720, but the present structure is mainly from 1868, and then immediately adjacent is the home of Dublin's Lord Mayor, **Mansion House** (20), dating back to 1710 and a study of Queen Anne- style architecture. It is not open to the public, but the fanciful exterior is well worth a look or a photograph.

Return to Grafton Street, continue northward, and on your left is **\*Bewley's Café** (21), 78/79 Grafton St., ☎ 677-6761. This three-story landmark is the city's quintessential coffee (and tea) house. Founded in 1840 by Quaker Joshua Bewley, it quickly became "the place" for Dubliners to meet and to enjoy a piping hot beverage, accompanied by freshly baked scones, pastries, or "sticky buns." There is also a coffee museum on the second floor and a lunchtime theater.

Leave Bewley's by the side exit (Johnson Court) and follow the narrow laneway to **St. Teresa's Church** (22), Clarendon St., ☎ 671-8466 or 671-8127. Dating back to 1793, this was the first post-Penal church to be legally erected in Dublin for Catholics. One of Dublin's busiest inner city churches today, St. Teresa's is known for its beautiful stained-glass windows. There is also a café within the church's enclosed cobbled courtyard, an ideal refreshment stop in an ecclesiastical setting.

While on Clarendon Street, take a few moments to enter the **\*Powerscourt Townhouse Centre** (23), stretching a full block from Clarendon Street to South William Street. Housed in a restored 1774 townhouse, this four-story complex consists of over 60 craft shops, boutiques, and art galleries. The wares include crafts from all over Ireland — knitwear, pottery, leatherwork, prints, jewelry, clothing, antiques, hand-dipped chocolates, and farmhouse cheeses.

Return to Grafton Street, in the pathway of leading department stores such as Brown Thomas and Marks & Spencer, to the end of the street, marked by a bronze statue of **Molly Malone** with her wheelbarrow. The statue was erected in 1988 as part of Dublin's celebration of its 1,000th anniversary as a city.

Take a left onto Suffolk Street and walk one block to **St. Andrew's Church** (24), a building dating back to 1866 and said to have Viking and medieval roots, now serving as the new **Dublin Tourism Centre.**

Undoubtedly an attraction in itself, the centre includes an information and reservations service in the original nave of the church, and an audiovisual presentation on Dublin in the former cloister. On the choir level, a new upper section was created to become "The Belfry," a coffee shop surrounded by stained-glass windows and overlooking the main floor. In addition, the facilities include a gift shop, book store, bureau de change, and booking desks for bus tours, transport and ferry services. With its formidable links to Dublin's past, the Dublin Tourism Centre, is an ideal place to finish this tour.

# Trip 3

# Temple Bar

In today's parlance, Temple Bar is cool, hip, and "where the action is" in the Irish capital. Described variously as Dublin's Greenwich Village, Left Bank, or Latin Quarter, Temple Bar is a magnet for the young and the restless, the avant-garde and the bohemian, and the artistic and the entrepreneurial. It is a melting pot, a hub of activity and creativity. Above all, Temple Bar is fun—and it is different!

More than any other part of Dublin, Temple Bar has been developing so fast that travel guidebooks (and some locals) can hardly keep up with it. Every month or two there is something new. Slightly off the beaten track in more ways than one, Temple Bar is a compact 10-block hodge-podge of narrow streets and alleys running between Westmoreland and Fishamble Streets, just south of the River Liffey. You can easily pass it by if you stick to the main streets between Trinity College and Christ Church Cathedral. But don't pass it by, even if you have to re-trace your steps or ask for directions.

Step into this ever-changing enclave and be ready for a shock— Temple Bar is more international than Irish. The names of restaurants and bars cry out for attention—*Bad Ass Café, Tante Zoe's, Poco Loco, Norseman, Omar Khayam, Fan's Cantonese, Il Pasticcio, La Med, Little Lisbon, Thunder Road Café, Turks Head Chop House, Les Freres Jacques, La Mezza Luna,* and *Wall Street Café.* All of these easily out-number more traditional establishments like *The Auld Dubliner, Eamonn Doran's, Fitzsimons, Gallagher's, Oliver St. John Gogarty, Daniel O'Connell,* and *The Old Mill.* Temple Bar is as multi-cultural as you can get.

Buildings are painted in bright primary colors, with heavy emphasis on garish yellow, purple, and orange facades; teenagers parade by with punkish pink-and-green hair; and loud music blares from New Age shops, coffee houses, pubs, studios, theaters, and more. People of all ages stroll the narrow alleys and streets, or browse in second-hand clothes shops, book stores, galleries, craft and specialty shops. Trick-cyclists whiz by, pavement artists chalk up smiling portraits, buskers play music on every corner, and students just "hang out" at the sidewalk cafés.

To anyone who has not visited Dublin in a few years, Temple Bar is amazingly new, yet in reality it is also quite old. The area dates back to the early 17th century when it was the home of Sir William Temple, Provost of Trinity College, who maintained a house and gardens here. During the next hundred years, Temple Bar evolved into a commercial district, synonymous with merchants, printers, and clockmakers. In time, warehouses and shops sprung up along the streets, imparting a distinctive blend of

Georgian and Victorian architecture that has survived.

By the 20th century, however, Temple Bar lost its luster and was avoided by almost everyone. A cluster of decaying warehouses, the area became an eyesore on the city landscape, earmarked to become a bus depot until 1991 when a group of preservation-minded local citizens stepped in and turned the tide toward urban renewal.

In less than a decade, Temple Bar has become the Cinderella of Dublin's inner city precincts — re-inventing itself as the city's long-needed "cultural quarter." A multi-million pound investment has transformed old warehouses into new apartments and living quarters, shops, galleries, and studios. Streets have been re-paved, re-cobbled, and pedestrianized; new street lighting has added a touch of class to every corner; new street sculpture, signage, and benches have been installed; and new cultural centers have opened their doors.

At last count, Temple Bar has more than a dozen hotels and hostels, including the Clarence Hotel, a luxury boutique hotel owned by the rock group U2, plus 40 restaurants, 20 cafés and sandwich bars, 25 bars and pubs, 15 music venues and dance clubs, and over 150 shops, studios, and galleries. It is home to the Irish Film Centre, Meeting House Square, and the Ark Children's Cultural Centre, and a few unique shopfronts not seen elsewhere in Ireland such as Africa Calls, Condom Power, Harley Davidson, Skate City, and Tambuli Tribal Carvings. And Temple Bar isn't finished yet...

### GETTING THERE:

Wedged into a rectangular 10-block area between Westmoreland and Fishamble Streets on the south bank of the River Liffey, Temple Bar is right in the heart of downtown Dublin. All city center buses stop near Temple Bar at Fleet Street, College Green or Dame Street. From the DART Station at Tara Street, walk two blocks west to Westmoreland Street to enter the Temple Bar district. You can enter Temple Bar from the quays or College Green, Dame Street, Lord Edward Street, or any of the smaller streets in between. There is no official entranceway or exit; just a network of streets and alleys. If you are coming from the north side, the most picturesque way to arrive is by crossing over the Liffey at Ha'penny Bridge, and entering via **Merchant's Arch**, a covered stone walkway dating back to 1821, into Temple Bar Square and Crown Alley in the heart of Temple Bar.

### GETTING AROUND:

Once you have entered Temple Bar's maze of narrow streets, cobbled alleys, and pedestrianized squares, walking is the only way to get around. Since it is only 10 blocks long and two blocks wide, it is the easiest area of Dublin to get to know.

### PRACTICALITIES:

Forget formalities. Wear casual clothes and comfortable shoes for a walk around Temple Bar. Watch where you are walking, since the cobbled pavements and uneven surfaces can cause unexpected stumbles and tumbles. Although most of the traffic is pedestrian, a constant flow of vans and commercial trucks make deliveries, so take normal precautions in crossing streets. Visit in the morning or mid-afternoon, when crowds are small, to get your bearings. The area can get very congested, especially at weekends and at night, so watch your wallets and handbags. If you need help, Temple Bar has its own tourist office—**The Temple Bar Information Center**, 18 Eustace St., ☎ 671-5717.

To avoid confusion, be forewarned that Temple Bar is not only the name of the district, but it is also the name of one of the major east-west cross streets, set between Fleet Street and Essex Street. So, if you ask for Temple Bar, you may be directed not only to the district but also to a specific street.

## FOOD AND DRINK:

It's no secret that Temple Bar has more restaurants per block than any other part of Dublin—indoor or outdoor, fast food or formal, riverview or basement, ethnic or internet, soul food or wholefood, steaks or stews, traditional or exotic, spicy or sweet, seafood or vegetarian, and lots more. Just about every nationality and cuisine is represented and most restaurants are in the moderate price range. Here is a meager sampling, to whet your appetite:

**Bad Ass Café** (9–11 Crown Alley) Housed in a former warehouse, this bright and colorful eatery has been a fixture here long before Temple Bar became an "in" spot (pop singer Sinéad O'Connor was a waitress here in the 1980s). It is known for pizzas, steaks, and burgers, all served to the beat of rock music from a jukebox. ☎ 671-2596. £ to ££

**Eammon Doran** (3A Crown Alley) A mural of Temple Bar blends harmoniously with posters of the US in this huge two-story pub/restaurant, known for its New York-style brunches and burgers, as well as traditional Irish specialties such as steak-and-kidney pie, shepherd's pie, fish-and-chips, and lamb stew. ☎ 679-9114. ££

**Gallagher's Boxty House** (20–21 Temple Bar, between Bedford Row and Aston Place) Crowds line up at this shopfront restaurant to sample the wide array of boxty, a sort of Irish-style crêpe. It's a traditional rolled potato pancake filled to order with meats, seafood, or vegetables, as well as combinations such as bacon-and-cabbage or beef-and horseradish. ☎ 677-27262. £ to ££

**Elephant & Castle** (18 Temple Bar, between Bedford Row and Aston Place) With a decor of modern art and statues of elephants and cartoon characters, this fun restaurant offers an eclectic menu of exotic multi-ingredient salads, omelets, and pastas, as well as the house special Elephant Burger, topped with curried sour cream, bacon, scallions, cheddar, and tomato. ☎ 679-3121. £ to ££

**Les Frères Jacques** (74 Dame St., next to the Olympia Theatre, between

Sycamore St. and Crampton Ct.) Another long-time mainstay of the Irish dining scene, this stylish two-story restaurant is known for its creative French cuisine, served in a relaxed Dublin atmosphere. ☎ 679-4555. X: Sun. £££

**Irish Film Centre Restaurant & Café** (6 Eustace St.) Dine here and feel like a star. Innovative Irish and international dishes are served at the mezzanine-level restaurant amid a black-and-white decor with photos of Hollywood icons. For lighter fare, there is also an informal café on the ground level offering choices such as seafood omelets, stir-fry dishes and salad-bar servings. ☎ 677-8788 or 677-8099. £ to ££

**Nico** (53 Dame St., at the corner of Temple Lane) Long a favorite with Dubliners, this simple shopfront restaurant is known for its authentic Italian fare, served with Irish flair and Puccini music in the background. ☎ 677-3062. X: Sun. ££

**Oliver St. John Gogarty** (57 Fleet St. at the corner of Anglesea St.) If you tire of the trendy, step into this pub/restaurant for a respite of Irish stews, steaks, seafoods, and snacks, usually served to the tune of Irish traditional music. ☎ 671-1822. £ to ££

**SUGGESTED TOUR:**

The best place to start a tour of Temple Bar is two blocks away at the **Dublin Tourism Centre** (1), Suffolk Street, to arm yourself with the latest information. From Suffolk Street, cross over Dame Street to Anglesea Street, one of Temple Bar's many gateways.

**Anglesea Street**, dating back to 1658, is named after Arthur Annesley, known as the Earl of Anglesea, who acquired the land on which the street was built in return for his work in behalf of the British monarchy. Like most of the area, the present layout dates from the 18th century, and was once a very fashionable address, especially after the Dublin Stock Exchange opened here. It is still a focal point of the street:

**DUBLIN STOCK EXCHANGE** (2), 24–28 Anglesea St., ☎ 677-8808. *Open for visitors Mon.–Fri. 9:30 to 10, and 2:15 to 3. Admission free.*

With bells ringing and computers flashing, this is Ireland's version of Wall Street, where stockbrokers monitor the rise and fall of stocks around the globe. Although stockbroking was established in Dublin in 1799, the present exchange dates from 1878. The exchange opens for visitors for a short time each morning and afternoon, allowing spectators to sit in a gallery on the third floor to enjoy an overview of all of the activity. Call in advance to arrange an admission ticket.

To the left of Anglesea Street, is **Cope Street**, home of Ireland's Central Bank, completed in 1978 and one of Ireland's most controversial modern buildings. At this point, you may wish to make a slight detour onto Cope Street and "through the arch" to visit the **Graphic Studio Gallery** (3), 8a Cope St., ☎ 679-6021. A veteran on the Temple Bar scene, it is the oldest

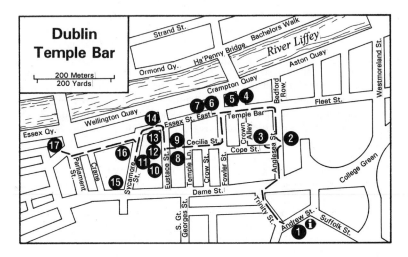

gallery in Dublin dealing exclusively with contemporary and original graphic prints by prominent and emerging Irish artists. *Open Mon.–Sat. 10:30–6.*

Return to Anglesea Street and follow it straight ahead and you will meet **Temple Bar**, the narrow central street that gave its name to the area.

Take a left onto Temple Bar, and you will pass **Merchant's Arch** (4) on the right, a covered passageway designed as part of the Merchant's Hall in 1821. The first street on the left is **Crown Alley**, setting for a strip of flamboyant shops, bars, and restaurants. Next is **Temple Bar Square** (5), a new public plaza and favorite meeting point for shoppers and tourists.

Coming up on the right are two leading galleries: **Temple Bar Gallery & Studios** (6), 5–9 Temple Bar, ☎ 671-0073, a complex of studios and display areas showing off the work of 30 emerging photographers, sculptors, and painters; and the **Original Print Gallery** (7), 4 Temple Bar, ☎ 677-3657, an exhibition of contemporary limited edition prints, etchings, lithographs, and woodcuts by Irish and international artists. *Both are open to the public on weekdays and Saturdays, usually from 11–5 or later.*

Take a left on **Lr. Fownes Street**, named after Sir William Fownes, one of Dublin's wealthiest merchants and Lord Mayor of Dublin (1708-09). His large house on Fownes Street was later used by Dr. Bartholomew Mosse as the first maternity hospital in the British Isles, and then it became the General Post Office (1755-83), followed by an infirmary, school, and finally a commercial building. Nothing of the original building remains today but memories. Turn right onto **Cecilia Street**, once the location of one of Dublin's earliest theaters, the Crow Street Theatre, opened in 1730. No trace remains.

Continuing westward, Cecilia leads into **Curved Street**, a brand new street and home of two new enterprises, **Arthouse** (8), Curved Street, ☎

605-6800, an innovative center for the creative arts, providing subsidized training for artists to use computer technology in their work. The building, an open-plan glass-house design with a central skylit atrium, is an attraction in itself, as is its cyber-themed café which is open to the public. *Open Mon.–Fri. 10–5:30.* Across the street is the **Temple Bar Music Centre** (9), Curved St., ☎ 677-7349, a learning and performance space for all types of Celtic, world, and popular music. Request a copy of the latest program of events open to the public.

Curved Street ends at **Eustace Street**, named after Sir Maurice Eustace, speaker of the House of Commons in 1639 who had a residence on this site. In later years, both the Quakers and the Presbyterians settled here, providing buildings that have been incorporated into several new and exciting developments on this street:

**\*IRISH FILM CENTRE** (10), 6 Eustace St., ☎ 679-5744 or 679-3477. *Open daily 10 a.m.–11:30 p.m. Admission free to center; film tickets cost £2–£4. Shop. Restaurant. Café.*

With a 100-year-old tradition of film production, Ireland is an appropriate setting for this vibrant "museum" of cinematic arts. A gathering place for film-makers, film stars, film scholars, and film fans, this complex is fast becoming the centerpiece attraction of Temple Bar, with its fascinating displays of photos, posters, and memorabilia of the Irish film industry. Under one roof, it houses two movie theaters (cinemas), the Irish Film Archive, a library, a film-themed bookshop, restaurant, café, and eight film-themed organizations. From June through September, there are regular screenings of the film Flashback, a documentary of Irish cinema since 1896.

On an historical note, the Irish Film Centre incorporates the site of the former meeting house of the Society of Friends (Quakers), and parts of the building date from the Quakers' arrival in 1692. As you exit the film centre, take a left for the entrance to:

**MEETING HOUSE SQUARE** (11), Eustace and Sycamore Sts., ☎ 671-5717. *Open as a public square and for scheduled performances. Admission for strolling and most events is free; call for schedule and ticket prices.*

Opened in 1996, this is a new public plaza, available for strolling anytime. It is also an open-air theater area, purpose-built as "the first outdoor performance space in Ireland." It hosts a mix of free and ticketed events, ranging from classical music to gospel and blues, as well as film screenings and family happenings. On Saturday mornings and afternoons, an open market takes place here—well worth a stroll.

The adjacent building is home to:

**THE GALLERY OF PHOTOGRAPHY** (12), Meeting House Square, Sycamore St., ☎ 671-4654. *Open Mon.–Sat. 11–6, Sun. noon–6. Shop.*

Touted as Ireland's only gallery devoted exclusively to photography, this thriving enterprise is a showcase for exhibitions of international and Irish contemporary photographs and posters, especially views of old and new Dublin. It also offers a fine selection of unusual postcards and specialist publications and books on photography.

Returning to Eustace Street, take a look at the stone facade of **The Ark—A Cultural Centre for Children** (13), 11 Eustace St., ☎ 670-7788. It was originally a Presbyterian Church built circa. 1725. Although The Ark is geared for programs for Irish children, it is open to adults on Thursday evenings from 5–7 and to visiting children on Saturdays by appointment.

Make a left onto East Essex Street and on the right is:

**DESIGNyard—THE APPLIED ARTS CENTRE** (14), 12 East Essex St., between Sycamore and Eustace Sts., ☎ 677-8467 or 677-8453. *Open Mon.–Sat. 10:30–5:30. Shop.*

The quality of the work on display within this building is evident from the moment you draw near to this converted Victorian warehouse. Visitors enter the building through a set of wrought-iron gates, designed by sculptor Kathy Prendergast and based on city maps of Dublin, Madrid, New York, and Vienna. The rest of the gallery is devoted to a display of the best in Irish-designed and-manufactured contemporary jewelry, furniture, ceramics, and glass, lighting, and textile products. The Crafts Council of Ireland is also housed here.

At this point, you may wish to take a stroll up Sycamore Street for a slight detour to the **Olympia Theatre** (15), 72 Dame St., ☎ 677-7744, Dublin's oldest surviving theater. It was opened in 1871 as The Star of Erin Music Hall. The decor includes an elaborate Victorian canopy of glass and iron and a flamboyant interior with tiered boxes. The program today includes an eclectic mix of variety shows, concerts, operettas, pantomimes, ballet, comedy, and drama.

Return to East Essex Street and continue in a westward direction. On the left is the:

**PROJECT ARTS CENTRE** (16), 39 E. Essex St., ☎ 671-2321. *Gallery open Mon.–Sat. 11–6; theater, Mon.–Sat. 8–11. Admission is free to the gallery.*

A combination of visual arts gallery and performing arts space, the Project Arts Centre is one of the original pioneers of Temple Bar cultural scene. By day, it is an airy exhibition space for avant garde paintings, free-expression sculpture, and other modern trends in the visual arts. Many established Irish artists staged their first show here. At night, it turns into a theater, providing a stage to various branches of the performing arts.

Continuing on E. Essex Street, on the right hand side is the back entrance to the **The Clarence**, a handsome Regency-style building that has been a fixture in this neighborhood since 1852. It was recently transformed into a luxury boutique hotel by its owners who include two members of the rock group U2.

Cross over to West Essex Street. Here you will see the entrance to **Dublin's Viking Adventure** (17) (described on page 32). End your tour here, with a choice of turning right onto Essex Quay to walk back along the riverside quays—to see Temple Bar from the different perspective of "outside-looking-in," or retrace your steps through Temple Bar for another look at your favorite shops and galleries.

**Trip 4**

# The North Side - Historic & Literary Hub

After several decades of stagnation, Dublin's historic North Side is enjoying a Renaissance—a new buzz of development, activity, and civic pride.

From O'Connell Bridge to Parnell Square and from the Abbey Theatre to The Gate, things are happening. It all started in 1988 as Dublin celebrated its 1,000th anniversary and opened its doors to hoards of visitors. All parts of the city vied to put on the "best face" for the world. Many of the North Side's great buildings—from the General Post Office to the Four Courts and The Custom House, were all restored and spruced up.

The early 1990s also brought a new source of commerce—the International Financial Services Centre at Custom House Quay, attracting dozens of multi-national financial and banking interests. A quintessential example of urban renewal at its best, the Financial Services Centre has injected new life into the once-seedy area around The Custom House, with high-rise office buildings, riverview hotel, restaurants, and shops.

In addition, new cultural attractions, such as the Dublin Writers Museum, the James Joyce Centre, The Point Depot, and the Temple Theatre, have opened to the public, bolstering the North Side's image as a literary and performing arts hub.

So, step out onto O'Connell Street's broad thoroughfare. Ignore the neon signs, cinema posters, and fast food shops. Follow the historic and literary footsteps, amble down a few rejuvenated riverside quays, and enjoy the "new face" of the North Side.

## GETTING THERE:

Irish Rail and DART trains stop at **Connolly Station**, Amiens Street. All buses coming into the city from other parts of Ireland stop just one block away at **Busaras**, the Central Bus Station. Most cross-city buses originate or stop at Eden Quay, a block from Busaras.

## GETTING AROUND:

The best way to get around the North Side is by walking. If you get tired, there are several taxi ranks along O'Connell Street. The offices of

**Dublin Bus** are at 59 Upr. O'Connell Street, if you need advice, but it would not be feasible to take public transport from one site to the next.

## PRACTICALITIES:

Avoid walking on the North Side during business rush hours, when traffic can be very heavy on O'Connell Street, or after dark. Pickpockets and purse-snatchers thrive in the crowded atmosphere of O'Connell Street and other congested shopping streets such as Abbey Street or Henry Street, so take normal precautions with handbags and wallets.

## FOOD AND DRINK:

**Beshoff** (7 Upr. O'Connell St.) For traditional fish-and-chips, try this busy self-service eatery, run by a family that has been in the seafood business in Dublin since 1913. The menu provides the freshest of fish (often as many as 20 varieties) and chips made from potatoes grown on their own farm. ☎ 874-3223. £

**Chapter One** (18/19 Parnell Square, in the basement of the Dublin Writers Museum) A literary theme dominates the decor of this elegant restaurant, and the menu offers a mix of Irish and Scandinavian dishes. The pre-theater menu is great value. ☎ 873- 2266. X: Sun. £££

**Chief O'Neill's Café** (Smithfield Village, off Bow St.) Named after a prime collector of Irish traditional music who is honored in the adjacent Irish traditional music museum (see "Ceol" on the suggested tour), this modern café has a music-themed setting and live music often fills the air. The menu offers traditional and modern Irish cuisine including freshly made soups and salads, and fresh local seafood. ☎ 817-3860. £ and ££

**Harbourmaster** (Custom House Dock, next to the Financial Services Centre) Situated in the restored Old Dock Office overlooking a riverside canal, this informal pub/restaurant is known for its seafood jambalaya and other fish dishes. ☎ 670- 1553. ££

**JAM Restaurant** (57 Middle Abbey St.) Located in the Irish Music Hall of Fame, this is a great spot for music-lovers to get anack, lunch, pre- or post-show dinner, or Sunday brunch. The food is international and eclectic, and the atmosphere and decor are music-filled. ☎ 874-9066. £ and ££

**John M. Keating** (14 Mary St., at the corner of Jervis St., two blocks west of the General Post Office) An ideal lunch stop, this pub offers an Old World atmosphere and a menu of homemade soups, stuffed baked potatoes, seafood platters, and unusual sandwiches such as sausage and pickles or tuna and sweet-corn toasties. ☎ 873-1567. £

**101 Talbot** (101 Talbot St, one block off O'Connell St.) With a bright decor featuring contemporary Irish art, this upstairs bistro provides just the right setting for a relaxing meal or a cappuccino or espresso. Light and healthy international dishes are featured with many vegetarian choices. X: Sun. ☎ 874-5011. ££

**The Winding Stair** (Lr. Ormond Quay at Ha'penny Bridge) For a good daytime meal in a literary milieu, step inside this three-story café/bookshop, a relaxing oasis with classical music playing in the background and wide windows overlooking the River Liffey. The three floors, connected by an 18th-century winding staircase, offer good books and a self-service menu of sandwiches, soups, natural juices, and additive-free meats and fruits. ☎ 873-3292. X: Sun. £

**Wright's Fisherman's Wharf** (Custom House Dock, next to Financial Services Centre) Situated beside a riverside canal, this contemporary wide-windowed bistro offers Dublin's best water views and a varied seafood menu including lobsters from the tank. ☎ 670-1900. ££

## SUGGESTED TOUR:

Start your tour at **Connolly Station** or **Busaras** (1), within a block of each other on the city's North Side. Walk in a westerly direction along Lower Abbey Street, a busy commercial thoroughfare, and on the left at Marlborough Street you will come to one of Dublin's premier entertainment venues, the ***Abbey Theatre** (2). Synonymous with some of Ireland's greatest writers, the Abbey was founded in 1904 as the national theater of Ireland by William Butler Yeats and Lady Augusta Gregory, and over the years has debuted classics such as *The Playboy of the Western World* by John M. Synge, *Juno and the Paycock* by Sean O'Casey, *Dancing at Lughnasa* by Brian Friel, and *Da* by Hugh Leonard. In recent years, the Abbey has been at the forefront of encouraging works by new Irish writers, such as Sebastian Barry, Marina Carr, Michael Harding, and Tom Murphy. The original playhouse, destroyed by fire in 1951, was replaced by a modern 600-seat building in 1966. Although the theater is not open for tours, the foyer area—with its colorful posters and portraits from past and present—is accessible during the day; reservations are a must, ☎ 878-7222.

Continue along Lower Abbey Street for one more block and you come to **O'Connell Street**, Dublin's broad main ceremonial boulevard. Originally known as Drogheda Street, Gardiner's Mall and then Sackville Street, in the mid-19th century it was renamed in honor of Daniel O'Connell, a former lord mayor of Dublin and the "Great Liberator" champion of Catholic emancipation in Ireland. The adjoining bridge over the River Liffey, to the left, was also re-named in tribute to O'Connell, and the monument beside the bridge is a statue of O'Connell. O'Connell Street garnered further national pride and honor during the Irish Rising of 1916 when it was the hub of patriotic activity.

Up until 30 years ago, O'Connell Street was considered the fashionable and historic focal point of Dublin, but today it is dominated by neon signs, fast-food restaurants, multiplex movie theaters, and unglamorous shops. Even the city's tourist office moved from the heart of O'Connell Street to the south side of the city in 1996. But all is not lost. At the start of the new millennium, preservation-conscious Dubliners are making efforts to curtail hodge-podge development and re-image O'Connell Street in all of its historic glory, with particular emphasis on O'Connell Street's role as

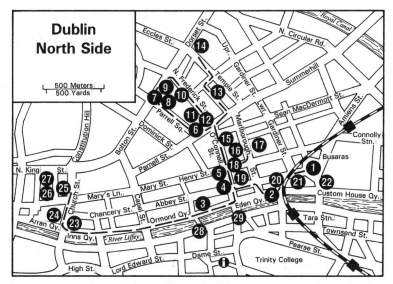

the gateway to the city's literary and theatrical attractions.

Cross to the far side of the street and enter Middle Abbey Street. Walk a block and on the left side of the street you will see one of Dublin's most fun-filled attractions for all ages:

**\*IRISH MUSIC HALL OF FAME** (3), 57 Middle Abbey St., ☎ 878-3345. *Open daily, 10–6. Adults £6, students and seniors £4. Shop. Café.*

For such a small country, Ireland has made a gigantic contribution to the world of music—from the original harp music of the bards, traditional tunes, classical airs, and folk music to pop, rock, punk, hip-hop, showbands, and more. Step inside this museum, put on an audio-headset and follow the trail of Irish music through the centuries, via a multi-media interactive tour, using touch-screens, soundtracks, and large-as-life visuals. It's a veritable alphabet of Irish/international music, from Altan and Boyzone to U-2, plus special sections on Irish women in music, Northern Ireland's finest, Irish composers, and international phenomenons like "Riverdance" and Lord of the Dance."

There lots of fun, too—step onto a simulated stage and pretend to be a rock star yourself, press touch screens and take an Irish music quiz (win an "award," too), or just browse among the marvelous collection of memorabilia donated by Irish musicians of all ages and era - classic records, guitars, original writings of songwriters, handprints, old photos, murals, tee shirts, costumes. It all ends in a theatre for a 15-minute "rockumentary" with interviews of many of the stars. The complete walk-through can be done in a breathless hour or you can take your time to explore your favorites in depth and fill a whole morning or afternoon. It's a great activity for a rainy day.

Return to O'Connell Street and walk in a northerly direction. On the left you will see **Eason & Son Ltd.** (4), 40–42 Lr. O'Connell St., operating as a book shop for over 100 years at this location. Continue for one block and you have arrived at one of Dublin's greatest historic shrines:

**THE GENERAL POST OFFICE (GPO)** (5), O'Connell St., ☎ 872-8888. *Open Mon.–Sat. 8–8, Sun. 10–6. Free. Philatelic Shop.*

Built between 1816 and 1818 according to the designs of noted architect Francis Johnston, this was one of the last great public buildings of the Georgian era, but its prime claim to fame is it was the pivotal point of the Irish struggle for freedom. The Republic of Ireland was proclaimed here in 1916 when the Irish Volunteers commandeered the GPO as their headquarters. Although the patriots put up a brave fight, the building was shelled by a British gunboat anchored in the River Liffey and completely gutted by fire. Now fully restored, the GPO commemorates the Irish Rising in one of its front windows with a huge bronze statue of the dying Cuchulainn, a legendary Irish folk hero. The building's outer façade still bears bullet holes, as well as the words from the Proclamation of the Irish Republic etched in stone. On an architectural note, the GPO is distinguished by its giant front Ionic portico, with six fluted columns topped by three stone figures, representing Mercury, Fidelity and Hibernia. It is a full-service postal office, as well as a revered landmark.

Take the next turn left onto Henry Street, a busy pedestrianized shopping thoroughfare, with several major department stores, such as Arnott's and Marks & Spencer, as well as ILAC Shopping Mall. A right turn off Henry will thrust you into one of Dublin's noisiest and most aromatic attractions—**Moore Street**, an open-air market for fresh fish, fruit, vegetables, flowers, and more. Molly Malone would be at home here, except nowadays the street vendors usually arrive each morning with their wares loaded onto four-wheel carts or baby carriages instead of wheelbarrows. You'll find it hard to resist the feisty salesmanship, sharp wit, and rich Dublin dialects.

Return to O'Connell Street, and continue northward. Straight ahead is the **Parnell Monument** and **Parnell Square**, dating back to 1748 and the oldest of the city's squares after St. Stephen's Green. In the mid-18th century, this was one of the most fashionable places to live in Dublin, with palatial town houses occupied by more peers, bishops, and members of Parliament than any other part of the city. Both the statue and the square are named after Charles Stewart Parnell, a 19th-century Irish Protestant leader and advocate of Irish Home Rule who is fondly referred to as "the uncrowned king of Ireland." Today Parnell Square is a mainly commercial area, with several notable landmarks.

On Parnell Square West is the **Rotunda Hospital** (6), the oldest maternity hospital in Britain and Ireland (built in 1751–55). Built in the Palladian style, it includes a chapel decorated in Baroque style with very ornate and figurative plasterwork.

As you approach Parnell Square North, a slight cut-off to Granby Row will bring you to the **National Wax Museum** (7), at Upr. Dorset St., ☎ 872-6340. It presents an interesting collection of Irish historical and political figures, as well as world leaders and contemporary music stars. It's a great refuge on a rainy day. *Open Mon.–Sat. 10–5:30, Sun. noon–5:30. Adults £3.50, students £2.50, children under 12 £2.* Return to the square and continue to two of the area's outstanding attractions:

**\*HUGH LANE MUNICIPAL GALLERY OF MODERN ART** (8), Parnell Square, ☎ 874-1903. *Open Tues.–Wed. 9:30–6, Thurs. 9:30–8, Fri.–Sat. 9:30–5, Sun. 11–5. Admission Free. Shop. Café.*

The first-ever public gallery of modern art in Ireland, the Hugh Lane collection opened in 1908 with over 300 works by Irish and continental artists. It was launched with the initiative and resources of art collector Sir Hugh Lane, who subsequently died in the sinking of the *Lusitania* in 1915. With the Lane collection as its core, this museum has continued to grow in the past century, with heavy emphasis on Impressionists including works by Manet, Monet, Degas, and Renoir. The Stained-Glass Room contains noteworthy works by Irish artists Harry Clarke, Evie Hone, and James Scanlon. In 1993 it moved to its present location—a building that is an attraction in itself—Charlemont House, one of Dublin's finest houses and often compared to a palace, erected between 1762 and 1765. Musical concerts are often given at the gallery, free of charge, on Sundays at noon.

In August of 1998, the Hugh Lane Gallery received word of the most important gift since its establishment—the studio of Francis Bacon, an internationally renowned artist who was born in Dublin in 1909 and lived in Ireland until 1925. The contents of his studio, reflecting the last 30 years of his life in London, includes drawings, canvases, and brushes as well as books and photographs. The re-assembled studio opens to the public in 2001 at the Hugh Lane Gallery, preceded by two major exhibitions of Bacon's paintings.

**\*DUBLIN WRITERS MUSEUM** (9), 18/19 Parnell Sq. N., ☎ 872-2077. *Open June–Aug., Mon.–Fri. 10–6, Sat. 10–5, Sun. 11–5; Sept.–May, Mon.–Sat. 10–5, Sun. 11–5. Adults £3.10, seniors and students £2.60, and children under 12 £1.45. Bookshop. Café.*

In tribute to Dublin's great literary traditions, this museum pays homage to Ireland's legendary and contemporary scribes. Housed in two restored 18th-century buildings, it offers literary exhibits focusing on Ireland's four Nobel Prize winners—Shaw, Yeats, Beckett, and Heaney, as well as other famous writers—from Swift and Wilde, to O'Casey, Joyce, Behan, and Binchy. Exhibits focus on the history of Irish literature over the past 300 years, with displays of rare editions, manuscript notes, and assorted memorabilia. There is also a gallery of portraits and busts, library, and meeting rooms for writers of today.

The distinctive spires of the **Abbey Presbyterian Church** (10) stand out at the juncture of Parnell Square North and North Frederick Street. Although the current Gothic-style building dates back only to 1864, the roots of the Presbyterian congregation in Dublin go back to at least 1660, and the current church contains many objects preserved from earlier times. Locals refer to it as Findlater's Church, because it was built with a large donation from Alexander Findlater, a local wine merchant. In the summer months, the church presents a free 20-minute audiovisual on the history of the Presbyterianism in Ireland. *Open Mon.–Sat. 11–3:30. Admission free.*

Cross over to the walkway beside Parnell Square to the entrance of the **Garden of Remembrance** (11), a tranquil setting blending flowers, shrubs, statuary, and water. Dedicated to all those who gave their lives in the cause of Irish freedom, it was created in 1966, on the 50th anniversary of the Easter Rising. The mosaics on the floor of the central pool depict broken and discarded weapons as a sign of peace.

Continue to follow the path along Parnell Square southward to the **Gate Theatre** (12), built in 1784-86 as an assembly room attached to the Rotunda Hospital. It was converted into a 370-seat theater in 1930 and run by Hilton Edwards and Michael MacLiammoir, pioneers in contemporary Irish theater who achieved an international reputation by reaching beyond Irish shores and introducing a wide array of European works. The Edwards-MacLiammoir team helped to launch the careers of many fledgling actors including Orson Welles and James Mason. Each summer the theater sponsors a Beckett Festival. Reservations are recommended for all performances, ☎ 874-4045 or 874-6042.

Continuing in a literary vein, take a slight detour by departing Parnell Square at its southeast corner (onto Summerhill Street) and walk two blocks to North Great Georges Street, proceeding to the:

**JAMES JOYCE CENTRE** (13), 35 N. Great Georges St., ☎ 878-8547. *Open Mon.–Sat. 9:30–5, Sun. 12:30–5. Adults £2.75, seniors and students £2, children 70p. Walking tours £3 extra. Shop. Café.*

Joycean fans and scholars from all over the world gather at this relatively new shrine celebrating the life and writings of James Joyce, one of Dublin's most creative 20th-century scribes. Housed in a restored 1784 Georgian town house, the exhibits include a variety of Joycean manuscripts, photos, documents, and other memorabilia, as well as a literary archive, reference library, and study area. At various intervals throughout the day, Joyce's relatives and other devotees give readings and conduct 45-minute tours of the house and one-hour walks through "Joyce Country" in the surrounding neighborhood.

*Ulysses,* Joyce's masterwork, has provided the inspiration for the on-premises coffee shop. The decor features a "Ulysses Experience" commemorative mural and the original Leopold Bloom door, from #7 Eccles Street. The door was a familiar sight for visitors for many years at The Bailey Pub on Duke Street before being transferred here.

Continuing the detour for one more block northeast to Temple Street, take a look at the **Temple Theatre** (14), a concert and entertainment center. It is housed in the former St. George's Church, a landmark Georgian building dating back to 1802. If the front columns look familiar, it is because the church was designed by Francis Johnston, the same architect who gave the General Post Office (GPO) its striking multi-columned façade. Topped by a six-chamber triple-tiered spire (the tallest in Dublin), the building was extensively restored in 1994–96 and transformed into a performing arts venue. Concerts and touring theatrical shows are presented in a series of rooms ranging from a huge main auditorium seating 1,000 to 2,000 persons, to four vaulted crypt-style rooms that can hold another 600 people.

Return to O'Connell Street, and walk southward on the opposite (east) side of the street. One block south of the Parnell Monument is the **Gresham Hotel** (15), a Regency-style building and one of the oldest hotels in the city, founded in 1817 by Thomas Gresham. Although the area around the hotel has had its ups and downs in recent years, the Gresham holds firm as a bastion of style, hospitality, and high standards. Step inside the lobby and view the panorama of Georgian elegance, with marble floors, molded plasterwork, and crystal chandeliers. Afternoon tea at the Gresham is a Dublin tradition not be to missed.

On the outside of the Gresham, in the central mall, is the Father Theobold Matthew statue, a monument erected in honor of a 19th-century priest who founded the Pioneer Total Abstinence Movement in Ireland. The "Pioneers," as they are commonly known, are a group of people who refrain from alcoholic beverages for religious reasons.

Also in a religious vein, turn left onto Cathedral Street for a visit to:

**ST. MARY'S PRO-CATHEDRAL** (16), Cathedral and Marlborough Sts., ☎ 874-5441. *Open Mon.–Fri. 8–6, Sat. 8 a.m.–9 p.m., Sun. 8–8. No admission charge, donations welcome.*

The main Catholic parish church of the city center, this is the equivalent of a cathedral for Dublin's Roman Catholic population, since the two main cathedrals (St. Patrick's and Christ Church) both belong to the Protestant (Church of Ireland) denomination. Dedicated in 1825, it combines two unique architectural styles for Dublin—a Greek Revival façade with a six-columned portico modeled after the temple of Theseus in Athens, and a Renaissance-style interior reflecting the design of the church of St. Phillippe-le-Roule in Paris. Dubliners and visitors alike flock here at 11 o'clock on Sundays to hear the church's noted Palestrina Choir, a group that gave the world the great Irish tenor John McCormack at the turn of the century.

Opposite the Pro-Cathedral on Marlborough Street is **Tyrone House** (17), an impressive 18th-century building erected for the Viscount Tyrone. It was acquired by the Irish government in 1835 and now is the headquarters of the Irish Department of Education. Of particular note is the marble *Pieta* statue outside, given to Ireland by the Italian government in gratitude for relief supplies sent during World War II.

Return to O'Connell Street at the juncture of North Earl Street to see the **Anna Livia Fountain** (18), a multi-spouted monument erected during the city's millennium celebrations in 1988. It was designed to represent the River Liffey ("Anna Livia" is the Irish name for the river popularized by James Joyce in his works). In the time since it has been installed, it has added a refreshing and tranquil tone to the bustle of busy O'Connell Street. A bronze statue of James Joyce himself stands approvingly on the corner at North Earl Street.

Continuing southward, the next building of note is **Clerys** (19), Ireland's largest department store, dating back to 1883. The monument in the central mall is a statue of **Jim Larkin**, champion of the working class and powerful orator, who organized the Irish Transport and General Workers Union of Ireland in 1924.

To see the eventual results of Larkin's efforts, continue one block to Eden Quay and turn left to **Liberty Hall** (20), the modern headquarters of the Irish Transport and General Workers Union. A 1960's addition to the Dublin scene, it's the closest thing to a skyscraper (16 stories) in this city. Straight ahead is one of the city's foremost public buildings:

**THE CUSTOM HOUSE** (21), Custom House Quay, ☎ 878-7660. *Open mid-Mar. to Nov., Mon.–Fri. 10–5, Sat.–Sun. 2–5; Nov. to mid-Mar., Wed.–Fri. 10–5, Sun. 2–5. Admission £1.*

The 200-year-old Custom House, one of Dublin's great landmarks designed by James Gandon and long regarded as a masterpiece of European neo-classicism, is at last open for tours, thanks to a new visitor centre located on the ground floor under the Dome.

Visitors assemble in the Clocktower area, which contains the most important interior features to have survived the destruction of the building by fire in 1921 during the War of Independence. The tour, which starts with a 10-minute introductory audiovisual, also includes a Gandon museum, a display on the history of the Custom House and profiles of the many important characters who have had offices in the building. You can also enjoy great views of Dublin and the River Liffey from the huge Georgian windows. In the exterior, be sure to see the 16-foot statue of *Commerce* atop the dome and surrounded by 14 "Riverine Heads," each representing one of the 13 rivers of Ireland plus the Atlantic Ocean.

In contrast, continue one block to see the green-tinted glass façade of the **International Financial Services Center** (22), a new government-sponsored development and the epitome of urban renewal, bringing new life to an area that stood for many years in dockside decay. It is now the sleek headquarters for an international assortment of banking and financial institutions. As is so often the case, a nest of new enterprises, ranging from a riverview hotel to wharfside restaurants and shops, is springing up on the 27-acre site around the new financial hub.

Retrace your steps slightly westward now, returning to Eden Quay, crossing O'Connell Bridge, and then along three more quays—Batchelor's Walk, Lower and Upper Ormond, to Inns Quay and **The Four Courts** (23), headquarters of the Irish justice system since 1796. Like The Custom House and other notable Dublin buildings of the Georgian era, this distinctive 440-foot long building was designed by James Gandon. To make it stand out on the Dublin skyline, Gandon gave it a massive 64-foot lantern-style dome with Corinthian columns flanked by statues of *Justice, Mercy, Wisdom* and *Moses.* One block farther west is:

**ST. MICHAN'S CHURCH** (24), Church St., ☎ 872-4154. *Open Mid-March through Oct., Mon.–Fri. 10–12:45 and 2–5, Sat. 10–12:45; Nov. to mid-March Mon.–Fri. 12:30–3:30; Sat. 10–12:45. Adults £2, seniors £1, children under 12 50p.*

This 17th-century Church of Ireland edifice has many historic claims to fame. Built on the site of an early Danish chapel (dating back to AD 1095), it gives Dublin's North Side one of its strongest Viking connections. It also has some very fine woodwork, including an organ dated 1724 and originally housed in a theater on Fishamble Street. This is the organ on which Handel is reputed to have played his *Messiah.* The most unique feature of this church, however, is the underground burial vaults. Because of the dry atmosphere, bodies have laid for centuries without showing normal signs of decomposition. The skin of these corpses has remained remarkably soft, even though it is brown and leather-like in appearance. It is said if you "shake hands" with the figure known as *The Crusader,* you will always have good luck.

Turn left at Mary's Lane north of St. Michan's and the next right will bring you to **Bow Street**, a cobbled passage that is one of the city's oldest thoroughfares. Legend has it that the street follows the line of a trade route known as *Slighe Mhidhluachra,* which was in existence before the foundation of the city. The street later belonged to the Bow Street Distillery, which ceased operations in 1972, but is now the home of:

**THE OLD JAMESON DISTILLERY** (25), Bow St., Smithfield Village, ☎ 807-2355. *Open daily 9:30–6. Adults £3.95, seniors £3, children £1.50. Shop. Restaurant. Café.*

Housed in the original Jameson Whiskey Distillery (circa. 1780), this visitor centre tells the story of one of Ireland's prime beverages—whiskey, originally known as *uisce beatha*—the water of life.

A tour starts with an eight-minute audiovisual which provides background on the great tradition of distilling in Ireland, dating back over 1,400 years to the days of the early monks. A 20-minute walk-around guided tour follows, with opportunities to view and smell the aromas of a working mash tun, an old wooden fermentation vessel, original copper pot stills, a re-created maturing warehouse, working bottling line, and more. The tour culminates in the "Tasting Room" with an opportunity to sample the finished product.

After visiting the distillery, if you are in a musical mood, follow the signs to the left through the courtyard to:

**\*CEOL** (26), Smithfield Village, ☎ 817-3820. *Open daily except Christmas Day and Good Friday, Mon.–Sat. 9:30–6 and Sun. 10:30–6. Adults £3.95, seniors and students £3.50, children £3. Shop. Café.*

If you've ever been charmed by the Chieftains or reveled in "Riverdance," then this museum is for you. It's devoted entirely to the development, influence and use of Irish traditional music. Aptly named "Ceol" (the Irish word for "music"), this new interactive museum presents the many aspects of Irish music from the instruments to the songs, dances, and practitioners. The wide range of interactive displays shows how Irish music has been interwoven with all of Irish history(from the earliest times, medieval era, bardic traditions, famine years, rebellion and independence, and post-war years), and cultural experiences (house dances, the advent of radio, 78 rpm records, and local sessions).

Many of the exhibits invite you to touch, listen, and participate in music, song, and dance. There are two song galleries for selecting tunes you want to hear and a dance floor that provides an opportunity to participate in an Irish set dance. The self-guided tour ends in the state-of-the-art theatre with an 18-minute film, shown on a panoramic 180-degree screen that makes you feel a part of the music and the scenery. A dazzling array of Ireland's top traditional musicians is presented in their native house or pub settings, including scenes from the Fleadh Cheoil, the Tulla Ceili Band, and a Knocknaree set dance in Kerry. It's no wonder the film leaves a lasting message emblazoned on the screen: "There's enough in Irish music to keep a person enthralled for a whole lifetime." And there's enough at this museum to keep you enthralled for several hours or more.

For a change of pace, step outside of Ceol and cross over a small courtyard to visit **The Chimney** (27), an observation tower that provides panoramic views of the whole city.

Return to the quays and walk the path beside the Liffey, enjoying riverside sights. Between Lr. Ormond Quay and Batchelor's Walk is the most picturesque of the Liffey's 14 bridges—**\*The Ha'penny Bridge** (28). Built in 1816 as the Wellington Bridge, it acquired its current nick-name because all users originally had to pay a toll of a half-penny to cross over from one side to the other. Don't worry about the toll, however—it was discontinued in 1919. For the record, it is also referred to as "the metal bridge" because of its sturdy cast iron construction, but its official current name is Liffey Bridge. Ask any Dubliner, however, and you'll hear it identified simply by its nick-name.

Follow Batchelor's Walk and Eden Quay back to Custom House Quay and make a left at Beresford Place to complete your tour back at Connolly Station or Busaras. Or, end your tour at **O'Connell Bridge** (29).

**Trip 5**

# West Side Wanderings

As tour buses drive toward Dublin's western fringe, they are usually heading for Phoenix Park, the city's huge enclosed natural oasis. Phoenix Park is to Dublin what Central Park is to New York, Fairmount Park to Philadelphia, Griffith Park to Los Angeles, Hyde Park to London, Bois de Boulogne to Paris, or Villa Borghese to Rome. It is the city's ecological centerpiece, a playground for young and old, native and visitor. No trip to Dublin is complete without a tour of the Phoenix Park, or at least a quick drive around the principal sites.

With a circumference of over seven miles, getting around Phoenix Park can easily take a day or more on foot, and that is why so many people choose to see the park from the comfort of a tour bus or a car.

If you have the time, however, it is worth devoting a day to the park and some of the West Side's other far-flung attractions, such as the Irish Museum of Modern Art, Kilmainham Gaol, the Guinness Hopstore, and the National Museum of Ireland at Collins Barracks.

### GETTING THERE:
From downtown, **Dublin Bus** operates three buses that go to Phoenix Park - #10 bus from O'Connell Street or buses # 25 and #26 from Middle Abbey Street. If you are coming from another city in Ireland, all **Irish Rail** trains from the west terminate at **Heuston Station**, a two-block walk from the Park.

### GETTING AROUND:
There is no one bus service that serves the various attractions of the west side. You can either take a bus to one site and walk to several others, or take taxis from one point to the next.

### PRACTICALITIES:
Of all sections of Dublin, the layout of the West Side requires the most walking—each site takes in a lot of territory and all are a good walking distance from each other. Wear comfortable and supportive shoes, if you intend to take in all or most of the sights in one day. If you don't want to spend a lot of time walking, then take a bus to one place and a taxi to the next. Taxis are readily available at Heuston Station, and you can engage a taxi for part of a day.

### FOOD AND DRINK:
With a relatively small number of attractions compared to the rest of

the city, Dublin's West Side sees fewer tourists and has less call for restaurants or coffee shops. In addition to the three places listed here, you'll find good cafés at the Phoenix Park Visitor Centre, Dublin Zoo, Museum of Modern Art, and the National Museum at Collins Barracks.

**Footplate Brasserie** (Heuston Station, St. John's Rd.) This Georgian-style dining room adds a lot of class to Dublin's West Side train terminal. Meals are served from noon to early evening each day, amid a decor of high ceilings, brass railings, and dark woods. The menu offers a mix of European, French, and Mediterranean dishes. ☎ 703-2100. ££

**Nancy Hands** (30–32 Parkgate St.) Situated a stone's throw from the main gate of Phoenix Park, this traditional pub is noted for its carvery buffet lunches, accompanied by house special treats—potato cakes, tomato-and-herb bread rolls, and homemade soups such as bacon and pureed turnip. The décor is full of conversation-starters, from curios to contemporary art to antiques such as the authentic Victorian bar featured in the film *Educating Rita.* ☎ 677-0149. £ to ££

**Ryans** (28 Parkgate St., at the entrance to Phoenix Park) This place offers two settings—an upstairs restaurant for formal dining and an Old World pub for snacks, soups, and light lunches. The pub has long been a favorite setting for Dubliners coming to spend a day in Phoenix Park, with mahogany bar, brass lamps, metal ceiling, domed skylight, beveled mirrors, etched glass, and two authentic "snugs." ☎ 677-6097 or 671-9352. X: Sun. ££

## SUGGESTED TOUR:

From downtown, head first to Phoenix Park via a taxi, rented car, or take bus #10 bus from O'Connell Street or buses #25 and #26 from Middle Abbey Street. Enter the park from Parkgate Street, and begin your tour:

**\*PHOENIX PARK** (1), Parkgate St., ☎ 677-0095. *Park: Open 24 hours a day. People's Gardens: Open Mon.–Sat. 10:30–dusk, Sun. 10–dusk, Admission is free. Visitor Centre: Open Sat.–Sun., Nov. to mid-Mar., 9:30–4:30; daily mid- to end-March 9:30–5, April–May 9:30-5:30, June–Sept. 9:30-6:30, Oct. 9:30–5. Adults £2, seniors £1.50, students/children £1. Café.*

As the largest urban enclosed park in Europe with a total area of 1,752 acres, this vast expanse of pasturelands, woodlands, nature trails, sports fields, and gardens is Dublin's playground. Opened in 1747, it is also the home of the Irish President and the US ambassador to Ireland, and the setting for a half-dozen monuments, statues, and forts. It is located two miles west of the city center, and is traversed by a network of roads and quiet pedestrian walkways.

A walking or driving tour, after entering from Parkgate Street, takes you via Main Road past the **People's Gardens** on the right, an ever-changing seasonal display of ornamental plantings; and the **Wellington Monument** on the left. This striking 205-foot obelisk, said to be the highest

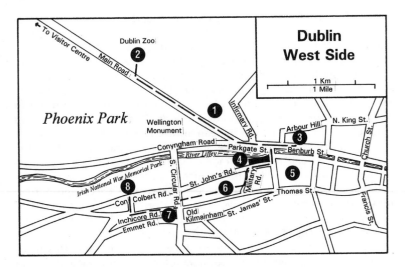

of its kind in the world, was erected in 1817 in tribute to the Duke of Wellington, who was born in Dublin. The next major area of interest, returning to the right, is the **Dublin Zoo**, a prime attraction in its own right (see below).

Continuing in a westerly direction, about a third-of the way into the park, you will see glimpses of *Áras an Uachtaráin, the sprawling white-pillared residence of the President of Ireland. Dating back to 1751, it was originally a private hunting lodge, then for 140 years (1782–1921) was the residence of the British viceroys, followed by 16 years of British Governors General, and finally in 1938 it became the home of Ireland's Presidents. Eight presidents have lived here to date.

Although the house is not normally open to the public, it is open for guided tours on Saturdays throughout the year. Tickets are free, but available only on a first-come basis at the Phoenix Park Visitor Centre (see below), where you will see a 10-minute audiovisual that gives background on the history and architecture of the house, followed by a 3-minute minibus ride to Aras. The guided tour of the house takes you through seven rooms including the newest section of the house, the State Corridor (1957), a long hallway decorated with stucco wall panels and displaying busts of all of Ireland's Presidents on Connemara marble pedestals; and then on to the State Dining Room (1849), containing a table of Georgian mahogany where the first-ever Irish cabinet meeting was held; and the State Reception Room (1802), where the Presidents greet guests.

Other rooms on the tour are The Council of State Room (1751); State Drawing Room (1751); the President's Study (1751); and the Entrance Hall (1751), a part of the original house, with many features dating back to 1751 including a magnificent coffered barrel-vaulted ceiling. The walk-around takes about 20 minutes, depending on questions and comments from the participants. If you are in Dublin on a Saturday, it is well worth a detour— a great experience. You may even get a glimpse of the President! For more information ☎ 670-9155.

Continuing on the Main Road, to the right you will see the **Phoenix Monument**, a 30-foot column of Portland stone erected in 1745 beside a natural spring. It is topped by an image of a mythological phoenix. It was originally thought that the park was named in honor of the bird, but the name "phoenix" actually comes from the Irish word *Fionn Usice* (pronounced "phoenix" in English), meaning "clear water."

To the left is a turn into the road for the **Papal Cross**, a huge white steel cross commemorating the visit of Pope John Paul II to the park in 1979. More than one million people crowded into the adjacent area, known as "The Fifteen Acres," to see the Pope celebrate Mass. In typical Irish understatement, this spot actually encompasses 200 acres. Legend has it that it was a dueling ground in the 18th century, but today it is normally used as sports playing fields.

Alternatively, take the roundabout from the Phoenix Monument to the **Phoenix Park Visitor Centre** which is housed at the former Ashtown Castle, a tower house believed to have been built in the early 1600s by John Connell. The site was used from 1929 to 1978 as the residence of the Papal Nuncio. Now it serves as an information center, with exhibits and an audiovisual show on the park's history and on the trees, plants, deer, and birds that have their habitats here.

Other important components within the Park include the American Ambassador's Residence, which is not open to the public, and the **Furry Glen**, a wildlife and waterfowl sanctuary.

No matter how much time you devote to touring Phoenix Park, be sure to save a couple of hours for a very special zoo. As noted above, this is one area of the park that is an attraction unto itself:

**DUBLIN ZOO** (2), Phoenix Park, ☎ 677-1425. *Open Mon.–Sat. 9:30–6, Sun. 10:30–6. Adults £6, seniors and children £3.50. Shop. Café.*

Established in 1830, the Dublin Zoological Gardens comprise the third-oldest public zoo in the world (after London and Paris). Famed for its breeding of lions, the zoo occupies 30 acres of Phoenix Park, providing natural living environments for over 250 species from snow leopards and gorillas to fruit bats. Two natural lakes also serve as a habitat for pelicans, flamingoes, ducks, and geese. The newest addition is the Reptile House, holding a collection of East African crocodiles, snakes, monitors, tortoises, terrapins, and locusts. Facilities include a passenger train which travels around the perimeter of the zoo and an information center that presents a slide show on endangered species. Visitors are encouraged to take part in the daily feeding program for gorillas, polar bears, reptiles, sea lions, and elephants.

After touring the park, return to Parkgate Street, and go one block east along Wolfe Tone Quay to Collins Barracks, until recently one of the oldest inhabited Army barracks in Europe and now home to:

**THE NATIONAL MUSEUM OF IRELAND** (3), at Collins Barracks, Benburb St., ☎ 677-7444. *Open Tues.–Sat. 10–5, Sun. 2–5. Admission is free. Shop. Café.*
Ever since it opened in mid-1997, this museum has been drawing many new visitors to Dublin's north side. The structure itself, with a sprawling quadrangle combined with esplanades, squares, and a clock tower, is a landmark dating back to 1701. Constructed of Wicklow granite and limestone, it was built for use by the British forces and it remained in continuous use for almost three centuries until it was demilitarized and acquired for the museum. Since 1922, the complex has been known by its present name, in honor or Michael Collins, one of Ireland's heroes and the subject of the 1996 film "Michael Collins." The interior is masterfully laid out on four levels, connected by stairs or elevator. The collection ranges from period furniture and Irish country furniture to weaponry and scientific instruments, as well as Irish silver, ceramics, and glassware. The Curators' Choice, comprising 25 unique objects rarely seen, is particularly intriguing as is the Fonthill Vase, presented in an exhibition that traces its journey from 14th century China to the present day. Plan to devote at least two hours to this excellent attraction.

Return to Wolfe Tone Quay and cross over to the south side of the Liffey at **Heuston Bridge**, opened in 1828 and originally known as King's Bridge, to **Heuston Station** (4) at St. John's Road West. Built of local stone, this impressive Georgian-era building was erected in 1844, according to the Act of Incorporation of the Great Southern and Western Railway.
The act authorized that the railway "commence in a field at or near King's Bridge in the city of Dublin between Military Road and the River Liffey." Although this part of Dublin was considered a rural area at the time, the plan to build a station here was a wise one, especially since one of Dublin's chief industries—the Guinness Brewery—was only a block away. Later a connecting line was run into the brewery, to facilitate transport of the famous brew. Because of its location next to King's Bridge, the depot was originally known as Kingsbridge Station. It was renamed Heuston Station in 1966 in honor of Sean Heuston (1891–1916), an employee of the Great Southern and Western Railway who was executed after the Easter Rising in 1916. One of three major train stations in Dublin, Heuston Station is the departure point for most trains to the south and southwest of Ireland (the three coats of arms carved on the front of the building are those of Dublin, Cork, and Limerick).
At this point, you may wish to visit the ***Guinness Hopstore** (5) (see page 33). Walk one long block south along Steven's Lane for a left turn onto James's Street and another block to the Crane Street entrance of the

Guinness Hopstore Visitor Centre.

Alternatively, from Heuston Station, you may wish to visit several of the attractions in the area known as Kilmainham. Cross over St. John's Road West to Military Road for a visit to one of the outstanding cultural attractions of the city:

**\*THE IRISH MUSEUM OF MODERN ART (IMMA)** (6), Military Road, Kilmainham, ☎ 671-8666. *Open Tues.–Sat. 10–5:30, Sun. noon–5:30. Guided tours on Wed. and Fri. at 2:30 and on Sun. at 12:30. Admission is free. Café.*

Contemporary creativity is the hallmark of this innovative museum, presenting a broad range of late-20th-century international and Irish paintings, sculpture, hangings, graphics, and three-dimensional art. Like the National Museum of Ireland's recent occupancy of the Collins Barracks, IMMA is housed in a building that is an attraction in itself—the former Royal Hospital Kilmainham. Considered as the finest 17th-century building in Ireland, it was built in 1684 by James Butler, Duke of Ormonde, who obtained a charter from King Charles II to create a hospice for retired soldiers. It continued in that use for almost 250 years. The style is based on Les Invalides of Paris, in the form of a quadrangle, with two stories, dormer windows, and a large central courtyard. Although it was vacant for several decades, the building was restored by the Irish government in 1986, at a cost of £21 million ($35 million). Highlights include a chapel with Baroque-style ceiling, stained glass, and intricate wood carvings. Outside there is a sculpture park and an 18th- century formal garden. The main building and grounds are also used for concerts and other cultural events. If you prefer to come here directly from downtown, take Bus #79 from Aston Quay.

After visiting the museum, walk straight through the central courtyard and exit via the rear of the property, through Johnston's Gate, to:

**KILMAINHAM GAOL (JAIL)** (7), Inchicore Road, Kilmainham, ☎ 453-5984. *Open April–Sept., daily 9:30–4:45; Oct.–Mar., Mon.–Fri. 9:30–4 and Sun. 10–4:45. Closed Sat. Adults £3.50, seniors £2.50, students and children £1.50.*

For insight into Ireland's long struggle for freedom, this building is a standout—more of a shrine than a jail. From 1796 to 1924, this was the place of detention or execution for the leaders of the rebellions of 1798, 1803, 1848, 1867, and 1916. Closed as a prison in 1924, it has since become the largest unoccupied jail in Ireland or Britain. Most of all, it is a monument to some of Ireland's greatest names—Robert Emmet, Thomas Francis Meagher, Charles Stewart Parnell, Padraic Pearse, DeValera, and a host of others who spent time in this jail. What was it like to be a prisoner here? Take a guided tour to see cells and other areas of confinement and punishment. A visit also includes exhibits and an audiovisual presentation on the history of the jail and its occupants. If you prefer to come here directly, take Bus #51 or #79 from Aston Quay or 51A from Lr. Abbey St.

To end your visit in this area, take Inchicore Road for one short block north to Con Colbert Road and the entrance to the **Irish National War Memorial Park** (8), Islandbridge, ☎ 661-3111, a two-block-long garden dedicated to the memory of 49,400 soldiers who died in World War I. Laid out in 1931, it contains a splendid blend of steps, statuary, flowers, shrubs and trees in a peaceful setting on the south bank of the River Liffey opposite the Phoenix Park. *Open Mon.–Fri. 8 a.m., Sat.–Sun. 10 a.m. till dark. Admission is free.*

To return to downtown, walk to Heuston Station for a taxi; or cross over Sarah Bridge to Parkgate Street for a bus #10 to O'Connell Street or buses #25 and #26 to Middle Abbey Street. If you are energetic, walk back to the city center in an eastward direction along the quays.

# *The Southern Suburbs

W hat is it like to live in Dublin? One of the best ways to find out is to head out into the suburbs. The southern suburbs are particularly fashionable—starting in Ballsbridge, home of many embassies, and stretching southward along the Dublin Bay coast into Dun Laoghaire, Dalkey, and Killiney.

Although there are relatively few tourist attractions here, the main draw is the natural beauty of the landscape and the gentle pace of life. The area is ideal for strolling, whether along a shady tree-lined residential street, in a village shopping center, or on a seafront promenade. It's a great way to get to know the Irish.

Many of Dublin's finest hotels are located in the southern suburbs, from the Berkeley Court, Jurys, and Herbert Park in Ballsbridge to the legendary Fitzpatrick's Castle in Killiney, as are many fine restaurants and friendly neighborhood pubs. You may even decide to base yourself in one of the southern suburbs, and commute into the city like most Dubliners.

## GETTING THERE:

Although you can easily walk to Ballsbridge from most parts of downtown Dublin, the other southern suburbs require some form of transportation. You can rent a car and drive around for a day, or you can take the **DART** from Connolly Station, Tara Street Station or Pearse Station southward into the suburbs. The **DART** stops at all of the major points including Dun Laoghaire, Sandycove, Dalkey, Killiney, and Bray.

**Dublin Bus** provides frequent service throughout the day to the suburbs. Here is a sampling of the most popular routes: bus #7 and 7A from Burgh Quay to Ballsbridge and Dun Laoghaire; bus #8 from Burgh Quay to Ballsbridge, Dun Laoghaire and Dalkey; bus #45 from Custom House Quay to Ballsbridge and Bray; and bus #46A from Townsend Street to Dun Laoghaire. If you intend to go to just one town or village, then the ordinary bus fare is the best buy, but if you want to go to several suburbs, taking the **DART** or a bus from one to the other, then be sure to buy a one-day bus or bus/rail ticket. You'll save money and you can enjoy unlimited travel from town to town. These special one-day tickets can be purchased from Dublin Bus, 59 Upr. O'Connell St. or at any Irish Rail or **DART** station.

**GETTING AROUND:**
Unless you rent a car or taxi for a day, you'll need to take public transportation to get from one town to the other (refer to the **Dublin Bus** and **DART** routes described above). If you only have a few hours or prefer an escorted tour, during the months of June-September, **Dublin Bus** offers the *South Coast Tour,* a four-hour drive covering Dun Laoghaire harbor, the Joyce Tower at Sandycove, and other scenic parts of the southern suburbs; departures are daily at 11 and 2 from **Dublin Bus**, 59 Upr. O'Connell St., ☎ 873-4222.

**PRACTICALITIES:**
When using public transport (buses and DART trains), avoid morning and evening business rush hours and school dismissal times, and then you'll be sure to get a seat and enjoy the ride to the fullest. Wear comfortable shoes, since it takes some walking to get around each town or area.
For on-the-spot information, **Dublin Tourism** has a branch office at the Ferry Terminal Bulding, St. Michael's Wharf, at The Pier, Dun Laoghaire, ☎ 280-6984.

**FOOD AND DRINK:**
Some of Dublin's best restaurants and pubs are in the southern suburbs, frequented by the people who live in the surrounding areas. Not surprisingly, many savvy visitors who are staying in downtown hotels often take a taxi or bus to Ballsbridge or an early evening's ride on the DART to Dun Laoghaire, Sandycove, or Dalkey, just to patronize one of the local restaurants. Here is a sampling:
**Brasserie na Mara** (1 Harbour Rd., Dun Laoghaire) Housed in a former Victorian rail station adjacent to the harborfront pier, this restaurant has recently been given a funky new look with a minimalist decor of plain white walls and massive mirrors. As to the food, it is not surprising that fish is the star of the menu, especially since the Irish name *na Mara* means *of the sea.* House specialty is seared tuna steak with warm salsa. ☎ 280-6767. X: Sun. ££
**DeSelby's** (17/18 Patrick St., off George's St., Dun Laoghaire) Situated on a side street in the center of a busy harbor town, this informal indoor/outdoor eatery is a favorite with the locals. The menu offers a half-dozen varieties of fresh fish plus Irish dishes (stews and mixed grills) and international fare (pastas and burgers). ☎ 284-1761 or 284-1762. £ to ££
**Guinea Pig** (17 Railway Rd., Dalkey) In spite of its name, this restaurant is known for seafood, such as *symphony de la mer* (potpourri of fish and crustaceans), as well as rack of lamb and game. All dishes are prepared with a French/Irish flair and served in a homey Victorian village inn atmosphere. Early-bird specials offer great value. Open for dinner only. ☎ 285-9055. ££ to £££
**Le Coq Hardi** (35 Pembroke Rd., Ballsbridge) A favorite with ambas-

sadors and business tycoons, this formal 50-seat restaurant occupies a Georgian house on the corner of Wellington Road. The menu blends the best of French and Irish cuisine, with dishes such as caneton à l'orange or steak flamed in Irish whiskey. The 700-bin wine cellar is an attraction in itself. ☎ 668-9070. X: Sun. £££

**The Queens Bar & Restaurant** (12/13 Castle St., Dalkey) An 18th-century atmosphere prevails at this three-story landmark, with open fireplaces, shelves lined with nautical memorabilia, beamed ceilings, antique furniture, and floors of polished tile, rough timber and coarse flag stones. At lunchtime enjoy a soup, sandwich, salad, or snack in the pub, or at dinner order a pizza, pasta, and other Italian/Mediterranean dishes in the on-premises restaurant. ☎ 285-4569. £ to ££

**Roly's Bistro** (7 Ballsbridge Terrace, Ballsbridge, one block south of the American Embassy) Getting a table at this trendy restaurant is considered a coup by Dubliners. The menu, dictated by what is fresh and seasonally best, presents imaginatively prepared cuisine, served with finesse and enthusiasm in a bright and airy atmosphere that is full of local buzz. Best of all, the prices are mostly moderate. It's hard to match. ☎ 668-2611. ££

**South Bank** (1 Martello Terrace at Islington Ave., Dun Laoghaire) Situated within walking distance of the James Joyce Tower at Sandycove, this restaurant occupies a seafront terrace house and offers views of the harbor from some upstairs tables. The menu features dependable Irish and Continental dishes. Open for dinner year-round; also for lunch during May–Sept. ☎ 280- 8788. X: Mon. in winter. ££

**Teddy's** (1A Windsor Terrace, Dun Laoghaire) Established in July of 1950, this local landmark is "the place" to go for take-out ice cream on a warm day. Dubliners flock here and then head for the Promenade to enjoy their frozen treats as they take a stroll or sit on a bench overlooking the waterfront. The menu offers ice cream only—it's a "tradition" not to be missed. ☎ 284-5128. £

## SUGGESTED TOUR:

Start your tour at **Pearse Station** (1), a stop on both the DART and Irish Rail systems. Spend the rest of the morning learning about three phases of Irish life—traditional craftwork, the nation's waterways, and the printing business. To begin, from Pearse Station, walk two blocks westward along Pearse Street to the:

**TOWER DESIGN CENTRE** (2), Pearse St., off Grand Canal Quay, ☎ 677-5655. *Open Mon.–Fri. 9:30–5:30. Admission is free.*

For an overview of some of Ireland's best products, stop into this thriving eight-story enterprise center, sponsored by the IDA, Ireland's industrial development authority. It is housed in a former sugar refinery dating back to 1862, restored in the early 1980s. Watch artisans at work and then purchase a special souvenir—from hand-made chocolates and candies to greeting cards, hand-marbled stationery, pewter, ceramics, pottery, knitwear, hand-painted fabrics, copper plate etchings, wall hangings, silver and gold Celtic jewelry, and heraldic gifts.

While you are at Grand Canal Quay, take time to visit one of Dublin's newest attractions:

**WATERWAYS VISITOR CENTRE** (3), Grand Canal Quay, ☎ 677-7510. *Open Oct.–May, Wed.–Sun. 12:30–5; June–Sept. daily 9:30–6:30. Adults £2, seniors and students £1.50, children, £1.*

Dating back to 1763, the Grand Canal was built to help provide a link between Dublin and the Shannon and Barrow Rivers. This new interpretative center, perched beside the Grand Canal Basin, tells the story of the adjacent canal and Ireland's other inland waterways. A great source of power, transport, and recreation, Ireland's waterways are an integral and important part of the country's history and development. A tour around the center includes an audiovisual show, demonstrations by working models of various engineering features of the inland waterways, and an interactive multimedia presentation on the diversity of activities and experiences provided by the waterways.

Continue to walk along Grand Canal Quay, turning left onto Upr. Grand Canal Street. Cross over the canal and you are now "officially" in Ballsbridge. Laid out and built between 1830 and 1860, Ballsbridge is one of Dublin's most pricey suburbs, with a fine selection of Georgian, Victorian, and Edwardian townhouses and mansions. Walk one block to Haddington Road, for a visit to the:

**NATIONAL PRINT MUSEUM** (4), Beggars Bush Barracks, Haddington Rd., Ballsbridge, ☎ 660-3770. *Open May–Sept., Mon.–Fri. 10–12:30 and 2:30–5, Sat.–Sun. 12–5; Oct.–April, Tues., Thurs., and Sat.–Sun. 2–5. Adults £2.50, seniors, students and children £1.50. Shop. Café.*

In this age of inkjets, lasers, disks, and the internet, this museum provides a nostalgic look back to the era of the printing press. Laid out in the format of a working printing office of a half-century ago, it displays a variety of printing artifacts, some of which date back to 1810, ranging from linotype and monotype machines, compositors' tools, wire stitchers, book-sewing gadgets, paper machines, and guillotines, to examples of hand-made paper and old magazine and newspaper pages. In addition, visitors can have their names set in print in a chosen typeface and printed, using the old hot-metal printing system. To add to the aura, this museum is housed in a restored 19th-century garrison chapel with lovely stained glass windows and a gallery.

Make a right onto Shelbourne Road and follow it for one long block to Lansdowne Road, distinguished as the entrance to **Lansdowne Stadium**, the home of the Irish Rugby Football grounds where the international and triple crown games are played. From here, you can board the DART at the

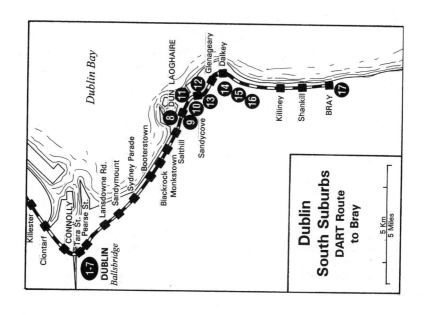

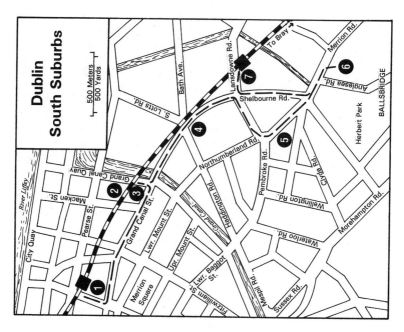

**Lansdowne Road Station** and continue southward to other suburbs, or you can continue to walk around Ballsbridge.

If you choose to continue walking around Ballsbridge, follow Lansdowne Road away from the stadium, passing the **Berkeley Court Hotel** and **Jurys Hotel** on your left, until you come to the intersection of Lansdowne and Northumberland Roads. This is the heart of Ballsbridge. Take a left and cross over to the other side of the street and you will come to the **American Embassy** (5), 42 Elgin Road, ☎ 668-8777, a round circular building patterned after a Celtic round tower. If you are fond of embassy-hopping, spend some time in this neighborhood. Within a radius of six blocks, there are at least a dozen other embassies including three on Ailesbury Road: Austria (#93), France (#36), and Switzerland (#6). Two are on Merrion Road: Britain (#31/33) and the Netherlands (#160), as well as Spain at 17a Merlyn Park, just off Merrion Road; plus the Belgian Embassy at 2 Shrewsbury Road and the Italian Embassy at 63/65 Northumberland Road.

One block south of the American Embassy are the **\*Royal Dublin Society Showgrounds (RDS)** (6), Merrion Road, Ballsbridge, ☎ 668-0645, a huge complex of indoor exhibition space, livestock areas, and parade grounds. The RDS is best known as the home for the annual *Dublin Horse Show* which takes place in early August, but it is also a setting for major music concerts and meetings.

At this point, it is no longer possible to continue the tour on foot since distances from place to place become much greater. You may wish to catch a southbound bus to reach other suburbs, or you can walk back to **Lansdowne Road Station** (7) to ride the DART to your next stop.

Depending on your time and interests, you may want to head to **Dun Laoghaire** (pronounced *Dunn-leery*), six miles south of the city center. All buses or the DART will let you off at **Dun Laoghaire Station** (8) on the harborfront. If your timing is right, you'll catch a glimpse of one or more of the new "super-ferries" that bring passengers across the Irish Sea from Britain to the Dun Laoghaire terminal.

Dating back at least to early Christian times, Dun Laoghaire is named after Laoghaire, a 5th-century Irish king who built a fort here. In 1821, the name was changed to Kingstown in honor of King George IV, but it reverted back to the original in 1920 after the Irish Rebellion. It prospered as a fishing village until the east and west piers were built in 1817-21 and it gradually became a viable port for shipping fleets. A car ferry service was introduced in 1965. Today Dun Laoghaire is a major yachting center and home of the Royal Irish Yacht Club, National Yacht Club, and Royal St. George Yacht Club. Sailboats dot the harbor throughout the year.

Step out onto Royal Marine Avenue, across from the train station. You can follow this street for one block up to Upr. and Lr. George's Street, the main thoroughfare of the town, to look at the shops and other enterprises. Alternatively, you can cross the street and take a stroll in **Moran Park** (9), which boasts lovely gardens and a bowling green laid out in 1903. To gain some insight into the maritime history of the area, walk a half-block to **Maritime Museum of Ireland** (10), off Haigh Terrace. Housed in the former Mariners Church (dating back to 1837), this museum presents a collection of maritime models, pictures, documents, photographs, charts, stamps, post cards, flags, badges, and other memorabilia. *Open Tues.–Sun. 1–5. Adults £1.50, seniors, students and children 80 p.*

Follow Queens Road southward to Windsor Terrace, with the bay on your left, for a bracing walk along the three-block-long **\*Promenade** (11) or "Prom" as the locals call it. From the south end of the Promenade, at Marine Terrace, follow the signs for two blocks to reach one of the most famous literary sights of the area:

**\*THE JOYCE TOWER** (12), Sandycove Point, Sandycove, ☎ 280-9265. *Open April–Oct. Mon.–Sat. 10–1 and 2–5, Sun. 2–6. Adults £2.70, seniors, students and children aged 12–18 £2.20, children aged 3–11 £1.40. Shop.*

For anyone with an interest in James Joyce, this is a "must see" attraction. Occupied by Joyce for a period at the turn of the century, the author made the tower the setting for the first chapter of his famous novel *Ulysses*. Understandably, it's been known as *Joyce's Tower* ever since. The rooms inside contain a collection of Joycean memorabilia including letters, photographs, documents, first and rare editions, and personal possessions including a vest, guitar, and death mask. Apart from its literary life, this 40-foot granite tower has an interesting history. It is one of a series of martello towers built in 1804 to withstand a threatened invasion by Napoleon. In 1904 it was rented from the army by Oliver St. John Gogarty, also a distinguished writer, for £8 (less than $15 today); and it was Gogarty who invited Joyce to be his guest. It sits on the edge of Dublin Bay a little less than eight miles south of downtown Dublin. The exterior gun platform offers panoramic views.

After visiting the Joyce Tower, you can catch a DART train at the **Sandycove Station** (13) or retrace your steps back to the Dun Laoghaire rail station for a bus or a DART train. Some buses also stop along Upr. or Lr. George's Street in Dun Laoghaire. Alternatively, if you are continuing on to Dalkey, walk two short blocks along Sandycove Avenue West to Sandycove Road to catch a #8 bus to Dalkey.

**\*Dalkey**, exactly eight miles from the center of Dublin City, is a very walkable small village. One of the most historic of the southern suburbs, Dalkey dates back to Norman times and incorporated as a town in 1358. It was a thriving port until the 17th century, and was once protected by seven castles, parts of which can still be seen on the main street, appropriately known today as **Castle Street**. A favorite residential area for writers, theater folk, and politicians, the streets of Dalkey are lined with an array of handsome Regency and Victorian homes.

To learn all about Dalkey, stop into the **Dalkey Castle Heritage Centre** (14), Castle Street, ☎ 285-8366, the town's centerpiece castle which has been totally restored and turned into a museum. It houses an exhibition tracing the history of the town and also features local art showings. *Open Mar.–Oct., Mon.–Fri. 9:30–5 and Sat.–Sun. 11–5; Nov.–Feb., Sat.–Sun. 11–5. Adults £2.50, seniors and students £2, children £1.50.*

If you'd like a good climb, walk up Dalkey Avenue to the **Hill of Dalkey** and **\*Killiney Hill Park** (15), both offering panoramic vistas of Dublin Bay. **\*Vico Road**, which runs behind these two parks overlooking the water, offers views that have often been compared to the Bay of Naples. The luxury hotel, **Fitzpatrick's Castle** (16), sits atop Killiney Hill, and is well worth a visit, a refreshment stop, or an overnight.

The final southern stop on the DART route is **Bray** (17), a typical Irish beach resort town, 12 miles south of Dublin and actually in County Wicklow. Bray has a mile-long beach, with a mile-long esplanade running its length to **Bray Head**, a cliff that rises from the sea to a height of nearly 800 feet. Take time to walk around and breathe the sea air and then board the DART or a bus for the return trip to Dublin city.

# Northern Suburbs

I f you fly into or depart from Dublin International Airport, you'll have a
taste of Dublin's northern suburbs. The airport, nine miles north of the
city center at Swords, sits amid a landscape of superhighway bordered
by sprawling inland communities with rows of attached and semi-attached
houses such as Artane, Beaumont, Coolock, Killester, and Santry.

To add a touch of class to the airport corridor, these densely populated districts are rimmed by a handful of older and more affluent residential neighborhoods such as Drumcondra, Glasnevin, Clontarf, and Marino,
and exclusive seafront enclaves at Malahide, Sutton, and Howth, as well as
the golfing Eden at Portmarnock. Farther out into the north of County
Dublin, there are also the coastal communities of Donabate, Rush,
Skerries, and Balbriggan.

Each section has its own personality but yet they all fit neatly together to provide an easy commute for many Dubliners. In addition, these suburbs offer a number of attractions of interest to the visitor—from wide
harbors and sandy beaches, to restored castles, award-winning gardens,
stately houses, and unique museums.

## GETTING THERE:

All of the city's northern suburbs are served by the **Dublin Bus** network, but not necessarily on the same lines which makes it difficult to get
from one attraction to the other. Here is a sampling of the most popular
routes: To the Botanic Gardens at Glasnevin, take #13 or #19 from
O'Connell St. or #34 from Middle Abbey St. To Glasnevin Cemetery take
#19 or 19A from O'Connell Street, #34 from Middle Abbey St., or #40, 40A,
or 40B from Parnell St. Board #31 from Lr. Abbey St. to Howth; #33 from
Eden Quay to Rush, Skerries, and Balbriggan; #42 from Beresford Place to
Malahide or Marino; or #33B from Eden Quay to Donabate.

The **DART** provides service to Sutton and Howth and other northern
suburbs near the sea from Connolly Station, Tara Street Station or Pearse
Station. For the more far-flung destinations such as Malahide or
Donabate, take **Irish Rail** from Connolly Station.

Note: If you intend to go to just one town or village, then the ordinary
bus fare is the best buy, but if you want to go to several suburbs, taking the
**DART** or a bus from one to the other, be sure to buy a one-day bus or
bus/rail ticket. You'll save money and you can enjoy unlimited travel from
town to town. These special one-day tickets can be purchased from
Dublin Bus, 59 Upr. O'Connell St. or at any Irish Rail or DART station.

## GETTING AROUND:

Unless you rent a car or taxi for a day, you'll need to take public transportation to get from one town to the other (refer to the **Dublin Bus**, **DART**, and **Irish Rail** routes described above).

If you only have a few hours or prefer an escorted tour, during the months of June–September, **Dublin Bus** offers the *Coast & Castle Tour*, a three-hour drive covering the National Botanic Gardens, Casino at Marino, Malahide Castle, Howth, and other scenic parts of the northern suburbs; departures are daily at 10 from Dublin Bus, 59 Upr. O'Connell St., ☎ 873-4222. From March to November, Gray Line Tours operates half-day sightseeing tours to Malahide Castle and North County Dublin (on Mon. and Wed. afternoons). For bookings and full information, visit the Gray Line Tours desk at the Dublin Tourism Centre, Suffolk St., ☎ 605-7705.

## PRACTICALITIES:

Dublin's northern suburbs are not tied up in a neat little package, and consequently do not lend themselves to one continuous itinerary, nor is it practical to walk from place to place. In fact, to do a complete tour of all of the northern suburbs, you would need to use a combination of public transport services, plus an occasional taxi. The only sure way to take in the whole area would be to rent a car for a day and plan a hopscotch-style of itinerary.

## FOOD AND DRINK:

The north side offers a fine selection of restaurants that cater for the resident population. Howth, with its seaside location, is undoubtedly the most popular choice for a meal, particularly on weekends. Since many of these restaurants are open primarily for dinner, the best bets for lunch are usually the cafés and tea rooms at attractions, such as Malahide Castle, Newbridge House, and Ardgillan Castle.

**Abbey Tavern** (Abbey St., Howth) With open turf fireplaces, stone walls, flagged floors, and gaslights, this Old World tavern is a cozy setting in the heart of the village. Seafood is the specialty here, whether you enjoy a snack lunch in the bar or a full dinner at night in the upstairs dining room. Each evening there is also a rousing session of traditional ballad music—a blend of fiddles, concertinas, tin whistles, pipes, spoons, and whatever else it takes to make foot-tapping music. ☎ 839-0307. £ to £££

**Bon Appetit** (9 St. James Terrace, Malahide) For nearly 20 years, this charming restaurant has drawn people to a Georgian terrace house setting beside the sea. The menu is a blend of French and Irish haute cuisine, with a house special of *Sole Creation McGuirk*, aptly named for owner-chef Patsy McGuirk. ☎ 845-00314. X: Sun. ££ to £££

**King Sitric** (East Pier, Howth) Named for the legendary Viking monarch, this bayfront restaurant occupies a 150-year-old harbormaster's building. Although steaks and game are available, the menu is synonymous with seafood. House specials are lobsters from the tank and *Howth fish ragout*, a combination of the best of the day's local catch. Open for dinner only except May–Sept. when a seafood-oyster bar is operated at lunchtime. ☎ 832-5235. X: Sun. £££

**Red Bank** (7 Church St., Skerries) In the center of town, this restaurant is located in a converted bank. The menu features local produce, from vegetables and meats to flours and cheeses, but the unmistakable star is fresh seafood. House specials include cockles and mussels soup, *Black Sole Red Bank* (stuffed with mussels and prawns) and *Baked Crab Loughshinney* (blended with dry sherry and served in its own shell. Open for dinner only except lunch on Sunday. ☎ 849-1005. X: Mon. year-round and Sun. night in Nov.–May. ££

### SUGGESTED TOUR:

To start a tour of the northern suburbs really depends on your own preferences. If you are interested in flowers and plants, start your tour by taking a Bus #13 or #19 from O'Connell St. or #34 from Middle Abbey St., to Glasnevin, for a visit to the:

**\*NATIONAL BOTANIC GARDENS** (1), Botanic Road, Glasnevin, ☎ 837-7596 or 837-4388. *Open May–Sept., Mon.–Sat. 9–6, Sun. 11–6; Oct.–April, Mon.–Sat. 10–4:30; Sun. 11–4:30. Free admission.*

Have you ever heard the song *The Last Rose of Summer?* Well, here's where you will find it—on a 50-acre expanse along the south bank of the River Tolka. In addition to the delicate bloom that inspired the famous ballad, you will also see other notable rare specimens, ranging from a weeping Atlantic cedar and Chusan palms, to native strawberry trees. Established by the Royal Dublin Society in 1795, now administered by the Department of Arts, Culture, and the Gaeltacht, these extensive horticultural displays include rock gardens and burren areas, herbaceous borders, and an annual display of decorative plants including a rare example of Victorian carpet bedding. In addition, a curvilinear range of glasshouses designed and built by Richard Turner between 1843 and 1869, houses large collections of palms, alpine plants, ferns, tropical water plants, and succulents. In all, more than 20,000 different plants and cultivars are on view.

The Botanic Gardens are adjacent to:

**GLASNEVIN CEMETERY** (2), Finglas Road, Glasnevin, ☎ 830-1133. *Open daily 8–4. Admission is free.*

Officially known as *The Irish National Cemetery,* this 124-acre expanse may not be the most popular place in Ireland, but it is one of the most fascinating for history buffs. Founded in 1832, it is the final resting place for legions of famous Irish people, from former Irish presidents,

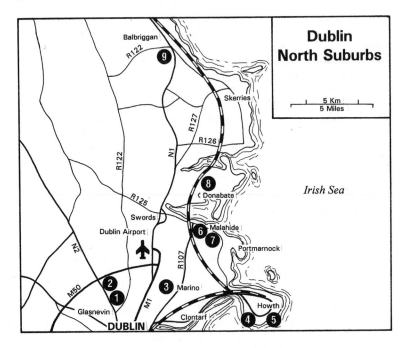

**Dublin North Suburbs**

Eamonn De Valera and Sean T. O'Kelly, to political heroes Daniel O'Connell, Roger Casement, Michael Collins, and Charles Stewart Parnell. In addition, the tombstones and Celtic cross markers list the names of literary figures such as poet Gerard Manley Hopkins, Christy Brown, and Brendan Behan. A *Heritage Map,* on sale in bookshops, serves as a guide as to who is buried where. Guided tours are offered by members of the Dublin Cemeteries Committee on Wednesdays and Fridays at 2:30. For details ☎ 830-1133.

From Glasnevin, it's about two miles east to Marino, but a difficult transfer via public transport. Unless you enjoy a good long walk, take a taxi to:

**CASINO AT MARINO** (3), Malahide Road, Marino. ☎ 833-1618. *Open Feb. to mid-June and Nov., Wed. and Sun. noon–4; mid-June to Sept. daily 9:30–6:30; Oct. daily 10–5. Adults £2, seniors £1.50, students and children under 12 £1.*

Architectural experts agree that it's worth the slightly out-of-the-way trip here to see one of Europe's best examples of an 18th-century garden temple—and one of Ireland's finest classical buildings. Designed in the Franco-Roman style of Neo-classicism by the Scottish architect Sir William Chambers, it was constructed over a 15-year period (1762–77) in the garden of Lord Charlemont's house by the English sculptor Simon Vierpyl. It is noteworthy for its elaborate stone carvings and compact structure, making it appear to be one story in height when it is actually two stories. It's located three miles north of downtown, off the Malahide road, and can be reached directly by taking the Malahide bus, #42 from Beresford Place near Busaras.

If you are driving from Marino, take Malahide Road north to Collins Avenue East which leads to Howth Road. Follow this road all the way to Howth. Alternatively, you can take the DART from any station north to Howth, the last stop, or take bus #31 from Lr. Abbey St.

*Howth (pronounced Ho-th) is a picturesque fishing village with a large marina, eight miles north of downtown. Sitting on an isthmus of hilly land, it is almost an island unto itself, with dozens of posh homes overlooking the water outside of the village. Howth Castle, which is not open to the public, dates back over 800 years and sits beside the Hill of Howth (4). Dubliners often take a morning or afternoon trip up to Howth, just to scale the Hill, stroll the village streets, or walk along the panoramic harborfront.

In the summer months, visitors flock to Howth Castle Gardens, off Howth Road, ☎ 832-2624, to see the peak blooms of more than 2,000 varieties of rhododendron. The 30 acres of gardens, which are set on a steep slope, were first planted in 1875. Open daily 8–sunset. Admission is free.

Another place of interest is the adjacent National Transport Museum (5), Howth Castle Demense, ☎ 288-3009. Staffed by a group of volunteers who are dedicated to the preservation and restoration of Ireland's transport heritage, this museum presents exhibits, photographs, and other memorabilia on buses and trams, as well as commercial, military, and public utility vehicles, plus fire-fighting appliances and horse-drawn carriages and vans. Open Sat.–Sun. 10–5. Adults £1.50; seniors and students 50p.

The northern suburbs' foremost cultural centerpiece is at Malahide, another nearby marina town. The best way to reach Malahide is via bus #42 from Beresford Place or via Irish Rail from Connolly Station.

*MALAHIDE CASTLE (6), Malahide, ☎ 846-2184. Open April–Oct., Mon.–Fri. 10–5, Sat. 11–6, Sun. 11:30–6; Nov.–March, Mon.–Fri. 10–5, Sat.–Sun. 2–5. Adults £3.15, seniors, students, and children 12–18 £2.65, children aged 3–11 £1.75. Shop. Café. Tours.

With a balanced array of turrets, towers, battlements, and mullioned windows, Malahide Castle is everything a castle should be, and well worth the eight-mile trip from downtown. Set amid 250 acres of parkland on the edge of the seaside town of Malahide, it was built by Richard Talbot in 1185 and was occupied by the Talbot family as a fortress and a private home for nearly 800 years. In 1973, when the last Lord Talbot died, the building was taken over by Dublin Tourism personnel who have fully restored it, opened it to the public, and filled it with a comprehensive collection of

Irish furniture, dating from the 17th century through the 19th. The walls are lined with Irish portraits and tableaux on loan from National Gallery. Each painting reflects a segment in the history of the Talbot Family including their involvement in the historic Battle of the Boyne in 1690.

The 250-acre Malahide Castle estate includes two other attractions—a 20-acre garden with more than 5,000 species of plants and flowers, and a unique museum:

**THE FRY MODEL RAILWAY MUSEUM** (7), Malahide, ☎ 846-3779. *Open April–Sept., Mon.–Sat. 10–5, Sun. 2–6, except closed Fri. in April, May, and Sept.; Oct.–March, Sat.–Sun. 2–5. Adults £2.90, seniors, students, and children aged 12–18 £2.20, children aged 3–11 £1.70. Shop. Café.*

For model railroad enthusiasts, this museum is a must. It is a collection of more than 300 model trains, reflecting the development of the Irish rail system from its inception in 1834 to the present. The model trains were built by hand in the 1920s and 1930s by Cyril Fry, a railway engineer and draftsman. In addition to models of the rolling stock, the display includes examples of stations, bridges, trams, buses, barges, boats, and the River Liffey and Hill of Howth.

From Malahide, it's four miles by car or taxi to Donabate. Alternatively, from downtown, you can travel north to Donabate via bus #33B from Eden Quay or Irish Rail from Connolly Station. In this quiet village, the main attraction is a beautifully restored 18th-century house with its own working farm:

**\*NEWBRIDGE HOUSE AND PARK** (8), Donabate, ☎ 843-6534. *Open April–Sept., Tues.–Sat. 10–1 and 2–5, Sun. 2–6, closed Mon.; Oct.–March, Sat.–Sun. 2–5. Adults £3, seniors, students and children aged 12–18 £2.60, children aged 3–11 £1.65. Shop. Café. Tours.*

Set on 350 acres of parkland, this two-story brick-faced Georgian gem was built in 1737 for the Archbishop of Dublin, Dr. Charles Cobbe, according to a design by Richard Castle. It served as the family home until 1984 when it was taken over by Dublin Tourism. Each room, which has been restored to look as it did 150 years ago, has its own style and decor. The Great Drawing Room, with its elaborate hand-carved furniture and original portraits, is considered one of the finest Georgian interiors in Ireland, while the downstairs area, originally occupied by servants, epitomizes a typical mid-18th-century kitchen and laundry room with all the appropriate and hand-operated machinery and utensils of long ago. Household items on display range from travel memorabilia to daybooks and dolls. The adjacent fully restored courtyard has a coachhouse, carpenter's shop, and blacksmith's forge, all displaying 19th-century tools and implements, while the grounds contain a 29-acre walk-around traditional farm with a dairy barn and farmyard animals.

The final loop on a tour of the northern suburbs takes you a further ten miles to the northernmost edge of County Dublin. If you are driving, it is easy to reach off the main N1 road, between Skerries and Balbriggan. On public transport, take bus #33 from Eden Quay. Once you reach Balbriggan, follow the signs to:

**ARDGILLAN CASTLE & PARK** (9), Balbriggan, Co. Dublin, ☎ 849-2212. *Castle open April–Sept., Tues.–Sun. 11–6; Oct.–March, Tues.–Sun. 11–4:30. Grounds open year-round daily 10–dusk. Castle admission: Adults £2.75, seniors and students £1.75. Grounds free. Café.*

Ardgillan, meaning *high wooded area* in the Irish language, is a perfect name for this beautiful 194-acre estate. Set on high ground overlooking the Bay of Drogheda on the Irish Sea, it comprises an idyllic blend of pasture, woodland, and gardens; and is a sanctuary for many species of animals and birds. The estate includes a castellated country house, the home of the Taylour family from 1738 until 1962. Admission to the house includes a tour of the four rooms on the ground level, which are furnished in period furnishings and antiques of the Georgian and Victorian styles. In addition, visitors also have access to the basement-level kitchen, a Victorian Conservatory, walled kitchen garden, and a permanent exhibition of maps including the 17th-century "Down Survey of Ireland." The main reason to come here, however, is the setting, ideal for enjoying a day in the country, with miles of walking paths, coastal views, picnic tables, rose gardens, and a herb garden. In June, July and August, guided tours of the gardens are given once a week, on Thursday at 3:30.

From Ardgillan, return to Dublin or continue on to tour other parts of Ireland.

## Trip 8

# The Boyne River Valley

Meandering in an east-west direction through the rich farming counties of Louth and Meath, the River Boyne has long been a pivotal setting in Irish history. Indeed if the river could speak, it would reveal many a spellbinding tale!

Follow the flow of the Boyne between Slane and Drogheda. The banks are lined with landmarks from almost every phase of Ireland's past—from the prehistoric passage tombs at Newgrange, to the legendary Hill of Tara, seat of the Irish High Kings, as well as monuments from the early days of Christianity. Above all, this land is remembered as the setting for the infamous *Battle of the Boyne* in July of 1690 when King William III defeated the exiled King James II for the crown of England—and changed the course of Irish history.

So come to the banks of the Boyne, to see history at every turn. While you are here, learn what life is like today by touring a working Irish farm. Lend a hand at the milking of the cows or feeding the baby lambs. It's all part of a daytrip to the bucolic Boyne River Valley.

### GETTING THERE:

The Boyne River Valley is 30 miles north of Dublin City. By car, depart the downtown area from the north side, via Parnell Square, following the signs for N2/N3. When the two routes split, stay on N3 heading toward Navan/Cavan. Stay on N3 until you reach Navan and then turn right to travel along N51 to reach Slane, Newgrange, and Drogheda. You can return to Dublin via N1, the main Dublin-Belfast road.

If you prefer not to drive, the best way to see the sights is to take an escorted sightseeing tour of the region. From February through November, the following choices are available:

**Bus Eireann**, Busaras/Central Bus Station, Dublin, ☎ 01-836-6111, operates full day trips to Newgrange and the Boyne Valley, departing at 10 and returning at 5:45.

**Gray Line Tours**, Dublin Tourism Office, Suffolk Street, Dublin, ☎ 01-605-7705, operates half-day trips to Newgrange and the Boyne Valley, departing at 10 and 2:30.

### PRACTICALITIES:

For visitor information, contact the **Tourist Information Office** at Brú na

Bóinne—Boyne Valley Visitor Centre, Donore, ☎ 041-988-0305, open all year. In addition, there is a seasonal (May–September) tourist office on West Street, Drogheda, ☎ 041-983-7070.

Note: Access into the Newgrange historic site is by guided tour only, and requires climbing down and up some steep underground stairways and walking through narrow passageways that can be a little claustrophobic. It is not recommended for everyone.

Area codes for the Boyne Valley are 041 and 046. To avoid confusion, each telephone number will be listed with its area code.

## FOOD AND DRINK:

**Conyngham Arms** (Main St., Slane) Dating back to 1850, this vintage inn blends an Old World ambiance with contemporary cuisine. During the day, enjoy Buffalo chicken wings, stir-fry dishes, pastas, stuffed baked potatoes, or other light meals in the bar, and by night feast on entrees such as sea trout Chablis, mushroom and chestnut Stroganoff or chicken with bacon, bananas, corn, and pineapple. ☎ 041-988-4444. £ to ££

**The Gateway** (15 West St., Drogheda) From mid-morning till early evening, this dependable self-service eatery serves a variety of light meals and snacks including homemade soups and vegetarian dishes. ☎ 041-983-8782. X: Sun. £

**Newgrange Farm Coffee Shop** (Newgrange Farm, Slane, Co. Meath) Housed in a converted 18th-century coachhouse on a working farm, this family-run café has a homey atmosphere, with white- washed walls, an open fireplace, local art, and assorted memorabilia. The self-service menu offers a wide array of homemade soups, baked goods, and snacks, prepared with ingredients produced by the farm. ☎ 041-982-4119. X: Oct.–Mar., and Mon. in April–June and Sept. £

## SUGGESTED TOUR:

The Boyne River Valley is rich in history at every turn. Begin your tour as you approach the town of Navan on N3. About five miles south of the town is one of Ireland's most historic sites:

**THE HILL OF TARA** (1), Navan, Co. Meath, ☎ 041-982-4488. *Open daily May to mid-June 10–5; mid-June to mid-Sept. 9:30–6:60; mid-Sept.–Oct. 10–5. Adults £1.50, seniors £1, students and children 60p. Tours.*

Perched 300 feet above the surrounding countryside, this impressive site has been a pivotal part of Irish history and legend since the late Stone Age when a passage tomb was constructed here. Tara is best known, however, as the seat of early Irish high kings and great open-air assemblies in the early centuries just before and after Christ.

Every three years Tara was the scene of a *feis* (great national assembly), when laws were passed, tribal disputes settled, and matters of peace and defense were decided. By the end of the 6th century, the Tara monarchy had become the most powerful in Ireland. Hence the name of *Tara,*

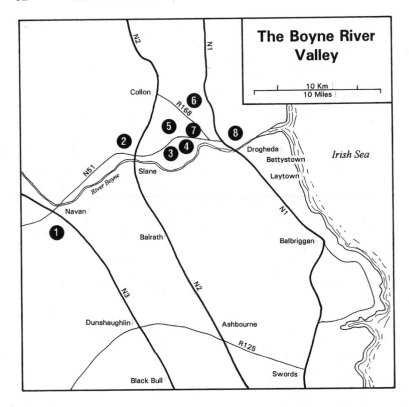

which means "elevated place" or "assembly hill." The words to the famous song, "The harp that once through Tara's halls, the soul of music shed..." still reverberate today.

Tara's fame was also perpetuated by Ireland's patron saint. St. Patrick preached here in the 5th century and used a simple three-leafed shamrock to illustrate the doctrine of the Trinity—and convert High King Laoire and his followers to Christianity. Little remains of Tara's former glory today except grassy mounds and earthworks that were used for ritual and burial purposes. Use your imagination to comprehend the full impact that Tara has had through the ages, or you can watch the audiovisual show called "Tara, Meeting Place of Heroes" shown continuously in the adjacent visitor centre on the grounds.

Continue on to **Slane**, a small crossroads village. It stands at the intersection of the Dublin/Derry and Drogheda/Navan roads, and is a unique example of an 18th-century planned town. The focal point is a group of four almost identical Georgian houses, standing at the four corners of the central intersection. These four houses and the openings to the four roads, make the eight sides of an octagon. Though commonly called the "village square," Slane's octagon is a one-of-a-kind architectural layout in Ireland.

Take a slight detour one mile north of the village to the **Hill of Slane** (2), a lofty 500-foot mound where St. Patrick lit the paschal fire in 433 and proclaimed Christianity throughout all of Ireland. It is not as famous or well-preserved as Tara, but still it is worth a look.

Slane is also the gateway to the passage grave site at Newgrange, considered one of the finest archeological wonders of Western Europe. Turn east on N51 and follow the signposts to:

**BRÚ NA BÓINNE—THE BOYNE VALLEY VISITOR CENTRE** (3), Donore, Co. Meath, ☎ 041-988-0300. *Open daily Mar.–April and Oct. 9:30–5:30; May and mid-Sept. to end-Sept. 9–6:30; June–mid-Sept. 9–7; Nov.–Feb. 9:30–5. Visitor Centre only: Adults £2, seniors £1.50, students and children £1. Visitor Centre & Newgrange: Adults £4, seniors £3, students and children £2. Visitor Centre & Knowth: Adults £3, seniors £2, students and children £1.25. Visitor Centre, Newgrange & Knowth: Adults £7, seniors £5, students and children £3.25. Shop. Café. Tours.*

If you have ever visited Newgrange before, be prepared for big changes on your next visit. And if you haven't visited before, look forward to a dazzling experience—a spectacular new circular rock-trimmed museum built to harmonize with the surroundings. Even the huge parking area is tastefully laid out with trellises and arbors, and stone walkways. The new centre is located two miles off the main N51 (Slane-Drogheda) road and all traffic for Newgrange is directed here, eliminating any direct access.

All visitors must register with the desk personnel for guided tours of Newgrange and in the busy summer months, the wait can be up to three hours for a tour (maximum of 25 persons). However, there is plenty to do at the centre, and some visitors will be satisfied to get their experience of Newgrange indoors and forego the on-site tour (which takes a full hour). The exhibits at the centre, which also take one hour to complete, range from a 7-minute introductory audiovisual to a walk-through replica of Newgrange that includes a simulation of the winter solstice and a thorough explanation of why Newgrange is Ireland's best-known prehistoric monument.

Built between 3500 and 2700 BC, it was used as a tomb in which Stone Age men buried the cremated remains of their dead. It is estimated that it took at least 40 years to build, the equivalent of the life's work of a whole generation. To illustrate its place in world history, scholars point out that Newgrange is 500 years older than the Pyramids, and 1,500 years older than Stonehenge.

If you choose to tour the Newgrange site itself, you will be transported there from the visitor centre by minibus. As you approach, you will see a huge mound made of quartz and granite—36 feet tall, with over 200,000 tons of stone including a 6-ton capstone, and other stones weighing up to 16 tons each. It covers almost one full acre of ground. The guide will take you down into the site itself, to see remnants of stone implements and fine examples of primitive carved stone artwork such as tri-spiral designs as well as chevrons, arcs, radials, and diamonds. Two other prehistoric passage graves are nearby, Knowth and Dowth. Knowth is also open for tours but Dowth is still under excavation.

For a totally different experience nearby, follow signs for:

*NEWGRANGE FARM (4), Slane, Co. Meath, ☎ 041-982-4119. *Open Easter–Aug., daily 10–5. Admission £2.50 per person. Shop. Café. Tours.*

For insight into Ireland's great agricultural heritage, this 330-acre mixed farm is a real gem. Willie and Ann Redhouse and their family welcome visitors to join in the daily chores such as milking the cows, feeding the ducks, bottle-feeding the baby lambs and kid goats, checking on the hatching chicks in the incubator house, or grooming a calf. A walk-around tour takes you through a courtyard to see the hen house, chicken house, rabbit den, dove/pigeon loft, and stables with horses, as well as a working forge and a rural life museum with demonstrations of spinning and making rush candlesticks. Step outside to see exotic pheasants, turkeys and other fowl; as well as sows and piglets, and sheep of all sizes being kept in order by working sheep dogs. In addition, there are horse-drawn farm vehicles, vintage farm machines, crop and wool displays, and an herb garden. To cap your visit, Farmer Willie will take you on a narrated tractor ride tour to see the fields of corn, wheat, oats, and barley, and other far-flung parts of the farm as it slopes down to the waters of the River Boyne. The tractor ride also provides sweeping "insider" views of the adjacent Newgrange prehistoric site, not normally seen from the road. Allow at least two hours for a full tour and to enjoy the indoor coffee shop in an old coach house, outdoor gardens, and picnic areas.

After visiting Newgrange, return to the main (N51) road and take a slight detour toward Collon, to visit two of Ireland's greatest Christian monuments in County Louth:

OLD MELLIFONT ABBEY (5), Collon, Co. Louth, ☎ 041-982-6459. *Open daily May to mid-June and mid-Sept. to end-Oct. 10–5; mid-June to mid-Sept. 9:30–6:30. Adults £1.50, seniors £1, students and children 60p.*

Nestled in the lush County Louth countryside, this peaceful setting beside the Mattock River drew St. Malachy of Armagh to found Ireland's first Cistercian monastery here in 1142. In time it grew so extensively that it became known as "The Big Monastery." Not too much remains of the abbey today, except for remnants of a 14th-century chapter house and several arches of Romanesque design. The most unusual feature is an octagonal lavabo, dating back to c. 1200.

Continue eastward for about two miles until you arrive at an equally impressive site:

**MONASTERBOICE** (6), off N1 (Dublin–Belfast Road), near Collon, Co. Louth (no phone). *Open during daylight hours. No admission charge.* Dating back to the early 6th century, Monasterboice was chosen as a monastic site by St. Buite, but it is best known as the home of a huge monument, known as **Muiredach's Cross.** One of the most perfect specimens of a high cross in Ireland, this 17-foot-tall cross can be traced back to 922. It is ornamented with sculptured panels of Biblical scenes from the Old and New Testaments including a Crucifixion on the west face and a Last Judgment on the east face. The latter is one of the earliest surviving representations of the scene, and also has the most figures in a single scene of any of the Irish high crosses. The west face of the shaft still bears a readable inscription asking for a prayer for a person named Muiredach who had the cross made. The grounds also contain a round tower, two early grave-slabs, and an early Irish sundial.

Return to the main N51 road and drive the remainder of the scenic route between Slane and Drogheda—this is the heart of the historic Boyne River Valley, the setting for the famous *Battle of the Boyne (7)* in 1690.

To finish this historic circuit, take N5 into **Drogheda,** an ancient walled town founded by the Danes in 911. A tableau of stone walls, gates, and churches, Drogheda ranked alongside Dublin and Wexford as a Viking trading center. By the 14th century, it was one of the four principal walled towns in Ireland, and Drogheda continued to prosper until Oliver Cromwell took it by storm in 1649 and massacred its 2,000 inhabitants. Happily, the population has grown to ten times that number today, and the town is a thriving port and industrial center. To learn more about the area, stop into the:

**MILLMOUNT MUSEUM** (8), Duleek St., Drogheda, ☎ 041-983-3097. *Open Mon.–Sat. 10–5 and Sun. 2–5. Admission £2.50 per person. Shop. Café.*
Housed in the courtyard of a 12th-century fort that later became an 18th-century army barracks, this museum presents historical and geological exhibits on Drogheda and the Boyne River Valley. The collections include medieval guild banners and kitchen items ranging from a traditional dresser to smoothing irons, a pot-oven, bellows, and an oil lamp. In addition, there is an industrial room with authentic equipment for spinning and weaving, brewing, shoe- and rope-making, shipbuilding and ironworks, as well as the genealogy center for all of County Louth.
To explore the town in depth, obtain a copy of the *Drogheda Tourist Trail* booklet, and follow the signposts marked "Tourist Trail" throughout the town.
From Drogheda, follow the main N1 road south into Dublin to complete your tour.

# County Kildare—Horse Country

With vast panoramas of open grasslands and limestone-enriched soil, County Kildare is the hub of Ireland's horse-breeding and racing country. Hundreds of stud farms dot the countryside and racing takes place regularly at three Kildare tracks—Punchestown, Naas, and The Curragh, home of the annual Irish Derby.

Check the Irish newspapers to see if a race is on during your visit, or simply come here to learn why Ireland and the horse have always been synonymous—in legend and lifestyle.

## GETTING THERE:

By car, Kildare is an easy drive, about 25 miles west of Dublin. Head west from downtown along the Grand Canal. Follow the signs for the Dublin/Limerick Road (N7), known locally as the Naas Road, one of Ireland's best roadways. It is considered a "dual carriageway" since there are two lanes running in each direction, with overhead bridges, hard shoulders and central dividers. It is Ireland's equivalent of an expressway or superhighway.

## PRACTICALITIES:

If there's a race on in Kildare when you are there, don't miss it! Going to the races is a way of life in Ireland—an integral part of the local lifestyle. Old and young mingle side-by-side at the races. More than a sport, racing is a day's outing—a time to meet friends and make friends and enjoy the fun. Consult the daily newspapers or call in advance to get the details: The Curragh, ☎ 045-441205; Naas Racecourse, ☎ 045-897391; and Punchestown, ☎ 045-897704.

If you go to the races, be prepared for crowds, and lots of walking. Be sure to take all-weather clothing and gear, since seating is limited at some tracks and many of the racing activities, such as betting and watching the horses parade in the ring, take place outside. Cars are usually parked on the grass, and sometimes at great distances away from the entrance gates.

For tourist information, stop into the **Kildare Tourist Office**, Town Square, Kildare, ☎ 045-522696, open from May through mid-September. The telephone area code for Kildare is 045.

## FOOD AND DRINK:

**Lawlors of Naas** (Poplar Square, Naas) A longtime favorite meeting place for trainers, owners, jockeys, and racing fans, this pub/restaurant offers a varied menu of snacks, homemade soups, and seafood including the house special of *Lawlors Fish Smokies*. ☎ 045-897332. ££ to £££

**The Manor Inn** (Main St., Naas) The racing set gathers often at this popular pub/restaurant known for its decor of equestrian pictures and memorabilia. Steaks are a specialty, but the menu also includes a wide array of pub grub, ranging from sandwiches and salads, to burgers, meat pies, omelets, pastas, and smoked fish. ☎ 045-897471. £ to ££

**Red House Inn** (Main Street, Newbridge) An Old World ambiance prevails at this restaurant known for its fine French and Continental cuisine as well as some traditional Irish favorites like colcannon. Open for dinner only, except lunch on Sunday. ☎ 045-431657. X: Mon. ££ to £££

**Silken Thomas** (The Square, Kildare) With an open fireplace and a decor of dark woods and brass, this historic pub/restaurant is named after a famous character in local history who led an unsuccessful rebellion against England. The menu features a blend of continental cuisine and Irish mixed grills, roasts, and fresh seafood platters. ☎ 045-521695. £ to ££

**SUGGESTED TOUR:**

Start your tour from **Dublin** (1) heading west via N7, often called the Naas Road, a swift and modern highway which bypasses many small towns. After traveling 21 miles, you will see signs for **Naas** (pronounced *Nay-se*), the chief town of County Kildare, and you may wish to get off the main road and take a slight detour through Naas. An ancient town that was one of the royal seats of the province of Leinster, Naas takes its name from the Irish *Nás na Ríogh,* meaning "the assembly place of the kings." It is said that Naas was the residence of local royalty and a great meeting place until the 10th century. Today Naas is a busy market town and little remains from those early glory days. The town's prime claim to fame is that it is home to two racetracks, the **Naas Racecourse** (2), for flat racing, and **Punchestown Racecourse** (3), a steeplechase track famed as the venue for the three-day Irish National Hunt Festival Races each April.

Continue for eight miles more and you will come to the town of **Newbridge**, often referred to in maps and books as *An Droichead Nua,* which literally means "the new bridge" in the Irish language. Situated at the crossing point of the Naas-Kildare road and the River Liffey, Newbridge is a small manufacturing town best known as the home of **Newbridge Cutlery** (4), Cutlery Rd., off the Dublin/Limerick Rd. (N7), Newbridge, ☎ 045-431301, one of Ireland's leading manufacturers of silverware for the past 60 years. The showrooms present a display of silver place settings, bowls, candelabras, trays, frames, and one-of-a-kind items. There is also a video on silver-making, a craft that has been practiced in the area since the time of Ireland's high kings. *Open Mon.–Fri. 9–5, Sat. 11–5, Sun. 2–5. Admission is free.*

Continue your drive for almost four miles and suddenly—appearing

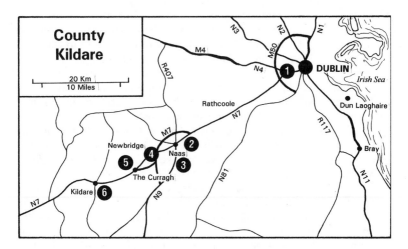

on both sides of the road—you will see the vast open spread of grasslands known as **\*The Curragh**, the largest area of arable land in the country (5,000 acres). In 1994, Mel Gibson used this panoramic expanse to stage some of the battle scenes in his movie, *Braveheart*. Even though the film was set in Scotland, the Irish scenery proved the perfect backdrop to re-create the sights and sounds of early Scotland.

On the north side of the road, you will see **The Curragh Racetrack** (5), famed as the "Churchill Downs of Ireland." It is one of Ireland's largest and most modern racetracks, the home of the annual Irish Derby and many other classic races throughout the year. In just over one mile, you will come to the town of **Kildare**, honored as the birthplace of St. Brigid, Ireland's second patron saint after Patrick. It is said that Brigid, who lived in the 5th or 6th century, made a lasting contribution to "women's lib" by founding a Kildare monastery that held the unique distinction of being a "double monastery"—one part for nuns, one part for monks, ruled jointly and equally by an abbess and abbot-bishop. The placename of Kildare comes from the Irish language *Cill Dara*, meaning "church of the oak"— the traditional location of St.Brigid's foundation in a sacred grove of oak trees. Above all, Kildare is distinguished as the epicenter of the Irish horse-breeding industry. To learn more about Ireland's equestrian endeavors, take a left at the town square and go for one mile southeast along a well-signposted route to the:

**\*IRISH NATIONAL STUD** (6), Tully, ☎ 045-521617. *Open Feb. 12 to Nov. 12, daily 9:30–6. Adults £6, seniors, students, and children over age 12 £4.50, children under age 12 £3. Shop. Café. Tours.*

Horses and more horses are the focus of this sprawling national stud farm, set on 958 acres of prime grasslands. It was established in 1945 to provide a government-sponsored prototype of ideal horse farm conditions for others to emulate throughout the land. Some of Ireland's most famous horses have been bred and raised on these grounds, and visitors are welcome to watch the horses being exercised and groomed.

A tour, which takes approximately 40 minutes to an hour, includes a visit to the Sun Chariot Yard which houses the mares and foals, the Foaling Unit, the Stallion Paddocks, Saddler Shop, and the Forge. In addition, there are two walks, *The Oak Walk*, which runs along the stallion paddocks, and *The Tully Walk* beside the mares' paddocks. From mid-spring to mid-autumn, mares and foals run freely in the verdant grassy enclosures. A converted groom's house serves as the setting for a horse museum with exhibits on equine pursuits in Ireland from the Bronze Age to the present. There are also displays of horses in transport, racing, steeplechasing, hunting, and show jumping, plus a skeleton of Arkle, one of Ireland's most famous equine heroes.

A visit here includes admission to the adjacent **Japanese Gardens**, laid out between 1906 and 1910 by the Japanese gardener Tassa Eida, to symbolize the Life of Man in 20 different stages from Oblivion to Eternity. The gardens, which are considered among the finest in Europe, include cherry blossoms, bonsai trees, and other exotic plantings, as well as a tea house and a miniature Japanese village.

Entrance to the National Stud is through a visitor center built in the style of a Japanese country inn. Facilities include a wide-windowed and skylit restaurant that has an outside deck overlooking the gardens. Even if your interest in horses is minimal, it is worth the drive to Kildare just to relax in this serene setting.

The newest development on the grounds of the Irish National Stud is an attraction in itself and well-worth some extra time—**St. Fiachra's Garden**, named in honor of the 6th-century Irish monk who is the patron saint of gardeners. This garden is a natural oasis of woodlands, waterfalls, and wetlands, along with aquatic plants, islands, and greenery of all types.

Designed to re-create the serene environment of Ireland of monastic times, the layout includes a sunken oak forest, filled with 5,000-year-old bog oak from the Bog of Allen; 1,200 tons of rocks and bolders from the west of Ireland; a splendid statue of St. Fiachra seated on a lakeside peninsula; and three replicas of early monastic cells or beehive huts.

Within the main cell is a unique flood-lit subterranean garden, featuring glass-shaped rocks and plants such as ferns and orchids, lit by fiber optics and fashioned as a Millennium centerpiece by Waterford Crystal. Allow at least an hour or more to walk and wander, reflect and relish. Admission to the garden is included in the general admission price of the Irish National Stud.

It's hard to imagine that it's only a 40-minute drive back to Dublin!

# *County Wicklow—
# The Garden of Ireland

Located directly south of Dublin, County Wicklow is nature at its best. Aptly described as "The Garden of Ireland," it offers a blend of verdant coastal and mountain scenery, quiet country lanes and tree-shaded walking trails, flower-filled glens and meandering rivers, sloping hills and sandy seascapes—all within a short drive from Dublin. Even the placenames of County Wicklow sound alluring—from Lugnaquilla and Lough Luggala, to Sally Gap, Devil's Punch Bowl, Glenmalure, and Glen of the Downs, as well as a host of villages with melodic names such as Annamoe, Enniskerry, Laragh, Ballinlea, Baltinglass, Glencree, Rathnew, and Shillelagh.

In addition to its incomparable scenery, Co. Wicklow presents a host of other sightseeing and cultural attractions, each worth a visit in its own right, from the 6th-century monastic settlement of St. Kevin at Glendalough, and historic 18th- and 19th-century country manors and estates, to the storied Vale of Avoca, literary setting for the poetry of Thomas Moore.

## GETTING THERE:

County Wicklow starts where County Dublin ends, just 12 miles south of Dublin City center. By car, take the wide main road (N11) south from Dublin, and then follow the signs for Enniskerry.

If you prefer not to drive, the best way to see the sights is to take an escorted sightseeing tour of the region. From April through October, the following companies operate half-day and full-day tours from Dublin to Glendalough and County Wicklow:

**Bus Eireann**, Busaras/Central Bus Station, ☎ 01-836-6111.

**Gray Line Tours**, Dublin Tourism Office, Suffolk St., ☎ 01-605-7705.

## PRACTICALITIES:

For travel information, contact the **Wicklow Tourist Office**, Fitzwilliam Square, Wicklow, ☎ 0404-69117, open June to September. In addition, there are seasonal tourist offices in these towns: Arklow, ☎ 0402-32484, open from May to October; and Glendalough, ☎ 0404-45688, open June to September.

The majority of telephone numbers in County Wicklow use the area code of 0404. However, some numbers that are close to Dublin use the 01 area code and a few others use the 0402 code. Unless shown otherwise, assume that numbers given belong to the 0404 area code.

Because of its proximity to Dublin, County Wicklow is at its busiest on weekends, particularly on Sunday afternoons, when it's customary for Dubliners "to take a drive in the country" after lunch. Try to time your visit for weekdays, to avoid crowded roads and long lines at attractions.

## FOOD AND DRINK:

**Cartoon Inn** (Main St., Rathdrum) Have a laugh or a chuckle as you enjoy homemade soups, sandwiches, and other light refreshments at this humor-themed pub. The walls are lined with the works of many leading Irish and international cartoonists. ☎ 46774. £

**The Coach House** (Main St., Roundwood) It's hard to pass this 1790's pub by without a drink or at least a photograph—the Tudor-style facade is adorned with baskets filled with colorful flowers. The interior is just as enticing - full of local memorabilia and antiques. Soups, sandwiches, and other light meals are served. ☎ 01-281-8157. £

**The Meetings** (at the Vale of Avoca, Avoca) Situated beside the storied "Meeting of the Waters" which inspired poet Thomas Moore, this Tudor-style pub is decorated with Moore memorabilia and other local treasures. Soups, salads, sandwiches, and other pub grub are on the menu and there is often traditional Irish music or an open-air *ceili* on weekends. ☎ 0402-35226. £

**Mitchell's** (Main St., Laragh) Housed in a former schoolhouse on the edge of town, this restaurant has a country kitchen ambiance with pine furniture, beamed ceilings, leaded window panes, and open fireplaces. The menu includes specialties such as bacon and cabbage, rack of Wicklow lamb, or roulade of chicken and smoked salmon. All breads and scones are made on the premises, as is the ice cream. ☎ 54302. £ to ££

**Roundwood Inn** (Main St., Roundwood) Antique furnishings, wooden floors, and open fireplaces add to the atmosphere of this 1750's coaching inn, known for its international cuisine with a German slant, ranging from Irish stew, Galway Bay oysters, and local lobster to weiner schnitzel, Hungarian goulash, pickled herrings, and gravlax. X: Mon. ☎ 01-281-8107. ££

## SUGGESTED TOUR:

Take the wide main road (N11) south from Dublin toward **Bray** (1), a popular seaside resort with a mile-long beach and esplanade. Just before you reach Bray, a well-signposted turn-off to the right will put you on the road to Enniskerry. **Enniskerry** is a beautiful little village set in a wooded hollow among the hills. Once you reach Enniskerry, follow the signs for one mile further south, to the:

**\*POWERSCOURT HOUSE & GARDENS** (2), Enniskerry, ☎ 204-6000. *Open daily March–Oct., 9:30–5:30; Nov.–Feb., 9:30–dusk. Adults £5, seniors and*

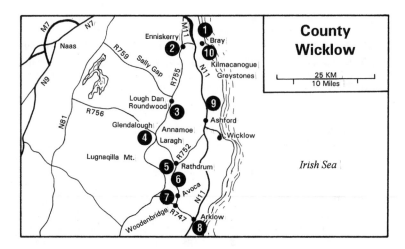

*students £4.50, children under 12 £3. Shop. Café. Tours.*

For almost 60 years, this 47-acre garden has been the epitome of County Wicklow's reputation as the home of Ireland's most beautiful and lush greenery. It is a fine example of an aristocratic garden with Italian and Japanese themes, plus herbaceous borders, ornamental lakes, splendid statuary, and decorative ironwork. In addition, the grounds hold a pet cemetery, a wildlife park, and a waterfall, the highest in Britain and Ireland, which tumbles downward from a 400-foot high cliff.

In recent years, the stately 18th-century Georgian-style house has been restored and re-opened to the public, adding a new dimension to a visit and making Powerscourt a truly all-weather attraction. The house offers a range of activities, from continuous audiovisuals and exhibits on the history and development of the house and gardens, to guided tours of the restored ballroom. For shoppers, there is an 11-unit craft center, offering knitwear, books, stationery, pottery, glass, cashmere, jewelry, and more, with many items designed specifically with a Powerscourt label. The restaurant, located in the original kitchen of the house, is divided into two sections—a fish bar and a café bar, with extensive indoor seating amid a sky-blue interior and outdoor setting on a large terrace.

Next head south for 10 miles over the mountains to **Roundwood**, reputed to be the highest village in Ireland (over 700 feet above sea level). Roundwood is home to a couple of atmospheric 17th-century inns, each worth a stop for a meal or light refreshment. On Sundays, the village hosts the **Roundwood Home Market** (3), an indoor gathering featuring an array of locally-made crafts from sweaters, woolens, and crochet-work to paintings, as well as preserves and baked goods. *Market open Sun. 2–5, admission is free.*

From Roundwood, continue southward on this winding mountain road, passing Lough Dan and the Wicklow Gap on your right, for nine miles to **Laragh**, at the junction of the Annamoe Valley, the Clara Valley, and Glendalough, Glendasan, Glenmacnass—a meeting place of roads that traverse some of the most scenic areas of County Wicklow. Follow the signposts for one mile to the most celebrated site within all of these directions:

**\*GLENDALOUGH VISITOR CENTRE** (4), Glendalough, ☎ 45325. *Open daily, mid-Oct. to mid-March 9:30–5; mid-March to end-May and Sept. to mid-Oct. 9:30–6; June–Aug. 9–6:30. Adults £2, seniors, £1.50, students/children £1. Shop. Tours.*

What was Ireland like during the "Golden Age of Saints and Scholars?" Thousands of visitors flock here every day to learn the answer to that question. Nestled in a glaciated valley between the Upper Lake and the Lower Lake of Wicklow Mountain National Park, Glendalough has a well-chosen name. In the Irish language, *Gleann Dá Loch* literally means "valley of (the) two lakes." It was here in the 6th century that St. Kevin founded a monastery that would become a leading center of learning for all of Europe, with thousands of students from Ireland, Britain, and the continent. Glendalough flourished until the 15th century, when it was plundered by Anglo-Norman invaders.

Although much of the monastic city is in ruins today, the site includes a visitor interpretative center with exhibits and an audiovisual that tell the story of St. Kevin and his many successor-abbots including St. Lawrence O'Toole. Tours of the grounds will show you the remains of a nearly perfect 103-foot round tower, hundreds of hand-carved Celtic crosses, and a variety of churches including St. Kevin's own chapel, a fine specimen of an early Irish barrel-vaunted oratory with a miniature round belfry.

Return to Laragh, and then head southward through the scenic wooded valley known as the **Vale of Clara**. Look west for expansive views of **Lugnaquilla Mountain** (3,039 feet), the third-highest mountain in Ireland, and the tallest outside of County Kerry. For a change of pace or to stretch your legs, stop for a while at **Rathdrum**, a village perched above the Avonmore River. Continue 1.5 miles south of the village to visit one of County Wicklow's historic houses:

**AVONDALE HOUSE AND FOREST PARK** (5), Rathdrum, ☎ 46111. *House: open Feb.–Nov., daily 11–6. Adults £3, seniors £2.50, students £1.75, and children under 12 £1.50. Grounds: open daily daylight hours. Admission is £1 per car. Café. Shop.*

Set beside the Avonmore River, Avondale is the birthplace and former home of Charles Stewart Parnell (1846-91), one of Ireland's great political leaders and affectionately called "the uncrowned king of Ireland." The house, built in 1779, is filled with Parnell memorabilia and furnishings. The main attraction is the surrounding 500-acre estate, with an internationally acclaimed arboretum, forest walks, and sign-posted nature trails. Developed as a training school for the Irish Forest and Wildlife Service, the park is considered as the catalyst and testing ground of modern Irish forestry.

This route continues south for 3.5 more miles, to the point where the Avonmore River meets the Avonbeg River to form the Avoca River—described idyllically as **The Meeting of the Waters** (6) by the 19th-century poet Thomas Moore. A lone tree, well-picked by souvenir hunters over the years, still stands on the spot where Moore is said to have spent long hours looking for inspiration before he finally penned the oft-sung words: *"There is not in this wide world a valley so sweet, as the vale in whose bosom the bright waters meet...."* The adjacent pub, known as **The Meetings** displays an interesting collection of Moore memorabilia including an 1889 edition of the poet's best works.

Follow the Avoca River for less than a mile south into the village of **Avoca**, crossing over the bridge to visit one of Ireland's oldest enterprises:

**\*AVOCA  HANDWEAVERS** (7), Avoca, ☎ 0402-35105. *Open  Mon.–Fri. 9:30–5:30, Sat.–Sun. 10–6. Admission is free. Shop. Café. Tours.*

See colorful hand-woven tweeds "in the making" at Avoca Handweavers, the oldest handweaving company in Ireland, dating back to 1723. Housed in a cluster of white-washed stone buildings, this enterprise invites visitors to take a walk-through tour to observe all stages of production—from wool preparation, spinning, carding, and dyeing, to the actual weaving process. The adjacent mill shop stocks the results—travel rugs, blankets, bedspreads, cushion covers, stoles, suits, coats, jackets, ponchos, and hats. Although all colors are available, the predominant tones of mauve, aqua, teal, and heather, are much in demand, often perceived as a reflection of the landscape of the surrounding countryside.

From Avoca, continue approximately five miles south via Woodenbridge and east to **Arklow** (8), a fishing port dating back to Viking times and long known for the building of small wooden ships.

From Arklow, follow the main road (N11) north back to Dublin via **Wicklow**, the chief town of the county and a small seaport and seaside resort at the mouth of the River Vartry. Less than four miles north is one of the area's great horticultural attractions:

**MOUNT USHER GARDENS** (9), Ashford, ☎ 40116. *Open daily mid-March to early-Nov. 10:30–6. Adults £3.50, seniors, students, and children £2.50. Shop. Café.*

For garden enthusiasts, this is a "must-stop." Set on 20 acres beside the River Vartry, Mount Usher is a paradise of over 5,000 types of plants, trees, and shrubs from all over the world, blending familiar species such as rhododendrons, magnolias, camellias, eucalyptus, and palms, with the exotic, such as Burmese jumpers, Chinese spindles, and North American swamp cypress. One of the best examples of a romantic Robinsonian garden, Mount Usher dates back to 1886. Water plays an essential part of the layout, with cascades and bridges, visible in just about every section.

From **Ashford**, the main road wends its way via towns with fanciful tongue-twister names like Newtownmountkennedy and Kilmacanogue and views of the **\*Great Sugar Loaf Mountain** (1,659 feet), toward Bray. Before completing your tour, you may wish to stop at another of County Wicklow's great houses, situated one mile south of Bray:

**KILLRUDDERY HOUSE & GARDENS** (10), Killruddery, Bray, ☎ 01-286-2777. *Open (House) May, June, and Sept. and (Gardens) April–Sept., daily 1–5 and by appointment. House & Gardens: Adults £4, seniors and students over age 12 £2.50; Gardens only: Adults £2, seniors and students over age 12 £1.50.*

Picturesquely ensconced between Bray Head and the Little Sugar Loaf Mountain (1,120 feet), this bucolic setting has been the seat of the Earl of Meath since 1818. The original part of the house dates back to 1820, with many additions including a 19th-century Victorian Conservatory that was modeled after the Crystal Palace in London. The gardens are even older, dating back to the 1680s, laid out in French style. The core of the garden is a pair of canals that connect the house at one end and an avenue of lime trees at the other. On one side, there is a series of radiating walks flanked by hedges of beech, hornbeam, and lime. On the other is a sylvan theater and a great circular pool enclosed by high hedges. The tableau is completed by an extensive natural rock garden.

Follow the main road (N11) back to Dublin, or take the scenic seafront route along Dublin Bay via the suburbs of Killiney, Dalkey, Dun Laoghaire (see page 82).

**Trip 11**

# Dublin's Fair City – Smart Shoppers' Tour

As the capital of Ireland, Dublin is an alluring shopping mecca, offering products from all over the Emerald Isle as well as many fine European goods.

Although there are great shopping opportunities throughout the entire city centre and its environs, the focal point of this tour is the Grafton Street area, between Trinity College and St. Stephen's Green. This area has more shops per square foot than any other real estate in the capital—and requires the least amount of walking for you, the visitor. We'll also suggest a short detour, for those who don't mind a few extra steps to seek out something not found elsewhere along the route.

**GETTING THERE:**

Located on Dublin's south side, the Grafton Street area is easily accessible. All cross-town buses stop at or near Trinity College, at the north end of Grafton Street. Dublin Bus's "Hop-On/Hop-Off Bus" also has stops at three points along this tour route—the Dublin Tourism Office, Trinity College, and St. Stephen's Green.

**GETTING AROUND:**

Because the scope of this tour is so compact and Grafton Street itself is pedestrianized, walking is the only way to follow the route.

**PRACTICALITIES:**

Unless you are only interested in window shopping, the best time to follow this tour is during normal shopping hours, usually 9 a.m. or 9:30 a.m. to 5:30 p.m. or 6 p.m., Monday through Saturday, except for Thursday when most shops stay open until 8 p.m. An increasing number of shops is also offering Sunday shopping hours, usually 11 a.m. or 12 noon until 5 p.m., especially in the months of April through December. In the peak summer months (June–August), shops that are geared particularly to tourists also stay open late on most weekday nights.

For tourist information, visit the **Dublin Tourism Office**, Suffolk St., Dublin, ☎ 01-605-7700, located one block west of Grafton Street.

The telephone area code for all numbers in this tour is 01.

## FOOD AND DRINK:

**AYA @ Brown Thomas** (48 Clarendon St.), located at the rear of the famous Brown Thomas department store, is no ordinary in-store café—it is instead a contemporary sushi bar and restaurant, with the finest of modern Japanese cuisine. There is also a deli for "orders to go" for picnickers or shoppers in a hurry. ☎ 677-1544. X: Sun. £ to ££

**Butler's Chocolate Café** (24 Wicklow St.), run by the famous Irish Chocolate company of the same name, is perfect for a snack or pick-me-up in the midst of shopping. The menu is sheer heaven for chocolate lovers—fudge shakes, cakes, brownies, truffles, and dozens of varieties of handmade chocolates. Beverages range from sinfully rich hot chocolate to coffee, tea, or cappuccino. ☎ 671-0591. £

**Café en Seine** (40 Dawson St.) is one of Europe's longest coffee bars, with a continental ambiance, making it popular with students and young professionals. Besides coffee and pastries all day, the menu offers an appealing variety of quiches, pastas, and salads. Brunch is available on Sundays with live jazz. ☎ 677-4369. £ to ££

**Captain America's Cookhouse & Bar** (44 Grafton St.), has been a fixture on Dublin's main shopping street since 1971. The menu offers over a dozen varieties of burgers plus steaks, Cajun chicken, and vegetarian dishes. The décor includes an eye-catching display of rock and roll and movie memorabilia, including guitars signed by U2 and Van Morrison and Debbie Harry's shoes. ☎   671-5266. £ to ££

**Dail Bia** (46 Kildare St.) is Dublin's first Irish-language café, serving breakfast lunch and evening early meals amid the soft tones of Gaelic chatter. The menu features wholesome and organic foods, such as marmalade scones, meusli rockbuns, salads, and baguettes freshly baked on the premises, as well as specialty dishes such as seafood bake, creamed turnip, or stuffed onions with spinach and parmesan. ☎ 670-6079. X: Sun. £ to ££

**Kilkenny Café & Restaurant** (5–6 Nassau St.) is situated on the 1st floor of the Kilkenny Shop, overlooking the playing fields of Trinity College. The self-service menu offers modern Irish and traditional Irish cuisine such as homemade soups, salads, quiches, casseroles, home-baked breads and cakes. Traditional lamb stew is a specialty. ☎ 677-7066. X; Sun. £

**Juice** (73 S. Gt. George's St.) If you crave freshly squeezed fruit and vegetable juices, this place is the answer. All kinds of juices are squeezed to order. The food menu presents an ever-changing array of fresh and modern vegetarian dishes. ☎ 475-7856. £ to ££

**Planet Cyber Café** (23 S. Gt. George's St.). If you are anxious to keep in touch with your e-mail or surf the Internet while shopping, this is a convenient stop. You can also enjoy sandwiches, coffee, and other light snacks while at the computer. ☎ 679-0583. £

## SUGGESTED TOUR:

Start this tour at the Dublin Tourism Office, Suffolk St., just a block

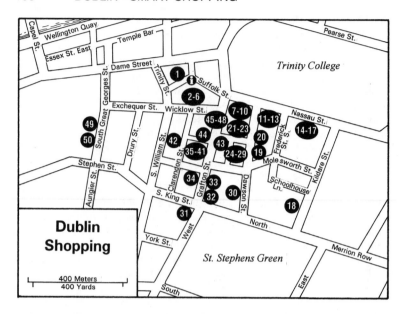

**Dublin Shopping**

400 Meters
400 Yards

west of Trinity College. From the front entrance of the Tourism Office, turn left and enter Andrew St. If you are interested in antique costume jewelry, stop into **Rhinestones** (1), 18 St. Andrew St., ☎ 679-0759. The wares range from Victorian and Art Deco jewelry, to American designer pieces and Mexican 1930's silver, as well as European art glass.

Continue for one short block to Wicklow St., and turn left. On the left is the **Sheepskin Shop** (2), 20 Wicklow St., ☎ 671-9585, a long-established shop that specializes in sheepskin, lambskin, leather, and suede clothing for men and women. They also operate a repair and alteration service.

Next is **Louis Copeland & Sons** (3), Burberry House, 18/19 Wicklow St., ☎ 677-7038), a master tailor for men, if you are staying for a few days and have time for several fittings. The racks also offer an unrivaled selection of gents' quality ready-to-wear suits.

A few doors on is **Past Times** (4), 13 Wicklow St., ☎ 671-7477, a unique shop featuring gifts and home accessories with Victorian, medieval, and Celtic themes. The assortment ranges from jewelry and clothing, to frames, posters, tableware, games, mugs, books, paper goods, baby gifts, stained glass, statuary, and music CDs.

For a colorful array of modern Irish sweaters, continue to The **Sweater Shop** (5), 9 Wicklow St., ☎ 671-3270, known as the "sweater specialists" for soft wool and cotton knitwear. All colors, sizes, and styles are on display.

As Wicklow St. comes to an end, you will see a landmark store, dating back to 1869—**Weir & Sons** (6), 3 Wicklow St. at 96–99 Grafton St., ☎ 677-9678. It's "the place" to go for new and antique jewelry and watches, as well as silver, china, and glass.

Straight ahead is **Grafton Street**, a complete shopping experience in itself. But before you enter the bustling shopping milieu of Grafton Street, turn first to the left, with the bronze statue of "Molly Malone" before you. With Molly as your landmark, walk to the corner facing Trinity College and make a fast right onto **Nassau Street**, another prime shopping street in Dublin. This street is popular because it faces the grounds of Trinity College, so many tour buses park along this thoroughfare and discharge their passengers to view the attractions of Trinity (on the left side) and, of course, to stroll along Nassau Street (on the right side) and shop.

One of the first shopfronts you'll see on Nassau Street is a familiar (and useful) one—**American Express Foreign Exchange** at 41 Nassau Street; make a visit here especially if you need to change some currency or cash a traveler's cheque.

Next door is **Monaghan's Cashmere Store** (7) 40 Nassau St., ☎ 679-4011, a branch of the original Monaghan's around the corner in the Grafton Arcade (see the Grafton Street section later in this tour). This store specializes in stylish cashmere sweaters and other fashionable woolen wear for women. Although the prices aren't cheap, it's the best place to go when cashmere is on your shopping list. Adjacent is **Kennedy & McSharry** (8), 39 Nassau St., ☎ 677-8770, a men's ready-to-wear shop established in 1890. It offers a wide range of jackets, suits and overcoats in cashmere, pure wool, and Donegal tweed including the famous Magee label, as well as formal and casual wear, including shirts, ties, gloves, scarves, hats, and caps.

One of Dublin's smallest specialist shops is **The Pen Shop** (9), 36 Nassau St., ☎ 679-1633, chock full of writing instruments of all sizes and types. It has been a reliable fixture here since 1935, but look out for it—it is so small, you could easily miss it!

Next is a shop that you surely won't miss—a large wrap-around establishment that occupies two full stores—**House of Ireland** (10), 35 Nassau St. at Dawson St. ☎ 679-5666. It is a well-known emporium for Irish and European high quality products—from designer fashions and linens to Waterford, Wedgwood, Belleek, and Lladro as well as all types of souvenirs.

From House of Ireland, cross over Dawson Street and continue eastward along Nassau Street. The next shop of particular interest is **Kevin & Howlin** (11), 33 Nassau St. ☎ 677-0257, is often referred to as a "tweed heaven" by men and women in search of fine Donegal tweed suits, overcoats, jackets, ties, and hats/caps. Tweed is also sold by the yard or metre. It's been pleasing customers for over 50 years.

Continue a few more doors to **Hanna's Bookshop** (12), 27–29 Nassau St., ☎ 677-1255, a shop favored by students and professors of Trinity College in search of academic texts, as well as new, used, and antiquarian volumes on all topics. There are strong sections on art, architecture, and "Irish Interests," as well as a paperback area.

The next shop of general interest is a branch of the famous Co. Cork institution of the same name, **Blarney Woollen Mills** (13), 21 Nassau St., ☎ 671-0068, offering a wide range of Irish hand-knit sweaters and other woollens at hard-to-beat prices, as well as gifts and souvenirs.

Cross over S. Frederick Street and on the facing corner is **Knobs & Knockers** (14), 19 Nassau St. ☎ 671-0288, an ironmonger's studio of quality European goods, trading on this spot since1972. It's the ideal place to shop if you find yourself enamored by the polished brass door knockers (particularly the Claddagh design) on the Georgian doors of Fitzwilliam St. or Merrion Square. The wares also include brassy door knobs and handles, Victorian cupboard knobs, and a large assortment of decorative furniture hardware.

The three remaining shops of interest along Nassau Street come in rapid succession. First you will see **Celtic Note** (15), 14–15 Nassau Street, ☎ 670-4157, known as "the home of Irish music" and a top source for thousands of Irish music CDs and cassette tapes.

The **Kilkenny Shop** (16), 6–10 Nassau St., ☎ 677-7066, is an outstanding showcase of Irish-made products, drawn from over 200 Irish companies and craftspeople. The wares range from the cream of Irish pottery, earthenware, ceramics and glassware, to hand-turned wood, handmade leather goods, jewelry, knitwear, and clothing from leading Irish designers such as Magee, Michael Mortell, Paul Costelloe, and Pat McCarthy. You'll also find unique gift items, kitchen accessories, candles, and creative stationery. It's a treasure-trove not to be missed!

Do you have Irish roots? Then you can't pass by the door of **Heraldic Artists** (17), 3 Nassau St., ☎ 679-5313, specializing in tracking down your ancestry and providing family trees, hand-painted coasts of arms, heraldic crests, and books on heraldry.

After Heraldic Artists, continue to the corner and make a right turn onto Kildare Street. This street is an important site of government buildings including the Office of the Chief Herald, the National Library, and the National Museum (see "Dublin—The South Side" daytrip for full details of these sites). Continue south on Kildare Street and on the right side, you will come to a gem of a shop known simply as **Cleo** (18), 18 Kildare St. ☎ 676-1421. For over 50 years (and three generations of the Joyce family), this shop has distinguished itself as a trendsetter for stylish traditional and contemporary Irish clothing for men and women, using natural Irish fibers of wool and linen. Proprietor Kitty Joyce aims to provide unique designer ready-to-wear fashions in patterns and colors not found anywhere else—often referred to a "wearable art." The goods range from poet shirts and grandfather shirts, Munster cloaks, and deerstalker hats to fishermen's waistcoats and trousers and traditional farmers' coats, as well as clothing inspired by the Aran Islands—hand-knit pullovers and jackets, crios, cuffed and tassel hats, and wool wraps.

After Cleo, you now approach St. Stephen's Green North. To the left is the revered Shelbourne Hotel. Take a right turn to continue the shopping tour, following St. Stephen's Green North for one block and you will come to Dawson Street. Turn right (a north direction) onto Dawson Street. The right side of the street is dominated by two impressive buildings— 18th century St. Anne's Church and the Mansion House, home of Dublin's Lord Mayor (not open to the public). Walk along until you come to the intersection of Molesworth Street. On the corner is a small book store that is popular with fans of mysteries and whodunits—**Murder Ink** (19), 15 Dawson St., ☎ 677-7570.

Continue toward the north end of Dawson and you will encounter one of Dublin's largest bookshops, **Waterstone's** (20), 7 Dawson St., ☎ 679-1415, a British-owned store know for its books on Irish topics. This large two-story store offers an amazing cross section of titles on art, antiques, biography, the classics, crime, gay literature, health, new age, religion, sport, travel, women's studies, and wine.

At the end of the street, cross over to the left side and retrace your route to the south end of Dawson. Along the way, you'll encounter a variety of fine shops, starting with **O'Farrell Workshops** (21), 62 Dawson St., ☎ 677-0862, a leader in Irish craftwork for over 40 years. The shelves are filled with unique hand-made crafts inspired by designs from the 5th to 15th centuries—from "Book of Kells" art to beaten copper wall hangings and brass door knockers, not to mention elegant stationery, posters, wall hangings, and handmade dolls and animals.

A few doors down is **Hodges Figgis** (22), 56-58 Dawson St., ☎ 677-4754, one of Europe's largest bookstores, established in 1768. It offers three floors of books including general literature and children's literature, but with a special proclivity for Irish and Celtic literature.

Continuing south, on the right side, Dawson Street is intersected by Duke Street. You may wish to take a detour of a few steps to **Cathach Books** (23), 10 Duke St., ☎ 671-8676, specialists in rare and antiquarian books, signed and first editions of Ireland's greatest writers, original maps, and prints.

Next major shopping point is the **Royal Hibernian Way** (24), 49–50 Dawson St., a courtyard cluster of shops standing on the site of the old *Royal Hibernian Hotel*. This ground level shopping mall houses about a dozen elegant stores and specialty boutiques, including **Monaghan's Men's Shop** (25) (☎ 677-0823), for top class men's sportswear; **The Custom Shop** (26) (☎ 677-4090) for classic and casual shirts both on the rack in made to order; and **Leonidas** (27) (☎ 679-5915), maker of handmade chocolates.

After this complex, on the corner is **Louis Mulcahy** (28), 46 Dawson Street, ☎ 662-8787. This is the Dublin sales outlet for a Dingle, County Kerry-based potter who has been producing colorful hand-thrown pottery since 1975. The wares include vases, platters, teapots, lamps, and doorknobs, all ideal as souvenirs, especially if your travels won't take you as far as Kerry.

At this corner, on the right, Anne Street intersects with Dawson Street. A short detour onto Anne Street will take you to a cluster of shops known for antiques and jewelry including **J. Byrne & Sons** (29), 23 S. Anne St. ☎ 671-8709, a specialist in diamond rings and quality souvenirs.

Returning to Dawson Street, next is an enchanting little shop that is favored by knitters and needle workers—Needle Craft (30), 27–28 Dawson St., ☎ 677-2493. If you want to knit your own Aran sweater, this is the ideal store to buy wool, buttons, stitching patterns, and accessories.

Next, on the corner, as Dawson Street ends, is the main Dublin City office of Aer Lingus, if you need help with airline arrangements.

This route has brought you back to St. Stephen's Green North; turn right and walk toward the **St. Stephen's Green Shopping Centre** (31) ☎ 478-0888, a large domed glass building in grand Victorian style. This Dublin city's largest shopping centre, with a wide array of shops, offering everything from tee-shirts and post cards, to hats, jewelry, clothing, and ice cream, as well as a branch of **Dunne's Stores**, one of the largest all-purpose chains in Ireland.

Directly in front of this shopping centre is the south end of Grafton Street, Dublin's prime shopping thoroughfare, often referred to as the "Fifth Avenue" of Dublin. By day it is a fully pedestrianized area that is ideal for strolling and browsing. The street is often lined with "buskers" (street musicians) who provide impromptu entertainment. Since it is pedestrianized, you can literally walk in the middle of the street, turning right or left as your shopping pattern requires. Even though I am providing street numbers in most cases, do not be perplexed if you can't see a number outside a door. Most Dubliners rarely use street numbers along Grafton Street, so if you get lost, just ask for the shop itself, rather than a number.

As you start to stroll, immediately to your right is a tempting little shop—**Butler's Handmade Chocolates** (32) 51A Grafton St., ☎ 671-0599, founded in 1932 by Mrs. Bailey-Butler, first and foremost chocolatier in Ireland. The goodies are handmade, using the finest chocolate with fresh Irish cream, butter, and eggs. The confections include fresh cream truffles, filled with famous Irish flavors such as *Baileys, Irish Mist, Jameson,* and *Irish Coffee*. Other tempting treats range from milk, dark, and white chocolate, to pralines, peppermint creams and fudges. Ice cream cones, made with Butler's ice creams, are also offered on warm summer days.

Next on the right is a landmark shop for fine men's wear—**F.X. Kelly** (33), 48 Grafton St. (☎ 677-8211). The stock includes designer names, with an emphasis on conventional clothing as well as creased-linen suits, painted ties, and trendy sportswear such as soft leather jackets. Almost across the street on the left is **Laura Ashley** (34), 60 Grafton St. (☎ 679-5433), a branch of the famous English designer products, offering a full selection of women's and children's clothes, home furnishings, and accessories.

Continue northward until you come to Harry Street and turn left into a small half-street that leads to the fashionable Hotel Westbury, Dublin's best located hotel for shoppers. On the left is a new shop, **Berry Bros & Rudd** (35), 4 Harry St. (☎ 677-3444). It is the Dublin branch of the famous

17th-century London wine shop that is the oldest independent family wine merchant in the world. Even if you are not interested in wine, it's worth a visit just to see how one of Dublin's finest Victorian buildings has been handsomely refurbished. The décor features paraphernalia from an old Weights & Measures office, pine shelf units made from pylons salvaged from Wexford harbor, a cellar floor of Donegal stone, plus the building's own original brick fireplaces and marble counters.

On the right is the entrance to the **Westbury Mall** (36), off Grafton St., (☎ 677-2083), an arcade of exclusive shops in a decorative Victorian skylit layout. The selection, which ranges from jewelery, crafts, and toys, to leather goods and wax candles, includes three shops of unique interest— **Magills** (37) ☎ 671-3830, one of Dublin's longest established food shops, offering cold meats, exotic spices and a wide range of Irish farmhouse and international cheeses (you are welcome to sample a few!); **St. Paul's Book Centre** (38) (☎ 671-7440), an outlet for spiritual books, cards, posters, videos, audio cassettes, wedding and christening gifts; and **Out of the Blue** (39) (☎ 671-6795), a specialty tee-shirt shop, using Irish designs, sayings, and characters.

If you walk all the way through the Westbury Mall, you will exit onto **Johnston's Court** (40), a narrow alley separating the Hotel Westbury from St. Teresa's Church. This small pedestrian street is also known as "jewelry row," housing a string of fine jewelry shops, from **Appleby**, **Gray's**, **Hardy's**, to **Sheeran** and **Sleater's**. In addition, there is a unique outdoor artist's gallery—the **Johnson Court Wall Gallery**, displaying the watercolors and pen-and-ink drawings of Dublin artist, Donal Branigan. Another indoor shop of note is **The Stencil Shop** (41), 9 Johnson Court (☎ 679-3487), selling a fine range of stencil products, with emphasis on Irish and Celtic designs.

If you take Johnson Court all the way to the end, it intersects with Clarendon Street and directly ahead of you is the entrance to one of Dublin's most appealing indoor malls—the **Powerscourt Centre** (42), between Clarendon St. and S. William St. (☎ 671-7000), an 18th century Georgian townhouse residence converted into a shopping centre in 1981. With over 50 shops and art galleries spread over three floors, it's an ideal shopping experience for a rainy hour or two. The wares range from antiques and crafts, to fashions, jewelry, perfumes, leather goods, toys, and heraldry. Background music is often played on the stage in the centre of the complex to enhance the elegant ambiance.

Returning to Grafton Street, on the right side is another leading Dublin jeweler, **Fields Jewellers** (43), 22 Grafton St. (☎ 671-2419), known especially for Claddagh rings and Claddagh-design pendants and Celtic-themed jewelry.

On the left is **Bewley's** (44), 78-79 Grafton St. (☎ 677-6761), a legendary Dublin café/restaurant that also houses an appealing shop, selling Bewley's own brands of coffee and tea as well as cookies, candies, and cakes and other confections.

Directly across on the right side of Grafton Street is **Marks & Spencer**

(45), 15–20 Grafton Street (☎ 679-7855), a branch of the famous British department store chain, known for competitive prices.

Next, on the right, is the Grafton Arcade, a small collection of enclosed shops, jutting off the main throughfare, so not always visible to passersby. But, it's well worth walking through the aracade to find **Monaghan's** (46), 15–17 Grafton Arcade (☎ 677-0823), a store that is synonymous with fine cashmere sweaters at affordable prices, for both men and women. Founded in 1960 and presided over by Tom Monaghan, this shop has the best selection of colors, sizes, and styles of cashmere in Ireland, plus Aran knits, lambswool, and more.

Tucked next to Monaghan's is a very small shop, **Helen McGroarty** (47), 7 Grafton Arcade (☎ 677-7508), run by Patricia McGroarty. It specializes in Irish tweeds, linens and mohair clothing for women. This is also a good source tartans and kilts, and for children's clothing, especially small-size Aran knits.

Opposite the arcade, at the intersection of Wicklow Street, is Dublin's legendary department store, **Brown Thomas** (48), 92 Grafton St. (☎ 605-6666), a showcase for Irish and international fashion, plus cosmetics and jewelry, as well as a large selection of gift items from Waterford Crystal, Wedgewood, and Belleek China to fine linens, pottery, leathers, and much more. It's considered the "Bloomingdale's" of Dublin.

Now that you have reached Wicklow Street, you have returned to the approximate starting point for this tour. Here's detour worthy of note if you are interested in dolls or music:

Cross over to Wicklow Street and follow it all the way till it changes its name and continues on as Exchecquer Street. Follow this street for one block till it meets South Great George's Street straight ahead. Turn left and cross over to the other side. Here you will find two shops worth the detour:

**The Dolls Store** (49), 62 S. Gt. George's St. (☎478-3403), is the top source for Irish and designer dolls and teddy bears, doll houses, doll house kits, and miniatures. It offers a full range of dolls including the largest collection of porcelain dolls in Ireland, plus prams, buggies and other doll furniture, clothes, and accessories. In addition, there is a *Dolls Hospital* and *Teddy Bear Clinic* on the premises, for the repair of broken toys.

If you are charmed by Irish traditional music and would like to learn to play some tunes yourself, head a few doors further to **Walton's** (50), 69-70 S. Gt. George's St. (☎ 475-0661). Here you can buy a variety of Irish instruments such as harps, bodhrans, tin whistles, pipes, flutes, fiddles, or concertinas. If you have a spare day, the *Walton School of Music* offers one-day crash courses in many instruments, or you can buy books on Irish music and teach yourself. For those who prefer to listen, there is also a wealth of Irish traditional music cassettes, CDs, and videos for sale.

# Section III

# THE SOUTHEAST

Ireland's Southeast is often missed by visitors in a rush to travel the fastest route between Dublin and Cork, or Dublin and The West. And this is a pity because Ireland's Southeast is a harmonious blend of some of the country's most picturesque and unspoiled scenery, fascinating Viking and medieval heritage, and fun-filled outdoor and indoor experiences. To top it off, statistics also tell us that this little corner of the Emerald Isle enjoys more hours of sunshine than the rest of Ireland, earning the title of "sunny Southeast."

A fertile and prosperous agricultural area, the Southeast takes in four counties—Waterford, Wexford, Kilkenny, and Carlow, and three magnificent rivers—the Barrow, the Nore, and the Slaney.

This section outlines four daytrips, starting with Waterford, the major seaport of Ireland's southeast coast and the city famous all over the world for its production of delicate hand-cut crystal. Waterford is also the gateway to the rest of the southeast coast, and the ideal starting point for each of the other tours.

# Waterford City

Say the word "Waterford" and many people think "glass." Without a doubt, the city's beautiful hand-cut crystal, produced since 1783 at the Waterford Crystal Factory, is known and treasured around the world. But the word "Waterford" symbolizes a lot more than glass—it is the name of one of Ireland's most historic maritime cities.

Stretching for over a half-mile along the southern bank of the River Suir (pronounced *Shure*), Waterford City sits at the point where the river opens into the estuary of Waterford Harbor. The city's name dates back to the 9th century, when it was an important Danish settlement known as *Vadrefjord*. A still earlier name for it in the Irish language was *Cuan na Greine* or "harbor of the sun." The city's present name in the Irish language, which you'll often see on buses and official government signs, is *Port Láirge* which means "Láirge's Landing Place."

In any event, it has always been a favorite landing place through the years, first for the Vikings who are credited with founding a settlement here in the 10th century, later by the Normans and the English, and still more recently by tourists from all over the world who come via cruise ships, buses, cars, and other modes of transport.

With a population of 50,000, Waterford is the main seaport of Ireland's southeast coast. In addition to glass-making, the city's traditional industries have included meat-processing, brewing, and iron-founding, along with newer trades such as making pharmaceuticals, optical products, electronics, and aerospace components.

Waterford's best-known citizens have included Luke Wadding (1588-1657), Franciscan priest, scholar, and historian, and the only Irishman who was ever a Papal candidate; Thomas Francis Meagher (1823-67), a Waterford-born Irish patriot who was condemned to death in 1848 but escaped to America where he founded the Irish Brigade and fought on the Union side in the Civil War, eventually heading West and becoming governor of Montana; and Edmund Ignatius Rice (1762-1844), a native of Callan, Co. Kilkenny, who became a wealthy Waterford merchant and then gave it all up to devote his life to the poor, founding the Irish Christian Brothers. He is currently on the path to sainthood, having been beatified by Pope John Paul II in October of 1996.

## GETTING AROUND:

By car, Waterford is 98 miles southwest of Dublin, via the main N7 and N9 roads, less than a three-hour drive. **Irish Rail** provides daily train service from Dublin's Heuston Station to Waterford, with at least two trains each morning and afternoon; travel time is about 2.5 hours. **Bus Eireann** provides daily service to Waterford from Dublin and all other major Irish cities; travel time from Dublin is about three hours depending on the route. Trains and buses all arrive at Plunkett Station in Waterford.

## PRACTICALITIES:

The best way to see downtown Waterford is on foot. All of the main sights are concentrated in a relatively small area along the quays, The Mall, and nearby streets. The only exception is Waterford Crystal which is about two miles south of town, about a half-hour walk. You can arrange to take a taxi from your hotel or hop on board Bus #1 at the Clock Tower on The Quay; the sign at the front of the bus will say *"Ballybeg"* as its destination, but the Waterford Crystal complex is one of its stops.

For visitor information, contact the **Waterford Tourist Office**, The Granary, The Quay at Hanover St., ☎ 051-875823, open year-round. From April to October, there is also a tourist information desk at the Waterford Crystal Visitor Centre, ☎ 051-358397.

Walking tours with a local guide are conducted by **Waterford Tourist Services**, departing every day from the foyer of the Granville Hotel. For the latest schedule or to reserve a place in advance, contact Jack Burtchaell, ☎ 051-873711.

A note to shoppers: Waterford Crystal is sold at the Waterford Crystal Visitor Centre Shop and at shops throughout Waterford City and the rest of Ireland. The suggested retail price for all Waterford Crystal products is identical at all outlets in the Republic of Ireland; it is not cheaper to buy it at the factory shop.

The telephone area code for all numbers is 051, unless otherwise indicated.

## FOOD AND DRINK:

**T & H Doolans** (32 George's St., next to the George's Court Shopping Centre) Situated beside a cobbled pedestrian pathway and fragments of the original city walls, this 200-year-old lantern-lit pub was once a stagecoach stop, and claims to be Waterford's oldest pub. It's a good stop for a drink, traditional Irish food, snacks, or evening sessions of traditional music. ☎ 872764. £

**Dwyer's Restaurant** (8 Mary St., off Bridge St.) Chef-owner Martin Dwyer has transformed an unlikely setting—a former barracks building on a back street—into a cozy haven of innovative international cuisine featuring local seafood and produce. Dinner only. ☎ 877478. ££

**Jade Palace** (3 The Mall, two doors from Reginald's Tower) This upstairs restaurant is one of Waterford's most surprising finds—top class Chinese food served in an elegant atmosphere of fine linens, antique furnishings, Waterford Crystal accessories, and silver cutlery (or chopsticks, if you prefer). ☎ 855611. ££

**McCluskeys Bistro** (18 High St., next to the parking entrance of the City Square Shopping Centre) Located on one of Waterford's oldest streets, this friendly shopfront bistro is known for its seafood dishes and unusual salads such as warm chicken with cashews and roasted peppers or rocket salad with local Knocklara cheese. In the evening, "early bird" menus offer exceptional value. X: Sun., Mon. ☎ 857766. ££

**The Olde Stand** (45 Michael St., at the corner of Lady Lane) A Victorian atmosphere prevails at this vintage pub, with a decor of paintings and maps of old Waterford. The downstairs pub offers snacks and carvery-style lunches by day, and the upstairs restaurant serves traditional Irish favorites such as steaks and chicken Maryland in the evening. ☎ 879488. £ to ££

**The Reginald** (The Mall, next to Reginald's Tower) Taking its name from the famous adjacent landmark, this pub-restaurant has a decor reminiscent of Viking times including alcoves, arches, and part of an old city wall (c. AD 850). The menu offers burgers, steaks, prime ribs, and seafood, as well as sandwiches and pub grub. ☎ 855087. £ to ££

**The Wine Vaults** (High St.) is housed in a 15th-century building, formerly the home of the mayor on one of Waterford's oldest streets. With such an atmospheric setting, it's no wonder that this is a favored spot for a special lunch or dinner. The menu, which features the best of local ingredients, is known for its seafood, pastas, char-grilled meats, game, and vegetarian dishes. X: Sun. ☎ 853444. ££

## SUGGESTED TOUR:

Start your tour at the bus and rail depot, **Plunkett Station** (1), on the north bank of the River Suir. Cross over the **Edmund Ignatius Rice Bridge**, named after one of the city's great altruistic citizens who devoted his life to the poor and who is currently a candidate for sainthood (see Barrack Street below). The south bank of the river is the city's main feature, known simply as **The Quay**, although it is in fact four quays (Gratton Quay, Merchant's Quay, Meagher Quay, and Parade Quay), stretching for 10 blocks or about a half-mile. Do as the Waterforders do—turn left and stroll along The Quay at a leisurely pace, looking at the distinctive shop windows and pub facades en route.

Proceed in an eastward direction, along Merchant's Quay to Hanover St. and you will see the main entrance to the **Waterford Tourist Office** at The Granary (see above). Turn right onto Hanover Street and visit Waterford's newest attraction:

**WATERFORD TREASURES** (2), The Granary, Hanover St., ☎ 304500, fax 051-304501. *Open June.–Aug., daily 9:30 a.m. to 9 p.m.; Sept.–May, daily 10–5. Adults £3, seniors and students £2.50, children aged 5–16 £2, and under 5 free. Shop. Café. Tours.*

Housed in a restored 19th-century six-story granary building, this new museum is the ideal way to get to know a lot about Waterford in a

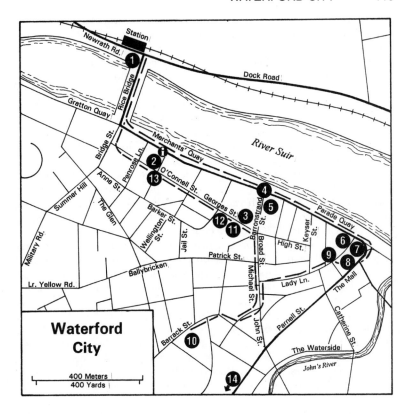

short time. It presents a one-stop rendezvous with some of Waterford's greatest people, places, and things, dating from Viking times to the present. All of the city's "treasures" (formerly housed at several smaller locations, are now united under this one roof—from Viking jewelry to medieval gold, bronze, and silver artifacts, as well as the city's original charter roll, civic regalia, and specimens of rare old Waterford glass.

Using a sound-guide headphone (available in adults' and children's versions), you'll also step back in time to enjoy a simulated eight-minute sea voyage on a Viking ship, observe the 12th-century wedding of Strongbow and Aoife, or savor the atmosphere of a Georgian society ball. The tour takes about one hour, but you are free to set your own pace. In addition, there is a 12-minute audiovisual and an art gallery displaying works of local artists.

Return to the Quay and continue to Meagher Quay. On the right is the **Granville Hotel** (3), a focal point of the city, incorporating several buildings that were once private Georgian-era residences including the birthplace of Waterford patriot Thomas Francis Meagher. The site was later purchased for use as a coaching inn by Carlo Bianconi who started the first public transport system in Ireland using a horsedrawn fleet of vehicles called *Bians.*

At the next intersection, Barronstrand Street, is the **Clock Tower** (4), a Victorian Gothic landmark of local cut stone that helped local sea captains keep their ships on schedule. Built in 1861, it once had troughs of water at its base for horses to drink, and was often referred to as the Fountain Clock. The original structure, with its troughs, was replaced with the present clock in 1954.

At this point, take a short detour for one-half block to the right to see the **Cathedral of the Most Holy Trinity** (5), Barronstrand St., ☎ 874757. Dating back to 1793, it was designed by Waterford-born architect John Roberts, with an austere Ionic-style facade. The interior, however, is rich and decorative, with a high vaulted roof, Corinthian pillars, carved oak pulpit, and a magnificent set of Waterford Crystal chandeliers donated by Waterford Crystal in 1979 after the church was renovated.

Continue along The Quay for five short blocks, passing the General Post Office and an assortment of shops, pubs, and department stores.

A sign indicates a lane to the right is known as Greyfriars Street, site of the Grey Friars ecclesiastical ruins, originally a Franciscan Abbey (founded in 1240). After it was disbanded by Henry VIII, the friary was used in turn as a hospital, burial place, and a parish church for French Huguenot refuges, and hence the site is usually referred to by the locals as **French Church** (6). Today it consists of the ruins of the nave, chancel, choir, and tower of the monastic church, a chapel, and many centuries-old tombs, such as that of John Roberts, the Waterford architect who is responsible for most of the city's fine buildings including its two cathedrals.

Turn the corner and you will see Waterford's most impressive Viking monument:

**\*REGINALD'S TOWER** (7), The Quay, ☎ 73501. *Open April–May and Sept.–Oct., Mon.–Fri.10–5, Sat.–Sun. 10–1 and 2–5; June–Aug. daily 8:30–8:30. Adults £1.50, seniors £1, children 60p.*

Built in 1003 by a Viking governor named Reginald, this 70-foot circular fortress gives Waterford its unmistakable Viking ambiance, with ten-foot-thick walls and a huge conical roof. It dominates the east end of The Quay, at the juncture of The Mall, and is considered the oldest urban civic building in Ireland and possibly the oldest tower of mortared stone in Europe. As the historic centerpiece of Waterford, it has served first as a fortress, then as a prison, military depot, mint, air-raid shelter, and now a museum of Waterford history.

After visiting the tower, turn right onto **The Mall** (pronounced *Maal*), Waterford's wide ceremonial street. In the center of the street is a statue of Luke Wadding, a local man who spent most of his life in Rome as a

Franciscan priest and scholar, the only Irishman ever to be a candidate for the Papacy. A half-block to the right is **City Hall** (8), The Mall, ☎ 873501, headquarters of the Waterford city government. An impressive 18th-century building designed by Waterford-born architect John Roberts, it houses a comprehensive collection of local art; a permanent exhibit of the battle flags, uniforms, and swords of local patriot-turned-Civil War commander Thomas Francis Meagher; some priceless antique Waterford crystal display pieces, and the ornate Victorian-style Theatre Royal. *Open June–Sept., Mon.–Fri. 9:30–5. No admission charge.*

After City Hall, turn right at the next street to see **Christ Church Cathedral** (9), Cathedral Square, ☎ 874119. Built 1770–79 to the specifications of John Roberts who also designed City Hall, the Catholic Cathedral of the Most Holy Trinity, and other notable Waterford landmarks, it occupies the site of an old Viking cathedral and its medieval successor that lasted until 1770. The present cathedral, which belongs to the Church of Ireland, still has some medieval monuments on view including a small crypt and 15th- and 16th-century tombs.

To the right is **Lady Lane**, a narrow passage that is considered as Waterford's best example of a surviving medieval street. It still serves as a through-street wending its way beside the modern City Square Shopping Centre, of 1990s vintage.

Follow Lady Lane to **Michael Street**, famed in the 19th century as the headquarters for the Waterford's guild of weavers, and today a busy main commercial strip. At this point, you may wish to detour to the left to New Street, for two blocks past Convent Hill, to visit the **Edmund Rice Centre** (10), Mount Sion, Barrack St., ☎ 874390. This museum is housed at the Christian Brothers School and focuses on the life of Waterford's spiritual hero—Ignatius Edmund Rice (1762–1844)—a local man who sold all his possessions to help the poor. Founder of the teaching order of the Irish Christian Brothers, he was declared blessed by Pope John Paul II in 1996. A visit includes a multi-image audiovisual presentation and a tour of the chapel where his tomb is enshrined. *Opening times vary; call in advance to check. No admission charge; donations welcome.*

Returning to **Michael Street** at the corner of Lady Lane, turn right and walk in a northerly direction, as Michael changes its name to Broad Street. Make a left at **Broad Street**, beside the Broad Street Shopping Centre, another 1990's commercial addition to the city.

Go on **Patrick Street** and **Little Patrick Street** to the **Waterford Heritage Genealogical Centre** (11), Jenkins Lane, ☎ 873711. If you have Waterford ancestry, this is the place for you. It contains a vast collection of Waterford records and its staff is trained in helping visitors to find their roots. *Open June–Sept., Mon.–Fri. 9–1:15 and 1:45–5; Oct.–May, Mon.–Thurs. 9–1:15 and 1:45–5 and Fri. 9–2. Admission is free, but a minimum search is £30.*

Even if you don't have Waterford connections, this centre is an interesting attraction since it is housed at **St. Patrick's Church**, Waterford's oldest church. Although its exact date of origin is unknown, it began as a

Penal Chapel in a corn store and was identified on a 1764 map as a "Mass House." Highlights include an 18th-century arch and bell tower and a unique U-shaped gallery inside.

Follow Little Patrick Street to George's Street, a pedestrianized shopping street. To the left is the **Chamber of Commerce Building** (12), a fine example of 18th-century Georgian architecture, designed by the ubiquitous John Roberts and open during normal business hours. At the intersection of Gladstone Street, George's Street becomes O'Connell Street. Coming up on the left is the **Garter Lane Arts Centre** (13), 5 O'Connell St. ☎ 855038, a contemporary art gallery and craft center. *Open Mon.–Sat. 10–6. Admission is free.*

One block farther is the **Garter Lane Theatre**, 22a O'Connell St., ☎ 855038, a 170-seat performing arts venue. It is housed in the former Friends Meeting House.

Walk three more blocks on O'Connell Street to Bridge Street and turn right to return to the Edmund Ignatius Rice Bridge and The Quay, the starting point of the tour.

But your tour is not yet over—the best is yet to come. From the Quay, take a bus, taxi, or drive to the final highlight of a visit to Waterford City:

**\*WATERFORD CRYSTAL VISITOR CENTRE** (14), Kilbarry, Cork Rd., ☎ 373311. *Open April–Oct. daily; tours 8:30–4, showrooms 8:30–6; Nov.–March, Mon.–Fri., tours 9–3:15, showrooms 9–5. Adults £3.50, seniors £2, children under 12 £1.75. Shop. Café.*

Founded in 1783, Waterford Crystal is the grand-dame of all Irish craft enterprises and one of the world's best-known names in genuine decorative hand-made glass production. A visit includes a 17-minute audiovisual and a walk-through tour of the factory to see the whole magical process—from the master blowers, shapers, and cutters to the engravers, including an interactive exchange and a time to ask questions. A visit also provides an opportunity to browse in the Waterford Crystal Gallery, the most comprehensive display of this glassware in the world, from stemware to trophies, globes, and chandeliers. Relax and listen to piano recitals or even play chess on a £2,000 Waterford Crystal chessboard. It's located about two miles south of the downtown area, on the Cork Road (N25).

Return to Waterford City or continue on to other parts of Ireland.

# Wexford Town

Wexford, a town of narrow streets, hidden laneways, original stone walls, and ancient abbeys, is one of Ireland's oldest settlements. Ideal for walking and meandering, it is situated on a sheltered inlet where the River Slaney, once known as the *River Garma*, meets Wexford Harbour.

The first reference to Wexford goes back to the second century AD when Ptolemy's maps marked the site as a place called *Menapia*, after a Belgic tribe who are believed to have settled here in prehistoric times. The Irish later called the area *Loch Garman*, which literally means "lake of the river Garma," but that name is so old that its origin was disputed even in pre-Christian times.

The Vikings, who founded a trading settlement in the area in the 9th century, called it *Waesfjord*, which means "esker fort" or literally "inland by the sandbank." Three centuries after the Viking sea-rovers claimed the land the Normans followed and took control, anglicizing the name to its current spelling. By the 14th century, they had added a new towered wall with five gates to the town layout, but it did not provide invincibility.

Like much of Ireland, Wexford struggled under English rule for many centuries, including a 1649 massacre by Cromwell's forces. Wexford's shining moment in Irish history came in 1798 when a group of local men rallied to lead a full-scale rebellion to protest the oppressive penal laws of the 18th century. The insurgents were mostly farmers armed only with their enthusiasm and pikes in hand. Eventually called the *Pikemen*, these brave rebels met success at first but were eventually defeated. Their glory lives on, as evidenced by many memorials and statues throughout the town and county of Wexford.

Because of its strategic location, Wexford has always been a busy seaport, and today is still a major shellfish port, especially for mussels. It is also an important marketing hub for the surrounding agricultural lands, and a manufacturing center. Famous Wexford area natives have included Sir Robert McClure (1807–73) who discovered the Northwest Passage; and Commodore John Barry (1745–1803) who emigrated to America and became "The Father of the United States Navy." The mothers of two famous 19th-century writers, Oscar Wilde and Thomas Moore, were also born in the town.

**GETTING THERE:**

By car, Wexford is 39 miles east of Waterford, via the N25 main road.

**Bus Eireann** provides daily express service from Waterford to Wexford, arriving at O'Hanrahan Station, at Redmond Square. The trip takes approximately one hour. Wexford can also be easily reached from Dublin, 88 miles away (approximately 2.5 to 3 hours), via national road, N11, or via daily services on **Bus Eireann** or **Irish Rail**.

## PRACTICALITIES:

Walking is the best way to see Wexford. There is no local bus transport in the downtown area. Park your car in the parking area beside Redmond Square, next to the bus/rail station.

For visitor information at any time of year, contact the **Wexford Tourist Office**, Crescent Quay, Wexford, ☎ 053-23111.

Wexford is at its best (and busiest) during the end of October and early November when it hosts the annual **Wexford Festival Opera**, a two-week program of world-class operas and many other musical and artistic fringe events. If you are interested in attending, advance reservations are a must (contact the Festival Office, ☎ 053-22400).

The telephone area code for all numbers is 053, unless indicated otherwise.

## FOOD AND DRINK:

**The Cape of Good Hope** (The Bull Ring, off N. Main St.) The sign outside of this pub tells of three services all under one roof: "Bar—Undertaker—Groceries." Step inside, pass by the funeral wreaths, and enjoy a drink amid an intriguing Old Wexford atmosphere. Long a favorite meeting place for local patriots and politicians, it is chock full of rebel souvenirs, weapons, and plaques. ☎ 22949. £

**La Cuisine** (80 N. Main St.) For a packed lunch or a light meal of freshly made soups or salads, this self-service delicatessen/coffee shop is a real find. Try locally-made chocolates and cheeses as well. ☎ 24986. £

**Oak Tavern & Riverside Restaurant** (Ferrycarrig Bridge, Ferrycarrig Rd.) One of Wexford"s best eateries is actually out of town, two miles to the north, adjacent to the Irish National Heritage Park. Originally a tollhouse, this 150-year-old tavern overlooks the River Slaney, with seating indoors and on a riverside patio. The menu features bar food by day, and evening meals that range from shepherd's pie to charcoal-grilled steaks. ☎ 20922. £ to ££

**La Riva** (2 Henrietta St., off Crescent Quay) With windows looking out onto Wexford Harbour and the River Slaney, this upstairs bistro offers the best dining views in town. The menu has a Mediterranean/Italian flair, with a wide choice of homemade pastas and pizza, as well as steaks and seafood. Open for dinner only. ☎ 24330. ££

**Tim's Tavern** (51 S. Main St., in the heart of town) A longtime favorite with the locals, this cozy tavern has an Old World decor and serves food all day—from an extensive range of hot and cold lunches and tea/sandwiches all afternoon to full dinners at night. Local seafood, homemade soups, Irish traditional dishes, and fresh fruit dishes are specialties. ☎ 23861. £ to ££

## SUGGESTED TOUR:

Start your tour at the **O'Hanrahan Station** (1) at **Redmond Square**, the bus/rail depot on the north side of the town. This square commemorates a prominent 19th-century Wexford family. Walk one block west from the station along Slaney Street to Westgate Street, site of the original western walls and west gate of the city. Here you can visit the:

*WESTGATE HERITAGE CENTRE (2), Westgate St., ☎ 46506. *Open Mar.–June and Sept.–Dec., Mon.–Sat. 9:30–1 and 2–5:30; July–Aug., Mon.–Sat. 9:30–1 and 2–5:30, Sun. 2–6. Adults £1, children 50p. Shop.*

See parts of Wexford's original west gate and walls and learn more about the town's colorful role in Irish history at this heritage center, formed by part of the original Viking/Norman walls. The layout includes displays, artifacts, and a continuous 27-minute audiovisual. Admission also provides access to the adjacent ruins of the 13th-century church of the Augustinian Priory of SS. Peter and Paul, commonly called Selskar (i.e. Holy Sepulchre) Abbey. This ruined abbey is believed to be the oldest place of worship in Wexford county. The first Anglo-Irish treaty was signed at St. Selskar's in 1169, and it is said that Henry II spent the Lent of 1172 here, doing penance for having Thomas à Becket murdered.

After visiting the Heritage Centre and abbey, follow George's Street to North Main Street. **Main Street**, both north and south, is the principal shopping thoroughfare of Wexford. It is narrow and irregular, having evolved over the centuries from a Viking market trail into a street, and personifies the friendly and close-knit atmosphere of this ancient town.

On the right is **White's Hotel** (3), an old coaching inn dating back to 1779 but renovated and enlarged over the years. The layout incorporates many former private houses and buildings, including the family home of Robert McClure, who is credited with discovering the Northwest Passage. Continue walking southward for two blocks until you come to the **Bull Ring** (4), a market square in the center of town. It dates back to 1621 when the local butchers' guild introduced the sport of bull-baiting for the amusement of resident Norman nobles. Over the centuries, the square evolved into a place of public assembly, including the occasion in 1798 when Wexford's local freedom fighters, called the Pikemen, boldly put forward Ireland's first declaration as a Republic. Today a statue in memory of the Pikemen stands in the center of the Bull Ring, which is now used primarily for a weekly outdoor market.

Now take a right and go one block to the **Cornmarket** (5), once the central marketplace of the town. Although it lost some of its prominence in the 19th and 20th centuries, the Cornmarket is slowly coming back through urban renewal, once again humming as a commercial center. The

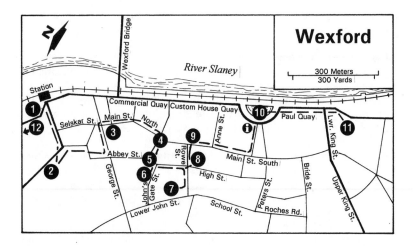

focal point is the market house, built in 1775, and now the **Wexford Arts Centre** (6), a showcase for art galleries and artistic events. Over the years this building served as a dance hall, concert venue, town hall, and municipal offices, before it was given new life as an arts milieu. The Cornmarket is also home of the **Thomas Moore Tavern**, originally known as The Ark, the house where poet and songwriter Thomas Moore's mother was born.

From the Cornmarket, follow High Street one block to Rowe Street, to see the Church of the Immaculate Conception, known as one of Wexford's **Twin Churches** (7). The other, five blocks away on Bride Street, is the Church of the Assumption. Both churches were built 1851–58 to the designs of the same architect, Robert Pierce, a pupil of Augustus Pugin. Their spires are an identical 230 feet in height.

Follow Rowe Street back to High Street. On the right-hand corner is the **Theatre Royal** (8), opened in 1832, and current the headquarters of the Wexford Festival Opera. Continue one block back to N. Main Street and directly ahead is **St. Iberius Church** (9), standing on an ecclesiastical site that dates back to St. Patrick's time (5th century). It is dedicated to a local saint whose name is used in various forms such as St. Ibar or St. Iver. Built in 1660, this church blends an elegant Georgian interior with a late 19th-century Venetian Renaissance facade. During late July and mid-August, every Wednesday and Saturday, the church presents *Music for Wexford,* a series of short classical concerts. *Open Mon.–Sat. June–Aug. 10–5; Sept.–May 10–3. Concerts start at 1:05. Admission is free to the church; concerts £5 per person.*

Continue along Main Street, passing Anne Street on the left. In the past, this was a street used for meat markets, and was consequently referred to as the Flesh Market and the *Shambles.* Anne Street marks the changeover from North Main Street to South Main Street. Coming up on the left is **\*Keyser's Lane**, one of the narrowest and the oldest thorough-fares in Wexford, dating back to Viking times. **Slegg's Lane**, across Main Street, is the inland continuation of this route. To the right is Allen Street, first paved in 1793.

Take a left at Henrietta Street, once lined by sawmills and timber yards, to the river. Here is **Crescent Quay**, a half-moon-shaped riverbank, and setting for the **John Barry Monument** (10), a modern statue of Commodore John Barry, born at nearby Ballysampson, 10 miles south of Wexford town. Barry left Wexford in his teens and volunteered in the cause of the American Revolution. One of the US Navy's first commis-sioned officers, he became the captain of the *Lexington*. In 1797 George Washington appointed him Commander-in-Chief of the US Navy, and thus he has been considered ever since as the "Father of the United States Navy." The statue, which faces out toward the sea, was a gift from the American people in 1956. Behind the monument is the **Wexford Tourist Office**.

If you wish to see the **Talbot Hotel** (11), long a fixture on the Wexford riverfront and originally a schoolhouse, detour two blocks south along Paul Quay, and then return to Crescent Quay.

From Crescent Quay, walk northward along the two remaining quays (Custom House Quay and Commercial Quay), returning to Redmond Square, the starting point of the walking segment of this tour.

To complete your tour of Wexford, now go by car or taxi two miles north of the town to spend the rest of the day at the:

**\*IRISH NATIONAL HERITAGE PARK** (12), Ferrycarrig, ☎ 20733. *Open Mar.–Nov., daily 9:30–6:30. Adults £5, seniors £4.50, students £4, children aged 13–16 £3, ages 4–12 £2.50. Café. Tours.*

You can literally walk through 9,000 years of Irish history at this 30-acre outdoor walk-around museum, starting with a camp site dating from the Mesolithic Period (7000 BC). The exhibits also depict an early Irish farmstead and a portal dolmen from the Neolithic Period (2500 BC) and a cist burial site and stone circle from the Bronze Age (2000 BC), as well as dwellings, vessels, and tools from the Celtic, Early Christian, and Early Norman Periods. Meander into a 10th-century monastery, cross over a Celtic crannog, explore a Viking boatyard, or a climb into a Norman fort. To add to the ambiance, there are demonstrations of age-old crafts, from pole lathe and weaving to pottery.

From the National Heritage Park, return to Wexford town and then via the N25 main road to Waterford, or continue on to other parts of Ireland.

# Trip 14

# *Kilkenny - Medieval City

Ireland's medieval heritage is the focus of this tour. It's just about an hour's drive from the Viking coastal port of Waterford to the inland "medieval city" of Kilkenny.

Founded in the 6th century by St. Canice, Kilkenny takes its name from the Irish *Cill Choinnigh*, which means "Canice's Church." Like most Irish cities, Kilkenny fell into Norman hands by the 12th century, but, thanks to its inland location beside the River Nore, became a prosperous walled medieval city and served as the venue for many parliaments. At one point, from 1642 to 1648, the Confederation of Kilkenny functioned as an independent Irish Parliament, and Kilkenny was briefly considered the capital of a united Ireland. Alas, Kilkenny fell into conquering hands in 1650 when Oliver Cromwell's army swept into town. Never again did the city rise above regional prominence, but it has earned great respect in the southeast as a marketing hub and an architectural gem.

Much of Kilkenny's 13th- and 14th-century character and layout remain today. Walk from one end of the city to the other, and encounter a continuous tableau of well-preserved medieval churches, public buildings, narrow streets, and arched laneways, many with descriptive names like Pennyfeather Lane, Horseleap Slip, Butter Slip, and Pudding Lane.

One of the most famous natives of Kilkenny was Dame Alice Kyteler, born circa. 1280, a local beauty who was accused of witchcraft but escaped to England. Her servant Petronella was not so lucky—she was burned at the stake in 1324. The legend of Dame Alice lives on at her original house which was restored in 1966, and is now a tavern.

In addition to its medieval ambiance, Kilkenny is also known as The Marble City—because fine black marble used to be quarried on the outskirts of town. Up until 1929, some of the streets had marble pavements.

## GETTING THERE:

By car, Kilkenny is 30 miles north of Waterford, via the N9 and N10 main roads. **Bus Eireann** provides daily service from Waterford to Kilkenny, arriving at McDonagh Station, Dublin Road. The trip takes approximately one hour. Kilkenny can also be easily reached from Dublin, 75 miles away (approximately two hours), via national roads, N7, 9, and 78, or via daily services on **Bus Eireann** or **Irish Rail**. The latter departs from Dublin's Heuston Station.

## PRACTICALITIES:

The best way to see Kilkenny is on foot. There is no local bus transport in the downtown area. Park your car at one of the designated parking areas, such as The Parade, next to the rail station, or at the Market Cross Shopping Centre Car Park.

Kilkenny is at its best (and busiest) during the last week of August when it hosts the annual **Kilkenny Arts Week**, a program blending classical and traditional music, plays, readings, films, poetry, art exhibitions, and many social events.

For visitor information at any time of year, contact the **Kilkenny Tourist Office**, Shee Alms House, Rose Inn St., Kilkenny, ☎ 056-51500.

Walking tours with a local guide are conducted by **Tynan's Walking Tours**, departing every day year-round from the Kilkenny Tourist Office. For the latest schedule or to reserve a place in advance, contact Patrick Tynan, ☎ 056-65929.

In the summer months, **Irish City Tours** operates "The Kilkenny Tour," a narrated hop-on/hop-off tour of the medieval city and environs, making stops at 14 leading sites and landmarks. The complete tour, without disembarking, takes 45 minutes and provides a good overview if you don't have time to walk around. Tickets are available from the driver or at the Tourist Office. For full details ☎ 71566.

The telephone area code for all numbers is 056, unless indicated otherwise.

## FOOD AND DRINK:

**Caisleán uí Cuain—The Castle Inn** (Castle St., at the corner of High St.) Founded in 1734 as a stagecoach inn, this pub exudes Old World charm with lots of memorabilia on display. Traditional music is on tap many nights and the Irish language is often spoken by patrons and staff alike. The Swiss-trained owner/chef is known for creative pub grub. ☎ 65406. X: Sun. £

**Edward Langton** (69 John St.) With its stained-glass windows, etched mirrors, polished granite tables, and brass globe-lamps, this pub has long been known for its "Old Kilkenny" atmosphere, as well as its award-winning soups, sandwiches, and casseroles. ☎ 65133. £

**Italian Connection** (38 Parliament St.) Wine casks and dark wood furnishings provide the backdrop for this informal shopfront eatery, popular for pizzas and pastas, as well as steaks and curries. ☎ 64225. £ to ££

**Kilkenny Design Restaurant** (The Parade, on second floor of Kilkenny Design Centre) Housed in the original coach house of Kilkenny Castle, this self-service café offers an ever-changing menu of freshly made soups, salads, casseroles, pastries, and breads, and other local goodies, all presented amid a welcoming atmosphere of white-washed walls, handcrafted furnishings, and local art. ☎ 22118. X: Sun. in Oct.–Mar. £

**Kyteler's Inn** (St. Kieran St.) Enjoy a drink or a meal at this bewitching local tavern. Dating back to 1324 and once the home of a witch, Dame

Alice Kyteler, it offers a menu of burgers, steaks, and simple fare served amid a decor of medieval stone walls, caverns, and arches. ☎ 21064. £

**Lacken House** (Dublin Rd., about a mile from center of town near railroad/bus station) For award-winning Irish and international haute cuisine, treat yourself to a night at this highly regarded restaurant, housed in an elegant Georgian house. Local ingredients are featured in specialty dishes such as baked crab au gratin or breast of pigeon with smoked bacon. Open for dinner only. ☎ 61085. X: Sun.–Mon. £££

**Lautrec's Wine Bar** (9 Kieran St.) is a casual and friendly bistro with an Old World decor including beamed ceilings, stone walls, and a potbelly stove. The modern menu offers international favorites all day, from pastas and pizzas to char-grilled meats, salads, and stuffed baked potatoes. ☎ 62720. £ to ££

**Ristorante Rinuccini** (1 The Parade, opposite Kilkenny Castle) With a formal candlelit decor, this classy restaurant offers Italian/Irish dishes, ranging from steak Diane and local seafood to homemade pastas. Quick-lunch specials offer exceptional value. ☎ 61575. X: Sun. ££

**Tynan's Bridge House** (2 Horseleap Slip, next to St. John's Bridge) A Kilkenny tradition for over 225 years, this classic pub once doubled as a grocery store and pharmacy. It is full of great conversation-starting pieces, from its horseshoe-shaped bar, to wide drawers marked mace, citron, and sago, as well as 17th-century weighing scales, shaving mugs, teapots, and vintage books including a time-worn copy of Chaucer's *Canterbury Tales*. Drinks only. ☎ 21291. £

### SUGGESTED TOUR:

Start your tour at the bus and rail depot, **McDonagh Station** (1), on the east edge of town at the junction of Upr. John Street and the Dublin Road. Walk west along Upr. John Street, a busy commercial thoroughfare that changes its name to Lr. John Street as it approaches the Nore River. Cross over the bridge and the street name changes to Rose Inn Street. On the right side is the **Shee Alms House** (2), built in 1582 by Sir Richard Shee to shelter paupers and now the city's tourist office. After visiting the tourist office and gathering the latest brochures, step upstairs to the **Cityscope Exhibition,** ☎ 63955, on the upper floor for some helpful background on Kilkenny's history. The layout includes a three-dimensional architectural scale model of Kilkenny with lighting and sound effects to re-create the city as it was in 1640. The program is run every half-hour. *Open May–Sept., Mon.–Sat. 9–5:30, Sun. 11–4:30; Oct.–April, Tues.–Sat. 9–4:30. Adults £1, children 50p.*

Continue on Lr. John Street for a half-block. To the left the road opens out onto the wide thoroughfare known as The Parade, with a parking area and the grounds of Kilkenny's centerpiece attraction:

**\*KILKENNY CASTLE** (3), The Parade, ☎ 21450. *Open daily April–May, 10:30–5; June–Sept., 10–7; and Oct.–March, Tues.–Sat. 10:30–12:45 and 2–5,*

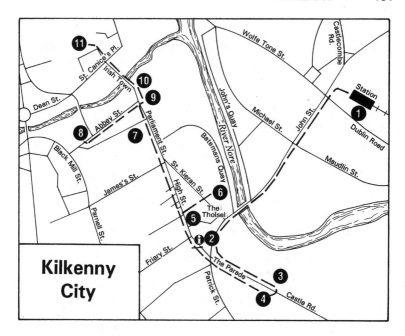

Kilkenny
City

and Sun. *11–12:45 and 2–5. Adults £3.50, seniors £2.50, children and students £1.50. Shop. Café. Tours.*

With a striking facade of huge towers and battlements edging the banks of the River Nore, Kilkenny Castle dominates the southern end of Kilkenny City. It dates back to 1192, built by the Norman leader Strongbow who eventually passed it to his son-in-law, but it was acquired in 1391 by the Butlers, the Dukes and Marquesses of Ormonde. The Butler family remained for over 500 years, in almost uninterrupted occupancy until 1935. The castle was eventually given to the Irish government to preserve as a national monument in 1967. Step inside and tour the library, drawing room, bedrooms, and sitting rooms, decorated in 1830's style with pieces from the National Furniture Collection of Ireland. In addition, the former servants' quarters have been restored as the Butler Art Gallery, a showcase for changing exhibitions of contemporary art. The old castle kitchen also operates as a tea room. Interior access is by guided tour only. The grounds include riverside walks and seasonal gardens.

Cross over the street to see another Kilkenny landmark:

**\*KILKENNY DESIGN CENTRE** (4), Castle Yard, The Parade, ☎ 22118. *Open April–Dec., daily 9–6; Jan.–March, Mon.–Sat. 9–5. No admission charge.*

A unique arched gateway and copper-domed clocktower beckon visitors to the entrance of this bustling complex. Inside is a world of creativity, a showcase for the best of Irish design and workmanship chosen from over 200 studios and workshops throughout Ireland. Built in 1760 as the coach house and stables for Kilkenny Castle, this design center consists of a central shop surrounded by a collection of workshops with artisans and craftspeople plying their trades each day.

Stroll from the castle grounds to the heart of the city, along High Street which becomes Parliament Street. On the right side is **The Tholsel** (5), with an arcaded front and clock tower. Erected in 1761, it served originally as a toll house, city hall, and exchange for local produce. It is now the town hall, open during normal business hours. The Tholsel contains municipal archives and charters including Kilkenny's first book of records, dating back to 1230, as well as the charter of 1609 elevating Kilkenny to the status of a city, the city's official sword (1609) and mace (1677).

The next right turn is **Butter Slip**, one of the city's many medieval passageways. It is a narrow covered lane with steps built in 1616 to accommodate people seeking a shortcut between the raised ground of High Street and the lower level of St. Kieran Street. Its name originated when a local woman used the lane as a market place to set up a stall and sell butter. If you follow the slip to St. Kieran Street, you can visit **Kyteler's Inn** (6), a 14th-century tavern that was reputedly the home of a witch (see Food and Drink above).

Moving along to the point where the street changes its name to Parliament, on the left you will see:

**ROTHE HOUSE** (7), Parliament St., ☎ 22893. *Open Jan.–Mar. and Nov.–Dec., Mon.–Sat. 1–5, Sun. 3–5; April–June and Sept.–Oct., Mon.–Sat. 10:30–5, Sun. 3–5; July–Aug., Mon.–Sat. 10–6, Sun. 3–5. Adults £2, seniors £1.50, children £1. Tours. Shop. Café.*

One of Kilkenny's oldest houses, this museum is a fine example of a Tudor-style middle-class home built in 1594 by a local merchant, John Rothe. It is actually three restored buildings, joined by cobbled courtyards. A tour includes a reception room with splendid hand-carved oak furniture and a collection of costumes, as well as a large common kitchen, bakery, and brewhouse. Throughout the house, there is an interesting panorama of pictures and artifacts of Kilkenny's past.

Walk one block and take a left to see one of the city's best preserved and restored churches:

**THE BLACK ABBEY** (8), Abbey St. ☎ 21279. *Open Mon.–Sat. 8–6, Sun. 9–7. No admission charge.*

Founded in 1225 by William Marshall, Earl of Pembroke, this abbey was formed as the Dominican Friary of the Most Holy Trinity. It was suppressed 300 years later and all of the property confiscated for Henry VIII. Subsequently, it was used as a courthouse until 1650 when Cromwell's troops reduced the abbey to a roofless ruin. In 1816 the local people revived it as a house of worship, and gradually began to restore it. A new nave was constructed by 1866 and the entire building fully restored by 1979. The abbey derives its name from the Dominicans wearing a black cappa over their white habit. Items of note include stone coffins from 13th century at the entrance; the great east window, measuring 500 square feet, depicting the 15 mysteries of the rosary (1892); a sculpture of the Holy Trinity, c. 1400, carved from alabaster on view in a glass case near the altar; and a pre-Reformation Irish oak statue of St. Dominic, believed to be the oldest of its kind in the world. Beside the abbey is Black Ferren Gate, Abbey Street, the last remaining gate of the original walls of the town.

Another ecclesiastical landmark, **St. Francis Abbey**, built in 1234, sits directly across Parliament Street to the right. Although this abbey no longer operates as a church, its walls and belfry tower live on as part of the facade of **Smithwick's Brewery** (9), Parliament St., ☎ 21014. The brewery, founded at this site by John Smithwick in 1710, now makes Budweiser for Irish markets as well as the original Smithwick's brand. *It is open for tours, May–Sept., Mon.–Fri. at 3. Admission is free.*

Next on the right is the **Watergate Theatre** (10), Parliament St., ☎ 61674, one of Ireland's newest theaters (1993). It presents a variety of shows in a contemporary setting.

Follow the street to the end, over the bridge at Irishtown, and you will arrive at St. Canice's Place, and the core of Kilkenny's origins:

**\*ST. CANICE'S CATHEDRAL** (11), Coach Rd., ☎ 21516. *Open April–Oct., Mon.–Sat. 9–1 and 2–6, Sun. 2–6; Oct.–April, Mon.–Sat. 10–1 and 2–4, Sun. 2–4. Admission is free.*

This is the place that gave Kilkenny its name—St. Canice founded a monastery on this site in the 6th century. The Irish word for Kilkenny—*Cill Chainnigh*—means St. Canice's Church. The present Gothic-style church was built mostly in the 13th century, but has been expanded over the years. It is the second-longest of Ireland's medieval cathedrals, measuring 212 feet in length. An equally imposing structure on both the exterior and the interior, St. Canice's has over 100 of the finest 16th-century funerary and sepulchral monuments of Ireland. Relatively modern highlights include a hammer barn roof that dates back to 1863, made from Canadian red pine timber; an organ dating back to 1854 and still in use; and a marble floor composed of the four marbles of Ireland. The grounds include steps that were constructed in 1614, and a massive 101-foot-high round tower that is believed to have survived from St. Canice's time.

Complete your tour by retracing your steps and strolling back along Parliament, High, Rose Inn, and John Streets, taking the opportunity this time to look at the many colorful shopfronts and perhaps stopping at one or more of the atmospheric pubs described above under Food and Drink.

**Trip 15**

# The Nore and Barrow River Valleys

The River Barrow and the River Nore are two of Ireland's most picturesque waterways, known for prolific salmon and trout fishing, yet their bucolic banks are seldom traveled by tourists, especially from North America. These two rivers meander in the shadow of the Blackstairs Mountains, beside some lovely little "undiscovered" towns with hard-to-pronounce names like Muine Bheag, Inistioge, and Graiguenamanagh, and an ever-changing landscape of fertile farm country. From Waterford, it's an easy day's drive to take in the best of the Barrow and the Nore.

## GETTING THERE:

By car, this route begins and finishes in Waterford via the main N25 road. It follows a combination of both main roads and secondary roads, taking in the scenic valleys of the Rivers Barrow and Nore. The basic route extends from New Ross to Carlow and back, a distance of about 30 miles each way.

## PRACTICALITIES:

This tour is "off the beaten track" at its best—not too many restaurants, pubs, visitor centers, or man-made attractions, just beautiful natural river valley vistas and non-touristy towns. The only way to do it is by car.

For visitor information, contact the **Carlow Tourist Office**, Kennedy Ave., Carlow, ☎ 0503-31554, open year-round; or the **New Ross Tourist Office**, The Quay, New Ross, Co. Wexford, ☎ 051-421857, open from mid-June through August only.

Since this tour covers parts of four counties (Waterford, Wexford, Carlow, and Kilkenny), telephone area codes are specified with each listing.

## FOOD AND DRINK:

**Café Nore** (Main St., Bennettsbridge, Co. Kilkenny) An ideal daytime stop, this modern skylit café is nestled on the main street of a town known for its great craftsmen and artisans, so the café's decor reflects the work of many local talents. The menu specializes in "made-to-order" items such as freshly squeezed juices, organic salads, herb teas, homemade soups, and unique sandwiches. Tempting desserts, muffins, and pastries are offered and designer coffees are also brewed. X: Mon., Jan. ☎ 056-27833. £

**Galley Cruising Restaurants** (New Ross Quay, New Ross, Co. Wexford) Cruise the rivers of the Nore and the Barrow on a double-deck barge while enjoying a narrated tour with lunch or dinner. Trips last from two to three hours, depending on time of day. ☎ 051-421723. X: Nov.–March. ££

**Lord Bagenal Inn** (Leighlinbridge, Co. Carlow) Situated on the banks of the Barrow, this Old World inn has long been a mecca for good food in a cozy atmosphere with open fireplaces and local memorabilia. The menu features steaks, seafood, and game, as well as hearty soups and sandwiches. ┃ 0503-21668. ££

**Waterside** (The Quay, Graiguenamanagh, Co. Kilkenny) Housed in a 19th-century granary with authentic dark wood beam ceilings, paned windows, and an imposing granite facade, this unique inn sits right beside the River Barrow. The rustic ground floor dining room is noted for innovative Irish cuisine using local ingredients. Choices range from homemade soups, fruit-and-cheese platters, pastas, and pita bread sandwiches to char-grilled vegetables and meats and free-range chicken. ☎ 0503-24246. £ to ££

## SUGGESTED TOUR:

Start out from **Waterford** (1), departing on the main N25 road toward **New Ross**, a busy port town on the east bank of the River Barrow. In the Middle Ages, New Ross rivaled Waterford as a seaport. New Ross, which is actually part of County Wexford, is the gateway to "Kennedy Country" — the ancestral homeland of John F. Kennedy, 35th President of the United States. If time allows, take a short detour 4.5 miles south via R 733 to the:

**JOHN F. KENNEDY ARBORETUM** (2), Dunganstown, New Ross, Co. Wexford. ☎ 051-388171. *Open daily Oct.–March 10–5; April and Sept. 10–6:30, May–Aug. 10–8. Adults £2, seniors £1.50, students and children £1. Shop. Café. Tours.*

As its name implies, this 600-acre park is dedicated to the memory of President John F. Kennedy. It is located near a hill known as Slieve Coillte, overlooking a simple thatched cottage at Dunganstown, one mile away, the birthplace of President Kennedy's great-grandfather. Opened in 1968, the park was a joint undertaking of the Irish government and a group of Americans of Irish origin. It is laid out and landscaped to provide for leisure, education, and research, with a lake and 200 forest plots, as well as over 4,500 species and varieties of trees, plants, and shrubs, from five continents. Thanks to Wexford's mild climate, it is expected that the number will eventually reach 6,000. Visitor facilities include a picnic area, self-guided walking trails, information center with audiovisual show, and a hilltop observation point that presents sweeping views of at least four Irish counties—Wexford, Waterford, Kilkenny, and Tipperary.

Return to the main road and follow signs for N79, making a left turn into a local road, R705, which runs along the west bank of the Barrow in

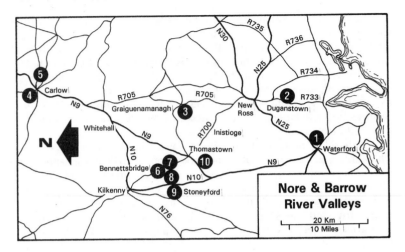

**Nore & Barrow River Valleys**

20 Km
10 Miles

County Kilkenny. The ride is particularly scenic, with panoramic farmland landscapes, rimmed by Brandon Hill to the left and the Blackstairs Mountains to the right. After 10 miles, this road curves into the village of **Graiguenamanagh** (pronounced *Gray-ge-na-maan-ah*), a name that means "village of the monks" in the Irish language. This is the home of:

**\*DUISKE ABBEY** (3), Graiguenamanagh, Co. Kilkenny, ☎ 0503-24238.

　　Founded by the Cistercians in 1204, Duiske (pronounced *Doo-shkaa*) Abbey took 40 years to build, and was considered a fine example of the style of architecture known as "Early English," as well as being the largest of the Irish Cistercian monastery churches (with a nave of over 200 feet long). It became a hub of ecclesiastic and scholastic activity in the Middle Ages, only to be suppressed by 1536 and eventually fall into ruin. It was fully restored in the 1970s, thanks to the efforts of the local community who pooled their talents and once again made the abbey the focal point of the area. Highlights from the 13th century include part of the original tiled floor and stone carvings on windows, doorways and arches, as well as rugged stone-faced walls lime-washed in the original manner. The great oak roof, although new, was constructed exactly as a medieval roof with dowels and wedges without a single nail. Celtic crosses on the grounds are believed to pre-date the foundation of the abbey as far back as the 9th century. A nearby visitor center offers a display of Christian art and artifacts.

　　From Graiguenamanagh, continue to follow R705 along the Barrow River via Borris and Muine Bheag (Bagenalstown), and then via N9 into **Carlow**, the chief town of County Carlow and the largest market center of the Barrow Valley. To learn more about Carlow, stop into the **County**

**Carlow Museum** (4), Town Hall, Centaur St., ☎ 0503-40730, just east of the River Barrow. Operated by the voluntary Old Carlow Society, this museum houses a representative sampling of 19th-century memorabilia and exhibits on local celebrities. *Open year-round Tues.–Sat. 10–1 and 2–5:30, Sun. 2:30–5:30. Adults £1, children 50p.*

The surrounding County Carlow area is often called "Dolmen Country" because it is rich in archaeological sites, particularly the **Brownshill Dolmen** (5), also known as the Mount Browne Dolmen, two miles east of town. Dating from 2000 BC, this is a very fine example of a portal-tomb or *cromlech,* thought to be the burial place of a significant prehistoric prince. Topped by a capstone that weights over 100 tons, it is considered the largest dolmen in Ireland and perhaps the largest in Europe.

Return to the main road N9 heading south via Leighlinbridge, Royal Oak and Whitehall, and Gowran, following a sign to the right for **Bennettsbridge**, on the banks of the River Nore and back into County Kilkenny. Originally known as St. Benet's Bridge, this small town sits beside a bridge on a route that was the medieval highway from Dublin to the South of Ireland, crossing the Nore at this point. For many years, the town's chief claim to fame was Mosse's Mill, a river-powered flour mill that produced the ingredients for the delicious brown bread synonymous with an Irish country breakfast. Because of its secluded yet convenient location (5 miles southeast of the city of Kilkenny), in recent years the town has drawn a number of artisans and craftspeople who have taken up residence and opened studios and craft shops that welcome visitors, including **Nicholas Mosse Pottery** (6), **Stoneware Jackson Pottery** (7), and **Chesneau Leather Goods** (8). Still another craft studio is located about five miles west and south of Bennettsbridge, via the main N109 road—the **Jerpoint Glass Studio** (9) at Stoneyford.

From **Stoneyford**, you can take a short detour, less than two miles west, to **Kells**, the only complete walled medieval town in Ireland. Although largely in ruins, the extensive curtain walls, seven towers, and some monastic buildings have been preserved.

Returning to Stoneyford, continue about two miles east along a deserted stretch of farming countryside where the road suddenly curves to reveal an imposing monument of long ago:

**\*JERPOINT ABBEY** (10), Jerpoint, Thomastown, Co. Kilkenny, ☎ 056-24623. *Open mid-April to mid-June, Tues.–Sun. 10–1 and 2–5; mid-June to end-Sept., daily 9:30–6:30; end-Sept. to mid-Oct., daily 10–1 and 2–5. Adults £2, seniors £1.50, students and children £1. Tours.*

In many ways, Jerpoint Abbey is an Irish version of a ghost town. Founded as a Cistercian Monastery in 1160, it became a thriving town, with infirmary, granary, stables, watermills, gardens, and various houses and buildings, flourishing well into the 15th century. Like most Irish religious foundations, it was suppressed in the 16th century and eventually fell into ruin by the 17th century. Highlights include original 12th-century Romanesque pillars, a medieval chancel, a 14th-century window with elaborate tracery, and one of the most decorative cloister arcades of any Irish church, partially reconstructed in 1953. The carvings are of great interest, ranging from human figures such as a bishop, a knight and his lady to grotesques and small unexpected figures in corners or on bases. There is also a remarkable collection of medieval glazed earthenware tiles, generally dated to the 14th and 15th centuries, with four design patterns—a lion rampant, fleur-de-lis, a naturalistic design on a cusped frame, and a border tile with a running vine-scroll motif.

Less than two miles eastward is **Thomastown**, Co. Kilkenny, a small market town situated at the head of Nore River Valley. It is named after Thomas FitzAnthony who founded the town in the 13th century. In the Middle Ages, it was a walled town but only the ruins of its walls and castles remain. The centerpiece today is Mount Juliet, originally a private estate and now a vacation resort with golf course and other sports facilities including Ireland's oldest cricket club.

Follow R700 south of Thomastown for about five miles, along a very scenic and verdant tree-shaded section of the River Nore Valley to **\*Inistioge**, Co. Kilkenny, a name derived from the Irish language, *Inis Tiog*, meaniong "Teoc's riverside meadow." It is pronounced *Innish-teague*. Aptly named, this beautiful little village is situated on the banks of the River Nore, with a romantic 18th-century bridge of nine arches in the center of town. This idyllic setting has been recognized often as a splendid location for movies including the recent *Widow's Peak*, starring Mia Farrow. From Inistioge, follow the scenic riverside route along the Nore for ten miles, returning to New Ross and the main road to Waterford.

# Section IV

# CORK

When it comes to ranking Ireland's 32 counties in order of size, Cork is #1. Not only is it the largest county, it is also one of the most varied. Warmed by Gulf Stream breezes, Cork is shaped by a 160-mile coastline of ocean, inlets, harbors, coves, and bays, including Bantry Bay, one of Ireland's most photographed bays, as well as a dozen others many with descriptive names such as Roaringwater, Castle Haven, and Ballycotton.

Three great rivers run through County Cork in an east-west direction—the Lee, Blackwater, and Bandon, with the Caha, Shehy, and Derrynasaggart mountains providing a dramatic backdrop. The Cork landscape is a veritable panorama of golden beaches, rocky headlands, fertile farmlands, and flower-filled valleys.

With the energetic Cork City as its hub, the county is a mix of busy market towns and secluded seaside villages, many with evocative place-names such as Ballydehob, Barleycove, Castletownsend, Crookhaven, Owenahincha, Oysterhaven, Courtmacsherry, and Belgooly. There's even the sound of the familiar in the Cork landscape—from Baltimore to Long Island, not to mention surprisingly unlikely names like Leap and Ovens.

Cork has many claims to fame, starting with two famous towns—Kinsale, an enchanting port that is considered the "gourmet capital" of Ireland, and Blarney, home of the legendary Blarney Stone. Cork is also the setting of the transatlantic port of Cobh and the world's oldest yacht club at Crosshaven, as well as Mizen Head, the most southerly point in the whole country.

## Trip 16

# Cork City

In the south of Ireland, it seems that all roads lead to Cork, a busy and burgeoning city with a history going back to the 6th century when St. Finbarr founded a monastery on this site. Sitting between two channels of the River Lee, Cork is a city of many riverfront quays and no less than 25 bridges.

Like other parts of Ireland, Cork experienced long periods of domination by outside forces, from the Viking raids in the 8th and 9th centuries, to Anglo-Norman invasions in the 12th century, and English suppression for hundreds of years afterward. Cork was granted a charter as a city as early as 1188 by Prince John of England and remained under English rule until this century.

The name Cork, which has nothing to do with bottles or drinking, dates back to earliest times. It is derived from the Irish language word, *Corcaigh*, which means "marsh." The 6th-century monastic settlement of St. Finbarr was built on the edge of a marsh, and until the 18th century, major thoroughfares, like St. Patrick Street and the Grand Parade, were built over steep stretches of muddy streams.

During Ireland's long struggle for independence, it was usually the Corkonians who led the way in self-reliance and spunk, earning the title of "Rebel Cork" for the city and county. Corkmen were at the forefront of Ireland's modern political formation, from local heroes Thomas MacCurtain and Terence MacSwiney, to charismatic national leaders like Michael Collins, recently immortalized in a major Hollywood movie bearing his name.

As the third-largest city in Ireland (after Dublin and Belfast), and with a population close to 150,000, Cork is an important seaport and manufacturing center, but most of all, it is a congenial city with a "hometown" atmosphere. The Corkonians are a friendly people with a delightful way of speaking that is all their own. The Cork accent is fast-paced and almost sing-song in style. It may take you a few hours to "tune in" your ears, but you'll be glad you did.

**GETTING THERE:**

By car, all main national roads do lead to Cork—this city is 160 miles southwest of Dublin via N8, 76 miles south of Shannon Airport via N18 and N20, 78 miles west of Waterford via N25, or 54 miles east of Killarney via N22. Follow signs for City Centre as you approach the city and you will find yourself in the heart of town on St. Patrick Street. From there, it is easy to find hotels or the tourist office which is well sign-posted. Cork has several very convenient parking garages along the quays, particularly at Merchant's, Lavitt's, and St. Patrick's Quays.

From Dublin and other major cities, **Irish Rail** provides daily service to Cork, arriving at **Kent Station** on Lr. Glanmire Road, which is on the eastern edge of the city. The usual journey from Dublin's Heuston Station takes from 2.5 to 3.5 hours, depending on the number of stops en route. From the station, take a taxi or bus to your accommodations, depending on where you have chosen to stay.

Similarly, **Bus Eireann** provides daily service to Cork from all major cities and smaller towns throughout Ireland. Depending on the route and number of stops, the journey time from Dublin takes from about 4 to over 6 hours. All buses pull into the **Bus Eireann Central Station** at Parnell Place which is in the heart of the city and within walking distance of many accommodations.

## PRACTICALITIES:

Cork is a big city, divided into three parts—the **South Bank** and the **North Bank** of the River Lee, and the main island or downtown area, usually referred to as the **Flat of the City**. Like most Irish cities, the best way to see Cork is on foot, although you may want to take a taxi from one part of the city to the other.

Local advice and information are available year-round at the **Cork Tourist Office**, Grand Parade, Cork, ☎ 021-273251.

For sightseeing in an independent style, **Guide Friday Tours** operates the *Cork City Tour*, a continuous bus service that stops at eight different points throughout the city including St. Finbarr's Cathedral, St. Patrick Street, Cork City Gaol, and Parnell Place (bus station). The tour provides a 70-minute guided tour plus on/off bus privileges all day at major sights. It departs daily, starting at 10 a.m., from the Grand Parade (opposite the Tourist Office), from the end of May through September, via a black-and-gold-colored double-deck open-top bus, ideal for picture-taking. For those who don't want to walk from one section of the city to the other, this tour can be used in conjunction with our walking tour. Get complete information on schedules at the Cork Tourist Office.

Cork is at its busiest during one of its many annual festivals, starting with the **Cork International Choral and Folk Dance Festival** in April or May, **Cork Folk Festival and Music Fair** in June, **Cork Film Festival** in September, and **Cork Jazz Festival** in October. Don't arrive without advance lodging reservations!

The telephone area code for all numbers in Cork City is 021 unless indicated otherwise.

## FOOD AND DRINK:

Cork is famous for some traditional and unique foods, such as tripe (animal stomach), crubeens (pigs' feet) and drisheen (local blood sausage). If any of those don't appeal to you, you can always try one of the local beers, *Beamish* and *Murphy's*. For tea drinkers, Cork is a mecca—the home base of *Barry's Tea*, blended here since 1901. All over Ireland but especially in Cork, the name *Barry* is to tea what *Bewley* is to coffee—simply the best!

**Bullys** (40 Paul St.) Wedged in the heart of a busy shopping street, this shopfront café offers a tasty selection of international fare, from chargrilled steaks and burgers, to pastas, omelets, and a dozen varieties of pizza made on a wood-burning stove. ☎ 273555. £ to ££

**Crawford Gallery Café** (Emmet Place next to the Opera House) A serene and artistic atmosphere prevails at this lovely restaurant, nestled on the ground floor of Cork's leading art gallery. The cuisine, provided by the Allen family of Ballymaloe Cooking School fame, is best described as "Cork country cooking" with choices such as chicken pie, Scotch eggs, stuffed filet of pork, spinach and mushroom pancakes, and Ballycotton Bay seafood. All breads and baked goods come from the Ballymaloe kitchens. Snacks and lunch only. ☎ 274415. X: Sun. £ to ££

**Farmgate Café** (Old English Market, Princes St.) After you enjoy the sights and aromas of Cork's prime indoor marketplace, savor the tastes at this restaurant upstairs. The ever-changing menu uses only the freshest produce, meats, seafood, and cheeses from the market stalls below. Open for daytime meals only. ☎ 278134. X: Sun. £ to ££

**Isaacs** (48 MacCurtain St.) Housed in a former 18th-century warehouse, this restaurant presents trendy food in a traditional setting of high ceilings, stone arches, and brick walls. The menu offers creative Mediterranean-style salads such as warm squid and almond salad, as well as pastas, seafood chowders, and unique items such as salmon and potato cakes. ☎ 503805. X: Sun. lunch. £ to ££

**Jacques** (9 Phoenix St., off Pembroke St. and the South Mall) Two members of the Barry family, famous for Cork's signature brand of tea, run this bright and modern bistro with Art Deco furnishings and citrus-toned colors. The menu is a blend of old Irish recipes, fresh local produce and seafood, and the chef's unbridled imagination. It's "the place" to go for Corkonians. ☎ 277387. X: Sun. and Sat. lunch. ££

**Mutton Lane Inn** (3 Mutton Lane, off St. Patrick St.) Step into this pub for a dose of Old Cork. Named after the adjacent laneway that was developed as a path for sheep going to market, it was opened as a public house in 1787 and still looks the same, with lantern lights, paneled walls, beamed ceilings, and lots of local memorabilia. The pub grub is hearty and standard—stews, soups, sandwiches. ☎ 273471. £

**Reidy's Wine Vaults** (Lancaster Quay, Western Rd.) Transformed from an old wine warehouse, this pub has an atmospheric decor of vaulted ceilings, traditional tiles, a massive mahogany bar, beveled mirrors, stained-glass windows, and a minstrels' gallery of antiques. The bar food features soups, meat pies, seafood platters, and savory pancakes, plus breads and quiches baked daily on the premises. ☎ 275751. £ to ££

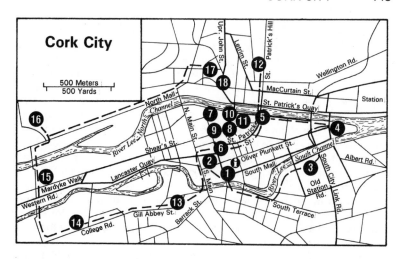

## SUGGESTED TOUR:

Since Cork's Kent Station is situated east of the city center, the best place to start a tour is in the heart of the city at the **Cork Tourist Office** (1) on the Grand Parade for basic local information, maps, and brochures.

Take time to stroll the **Grand Parade**, a wide thoroughfare that blends the remains of the old city walls and 18th-century bow-fronted houses with modern offices, shops, and the *Bishop Lucy Park** (2), a welcome patch of greenery with benches and a fountain, named for a local prelate. Parts of the old city walls can still be seen on the perimeter of the park.

On south end of the Parade is the junction with the **South Mall**, the fiscal hub of the city, with many well-preserved Georgian buildings now occupied by banks, stockbrokers, and other financial institutions. Follow the South Mall to Lapp's Quay along the South Channel of the River Lee. On the opposite side of the river is the classical domed facade of **City Hall** (3), on Albert Quay, Cork's chief administrative center. Dating back only to 1936, it was built on the site of a previous structure that was burned down during the Irish War of Independence in 1921. In 1852, the earlier building had been the setting of the first-ever national Industrial Exhibition in Ireland, modeled after a similar event held at the Crystal Palace in London. The interior of the present building houses a 2,000-seat concert hall, a popular venue for major shows and events.

Continue along Lapp's Quay to Custom House Quay and the **Custom House** (4), on Albert Street, now the Harbour Board Office, a classical structure (built 1814–18) that many people consider to be Cork's finest building. The defining features of its exterior include a pale gray limestone facade, Palladian windows, and the Cork coat of arms.

Follow Albert Street north for one block to Michael Collins Bridge and make a left, walking west to Merchant's Quay. On the left is the Bus Eireann Central Bus Station. The next block is devoted to Merchant's Quay Shopping Centre, a two-story enclosed shopping mall housing over 20 Irish and international shops. Straight ahead is St. Patrick's Street Bridge, opened in 1859. Take a left onto **St. Patrick's Street**, known locally as **Patrick Street**, or colloquially "Pana," the city's main street. This broad avenue was formed in 1789 when an open channel of the river was filled in on the marshy land. In the center of the street is one of Cork's best-known landmarks, the **Fr. Theobold Matthew Statue** (5), a monument to a 19th-century priest who led a crusade against alcoholic drink, and is fondly called "the apostle of temperance." The statue, or "stacha" as the locals call it, stands at the juncture of Patrick Street and Patrick Bridge, considered the city's central point, and a favorite meeting place for Corkonians.

Not known particularly for great monuments or museums, Patrick Street is unabashedly a shopping street—sometimes called the Regent Street or Fifth Avenue of Cork. Stroll along the street, looking at the great variety of department stores and specialty shops. Make a left on Princes Street into one of Patrick Street's great institutions—the **\*Old English Market** (6), more recently known as the City Market, a huge indoor marketplace dating back to 1610, although the current building dates only to 1786. Browse amid the colorful stands brimming with vegetables, fish, and fruit as well as traditional Cork foods.

Return to Patrick Street, crossing over to the right onto Cornmarket Street. On Saturdays only, this is the scene of **Coal Quay Market** (7), Cork's original outdoor street market beside the River Lee. Rejuvenated in recent years as part of an urban renewal project, the Coal Quay Market is a colorful and aromatic shopping experience overflowing with delicacies such as sun-dried tomatoes, smoked fish, olives with anchovies, marinated feta with chilis and stuffed vine leaves, mustards, relishes, farmhouse cheeses, and herb oils. It isn't a place to find the usual souvenirs, but it is the ideal spot to rub shoulders with Corkonians, bask in the local ambiance, and perhaps get a great photo.

From Cornmarket Street, make a right onto **\*Paul Street** (8), in the heart of Cork's Huguenot Quarter, originally populated by French Huguenot merchants and craftsmen. Today the Huguenots are gone, but their cobbled streets and tiny shopfronts remain. This is now Cork's newest "in" place to shop, a solid block of craft, fashion, and souvenir enterprises. It is also a veritable "bookshop row," with a branch of the international Waterstone's as well as specialty book stores such as Mainly Murder, 2a Paul St., a storehouse of Irish and international mysteries and curious tales ideal for rainy days. A half-block away is Mercier Press, French Church St., Ireland's oldest independent publishing house, and a prime source for hard-to-find Irish history and folklore titles.

**Paul's Lane** (9), a narrow off-shoot to the left, is lined with a handful of antique shops, and fast becoming Cork's "antique row."

At the end of Paul Street is Emmet Place, home of two of Cork's main cultural keystones. To the left is the:

**\*CRAWFORD MUNICIPAL ART GALLERY** (10), Emmet Place, ☎ 273377. *Open Mon.–Sat. 10–5. Admission is free.*

With a striking classical facade of red brick dressed with limestone, this impressive building was erected in 1724 as the Custom House, but as the port of Cork expanded the Custom House was moved less than 100 years later to its present location and the art gallery was born. The collections include paintings by some of Ireland's finest masters, from Jack Yeats to Nathaniel Grogan, James Barry, William Orpe, and Daniel Maclise, and sculptures by John Hogan. In addition, there are casts from antique sculptures from the Vatican Galleries, given to Cork in 1818; hand-crafted silver; and antique glass pieces.

The adjacent building is the **Opera House** (11), Emmet Place, ☎ 270022, a relatively new addition (1963–65) to the Cork scene, and the major venue in the southwest for opera, drama, musicals, concerts, and more. Reservations are a must.

From Emmet Place, make a left onto Lavitt's Quay and walk one block to **St. Patrick's Bridge**, crossing over the River Lee to the **North Bank** of the city. Opened in 1859, the bridge leads to the north side of the city, a hilly and terraced section where the continuation of St. Patrick Street is called Bridge Street and then **\*St. Patrick's Hill** (12). Aptly named, St. Patrick's Hill is an incline so steep that it is usually compared to the hills of San Francisco. Climb the stepped sidewalks for incomparable views of the Cork skyline.

At this point of the tour, it is best to take a refreshment break or return to your place of lodging for a short rest. Depending on where that takes you, it might be best to take a taxi or the Cork City tour bus (as mentioned above) to commence the rest of this tour. The second part of the tour, which explores some of the more far-flung attractions, involves more extensive walking.

Start on the **South Bank** of the river at a structure that has come to be symbolic of Cork:

**\*ST. FINBARR'S CATHEDRAL** (13), Bishop St., ☎ 963387. *Open Mon.–Fri. 10–1 and 3–5:30. Admission is free.*

Named after the saint who is credited with founding Cork, this impressive Church of Ireland cathedral is of fairly recent vintage (1867–79), but it stands on ground said to be the site of St. Finbarr's monastic settlement (circa. 650). In the 8th and 9th centuries, it was a focal point during Ireland's period as "the isle of saints and scholars" as students from all parts of Europe gathered here to immerse themselves in Christian scholarship. Ever since the Reformation, the church has been the seat of the bishopric of the Church of Ireland. The present structure is a multi-spired early French Gothic edifice known for its elaborate scriptural carvings, mosaic pavements, and a great rose window. The graveyard outside holds many interesting hand-carved monuments.

Make a right turn onto Gill Abbey Street, which then becomes College Road and visit:

**UNIVERSITY COLLEGE—CORK** (14), Western Road, ☎ 276871. *Open June–Sept., Mon.–Fri. 9–5. Tours.*

Dating back to 1845, this college is a component of Ireland's National University, and intellectually nurtures over 7,000 students. It is set in a riverside quadrangle, with several interesting Gothic Revival-style buildings as well as the Honan Chapel, added in 1915 and modeled after Cormac's Chapel at the Rock of Cashel. It contains a splendid collection of stained-glass windows including works by Harry Clarke and Sarah Purser. Outside there is an area known as the Stone Corridor, a collection of stones inscribed with the Ogham style of writing, an early form of the Irish language. Tours of the campus are conducted Monday through Friday at 2:30 p.m., departing from the main gate.

Cross over the River Lee from the Western Road to the Mardyke Walk in the **Flat of the City**. Here you can stroll through *Fitzgerald Park, an 18-acre site named after Edward Fitzgerald, former Lord Mayor of Cork. On the grounds of the park, visit the:

**CORK PUBLIC MUSEUM** (15), Fitzgerald Park, ☎ 270679. *Open Mon.–Fri. 11–1 and 2:15–5, Sun. 3–5. Admission is free, except on Sunday, £1 per person. Café.*

An elegant Georgian house serves as the setting for this museum, opened in 1945. The collections provide insight into the city's colorful political and social history, with artifacts from recent excavations within the city, and an archive of photographs and documents relating to Cork-born Irish patriots, Terence MacSwiney, Thomas MacCurtain, and Michael Collins. In addition, there are noteworthy collections of civic regalia, as well as Cork silver, glass, needlepoint lace, and other crafts practiced locally during the 19th and 20th centuries. Modern Irish sculptures are displayed outside including works by Oisin Kelly and other noted sculptors.

From the Park, take Ferry Walk north, crossing over the Lee to the North Bank to Sunday's Well Road, and an area of the city known simply as Sunday's Well. Turn right and walk for one block to:

**CORK CITY GAOL (JAIL)** (16), Convent Avenue, Sunday's Well, ☎ 305022. *Open March–Oct., daily 9:30–5; Nov.–Feb., Mon.–Fri. 10–4, Sat.–Sun. 10–5. Adults £3.50, seniors and students £3, children £2. Shop. Café. Tours.*

In spite of its castle-like facade, this impressive 19th-century prison building treated its occupants more wretchedly than royally. Indeed many a Cork patriot served time within these walls under miserable conditions in the cause of Irish freedom. The layout includes furnished cells, life-like animated figures, sound effects, and an audiovisual show, all of which re-create prison life in Cork.

Also within the Gaol's complex, in the former jail governor's house, is the **Radio Museum Experience**, a museum that spotlights the impact of radio on all of our lives, with various exhibits on the early days of Irish and international radio broadcasting. *Open daily, March–Oct. 9:30–6 and Nov.–Feb. 10–5. Adults £3.50, seniors and students £3, children £2. A joint ticket to both the Gaol and the Radio Experience Museum is available at a discounted price.*

Ramble back toward the city along the North Bank of the river, following Sunday's Well Road to the North Mall. Take a left at Shandon Street and follow it north into one of the city's oldest neighborhoods north of Pope's Quay. The centerpiece is:

**\*ST. ANN'S SHANDON CHURCH** (17), Church St., ☎ 501672. *Open Mon.–Sat. 9:30–5. Admission £1.50 per person.*

Dating back to 1722, this Church of Ireland edifice is the North Bank's prime landmark, synonymous with the Cork skyline. From almost anywhere downtown, you can see the church's tower, a giant pepperpot steeple, two sides of which are made of limestone and two of sandstone, with a top crowned by a gilt ball and an 11-foot salmon-shaped weathervane. Each side of the steeple also boasts a clock. Most of all, this church is known for its eight melodious bells, which echo throughout the city. Visitors are encouraged to climb up to the belfry and play a tune or at least enjoy panoramic views of the city. Corkonians are always raising their heads up toward Shandon, if not to hear the bells, then to set their watches by one of the clocks, or to check the fish weathervane for a weather forecast.

Directly opposite the church is a unique new visitor museum:

**CORK BUTTER MARKET** (18), O'Connell Square, Shandon, ☎ 300600. *Open May–Sept., Mon.–Sat. 10–5. Adults £2.50, seniors, students, and children £2.*

Housed in the original Cork Butter Exchange building, this museum tells the story of Cork's eminence in the 18th and 19th centuries as a major producer of butter. In its day, the Cork market was the largest market of its type in the world and Cork-branded butter set the standards for quality and price around the world. The exhibits trace the whole story of butter production in Ireland, from the origins of dairying and the Irish practice of preserving butter in bogs to the importance of "milch cows" in medieval Ireland and the development of "butter roads." One whole floor of the museum is devoted to displays of butter-making equipment, and there is also a audiovisual that explores the butter industry in modern times.

Make a right and follow John Street back to the quays and walk eastward along Camden Quay, which leads to St. Patrick's Bridge. Cross over to Patrick Street, back to the heart of Cork, to complete your tour.

# *Kinsale

S itting on the gentle slope of Compass Hill beside the Bandon Estuary, Kinsale is a picturesque seaport with a wide sheltered harbor. This little town of 2,000 residents, less than 20 miles from Cork City, is a favorite haunt for Corkonians and worldwide visitors alike, especially those who have a penchant for boating, fishing, or just strolling along the wide marina. The placename of Kinsale is indeed fitting, derived from the Irish language *Cionn tSáile*, meaning "head of (the) sea."

Historically, Kinsale traces its origins back to 1177 when the Anglo-Normans founded a town in a small walled area close to the water. The town received its first royal charter from King Edward II in 1335. Almost 300 years passed before Kinsale achieved its moment of fame in the long struggle for Irish freedom. In September of 1601, an Iberian fleet of masted warships, known as the Spanish Armada, pulled into Kinsale Harbour to help the Irish chieftains O'Neill and O'Donnell from Ulster in their quest to win the town from the English. Unfortunately, the Spanish-Irish alliance was betrayed from within and attacked at The Battle of Kinsale, turning the joint effort into defeat. Afterwards, Kinsale became an important British Naval base.

Rather than submit to the Crown, many of the Irish clan leaders fled to the Continent, signaling the end of the old Gaelic order in Ireland. Their escape from Ireland, which is referred to variously as The Flight of the Earls or The Flight of the Wild Geese, provided mainland Europe with many legacies including the establishment of Irish colleges and regiments in France, Italy, Spain, and France, and development of the wine and spirits industry in Europe. Few have not heard of *Hennessy* brandy, but there are also Irish names on some of France's best wines, such as *Château McCarthy*, *Château Dillon*, *Château Barton*, *Château Kirwan*, *Château Phelan*, *Château Lynch*, and *Château Clarke*. In time, Kinsale benefited from these connections and became one of Ireland's principal wine ports in the 17th and 18th centuries.

Kinsale's other significant rendezvous with history was on a more tragic note. In 1915, just off the coast of Kinsale, the *Lusitania* was sunk by a German submarine, with the loss of over 1,500 lives, many of whom were buried in a local cemetery.

Today Kinsale is best known for its well-maintained waterside setting, consistently winning national and international awards for the quality of its environment, and use of trees and flowers. Thanks to the abundance of fresh seafood at its doorstep, Kinsale has also made a big name for itself as "the gourmet capital" of Ireland. Home to more than a dozen award-winning restaurants and pubs, Kinsale draws lovers of good food year-round and particularly each October when it hosts a three-day gourmet food festival.

## GETTING THERE:

From Cork City, it's 18 miles south to Kinsale, an easy half-hour drive on local road R600. Follow signs for the airport, on leaving the city center, and once on the airport road, you will see signposts for Kinsale.

From Cork's Central Bus Station, **Bus Eireann** operates regular service to Kinsale. The trip, making various stops en route, takes approximately 45 minutes. The bus depot is on Pier Road, opposite the tourist office.

## PRACTICALITIES:

Kinsale is a small town that is very popular with Irish and European vacationers, so be sure to have advance reservations in the busy May–October season. Walking is the only way to explore it as there is no local transport. Most streets are quite narrow, and some are steep or cobbled. Parking is limited, so leave your car near the pier and walk everywhere.

For information, contact the **Kinsale Tourist Office**, Pier Rd. at Emmet St., ☎ 021-772234, open from March through November.

Kinsale is at its busiest during the first weekend of October, when the **Kinsale Gourmet Festival** is held. For advance information about the festival, contact the tourist office.

**Herlihy's Guided Tours**, one-hour walking tours around the historic sections of Kinsale, are operated on weekends, departing from the tourist office. Advance reservations are suggested, ☎ 772310 or 772873.

The telephone area code for all numbers is 021, unless indicated otherwise.

## FOOD AND DRINK:

As the "gourmet capital" of Ireland, Kinsale offers a wide choice of restaurants, from village shopfronts to harborside settings, with cuisine from local seafoods to international favorites. At least a dozen of Kinsale's restaurants belong to the "Good Food Circle." A complete list is available at the local tourist office.

**The Blue Haven** (3 Pearse St.) Known as the "seafood specialist," this award-winning inn has been featured in leading food magazines and major television programs including *The Today Show*. Specialties include oak-smoked salmon, seafood thermidor, garlic mussels, and fishermen's platters. Bar food ranges from seafood pastas and chowders to quiches and pancakes. Dining areas include an indoor/outdoor café, fireside pub, and full-service skylit restaurant. If you are in the mood for a picnic, the inn's gourmet shop also stocks Irish-produced foods such as smoked salmon, brown bread, patés, jams, and cheeses. ☎ 772209. X: early Jan. ££

to £££

**Cottage Loft** (6 Main St.) As its name implies, this little restaurant has a cottage-style ambiance, housed in a 200-year-old shopfront building, with a decor of antiques, caned chairs, and beamed ceilings. The menu offers a mix of Irish and international dishes, from farmyard duck and rack of lamb, to a house specialty of *seafood Danielle*—salmon stuffed with crab, prawns, and peppers in a nettle sauce. Dinner only. ☎ 772803. X: Mon. in Nov.-Apr. ££

**The Dock** (Castlepark, en route to James Fort) On a warm sunny day, it's hard to find a table at this pub. It has one of the best locations in town, on the harborfront on the outskirts of town. The interior has a homey atmosphere with windows overlooking the water, and there is patio seating outside for sunny days. The menu offers light meals and snacks, such as smoked salmon and crabmeat platters and a variety of open-faced and toasted sandwiches. ☎ 772522. £

**Jim Edwards** (Market Quay, off Emmet Pl.) For over 25 years, this restaurant-pub has earned a reputation for fresh seafood served in an authentic nautical atmosphere. The menu offers lobster and oysters from the tank, as well as the best of the local catch and a variety of steaks, poultry and lamb dishes. Don't miss the distinctive clock at the entrance; instead of numbers, the time is shown in letters which spell out the owner's name. ☎ 772541. ££

**Max's** (Main St.) Housed in a cozy shopfront setting, this little wine bar offers light and healthy meals with emphasis on fresh seafood and vegetarian dishes. Specialties include grilled mussels, beefburgers, Mediterranean-style salads, and creative pastas. The early-bird menu offers very good value. ☎ 772443. X: Nov.–Feb. £ to ££

**Spaniard** (Scilly, on the road to Charles Fort) Set high above the harbor en route to an area known as Summercove, this pub exudes an early 17th-century atmosphere, harking back to the days of the Spanish Armada, with low beamed ceilings, stone floors, and lots of seafaring memorabilia. The food is simple pub grub, from soups, salads, and sandwiches to Irish stew. There is traditional Irish music session every Wednesday and light jazz and contemporary folk music on other nights. ☎ 772436. £

**1601** (Pearse St.) Situated in the heart of town near Market Square, this restaurant is named after the year of the Battle of Kinsale and the decor reflects that theme, with a wall-size mural of the event. The eclectic menu offers chowders, salads, seafood platters, quiches, steaks, and Irish traditional dishes such as bacon and cabbage and Irish stew. ☎ 772529. £

## SUGGESTED TOUR:

Start a tour at the bus deport, opposite the tourist office, on **Pier Road** (1) at Emmet Street, also known as **Emmet Place**. The town's original Water Gate stood here, as part of the original city walls built by the Normans. To the left is the Temperance Hall, the first building of its kind to be built for

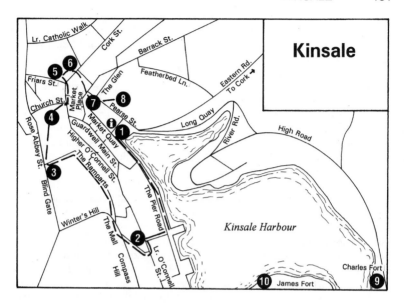

Kinsale

the purpose of discouraging drink by the local folk.

Turn right and walk along *The Pier, built in 1890, with Kinsale's vast marina and harborfront on the left. On the right are rows of lovely Georgian homes and gardens, some now serving as hotels and guest-houses. Make a right at **Denis Quay**, one of 15 original quays that served the harborfront before the Pier was added. In the 17th and 19th centuries, these quays were not only moorings for huge cargo ships, but also pro-vided workshops for fish coopering and net repairing, sail making, and other nautical trades. Denis Quay, like the others, is now a road.

Cross over Lr. O'Connell Street, a busy thoroughfare now housing an assortment of restaurants, guesthouses, and shops. Turn left, and then make a quick right, to climb St. John's Hill. On the right is the Bowling Green, now known simply as **The Green** (2), used as a place of social gath-erings and assemblies in the 18th century. It is said that William Penn vis-ited and that John Wesley preached about Methodism here.

Continue to **The Mall** and make a left turn onto *Compass Hill, the highest point on this walk, with sweeping views of the houses and harbor below. Return to The Mall, which was the fashionable walkway of 18th-century Kinsale. Stroll along The Mall, passing the old Municipal Hall on the right, and some 17th-century almshouses, known locally as the Gift Houses on the left. These have been restored in recent years. This walk-way then changes its name to **The Rampart** because it is on the site of the upper wall of the old walled town.

Take a left at Rampart Lane and then a right at **Blind Gate** (3). The gate derived its name from having been walled or "blinded" up in 1695 since it was proving convenient for smugglers. Blind Gate merges into Rose Abbey Street and then Church Street. Here to the right is **St. Multose Church** (4), Church St., a Church of Ireland edifice and one of the two significant medieval buildings still left in Kinsale. Built in 1190, it has changed over the years, but still retains many of its original features including black letter inscriptions in Norman French, an Easter sepulchre, carved memorials and reredos, and a wooden coat of arms.

Follow Church Street to Cork Street, making a left to see the **Church of St. John the Baptist** (5), Friars Street. This Classical-style Catholic church is of more recent vintage, built shortly after Catholic Emancipation Act of 1829. The walls were built of local shale and limestone.

Returning to Cork Street, on the left stands Kinsale's other significant medieval building—**\*Desmond Castle** (6), Cork St., ☎ 774855, replete with mullioned windows and stepped battlements. Built by the Earl of Desmond, c. 1500, this castle has had a long and colorful history. It served first as a customs house for wine, wool, and tobacco. During the Battle of Kinsale in 1601, it was used by the Spanish to store ammunition. In the mid-18th century, it became a prison for French men captured during the Napoleonic wars, and was known locally as French Prison. Declared a national monument in 1938, it is currently being adapted to house one of Ireland's newest epicurean attractions—a unique wine museum. The displays and exhibits will recall Kinsale's days as a leading wine port and Ireland's contributions to the wine industries of Europe. *Open mid-April to mid-June, Tues.–Sun. 10–6; mid-June to early-Oct., daily 10–6. Adults £2, seniors £1.50, students £1. Tours.*

Turn right and follow Chairman's Lane down the hill to **Market Square**, the heart of Kinsale. The centerpiece of this commercial square is **Market House** (7), erected c. 1600 as a traditional two-story building with arches on all four sides, and a brick facade with Dutch gables, a clock, bell cote, and turrets. There were offices upstairs and markets below. In 1706 the building added a new dimension as the town courthouse and official meeting rooms. More recently, in 1940, the building was "born again" as the **Kinsale Regional Museum**, Market Square, ☎ 772044. The museum has a display of old Kinsale craftwork and other memorabilia including an exhibit on the legendary Kinsale Giant. He was Patrick Cotter O'Brien, reputed to have been over eight feet tall. *Open daily 10–6. Adults 50p, children 20p.*

Bear left onto Pearse Street, originally part of Long Quay and lined with merchant's residences and warehouses. On the left is the **\*Blue Haven Hotel** (8), originally the Old Fish Market and now a much-heralded seafood restaurant and inn. The street was re-named in honor of the Irish patriot Padraic Pearse after the Irish Rising of 1916.

From Pearse, take a right onto Emmet Street, named after another Irish patriot, Robert Emmet, and the completion of the walking portion of the tour.

The remainder of Kinsale is best done with the help of a car or taxi.

Two forts are worth exploring, each situated on one side of the harbor entrance. Both forts, now in ruins, were built by the British to protect their interests in Kinsale, and remained in British hands until 1922. First, follow Long Quay and the High Road to **Charles Fort** (9), ☎ 772263, a unique star-shaped fort built c. 1677. Across the harbor, via the Pier Road, is **James Fort** (10), built in 1602. Both are fine examples of 17th-century military architecture, offering sweeping views of the harbor, the town, and each other. Only Charles Fort is fully accessible to the public. *Open mid-March to Oct., daily 10–6; Nov. to mid-March, Sat.–Sun. 10–5. Adults £2.50, seniors £1.75, students £1.*

Return to the heart of Kinsale and complete your tour by strolling along Main Street, lined with local craftshops, or return to The Pier Road, to watch the fishing boats unloading their daily catch or sail boats gliding into the marina.

**Trip 18**

# From Blarney to East Cork

A visit to Cork is not complete without an hour or two at Blarney, a lovely Tudor-style village five miles northwest of downtown. Aside from Killarney, Blarney is probably the most popular place in Ireland—because almost every tourist wants to kiss the famous Blarney Stone.

Ideally, a brief sojourn in Blarney can be combined with a drive around the eastern part of County Cork, an often-overlooked area that is well worth a detour. East Cork is the home of Cobh, Ireland's chief port and departure point for millions of emigrants before air travel; Fota Island, a delightful harborside wildlife park and arboretum; Midelton, the hub of Ireland's whiskey-distilling industry; Shanagarry, setting for Ireland's premier cooking school; and Youghal, a fishing port immortalized in the movie Moby Dick.

## GETTING THERE:

From Cork's Central Bus Station, **Bus Eireann** offers frequent service to Blarney, a 20-minute ride. Bus Eireann also operates service to Midelton and Youghal, but this would only be practical if you wanted to explore only one of those towns for an afternoon. To do a tour of East Cork, you need a car, traveling out of Cork City or Blarney to link up with the main N25 road in an eastward direction. From N25, you can take the turn-offs as sign-posted for Cobh, Fota, Midelton, Shanagarry, and Youghal.

## PRACTICALITIES:

The best way to see Blarney and East Cork is by car. Individual round-trips to Blarney, Midelton, or Youghal can be made by bus, but to cover the whole circuit of East Cork requires driving from place to place.

At least two of the East Cork attractions, the Cobh Heritage Centre and the Old Midleton Distillery, are very popular and require at least an hour or more to see and perhaps some waiting time, so you may need to pick-and-choose what interests you most, rather than trying to do everything in one day.

For on-the-spot help, stop into the **Blarney Tourist Office**, Main St., Blarney, ☎ 021-381624, open all year; and the **Youghal Tourist Office**, Market Square, Youghal, ☎ 024-92390, open from June through mid-September. In addition, there is a tourist information desk at the Old Midleton

Distillery, Midleton, ☎ 021-613702, open from April through September. The telephone area code for all numbers is 021, unless indicated otherwise.

## FOOD AND DRINK:

**Aherne's** (163 N. Main St., Youghal) Situated in the heart of town, there are no sea views at this Old World inn, but the best of the local catch is always on the menu—from lobsters and oysters out of the tank, to crab claws and giant prawn tails, as well as seafood chowders, pies, and salads. The menu offers a choice of pub meals by day and full à la carte dinners at night. ☎ 024-92424. £ to £££

**Ballymaloe House** (Shanagarry, Midleton) Housed in a Georgian country house in an off-the-beaten path setting, this restaurant is known for top class cuisine, using the freshest produce from its own farm, gardens, and nearby waters. The food is so good that it has inspired an on-premises cooking school and a half-dozen cook books. Reservations are a must. ☎ 652531. ££ to £££

**Christy's Restaurant** (Blarney) Operated by the Kelleher family, who also own the adjacent Blarney Woollen Mills, a huge shopping emporium, this restaurant is a favorite with tour buses. It offers a good choice of pub meals and full-service dining. ☎ 385011. ££

**Farmgate Restaurant & Country Store** (Coolbawn, Midleton) Fresh locally produced foods are the mainstay of this cozy restaurant. Specialties include free-range duck and fresh fish, as well as farmhouse cheeses. Open for daytime meals plus dinner on Fri.–Sat. ☎ 632771. X: Sun. ££

**Longueville House—President's Restaurant** (Mallow, Co. Cork) Although this country house restaurant is technically in north Co. Cork, it is worth a slight detour when in the Blarney-Midleton environs. Long a benchmark of fine food, Longueville is nestled on a 500-acre wooded estate and farm which also includes vineyards and a winery that produces lovely Irish white wine. The O'Callaghan family provide a warm welcome and outstanding cuisine, including lamb raised on the estate, fresh salmon and trout from the river, and vegetables from the garden. ☎ 022-47156. X: mid-Dec. to mid-Feb. ££ and £££

**Stephen Pearce Café** (at the Stephen Pearce Emporium, Shanagarry) Surrounded by pottery and the latest in Ireland's ceramic creations, this self-service restaurant offers seating indoors and on an outdoor patio. The menu changes daily but includes homemade soups, pies, and traditional dishes, as well as freshly made salads. Open for daytime snacks and light meals. ☎ 646807. £

## SUGGESTED TOUR:

Start the day with a visit to the village of **Blarney**, five miles northwest of Cork City via local road R617. Designed in the Tudor style, around a village green, Blarney sits on the edge of the Shournagh River, surrounded

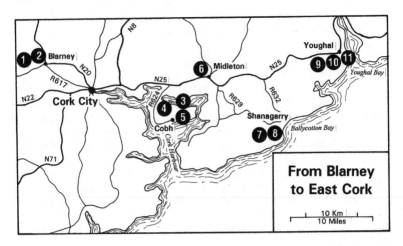

by wooded countryside and quiet country lanes. It was planned as a water-powered linen-and-wool-processing center, the latter of which still flourishes today at the Blarney Woollen Mills, a local enterprise that produces and stocks knitwear of all kinds plus a wide range of souvenirs and gifts. Although historical details on the origins of Blarney are a little sketchy, legend and tradition have filled in the gaps and made the "stone" at Blarney Castle a sine qua non of a visit to Ireland. Park your car and follow the signs for the short walk up the path to:

**BLARNEY CASTLE** (1), Blarney, ☎ 385252. *Open daily 9–5:30. Adults £3.50, seniors and students £2.50, children £1. Shop. Tours.*

In many ways, Blarney Castle is to Ireland what Big Ben is to Britain or the Eiffel Tower to France. Just about everyone in the Western world has heard of the castle's Blarney Stone and identifies it with the Emerald Isle. It is just an ordinary gray stone, yet people believe that a quick kiss on the old cold rock will impart magical powers and particularly the gift of eloquence or "the gift of the gab."

The centerpiece of the village of Blarney, this storied castle was built circa 1446. Originally the stronghold of the MacCarthys, the castle is long since gone, except for its massive square keep, a tower with a battlemented parapet rising 83 feet high. The fabled Blarney Stone is wedged underneath the battlements, and, in order to kiss it, visitors must lie down on the ground and bend backwards into a trench where the stone awaits. It sounds awkward, but the area is fully protected and a trained guide supervises all the kissing. The hardest part of the whole experience is climbing up the ancient curved stone steps to the parapet.

The legend of the Blarney Stone goes back to the days of Queen Elizabeth I, when the castle and lands of Blarney belonged to a local Irish family, the MacCarthys. The head of the clan, Cormac MacDermott MacCarthy, the Lord of Blarney, did not want to swear allegiance to the Queen, but he also did not want to loose his land. He was completely evasive when asked by the Queen's deputy to renounce the traditional systems and take the tenure of his lands from the Crown. While seeming to agree to the proposal, he put off fulfilling his promise from day to day with "fair words and soft speech." Finally, the Queen is reputed to have declared *"This is all Blarney—what he says, he never means!"* And thus the word Blarney came to mean pleasant talk intended to deceive without offending, and in its modern interpretation, as a clever and intense form of flattery. Somewhere over the centuries, the tradition evolved that anyone who kisses the Blarney Stone will obtain the everlasting eloquence of Cormac MacDermott MacCarthy. And thus all the tour buses and crowds who flock to Blarney.

After kissing the stone, you may wish to stroll through the gardens and nearby dell beside Blarney Lake. You can also visit the adjacent **Blarney House** (2), ☎ 385252, a Scottish baronial mansion dating back to 1874, with a unique facade featuring corner turrets and bartizans with conical roofs. Recently restored, it contains a collection of ancestral paintings, tapestries, and heraldic decorations. *Open June–Sept., Mon.–Sat. 12–6. Adults £2.50, seniors and students £2, and children £1.50. Note: Reduced rate combination tickets are available for anyone visiting both Blarney Castle and Blarney House.*

From Blarney, return to Cork and follow the signs for N25, the main eastbound road. Drive for 10 miles to Carrigtohill, and make a right turn onto local road R624. From the round-about, follow signs slightly to the left to **Barryscourt Castle** (3), Carrigtwohill, ☎ 021-882218, a newly restored castle dating back to the 12th century, and the seat of the Barry family for over 500 years. The present castle is a fine example of a 15th-century tower house with 16th-century additions. The adjacent stone coach house contains an Old World tearoom/craft shop featuring homemade soups, snacks, and desserts. *Open June–Sept., daily 10–6. Adults £1.50, seniors £1, students and children 60p.*

Continue for one mile south and cross the causeway onto Fota Island to visit one of Ireland's most exotic little corners:

**FOTA ISLAND WILDLIFE PARK & ARBORETUM** (4), Fota Island, Carrigtohill, ☎ 812678. *Open April–Sept., daily 10–6; Oct., Sat. 10–5., Sun. 11–5. Adults £4.40, students £3.50, seniors and children under age 14 £2.50. Arboretum open year-round in daylight hours, free admission. Café. Tours.*

Conservation and ecology are the buzz words on this island paradise. The Fota Wildlife Park, established in 1983, is considered one of the most modern of its kind in Europe. It provides a habitat for more than 70 species of exotic animals and birds in open natural surroundings with no obvious barriers. Giraffes, ostriches, and antelope roam together in 40 acres of grasslands, similar to the setting of an African savannah. Monkeys swing through trees, while kangaroos, macaws, and lemurs tread nearby. Only the cheetahs are secluded by a fence. It is interesting to note that, in recent years, Fota has become the world's largest breeder of cheetah, a species endangered in its own homelands.

In addition, Fota leads the way in the breeding of other endangered species including Scimitar horned onyx from North Africa; the liontailed macaque from India; and the white tailed sea eagle, being reintroduced into the wilds of County Kerry.

The remainder of the Fota expanse is an arboretum, home to trees and shrubs from every continent, with outstanding collections from China, Japan, and Chile. Each plant is labeled, giving country of origin, date of planting, and heights in recent years. The collection, which flourishes in the mild and sheltered micro-climate of this island, includes the tallest specimen of "spiralis" in Europe, a pine from Tasmania believed to be the largest in the British Isles, and a unique "handkerchief" tree. The admission charge provides access to both the wildlife park and the arboretum.

From Fota, continue southward via R624 and onto another island, known as the Great Island. It is less than four miles to Ireland's chief transatlantic port of **Cobh** (pronounced *Cove*), a word that means "haven" in the Irish language. In its earliest days, the town was referred to as "the Cove of Cork," but the name was changed to Queenstown in honor of Queen Victoria in 1849.

For many years, Queenstown was a British Naval Station, and during World War I it was also used by the US Navy as its principal base in European waters. The town's name was restored to Cobh in 1922 after the Irish achieved independence from Britain.

In the days before airline travel, Cobh was Ireland's chief port of entry or exit, with up to three or four transatlantic liners calling here per week. Records show that from 1848 to 1950 more than 2.5 million people emigrated from the port of Cobh. For those who left in poverty during the famine years and the early part of the 20th century, Cobh was the last glimpse of Ireland they would ever see. For an overview of Cobh's heyday as a transatlantic port and emigration depot, follow the signs to:

**\*COBH: THE QUEENSTOWN STORY** (5), Cobh Railway Station, Cobh, ☎ 813591. *Open March–Dec., daily 10–6. Adults £3.50, seniors and students £3, children under age 16 £2. Shop. Café.*

Housed in Cobh's former railway station, this relatively new heritage center focuses on the town's role as a major seaport and emigration center. Step inside and take a "walk-through" tour of Ireland in the mid-19th century when people were forced to starve or leave home for a better life in a new country. The life-size exhibits and tableaux include scenes of dockside departures and prototypes of emigrant cabins aboard the crowded ships. Cobh's role as a major port for luxury ships is also presented, with re-creations of interiors of great ocean liners, and scenes from historic events in the waters nearby including Cobh's connections to the ill-fated *Titanic* which sank in Atlantic waters on her maiden voyage in 1912, and Cobh's rescue efforts during the sinking of the *Lusitania* off Cork Harbour during World War I. For anyone with an Irish name or Irish roots, this center also houses an emigration museum with genealogical information and passenger manifests from ships that called at Cobh over the years.

Return to the main N25 road, turn right, and continue in an eastward direction for six miles to Midelton, a busy market town dating back to the 17th century. Make a left and follow the signs for a visit to Ireland's largest whiskey distillery at the:

**\*OLD MIDLETON DISTILLERY** (6), Midleton, ☎ 613594. *Open March–Oct., daily 10–6 (last tour at 4:30); Nov.–Feb., Mon.–Fri. for tours at 12 and 3, and Sat.–Sun. tours at 2 and 4. Adults £3.95, seniors and students £3.50, children £1.50. Shop. Café. Tours.*

Dating back to 1825, this landmark complex focuses on one of Ireland's foremost products, Irish whiskey, including leading brands such as John Jameson, John Power, Tullamore Dew, and others. A tour of the distillery provides close-up views of the mill building, maltings, corn stores, still houses, warehouses, kilns, water wheel, and copper stills, including the largest pot still in the world, with a capacity of 31,648 gallons. To illustrate the step-by-step whiskey-making process, there is an audiovisual presentation, as well as demonstrations and working models. Afterward, enjoy a sampling of the various brands of whiskey produced at this facility.

Depart Midleton and return to the main N25 road, continuing eastward for six miles to Castlemartyr, a small market town. At this point, if you are interested in a culinary detour, take a right, following the signposts for five miles to **\*Ballymaloe House** (7), Ballycotton Rd., Shanagarry, ☎ 652531. A founding member of the Irish Country Houses & Restaurants Association, Ballymaloe has been a prime mover in the emergence of top-class Irish country cuisine. Relying on local seafood and produce, accompanied by fresh vegetables from the garden, the Allen family has drawn connoisseurs of fine food from all parts of the world to this remote spot near Ballycotton Bay. The success of the Ballymaloe restaurant has spawned the trend-setting **Ballymaloe Cookery School**, offering more than 35 different courses a year ranging from one day to 12 weeks in duration. Designed for amateur and professional chefs of all levels of proficiency, the courses cover topics such as bread-making, weekend entertaining, hors d'oeuvres, seafood, vegetarian, family food, barbecue food, mushroom cookery, and Christmas recipes. If you don't have time to take a course, the Ballymaloe Shop offers a wide range of cookbooks by members of the Allen family as well as a wide array of cooking utensils, accessories, preserves, and other foods.

Take time to stroll in the adjacent **Kinoth Garden**, the epitome of a cooking school plantation, with an extensive herb garden and a potager or vegetable garden laid out on a strict geometric pattern with many traditional and exotic vegetables. There is also a formal fruit garden, with apples, pears, plums, peaches and cherries, many cultivated in arches. A rose garden, herbaceous borders, specimen trees and shrubs, and a small lake complete the setting. *Garden ticket £3.*

Before leaving **Shanagarry**, you should know that William Penn, founding father of the state of Pennsylvania, made his home for a time in the 1660s at Shanagarry House on the Cloyne Road. His father, Admiral Sir William Penn had been granted the lands of East Cork and sent his son to administer his estates. Descendants of Admiral Penn held the Shanagarry estate until 1903. The house has been in ruins for some time, but it is currently being reconstructed to form part of a new interpretative center focusing on the Penn family connections between Ireland and the US.

While in Shanagarry, if you are interested in crafts, visit the **\*Stephen Pearce Emporium** (8), Shanagarry, ☎ 646807. A native of this area, Pearce is one of Ireland's master ceramic craftsmen, distinguished for his earth-toned tableware and furnishings. This huge skylit factory/showroom is a retail outlet and demonstration center for this well-known potter's work.

Returning to the main N25 road, it's just over 10 miles to **Youghal** (pronounced *Yawl*), East Cork's major coastal town, situated right on the County Waterford border at the mouth of the River Blackwater.

Youghal, a town known for its yew trees, takes its name from the Irish language word *Eochaill*, meaning "yew wood." A leading beach resort, Youghal is loosely identified with Sir Walter Raleigh, who was the mayor of the town from 1588 to 1589. According to local lore, it was here that Raleigh, fresh from a visit to Virginia, smoked the first tobacco in Ireland and grew the first potatoes in Ireland. His house, Myrtle Grove, dating back to 1462, is still occupied today but not open to the public.

Historically, very little is known about Youghal until the 13th century when the Anglo-Normans founded a baronial town that evolved into a busy walled port. Follow the signs to the strand or promenade and park your car along Strand Street or The Mall, in the public parking area. Then take a left turn and walk one block up to Main Street, a long and narrow one-way thoroughfare, to see the **\*Clock Gate** (9), a five-story arched red sandstone building spanning over South Main St. Erected in 1777 to replace an earlier medieval iron gate, it served as the town jail until 1837.

Around the corner, on Market Square, is the **Moby Dick Pub**, the last visible reminder that in 1954 the town of Youghal served as the setting for the Hollywood-produced movie, *Moby Dick*, starring Gregory Peck. Market Square is also home to the **Youghal Heritage Centre** (10), an exhibit inside the local tourist office that tells the story of the development of Youghal from earliest days.

On the north end of Main Street is **St. Mary's Church** (11), erected about 1250 and restored in the mid-19th century. It is a cruciform structure, with an aisled nave of five bays, massive bell-tower, candle-snuffer roof, and a fascinating collection of tombs and monuments including 14th- and 15th-century effigies. Just off North Main Street are portions of the original city walls.

End your walk at Strand Street or The Mall and take a seaside stroll along the promenade to enjoy views of Youghal's wide and sandy four-mile beach.

From Youghal, take the main N25 road back to Cork, a straight run of 31 miles, or continue on to other parts of Ireland.

# *Bantry Bay

I n a county known for its beautiful bays, Bantry is the benchmark of Cork's waters. Nestled off the Atlantic between the Beara and Sheep's Head peninsulas, Bantry Bay is nature at its best—glistening and pure waters rimmed by lush and colorful foliage. Time after time, it inspires an artist's best impression or a photographer's finest frame. It provides the perfect backdrop for a scenic tour or a romantic rendezvous.

The Irish language place name for Bantry, *Beanntraighe*, describes it very well, with a meaning of "head land of the shore." The name Bantry also belongs to the adjacent market town, distinguished as the home of the Earls of Bantry since 1739.

Historically, Bantry Bay played an important role in Ireland's struggles to gain independence from Britain. French fleets, in support of the Irish, twice entered Bantry Bay. In 1689 they came to help James II in his unsuccessful campaign against William of Orange, and in 1796 the French Armada returned to aid Wolfe Tone and his United Irishmen in their abortive efforts to overthrow British rule.

To say that Bantry Bay is beautiful is trite. It is awesome, and yet simple—pristine and natural. It is worth a drive from Cork or any part of Ireland to spend a day drinking in the ageless wonders of Bantry Bay. Bring your camera, pen, paintbrush, or camcorder. Take it all in, and then take home fond memories.

## GETTING THERE:

By car, Bantry Bay is approximately 60 miles southeast of Cork, via the main N22 road to Macroom and then through the Shehy Mountains on the R584 road. Allow at least two hours, making stops at various towns en route.

Public transport is also available. From Cork's Central Bus Station, **Bus Eireann** operates daily service to Bantry. Travel time by bus is about two hours, depending on local stops.

## PRACTICALITIES:

The best way to travel to Bantry is by car. The route is a very pleasant drive, wending through rich agricultural lands and then a series of mountains and valleys. Since Bantry Bay is relatively isolated compared to the rest of Cork, it is wise to combine a visit to Bantry with a drive around one or both of the adjacent peninsulas—Beara and Sheep's Head.

For information, contact the **Bantry Tourist Office**, Old Courthouse,

Bantry, ☎ 027-50229, open from June to September. In July and August, there is also a small trailer dispensing visitor information next to the Eccles Hotel, Glengariff, ☎ 027-63084. The telephone area code for all numbers is 027, unless indicated otherwise.

## FOOD AND DRINK:

**Auld Triangle** (Main St., Macroom) For over 300 years, this stone-faced pub-restaurant has been a favorite with the locals and as a stopping place on the main road from Cork. Bar food, from soups and salads to sandwiches, is served all day. ☎ 026- 41940. £

**Ballylickey Manor House** (Ballylickey, Bantry) French-Irish cuisine is served at this 300-year-old manor house, in a restaurant overlooking 10 acres of gardens and views of Bantry Bay. X: Dec.–Jan. ☎ 50124. ££ to £££

**Blair's Cove** (Durrus, Bantry) For fine food in a romantic setting, it's hard to beat this long-established culinary outpost overlooking Dunmanus Bay. This Belgian-owned restaurant is housed in a restored and modernized 250-year-old stone barn. The menu is international, with emphasis on meats and fish cooked slowly and succulently on an open wood fireplace. Open for dinner only. X: Nov.–Mar. and Sun. ☎ 61127. £££

**Blue Loo** (Main St. Glengariff) In spite of its curious name ("loo" usually refers to a toilet), this little pub offers a welcoming traditional country atmosphere, with seating indoors and outside beside the road. Bar food items, such as fresh crab or smoked wild salmon sandwiches, are served only during peak season, otherwise it's a great spot for a drink. ☎ 63167. £

**Johnny Barry's** (Main St., Glengariff) This friendly pub offers a relaxing Old World setting and hefty portions of bar food all day, from soups and sandwiches, to seafood platters and steaks. There is music at night from May to October. ☎ 63315. £ to ££

**Sea View House** (Ballylickey, Bantry) Set overlooking Bantry Bay amid its own lush gardens, this Georgian-style country inn has won many awards for its creative cookery, using the best of local seafood and produce. Even the ice creams for dessert are homemade! Enjoy freshly made soups, salads, and sandwiches by day in the bar or a full five-course dinner in the antique-filled formal Georgian-era dining room at night. ☎ 50462. X: Nov. 15–Mar. 14. ££ to £££

**Shiro** (Ahakista) The secluded Sheep's Head Peninsula is an unlikely place to find world-class Japanese cuisine, but this 12-seat restaurant falls into that category. Run by Kei and Werner Pilz, it offers an array of authentic Japanese treats using local ingredients, from sushi and sashimi to zensai (flower-flecked appetizers) and suimono (seasonal soup). Dinner only; reservations are essential. ☎ 67030. X: Jan. £££

## SUGGESTED TOUR:

Depart **Cork** (1) on the main N22 road, heading west, following the path of the River Lee. After traveling 23 miles, you will go through **Macroom**, a busy market town at the confluence of three rivers—the Lee,

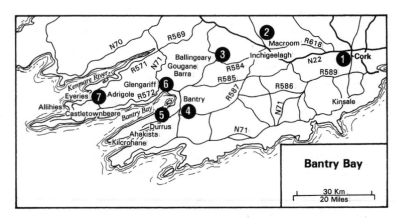

Laney, and Sullane. In the center of the town stands the remains of **Macroom Castle** (2), a 13th-century fortress that was granted in 1654 by Oliver Cromwell to Admiral Sir William Penn, father of the founder of Pennsylvania. It is said that young William spent much of his childhood here, before he left to study at Oxford in 1660. Over the years, the castle has endured many pillages and was finally burned for the last time during the Irish Civil War in the early 1920s. The ruins have been declared a national monument, and the entrance gateway restored.

After passing through Macroom, follow the sign-posts for local road R584 and begin a scenic drive through the Derrynasaggart Mountains. This is a *Gaeltacht*—an Irish or Gaelic-speaking area, and the signs indicate placenames in Irish first, and then in English, if at all. After 10 miles, the village of **Inchigeelagh** appears. The placename is so old that it rarely is given an English translation. Next, after 5.5 miles, is *Béal Átha an Ghaorthaidh* (**Ballingeary**), a name that means "ford-mouth of the wooded valley." It is a popular place for students to come in the summer to immerse themselves in the Irish language. The local enterprise, **Quills Woollen Market** (3), Main St., ☎ 026-47008, has long brought employment to this remote area, producing a wide range of sweaters, knitwear, and crafts, using the skins of sheep and goats.

About four miles west beyond Ballingeary, make a right turn following the signs for \***Gougane Barra**, a national park and the source for the River Lee. Legend has it that St. Finbarr, the founder of Cork City, also had a hermitage here in the 6th century, and hence it's Irish language name, *Guagán Barra*, which means "Finbarr's rocky cave." It's a beautiful spot, a glistening clear-blue lake, enhanced by cascades from the cliffsides, and surrounded by mountains, ancient trees, and lush flora.

Return to road R584, and continue southwest as the road descends via Keimaneigh Pass (which means "The Pass of the Deer's Step") and the Ouvane Valley, beside the Shehy Mountains, into Ballylickey, a scenic district at the head of **Bantry Bay**. Make a left and drive southward along the main N71 road, with glorious ever-changing vistas of Bantry Bay on the right and lush hilly greenery on the left. The temptation is to stop the car at each turn of the road, to look out on the bay and take pictures. One lovely scene follows another, but, then, this is the sine qua non of Bantry Bay. In just five miles, the road dips into the town of **Bantry**. Nestled beside Bantry Bay, this town has long been identified as the home of the Earls of Bantry. At the south end of the town is one of Ireland's grandest 18th-century houses:

***BANTRY HOUSE** (4), Bantry, ☎ 50047. Open daily 9–6. Adults £6.50, seniors and students £4.25, children under age 14 free. Shop. Café. Tours.*
    Built c. 1740 for the Earls of Bantry, with a mostly Georgian facade with Victorian additions, this house sits right on the edge of Bantry Bay, encircled by mountain vistas. A tour of the house includes many items of furniture and objets d'art from all over Europe, collected by the Earls of Bantry, including four panels of Aubusson tapestry made for Marie Antoinette and wainscotting of 17th-century Spanish leather, chests from the Indies, and urns from the Orient. The extensive gardens, with original statuary, are beautifully kept and offer several walking paths. Climb the steps behind the house for a panoramic view of the house, gardens, and Bantry Bay.

    The Bantry House stables contain the **1796 Bantry Exhibit**, Bantry, ☎ 51796. It commemorates the 1796 visit of the French Armada into Bantry Bay, in support of the Irish patriot Theobold Wolfe Tone, leader of the United Irishmen. This historical vignette is told by a walk-through tour, enhanced by music and sound effects, scale models, and interactive displays, all depicting life in Bantry over 200 years ago. *Open April–Oct., daily 10–6. Adults £3, seniors and students £1.75, children under 14 free. Reduced-rate combination tickets for visits to both Bantry House and the 1796 Exhibit are available.*

    From Bantry, you can take a short 30-mile detour around the **Sheep's Head Peninsula**, a thin strip of land wedged between Bantry and Dunmanus Bays. This is the least traveled of all the southwestern peninsulas in either Cork or Kerry. Remote and undeveloped, it is a haven for those who appreciate superb seascapes and mountain scenery. The journey begins five miles south of Bantry at Durrus, a tiny village known for fresh local farm products including **Durrus Cheese** (5), Hill of Coomkeen, Durrus, ☎ 61100. Cheesemaker Jeffa Gill produces a semi-hard cheese made from fresh milk, provided by a herd of fresians that graze among luxuriant meadows. Visitors are welcome on the farm, located 2.5 miles outside of town, a right turn (and a winding path) off the Ahakista road; phone in advance.
    Follow the road west to **Ahakista**, a unique name derived from the

Irish language *Áthan Chiste*, meaning "ford of the treasure." No one knows where the treasure is today, but this small village does have a memorial garden and sundial by Cork sculptor Ken Thompson, dedicated to the victims of the 1985 Air India disaster off the Irish coast. The garden leads within stone walls down to the water's edge.

The last village on the peninsula is **Kilcrohane**, and then the road ends. If you are fond of hiking, walk out along the pathway to the tip of the peninsula, known locally as "the edge of the known world," with only the ocean below and beyond.

Continue the drive by making a right turn back toward Bantry on the road that runs along the north coast of the peninsula—a route known as the **Goat's Pass**. It's a scenic secondary road that rises gently and then plunges steeply down the other side, opening to views of Bantry Bay and the Caha Mountains in the distance. Continue eastward through the village of Gerahies and, on the approach to the town of Bantry, look left for views of **Whiddy Island**, a small parcel of land floating in the bay 1.5 miles west of Bantry town. Once a British Naval Station, it is now an oil terminal. Return to Bantry.

For still more views of Bantry Bay from a different angle, retrace your steps through the Ballylickey district, driving 10 miles northward along the main N71 road, surrounded by a profusion of tall and shady trees and lush greenery, to **\*Glengariff**, a placename derived from the Irish language, *An Gleann Garbh*, meaning "the rugged valley."

As its name implies, Glengariff is a village in a beautiful glen—thickly wooded with oak, elm, pine, yew, holly, and palm trees, rimmed by Bantry Bay. The mild climate, influenced directly by the warm breezes of the Gulf Stream, favor the growth of luxuriant Mediterranean flora, such as arbutus, eucalyptus, rhododendron, fuschia, and blue-eyed grass. The unbridled beauty of the area has always attracted visitors from near and far, including artists, writers, and show business folk. Don't be surprised if you see Maureen O'Hara strolling along the bay. The famous Dublin-born movie star has a summer home in the area and serves as honorary president of the Glengariff Golf Club. Offshore lies a famous island:

**\*GARINISH ISLAND** (6), off Glengariff, ☎ 63040. *Open Mar. and Oct., Mon.–Sat. 10–4:30, Sun. 1–5; April–June and Sept., Mon.–Sat. 10–6:30, Sun. 1–7; July–Aug., Mon.–Sat. 9:30–6:30, Sun. 11–7. Adults £2.50, seniors £1.75, students and children £1.*

From Glengariff harbor, take a 20-minute boat ride (extra charge, averaging £4–5 round-trip), to an offshore island called Ilnacullin, known locally as Garinish. The island is home to an Italian Garden of rare and tender tropical plants, not usually seen in Ireland or northern Europe. It was here that George Bernard Shaw is reputed to have written St. Joan. The paths around the gardens, ideal for strolling, include ponds and pedimented gateways, a Martello tower, and a Grecian temple overlooking the sea. You can easily spend a morning or afternoon here.

From Glengariff, if time allows, take a detour drive around the **Beara Peninsula**, locally referred to as the Ring of Beara Drive. The full circuit is over 80 miles, but it can be cut in half by following the Tim Healy Pass through the Caha Mountains for a total drive of less than 50 miles.

Like the Sheep's Head peninsula, the Ring of Beara covers some of the most remote and undiscovered scenery in Ireland. From Glengariff, make a left turn onto local road R572 at the north end of town. Follow the shores of Bantry Bay for 11 miles, with the Caha Mountains rising on the right, to **Adrigole**, a small village famous for its nearby mountain, Hungry Hill (2,251 feet), a reminder of the famine of 1845. The highest peak in the Caha range, this mountain gave its name to the Daphne Du Maurier novel about local copper-mining barons of the 19th century.

Continue west for nine miles to **Castletownbeare**, the principal town of this peninsula and home of Ireland's largest whitefish port. Often referred to as Castletown Bearhaven, the town takes its name from the Irish language, *Baile Chaisleáin Bhéarra*, meaning "the town of (the) castle of Bear." Bear (or Bere) Island, formerly a fortified anchorage for the British Atlantic fleet, sits off the coast sheltering the town.

Three choices in routing arise now. If you are fond of the wilderness, continue 11 miles west on R572 to the very tip of the peninsula, to the remote village of **Allihies**, surrounded by copper mines that have existed here for over 3,000 years. The peninsula ends with the remote outposts of Dursey Island, Crow Head, and Cod Head.

Alternatively, turn right onto R571 which leads to **Eyeries**, a village of gaily painted houses that served as a setting for the French film, *The Purple Taxi*, shot on location here in 1975. This village is also home of another of Ireland's leading dairy products, **Milleens** (7), Eyeries, ☎ 74079, a soft washed-rind cheese. Cheesemaker Veronica Steele was the first in Ireland to develop and market a farmhouse cheese over 20 years ago, and has since inspired many others. The Steele family welcomes visitors to the farm and cheese plant, but please phone in advance.

The third routing is the most popular for visitors in search of a scenic drive. It requires going back to Adrigole, for a turn north onto local road R574 to follow the *****Tim Healy Pass** through the Caha Mountains. It is a spectacular route with Glanmore Lake below and great chasms and ravines opening on either side. The road, which reaches a height of 1,084 feet, is named after Tim Healy, a one-time governor-general of the Irish Free State and a native of Bantry.

The route descends gradually to Lauragh and the County Kerry border, joining local road R571. Make a right and follow this winding and twisty road as it wends its way along a scenic stretch of the *****Kenmare River Estuary**, with the Ring of Kerry in the distance, into Kenmare. At this point, you can travel onward in County Kerry or to other parts of Ireland, or return to Cork using the local road R569 via Kilgarvan to link up with the main road N22 eastward via Macroom to Cork City.

**Trip 20**

# The West Cork Coast

S tretching from Courtmacsherry to Mizen Head, the West Coast of
Cork is a happy mix of bays and coves, inlets and islands. The landscape presents a rainbow of constantly changing colors, warmed by
Gulf breezes and fanned by palm trees and lush subtropical foliage. It's a
magical place, attractive to fishermen, yachtsmen, tourists, retirees, artists,
craftspeople, and weekenders from Cork and other Irish cities.

Unlike the more traveled parts of Ireland, there are relatively few
"must-see" man-made attractions in West Cork. It's simply a place for
incomparable "wide-open-spaces" scenery, "let's get away from it all"
country lanes, new discoveries at every turn, and a surprising cornucopia
of great food, from locally-caught seafood and organically-grown vegetables to farmhouse-made cheeses.

### GETTING THERE:

This is a tour that requires use of a car. Depart Cork City on the main
N71 road and follow it throughout the day, taking occasional side trips and
detours on country roads. The normal run is approximately 75 miles each
way.

### PRACTICALITIES:

The only way to tour West Cork is by car. The route is a very pleasant
drive, wending through far-flung yet bustling market towns and beside
outstanding coastal scenery. It is not a drive that can be rushed; roads can
be narrow, hilly, and curvy at times.

For information, contact the **Skibbereen Tourist Office**, North Street,
Skibbereen, ☎ 028-21766, open all year. In July and August, there is also a
small visitor information office on Ashe Street, Clonakilty, ☎ 023-33226;
and a tourist information desk at the Mizen Telecottage, Main St., Goleen,
☎ 028-35225 or 028-35115.

Since there are at least two area codes operable in this area (023 and
028), all numbers will be preceded by their area code to avoid confusion.

### FOOD AND DRINK:

**Adèle's** (Main St., Schull) The creative cookery of Adèle O'Connor is
the big draw at this shopfront café, for a snack or light meal in the heart of
Schull. The menu changes daily but often includes homemade soups, salads, quiches, fish pies, chilli, and pastas. All breads and desserts are made
on the premises including chocolate squiggle flapjacks and cherry buns.

☎ 028-28459. X: Mon. and Nov.–March. £ to ££

**The Altar** (Toormore) Situated next to the Altar Church, built in the 1840s by a legendary local clergyman, this cottage-style restaurant is a surprising find deep in the countryside. It specializes in serving vegetarian dishes using organic produce and local seafood including lobster and crab from Toormore Bay. ☎ 028-35254. X: Sun. and Nov.–Apr. ££

**Annie's** (Main St., Ballydehob) This little shopfront restaurant of Annie Barry fits right into a vibrant and creative village. The menu features flavorful home cooking, freshly baked breads, farmhouse cheeses, and local produce, with choices such as seafood salads, steak and kidney pie, and lamb kidneys in pastry. Dinner only. ☎ 028-37292. X: Sun., Mon. and 1st 3 wks. Oct. £ to ££

**Bunratty Inn** (Main St., Schull) Long a fixture in the heart of this seafaring town, this white-washed pub has a nautical decor. Bar food is served all day in a choice of settings—from the cozy lounge to the bright conservatory, as well as outdoors in the stable yard beer garden or the front patio. The menu offers seafood chowders, seafood pies, shepherd's pie, ploughman's platters (assorted local cheeses and patés), and all types of sandwiches. ☎ 028-28341. £

**Casey's Cabin** (Baltimore) Great views of the bay are part of the atmosphere at this cottage-style pub. Quite fittingly, the decor has a nautical theme and the menu offers the best of the local seafood catch. For non-fish eaters, there are always steaks and vegetarian dishes. ☎ 028-20197. £ to ££

**Chez Youen** (The Pier, Baltimore) Shellfish is the star of this little restaurant overlooking the harbor. Brittany-born Youen Jacob, chef-owner since 1978, adds a touch of France to every dish. "Seafood in the shell" is the house specialty, including lobster from local waters, Dublin Bay prawns, Baltimore shrimp, and velvet crab. Dinner is served nightly but lunch only in summer. ☎ 028-21036. X: mid-Nov. to mid-Feb. ££ to £££

**Heron's Cove** (Goleen Harbour) With wide-windowed water views, this restaurant offers hearty soups, homemade breads, farmhouse cheeses, and other snacks by day, while in the evening it serves full dinners in a romantic candlelit atmosphere. The menu emphasizes fresh local produce; lobsters and oysters from a seawater tank; prawns, crab, and fish from the Goleen fleet; plus homemade desserts and ice cream. ☎ 028-35225. In Oct.–May, it is open only according to demand. Phone ahead. £ to ££

**Leap Inn** (Main St., Leap) This traditional pub is the centerpiece of the village of Leap (pronounced *Lep*). Ask a local person to explain the story behind the village's name—it's a real conversation-starter. While you listen, raise a toast or have a sandwich. ☎ 028-33307. X: Nov.–Easter. £

**Mary Ann's** (Castletownsend) Situated in the heart of town, this Old World pub dates back to 1844. Enjoy homemade soups, sandwiches, West Cork cheese platters, or local seafood amid a nautical decor of ship's wheels and lanterns, or step outside to a picnic table in the courtyard. ☎

028-36146. X: Sun. £ to ££

**Wine Vaults** (73 Bridge St., Skibbereen) A wine cellar ambiance prevails at this popular bistro, in the heart of town. The menu offers an international mix of soups, sandwiches, salads, crépes, and pizzas with eclectic toppings of choice. ☎ 028-22743. £

## SUGGESTED TOUR:

Depart **Cork City** (1) on the main N71 road, heading south via the local villages of Ballinhassig, Halfway, and Inishannon, to Bandon, a small market town dating back to the early 17th century. About a mile outside of Bandon, you may wish to take a left and detour on local road R602 to **Timoleague**, a small village that takes its name from the Irish language words *Tigh Molaige*, meaning "St. Molaga's house." A monastery was founded here in the 6th century by St. Molaga, a disciple of St. David of Wales. It was replaced in the 13th century by a new monastery, built for the Franciscans, which became one of the largest and most important religious houses of Ireland in medieval times. Continue for three miles to **Courtmacsherry**, an attractive fishing village on Courtmacsherry Bay, with lovely cliffside walks including an area of seven indentations, known as The Seven Heads. This placename has nothing to do with sherry, but is instead derived from the Irish language *Cúirt Mhic Shéafraidh*, meaning "residence of the sons of Geoffrey," apparently an Anglo-Norman family who settled the area long ago.

From Timoleague, continue on local road R600 for five miles to link up with the main N71 road and arrive in *Clonakilty, a busy and colorful market town dating back to the 13th century with a placename derived from the Irish language, *Clioch na Coillte*, meaning "stone (fort) of the woods."

Clonakilty is a delight to the senses — a series of narrow streets, overflowing with flowers in hanging pots and on stanchions, and lined with traditional hand-painted shopfronts, many displaying signage in Gaelic lettering. Local planning authorities have encouraged the use of older buildings for 21st-century purposes — a 19th-century mill has been adapted for use as the town library; a small Presbyterian church has been "born again" as the post office; a disused linen hall dating back to 1819 now serves as a bakery; and the former Methodist National School is now the home of the West Cork Regional Museum.

In addition, the defunct West Cork Railway station on the edge of town has been imaginatively transformed into the **West Cork Model Railway Village** (2), Inchydoney Rd., Clonakilty, ☎ 023-33224. A special delight for children, this is a miniature walk-around version of Clonakilty as it appeared in the 1940s, enhanced by a full-sized station, locomotive, and sample rail cars now used as shops. *Open Feb.–Oct., daily 11–5. Adults £3, seniors and students £1.50, children aged 5–12 £1.25, children under age 5 50p. Shop. Café.*

From Clonakilty, wend your way westward. Woodfield, four miles

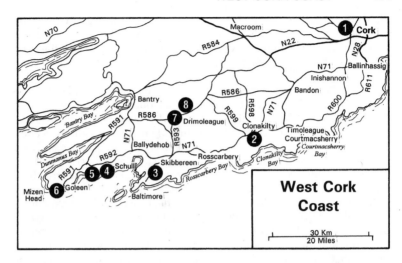

West Cork Coast

30 Km
20 Miles

down the road, is the birthplace of Michael Collins (1890–1922), recently immortalized in the movie of the same name. One of Ireland's great political heroes during the 1916–22 period of rebellion, Collins was a General of the Free State Army, and his powerful personality made him a legend in his own time. There is a memorial to his memory at Sam's Cross, Woodfield.

From this point, the route becomes more rugged, with the sea carving deep inlets and bays as it rolls in from the Atlantic. For the next 15 miles, the route passes through a series of picturesque harbor villages with melodic and curious names—Rosscarbery, Glandore, Leap, and Union Hall.

The next major town is **Skibbereen**, fondly referred to as the "capital of West Cork." Its placename is very fitting, derived from the Irish *An Scionairin,* meaning "the place of the little boats." Sitting on the banks of the Ilen River near Roaringwater Bay, Skibbereen is a popular hub for fishermen and yachtsmen. It is also the home of the West Cork Arts Centre, a haven for artists and craftspeople from all parts of rural Ireland.

A lively market center, Skibbereen is the gateway to several more remote towns and attractions. Take local road R596 to **Castletownsend**, an English name commemorating a castle built by an English settler, Col. Richard Townsend. The castle is now in ruin, but the town has survived very well, thanks to the prominence it received as the home of Edith Somerville and "Martin" (Violet Mary) Ross, the 19th-century writing team who penned *The Experiences of an Irish R.M.,* a classic book adapted for an award-winning public television series in the 1980s.

The small fishing and sailing port of **Baltimore** is seven miles southwest of Skibbereen, and well worth a short detour. It is generally acknowledged that the placename is derived from the Irish language, *Baile na*

*Tighe Mór,* meaning "townland of the big house." The big house, in this case, belonged to Lord Calvert whose family seat was the barony here. The American city of Baltimore, Maryland, derives its name from this Irish place. From Baltimore, boat trips are available to the islands of Cape Clear and Sherkin.

En route back to Skibbereen, you may wish to stop at **Creagh Gardens** (3), Skibbereen, ☎ 028-22121. Inspired by a Douanier Rousseau painting, these gardens have a romantic aura, set amid 20 acres of woodland glades and a serpentine millpond. Highlights include many wooded walks and a traditional walled organic kitchen garden. *Open Mar.–Oct., daily 10–6. Adults £3, seniors and students £2, children £1.50. Café. Tours.*

From Skibbereen, the N71 passes through an open scenic stretch for eight miles, with various inlets of Roaringwater Bay on the left and Mount Gabriel rising on the right (1,339 feet). The next spectacle is man-made—a beautiful 12-arch bridge leading into *Ballydehob, a cheery village of brightly colored shopfronts, each one trying to out-do the other. Many of the shops and pubs have murals and wall art on their facades. It is not surprising that this remote village is a popular retreat for artists, poets, and writers who have come to live among the farming community. Ballydehob's artisans often exhibit their works in the local craft shops and galleries as well as museums in Dublin, London, the U.S., and throughout Europe. The curious sounding placename is derived from the Irish *Béal an Dá Chab,* meaning "entrance of the two mouths," usually interpreted as Ballydehob's position on the shores of the bay and base of the mountain.

Although Ballydehob will probably win your heart, this tour is not yet over, although our use of N71 is. Switch now to local roads R592 and R591, continuing along the rim of Roaringwater Bay for five miles, to *Schull, pronounced *Skull,* from the Irish word *An Scoil,* meaning "school," and relating to an early school founded by the monks at this site. It is one of the most popular resorts on the West Cork coast for yachting. The island of Cape Clear, as mentioned above under Baltimore, lies across the bay while at the west of the harbor's mouth are Long Island, Horse Island, and Castle Island, all thriving centers of the fishing industry of long ago and now almost deserted. In the summer months, all types of water sports activities and boating trips are available from Schull Harbour and nearby Colla Pier including a coastal ferry service between Schull and Baltimore.

For a slight diversion with a celestial theme, make a left from Main Street, onto Colla Road. Three blocks down the road beside the bay is the **Schull Planetarium** (4), Schull Community College, ☎ 028-28552. Touted as the only planetarium in southern Ireland, this star-gazing center invites visitors to view the heavens under optimum conditions. At least once a day (schedule varies), there are "star shows" lasting approximately 45 minutes. *Open March, Apr.–May, Sun. 2–5; June, Tues., Fri.–Sat. 2–5; July–Aug., Tues.–Sat. 2–5 and 7–9. Adults £1, children 50p. Star shows: Adults £2.50, children £1.*

One of Ireland's most highly acclaimed dairy products—Gubbeen

Farmhouse Cheese—is made on the western fringe of Schull at **Gubbeen House** (5), Schull, ☎ 028-28231. This well-matured cheese, with a soft pinky-brown rind and soft center, is manufactured as a cottage industry by Tom and Giana Ferguson. A smoked version is also available, with the smoking done by Chris Jepson. Visitors are always welcome; phone in advance.

From Schull, it is just over seven miles to the remote resorts of Toormore, Goleen, Crookhaven, and Barleycove, the latter of which is known for its golden beaches, and finally to land's end—**Mizen Head**, the most southerly point on the island of Ireland.

Walkers and hikers will particularly enjoy the trek out to this wind-swept outpost. Park your car at the end of R591 and embark on a tour of ***Mizen Vision/The Mizen Head Signal Station Visitor Centre** (6), Harbour Rd., Mizen Head, Goleen, ☎ 028-35225. Walk (for approximately 20–30 minutes) along the well-fenced coastal precipice, passing over a suspension bridge and going down a cliff for 99 steps, to gain access to the signal station. Once you have arrived, you can use telescopes outside to look far out to sea and distant views of the **Fastnet Lighthouse** standing on a rock seven miles off the coast, take coastal pictures to your heart's content, or examine the various indoor displays set up within the lighthouse. The return trip retraces your steps, although there is a graded walkway back up, if you prefer not to climb up the 99 steps. Dress warmly, wear comfortable shoes, be prepared for brisk and bracing ocean breezes at every turn, and you'll have a once-in-a-lifetime experience. *Open June–Sept, daily 10–6; mid-March to May, daily 10:30–5; Nov. to mid-March, Sat.–Sun. 11–4. Adults £2.50, seniors and students £1.75, children age 5–12 £1.25.*

Now that you have "gone to the end of the world," as the Irish call it, there is only one way back—retrace your steps in an easterly direction via local road R591 and then via the main N71 road through Skibbereen all the way back to Cork, stopping at places that you might have missed on the westward leg of the tour.

As an alternative route, if time allows (and to add a little variety to the return journey), go north from Skibbereen and follow local roads R593 and R586 via Drimoleague and Dunmanway, two small market towns, back to Bandon to rejoin N71. En route, stop at Drimoleague to see two local enterprises that draw visitors in search of unique Irish souvenirs. **Methuselah Stained Glass** (7), The Old Corn Mills Building, Drimoleague ☎ 028-31723, produces individually designed and hand-made stained-glass jewelry, lamps, and glassware. **The Roadside Studios** (8), The Mill, Drimoleague, ☎ 028-21666, feature the work of Jeanne Rynhart, one of Ireland's foremost figurative sculptors. She creates artistic coldcast bronze sculptures with Irish themes, such as craftsmen of yesteryear, traditional musicians, and children at play.

Continue to Bandon and follow main road N71 into Cork City, or continue on to other parts of Ireland.

# Cork City—
# Smart Shoppers' Tour

I t is not surprising that Cork City, as one of Ireland's largest metropolitan areas, is a popular shopping hub. Thriving shops line the major streets and quays on all sides of the River Lee. For this tour, we are isolating the main shopping thoroughfare—Patrick Street, along with several streets around it.

Patrick Street, officially known as St. Patrick Street, is a wide avenue that makes a sweeping curve through the middle of the city. The surrounding area is composed of a network of narrow streets and alleyways, many of which are pedestrianized, such as Winthrop St., Cook St., Marlborough St., Prince's St., Paul Street, Carey's Lane, and French Church St.

All of the shops outlined on this tour can be easily visited on one continuous walk.

## GETTING THERE:

Running right through the middle of downtown Cork City, the St. Patrick Street (normally referred to simply as "Patrick Street") area is easily accessible. Once you approach Cork City, just follow signs for the "City Centre" or Patrick Street.

## GETTING AROUND:

Because the scope of this tour is so compact, walking is the ideal way to follow the route.

## PRACTICALITIES:

The best time to follow this tour is during normal shopping hours, usually 9 a.m. to 9:30 a.m. to 5:30 p.m. or 6 p.m., Monday through Saturday, except for Thursday when most shops stay open until 8 p.m. or 9 p.m.

For information, stop into the Cork Tourist Office, Grand Parade, Cork City, ☎ 021-273251. The telephone code for all numbers on this tour is 021.

## FOOD AND DRINK:

**Brown Thomas Café** (18 Patrick St.) This is the café of choice for Cork's most fashionable shoppers—an oasis of freshly brewed coffees, gourmet teas, pastries, and creative lunch choices. ☎ 276771. X: Sun. £ to ££

**Gingerbread House** (20 Paul St.) Housed in a former tea warehouse, this high-ceiling restaurant conveys an "old Cork" ambiance with sugan woven chairs and pine wood stools and tables. It is known for its freshly baked breads, made-to-order sandwiches, and gourmet milk shakes as well as fresh salads, soups, quiches, and casseroles. ☎ 276411 £

**Kylemore Café** (Merchants Quay, off Patrick St.) is part of a popular chain, known for its delicious cakes, pastries, and other baked goods, located throughout Ireland's major cities. This particular spot does not have a street entrance, but instead is reached via escalator on the upper level of the Merchants Quay Shopping Centre. With a bright and airy setting, this self-service restaurant draws Corkonians at all time of day for coffee, tea, lunch, homemade soups, salad bar, or a snack. There are also convenient rest rooms here, which are popular with shoppers. ☎ 275026. £ to ££

**The Long Valley** (10 Winthrop St.) If you are searching for a hearty well-stuffed sandwich in a traditional Cork pub setting, turn off Patrick Street and head to this long-established watering hole. It's on the left side as you approach the post office. ☎ 272144. £

**Meadows & Byrne** (Academy St.) is a small café at the back entrance (French Church St.) of this popular home furnishings store. The menu includes freshly made soups, salads, and sandwiches, and an assortment of fine coffees and teas. In fine weather, there is also seating outside on French Church St., a pedestrian area. ☎ 272324. £

**The Vineyard** (Market Lane, off Patrick St.) Tucked into a small pedestrian Lane, this inviting pub is known for its tasty sandwiches with many ingredients and international themes, such as New York Reuben, Smouldering Hoagie, and Musketeer, as well as hot dishes such as seafood gumbo; lamb shank osso bucco; and duck liver sausages. X: Sun. ☎ 274793 £ to ££

### SUGGESTED TOUR:

Start this tour at **Patrick Street** beside the River Lee, just south of the Patrick Bridge. Cross over the street to the left side and you will be at the corner of Patrick Street and Merchant's Quay, one of the many picturesque riverfront quays in Cork. In the center of the street is a local landmark, a statue of Fr. Theobold Matthew, a mid-19th century Cork cleric who distinguished himself in the cause of temperance. The statue is a point of reference for many Corkonians in giving directions or telling where to meet each other. In this case, it's the starting (and finishing) point for our tour.

Immediately on the left is a block-long brick building, a former warehouse, that has been transformed into a bi-level indoor shopping mall known as **Merchant's Quay Shopping Centre** (1) 1 Patrick, St., ☎ 275466, with an adjacent multi-story car park. It offers almost 40 different retail outlets including a branch of the British-owned department store, **Marks & Spencer**, as well as local Irish chains such as **Roche's Stores** and **Dunne's**

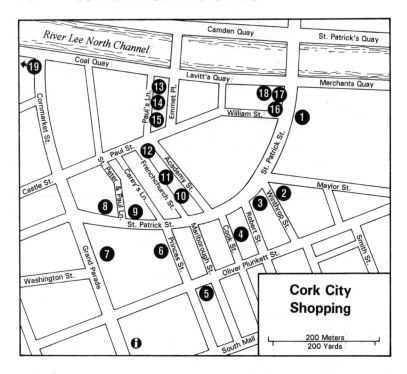

Cork City Shopping

200 Meters
200 Yards

**Stores.** There are also many boutiques and specialty shops for clothing, jewelry, perfume, books, music, and fashion including a Cork branch of **Laura Ashley.**

After spending time within the complex, return to the Patrick Street exit and then make a left onto the main thoroughfare. To the left is Maylor Street, and on the corner is **Brown Thomas** (2), 18 Patrick St., ☎ 276771, Cork's leading department store and a branch of the original Dublin store of the same name. This particular store, before it was linked by name and management to Brown Thomas, operated independently as "Cash's" dating back to 1830. So, it's a Cork tradition, by any name! It offers three floors of stylish and contemporary clothing and other wares, ranging from tweeds and knits to Irish linen, Waterford Crystal, and more.

Next, on the left, is the first of the pedestrian streets, Winthrop Street. If you take a left here, this street leads directly to the main Cork post office, passing one of Cork's oldest pubs en route, The Long Valley (see "Food and Drink" above).

Returning to the main thoroughfare, on the left is a Cork shopping landmark—**Fitzgerald** (3), 24 Patrick St., ☎ 270095, established in 1860. It is a stylish specialty shop for men, featuring Burberry coats and Bally shoes at considerably less than U.S. prices, as well as Irish tweeds, and cashmere and knitwear.

The next pedestrian street to come up on the left is Cook Street. Take a left here to visit **Carraig Donn** (4), 5 Cook St., ☎ 274050, a mecca for traditional Irish woolen knitwear, especially Aran fishermen sweaters and fishermen's jerseys. In addition, there is a wide selection of stylish and contemporary designs in boucle wool and cotton chenille cardigans and capes, wraps, scarves, jackets and hats.

Continuing along Patrick S., next on the left is the pedestrianized Marlborough Street. Turn in here and follow the street all the way to the end, to meet Oliver Plunkett Street. Here, on the far right corner is **Liam Ruiseal** (Russell) (5), 49–50 Oliver Plunkett St., ☎ 270981, a very good source for books and pamphlets on the history, literature, and social fabric of Cork City.

Retrace your steps to Patrick Street, and then continue on to the next pedestrian street, Prince's Street. Walk a few paces on the right and you will see the decorative 18th-century entrance to the **City Market** (6), Patrick Street, a definite highlight for shopping or just browsing to soak up some genuine Cork ambiance. Equally known by its original name—the Old English Market—this huge indoor marketplace was started in 1610 although the current building only dates back to 1786. Some of the favorite stalls include **Stephen O'Reilly**, ☎ 966397, purveyor of original Cork delicacies such as drisheen (a sheep's blood and beef blood pudding); **On the Pig's Back**, ☎ 279232, (offering a tasty selection of cooked meats, breads, cheeses, and pates); **The Real Olive Company**, ☎ 270842, (olives, artichoke hearts, white bean salads, wild garlic pesto, capers, and rich olive oils); **The Garden**, ☎ 272368, (organically grown vegetables, quality nuts, and dried fruits); **Mr. Bells**, ☎ 885333, (Oriental spices and foods); **P. Bresnan & Son**, ☎ 271119, (beef and lamb from their own farms); **Iago**, ☎ 277047, (pastas, pestos, cheeses and other specialist foods); **Stephen Landon**, ☎ 086-2266320, (bacon and ribs); and (fish and shellfish). Even if you make no purchases, this market provides a great sampling of typical Cork aromas, sounds, and sights.

Walk all the way through the market to the Grand Parade exit. To the right is a store that is favored by anyone in Cork who enjoys Irish music, both listeners and players. Step into **Kelly's Ceol** (7), Grand Parade, ☎ 272355, a small shop ("ceol" is the Irish word for music) specializing in the sale of traditional Irish music instruments, accessories, and music books, as well as a wide assortment of traditional music and dance CDs and cassettes.

The Grand Parade leads back to Patrick Street. Cross over the street now to visit some of the shops on the other side of Patrick Street.

The first shop of note is **Waterstone's** (8), 69 Patrick St., ☎ 276522. Part of a British-owned chain, this large shop is known for a wide selection of books about Ireland and especially Cork. It also stocks a variety of other topics—from art and antiques, to biography, the classics, crime, gay literature, health, new age, religion, sport, travel, women's studies, and wine.

Next on the left is Paul's Lane, leading to Sts. Peter & Paul Church. Continue along on Patrick Street and you will see another interesting British-owned shop—Past Times (9), 75 Patrick St., ☎ 270756, a unique shop featuring gifts and home accessories with Victorian, medieval, and Celtic themes. The assortment ranges from jewelry and clothing, to frames, posters, tableware, games, mugs, books, paper goods, baby gifts, stained glass, statuary, and music CDs.

On the left emerges the first of three pedestrian streets on this side of Patrick Street—Carey's Lane, lined with a parade of Irish and international cafés and fast-food shops. Continue to the next pedestrian street, French Church Street, and make a left onto it. Two shops are worth noting on the right side. The first is **Mercier Bookshop** (10), 5 French Church St., ☎ 275040, a large shop with entrances/exits on French Church and Academy Streets. It stocks a variety of books from art, humor, and drama, to politics, current affairs, law, and religion, but with special emphasis on Irish interest topics such as Irish history, literature, folklore and music. It is best known for books bearing the imprint of Cork-based *Mercier Press*, founded in 1944 and now the oldest independent Irish publishing house.

Two doors away is **Meadows & Byrne** (11), French Church St. and Academy St. ☎ 272324. This contemporary store is a not a typical haunt for tourists, but a stroll around may help you to find a unique souvenir in smart Irish style for your home or a friend's. The goods include include designer pottery, ceramics, carved wood accessories, frames, glassware, kitchenware, statuary, and more.

Straight ahead is Paul Street, another pedestrian street that is the entrance to a large Tesco grocery shopping centre, complete with multistory car park, so it's a handy place to park for access to this area. Paul Street offers an assortment of book shops and cafés and is sort of the "left bank" of Cork.

One of the smallest yet most intriguing shops is **Mainly Murder** (12), 2A Paul St, ☎ 272413, a treasure-trove of volumes on murder, mystery, and mayhem from Ireland, England, and many other English-speaking lands. It's an ideal stop for amateur sleuths or anyone looking for a good read. This shop also stocks complete "back lists" from all well-known writers. You'll also find an "Irish Detection" Section—admittedly small, because there are too few Irish crime writers! There is a strong Historical Crime Writers Section—covering all periods from ancient Rome to Victorian England; and a "First in Series" Section—a thoughtful touch that enables customers to start a new series in the right order!

An off-shoot of Paul Street is Paul's Lane, home to many antique shops, including **Mills**, 3 Paul's Lane (13), ☎ 273528; **Anne McCarthy** (14), 2 Paul's Lane, ☎ 273755; and **O'Regan's** (15), 4 Paul's Lane, ☎ 509141. Stop into to see one or all of them is you are interested in antique and heirloom jewelry, silver, curios, and art.

As Paul Street ends, take a right onto Academy Street which leads past the front entrances of Meadows & Byrne and the Mercier Bookshop, and back again to Patrick Street.

Turning left onto Patrick Street, head back toward the Fr. Matthew statue. After passing the intersection of William Street, you will come to **Quills** (16), 107 Patrick St., ☎ 271717, another Cork tradition—a family-run enterprise originally started deep in the heart of West Cork's Gaelic-speaking region at Ballingeary. Best items to look for are hand-knit sweaters and other hand-loomed knitwear, as well as garments using the skins of sheep and goats. Stylish contemporary clothing for men and women is also offered.

Next is one of Ireland's oldest leading booksellers, **Eason's** (17), 113–115 Patrick St. ☎ 270477, established over 110 years ago. It is a prime source of books, maps and magazines about Ireland as well as foreign newspapers, postcards, and stationery, plus books on literary, historical and cultural topics.

Continue to the Art Deco-style **Savoy Centre** (18), 117–119 Patrick St., a former cinema and now an indoor shopping mall with a variety of small specialty shops and boutiques, such as **Forgotten Cotton**, ☎ 276098, a specialist in Irish linen, handmade laces, pure cotton and lace duvet covers and bedspreads in antique designs, tablecloths, and small gift items; **Dineen Designs**, ☎ 272129, a small studio shop displaying the craft work of John Dineen and other local artisans in decorative candles, pottery, bog oak, banners, woolens, and note cards; and **Love Knot**, ☎ 272186, a small boutique selling handmade jewelry from all parts of Ireland and Celtic-style jewelry from Scotland.

From the Savoy Centre, turn left and you'll be facing the starting point of your tour, having completed the full scope of Patrick Street and its environs in one large oval pattern.

No shopping tour of Cork is complete, however, without mention of **Blarney Woollen Mills** (19), Blarney, ☎ 385280. Located next to Blarney Castle, it is one of Cork's (and Ireland's) most renowned shops—yet it is not on Patrick Street, nor is it in downtown Cork—it is five miles northwest of Cork City and requires a car, taxi, or bus ride to reach. It is a one-stop source for all types of Irish products and souvenirs, from cashmere and crystal to china, dolls to damask linen, kilts to keychains, as well as handknits to heraldry, tweeds suits to tee shirts, and the trademark bright green Blarney Castle-design wool sweaters, made on the premises.

# Section V

# KERRY

Kerry, the fifth largest county in Ireland, is fondly called "The Kingdom" by its inhabitants. And why not? It is as majestic and regal as Ireland can be. Even Queen Victoria extolled the virtues of Kerry, as have poets, writers, artists, photographers, and tourists ever since.

Rimmed by Ireland's tallest mountains and splashed by her loveliest lakes, County Kerry is indeed a kingdom of scenic delights, from the Lakes of Killarney, Tralee Bay, and Dingle Bay, to MacGillycuddy's Reeks, Mount Brandon, the Gap of Dunloe and Connor Pass, as well as two of Ireland's most popular drives—the Ring of Kerry and the Dingle Peninsula.

Kerry is home to boglands and beaches, gardens and woodlands, seacoasts and waterfalls, jaunting cars and windmills, remote islands and festive towns, and above all a warm and friendly people who treasure their heritage and every facet of their "kingdom."

Even the weather is magical—or at least mystical—in County Kerry. Nestled on Ireland's extreme southwest coast, Kerry is warmed by the Gulf Stream yet cooled by brisk Atlantic breezes. It can be beautiful in the morning and wet in the afternoon. You can start out in heavy mist and drive 10 miles and find sunshine. Stand still and feel rain one minute and sunshine the next. The weather is a constant topic of conversation in Kerry. Of course, all the rain and mist make the county lush and colorful, a nurturing habitat for palms, rhododendrons, strawberry trees, and so much more.

This is the county of the most westerly points of Europe, not to mention the Purple Mountains, Shamrock Hill, Slea Head, Moll's Gap, the Puck Fair, Fungie the Dolphin, and the Rose of Tralee. Come and explore ...the "kingdom" awaits...

# Killarney Town

Killarney is Ireland's Camelot, a place of rare natural beauty. Mention Killarney and people automatically conjure up images of glistening lakes, cascading waterfalls, majestic mountains, legendary islands, ancient trees, lush foliage, rare birds and wildlife, and endless romantic trails. Poets have strained to find adequate words to describe it, lamenting that even "Heaven's Reflex" or "Beauty's Home" fail to convey the grandeur of Killarney.

The good news is that all of this is true. Killarney is a natural treasure. There may not be gold in the hills but there certainly is unparalleled peace and pristine beauty. The bad news is that all of this is no secret—Killarney is popular and usually crowded except in the depths of winter.

Killarney is divided into two parts—a compact little town and an expansive national park. The town is rather ordinary, with no outstanding landmarks other than a fine cathedral. Its streets are lined by hotels, guesthouses, restaurants, and shops, all geared to the buoyant tourist trade. The adjacent national park, in striking contrast, is a spectacularly scenic 25-mile-square area, the magnet for artists, photographers, poets, and tourists.

Like many Irish towns, Killarney probably originated during or before the 9th century as a religious site. Its name in the Irish language, *Cill Áirne*, literally means "The Church of the Sloe," because there were many sloe woods in the area. It is not know exactly when Killarney began, but the growth and development of the town was tied closely to the fortunes of the local landlord, the Earl of Kenmare, Sir Valentine Browne. In 1588, he was granted 6,560 acres of land by the Earl of Glencar. Browne also purchased much land and added greatly to his estate. The family lived at Ross Castle until 1721 when they moved to a new home near what is now Killarney town. Surveys conducted prior to this time did not mention a town or village called Killarney.

By 1747, however, a survey showed that a small town had been born, consisting of the Earl's mansion, four slated houses, and 100 thatched cabins. In less than 10 years, a new street with a large inn was added and visitors were warmly welcomed. At this stage, Lord Kenmare realized that a tourist industry could be profitable and he encouraged building more inns and a series of colorful laneways. The railroad reached Killarney in 1853 and the Great Southern Hotel, known then as the Killarney Railway Hotel, opened in 1854. Surprisingly, though, it is Queen Victoria who is credited with putting Killarney on the map as a tourist mecca. When she visited the town with a large entourage in 1861, she made Killarney instantly fashionable and it has been a thriving destination ever since.

Although most of Killarney's charms lie on the outskirts of town in the National Park district, the town itself is well worth a walk, for at least an hour or two.

## GETTING THERE:

By car, Killarney is 54 miles west of Cork, via the main N22 road, 84 miles southwest of Shannon, via Limerick and the main N21 and N22 roads, or 192 miles southwest of Dublin, via Limerick or Cork. **Irish Rail** and **Bus Eireann** provide daily service to Killarney from Dublin and Cork and other major cities throughout Ireland. Trains arrive at the Killarney Railway Station, Railway Rd., off East Avenue Rd., and buses arrive at the Bus Eireann Station at the rear of the Killarney Outlet Centre, Fair Hill, also off East Avenue Rd., beside the Great Southern Hotel.

## PRACTICALITIES:

The best way to see Killarney town is on foot. Park your car at your hotel or at one of the town's designated public parking areas. There is no local transport within the town center, although there are various modes of conveyance to take you out into the national park area including the famous jaunting cars (see *Killarney Lake District*).

Killarney is at its best and busiest during **Killarney Race Weeks** (May and July) and during the **Roaring 1920's Festival**, an annual mid-March three day event around St. Patrick's Day. Advance reservations for accommodations are needed at these times.

For visitor information at any time of year, contact the **Killarney Tourist Office**, Beech Road, Killarney, ☎ 064-31633. The telephone area code for all numbers in Killarney town is 064.

## FOOD AND DRINK:

As befits a major tourist center, Killarney has many fine restaurants, with international cuisine ranging from French and Italian to Austrian, Swiss, and German, as well as superb Irish seafood restaurants, offering Kerry lobster, Valencia scallops, and other local fish.

**Bricín** (26 High St.) Named after a local bridge, this rustic enclave is housed in one of the town's oldest buildings, dating back to the 1830s, with original stone walls, pine furniture, and turf fireplaces. It is a combination restaurant-craft shop-bookshop; inviting guests to dine amid a creative selection of Celtic art work and books. The menu, which offers snacks throughout the day and full dinners at night, presents traditional Kerry boxty dishes (potato pancakes with various meat and vegetables fillings), as well as a variety of seafood choices, Irish stew, and a house specialty of chicken Bricín (breast of chicken in red currant and raspberry sauce). X: Sun. and Nov.–Feb. ☎ 34902. £ to ££

**Dingles** (40 New St.) Situated near St. Mary's Cathedral, this basement bistro is furnished with a variety of church accouterments, from church pews, wooden benches, and choir stalls, to arches and alcoves. The menu is international, with choices such as chicken curry, beef Stroganoff, Irish stew, vegetable casserole, and Dingle Bay prawns in Creole sauce. Dinner only. X: Sun. and Nov.–Feb. ☎ 31079. ££

**Foley's** (23 High St.) For over 30 years, this Georgian-style pub-restaurant has been a Killarney mainstay. The menu features local favorites such as Dingle Bay scallops, rainbow trout, breast of pheasant, Kerry mountain lamb and steaks. Don't miss the homemade brown bread scones. X: Mid-Jan. to mid-Feb. and Dec. 24–27. ☎ 31217. ££

**Gaby's** (27 High St.) When it comes to seafood, this nautically-themed restaurant is the benchmark, and well worth a big splurge, particularly for the Kerry shellfish platter, a cornucopia of fresh prawns, scallops, mussels, lobster, and oysters, or the house specialty of *Lobster Gaby,* served grilled in a sauce of cognac, wine, cream, and spices. X: Sun. and 3 wks. in Feb. ☎ 32519. ££ to £££

**Jimmy O'Brien** (College St.) Small and simply furnished, this cozy pub is a haven for those who eschew the touristy, and instead seek a quiet drink in an "Old Killarney" atmosphere. Amble in and chat with the ever-present and warm-hearted publican of the same name, or listen in as "spontaneous" Irish traditional music sessions inevitably erupt at this hidden treasure. ☎ 31786. £

**The Laurels** (Main St. at Market Cross) For a lively evening of local entertainment, this huge pub draws big crowds. The repertoire ranges from Irish ballads to an international cabaret of song and dance. Light meals such as Irish stew and bacon and cabbage are also served. ☎ 31149. ££

**Robertino's** (9 High St.) Operatic arias and a Mediterranean-style decor convey the ambiance of Italy at this mid-town spot. There are five separate dining areas including a "green zone" for non-smokers. The menu features a variety of pastas plus veal saltimbocca, roast rib of lamb flamed in Marsala wine sauce, and local seafoods. Dinner only. ☎ 34966. ££

**Swiss Barn** (17 High St.) If you are fond of fondue, this is the place to go. This Alpine-themed restaurant also offers dishes such as veal Zurichoise, beef stroganoff, veal cordon bleu, pork filet in morrel sauce. ☎ 36044. ££

## SUGGESTED TOUR:

Start your tour at the **Railway Station** (1) on the eastern edge of the town. The rail depot is one of Killarney's oldest buildings, dating back to 1853 and made of local stone, built as the terminus for the Killarney Junction Railway. It was the first railway company in Ireland to own and operate its own hotel, **\*The Great Southern** (2), which opened in 1854. You may wish to stop into the hotel and sample some of its 19th-century atmosphere, particularly in the grand lobby with its marble columns,

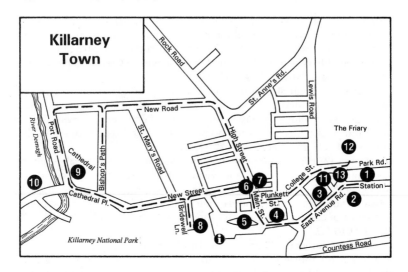

ornate ceilings, and warming open fireplace.

From the grounds of the Great Southern, turn left onto East Avenue Road. On the right is Killarney's only purpose-built museum, the:

**MUSEUM OF IRISH TRANSPORT** (3), East Avenue Rd., ☎ 34677. *Open daily 10–6. Adults £3, seniors and students £2.50, children £1.50.*

An ideal activity for a rainy day, this museum presents a unique collection of Irish veteran, vintage, and classic cars, as well as bicycles, motorcycles, carriages, and fire engines. The exhibits include the rarest car in the world—a 1907 Silver Stream, the only model ever built; a 1910 car driven by William Butler Yeats; and a DeLorean. The walls are lined with early motoring and cycling periodicals and license plates from all over the world.

Return to East Avenue road, and coming up on the right is **Brewery Lane**, one of Killarney's many colorful and often still- cobbled 18th- and 19th-century laneways. As its name implies, it was the site of at least one brewery over 100 years ago. The locals say that hops continued to grow all along the wall until a few years ago. This lane also earned fame in 1936 as the setting for a locally-produced film known as *The Dawn*.

Continue toward town and look to the left. At this juncture, intersected by Muckross Road, is one of the town's main jaunting car stations. During all daylight hours, there is usually a fleet of horse-driven jaunting cars assembled here, at the ready to take tourists on trips around the National Park area. The *jarveys* (drivers) can be a little aggressive in soliciting business, but will always accept a polite "no, thank you," if you wish to walk by and continue on your way.

Next on the right is one of the town's prime landmarks:

**ST. MARY'S CHURCH** (4), Church Place, ☎ 31832. Open: *Sun. 10:30–7. Admission free, donations welcome.*
This building is revered not for what it is, but where it is. Standing on the site of the original *Cill Airne* (The Church of the Sloe Woods), this small Church of Ireland edifice is the latest of a number of churches built on this hallowed ground since the 9th century. This neo-Gothic structure, which dates back to 1870, has an interior that includes a 19th-century organ and a mural commemorating Rev. Arthur Hyde, vicar of Killarney in 1808 and great-grandfather of the first President of Ireland, Douglas Hyde.

Opposite the church is the **Town Hall** (5), seat of the Urban Council. Although the building itself is not very notable, there is an old stone-covered well at the rear. For many years, this "holy well" was a center of local devotion, particularly because it was so near to the church. The name of the street has now become Main Street.

Continue on **Main Street** for one block, passing a variety of shops and fast-food eateries, to the intersection of New and High Streets. This is the center of town, known as **Market Cross** (6). Many different kinds of markets were originally held here, selling everything from butter to turf. On the right is the **Old Town Hall** (7), a red brick building erected by Lord Kenmare with bricks left over from his mansion.

Take a left and walk down **New Street**, Killarney's youngest thoroughfare, as its name implies. On the left is the Post Office and the entrance to **Bridewell Lane**, considered Killarney's most beautiful lane and the only lane where all of the houses are still occupied. The focal point is the *****Frank Lewis Gallery** (8), 6 Bridewell Lane, ☎ 34843. Set in a restored artisan's dwelling, this gallery presents an ever-changing display of paintings, photographs, and sculptures of leading and emerging Irish artists. *Open Mon.–Sat. 9–6. Admission is free.*

Return to New Street and continue in a westward direction to Killarney's ecclesiastical hub:

*****ST. MARY'S CATHEDRAL** (9), Cathedral Place, ☎ 31014. *Open daily 10:30–6. Admission is free, donations welcome.*
This is Killarney Town's centerpiece, considered as one of the most beautiful Gothic-Revival cathedrals in Europe. Built of limestone and designed by the noted architect Augustus Pugin, the building is cruciform in shape. Although construction started in 1842, it was interrupted by the Great Famine and used as a hospital during the famine years. A great redwood tree near the western doorway marks a mass children's famine grave. Eventually completed in 1855, the cathedral is officially known as the *Catholic Church of St. Mary of the Assumption.* Highlights include a giant spire reaching 285 feet in height that was added in 1912; lovely rose windows over the north and south transepts; and other stained-glass windows that tell stories from the Bible and illustrate the lives of Irish saints.

Directly opposite the cathedral, across the Deenagh River, is the entrance to the *Knockreer Estate (10), Cathedral Place, off New Street, ☎ 31440, an easily accessible part of the National Park grounds and ideal for long nature walks. Once part of Lord Kenmare's home, the estate has a turn-of-the-century house, now used as a field study center (not open to the public), a pathway along the River Deenagh, and gardens with 200-year-old trees and flowering shrubs. Opened to the public relatively recently (1986), this stretch of parkland offers lovely views of Killarney's Lower Lake. *Open daily during daylight hours; admission is free.*

Returning to Cathedral Place, follow **Port Road** north for one long block along the extensive cathedral grounds to **New Road**, lined with lovely lime trees, and make a right. This area is known as Killarney's educational district since it is the home of St. Brendan's College, Killarney Community College, Presentation Monastery, and Mercy Convent Schools. Take a right at **Bishop's Path** to see the Bishop's House and more schools including the Presentation Convent which dates from 1793, and was the hub of Killarney's lace-industry for many years. Note: These buildings, not open to the public for tours, can be viewed only from the outside.

Continue on New Road for one block. To the right is **St. Mary's Road**, alternately known as St. Mary's Terrace, the setting for a row of houses with colorful gardens known as the Castlerosse Cottages. These houses, originally built by Lord Kenmare for the workers on his estate, have been well preserved and enlarged by the current owners.

Continue on New Road to the traffic light and turn right onto **High Street**, one of Killarney's busiest commercial thoroughfares, with a variety of shops, many of which have fine examples of scroll-work fascias and late-19th-century traditional carvings. High Street also has 11 laneways, the greatest number of any Killarney street—Dodd's, Pawn Office, Barry's, Fleming's, Bower's, Brasby's, Huggard's, Ball Alley, Duckett's, Hogan's, and New Market. Many are named after sub-landlords who received use of the lanes from Lord Kenmare. Ball Alley Lane was the local site for handball games.

High Street leads back into Main Street. Continue for one block and then make a left onto **Plunkett Street**, originally known as Henn Street, the narrowest street in town. Take a sharp left to see some more of the town's original commercial lanes, with names ranging from Old Market Lane to Glebe Place. They were the early settings for the local post office and craftsmen's shops, such as cart-makers, bakers, harness-makers, coopers, flour and grain merchants, and tweed suppliers. The old Milk Market also took place here.

Plunkett Street leads to **College Street**, so named because it was the site for colleges run by the Franciscans, Mercy Sisters, and Presentation Brothers, operated at one time or another up until 1850. At the far end of the street, on the right, is the local **Court House** (11).

As College Street merges into Park Road, this area is known as **Fair**

**Hill**. It was originally called Martyr's Hill, because it was a place of execution in the 17th century. On the left side of the street is the **Franciscan Church and Friary** (12), Fair Hill, ☎ 31066. This church is relatively new, dating back only to 1860, although the tradition of Franciscan service in Killarney goes back to 1440 when friars made a foundation at Muckross Abbey. Officially known as the *Church of the Most Holy Trinity*, this building is attributed to Eugene Pugin, eldest son of the famous Augustus Pugin who designed the cathedral. It is simple in style, with a lofty arched ceiling and oak paneling. Highlights of the interior include a beautifully hand-carved wood altar and a stained-glass window over the entrance designed by the famous Irish artist Harry Clarke.

Opposite the church grounds, overlooking the left side of the road is a local landmark—the statue known as the **Spéir Bean** (13) (Spirit Woman), representing the spirit of Ireland. It commemorates the four Kerry poets of the Irish language, Pierce Ferriter (1616–53), Geoffrey O'Donoghue (1620–90), Egan O'Rahilly (1670–1726), and Eoin Rua O'Sullivan (1748–84).

Directly to the left is Railway Road and the Railway Station, where our tour began. At this point you might like to get your car or take local transport to see some of the surrounding areas of the Killarney National Park and beyond.

# Trip 23

# *Lakes of Killarney

How Can You Buy Killarney? That's the question the old song asks. The answer is simple. You can't. In fact, no one can buy Killarney—it belongs to the people of Ireland as the country's leading national park. Happily, the Irish are very willing to share their treasure with visitors.

The Killarney National Park consists of a 25-square-mile area of unspoiled and unpolluted lakes, mountains, and woodlands—a "green zone" in the truest sense. The Lakes of Killarney, as the district is collectively known, are carefully protected by the government which means no billboards, no fast-food chains, no rows of condominiums, no commercial developments, and no motorized traffic within parklands and along the lakeshores.

The layout includes three major lakes, surrounded by Ireland's highest range of mountains, MacGillicuddy's Reeks. Nearest the town is the Lower Lake (also known as Lough Leane, meaning "Lake of Learning" in the Irish language). It is the largest lake (5,000 acres) with about 30 islands. On the eastern shore of the Lower Lake are two popular historic sites, Muckross Abbey and Ross Castle.

The wooded peninsula of Muckross separates the Lower Lake from the Middle Lake (680 acres), sometimes called Muckross Lake. On the eastern shore of this lake are Muckross House and Torc Waterfall.

A narrow strait known as the Long Range leads to the third lake, the slender and finger-like Upper Lake (430 acres), which is almost embedded in the mountains. The upper lake is the smallest but often deemed the most beautiful of the Killarney trio. In addition, there are many smaller lakes in the folds of the mountains as well as numerous waterfalls and cascades.

Plant and animal life enhance Killarney's landscape. The woodlands thrive with a luxuriant medley of oak, birch, yew, ash, cedar, and juniper. The smaller flora include holly, fern, rhododendron, and arbutus (the strawberry tree), Killarney's native plant. Red deer, black Kerry cattle, and other animals roam freely while over 100 species of birds fly amid this wide natural expanse. For the human species, there are at least four signposted nature trails and countless garden-rimmed paths and walks.

It's paradise—and it's waiting for you!

**GETTING THERE:**

Access to Killarney National Park is available on foot from the town via the Knockreer Estate off Cathedral Place. By car, there are several entrances along the Killarney–Kenmare Road, particularly beside or near Muckross House. In every case, you'll have to park your car and do your touring on foot, bicycle, or via horse-drawn jaunting car. No motorized traffic is allowed within the park grounds and along the lakes.

## PRACTICALITIES:

The best way to see **Killarney National Park** is the traditional way—via a horse-drawn jaunting car. The jaunting car is to Killarney what a cable car is to San Francisco or a subway to New York—it's simply the best way to get around, unless you are an avid walker or biker. Park your car at your hotel or one of the town's designated public parking areas. You can arrange to hire a jaunting car in town or at major tourist sites within the park such as Muckross House, Muckross Abbey, Ross Castle, and Kate Kearney's Cottage. Rates, which are fixed and carefully monitored by the Killarney Urban District Council, depend on the duration of the tour and number of passengers.

As soon as you agree on the rate and board a jaunting car, you'll have a tartan blanket tucked on your lap, to protect you from "the mist" or a cool breeze. The driver, known as a jarvey, is both a guide and story-teller, often with a John McCormack streak to add a few tunes to the clip-clop of the horses.

More information on all modes of transport is available at the **Killarney Tourist Office**, Beech Road, Killarney, ☎ 064- 31633. The telephone area code for all numbers in Killarney is 064.

## FOOD AND DRINK:

**Frederick's** (Aghadoe Heights Hotel, Aghadoe) For sweeping views of the whole Killarney Lake District panorama, this upstairs restaurant cannot be beat. It offers a wide array of French food using local Irish ingredients, with dishes such as cassoulet of Kerry seafood, tournedoes of cod, grilled lamb cutlets, and mixed fruit fritters for dessert. ☎ 31766. £££

**Kate Kearney's Cottage** (Gap of Dunloe) Named for a local resident who used to run a speakeasy for poitin (the local potato brew) on this site, this former coaching inn has a lot of atmosphere and local memorabilia. Snacks are served throughout the day and Irish coffee is a specialty. Traditional music is on tap from May through September on Sunday, Wednesday, and Friday evenings. ☎ 44146. £ to ££

**Killarney Manor** (Loreto Rd.) For a special evening splurge, this former mansion provides a five-course dinner in 19th-century style with complete program of song, ballads, and dance. The menu offers a choice of traditional Irish spiced sirloin of beef, roast Kerry lamb, or poached local salmon, with all the trimmings; and the music includes the melodies of Thomas Moore, Percy French and other celebrated Irish songwriters. X: Sun. and Thurs. and Nov.–March. ☎ 31551. £££

**Molly's** (Muckross Rd., Muckross Village) Situated across from the entrance to Muckross House, this traditional thatched-roof pub offers a real country atmosphere, with stone walls, oak-beamed ceilings, open fireplaces, alcoves, snugs, and local memorabilia. The menu offers home-made soups, salads, sandwiches, and seafood platters. ☎ 31938. £ to ££

## SUGGESTED TOUR:

Although you may take all or part of this tour via a horse-drawn jaunt-ing car, this route is designed for departure from Killarney town by car. Depart Killarney via the main Kenmare Road, and take the first turn right to:

**ROSS CASTLE** (1), Ross Road, off Kenmare Road, ☎ 35851. *Open daily April 11–6; May and Sept. 10–6; June–Aug. 9–6:30; Oct. Tues.–Sun. 9–5. Adults £3, seniors £2, children and students £1.25. Tours.*

Once the home of the Earl of Kenmare who built Killarney town, this castle actually dates back to the 15th century and was probably built by one of the O'Donoghue chieftains, a local clan. Perched overlooking the Lower Lake, it is surrounded by a fortified bawn, with curtain walls and two circular towers. The interior, enhanced with samplings of 15th- and 17th-century furniture, has a stone staircase leading to upper chambers including a minstrels' gallery and a Great Hall with two large six-light win-dows. Climb to the parapets to enjoy sweeping views of the lake and sur-rounding countryside.

From the pier beside the castle, you can take a one-hour boat cruise on the lakes aboard a glass-enclosed waterbus or a boat trip to **Innisfallen**, a 21-acre island floating one mile from shore in the midst of the Lower Lake. St. Fallen founded a monastery here in the 7th century and it flour-ished for 1,000 years. Brian Boru, the great Irish chieftain, and St. Brendan the Navigator, are said to have studied here. From 950 to 1320, the *Annals of Innisfallen,* a chronicle of early world and Irish history, was written in Irish and in Latin on this island by a succession of 39 monastic scribes; it is now housed in the Bodleian Library at Oxford University. Traces of an 11th-century Hiberno-Romanesque church and a 12th-century Augustinian priory can still be viewed today. Evergreens and holly flourish all over the island.

Returning to the main Kenmare road, continue for 2.5 miles to the entrance to the Friary of Muckross, popularly known as **Muckross Abbey** (2), Muckross Estate, a well-preserved ruin on the shores of the Lower Lake. Founded in the 1440s by the Franciscans, this abbey flourished for more than 300 years, until it was suppressed by the Penal Laws. The remains include a church with a wide belfry tower and an intact vaulted cloister, with an arched arcade surrounding a square courtyard. The cen-terpiece of the courtyard is an ancient yew tree, said to be as old as the abbey. Through the years, the abbey property and grounds have served as a burial place for local chieftains and also for the four of Kerry's famous

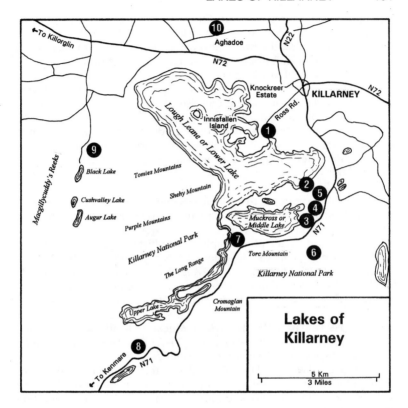

Lakes of Killarney

5 Km
3 Miles

Gaelic-language poets—Pierce Ferriter (1616–53), Geoffrey O'Donoghue (1620–90), Egan O'Rahilly (1670–1726), and Eoin Rua O'Sullivan (1748–84)— who are also commemorated by the statue in the middle of Killarney town. A visit to the abbey is a favorite stop on the jaunting car route. *Open mid-June to early-Sept., daily 10–5; admission is free.*

Return to the main road and continue for 1.5 miles to the entrance to one of the premier focal points of the lakeshore on the Middle Lake:

**\*MUCKROSS HOUSE & GARDENS** (3), Muckross Road, ☎ 31440. *Open daily Nov. to mid-March, 9–5:30; mid-March–June and Sept.–Oct., 9–6; July–Aug., 9–7. Adults £4, seniors £3, students and children £1.60. Tours. Shop. Café.*

Often called "the jewel of Killarney," this splendid 20-room Victorian mansion, built in 1843, provides a glimpse of the lifestyle of the landed gentry of Killarney in the 19th century. The house is adorned with elaborate architecture, from mullioned and stepped windows to 62 chimneys, and decorated with locally-made period furniture and needlework, as well as imported treasures such as Oriental screens, Venetian mirrors, Chippendale chairs, curtains woven in Brussels, and Turkish carpets. To give a balanced view, the house also has a "downstairs"—the area once used by the servants. It has been converted into a nest of workshops for traditional crafts, with working craftsmen giving demonstrations of weaving, pottery-making, book-binding, spinning, basket-making, and blacksmithing. The display areas also comprise a folk museum, with exhibits of County Kerry folklife, history, cartography, geography, geology, flora, and fauna. In addition, the well-manicured gardens outside are renowned worldwide for their collections of azalea and rhododendron. There is also an extensive water garden and a rock garden hewn out of natural limestone.

Next to the house is the **Killarney National Park Visitor Centre** (4), a separate building that serves as an orientation point for exploring the surrounding parklands. There are continuous showings of an audiovisual, *Mountain, Wood, Water,* plus exhibits, visual histories, and scale-models on the trees, birds, and wildlife. *Open daily Nov. to mid-March 9–5:30; mid-March–June and Sept.–Oct. 9–6; July–Aug. 9–7. Admission is free.* Seventy acres of adjacent land is devoted to an open farm. Touring requires several hours, but it is well worth it, especially for families to explore:

**\*MUCKROSS TRADITIONAL FARMS** (5), Muckross Road, ☎ 31440. *Open May and Oct., daily 2–6; June–Sept., daily 10–5; mid-March–April, Sat.–Sun. 2–6. Adults £4, seniors £3, students and children £1.60.*

This is a real working farm, although different from many of the other modern "open farms" in Ireland today. On this site, farming is done in the style of the 1930's with horse-drawn equipment and pre-electrification methods. Visitors can watch sowing and harvesting or potato-picking and haymaking, depending on the season. Farmers tend the livestock, while the blacksmith, carpenter, and wheelwright ply their trades. It is necessary to walk from farmhouse to farmhouse, and among the various cottages, outbuildings, and workshops, along a mile-long boreen (unsurfaced country road) that has some steep hills, so this tour is best done in good weather by those with a lot of time, stamina, and energy.

Returning to the main Kenmare road, continue for another mile to the signs for **\*Torc Waterfall** (6), one of the area's natural wonders and among the finest waterfalls in Ireland. Surrounded by tall shady trees, a footpath winds its way up beside 60 feet of cascading waters, affording magnificent views of the lake district from the upper end. The area is well sign-posted and has its own parking lot.

Return to the main Kenmare road. On the right, along the lakeshore, is an area known as the **Meeting of the Waters** (7), the point where the waters of the Upper Lake meet the other two lakes, the Middle (or Muckross) Lake and the Lower Lake (Lough Leane). It is spanned by the

Old Weir Bridge, known for its swirling rapids.

Continue for another seven miles to an area known as **Ladies' View** (8). From this high vantage point, all three lakes can be viewed in one sweeping panorama. It derives its curious name from the days of Queen Victoria's visit to Killarney over 100 years ago. It is said that, as the royal entourage approached Killarney, the queen's ladies-in-waiting called out for the coaches to stop so they could admire the view. Hence it has since been known as Ladies' View. Today it is still an ideal spot for a picture.

From this point it is necessary to backtrack through Killarney to take in the rest of the lakeland sights. After passing through the town, follow the signs for the Killorglin road for four miles and then take a left at the sign for the *Gap of Dunloe (9). This is a natural mountain wonder, but requires the better part of a day to explore fully. The typical Gap of Dunloe trip starts with a seven-mile trip through the Gap, a great glacial breach valley. There are four ways of doing the trip - walk, cycle, ride on horseback or take a seat in a horse-drawn trap. The route passes beside Black Lake, otherwise known as Serpent Lake, where St. Patrick is reputed to have drowned the last snake in Ireland. Then it's on via Cushvalley and Augur Lakes, with the Tomies and Purple Mountains on the left and MacGilllycuddy's Reeks on the right. The trek ends on the shore of the Upper Lake at Gearhameen, for a picnic lunch or refreshment at Lord Brandon's Cottage. Afterwards it's time to board a boat for a trip on the Upper Lake, through the Long Range to Meeting of the Waters under Brickeen Bridge. Here you shoot the rapids and go through Lough Leane to Ross Castle, and back to Killarney.

If you don't take the Gap of Dunloe tour, return from here to the Killorglin road and take the first turn on the left sign-posted to Aghadoe. Continue for 1.5 miles to *Aghadoe Hill (10), at 400 feet one of the highest points in the Killarney Lake District, affording sweeping views of the whole area with a panorama of mountains and lakes. From here, it is 2.5 miles back to Killarney town.

# *The Ring of Kerry

Extending westward from Killarney, the Iveragh Peninsula—or the Ring of Kerry as it is commonly known—is assuredly Ireland's most popular scenic drive. It is an ever-changing panorama of seacoast, bogland, mountain, and lakeside vistas. Not only does it start with the glistening waters of the Lakes of Killarney and reach out beyond boglands and beaches to the splashing surf of the Atlantic, but it also includes the profiles of Ireland's four highest mountains—Carrantuohill, rising to a height of 3,414 feet, followed by Beenkeragh (3,314 feet), Caher (3,200 feet), and an unnamed peak southwest of Carrauntohill (3,141 feet).

Unlike some parts of Ireland, there are no great museums or man-made landmarks along the Ring of Kerry, although some attractions and heritage centers are well worth a visit. Primarily, the Ring is a continuous 110-mile circuit of natural wonders and views. The drive itself is the attraction.

**GETTING THERE:**

The official start and end to the Ring of Kerry drive is Killarney, although Kenmare can serve equally well as a base. With one small exception between Killarney and Killorglin, the route follows the main N70 route in a complete circuit.

**PRACTICALITIES:**

The Ring of Kerry drive can be undertaken in either direction, but the normal route is in a counter-clockwise pattern. The duration can be anything from four or five hours to a full day, depending on how many stops you make for exploring heritage centers and attractions, taking pictures and videos, visiting pubs and cafés, chatting with the local farmers and turf-cutters, beach-walking, hill-climbing, shopping and craft-hunting, and detouring down the side roads. Plan to cover 20 miles an hour or less. This is a drive to be relished, not rushed.

Although a little rain or passing showers should not deter you, it is best not to set out in heavy sea mist, fog, or socked-in rain. If the clouds are moving, however, that usually means a good day on the Ring will follow.

The road is well-paved and easy to follow, but it is a slow and tedious drive for several reasons. The route takes concentration and is not meant for speed - it curves around seafront cliffs, over the boglands, and through mountain passes. Vehicular traffic can be heavy as many buses and cars set out to do the same thing; and animals, particularly sheep, meander lazily along the roads. Be sure to time your drive for daylight hours only since there is no roadside lighting and driving through the mountains can be difficult at night. All of that said, it's well worth the drive. For local guidance about road conditions and weather, tune into Radio Kerry (97 FM) as you drive. News and weather reports are given on the hour.

If you prefer not to drive, however, there are escorted sightseeing tours. From May through September, **Bus Eireann** operates daily sightseeing tours around the Ring of Kerry, departing from Killarney Bus Station, Railway Rd., ☎ 064-34777. In addition, several Killarney-based travel companies offer trips, including **Castlelough Tours**, 7 High St., Killarney, ☎ 064-32496; **Cronin's Tours**, College St., ☎ 064-31521; **Dero's Tours**, Main St., Killarney, ☎ 064-31251; and **O'Donovan's Tours**, Innisfallen Mall, Main St., Killarney, ☎ 064-54041.

For tourist information on the Ring, visit the **Killarney Tourist Office**, Beech Road, Killarney, ☎ 064-31633. In addition, seasonal offices are operated as follows: **Cahirciveen Tourist Office**, The Barracks, Cahirciveen, ☎ 066-947-2589 (open June–Sept); and Kenmare Tourist Office, The Square, Kenmare, ☎ 064-41233, (open April–Sept).

There are two area codes used for telephone numbers on the Ring of Kerry—064 and 066, so each number that follows includes its area code.

## FOOD AND DRINK:

**Blue Bull** (South Square, Sneem) With a blue straw bull's head resting over the doorway, this pub/restaurant exudes an "Old Kerry" ambiance, with open fireplaces and old prints of local scenes and people. Soups, sandwiches, and snacks are served all day, and full dinners at night. Specialties include local seafood, steaks, and Irish stew. ☎ 064-45382. £ to ££

**Fionan's Kitchen** (Skellig Heritage Centre, Valentia Island) With a rustic decor of sugan chairs, pine tables, and stone floors, this self-service eatery is an ideal spot for sandwiches, soups, salads, pastas, Irish stew, or quiche, all enhanced by stunning floor-to-ceiling views of the Portmagee Habour. X: Oct.–April. ☎ 066-947-6306. £

**The Huntsman** (The Strand, Waterville) With picture windows facing Ballinskelligs Bay, this is one restaurant that really makes the most of its waterfront location. The menu offers the best of the local catch including Skellig lobster and Kenmare Bay prawns, as well as Irish stew, rack of lamb, and seasonal game. Daytime snacks include burgers, omelets, pastas, and seafood salads. X: Nov.–March and Mon.–Tues. in April and Oct. ☎ 066-947-4124. ££ to £££

**Lime Tree** (Shelbourne Rd., Kenmare) Innovative "New Irish" cuisine presented in a charming setting is the secret of success at this restaurant, housed in a former schoolhouse dating back to 1821, with a lime tree out front. The ever-changing menu offers choices such as warm salad with prawns, Kenmare seafood en papilottte, oak planked Kenmare salmon, or roast herb-crusted Kerry lamb, all accompanied by a basket of barbecued bread with sundried olive oil spread. Dinner only. X: Nov.–Feb. 064-42225. ££

**Packie's** (Henry St., Kenmare) With a traditional decor enhanced by colorful Irish art, this shopfront bistro is known for its creative menu, making use of herbs and produce from its own garden. Irish stew, rack of lamb, braised beef in Guinness, gratin of crab and prawns are house specials. Dinner only. X: Sun. and mid-Nov.–Easter. ☎ 064-41508. ££

**The Park Hotel** (off Shelbourne Rd., Kenmare) A tour of the Ring is not complete without a meal or a drink at this luxury Victorian-style chateau-style hotel, dating back to 1897. Deemed to be the finest hotel in Ireland, it has a highly honored restaurant with a romantic setting overlooking palm tree-lined gardens and the Kenmare Estuary. The menu is as dazzling as the setting—choices such as ravioli of lobster and prawns, terrine of guinea fowl and pigeon with a truffle vinaigrette, and panfried filet of beef with a chartreuse of oxtail, onion confit, and red wine glaze. Finish with a selection of local cheese served with walnut bread. X: Jan.–Feb. ☎ 064-41200. £££

**The Quarry Restaurant** (above Pat's Shop and Post Office, Kells) Panoramic views are the big draw of this second-floor restaurant-in-the-round. The self-service menu offers an international selection of dishes ranging from Greek salads and moussaka, to quiches, pastas, curries, and Irish stew. ☎ 066- 947-7601. £ to ££

**Scariff Inn** (Caherdaniel) Perched on a cliff overlooking the Atlantic, this pub-restaurant is known for its picture-window views. The self-service menu offers sandwiches, soups, salads, Irish stew, bacon and cabbage, seafood salads, shepherd's pie, pastas, and curries. ☎ 066-947-5132. £

**Smuggler's Inn** (Cliff Rd., Waterville) Located a mile east of town overlooking Ballinskelligs Beach, this converted farmhouse restaurant is a favorite with golfers (it sits opposite the Waterville Golf Course). The decor and menu favor the nautical, offering lobsters from the tank, local seafood, and fish brochettes, as well as steaks. X: Nov.–Feb. ☎ 066-947-4330. ££

**The Thatch** (Strandsend, Cahirciveen) Home-baking is a specialty at this authentically thatched-roofed cottage, set on its own grounds along the main ring of Kerry road. The menu is self-service, offering soups, salads, sandwiches, traditional casseroles, pastries, scones, and pies. Seating is also available at picnic tables outside. ☎ 066-947-2316. £

**The Vestry** (Templenoe, four miles west of Kenmare) Savor a snack, drink, or a meal amid choir stalls and stained glass at this restaurant in a former church dating back to 1710. The menu offers bar food, such as soups, salads, steaks, and seafood, during the day and full dinner at night. ☎ 064-41958. £ to ££

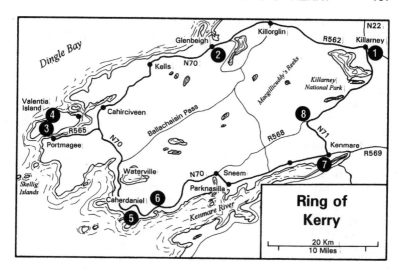

Ring of Kerry

20 Km
10 Miles

## SUGGESTED TOUR:

The Ring of Kerry is splendidly signposted. You can set out from **Killarney** (1) or Kenmare in either direction and follow "The Ring of Kerry" signs without ever having to know the names of the towns or mileages. A map adds to the enjoyment, but it is not necessary.

Assuming that you are setting out in a counter-clockwise direction from Killarney, you will depart the main N70 road for 15 miles as you head out onto the Ring via local road R562. This route presents lovely views of the River Laune to the left, as you approach the small marketing town of **Killorglin**, a name derived from the Irish *Cill Orglan,* meaning "Orgla's Church." No evidence is left of the namesake, but instead this town is celebrated today as the home of the annual Puck Fair, a mid-August horse, sheep, and cattle fair that is presided over by a wild goat. The animal, captured from the nearby mountains by the local folk, is enshrined in the center of town as a catalyst for three days of festivities. Depart Killorglin and the route links up with the main N70 road.

As you drive westward on N70, the road soon presents vistas of Dingle Bay on the right and **\*Carrantuohill**, Ireland's tallest mountain (3,414 feet) on the left. Vast open expanses of open bogland also come into view. Bogs, which cover much of the Kerry landscape, are an important source of fuel for the farm families who live on the Ring. Local residents spend much of the summer digging up pieces of "turf" (dried brick-like wedges of peat), to burn in their fireplaces for warmth. These boglands, formed thousands of years ago, are mainly comprised of decayed trees and foliage. Because of uneven surfaces, the roads built over the bogs tend to be bumpy and hard on cars. Take caution when driving over bog roads.

In addition to the bogs, the Ring of Kerry landscape winds around cliffs and the edges of mountains, with nothing but the sea below. The countryside is also dotted with the remains of many abandoned cottages dating from the famine years, in the mid-1840s, when the Irish potato crop failed and millions of people either starved or were forced to emigrate. This peninsula lost three-fourths of its population during the famine and emigration era.

One of the best ways to revisit what the Ring of Kerry was like in the 19th century is at the **Kerry Bog Village Museum** (2), Ballycleave, Glenbeigh, ☎ 066-976-9184, a cluster of thatched-roof buildings including a turf cutter's house, working forge, laborer's cottage, and thatcher's home, plus a stable, dairy house, and hen house. Visitors are encouraged to walk through the interiors of each building to see authentic furnishings, household implements, and farming tools. Turf fires burn in the small hearths and piles of turf are stacked at the entrance to the village. *Open March–Nov., daily 8:30–7. Adults £2.50, students £1.50, and children £1.*

The road leads next to the village of **Glenbeigh**, a tree-lined fishing resort, with a lovely dune-filled beach called Rossbeigh Strand. The name Glenbeigh comes from the Irish language, *Gleann Beithe,* meaning "The Valley of the Beech Trees." You may wish to stop here or continue for 17 more miles via the wide sweep through the mountains and along the sea's edge. On clear days, the horizon to the right reveals spectacular views of the Dingle Peninsula and the Blasket Islands.

The road now merges with the main street of **Cahirciveen**, also spelled Cahersiveen. Either way, it is derived from the Irish word *Cathair Saidhbhín,* meaning "little Sabina's fort." Not too much is known about Sabina or her fort today, but the town is particularly colorful and well-kept, consisting of one long main street.

Off the coast of Cahirciveen, you can often see the **Skellig Islands—** Skellig Michael and Small Skellig—sitting eight miles out in the Atlantic Ocean. In the 6th century, St. Fionan founded a monastery on these rocky outposts. Considered among the best preserved early Christian sites of its kind in the world, the Skelligs contain six corbelled stone beehive huts and two boat-shaped oratories, plus stone-built terraces, retaining walls, and stairways. Today the Skelligs are home to rare colonies of sea birds. To learn more about these storied islands, take a slight detour to Portmagee and follow the signs over the bridge to the:

**\*SKELLIG HERITAGE CENTRE** (3), Valentia Island, ☎ 066-947-6306. *Open daily March to mid-Nov., daily 9:30–7. Adults £3, seniors and students £2.70, children £1.50. Admission with boat cruise, adults £15, seniors and students £13.50, children £7.50. Tours. Shop. Café.*

With a stark stone facade framed by grassy mounds, this modern interpretative center blends in with the local landscape. Through a series of interactive displays and a 16-minute audiovisual, it conveys *The Skellig Experience*—what life has been like on the Skellig Islands through the ages—from the scholarly pursuits at St. Fionan's 6th-century clifftop monastery until today as the islands serve as a habitat for seabirds. In addition, exhibits cover underwater life around the islands and the history of local lighthouses and their crews. The center also provides sweeping views of the two islands. For a supplementary fee, visitors can take a 1.5-hour boat cruise from Valentia to circle the rocks and get close-up views—a chance to see, hear, and smell the Skellig world as it sits peacefully in the midst of the roaring seas.

Alternatively, rather than driving the full route from Cahirciveen to Valentia Island by land and bridge, you can save time and mileage by taking the Valentia Island Ferry from Renard Point near Cahirciveen to Knightstown on Valentia Island. This service operates from April through September, every day from early morning to late evening, on a drive-on/drive-off basis. The trip takes just five minutes. For more information on schedules and fares, call ☎ 066-947-6141.

While here, spend some time exploring **Valentia Island**, seven miles long and one of the most westerly points of Europe. Connected to the mainland by the bridge at Portmagee, this island was the site of the first telegraph cable laid across the Atlantic in 1866. In addition, the Valentia harbor was infamous in the 18th and 19th centuries as a refuge for smugglers and privateers; it is said that John Paul Jones also anchored here quite often.

On a gentler note, if time allows, visit the **Glanleam Subtropical Gardens** (4), Valentia Island, ☎ 066-947-6176. Created over 150 years ago by the Knight of Kerry, this site includes a collection of rare and tender Southern Hemisphere plants, such as palms, ferns, bananas, bamboo, and myrtles. *Open mid-June to mid-Sept. daily 11–7. Adults £2.50, seniors, students, and children £1.50. Tours. Shop. Café.*

Returning to the main N70 road, it is just 11 miles to **Waterville**, a narrow strip of land on Ballinaskelligs Bay between the Atlantic and Lough Currane. For many years, this town was the favorite summer hideaway for Charlie Chaplin, who helped to popularize it as a beach, golfing, and fishing resort.

After departing from Waterville, the road then passes through Coomakista Pass, the crest of which looks out onto beautiful views of the Kenmare River, and the Scariff and the Deenish Islands. After traveling seven miles, signposts lead to the former home of one of Ireland's great historic figures:

**\*DERRYNANE NATIONAL HISTORIC PARK** (5), Caherdaniel, ☎ 066-947-5113. *Open April and Oct., Tues.–Sun. 1–5; May–Sept., Mon.–Sat. 9–6, Sun. 11–7; Nov.–March, Sat.–Sun. 1–5. Adults £2, seniors £1.50, students and children £1. Tours. Café.*

Set on 300 acres of wooded and dune-filled lands along Derrynane Bay, this is the ancestral home of Daniel O'Connell, lawyer, politician, statesman, and one of Ireland's major leaders of the 19th century, known as "The Great Liberator." With a unique facade of turreted slate and stone, the house is laid out as it was in O'Connell's time, including the family portraits and silver, and an assortment of Victorian furnishings. The most unique room is the chapel, complete with altar, confessional, pews, colored glass windows, and a variety of ecclesiastical vessels and vestments. A tour includes a 25-minute audiovisual profile of O'Connell, *Be You Perfectly Peaceable*. In addition, the coach house displays O'Connell's triumphal chariot, while the grounds include extensive gardens with rare plant collections, plus a ring fort and a variety of self-guided beach and nature trails.

A little over a mile to the east is the hamlet of **Caherdaniel**. Although most people assume that it was named in honor of Daniel O'Connell, the placename is instead derived from the Irish language *Cathair Dónall*, meaning "Dónall's fort," and the fort of the same name is beside the road about a half-mile west of the village. Not too much is known about this old stone fort except that it was probably built by a man named Dónall as far back as 600 BC.

A little beyond Caherdaniel are the sandy beaches of Westcove and Castlecove and beyond these is the signposted left turn for **Staigue Fort** (6), a large stone circular structure, reputed to date back to 1000 BC. Although little is certain about its origins, Staigue is one of the largest and best preserved forts of its kind in Ireland, a fine example of dry-stone construction (no mortar is used). The area enclosed is a massive 90 feet in diameter, with walls as high as 18 feet, a base that is 13 feet thick, and a set of steps up to what was once a rampart. The fort, which sits on private land, is accessible at the discretion of the owner. There are no set admission charges, but contributions toward the upkeep can be made at the "honesty box" at the gate.

Return to the Ring road and continue to the village of *Sneem, a name derived from the Irish word *An tSnaidhm*, meaning "the knot" or "a junction." It is thought that Sneem earned this name because it sits at the head of an inlet where the Kenmare River meets the Sneem and Ardsheelhane Rivers. Sneem is a colorful little hamlet with twin parklets and houses painted in vibrant shades of blue, pink, yellow, purple, and orange, almost like a Mediterranean cluster. Because this area is a good fishing spot, the local church sports a salmon-shaped weather vane on its steeple. There is a sculpture park in town featuring a collection of international works such as the *Peaceful Panda* (a white marble statue from China); *Metal Tree* (a stainless steel sculpture from Israel); *Angry Christ* (from Singapore); and *The Goddess Isis* (from Egypt).

Continue in an eastward direction on the main road. The foliage becomes richer and more extensive, thanks to the warming waters and winds of the Gulf Stream. When you begin to see a profusion of palm trees and other subtropical vegetation, you'll know that you are in *Parknasilla, one of Ireland's lushest resorts. The exotic-sounding placename is actually derived from the Irish language, *Páirc na Saileach*, meaning "Field of the Willows." It has long been a favored resort of the rich and famous, princely and regal, presidential and political vacationers who seek sheltered seclusion. George Bernard Shaw is reputed to have written *St. Joan* here. Take time to visit the Great Southern Hotel, to see one of the loveliest seascape settings in Ireland, nestled amid 300 acres of lush foliage, palms, and flowering shrubs.

From Parknasilla, follow the main road, which runs on the north shore of the Kenmare River, for 14 miles into ***Kenmare**, the final town on the Ring of Kerry circuit, and by far the most captivating. The placename is derived from the Irish language, *Neidín*, meaning "Little Nest."

Kenmare is indeed a little nest—a well-maintained town amid lush foliage nestled between the Kenmare River and the River Roughty. Founded in 1760 by Sir William Petty, the town streets are laid out in an intriguing X-shaped pattern, with a central Market Place and Fair Green, a park for markets and fairs, in the heart of the town. In the mid-19th century Kenmare also became a hub of Irish lace-making, thanks to a local nun who set up a thriving industry by training local women in the work of fine needlepoint. Samples of Kenmare lace have since been exhibited at the Victoria and Albert Museum in London and the National Gallery in Washington.

The many facets of Kenmare history and enterprise are portrayed graphically at the **Kenmare Heritage Centre** (7), The Square, Kenmare, ☎ 064-41233, using a walk-through display, with individual cassette commentaries. The center also includes an exhibit and demonstrations on the art of lace-making. In addition, beautiful lace tablecloths, place settings, and decorative items are on view and for sale. *Open Easter–Sept. Mon.–Sat. 10–6. Adults £2, seniors and students £1.50, children under 12 £1. Tours. Shop.*

From Kenmare, it is just 20 miles back to Killarney, but the journey averages at least an hour. The route is particularly scenic, beginning with panoramas of wild heather, followed by winding mountain turns. The road swings northeast around Peekeen Mountain, and then the lake-filled vistas of Killarney come into view at **Moll's Gap** (8), a high look-out point. From the Gap, the road descends to Ladies View, Torc Waterfall, and Muckross, and the heart of the Killarney Lake District.

# Tralee

Almost everyone who approaches the town of Tralee starts to hum the lilting melody of *The Rose of Tralee*. Although there isn't always music in the air, Tralee is a town that owes much of its fame to music. The signature song, written by local resident William Mulchinock over 100 years ago, was composed in honor of a young woman named Mary who had won his heart, and every time it is played throughout the world (especially around St. Patrick's Day), it conjures up idyllic images of Tralee. And each August the Rose of Tralee Festival brings thousands of visitors and media attention to this simple market town for music, song, dance, merriment, and to pay homage to modern-day *Roses*.

Even if there was no Rose, Tralee would be an alluring town to visit. With a population of 17,225 people, Tralee is the largest town in County Kerry, the county seat, and a major shopping and industrial center. It sits at the head of Tralee Bay and the northeast corner of the Dingle Peninsula. The placename Tralee, in the Irish language *Trá Lí* which means "strand or beach of the River Lee," comes from the River Lee which flows into Tralee Bay.

Historically, the town grew up around a castle built in 1243 by John Fitzthomas Fitzgerald, one of the many Earls of Desmond. Much of the present town of Tralee dates from the 18th and 19th centuries and the streetscapes have a distinctive Georgian flavor.

In recent years, the people of Tralee have made concerted efforts to preserve their heritage and to "package" their attractions for visitors, making it an ideal destination in all kinds of weather. Ashe Memorial Hall houses a trio of activities showcasing the history and lifestyle of Tralee and County Kerry, and nearby an old windmill and narrow-gauge railway have been restored as attractions. To sustain its musical aura, Tralee is also home to *Siamsa Tíre*, the national Folk Theatre of Ireland, a venue that has fostered authentic Irish traditional music, song, and dance as an everyday occurrence in Tralee.

## GETTING THERE:

By car, Tralee is 20 miles north/northwest of Killarney, via the main N22 road. **Bus Eireann** and **Irish Rail** provide daily service from Killarney and other parts of Ireland into the Bus and Rail Station, John Joe Sheehy Road, Tralee.

## PRACTICALITIES:

The best way to see the main streets of Tralee is on foot. Park your car at your hotel or in one of the designated parking areas and walk through the heart of town. For sightseeing outside of the town, such as an excursion to Blennerville, you'll need a car.

The best and busiest time of year in Tralee is during the **Rose of Tralee Festival** in late August or early September. This six-day event is a sort of Irish *Mardi Gras*, with all kinds of entertainment, horse racing, other sports, and an international beauty pageant competition to select an annual "Rose" to reign over the festivities. More than 100,000 people converge on the town, so don't come without advance reservations.

For information, visit the **Tralee Tourist Office**, Ashe Memorial Hall, Denny St., ☎ 066-712-1288, open all year. Area codes for all telephone numbers in the Tralee area is 066, unless indicated otherwise.

## FOOD AND DRINK:

**Harty's** (Castle St., Tralee) A favored rendezvous for the locals, this pub in the center of town is credited with inspiring the idea for the *Rose of Tralee Festival*. Hearty pub food, such as Irish stew, steak and kidney pie, or shepherd's pie, is served all day and steaks are a specialty. ☎ 712-5385. £ to ££

**Kirby's Brogue Inn** (Rock St., Tralee) With a barn-like facade and interior, this long-standing pub offers an Old World atmosphere, with lots of Tralee memorabilia on the walls, agricultural implements, and rushwork furnishings. Steaks and seafood are the specialties, and Irish traditional music is often played on summer evenings. ☎ 712-3221. £ to ££

**The Old Marketplace** (Abbey Gate Hotel, Maine St., Tralee) Seldom does a hotel pub have as much atmosphere as this local favorite. It re-creates an "Old Tralee" setting with open fireplaces, natural wood and stone walls, beamed ceilings, brass lanterns, and shelves of local heirlooms. Soups, sandwiches, salads, stews, and seafood platters are served. ☎ 712-9888. £ to ££

**Oyster Tavern** (Fenit Rd., Spa, Tralee, three miles west of town) Sit indoors or outdoors to enjoy a drink or a meal overlooking Tralee Bay at this rustic pub. Specialties include oysters, lobsters, sole, scallops, and steaks. ☎ 713-6102. £ to ££

**Pocotts** (3 Ashe St., Tralee) Designed in a loft and courtyard format with paneled walls and brass lanterns, this full-service shopfront restaurant offers snacks during the day and full meals in the evening, with piano music in the background. Specialties include steaks and seafood, with breads, biscuits, and cakes from the restaurant's own bakery across the street. X: Sun. ☎ 712-9500. £ to ££

**The Tankard** (Kilfenora, Fenit) See the sun set on Tralee Bay through picture windows at this contemporary waterside restaurant located six miles northwest of Tralee. The menu offers fresh local shellfish and seafood as well as steaks, game, and rack of lamb. Dinner only. ☎ 713-6164. ££ to £££

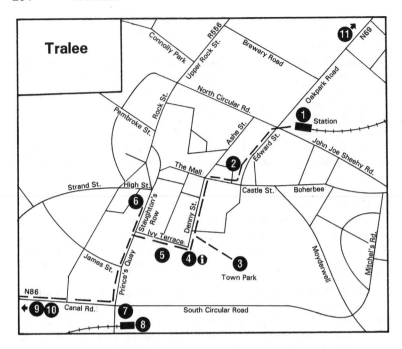

## SUGGESTED TOUR:

Start a tour at the **Tralee Bus and Rail Station** (1), officially named Casement Station. Turn left onto Edward Street which leads to **Castle Street**, part of the original 13th-century settlement of Tralee by the Fitzgerald family, the Earls of Desmond, also known as the "Geraldines." In those medieval days, Castle Street was surrounded by a moat and five satellite castles that were occupied by family members and friends of the Geraldines. Today it is lined with stores and businesses.

Turn right onto Castle Street. The next turn to the right, Ashe Street, is the home of the **Court House** (2), one of Tralee's finest buildings of a much later era. Built in the 1830s, it has a fine Ionic portico. Straight ahead is **The Mall**, a busy commercial and shopping area.

Take a left onto **Denny Street**. This is one of the principal streets of the town, constructed in 1826 and named after a family that was prominent in the town for over 300 years. It is said that the Great Castle of the Geraldines stood on this site in medieval times. Unfortunately, almost all traces of the castle have disappeared.

Today Denny Street is rimmed by lovely 18th- and 19th-century Georgian terraces and townhouses. Midway in the street begins the \***Town Park** (3), which extends for 75 acres. It is a haven for outdoor activity, with a series of leisure walks, rose gardens, and a fountain commemorating

William Mulchinock who composed the song, *The Rose of Tralee. Open during daylight hours; admission is free.*

At the end of Denny Street is Ashe Memorial Hall, an impressive three-story Georgian public building. It is home to the Tralee Tourist Office and to three of the town's prime attractions:

**\*KERRY THE KINGDOM** (4), Ashe Memorial Hall, Denny St., Tralee, ☎ 712-7777. *Open March 17–July and Sept.–Oct. 31, 10–6; Aug. 10–7; Nov.–Dec. 23, 2–5. Adults £5.50, seniors and students £4.75, children under 16 £3. Tours. Shop. Café.*

Ideal for a rainy day indoor visit, this building presents three different attractions that tell the story of County Kerry all under one roof. The first section is devoted to *Kerry in Colour,* a multi-image audiovisual display on County Kerry's scenery, historic monuments, and traditions. The second part is the Kerry County Museum, an interactive exhibition tracing human history in Kerry from 5000 BC to the present, featuring archaeological displays from the National Museum of Ireland, as well as slide presentations, scale models, and audio and visual gadgets. A "Kerry Today" section has live link-ups with *Radio Kerry* and the Irish-language station *Radio Na Gaeltachta.* The final stage is *Geraldine Tralee—The Irish Medieval Experience,* an action-packed time-car ride through Tralee as it looked, smelled, and sounded in the Middle Ages.

Departing Ashe Memorial Hall from the front door, turn left onto Ivy Terrace and walk one-half block to the town's cultural mecca, **\*Siamsa Tíre** (5), Town Park, Tralee, ☎ 712-3055. Founded in 1974, Siamsa Tíre (pronounced *Sheem-sah teer*), is the National Folk Theatre of Ireland, specializing in a form of entertainment that flourished when Irish (Gaelic) was the spoken language of the land. A mixture of music, dance, and mime, the program includes scenes that depict folk tales and farm life, such as the thatching of a cottage roof, flailing a sheaf of corn, twisting a sugan rope, and making a butter churn. The cast wears traditional costumes and dances to the music of tin whistles, concertinas, pipes, flutes, spoons, and fiddles. Although performances are slated only in the evening, the public areas of the theater are usually open during normal business hours and often contain displays of local art work and posters depicting the musical themes. If you can spend a night in Tralee, Siamsa is not to be missed.

Straight ahead is Princes Street; take a right. On the left is the **Holy Cross Dominican Church** (6), Day Place. Although it is relatively modern, dating back to 1861, it carries on the tradition of an earlier foundation that thrived during medieval times. A turn slightly to the right brings you back to The Mall and the heart of Tralee's commercial activity.

The remainder of the tour requires use of a car. Depart the town from Prince's Street, following signs for Blennerville. Straight ahead on the left is the **Tralee Aqua Dome** (7), Dan Spring Rd., ☎ 712-8899, an indoor swimming complex with water slides, waves, rapids, whirlpools, and more.

*Open Mon.–Fri. 10–8, Sat.–Sun. 10–7. Adults £4, seniors and children £3.*
Adjacent is the boarding station for the **Tralee & Dingle Steam Railway**
(8), Ballyard, Tralee, ☎ 712-8888. This vintage train uses equipment and
tracks that once comprised the Tralee & Dingle Light Railway (1891–1953),
one of the world's most famous narrow-gauge railways in its heyday. The
trip takes 20 minutes and runs along a scenic 19th-century canal route to
Blennerville, about two miles west. Trains depart every hour on the hour;
return trip from Blennerville runs every hour on the half-hour. *Open
April–Sept., daily 10:30–5:30. Adults £ 2.50, children £1.50.*
Whether you take the train or drive a car to Blennerville, don't miss
the area's centerpiece:

**\*BLENNERVILLE WINDMILL** (9), Windmill Street, Blennerville, Tralee, ☎
712-1064. *Open April–Oct., Mon.–Sat. 10–6, Sun. 11–6. Adults £3, seniors
and students £2.50, children £1.50. Tours. Shop. Café.*
It may look like something from the Netherlands on the horizon, but
this 60-foot-high tower mill has been a fixture on the Tralee horizon since
1800. Reputed to be the largest working windmill in Ireland or Britain, it
produces five tons of ground wholemeal flour per week. Take a guided
tour of the inside of the windmill and join in "hands-on" demonstrations
of the wind-driven milling process, or watch an audiovisual on the history
of milling. In addition, since the Tralee/Blennerville area was once a leading port along the Kerry coast, there are exhibitions on 19th-century emigration.
Beside the windmill is the area's most exciting seafaring project:

**THE "JEANIE JOHNSTON" VISITOR SHIPYARD** (10), Blennerville, Tralee, ☎
712-8888. *Open daily 9:30–5:30 except Dec. 21–Jan. 3. Adults £3, seniors and
students £2.50, and children £1.50. Café. Shop. Tours.*
This purpose-built shipyard is home port to the "Jeanie Johnston," a
triple-masted 135-foot tall ship built by a team of over 200 Irish and international students and shipwrights. It was built as an exact replica of a
Famine Era immigrant ship (1847–58) of the same name.
From April, 2000, the ship will sail across the Atlantic on a
"Millennium Voyage" to North America. She will follow the route taken by
the Irish Famine ships of the 19th century, calling at 20 U.S. and Canadian
cities over a nine-month period.
The original "Jeanie Johnston" carried a full passenger complement
of 200 passengers and 17 crew. The "new" ship is licensed to carry 40 peo-
ple: 10 professional crew, 18 volunteer crew, and 12 paying passengers.
The volunteer crew will include young people from Ireland North and
South, plus the U.S. and Canada.
After its North American sojourn, the "Jeanie Johnston" will return to
Ireland and be permanently docked at its Tralee Bay home as a floating
museum. Other ship reconstruction projects will follow, so there will
always be some work-in-progress for visitors to see.

From Blennerville, head westward exploring the Dingle Peninsula, return to Tralee, or perhaps continue on to other parts of Ireland. If you are heading northward toward Listowel, here's a new development that merits a stop:

**A DAY IN THE BOG** (11), Leam, Kilflynn, Tralee, ☎ 066-713-2555. *Open March–Oct., 10–6 and shorter hours in the off-season. Adults £2.50, seniors and students £1.50. Café. Shop.*

See a local community in action—and learn about Ireland's ubiquitous bogs, at this excellent new museum right in the heart of the North Kerry bog land. Motivated by a resident priest (Fr. Maurice Brick), this museum is the result of people pulling together to design, furnish, and staff a typical thatched cottage as a museum.

The walk-around exhibits are really informative—illustrating the ABCs of bogs, from bog formation and types of bogs to the uses of turf, as well as the flora, fauna and findings in the bogs. The story of bog cotton is also featured including items made from bog cotton. To top it off, there's a 15-minute video describing how turf is cut and the lifestyle of the people who work and use the bogs. Turf-cutting machines and equipment are on display outside as is a collection of farm animals (goats, hens, geese, pigs, rabbits and more), always a big draw for younger visitors.

# Trip 26

# *Dingle Peninsula

Long before Ireland became fashionable as a movie setting, the Dingle Peninsula was flashed across the silver screen throughout the world in the David Lean film *Ryan's Daughter*. Although the movie itself was soon forgotten, the cinematic seascapes of Dingle have long lived on in memory and tourist promotional blurbs. The rustic cottages, the endless beaches, the rhythmic cadence of the native Irish language, and the romantic mist-laced mountains of Dingle are still fondly referred to today as *"Ryan's Daughter country."* Before the movie, the Dingle Peninsula was completely undiscovered. Now, over 25 years later, it is still a well-kept secret, but can get downright crowded in the peak of summer.

Reaching out from Tralee like a thumb plunging into the Atlantic, the Dingle Peninsula (sometimes called The Ring of Dingle) is County Kerry's "other" peninsula, after the Ring of Kerry. More rugged and remote than its neighbor, Dingle is less than 40 miles long, but it seems much larger because there is so much to see and do.

Like the Ring of Kerry, Dingle is rich in seacoast vistas and mountain passes. It is rimmed by water on three sides (the Atlantic, Tralee Bay, and Dingle Bay), and overshadowed by the Slieve Mish Mountains and Mount Brandon, the fifth-highest mountain in Ireland (3,127 feet). Named after St. Brendan who had an oratory here in the 6th century, Mount Brandon is the highest peak in Ireland outside of the MacGillycuddy's Reeks, the range to the south.

The western tip of the Dingle Peninsula is also home to the West Kerry Gaeltacht, an area known as *Corca Dhuibhne*, where the Irish language (Gaelic) is readily spoken in everyday communication. Along with the language, native Irish traditions, folklore, crafts, and music flourish throughout the Dingle Peninsula.

Without a doubt, the peninsula's most famous "personality" in recent years has been Fungie, an adult male bottlenosed dolphin who swam solo into the waters of Dingle Harbour in 1984 and has thoroughly endeared himself to local residents and visitors alike.

## GETTING THERE:

By car, the Dingle Peninsula is best reached from Tralee via the main N86 road; it can also be approached from Killarney, 20 miles to the southwest, via Castlemaine and local road R561. From May through September, **Bus Eireann** operates sightseeing tours around the Dingle Peninsula, departing from Tralee Bus Station, Monday though Saturday, ☎ 066-712-3566.

## PRACTICALITIES:

The best way to explore the Dingle Peninsula is by car, but the roads are narrow and the driving can be slow, averaging 20 miles or less per hour, particularly over the mountain passes. Even though it is only 40 miles long, it takes a day "to do" Dingle.

The summer months, particularly August, can be very crowded in the major centers of population such as Dingle Town. Traffic moves slowly and parking is at a premium on the streets. Look for designated parking areas.

For information, visit the **Tralee Tourist Office**, Ashe Memorial Hall, Denny St., ☎ 066-712-1288. From March through October, the doors are also open at the **Dingle Tourist Office**, The Quay, Dingle, ☎ 066-915-1188. The area code for telephone numbers on the Dingle Peninsula is 066, unless indicated otherwise.

## FOOD AND DRINK:

In some ways, Dingle Town is the Kinsale of Kerry—a gourmet capital. Thanks to its position on Dingle Bay, the town has ready access to bountiful fresh seafood and many fine restaurants to serve it. In the past 25 years, the town has multiplied its eating choices many times over—and built up a reputation for top class cuisine in the process.

**An Café Liteartha** (Dykegate St.) With a name that literally means "the book café," this place is a combination bookstore/restaurant. The front section offers shelves of books, particularly on Dingle and Kerry topics. The café at the rear features freshly baked goods, salads, seafood, and traditional dishes such as Irish stew. X: Sun. ☎ 915-1380. £

**Beginish** (Green St.) With a stone facade, arched windows, and colorfully painted doorway, this restaurant exudes a Georgian townhouse atmosphere. Named after one of the Blasket Islands, it offers seating in an elegant dining room with seascape paintings or in a skylit conservatory overlooking the back garden. The menu features seafood with house specials such as smoked mackerel paté, mussels beurre blanc, poached lobster, and pan-fried medallions of monkfish. Save room for dessert—the hot rhubarb soufflé tart is a real treat. X: Mon. and mid-Nov. to mid-March. ☎ 915-1588. ££ to £££

**The Chart House** (Mail Road) Situated at the east entrance to town beside the harbor, this restaurant blends creative Irish cooking with attentive service. The menu features local fresh seafood plus steaks, and specialty dishes such as roast breast of duck with savory cabbage, pan-fried escalope of pork with vanilla risotto, roast shallots, grapes, and wild mushroom sauce, or local Annascaul grilled black pudding with baked apples and bacon. X: Wed.–Thurs. in winter. ☎ 066-915-2255. ££

**Doyle's Seafood Bar** (4 John St.) In this town of great restaurants, this is the benchmark. With walls and floors of stone, pine furnishings, shellfish tanks, and "Old Dingle" art, this place has a homey nautical town atmosphere. The small kitchen produces an amazing array of dishes, using ingredients from sea and nearby farms and gardens. Specialties include nettle soup, crab claws beurre blanc, seafood mornay, grilled mussels with garlic stuffing, oysters in Guinness, and rack of lamb for landlubbers. The early-bird menu offers great value. Dinner only. X: Sun. and mid-Nov. to mid-March. ☎ 915-1174. ££ to £££

**Half Door** (3 John St.) Carrying on the welcoming Irish tradition of a partly opened doorway, this restaurant conveys a country cottage atmosphere, with exposed stone walls, copper pots, and original tile work. Lobster and salmon dishes are featured, but the menu also includes grilled brill, baked filet of plaice, and seafood bisque. X: Tues. and Jan.–March. ☎ 915-1600. ££ to £££

**Lord Baker's** (Main St.) Incorporating the oldest tavern in Dingle, this pub-restaurant is named after a 19th-century Dingle poet, politician, and publican. Bar food is served throughout the day and formal dinners at night. The menu offers seafood chowders and platters, and "finger-food" such as scampi, Kerry oysters, and garlic prawns, as well as steaks and game. X: Dec. 24–26. ☎ 915-1277. £ to £££

**Ocean World Café** (Strand St, at the Dingle Aquarium) Whether you tour the aquarium or not, this harborview setting is ideal for a snack or light meal. Savor views of Dingle Bay through circular and picture windows in a setting of contemporary local art on white-washed walls, or sit outside amid the sea breezes under colorful umbrellas. The menu offers soups, sandwiches, salads, and home-baked goods. Unlike most Dingle eateries, this one has its own large parking lot. X: Nov.–March. ☎ 915-2111. £

**Old Smokehouse** (Main St.) For snacks and light meals throughout the day, this shopfront café is a local favorite. Nestled in the center of town beside a flowing stream, it is housed in an old stone building, with a country kitchen decor and an outdoor patio. The self-service menu offers made-to-order salads and sandwiches as well as soups and hot dishes. ☎ 915-1147. £

**Waterside** (Strand St) Views of the marina give this restaurant a seafront charm. Seating is available on an outside terrace or in a conservatory-style dining room. Snacks are available by day and full service dinners by night. The selection includes cockles and mussels sandwiches, shellfish salads, soups, quiches, crépes, and pastries. X: Oct.–Easter. ☎ 915-1458. £ to ££

### SUGGESTED TOUR:

Depart from Tralee via the main N86 road. After Blennerville (see page 206), the scenic drive starts to unfold immediately—with Tralee Bay on the right and the Slieve Mish Mountains rising on the left. Ahead on the right is a golden stretch of sandy beaches as you approach the village of **Camp**. The un-Irish-sounding name has nothing to do with outdoor living, but is instead derived from the Irish language *An Com*, meaning "The Hollow." You'll understand that it is aptly named as you drive through this

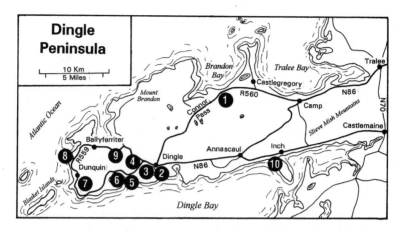

pleasant area with wild fuschia bushes growing on either side of the road. From Camp, the road branches right and left. The left route goes through the mountains into Annascaul, while the right road leads to Connor Pass. Unless it is raining heavily or deeply misted, opt for the latter route which is by far the more scenic and challenging for a driver, often described as a rugged "stairway to heaven." The second route, local road R560, swings westward and hugs the shore on high ground, overlooking the beachside village of **Castlegregory**, named after a 16th-century castle built on the site by a man named Gregory Hoare. The village is at the neck of a narrow spit of land that separates Tralee Bay from Brandon Bay.

Two miles farther on, turn left at Kilcummin to start the ascent up **\*Connor Pass** (1) (also spelled Conor), cutting through the mountains between the north and south sides of the peninsula. The placename comes from Irish language, *An Chonair,* literally meaning "The Path." And what a path it is!

A winding and twisting route rising to 1,500 feet above the boglands and beaches, Connor is the highest mountain pass in Ireland. It requires cautious driving, but is well worth the effort. On a clear day. the views are spectacular—from Tralee Bay and Mount Brandon to North Kerry and the mouth of the Shannon River. Rising steeply, this road curves and twists, dips and rises, presenting constantly changing panoramas of rocky mountain slopes and cliffs, including one point named *Faill na Seamrog,* meaning the "Shamrock Hill." At the summit, a car park affords sweeping views of both sides of the peninsula. The final descent brings you to the sheltered fishing port of Dingle.

**\*Dingle**, the main town of the peninsula and the most westerly town in Europe, is a picturesque fishing port, an attraction in itself. The placename derived from the Irish language *An Daingean,* meaning "The Fortress." Historically, not too much is known about Dingle except that it was the principal harbor in County Kerry during medieval times and it became a borough at the end of the 16th century.

Follow signs for the pier and leave your car in one of the designated parking areas. Dingle town is best explored on foot. Take time to walk along the marina area and see the large fishing fleet and sporting craft.

To learn more about local waters, visit Dingle's prime indoor attraction:

**MARA BEO/OCEANWORLD** (2), Strand St., ☎ 915-2111. *Open daily July–Aug., 9–8:30; May–June and Sept., 9:30–6; Oct.–April, 9:30–5. Adults £4.50, seniors and students £3.50, children £ 2.75. Tours. Shop. Café.*

Housed in a modern complex overlooking Dingle Harbour, this aquarium tells the story of the mariculture and fish farming along the west coast of Ireland. Using a unique walk-through undersea tunnel for up-close views of fish and other sea creatures, visitors can see more than 100 species of fish, both rare and common, including the only red lobster in Ireland, "vampire" fish (lampreys), box crab, and blue mouth, a type of redfish living in deep waters. In addition, the 37 tanks hold sea cucumber, cuttle-fish, conger eels, starfish, and the freshwater Arctic char. The exhibits also profile the life and voyages of St. Brendan who is said to have lived in the area and set sail from Dingle waters to cross the Atlantic and discover America.

Surprisingly, the town's main claim to maritime fame, *Fungie*, an adult male bottlenose dolphin, does not reside at the aquarium, but frolics freely in Dingle Harbour. Fungie swam solo into local waters over a dozen years ago and took up residence, although no one knows where he came from, how old he is, or how long he will stay. He is a born exhibitionist and swims regularly almost on cue beside local boats. Like most dolphins, Fungie is sensitive and gentle and eagerly interacts with people in the water. Several local companies offer boat trips to see Fungie, and usually give refunds if the dolphin does not appear. Inquire at the pier office for the next boat trip. Fishing and sailing trips are also readily available from the pier.

Take a left off Strand Street onto **Green Street** to see a few of Dingle's many craft shops. On the left is St. Mary's Church, refurbished in 1967, and to the right is **Lisbeth Mulcahy—The Weaver's Shop** (3), Green St., ☎ 915-1688, the peninsula's leading weaving center. Step inside and watch as skilled craftspeople create a wide range of fabrics, wall-hangings, scarves, shawls, rugs, and tapestries, all  reflecting the colors of the Kerry landscape and seasons. *Open Sept.–June, Mon.–Sat. 9–6; July–Aug., Mon.–Sat. 9–9 and Sun. 10–4. Admission is free.*

Green Street leads to Main Street, lined with colorful shops, restaurants, pubs, and local businesses. To the right is the **Post Office**. Main Street leads to John Street, home of some of the town's premier restaurants. From Main, turn right onto The Mall, an unusual street with a small stream running alongside the sidewalk on the right. This leads back to Stand Street and the pier. Return to your car for the remainder of the tour.

Head west out of town on local road R559, signposted for Ventry and Dunquin. For a look at some of the area's best crafts, turn right into **Ceardlann Na Coille—The Dingle Craft Centre** (4), The Wood, ☎ 915-1797. Laid out in a circular cluster of traditional cottages, these workshops present emerging local artisans at work on crafts such as knitwear, pottery, feltwork, leather goods, hand-weaving, and wood-turning, and making musical instruments. *Open March–Oct. daily 10–6. Admission is free.*

Returning to the road, on the left is the workshop of one of Ireland's top goldsmiths, **Brian De Staic** (5), The Wood, ☎ 915-1298. This artisan and his staff specialize in unusual Irish jewelry, handcrafted and engraved with the letters of the Ogham alphabet, an ancient Irish stick-form of writing dating back to the 3rd century. The collection includes pendants, bracelets, earrings, cuff links, and more. *Open Nov.–May, Mon.–Sat. 9–6; June–Oct. daily 9–6. Admission is free.*

Continue on the R559 for three miles. To see yet another of Dingle's specialty craft workers, take a left for **Holden Leathergoods** (6), Burnham, Dingle, ☎ 915-1796. Remotely set in an old schoolhouse beside Dingle Bay, this is one of the area's newest enterprises, established in 1989 by Conor Holden, one of the few Irish-born leather artisans in the country. Conor and his staff take the best of local hides and skins to hand-cut and stitch luggage, briefcases, bags, belts, and more. *Open June–Sept. daily 9–6; Mar.–May and Oct.–Nov., Mon.–Sat. 9–6:30; and Dec.–Feb., Mon.–Fri. 9–5:30. Admission is free.*

Returning to R559 puts you on a slow and scenic drive of less than 10 miles to the edge of the peninsula. En route you will pass **Ventry**, a lovely harborside village with a name that means "Head of (the) Strand" in the Irish language *(Ceann Trá)*, a graphic reference to its position overlooking the beach. To the west of Ventry Harbour rises **Mount Eagle** *(Sliabh an Iolair)* to a height of 1,695 feet. This area is rich in early Christian monuments, most of which date back to at least the 6th century. There are good examples of standing stones, bee-hive huts (called *clochans*), churches, stone crosses, and forts of various sizes and types.

As the road continues westward around Eagle Mountain, vast panoramas reveal the gentle profile of *Slea Head sweeping down to the sea. This dramatic mountain and seascape comprise one of the most photographed scenes in Ireland. The road then follows the curve Dunmore Head on the way to Dunquin. This is said to be the most westerly point on mainland Ireland.

Next stop is **Dunquin**, a townland that is known in the Irish language as *Dun Chaoin*, meaning "Pleasant Fort." In the summer, the many homes of the area play host to students who come to learn the Irish language. Dunquin's main claim to fame, however, is that it was for many years the chief port for crossings to the **Blasket Islands**, a cluster of seven offshore islands that resemble giant rocks lying two miles out on the horizon of the

Atlantic. There are four big islands, Inishmore, the Great Blasket, Inishvickillane, Inishtooskert, and Inish na Bró; and three smaller ones: Beginish, Young's Island, and Illaunboy. A great sea rock, Tearaght, and a multitude of lesser rocks and reefs also form part of the group. It is hard to imagine that anyone lived on these remote and rocky outposts, but historians believe that monks probably inhabited them in the 5th or 6th centuries and the Vikings may also have used the islands as jumping-off points for mainland raids in the 9th and 10th centuries. More recently, the largest of the islands, the Great Blasket, was occupied by a hardy assortment of fishing families until the population was reduced to 22 and they were forced to abandon the island in 1953. Not surprisingly, the solitude and setting of the island produced several notable poets and writers of the Irish language. The lives of these island people are chronicled in a creative and informative way at the area's only interpretative center:

*Ionad an Bhlascaoid Mhóir, the Blasket Centre (7), Dunquin, ☎ 915-6371. *Open Easter–June and Sept.–Oct. 10–6; July–Aug. 10–7. Adults £2.50, seniors £1.75, children and students £1. Bookshop. Café.*

What was it like to live on the Blasket Islands? This contemporary T-shaped center provides sensitive and introspective answers, through a series of exhibits and an audiovisual. Perched on the edge of the Atlantic with unobstructed views of the Blasket Islands, this living history museum explores all the dimensions of island-living, from the land, the sea, and the language, to the weather and the seasons, as well as the distinctive character of the Blasket Islanders. In addition, there are reviews of the far-reaching achievements of the Island writers, along with capsule biographies and moving descriptions of island life in their own words. To augment the cultural theme, contemporary art works depicting the harshness and joys of island life have been incorporated into the building and grounds. In the entrance is a work in stained glass that is reputed to be the largest secular work of its kind in Ireland, and statues, photographs, and paintings complete the layout.

Beyond Dunquin is the dramatic protrusion known as Clogher Head where brisk winds churn up the seas in a constant splash. For a look at the most westerly craft enterprise in Ireland, stop at **Louis Mulcahy Pottery** (8), Clogher, Ballyferriter, Dingle, ☎ 915-6229. This working pottery and studio produces a range of creations using local clay and glazes devised at the shop. The finished wares range from vases and teapots to platters. *Open every day, but hours vary with the seasons. Admission is free.*

Two miles northeast is **Ballyferriter**, a village that simply means "Ferriter's townland," from the Irish language *Baile an Fheirtéaraigh*. It is named after the Irish poet-soldier Pierce Ferriter (1616–53) who was born near here.

Continue on the R559 for four miles to one of the best preserved early Christian church buildings in Ireland, **Gallarus Oratory** (9), a beehive-hut built of unmortared stone. Although the exact date of its foundation is unknown, it has remained watertight for more than 1,000 years. To the left rises *Mount Brandon, at 3,127 feet the tallest peak on the peninsula and the 5th-highest mountain in Ireland. Named after St. Brendan, it is said that Brendan had a religious settlement here in the 6th century and set forth on his transatlantic voyage in a leather boat from Brandon Point. Continue on the R559 road back to Dingle.

From Dingle Town, the shortest way to return to Tralee or Killarney is on the Dingle Bay coast, via the main road N86 as far as the town of Lispole, and then along the coast road R561 from Annascaul to Castlemaine. The highlight of this 20-mile stretch of road is *Inch Strand (10), well sign-posted on the right. Featured prominently in the film Ryan's Daughter, Inch has also caught the imagination of other film-makers (Playboy of the Western World and the recent Tom Cruise epic Far and Away), and countless postcard-makers and photographers. Stop and take a picture or just admire the vast four-mile expanse of sandy beach. It is one of Dingle's—and Ireland's—most beautiful seascapes.

# Killarney—
# Smart Shoppers' Tour

Long acknowledged as one of Ireland's top scenic treasures, Killarney is now aiming for a new commercial title—"outlet capital" of the Emerald Isle. In Fall of 1999, the town unveiled the Killarney Outlet Centre, a purpose-built two-story shopping mall housing dozens of outlet stores. This new facility makes Killarney attractive as a shopping destination in the off-season as well as the peak season, for both tourists and residents of Ireland. Outlet shopping provides Killarney with a diverse all-weather activity, conveniently under one roof.

As a popular vacation resort, Killarney has always had a major share of seasonal tourist-orientated craft and souvenir stores, offering products that are popular throughout Ireland from woollens and tweeds to crystal and china, and, of course, leprechauns and shamrock coffee mugs. Because of the variety of lakeland, coastal, and mountain scenery in the area, items with an artistic slant consistently find favor with shoppers in Killarney. Many stores feature the same items, so prices have always been competitive as well. But none of this made Killarney stand out as a year-round shopping mecca until the advent of the outlets.

This tour starts and finishes at the outlet centre, but it also will take you to a cross-section of traditional Killarney shops. All of the shops outlined on this tour can be easily visited on one continuous walk.

## GETTING THERE:

Killarney is the hub of County Kerry, on Ireland's southwest coast. It is 84 miles southwest of Shannon Airport or 192 miles southwest of Dublin. Irish Rail and Irish Bus provide daily service into Killarney from all major cities and towns. The Killarney Rail Station and the Killarney Bus Station are both adjacent to the new Killarney Outlet Centre.

## GETTING AROUND:

Small and compact in layout, Killarney has no public transport, so walking is the ideal way to follow the route.

## PRACTICALITIES:

The best time to follow this tour is during normal shopping hours, usually 9 a.m. to 9:30 a.m. to 5:30 p.m. or 6 p.m., Monday through Saturday, except for summer when most shops stay open until 10 p.m. or 11 p.m. every day.

For visitor information at any time of year, contact the **Killarney Tourist Office**, Beech Rd., Killarney, ☎ 064-31633. The area code for all phone numbers on this tour is 064.

## FOOD AND DRINK:

**Buckley's** (2 College St.) is a traditional pub dating back to 1926. Relax and enjoy a drink or bar food made with fresh produce amid an "old Killarney" setting of an oak paneled bar, turf fire, and photos and paintings of yesteryear. ☎ 31037. £

**Café Internet** (49 Lr. New St.) If you want to check your e-mail or surf the Internet amid your shopping tour, this is an ideal stop—serving sandwiches, light snacks, fresh-baked scones, and plenty of coffee and tea, too. ☎ 36741. X: Sun. £

**Coopers Restaurant & Café** (Old Market Lane) Tucked in a little alley off Main Street, this newcomer presents modern Irish cuisine in a contemporary "funky" setting complete with photos of the chef at work on the walls. The menu offers fresh local seafood and organically grown produce and vegetables. ☎ 37716. X: Sun. £ to ££

**Foleys** (23 High St.) Decked out with flowers, fine linens, and antiques, this family-run restaurant offers full lunches and dinners in a Georgian country inn atmosphere right in the heart of town. The menu offers prime beef, Kerry mountain lamb, farmhouse cheeses, locally-grown vegetables, and Kerry seafood specialties such as mussel soup, Dingle Bay scallops, and wild salmon. The homemade pastries, breads and scones should not be missed. ☎ 31217. ££

**Great Southern Hotel** (Railway Rd., off East Avenue Rd.) What better way to cap off a day's shopping than to pamper yourself with a proper afternoon tea at this landmark 1854 hotel—served under Waterford Crystal chandeliers beside an open fireplace in the high-ceilinged lobby, with live piano music (Thurs.–Sun.). Conveniently located next to the Killarney Outlet Centre, this Old World hotel also offers bar food throughout the day or dinner in the main dining room. ☎ 31262. £ to ££

**Greens** (7 Bridewell Lane) For creative and colorfully presented salads and vegetarian meals, this is the place to come. Located near the post office, off New St. ☎ 33083. X: Mon. £ to ££

## SUGGESTED TOUR:

Start the tour at the **Killarney Outlet Centre** (1), Fair Hill, ☎ 36744 or 36663, on the east edge of town, with extensive free car parking adjacent to the bus and rail stations and beside the Great Southern Hotel. This is Ireland's first manufacturers' outlet centre, where customers can buy international and Irish name brands for much less than the usual ticket prices—averaging discounts of 30% to 50% and sometimes as much as 70% on out-of-season or over-run stock. It is laid out in an attractive two-story skylit format, and fully accessible via stairway, escalator, and elevator. There are well-maintained rest rooms and a sandwich bar on the premises.

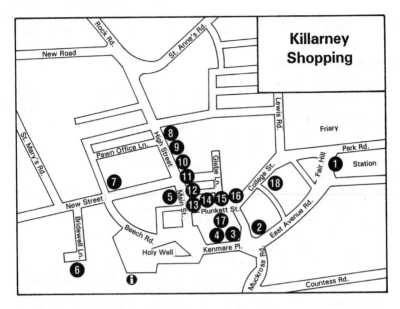

Geared to attract customers from near and far, the shops range from international brands such as **Nike, Ralph Lauren, Calvin Klein, Hilfiger,** and **Paco Sport & Leisure,** to Irish craft products such as **Brian de Staic,** the Kerry-based jewelry specialist and goldsmith. Other outlets feature many brands in a certain category, such as **Book Depot, Jean Scene, Leading Labels, Shoe Collections** and **Travel Accessories.**

After you have completed shopping in the outlet setting, take time to head into the main part of town for some typical Killarney souvenir shopping. Exit the outlet centre and turn left, passing the grounds of the Great Southern Hotel, and cross over to the right side of East Avenue Road. You will pass three more hotels and then arrive at the intersection of the Kenmare Road on the left. Horse-drawn jaunting cars are often lined up waiting for passengers at this junction. Continue on the right side of East Avenue Road (which now becomes Kenmare Place) and you will come to three popular craft shops in a row:

**Shades of Erin** (2), East Avenue Rd., ☎ 35959, specializing in dolls, crafts, linen, lace, hand-knits, and large selection of children's clothing.

**Viking Crafts** (3), Kenmare Place, ☎ 33820. The shelves here are stocked with an eclectic mix of tweed, china, silver, and lace, as well as fishing flies, shamrock seeds, heraldic crests, rugby shirts, Irish ballad books, local shell crafts, Irish coffee mugs, and leprechauns of various sizes and shapes.

**Country Crafts** (4), Kenmare Place, ☎ 36088, offering a variety of unique crafts, as well as hand-knits, woollens, jewelry, and crystal.

Follow Kenmare Place straight ahead as it takes a turn to the right and becomes Main Street, and the start of the main commercial strip of shops. Cross over the street and on the left side is **Anu Crafts** (5), 8 Main St., ☎ 34799, a small shop offering crafts decorated with Celtic design imprints and engravings, inspired by the art from *The Book of Kells*, Newgrange, and other historic symbols. The items range from jewelry and note cards to colorful tee-shirts and hand-knit clothing.

Continue on Main Street until the intersection of New Street, and turn left onto New Street. Follow this street, past the post office, to Bridewell Lane and make a left. Tucked at the end of the lane is the **Frank Lewis Gallery** (6), 6 Bridewell Lane, ☎ 34843, a local art mecca. With so much glorious scenery in the area, it is not surprising that Killarney inspires many artists to capture nature's beauty on canvas and paper and in clay. This modern gallery features monthly exhibits of the latest in County Kerry art—paintings, line drawings, sculptures, photographs, and other artistic works. Even if you are not in the mood for buying, you are welcome to browse.

Return to New Street and cross over to other side of street, heading back toward Main Street. On the left is the **Music Centre** (7), 6 New St., ☎ 33737, just the spot to find some local Kerry music CDs and cassettes as well as all the latest in Irish traditional music.

Back at Main Street, take a left as the street now becomes High Street. Walk along High Street almost to the end and then cross over to the other side. Here you will find **Bricin** (8), 26 High St., ☎ 34902, an interesting shop housed in one of Killarney's oldest buildings, dating back to the 1830's and retaining much of its original charm with stone walls, pine trim, and a turf fireplace. Named in Irish for a small bridge over the Killarney Lakes, this shop sells a variety of local crafts reflecting the Killarney countryside, from small ceramic birds and animals, to artistic wind chimes and mobiles, hand-crafted jewelry with floral or animal motifs, and books on local topics.

Continue along High Street, passing a string of international restaurants, and you will come to **Brian de Staic** (9), 18 High St., ☎ 33822, a Dingle-based jeweler and one of Ireland's leading goldsmiths. He sells a wide range of original hand-crafted jewelry, based on old Celtic patterns and ogham script designs and inspired by the natural beauties of Co. Kerry.

High Street changes back to Main Street at Market Cross. Here you will find **Quills Woollen Market** (10), Market Cross, ☎ 32277, situated right in the center of town where Main Street meets High Street and is intersected by New Street. This large and attractive shop is an off-shoot of a family business founded in 1939 at Ballingeary, in the west Cork Gaeltacht. It specializes in selling quality hand-knit sweaters of all colors, sizes, textures, and style. In addition, there is a wide array of Irish goods, including designer fashions, Donegal tweeds, linen, cashmere, as well as Waterford Crystal and other popular souvenirs in all price ranges.

Two long-established local shops are next: **J. O'Leary** (11), 33 Main St., a small antique store that is well-stocked with heirloom silver, brass, glass, and china as well as antique prints and vintage post cards; and the **Killarney Book Shop** (12), 32 Main St., ☎ 34108, a reliable source of Kerry maps and travel guides as well as books on Irish history, folklore, and fiction.

After a few more paces, one of Killarney's largest emporiums comes up on the left—**Blarney Woollen Mills** (13), 10 Main St., ☎ 33222, a branch of the highly successful Cork enterprise of the same name, specializing in hand-knit or hand-loomed Irish sweaters, tweeds, crafts, crystal, china, and souvenirs of all kinds.

Next turn left onto Plunkett Street. On the left are three stores that purvey the fine artistry and craftsmanship of the area: **The Killarney Art Gallery** (14), 3 Plunkett St., ☎ 34628, offering a fine assortment of paintings and other art work; **Memories** (15), 4 Plunkett St., ☎ 34447, a treasure-trove of Irish linen and lace products and accessories, both new and antique; and **The Artist** (16), 5 Plunkett St., ☎ 32273, the domain of local artist Stephen Doyle who produces colorful paintings, drawings, prints, and graphics reflecting the Celtic designs of Ireland.

Across the street on the right is **Celts** (17), 33 Plunkett St., ☎ 34200, specialists in Irish traditional music, selling instruments and instructional books, as well as CDs, cassettes tapes, and music-themed tee-shirts.

Remain on the right side of the street and follow it as Plunkett Street merges into College Street. On the right is one of Killarney's oldest shops—**Serendipity** (18), 15 College St., ☎ 31056. This aptly-named shop features a potpourri of knitwear in alpaca, mohair, and cashmere, as well as hand-thrown pottery, studio glass, linen, hand-woven fabrics, antique prints, paintings, copper, and hand-crafted silver and gold jewelry.

Follow College Street to the end and straight ahead is the Killarney Outlet Centre, the starting point and ending point of our tour.

# Section VI

# SHANNON REGION

S hannon—a name that is known the world over for duty-free shopping—is a lot more than an international airport. First and foremost, it is a river, the longest in Ireland, stretching for over 230 miles.

As the River Shannon approaches the Atlantic, it is the focal point of Ireland's midwest coast. The river cuts through the counties of Limerick and Clare, and touches parts of north Tipperary and east Galway.

Popularly called the Shannon Region, these counties offer an inviting combination of a major city, Limerick, surrounded by country towns and hamlets, mountains and seascapes, historic sites and craft centers—all close enough to the airport to be a daytrip.

Indeed this is the home of Bunratty Castle and Folk Park, Ireland's most popular attraction outside of the capital city, as well as Adare, the "prettiest village" in Ireland, plus the legendary Cashel of the Kings; the Brian Boru Oak, Ireland's tallest tree; Yeats' literary tower at Thoor Ballylee; the majestic Cliffs of Moher; the unique rock-strewn landscape of The Burren; and the Lough Derg Drive, Ireland's best-kept scenic secret.

No wonder so many people land at Shannon Airport. They can't wait to step off the plane to experience the Shannon Region.

# Trip 28

# Limerick City

A s the closest city to the international jetways of Shannon Airport, Limerick is often the first Irish city that transatlantic visitors encounter. Happily, it does make a good first impression.

Picturesquely situated beside the Shannon River, Limerick is rich in Viking, Norman, medieval, and Georgian traditions, making for an interesting and varied landscape. As the fourth-largest city in Ireland, it is a busy seaport and manufacturing center, as well as an important market and communications hub. Limerick is also a key learning center, home to the University of Limerick and an array of regional, technical, business, and language colleges, as well as music academies. In spite of its many facets, however, Limerick is a relatively small and compact city, easy to walk around and to get to know—a fitting introduction to Ireland.

Most people associate Limerick with a five-line rhyme known as a *limerick*, although no one knows for sure how or if it originated here. The name Limerick itself is derived from the Irish language *Luimneach*, meaning "bare area of ground." Linguists interpret this definition as being the land beside the lower reaches of the Shannon, with the "bare" understood to denote an unprotected and vulnerable location. And indeed Limerick was open to attack when it was plundered by the Vikings in the 10th century and later by the Anglo-Normans in the 12th century. The Norman conquerors made sure that Limerick would no longer be defenseless by building a mighty castle fortress that survives to this day on the banks of the Shannon.

The castle is only one of Limerick's many buildings and areas, recently renewed and restored, and constantly striving to make a good first—and lasting—impression.

In recent years, Limerick has also benefited from world-wide publicity as the setting for Frank McCourt's Pulitzer Prize-winning and best-selling biographical novel, *Angela's Ashes*, and the spin-off movie of the same name. Although most of the places depicted in McCort's depressing memoir have since been replaced or revitalized, many people now come to Limerick to retrace scenes from the book and movie. Even *"Angela's Ashes tours"* have been invented by enterprising local travel companies!

## GETTING THERE:

**Irish Rail** and **Bus Eireann** provide daily service from all major Irish cities into Limerick's Colbert Station, Parnell St. There is also regular bus service into Limerick from Shannon Airport. By car, many main roads converge on Limerick—N7 from Dublin and the east; N24 from Waterford and the southeast; N21 from Killarney and Tralee; N20 from Cork; N69 from the west; and N18 from Shannon, the west, and northwest.

## PRACTICALITIES:

Although Limerick spreads out into the suburbs on all sides, the core of the city is compact and walkable. There is a local bus service, but walking is the best way to see the major sites. The city is divided into three parts—King's Island, the older north end or medieval quarter, sometimes called Englishtown; downtown, the main commercial hub, formerly called Irishtown; and Newtown Pery, the newer Georgian corner of the city, added in the 19th century. You may wish to take a taxi from one section to the other, although it is not difficult to cover all three sections on foot. There are taxi ranks at the bus/rail station and on all main thoroughfares.

Driving around Limerick can be confusing because most of the streets are one-way. A good plan is to drive to King's Island, park your car, and see all of the sights in the medieval quarter, and then drive to the Tourist Office at Arthur's Quay, in the heart of the city, and park your car again to see the downtown sights.

In the summer months, Bus Eireann, ☎ 061-31333, operates **The Great Limerick Tour**, a 1.5-hour narrated open-top bus tour of all of the prime places of interest in the city, from medieval and Georgian quarters, to King's Island and the *Angela's Ashes* neighborhoods. There are two tours daily, at 11 a.m. and 2:30 p.m. Gray Line Tours, ☎ 061-413088, offers the **Limerick Panoramic City Tour**, a guided hop-on/hop-off tour that allows you to tour the city and disembark to see an attraction and then re-board again throughout the day (10 a.m. to 4 p.m.). You can buy tickets from the driver and join this tour at any of the pick-up points along the route.

Two walking tours are conducted by local guides departing daily from St. Mary's Action Centre, 44 Nicholas Street, ☎ 061-318106. The **Historical Walking Tour** covers Limerick's most historical area—Kings Island and St. Mary's Parish (departures at 11 a.m. and 2:30 p.m.), and the *Angela's Ashes* **Tour** traces the footsteps of Frank McCourt's novel (departures at 2:30 p.m.). Further information on all of these tours is available from the Limerick Tourist Office (see below).

It is always wise to have advance reservations, but especially at festival times in Limerick, such as **Limerick Civic Week** and the **Church Music/International Choral Festival**, both in March; and the **Limerick Food Fest** in mid-August.

For information, contact the **Limerick Tourist Office**, Arthur's Quay Park, Limerick ☎ 061-317522, open all year. The area code for all telephone numbers in the Limerick area is 061 unless indicated otherwise.

## FOOD AND DRINK:

**Bewley's** (10 Cruises St.) Situated in the heart of the Cruises Street Shopping complex, this dependable café is a branch of the Dublin landmark dating back to 1840. It's a convenient spot for coffee, tea, pastries, soups, sandwiches, or hearty hot dishes. X: Sun. ☎ 414739. £

**Castle Lane Tavern** (Nicholas Street) Sitting beside the riverfront in a reconstructed medieval laneway adjacent to King John's Castle, this pub-restaurant offers lots of atmosphere and good food in the heart of the historic district. Bar food is available throughout the day and full dinners with entertainment upstairs in the evenings. ☎ 318044. £ to ££

**La Piccola Italia** (55 O'Connell St.) The aura and aromas of Italy draw people to this long-established basement bistro on the edge of the Georgian district. The menu features pastas, lasagne, canelloni, steak pizzaiola, and Neapolitan specialties. Dinner only. ☎ 315844. ££

**Limericks** (Jurys Hotel, Ennis Rd) Come here for refreshment, and to learn about Limerick's limericks. A wall-long mural illustrating Limerick's "rhyming duels" is the focus of this pub, as is its carvery-style lunches with bountiful salad selections. ☎ 327777. £ to ££

**Moll Darby's** (7–8 George's Quay) Wedged beside the Shannon a block from St. Mary's Cathedral, this restaurant offers an Old World setting of beamed ceilings, brick walls and arches, bent-wood chairs, sconce lighting, and antiques. The menu specializes in seafood and steaks, with added choices of pastas, pizzas, and vegetarian dishes. Save room for homemade desserts and ice creams. Dinner only. ☎ 411511. ££

**Nancy Blake's** (19 Denmark St) Located just off Patrick Street, this popular pub is known for traditional music sessions in the evening, but is a fun place for a drink or snack at any time of day. ☎ 416443. £

**Patrick Punch's** (O'Connell Ave., Punch's Cross) It's worth a car or taxi ride to the south edge of town to dine at this popular pub-restaurant. The decor features the best of "Old Limerick" with Tiffany-style lamps, dark woods, open turf fireplaces, and a tin ceiling bedecked with antique model airplanes and unicycles. The menu offers Irish and international favorites—steaks, prime ribs, burgers, fresh fish, and pastas. ☎ 229588. ££

## SUGGESTED TOUR:

Start your tour at **Colbert Station** (1), Limerick's bus and rail depot on Parnell Street. By starting here, we are recalling Limerick's history in reverse since this area is the city's *newest* section, far from the historic original north end of town. If you are a history buff who prefers to retrace a city's progress in chronological order, this tour might best be done in reverse (i.e. starting with King's Island).

Having made that point, we'll continue from the front entrance of the station. Cross over to David Street and walk one block. On the right is the **Tait Clock**, a Gothic octagonal tower with a four-faced clock erected in 1867. Its decorative style sets the tone for the adjacent neighborhood.

Turn left at the clock and walk one block to an area known as **Newtown Pery** (2). Historically, this is Limerick's Georgian quarter and youngest development, compared to the rest of downtown. Built over a period of 80 years (1760–1840), Newtown Pery was the brainchild of

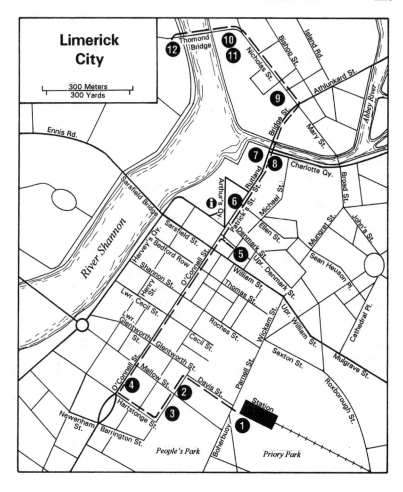

Edward Sexton-Pery, a local gentleman who inherited a large estate and proposed to develop his lands, virtually building a new city, based on a grid of wide streets and squares in the Georgian fashion.

The core of this area, **Pery Square**, contains six houses, numbers 1 through 6. Taken collectively, they are the finest example of Georgian architecture in Limerick, and comprise the only terrace of the city that is symmetrically designed. Notice that the houses at either end have gable entrances. One of the houses, #2 Pery Square, has been restored by the Limerick Civic Trust as a "Georgian show house" for visitors, similar to #29 Fitzwilliam Street in Dublin. The Pery Square house contains an illustrated history of Georgian Limerick.

On the east side of the square is the **Limerick City Gallery of Art** (3), Pery Square, ☎ 310633, housed in an attractive Romanesque-style building. Enter through a Celtic-patterned door with a stained-glass fanlight incorporating the city arms, a preview of the artistic flair of this establishment. Like many galleries and libraries in the US and Britain, it got off the ground with a little help from Andrew Carnegie who contributed £7,000 toward the construction of the building. The cultural hub of Limerick, this gallery contains a permanent collection of 18th-, 19th-, and 20th-century Irish art from acclaimed artists such as Jack Yeats and Sean Keating. There are also ever-changing exhibitions of paintings, patchwork, architecture, and sculpture. *Open Mon.–Wed. and Fri. 10–1 and 2–6; Thurs. 10–1 and 2–7; Sat. 10–1. Admission is free.*

The gallery is surrounded by the **People's Park**, a tree-shaded square of greenery with a Victorian-style drinking fountain. Walk along the edge of the park or take some time to explore the area. Then continue to Barrington Street and turn right; walk for two blocks to **O'Connell Street**, a wide thoroughfare that runs through the heart of Limerick. Like its counterpart in Dublin, it is named after Daniel O'Connell, the 19th-century Kerry-born lawyer, politician, and statesman who is known as "The Great Liberator." A statue of O'Connell stands in the center as the street splits in two for one block and forms **The Crescent**. Built in the early 1800s and originally known as Richmond Place, it was designed to be the principal feature of Newtown Pery. The unique design of a double crescent is rare in Ireland. From the Crescent, there is a clear view down O'Connell Street toward the rest of the city.

Walk along O'Connell Street, lined on both sides by Georgian town houses. To the right on the next block is the **Belltable Arts Centre** (4), 69 O'Connell St., ☎ 319866, a hub of Limerick's performing and visual arts. It contains a 315-seat theater and two gallery exhibition areas. In addition to evening performances, there are frequent daytime operatic recitals, traditional Irish music sessions, classical concerts, poetry readings, or drama workshops. *Open Mon.–Fri. 9–9, Sat. 10–9. Admission charges vary.*

If you are walking, follow O'Connell Street for seven blocks in a northerly direction, passing a variety of shops, fast-food eateries, and department stores. If you are in a car, this is not possible, since traffic flows one-way to the south. You may wish to take a few detours along the route. A left on Mallow Street brings you to the **Shannon Bridge** over the River Shannon, or a left on Sarsfield Street will bring you to the **Sarsfield Bridge**, also providing good views of the river.

A right on Cecil Street leads to the **Theatre Royal**, Upr. Cecil St., ☎ 414224, the oldest concert hall in Ireland and Limerick's main live-music venue for evening concerts. A right on Sarsfield takes you to **Cruises Street** (5), a shopping complex designed in an "Old Limerick" theme with 55 shops, restaurants, and other enterprises.

As O'Connell Street merges with **Patrick Street**, straight ahead is the **Arthur's Quay Shopping Centre** (6), an enclosed multi-story shopping com-

plex with 30 different shops and restaurants.

The adjacent **Arthur's Quay Park**, built on land reclaimed from the river, has a large central paved space for bands and outdoor festivals, and a riverside walk overlooking the Shannon. It is also the setting of the Limerick Tourist Office, well worth a stop for the latest touring information. This section of Limerick south of the turn of the river was the original **Irishtown**.

At this point, you may wish to return to Patrick Street for a detour. Take a right onto Ellen Street, and follow it eastward to Sean Heuston Place, passing the old **Milk Market** en route. Dating back to 1830, this outdoor market was once the thriving hub of Limerick's Irishtown. It was begun as a selling area for corn and later evolved for dairy products. Today it is the site of a country market for mixed vegetables, flowers, cheeses, home- baked goods, jams and preserves, on Saturdays from 8 to 1. On Fridays, there is an arts and crafts market from 11–6, complete with buskers and street entertainers.

Retrace your steps to Patrick Street and take a right to see one of the city's oldest attractions in a new setting:

**\*HUNT MUSEUM** (7), Custom House, Rutland St., ☎ 312833. *Open Mon.–Sat. 10–5. Adults £4, seniors & students £3, children £2.*

The cultural centerpiece of Limerick, this world-class collection of historic and archaeological artifacts, fine arts, and decorative arts is on display at the city's former Custom House, which has been totally restored. The collection contains more than 3,000 art objects, valued at over £50 million. The scope includes statues in stone, bronze and wood; panel paintings; metalwork; jewelry; enamels; and ceramics. Irish archaeological material includes Neolithic flints, and Bronze Age gold. Rare pieces range from the unique 8th-century *Antrim Cross,* to penal crucifixes of the 18th- and 19th-centuries, and the gold cross worn by Mary, Queen of Scots on the day of her execution; as well as works by Picasso and Leonardo de Vinci. The Hunt Collection is widely acknowledged as one of the foremost private medieval art collections made in this century. The Custom House itself is worth a visit in its own right. Designed by Italian architect Daviso de Arcort (Davis Ducart), it is a handsome 18th- century Palladian-style edifice, standing at the point where the Shannon River meets its tributary, the Abbey River.

For anyone with Limerick roots, turn right onto Charlotte Quay to visit the **Limerick Archives** (8), The Granary, Michael St., ☎ 410777. This civic office contains a collection of sources for tracing ancestry including newspapers, wills, cemetery records, trade directories, baptismal and marriage records, and detailed maps of parishes. *Open Mon.–Fri. 10–5. No admission charge, but charges for searches.*

Cross over the Shannon from Irishtown at **Mathew Bridge** and enter the area known variously as **King's Island** or Englishtown. On **Bridge Street,**

walk in a northerly direction. On the left is the heart of Limerick's medieval quarter or "Old City." On this site, in 922 the Vikings had pushed their beaked longships ashore to build their meeting place, *Thingmote*, their most western European stronghold. Two centuries later, Donal Mór O'Brien, the Irish King of Munster, built a palace on this site. In 1171, he donated it for use as a church. Today this historic ground serves as the setting for the:

**\*CATHEDRAL CHURCH OF ST. MARY THE VIRGIN** (9), Bridge St., ☎ 416238. *Open June–Sept., Mon.–Sat. 9–1 and 2:30–5; Oct.–May, Mon.–Sat. 9–1. Admission £1 per person. Sound-and-light show, £2.50. Tours. Shop.*

Customarily known as St. Mary's Cathedral, this massive Romanesque and Gothic Church of Ireland edifice was completed around 1194, and is Limerick's prime ecclesiastical landmark. It contains many fine antiquities including a coffin lid reputed to be that of Donal Mór O'Brien, the king who donated the property to the church and who died in 1194; and an original pre-Reformation stone altar, 13 feet long and weighing three tons, reputed the largest in Ireland or Britain. The Great West Door is Romanesque in style, and tradition claims it was King Donal Mór O'Brien's palace entrance. In addition, there is a reredos erected in 1907, carved by Michael Pearse, the father of 1916 Rising patriot Padraic Pearse; a wealth of stained-glass windows; a 14th-century tower rising to 120 feet in height; and a set of 23 misericords, medieval carved seats that are the only examples of their kind of furniture preserved in Ireland. The word *misericord* comes from the Latin meaning "act of mercy." Carved from oak, between 1480 and 1500, the seats, which were designed to be raised, each have a lip or ledge that allow the occupant, though standing, to rest during long services. On summer evenings, from mid-June to mid-September, the cathedral presents *Son et Lumiere*, a 45-minute sound-and-light show illustrating the story of the cathedral and the city.

Depart the cathedral and turn left onto **Nicholas Street**. Inset into the boundary wall of St. Mary's and Nicholas Street is a row of Tuscan columns, the only surviving element of **The Exchange**, built in 1702, a prominent market building in medieval Limerick. To the left also are the Limerick Civic Offices, on the site of the Old Courthouse and city jail. Next is the city's signature fortress, erected as a protection beside the Shannon River by the Anglo-Normans in 1210:

**\*KING JOHN'S CASTLE** (10), Nicholas St., King's Island, ☎ 411201. *Open mid-April to Oct., daily 9:30–5:30; Nov. to mid-April, Sun. 11–4. Adults £4.20, seniors and students £3.30, children £2.60. Tours. Shop. Café.*

Officially known as Limerick Castle and considered one of the finest examples of fortified Norman architecture in Ireland, this sprawling stone structure was built in 1210 under orders from King John of England to protect the settlement beside the River Shannon. The castle incorporates

some unique features for its time, such as curtain walls; D-shaped towers protecting the castle on the north side; and rounded gate towers. Now the focal point of Limerick's historic quarter, it comprises an on-site visitor center with displays, artifacts, and a multi-vision show that tells *The Story of Limerick*. The towers and battlements provide spectacular views of the River Shannon, and the undercroft invites visitors to watch the progress of current archaeological digs.

In addition, the grounds of the castle beside the river have been restored to include a cobbled courtyard and a cast of costumed characters who practice medieval trades and crafts including the minting of ancient coins and making charcoal. Stroll at your own pace beside the Shannon River and chat with each craftsman along the way.

Adjacent is Castle Lane, an authentic 18th- to 19th-century street, lined with buildings that represent Limerick's architectural heritage—a granary, two Dutch gable-fronted houses, a laborer's cottage, and a tavern. Thousands of bricks from original 18th century Limerick city buildings were used in the construction of Castle Lane to insure an authentic streetscape.

On the edge of this ancient street is **Limerick Museum** (11), Castle Lane at Nicholas Street, ☎ 417826, occupying a restored four-story granary building. This museum presents a collection illustrating the long history of Limerick City and the surrounding areas, from 5000 BC to the present. The exhibits range from Stone Age, Bronze Age, and medieval times, to examples of Limerick lace, a local enterprise. There is also a trades history display and a currency exhibit, as well as civic artifacts—the city's official sword, maces, and charters. *Open Tues.–Sat. 10–1 and 2:15–5. Admission is free but donations are welcome.*

To the left of the castle is Thomond Bridge, also built by the Normans. Cross over the bridge. To the left is the symbol of Limerick—the **Treaty Stone** (12), a rock on a pedestal whereon was signed the 1691 treaty between England and Ireland, a treaty that was never kept by England. Afterward Limerick was referred to as "the city of the violated treaty."

Stroll southward along the west banks of the River Shannon via Clancy's Strand, for fine views of King John's Castle and the city's other major historic landmarks to the left. Cross over Sarsfield Bridge back to the heart of downtown to complete your tour.

# Trip 29

# *Adare

**B**eing called "the prettiest village in Ireland" is a tall order, but one that Adare relishes. Set amid lush countryside beside the River Maigue, Adare is a model estate village lined with ornate thatched cottages, colorful walled gardens, distinctive Tudor-style stone buildings, and historic abbey ruins. It is cheery and slow-paced, with hardly a trace of the 20th century marring the village's "Old World" image.

No wonder Adare has always been a popular stop for travelers along the busy main N21 road between Limerick and Killarney/Tralee. Indeed photographers, film-makers, postcard-manufacturers, and artists have elevated Adare to the status of a tourism icon.

Not only does Adare look good, but it is genuine, not a reconstruction or a prototype. The placename Adare comes from the Irish language, *Áth Dara,* meaning "Ford of (the) oak grove." It aptly describes the village's bucolic setting, which is still shaded by great old oak trees beside the river. The rest of Adare's charm comes from its history, dating back to Norman foundations in the 13th century and enhanced over the years by the building of castles, manors, abbeys, and monasteries. The town owes much to the planning and benevolence of the Earls of Dunraven (Quinn family) who have made Adare their home for over 300 years.

So, if you are coming to this part of Ireland, put Adare on your itinerary. Whether you are just passing through or lingering awhile, be sure to walk along the wide flower-rimmed main street—relax, adjust to the local pace, and step back in time. Just being in Adare is part of the fun.

## GETTING THERE:

By car, Adare is 10 miles south of Limerick on the main N21 Limerick-to-Killarney/Tralee road. You can't really miss Adare, since the main road goes right through the middle of the town. **Bus Eireann** provides daily service from Limerick to Adare, a half-hour's ride.

## PRACTICALITIES:

Since Adare is on a main road, most people enter this little village when they are en route to some place else, and consequently they rush through the village with a promise to themselves to return someday and savor it. If you are staying in Limerick or other parts of the Shannon area, Adare is a worthy destination in its own right, for a relaxing morning or afternoon.

The best way to reach Adare is by car. Once you have arrived, see the

village on foot. Be warned, however, that Adare's wide main street is also a national road (N21), so traffic is constant. Take care when crossing from one side of the street to the other. Parking on the main street can be difficult at busy times of day, so head to the heritage center first and leave your car in the parking lot.

The village consists of one long street and a large walled area that belongs to Adare Manor, a hotel and golf resort. Many of the historic sites are in ruin and some structures do not provide public access. The appeal of Adare is not in touring its specific buildings or visitor attractions, but in the overall ambiance and lifestyle of the village itself. You can walk through the town in 15 minutes and move on, or you can take your time, enjoying the architecture, the gardens, the local craft shops, galleries, and pubs to your heart's content. It's up to you. Adare is not for everyone, but it is a one-of-a-kind experience in Ireland. Few can deny that it is certainly worth a picture stop.

For information, visit the **Adare Tourist Office**, Adare Heritage Centre, Main St., Adare, ☎ 061-396255, open March through November. The area code for all telephone numbers in Adare is 061 unless indicated otherwise.

## FOOD AND DRINK:

**The Dovecot Restaurant** (Adare Heritage Centre, Main St.) With a modern skylit decor, this bistro-style café offers snacks and full meals, both indoors and outside under colorful umbrellas. The menu is international, with a wide array of finger foods, from stuffed potato skins and open-faced sandwiches to Buffalo wings, as well as seafood platters, soups, salads, pizzas, burgers, steaks, and vegetarian dishes such as carrot and almond bake. ☎ 396449. £ to ££

**Inn Between** (Main St.) Wedged amid a row of colorful cottages, this thatched-roof restaurant specializes in innovative Irish cuisine, especially seafood and game dishes. Light choices—from burgers to salads and soups, are also offered. There is a choice of seating in cozy rooms inside or on a courtyard outside. ☎ 396633. £ to ££

**The Maigue** (Dunraven Arms Hotel, Main St.) Named after the local river, this restaurant exudes an 18th-century ambiance, and serves award-winning cuisine, with emphasis on local produce and vegetables from the hotel garden. Specialty of the house is roast prime ribs of beef, cut-to-order from a rolling silver trolley, although seafood and game are also featured. ☎ 396633. ££ to £££

**The Mustard Seed** (Echo Lodge, Ballingarry, about 12 miles southeast of town) Until 1996, this restaurant was the pride of Adare; now it has taken its prize-winning reputation out of town but still within reach. Housed in a lovely Georgian-style house, it offers two dining rooms, each decorated in bold blue and yellow colors, modern art, velvet drapes, tapestries, antiques, and flowering plants. The menu, as always, presents an array of creative cookery, such as wood pigeon on braised lentils;

spring lamb on curried pasta; beef with peppercorn crust; and homemade ice cream. Dinner only. X: Sun. ☎ 069-68508. ££ to £££

**Wild Geese** (at the Rose Cottage, Main St.) Named after the 17th-century legendary Irish chieftains and patriots who fled to France and Spain, this Tudor-style cottage sits in the heart of town. Bedecked by rose bushes outside and a cheery Victorian decor inside, it offers classical French-inspired food with an Irish twist. House specialties are lobster and oyster dishes. X: Mon. ☎ 396451. ££ to £££

## SUGGESTED TOUR:

The logical place to start a tour is at the **Adare Heritage Centre** (1), Main St., Adare, ☎ 396666, a relatively new development but built with the goal of blending into the local environment and architecture. It looks like it has been here for years, but it only opened in mid-1994. Documenting the historical events of Adare from the 13th century to the present day, this center does a good job in setting the tone for a visit to Adare. The layout uses a comprehensive exhibit with murals and realistic model enactments, along with a short 14-minute audiovisual, to profile the Earls of Dunraven and to tell the stories of Adare Castle and Manor and the village's three medieval monasteries—the Trinitarian Monastery, the Augustinian Friary, and the Franciscan Friary. *Open daily 9–6. Adults £3, seniors and children £2. Tours. Shop. Café.*

Take time to explore the other facilities of the heritage center including the **Adare Tourist Office**, craft shops, and a public library or stroll outside amid the well-manicured gardens. Directly across the street is an interesting feature of early village life, *"An Droichidin"* or the **Little Bridge** (2) over the Drehideen Stream, a tributary of the River Maigue that runs under the road. Used long ago as a watering place and washing pool, this small two-arched stone bridge was restored in 1975 by the Limerick County Council.

From the heritage center, make a left and enter the grounds of one of the village's trio of church landmarks—**Trinitarian Priory** (3), Main St., ☎ 396177 or 396172. Officially named Holy Trinity Church, this church incorporates the 13th-century nave, chancel, north transept and other parts of the Church of the White Monastery, a house of the Trinitarian Canons of the Order of the Redemption of Captives, the only branch of this order in Ireland. The work of these friars was the ransoming and liberation of Christian captives during the wars of the Crusaders. Why they came to Ireland is uncertain, but they established this monastery in 1230. It is commonly referred to as "The White Abbey" because of the white habit worn by monks. Like many similar Catholic establishments, it was suppressed in 1539 during the reign of Henry VIII. It remained in ruins until 1811 when it was restored by the 2nd Earl of Dunraven, given to the Catholics of Adare as their parish church, and it remains in that usage to this day. In 1852 it was enlarged by the 3rd Earl of Dunraven. One of the highlights of the layout is a fine circular dovecote or columbarium behind

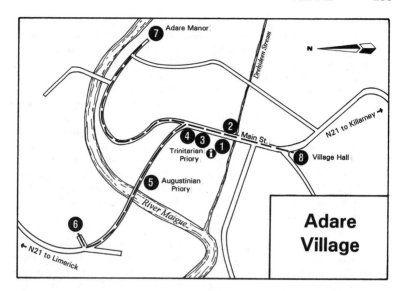

**Adare Village**

the church. *Open daily; hours vary, check the sign outside. Admission is free; donations welcome.*

Continue left walking up Main Street. The next building is the Parochial House, a fine stone building dating back to 1852, followed by the **Dunraven Arms Hotel** (4), Main St., ☎ 396633, a yellow-toned stone inn set amid palm tree-lined gardens. Dating back to 1792, it is furnished with local memorabilia and antiques and is well worth a visit for refreshment or overnight.

After the hotel, continue to the outskirts of town to the **Church of Ireland** (5), founded in 1316 as an Augustinian Priory, but converted into use as a Protestant place of worship (in 1807) and school (in 1814). Known locally for centuries as "The Black Abbey," it was suppressed by the forces of Henry VIII in the mid-16th century. The interior contains many interesting features including a 15th-century tower and cloister. *Opening times vary, check the sign outside. Admission is free; donations welcome.*

Moving to the left of the church, the River Maigue comes into view. Cross over the bridge, a fine stone work built by the Earl of Kildare in the 14th and 15th centuries, replacing an earlier wooden one.

Across the street is the entrance to the **Adare Golf Club** (6), part of the Adare Manor estate. Within the golf club grounds are three significant ruins—**Adare Castle**, also known as the Desmond Castle, dating back at least to 1227, built by the Normans and dismantled by Cromwellian forces in 1657; the Franciscan Friary, dedicated in 1464 and burned in 1646 by parliamentary forces; and the Old Parish Church of St. Nicholas, in use from the 12th century until 1806.

Return to the village, crossing back over the bridge, and to the left is the entrance to **Adare Manor** (7), Adare, ☎ 396566, nestled amid an 840-acre estate beside the River Maigue. The former home of the Earls of Dunraven and now a luxury hotel and golf resort, Adare Manor is a 19th-century Tudor Gothic mansion. The building of the manor in its present format, which spanned the period 1832 to 1862, under the direction of the 2nd Earl of Dunraven, provided work for the villagers during the disastrous potato famine. Walk around outside to see the many unique features—a turreted entrance tower, 52 chimneys to commemorate each week of the year, 75 fire places, and 365 leaded glass windows, and elaborate decorative stonework—arches, gargoyles, bays, and window frames. The interior is equally dazzling, with a 132-feet-long minstrel's gallery, inspired by the Hall of Mirrors at Versailles, lined on either side with 17th-century Flemish choir stalls. It remained in the hands of the Dunraven family until 1982, and opened as a hotel in 1988.

The grounds are a joy for strolling. The formal gardens, which were laid out in geometric box patterns in the 1850s, comprise an assortment of trees including a copious 300-year-old Cedar of Lebanon tree on the river bank, 180-year-old beeches, monkey puzzle trees, cork, and flowering cherries. There is also a display of Ogham stones from County Kerry, dating from the early 5th century to mid-7th century, and an animal cemetery with carved memorials to the Dunraven pets. *Gardens open all year, but hours vary. Admission is £2 per person or £5 per car.*

Return to the main road and turn left, strolling along the wide central thoroughfare which also doubles as the main national road (N21). To the left are two groupings of thatched cottages, preserved as originally built about 1828. Many of these now serve as restaurants, galleries, and shops.

Continue through the village, passing pubs, antique shops, and other local enterprises, until you come to the "top" or end of the street, as the road branches off in two directions (to Rathkeale or Askeaton). Here, at the apex of the two roads, stands the **Village Hall** (8), built by the 4th Earl of Duraven in 1911, on a site formerly the Fair Green. The Earl gave it to the people of Adare as a community center.

Cross to the other side of the main road and walk back to the Heritage Centre, the starting and finishing point of the tour.

# Killaloe

F ew towns in Ireland can rival Killaloe for its picture-postcard Shannon River setting. Encircled by a patchwork of green and golden fields with Slieve Bernagh and the Arra Mountains on either side, this little town is nestled on the southwestern shore of the Shannon's largest and most beautiful lake, Lough Derg (see page 241).

But, as the old saying goes, Killaloe is more than just a pretty face. It is also an historic town that forthrightly claims to have been the capital of Ireland during 1002-14 when Brian Boru reigned as High King of Ireland. Legend has it that Brian made Killaloe one of his chief bases of operations and built a palace on high ground here called *Kincora*. Even before Brian Boru, Killaloe was making history—and a name—for itself.

Earliest records of the area say that St. Lua founded a monastery here in the 6th century. Hence the name Killaloe or *Cill Dalua*, which in the Irish language means "St. Dalua's Church." Dalua is sometimes spelled *Do-Lua* or *Mo-Lua*, or simply *Lua*. The oratory that he built was originally on Friars Island, in the middle of the lake, but it was moved to Killaloe's mainland many centuries later.

Surprisingly, the patron of Killaloe is not St. Lua but St. Flannán, a 7th-century prince and bishop of the church, for whom the cathedral of the town is named.

Because of its enviable position on Lough Derg, Killaloe also gained prominence in the 18th and 19th centuries, when canal and river commercial traffic was at its height. Killaloe was then considered a key point on the main inland waterway trading route between Dublin and Limerick. In recent years, thanks to its wide and well-maintained marina, it has achieved favor as a boating and fishing center. Although popular with Irish visitors, Killaloe remains virtually "undiscovered" by many tourists, even though it is less than five miles off the main Limerick–Dublin road.

With lakeside views at almost every turn, Killaloe is a compact town of narrow and hilly streets with a medieval ambiance. Cross over the town's magnificent 13-arch stone bridge and you are technically no longer in Killaloe but in Ballina, County Tipperary.

Ballina, which offers dramatic views of Killaloe from its riverside banks, derives its placename, *Béal an Átha* in the Irish language, from its position on the water, meaning "(Place at the) Mouth of the Ford." Because they sit side-by-side on opposite sides of the river as one intertwined community, it is hard to distinguish between the two towns, so they have adopted a "twin town" approach, calling themselves Killaloe/Ballina.

## GETTING THERE:

By car, Killaloe is 13 miles northeast of Limerick, about a half-hour's drive. If you are traveling between Limerick and Dublin on the main N7 road, Killaloe is less than five miles to the north, via the Birdhill cut-off. **Bus Eireann** offers daily round-trip bus service from Limerick to Killaloe, about a 45-minute run depending on the stops en route.

## PRACTICALITIES:

Walking is the best way to see Killaloe. Park your car at the public parking area along the canal opposite the tourist office or along the riverside rest areas on the Ballina side. The streets in Killaloe are narrow and uneven in some sections. One-way traffic prevails on the long and hilly main street. The Killaloe Bridge, although very picturesque, is woefully narrow and inadequate for two-way 21st-century traffic, especially if a large truck, bus, or van is making its way across. Cars regularly have to stop and pull close to the side of the bridge to yield to larger vehicles. Be prepared for delays when crossing the bridge at busy times, and be cautious if crossing over on foot.

The Ballina side of the river has one relatively wide main street which is also a busy local road, so take care in crossing. For sweeping views of the entire Killaloe panorama, there is a series of benches in a park-like setting on this side of the river. Public access is free, making the benches ideal for picnics or just relaxing.

Killaloe is busiest in July and August when pleasure boat traffic on the Shannon is at its peak. The major annual festival is **Féile Brian Boru** (The Brian Boru Festival), a mid-July weekend recalling local hero Brian Boru's reign as High King of Ireland, with music, song, pageantry, fancy dress parades, and more.

For information, contact the **Killaloe Tourist Office**, The Bridge, Killaloe ☎ 061-376866, open May through September.

During the months of May through October, you can take a one-hour cruise of Lough Derg via the *Derg Princess*, a glass-enclosed riverbus, departing from Killaloe's north marina beside the Lakeside Hotel. For latest schedules or reservations, contact **Derg Marine**, ☎ 376364.

The area code for telephone numbers in Killaloe and Ballina is 061, unless indicated otherwise.

## FOOD AND DRINK:

The best views of Killaloe are enjoyed from the Ballina side of the river, so it is not surprising to find a fair share of the best restaurants and pubs on the east bank.

**Goosers Bar and Eating House** (Main St., Ballina). Situated across the road from the riverbank, this thatched-roof pub-restaurant offers seating outside overlooking the water or inside in a series of homey fireplace-warmed rooms filled with nautical and fishing memorabilia. Bar food is served all day and full dinners at night. Specialties include seafood soups and platters, bacon and cabbage, Irish stew, burgers, and steaks. ☎ 376792. £ to ££

**Liam O'Riain** (Main St., Ballina) For a sampling of "Old Killaloe" lifestyle, step into this riverside pub-grocery-newsagent. It's the ideal place to meet the locals and join a spontaneous session of traditional music, song, or poetry readings. ☎ 376456. £

**Molly's** (The Quay, Ballina) Perched at the foot of the bridge on the east bank, this informal plant-decked pub has a country cottage atmosphere with dozens of pictures and prints of Killaloe in its glory days. House specials include open-faced prawn or crab sandwiches, served on homemade brown bread, as well as seafood chowders, steaks, and burgers. Seating is also available at picnic tables outside overlooking the water. ☎ 376632. £ to ££

**Simply Delicious** (Main St., Ballina) The name of this shopfront café is an understatement. For a snack, light meal, or picnic ingredients, this is the place to know. Step inside and savor the tempting aromas of freshly baked breads, pastries, scones, fruit tarts, and cheese cakes, as well as a wide choice of soups, sandwiches, meat pies, quiches, and stuffed baked potatoes. X: Sun. ☎ 376883. £

## SUGGESTED TOUR:

Start at the Killaloe Tourist Office, on the west side of the bridge on the Killaloe Canal. It is quartered in the original lock house, and shares space with the **Killaloe Heritage Centre** (1), The Bridge, Killaloe, ☎ 360789. Through a series of walk-through exhibits, this center tells the story of Killaloe from its earliest days of St. Lua and Brian Boru to the town's heyday as a hub of inland waterway activity in the 18th and 19th centuries. One section of the center, designed to re-create the inside of a canal boat, conveys the sights and sounds along the canal waters, using a port-hole-shaped audiovisual. You can also "step out" onto a lakeside veranda and imagine yourself visiting the local hotel during its early days at the last turn-of-the-century. Pick up a vintage telephone and listen to local lore. In addition, the center has exhibits on fishing in the lake and on the town's hydro-electric scheme of 1929, which diminished the role of the canal and the lock keeper. *Open daily May–Sept. 10–5. Adults £2, seniors £1.50, and children £1. Shop.*

Now that you have a good grasp of Killaloe's history, step outside and see some of its sights first-hand. Start at the *\*The Bridge* (2), a handsome and symmetrical stone viaduct with 13 arches, linking Killaloe and Ballina, the "twin" towns. Although there is evidence that a wooden bridge existed here as early as the 11th century, the present stone bridge had its origins in the 17th century and had 19 arches. The west end of the bridge was altered in the late 18th century, deleting some arches when the canal was built. The most significant alteration was made in 1929 when a metal navigation arch was inserted to allow vessels to travel under the bridge.

Beside the bridge is the **Canal** (3), opened in 1799 to bypass the rapids

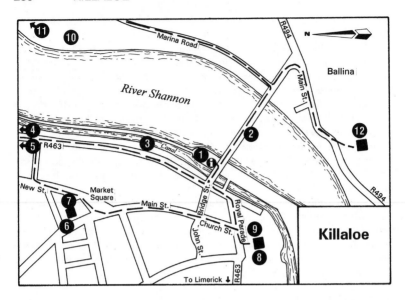

on the river. For over a century it provided a vital link in the navigation route between Limerick and other ports on the Shannon. In 1929 the canal fell into disuse when a hydro-electric station was opened at Ardnacrusha, 12 miles downstream, and the water level of the river was raised over the rapids. Beside the canal is the lock, which controlled the water levels and allowed passing craft to move from one level to another. The lock keeper lived in the house which is now the heritage center.

Walk along the canal to the edge of town to **Pier Head** (4), at the junction of the canal and the river. This is the spot where vessels could safely pull in and load and unload goods and passengers. The Lakeside Hotel opened next to Pier Head in 1897, but it burned down in 1922 and moved to its present location on the opposite side of the lake.

A slight detour of about one mile north of town leads to a site associated with Brian Boru, Ireland's High King and chieftain of this area. Take a right at the sign, **Brian Boru's Fort** (5), and park your car along the side of the road. Cars are not allowed beyond this point. Walk along the grassy, over-grown, and often muddy path until you see a massive earthen ringwork. This mound is said to cover an earlier ring fort, reputed to have been built in the 11th century by Brian Boru.

Return to the town and follow New Street up the hill to one of the town's chief landmarks, **St. Flannán's Church** (6), The Green, Killaloe, ☎ 376137 or 376633. Although this stone church is relatively new, built in 1836–37, the site is one of Killaloe's oldest. Local lore says that, on this high ground, once stood Kincora, the 11th-century palace of Brian Boru. It was totally destroyed in 1119. *Open daily 8:30–5 or later. Admission is free.*

To the right of the church entrance is Killaloe's oldest standing monument—*St. Lua's Oratory (7), a small stone chapel built in honor of the 6th-century founder and namesake of Killaloe. The oratory, which originally stood on Friars' Island in the Shannon, was moved and rebuilt here in 1929 when the local hydro-electric scheme that raised the water level of the river flooded the island. The nave can be verified as mostly 9th-century work, while the stone-roofed chancel is thought to be a 10th-century replacement of an earlier timber roof. *Open during daylight hours. Admission is free.*

In front of the church grounds is an area known as **Market Square**. For centuries, it has been the scene of local markets and exchanges for produce, animals, and other goods.

Walk down the steep hill of **Main Street**, passing the local post office and a parade of shops and local commercial enterprises. At the bottom of the hill, as Main Street changes its name to Church Street, straight ahead is *St. Flannán's Cathedral—Church of Ireland (8), Royal Parade, Killaloe, ☎ 376687. Like the landmark cathedrals at Limerick, Cashel, and Holycross, it was built in the 12th century by King Donal Mór O'Brien, one of the great benefactors of the church, but unlike the others, it has been in continuous use as a church ever since, first as Catholic and now as Protestant. It is named after St. Flannán, who became the first bishop of Killaloe in 639. Built in a simple cruciform style, it is designed with an aisleless nave. Decorative features include an elaborate Romanesque doorway; a medieval font, and a 12th-century high cross, transferred from Kilfenora in 1821, with engravings in ogham and other ancient writings. To the right of the cathedral is **St. Flannán's Oratory** (9), a well-preserved stone-roofed chapel of Romanesque design, also dating back to the 12th century. *Both sites open during daylight hours. No admission charge.*

From the cathedral, take a right on the **Royal Parade**. This street leads to the canal and back to the bridge. For the remainder of the tour, cross over the bridge to the **Ballina** side of the river. Once there, turn left and follow the path along the river. On the left is a red brick building, now a restaurant, but formerly the train station. The Irish railway served Ballina from 1862 to 1944. Coming up on the left are some private homes and the **Lakeside Hotel** (10), dating back to 1897 and on this site for over 70 years.

Ahead is the **Killaloe Marina** (11), home to an assortment of boats, yachts, and holiday cottages. Sightseeing cruises along the river depart from the marina dock.

Return to the bridge and walk southward along Main Street, lined with colorful pubs, restaurants, and shops. To the left is the **Church of Our Lady and St. Lua** (12), Main St., Ballina, ☎ 376178 or 376430, the final member of Killaloe's trio of churches. Compared to the other houses of worship, it is a young cousin, but it does have impressive stonework, stained-glass windows, and expansive views of the river from its front doorstep. *Open daily 9–6 or later. Admission is free.*

Beyond the church, on the right side, is a riverbank park with picnic benches. It provides the best views of the Killaloe tableau—tree-shaded steeples and rooftops, the bridge and the canal, sail boats and cruisers, and above all, the ever- meandering waters of the Shannon. It's an ideal spot for a picture or a picnic!

Cross back over the bridge to complete your tour.

# *Lough Derg Drive

L ough Derg is one of Ireland's best-kept secrets—scenically splendid and commercially unspoiled, yet rarely crowded. A body of water that is bigger than most cities, it is the Shannon River's largest lake, 25 miles long and almost 10 miles wide.

Often referred to as an inland sea, Lough Derg is touted as "Ireland's pleasure lake," because of all the recreational and sporting opportunities it provides—boating, fishing, hiking, water-skiing, kayaking, wind-surfing, canoeing, tubing, and jet-skiing.

For walkers and motorists, Lough Derg is a three-county experience, blending the best of the riverside back roads of Clare, Tipperary, and Galway. The road that rims the lake, appropriately dubbed the Lough Derg Drive, presents ever-changing views at every turn. The silvery blue waters of the Shannon are framed by a rolling patchwork of green fields, dotted by colorful fields of wildflowers and white-washed farmhouses, while the Slieve Aughty and Arra mountains and Slieve Bernagh slope in the background. It is one uninterrupted natural panorama—no billboards, no neon signs, no fast-food chains, no condominiums, no tacky amusement parks. Just the Shannon at its best.

Many of the most idyllic spots are designated as "lay-bys" (scenic look-outs) for visitors to stop and relax, with picnic tables and benches. Linger for a while and drink in the scenery or bring a picnic and feast amid the rolling green lawns with the Shannon ever in view. The resident birds provide a chorus of harmonious music, interrupted only by the buzz of a bee, the bleat of grazing sheep, the gentle splash of waves as boats cruise by, or perhaps another tourist or two.

The roads that rim the lake, a perimeter of 95 miles, comprise a well sign-posted circuit. In addition to the riverside scenery, the Lough Derg Drive is replete with well-kept marina towns and harborside villages, craft centers, monuments and castles, and a fair share of beguiling pubs.

The origin of the name Lough Derg is uncertain. It is derived from the Irish language words, *Loch Deirgeirt,* meaning "Lake of (the) red eye." Some placename experts maintain that the "red eye" refers to the color of a deep point or whirlpool somewhere in the water. For many, the mystery of the name just adds to the magic of the lake.

## GETTING THERE:

The Lough Derg Drive can be joined at any point along its 95-mile route, but the best starting point is Killaloe, on the south side of the lake,

13 miles northeast of Limerick. If you are traveling between Limerick and Dublin on the main N7 road, Killaloe is less than five miles to the north, via the Birdhill cut-off. On the north side of the lake, Portumna, about 35 miles southeast of Galway, is the best starting point.

The route is primarily a combination of five local roads—R463 and R352 on the west bank of the lake and R493, R494, and R495 on the east bank.

### PRACTICALITIES:

You'll need a car to do the Lough Derg Drive, since there are no local tours. Besides the ever-changing scenery, part of the fun of this tour is stopping at unusual craft centers, pubs, and historic sites en route. You might also like to rent a boat or wind-surfer and spend a few hours on the lake, or hike along one of the many wooded trails, or take a boat trip to Holy Island. All of these add to the enjoyment of the tour, but lengthen travel time as well.

So, while you might estimate that 95 miles should be a three-hour drive, it is more likely to take you a whole day, or at least five to six hours, to do justice to the whole Lough Derg circuit.

For information, start at the **Killaloe Tourist Office**, The Bridge, Killaloe ☎ 061-376866, open May through September. As you drive around, stop also at the **Portumna Tourist Office**, Gate Lodge at Portumna Castle, Portumna, ☎ 0509-41644, open in the June–August summer period only.

There are at least three area codes for telephone numbers in the Lough Derg area: 061, 067, and 0509, so area codes will be specified for each number, to avoid confusion.

### FOOD AND DRINK:

**An Cupán Caifé** (Main St., Mountshannon) Positioned on the main street of a flower-filled riverside town, this informal art-filled bistro features home cooking with a continental flair, as well as traditional soups, salads, and steaks. In the summer, there is seating outdoors with a view of Lough Derg and Holy Island. ☎ 061-927275. £ to ££

**Brocka-on-the-Water** (Kilgarvan Quay, Ballinderry) It may not overlook the water, but this small country house merits a devoted clientele who appreciate fine cuisine in an elegant candlelit setting of crisp linens and heirloom silver. The ever-changing menu features local produce, fresh seafood, and farmhouse cheeses, all enhanced by edible flowers and herbs from the garden. Dinner only. X: Sun. and Nov.–April. ☎ 067-22038. ££ to £££

**Ciss Ryan's Pub & Beer Garden** (Main St., Garrykennedy) Overlooking a picturesque harbor, this stone-faced pub has long been a tradition for evening traditional music sessions and piano sing-alongs. By day, it's a relaxing spot for soups, sandwiches, and local seafood. Outdoor seating is available on the front deck with water views. ☎ 067-23364. £

**Dan Larkin's Pub** (Main St., Garrykennedy) With a thatched roof and white-washed walls outside, this inviting Old World pub has a country kitchen atmosphere inside, with a traditional half-door, old hutch, open fireplace, vaulted pine ceiling, floors of stone and wide planks, and shelves filled with jugs, crocks, and memorabilia. The menu emphasizes seafood, with fish chowders, smoked salmon or trout platters, crab or prawn salads. ☎ 067-23232. £ to ££

**Derg Inn** (Main St., Terryglass) Nestled in a lane off the main road, this homey pub is filled with Tipperary memorabilia from horse pictures and ale posters to vintage bottles, fishing flies, and antique baskets, but the menu is the focal point. Creative pub cuisine choices include a unique warm salad with avocado, bacon, and walnut dressing, as well as open crab sandwich, smoked fish platter, mussels in vermouth, Irish cheese plate, chicken and mushroom pie. Seating is also offered on a large deck outside. ☎ 067-22037. £ to ££

**The Friars Tavern** (Main St., Lorrha) Join the locals for a set dance or session of traditional music at this shopfront pub, named after a 6th-century monastery founded by St. Ruadhan and nearby Friars Lough. Owner Dick Bourke, who extends a special welcome to visitors, is a top class musician and singer. He also serves a good selection of snacks and sandwiches during the day. ☎ 0509-47005. £

**Lantern House** (Ogonnelloe, nr. Killaloe) Panoramic views of Lough Derg and the verdant countryside draw people to this restaurant, set amid palm tree-lined and flower filled gardens. The views are exceeded only by the warm hospitality from Liz and Phil Hogan and their fine Irish cuisine featuring the best of local ingredients and home-baking. The varied menu ranges from duck à l'orange and pepper steak to fresh wild salmon. Dinner only. X: Nov. to mid-Feb. ☎ 061-923034. ££

**Moran's** (Main St., Woodford) In the heart of a town known for traditional Irish music, this pub offers music a-plenty and lots of atmosphere, along with an outdoor patio beside the river. Soups, sandwiches, and snacks are served. ☎ 0509-49063. £

**Paddy's** (Main St., Terryglass) With a lovely cottage decor, this pub is noted for its extensive collection of local antiques, as well as nightly sessions of traditional music. The pub grub features steaks, sandwiches, salads, and seafood. ☎ 067-22147. £ to ££

## SUGGESTED TOUR:

Start the tour at **Killaloe** (1), the historic marina town on the southern shore of Lough Derg (see page 237). The drive can be undertaken in either direction, but the route outlined here follows a clock-wise pattern. Leave Killaloe heading north, beside the canal on the western shore of the lake, via local road R463. After you exit the well-forested town limits of Killaloe, the road hugs the shore and reveals a continuous tableau of lakeshore scenery on the right.

Two miles north of town is the **University of Limerick Activity Centre** (2), Twomilegate, Killaloe, ☎ 061-376622, a watersports enthusiasts' haven.

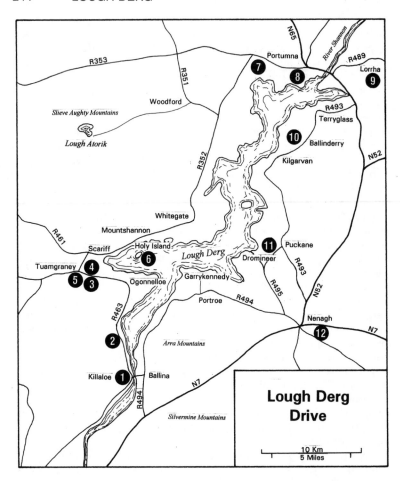

Lough Derg
Drive

10 Km
5 Miles

Join the locals for boating, fishing, tubing, waterskiing, windsurfing, canoeing, and other water-based sports. *Open May–Sept., Mon.–Fri. 10–9, Sat.–Sun. 10–8. Rental charges for most sporting equipment starts at £10 per hour.*

The route passes through the small hamlet of **\*Ogonnelloe**, a place of particularly scenic views, and then turns inland for several miles until you reach **Tuamgraney**, a small tree-shaded village that is well worth a stop or two. On the left is the **East Clare Heritage Centre** (3), Tuamgraney, ☎ 061-921351, housed in one of Ireland's oldest churches. It was built in the year 930, reputedly on the site of a monastery founded by St. Cronan in the 6th century, and has been in continuous use ever since, although not always as a church. Through a series of exhibits and an audiovisual, the center illustrates the history of the East Clare area and also provides a genealogical service, for those who can trace their family names to this area. *Open June–Sept. daily 9–6. Adults £2, seniors, students, and children £1. Tours. Shop.*

On the right is a turn-off for **Raheen Oakwoods**, Tuamgraney, ☎ 061-923010, an ancient forest that is part of a 500-acre estate on the shores of the lake. Recognized as one of the last primeval woods in Ireland, this estate was once the home of the late Edward MacLysaght, a leading authority on Irish names and author of *Surnames of Ireland.* The setting includes all types of trees, from oak, holly, ash, hazel, birch, and alder, blending with a carpet of mosses, ferns, and wildflowers. The centerpiece is the **Brian Boru Oak**, Ireland's oldest documented tree, estimated at 1,000 years old, with a massive 32-foot circumference at its base. Legend has it that the tree was sown by the High King of Ireland who ruled from his nearby fort at Killaloe. A guided tour of the forest starts at Tuamgraney Pier, which is sign-posted from the road, and includes a boat ride on the Graney River from the pier to the site of the giant oak. This trip is ideal for experienced walkers and hikers. It requires good walking footwear. *Open July to early Sept., daily 10–5:30. Adults £2, children £1. Tours.*

Continue into the town and follow the bend of the road to the right. On the left side of the road is a colorfully illustrated sign beckoning visitors to *Anke and Eugene McKernan—Handweavers (5), Tuamgraney, ☎ 061-921527. This husband-and-wife team has converted the town's former police barracks into a working weaving studio with a half-dozen looms of various sizes. Watch as Anke and Eugene work at creating a colorful array of tweed scarves, jackets, vests, and blankets. Many items are one-of-a-kind or made-to-order. *Open daily May–Sept. 10–6 or later, hours vary Oct.–April. Admission is free.*

From Tuamgraney, the road number changes to R352. Two miles north is **Scariff**, a small market town perched on a hill above Lough Derg. Literary enthusiasts often make a slight detour here, driving six miles inland to the town of **Feakle** in the remote southern foothills of Slieve Aughty Mountains. The full-time teacher and sometime poet Brian Merriman (1757–1805) is buried in the local churchyard, although no monument marks the spot. Instead a plaque outside of the graveyard celebrates the poet and his great opus, *The Midnight Court,* a single poem of 1,206 lines written in the Irish language. Merriman was a teacher at a nearby school.

Return to Scariff and continue to follow the road north. From Scariff, the road wends its way along the lakeside to the village of *Mountshannon, known for its lovely public gardens and picturesque harbor. Take a right at the sign for "Marina" and follow the road to the water's edge. Park your car and enjoy the walks and flower gardens that encircle the marina.

The Mountshannon marina is the departure point for boat tours to *Holy Island (6), known in the Irish language as *Iniscealtra,* meaning "Island of the Churches." Home to no less than five ruined churches, this five-acre island was the outpost of St. Caimin who founded a monastery here in the 7th century. The monks suffered repeatedly at the hands of the Vikings during the 9th and 10th centuries, but local lore says that the settlement was restored by King Brian Boru.

The main group of buildings centers on **St. Caimin's Church**. It contains a fine Romanesque doorway and chancel that were probably inserted in the 12th century. West of the church is a roofless round tower believed to have been contemporary with the church, and to the east is a burial ground known as "the saints' graveyard" which has grave slabs with 12th-century inscriptions in the Irish language. In addition, the island has a holy well, confessional, stone shrine, and several high crosses. Excavations in 1970-80 produced material dating from the 7th century, including traces of the original monastery.

Although the island is no longer inhabited, except by a roaming herd of cows and a bull, it is accessible by boat. To make the two-mile trip, contact the **Holy Island Ferry Service**, Mountshannon Marina, ☎ 061-921351 and 061-921615; mobile phone ☎ 088-601173. A round-trip lasts approximately 1.5 hours, including a guided tour and time to explore the island or have a picnic. *Open May–Sept. daily 10–5, with departures on the hour or by appointment. Adults £4, children £2.*

From Mountshannon, the road continues north via a well-forested area, with the Slieve Aughty Mountains rising on the left. At the next town, **Whitegate**, a popular base for boat cruisers, the road forks to the left and continues northward, entering County Galway. At Clonco Bridge, take a slight detour for *Woodford, a well-forested inland town on the Woodford River. The meadows beside the river banks are known for several rare kinds of flora including blue-eyed grass, a species that flowers in July with a pale blue color. Although historical records show that Woodford as a town dates back to the latter half of the 17th century, some archaeological sites can be traced to 1200 BC. A very musical town, Woodford is a mecca for Irish traditional music in its pubs. Each December this town holds a *Mummers' Féile*, a two-day festival of traditional music, song, dance, and mime performed by local mummers in colorful costume. From Woodford, a local road leads to *Lough Atorik, a beautiful and deserted lake hidden in the Slieve Aughty Mountains.

From Woodford, it is nine miles northeast to **Portumna**, the chief town at the northern head of Lough Derg. As you approach the town, R352 merges to become part of N65. With a wide and busy bridge crossing over the Shannon, Portumna is a popular berthing place for cabin cruises plying the waters of the Shannon. The placename for Portumna, which comes from the Irish language words *Port Omna*, means "Landing place of (the) oak tree." And it's a very appropriate name since the town signature attraction is *Portumna Forest Park (7), offering 1,400 acres of nature trails and sign-posted walks, amid lush riverside woodlands and foliage. *Open daily dawn to dusk. Admission £1 per person.*

For lovely views of Lough Derg, make a right off N65 onto the marina road to visit **Portumna Castle** (8), Portumna, ☎ 0509-41658, built before 1618 by Earl Richard Burke and recently restored. It is one of the finest 17th-century manor houses ever constructed in Ireland, with rows of stone mullioned windows and Dutch-style decorative gables. The grounds include a formal geometric-style garden. *Open daily mid-June to mid-Sept. 9:30–6:30. Adults £1.50, seniors £1 and children 60p.*

From Portumna, follow the main N52 road south, entering County Tipperary. At the cut-off for local road R489, take a one-mile detour to **Lorrha**, a small village that was the site of a monastery founded by St. Ruadhan in the 6th century. Even the local lake—Friars Lough—is a reminder of the early settlement, although no remnants remain.

**St. Ruadhan's Church of Ireland**, which stands today on the original site, does contain a ruin of a later foundation of the same name built around 1000. The town is also home to **Redwood Castle** (9), a private residence and one of the oldest occupied Norman castles in Ireland (built in 1210). Fully restored in recent years, it is owned by the kinsfolk of the original owners, the MacEgans. It contains 20 rooms spread over five stories—the top floor is confined to family use. Its features include a 13th-century-style banqueting hall, a small oratory, and a unique *Sheela-na-gig* (a female figure of uncertain significance) over the main entrance. It is used every alternate year for Egan family clan gatherings from around the world. *Open July–Aug. daily 2–6. Adults £2, seniors and students £1.*

Returning to the main N52 road, the next stop is \*Terryglass, a hamlet on a stream near the upper reaches of Lough Derg. Its placename—*Tir Dhá Ghlas,* meaning "Land of (the) two streams" in the Irish language, describes it perfectly. Although Terryglass is the site of a monastery founded by St. Colman in the 6th century, little remains of its early days except part of the abbey wall. There are, however, two exceptional pubs, and a picturesque marina.

From Terryglass, follow local road R493 which rims the shoreline of Lough Derg, offering frequent lakeside views and a series of charming small towns and villages including Ballinderry and Puckane. Shopping is the specialty of these two towns. The opportunities include **Lakeshore Foods** (10), Ballinderry, ☎ 067- 22094, a mustard and honey factory gift shop; and **\*Walsh Craft** (11), Puckane, ☎ 067-24229, a wood-carver's workshop. The latter enterprise, housed in a rustic white-washed cottage, produces unique hand-carved plaques depicting Irish rural, sporting, and religious themes, all reflecting the moods and colors of Ireland. The pieces range from pendant-style figurines and symbols, to portrait-sized scenes of Irish music sessions, pub facades, farmyards, cottages, castles, and villages.

From Puckane, the road dips eastward toward **Nenagh**, the chief town of north Tipperary, lying in a fertile valley between the Silvermine and Arra Mountains. Nenagh takes its name from the Irish language word *An tAonach,* meaning "The assembly place." In early Christian times, Nenagh was a major place of gathering. Later, the assemblies took the form of horse fairs that are still prevalent today in this horse-happy county.

Stop at the **Nenagh Heritage Centre** (12), off Kickham St., Nenagh, ☎ 067-32633, for an overview display on the whole Lough Derg area. Located in two stone buildings, dating from 1840–42, this site was once a jail, then a convent, and a school. Now, as a museum, it showcases collections of local arts, crafts, photography, and memorabilia. *Open mid-May to Oct., Mon.–Fri. 10–5, Sun. 2:30–5. Adults £2, seniors, students, and children £1.*

Depart Nenagh and follow the R495 road to *****Dromineer**, a major boating and fishing center with a wide marina, and then over to R494 to **Portroe**, a pleasant town on high ground. Follow a short detour off the main road to *****Garrykennedy**, to see one of the smallest harborfront towns on Lough Derg with a flower-filled marina and two inviting pubs, almost side-by-side and known for their impromptu sessions of Irish traditional music beside the water.

Return to R495 and follow it south, with wide-open vistas of the Lough Derg shoreline on the right. About three miles down there is a well-placed scenic look-out, with an ample parking area and picnic benches. It affords some of the best picture-taking angles of the whole Lough Derg Drive circuit.

Continue for less than five miles to Ballina and then cross over the bridge into Killaloe to complete your tour.

# West Clare

Contrast is the buzz word for the western half of County Clare. Facing the churning waves of the Atlantic and edged by the gentle waters of Galway Bay and the Shannon Estuary, this region is naturally diverse. It is rural and rugged, yet it provides a nurturing habitat for rare flora and fauna. Wide stretches of beach and mighty cliffs rim the coast, while a rock-strewn limestone plain known as The Burren dominates the interior. The roar of jets fills the sky as the silent aura of ancient prehistoric monuments pervades the countryside below. Craftsmen and artists rub shoulders with matchmakers and musicians, and underground caves are as popular as coastal marinas. The Corkscrew Road is as challenging as the championship Lahinch Golf Courses.

Literally at the back door of Shannon International Airport, this western half of County Clare is often the first or last glimpse of Ireland that transatlantic visitors see. And indeed it is a fitting introduction or finale—small and easy to tour, West Clare provides a kaleidoscopic experience of all that is best in the Emerald Isle.

## GETTING THERE:

By car, the Clare coast is within 15 miles of Shannon Airport or 25 miles from Limerick City, via the main N18 road in both cases. From May through September, **Bus Eireann** operates a series of "Summer Day Trips" including half-day or full-day tours of Lahinch, Cliffs of Moher, Doolin, and Lisdoonvarna, departing from Limerick's Colbert Station; and **Gray Line Tours** offers one-day sightseeing bus trips to the Cliffs of Moher and the Burren, departing from the Limerick Tourist Office at Arthur's Quay.

## PRACTICALITIES:

The ideal way to tour the Clare coast is by car, allowing flexibility to stop and enjoy the various attractions along the way. The basic tour follows two major national roads, N67 and N68, for most of the way. The route does go through vast and sometimes hilly stretches of rocky land, so the driving can be slow, averaging 25 to 30 miles per hour. The total mileage falls between 80 to 100 miles, depending on detours and diversions. Traffic can be very heavy, particularly on summer weekends in the Cliffs of Moher area, and within small and popular towns like Ballyvaughan and Doolin.

For the Cliffs of Moher, wear comfortable shoes for walking up the hill to the viewing areas. It can also be extra cool and windy along the edge of the Cliffs, so wear adequate clothing and be cautious as you walk.

For information, stop en route at the **Shannon Airport Tourist Office**, Arrivals Hall, Shannon, Co. Clare, ☎ 061-471664; **Limerick Tourist Office**, Arthur's Quay, Limerick, ☎ 061-317522; or **Ennis Tourist Office**, Arthurs's Row (off O'Connell St.), Town Centre, Ennis, Co. Clare, ☎ 065-682-8366, all open year-round. Seasonal tourist offices in West Clare are maintained as follows: **Cliffs of Moher Tourist Office**, Cliffs Visitor Centre, Co. Clare, ☎ 065-708-1171, open April to October; **Kilkee Tourist Office**, O'Connell St., Kilkee, Co. Clare, ☎ 065-905-6112, open late May to August; and **Kilrush Tourist Office**, Town Hall, Kilrush, Co. Clare, ☎ 065-905-1577, open June to early September.

Telephone numbers in west County Clare area use the 065 area code, unless indicated otherwise.

## FOOD AND DRINK:

**Bruach na hAille** (Roadford, Doolin) Espousing a name that means "Bridge over the River Aille" in the Irish language, this cozy cottage-style restaurant sits beside the river. The menu has a Continental flair, with dishes such as filet of sole in cider with shellfish cream; ragoût of seasonal fish; and seafood au gratin. Dinner only. X: Nov.–Mar. ☎ 707-4120. ££

**Captain's Deck** (Main St. Liscannor) With views of Liscannor Bay, this nautically-themed eatery offers snacks, soups, and sandwiches by day and full dinners at night. Specialties include lobster thermidor, medallions of monkfish, and sautéed skate with lemon and capers, as well as steak au poivre and honey-baked duckling. X: Nov.–April. ☎ 708-1666. £ to ££

**Gus O'Connor's** (Pier Rd., Doolin) Sitting amid a row of fishermen's cottages less than a mile from the roaring waters of the Atlantic, this historic (c. 1832) pub offers daytime snacks and evening sessions of Irish traditional music in the best of the old West Clare-style. ☎ 707-4168. £

**Manuel's** (Corbally, Kilkee) Situated on a hill overlooking the ocean and the rocky countryside, this cottage-style restaurant is run by Manuel and Doris Di Lucia. Manuel goes out in his boat every day to catch the best of local seafood and Doris does the cooking. Specialties include Clare lobster, served grilled or thermidor; and baked Atlantic salmon; and black sole on the bone. Dinner only. X: Oct.–March. ☎ 905-6211. ££ to £££

**Monks Pub** (The Pier, Ballyvaughan) Hugging the harbor, this old fishermen's pub offers a briny atmosphere and great seafood, with indoor or outdoor seating, and views of the water. House specialties are fresh mussels, seafood chowder, and fresh crab. X: Dec.–Feb. ☎ 707-7059. £ to ££

**Whitethorn** (Ballyvaughan, 1 mile east of the village) If location is everything, this restaurant, sitting right on the southern edge of Galway Bay, scores a 10, especially at sunset time and on sunny days. With an all-rock Burren-inspired exterior except for floor-to-ceiling picture windows, this contemporary eatery is self-service by day and full-service in the evening. Snack items include soups, seafood salads, pastas, meat casseroles, and yummy home-baked scones, while dinner entrées range from steaks and seafood to wholemeal crêpes filled with mixed vegetables. X: Nov.–Feb. ☎ 707-7044. £ to ££

## SUGGESTED TOUR:

From **Shannon Airport** (1) or Limerick City, drive north on national road N18 as far as Ennis (see page 266), and then turn left onto N85 for three miles, breaking off to the right at local road R476, for just over five miles into **Corofin**, a small market village near Lake Inchiquin. The place-name Corofin comes from the Irish language *Cora Finne,* meaning "Finne's weir."

In the center of the town is the **Clare Heritage & Genealogical Centre** (2), Main St., Corofin, ☎ 683-7955. Housed in the former St. Catherine's Protestant church dating back to 1718, this center is an ideal place to stop and learn some background about the area. Its main display, *Ireland West 1800–1860,* portrays the traumatic period of Irish famine, emigration, and land tenure. In addition, there are exhibits on Clare farming, industry, commerce, education, forestry, language, and music, all designed to portray life in this area during the past 300 years. Visitors with Clare roots can also consult with the on-site genealogical service. *Open April–Oct. daily 10–6. Adults £2, children under 12 £1.*

After passing through Corofin, you have now officially entered **\*The Burren** (3), sometimes referred to as Ireland's "rock desert." It is an amazing 100-square-mile-area covered with a barren lunar-like landscape. It is not surprising that the Irish language word for Burren is *Boirinn,* meaning "Stony place." Massive sheets of rock, craggy boulders, and potholes are visible for miles in an almost moonscape-style pattern, yet this area is also a setting for pocket lakes and streams, set amid hills, turloughs, valleys, and mountains, as well as an amazing assemblage of wildlife and greenery.

Experts say there is always something in bloom, even in winter, from ferns and moss to orchids, rock roses, milkworts, wild thyme, geraniums, violets, and fuschia. This area is also famous for its 33 species of butterflies. Animals such as the pine martin, stoat, and badger, not often seen in the rest of Ireland, are common here.

The story of The Burren began millions of years ago when layers of shells and sediment were deposited under a tropical sea, only to be thrust above this surface years later and left exposed to the erosive power of Irish rain and weather, producing the limestone landscape that appears today.

As the locals will tell you, however, the word "Burren" should not be confused with  barren. As early as the Stone Age, man has settled in this curious area. Evidence of human habitation is all around—massive dolmens and wedge tombs, and hundreds of stone forts, known as *cahers,* which were the homesteads of farmers long ago. The area is also rich in Christian ruins—round towers, churches, high crosses, monasteries, and holy wells. In recent years, the Burren area has been designated as a national park.

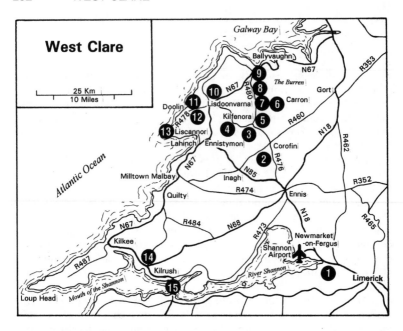

Continue on R476 north for five more miles and then make a right to R480 which goes north. R476 turns westward at this point. You may wish to take a slight detour by continuing instead on R476 as it goes west for about three miles, to see the **Burren Centre** (4), Kilfenora, Co. Clare, ☎ 707-8030, to learn more about the amazing facets of the Burren. Established in 1975 as a community development cooperative, this facility presents a 25-minute audiovisual plus landscape models on the geology, geography, flora, and fauna of the area. The on-premises shop features crafts that are native to the area. *Open daily Mar.–May and Sept.–Oct. 10–5; June–Aug. 9:30–6. Adults £2, seniors £1.50, children over age 8 £1.*

Return eastward to the start of R480, otherwise known as the *****Corkscrew Road** (5) because it literally twists and turns like a corkscrew as it wends its way down the hillside to Ballyvaughan. At its highest point here, the road overlooks panoramic views of the Burren and Galway Bay in the distance.

One mile down the road there is a right turn for **Carron**, a small hamlet lying on the edge of some of the Burren's best karsts. The placename comes from the Irish language *An Cairn*, meaning "The cairn." To learn more about the area's wild and fragrant plantings, visit the **Burren Perfumery & Floral Centre** (6), Carron, Co. Clare, ☎ 708-9102. The complex includes a laboratory, displays, and an audiovisual presentation, all designed to illustrate how the natural alpine and arctic flowers of the Burren are transformed into perfumes, bath oils, and bubble baths. *Open* *daily, hours vary; call ahead. Admission is free.*

Continue via R480 for the remainder of this drive through the heart of the Burren. Approximately 5 miles north of Ballvaughan, off to the right in a private field is the much-photographed **Poulanabrone Dolmen** (7), a portal dolmen. Nearby is **Gleninsheen** (8), a wedge tomb and several ring forts, all sign-posted and visible from the main road.

Approacing Ballyvaughan, there is a sign for a right turn to one of the area's great natural wonders:

**\*AILLWEE CAVE** (9), Ballyvaughan, ☎ 707-7036. *Open mid-Mar. to June and Sept. to early Nov., 10–5:30; July–Aug. 10–6:30. Adults £4, children aged 4–16 £ 2.50. Tours. Shop. Café.*

Formed hundreds of centuries ago yet discovered only in the last 60 years, this cave is one of Ireland's oldest underground sites. The cave has over 3,400 feet of passages and hollows running straight into the heart of a mountain. Highlights include subterranean rivers, bridged chasms, deep caverns, a frozen waterfall, and an assortment of stalactites and stalagmites, some of which have been given descriptive names such as "The Praying Hands" or "Bunch of Carrots."

In addition, many bones, including those of bears, horses, pigs, and badgers, have been found inside, showing that the cave provided a refuge for man and animal over the centuries. Unique features include the bear pits, hollows that were scraped out by the brown bear, one of the cave's many inhabitants. This explains why Aillwee uses a silhouette of a bear as its mascot on signage and literature. Guided tours, which last about one-half hour, are conducted continually.

At the entrance to the cave, there is a small local cheese-making enterprise known as "Burren Gold." Step inside to sample local cheeses and honeys.

Straight ahead is **Ballyvaughan**, a small village and port on the southern shore of Galway Bay. The placename, which in the Irish language is *Baile UíBheacháin*, means "Townland of the descendants of Behan." It is a popular vacation village today for all names and nationalities.

From Ballyvaughan, depart in a westerly direction on the main N67 road to **Lisdoonvarna**, a popular resort town that sits at a height of 400 feet above sea level, unusual for this area. "Lisdoon," as it is called by the locals, has been famed since the 18th century for its Victorian-style spa complex, sheltering a natural mineral spring of sulphur, magnesium, and chalybeate (iron). Each summer thousands of people come to bathe in the therapeutic waters.

Adjacent to the spa is the **Burren Smokehouse** (10), Lisdoonvarna, ☎ 707-4432, a local fish-smoking enterprise. Step inside and watch an audiovisual and hands-on demonstrations that illustrate how fresh Atlantic salmon is slowly cold-smoked over oak chips to produce one of Ireland's tastiest delicacies. *Open daily 10–7. Admission is free.*

Lisdoonvarna, which promotes itself as a match-making center, is the setting each September for Europe's largest "singles" match-making festival. The fanciful placename comes from the Irish language *Lios Dúin Bhearna*, which means "Ring-fort of the gapped fort." The particular fort in question is the ruin on the right as you enter Lisdoonvarna from Ballyvaughan.

Five miles southwest is **\*Doolin**, a remote fishing village that is famed as a haunt for Irish traditional musicians. It is also the departure point for **Doolin Ferries** (11), The Pier, Doolin, ☎ 707-4455, operating regularly scheduled crossings to the Aran Islands of Inisheer (30 minute ride) and Inishmore (50 minute ride). It presents a convenient alternative for those who are not going to be in the Galway area. *Operates daily mid-April to Oct. Hours and fares vary.*

Surrounded by lovely gardens, the **Doolin Crafts Gallery** (12), Church Rd., Doolin, ☎ 707-4309, is worth a slight detour to the north end of the village to see two local artisans at work. Mary Gray makes gold and silver jewelry, inspired by the rocks and flora of the Burren and traditional Celtic designs, as well as a range of jewelry using wood, brass, glass, soapstone, bone, and beads. Her partner Matt O'Connell produces a colorful array of batik art and wall hangings. The shop stocks the work of other Burren-based craftspeople. *Open daily 10–6 or later. Admission is free. Shop. Café.*

Return to R478 and follow signs for the area's signature scenic attraction:

**\*THE CLIFFS OF MOHER** (13), Co. Clare, ☎ 708-1171. *Visitor Centre open May–June 9:30–6, June–Aug. 9–6:30, Sept.–April 10–6. Admission free. Charge for tower: Adults 75p, children 50p. Shop. Café.*

Acclaimed as one of Ireland's greatest natural wonders, these dramatic cliffs rise to a height of 668 feet above the Atlantic Ocean, stretching for five miles along the windswept open coastline. The visitor center provides basic information and background, and then it's necessary to climb a steep but graded hill up to the edge of the cliffs to enjoy sweeping views of the coastline. Surprisingly, most of the cliffside terrain is not protectively fenced in, so be careful and cautious since pavement or grass can be slippery, especially after rain. For the highest perspective, follow the signs to O'Brien's Tower, a Victorian-style viewing point erected in the 19th century.

Return to R478 and travel three miles to **Liscannor**, a small fishing village overlooking Liscannor Bay. Its main claim to fame is that is was the birthplace of John Holland (1841–1914), pioneer of the submarine. The road then leads to **Lahinch**, a dune-filled beach resort that is home to one of Ireland's most challenging golf courses. There are actually two 18-hole courses here, but the longer championship links course is the one that has given Lahinch its far-reaching reputation. The course elevations, such as the 9th and 13th holes, reveal open vistas of sky, land, and sea; they also make the winds an integral part of the game. Look out for the goats—they are Lahinch's legendary weather predictors. If they huddle near the clubhouse, a storm is brewing.

At Lahinch you can join the main N85 road and follow it for 20 miles back to Ennis to complete your tour. Alternatively, if you are fond of beaches and time allows, continue south on N67, passing some beautiful coastal scenery to the right, via the resort towns of **Miltown Malbay, Quilty,** and **Kilkee.**

Eight miles southeast via the main N67 road is **Kilrush,** fondly called the "capital" of West Clare. The focal point is the Town Hall, built in 1808 as the market house. It burned to the ground in 1922 and was reconstructed in its original style in 1931. Today it houses the **Kilrush Heritage Centre** (14), Market Square, off Henry St., Kilrush, ☎ 905-1577, a hub for information on historical and cultural developments of the area. An audiovisual, *Kilrush in Landlord Times,* tells of the struggles of the tenant farmers of West Clare during the 18th and 19th centuries, particularly during the famine years. *Open May–Sept., Mon.–Sat. 9:30–5:30, Sun. noon–4. Adults £1, children 50p.*

From Kilrush, it is less than five miles to **Killimer,** departure point for a ferry service to Tarbert in north County Kerry. Crossing time is just 20 minutes and ferries depart on a drive-on/drive-off basis every hour on the hour from the Killimer side, starting at 7 a.m. Mon.–Sat. and from 9 a.m. on Sun. If you are traveling on to Kerry, it can be a real time-and mileage-saver, rather than returning via Shannon and Limerick. For more information, contact **Shannon Ferry Ltd.,** Killimer, Co. Clare, ☎ 905-3124.

If you are not going on to Kerry, take the main N68 road back for 20 miles through the rocky West Clare farmlands to Ennis and on to Shannon or Limerick, to complete the tour.

# The Tipperary Trio—Cashel, Holycross, and Cahir

Directly east of Limerick, County Tipperary is one of Ireland's most verdant and undulating areas. Like Clare and Limerick, Tipperary is also rimmed by the Shannon River, along its northwest corner. As Ireland's largest inland county—and sixth in overall size—Tipperary is rich in pastoral scenery, with green hills and fertile river valleys. The Tipperary tableau includes the Galtee and Knockmealdown Mountains, and in the middle of the county a broad plain is traversed by the River Suir (pronounced *Sure*).

In many ways, Tipperary rivals Kildare as the home of the horse. There are three race tracks in the county (Clonmel, Thurles, and Tipperary), and stud farms dot the countryside. There is even a town on the main N8 road, mid-way between Cashel and Thurles called Horse and Jockey.

Tipperary's stand-out attractions, however, are historic and man-made—three national monuments that transformed this rural county into one of Ireland's most pivotal gathering areas for well over 1,000 years—the Rock of Cashel, Holycross Abbey, and Cahir Castle.

## GETTING THERE:

It's not such a long way to Tipperary—from Shannon or Limerick. Just follow the main N24 and N74 roads southeast to Cashel, about a 35-mile drive southeast of Limerick. **Bus Eireann** operates daily service to and through Cashel or Cahir from Limerick, Dublin, Cork, Waterford, and most major cities.

## PRACTICALITIES:

Tipperary's three key places—Cashel, Holycross, and Cahir—are all within 25 miles of each other, sitting right in the heart of Ireland. Visited together, they make a memorable daytrip from the Shannon area. And since they are all located on or near the junctions of several main roads, they can be easily visited en route from Shannon or Dubin to the south. Although Cashel or Cahir could be reached separately by bus, to do this entire tour requires use of a car.

For information, contact the **Cashel Tourist Office**, Cashel City Hall,

Main St., Cashel, ☎ 062-61333, open April through September; and the **Cahir Tourist Office**, Castle Car Park, Cahir, ☎ 052-41453, open April to September.

There are at least three different telephone area codes in this region, so the appropriate code will be specified with each number, to avoid confusion.

## FOOD AND DRINK:

**Brú Ború** (Rockside, Cashel) Sitting at the foot of the Rock, this modern building with its own natural outdoor amphitheater is more than a restaurant. It is musical heritage center, with frequent performances throughout the day of native Irish music, song, and dance. The café offers a variety of freshly made soups, salads, sandwiches, and baked goods. Full dinners are also served on summer evenings. X: Sat.–Sun. in Oct.–April. ☎ 062-61122. £ to ££

**The Buttery** (Cashel Palace Hotel, Main St., Cashel) Located in the basement of the town's best hotel, a former Bishop's palace, this pub-restaurant has a country kitchen atmosphere with open fireplace, white-washed walls, and local memorabilia. The menu offers soups, sandwiches, seafood platters, salads, and hot casseroles. ☎ 062-61411. £ to ££

**Chez Hans** (Rockside, Cashel) For over 25 years, this former Wesleyan chapel in the shadow of the famous Rock has been the culinary domain of Hans-Peter Mattiá. The setting provides a romantic atmosphere—with a cathedral-style ceiling, original stone walls, and candlelight, while the menu features Irish ingredients with a French/Irish twist. Specialties include local seafood such as oak-smoked salmon and Rossmore oysters, as well as free-range chicken with Cashel Blue cheese and leek sabayon. Dinner only. X: Sun.–Mon. and Jan. ☎ 062-61177. ££ to £££

**Crock of Gold** (1 Castle St., Cahir) Across the bridge from Cahir Castle, this multi-level enterprise is a café amid a creatively-stocked craft and book shop. It offers an all-day menu of fresh salads, soups, sandwiches, and home-baked goods. ☎ 052- 41951. £

## SUGGESTED TOUR:

When it comes to majestic sights, all roads seem to start in Cashel. Depart the **Limerick** (1) area and follow signs for the main N24 road toward **Tipperary**, the busy marketing town that gives the whole county its name. In the Irish language, Tipperary is known as *Tiobraid Árann*, meaning "Well of (the) river Ara." Although the River Ara still runs through the town, the original well on Tipperary's long main street has long since been covered over. From Tipperary, go east (a left turn) onto the N74 main road and travel 12 miles.

This road brings you to the historic hub of the county, **Cashel**, seat of Ireland's kings for over 900 years, and often referred to as "Cashel of the Kings." The word Cashel, which comes from the Irish language *Caiseal*, means "circular stone fort."

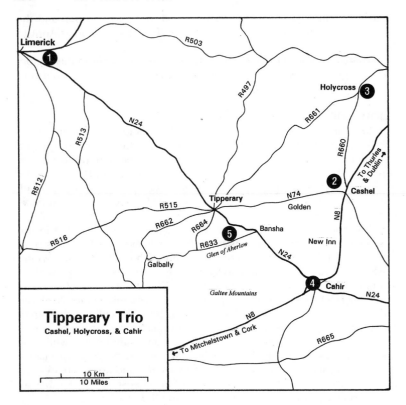

**Tipperary Trio**
Cashel, Holycross, & Cahir

10 Km
10 Miles

The focus of the town is the **Rock of Cashel**, a commanding hill of limestone rising over 200 feet above the surrounding Tipperary country-side. Follow the signs to the "Rock" and park your car in the ample parking area.

Start your tour by climbing the steep hill to the entrance. But before you start your visit to this stunning sight, you might ask yourself: Just what is the Rock?

The Rock of Cashel has been modestly called Ireland's Acropolis. It is the sky-high outpost from whence Ireland's early kings ruled. To enhance it further, Cashel later became intertwined with Ireland's ecclesiastical history.

Cashel's long tale began in the 4th century when local kings chose it to set up a fortress. Even St. Patrick came to Cashel. Legend has it that in 448 he baptized King Aengus here. Over the centuries kings from Cashel conquered much of the surrounding area and were declared rulers of the entire province of Munster. In addition, it is commonly accepted that Brian Boru declared himself the undisputed King of Cashel and was crowned the High King of Ireland here in 977.

Cashel remained a royal capital until the reign of Muirchertach O'Brien who handed over Cashel in all its glory to the Church in 1101. Ten years later the archdiocese of Cashel was formally constituted and a cathedral was built in 1127-34 by Cormac McCarthy, another king, on the site of the former royal palace. By 1169, the cathedral was deemed too small and Donal Mór O'Brien, King of Thomond who also built great cathedrals at Limerick and Killaloe, began to build a new cathedral. This was followed by yet another cathedral in the 13th century. But alas, Cashel's expansions were slowly stymied in the Middle Ages as English rulers suppressed the power of the Catholic church in Ireland. The main buildings were burned in 1495 and yet again in 1647. The structures remained derelict until 1686, when the cathedral was repaired for Protestant use. In 1729, it was re-edified, only to be abandoned again in 1749. In 1874 the ruins were handed over to the Irish government, to be preserved as a national monument. And what a monument it is!

A walk through Cashel is a walk through the centuries. Enter the main gateway and this is what you will see:

**\*ROCK OF CASHEL** (2), Cashel, ☎ 062-61437. *Open daily mid-Sept. to mid-March 9:30–4:30; mid-March to mid-June 9:30–5:30; mid-June to mid-Sept. 9–7:30. Adults £3.50, seniors £2.50, students and children £1.50. Tours.*

A visit to this spectacular group of medieval ruins starts with a 17-minute audiovisual presentation, *Stongholds of the Faith,* presented in the recently restored **Hall of Vicars Choral**, a 15th-century building with some 17th-century features. To the right of the entrance is **St. Patrick's Cross**, reputed to date back to 1150, and which stood for 800 years outside. For safety, it has been brought indoors and a replica stands outside. It is a rare cross of intricate designs. The carvings include a Crucifixion, and interlacing figures of ribbon-beasts and birds as well as a Romanesque lion ringed by pellets and concentric circles. Upstairs is a restored dining hall with a minstrel gallery and kitchen, and 15th-century furniture.

Nearby is the 13th-century **Cathedral**, the largest of the buildings. Standing over the earlier cathedral built in 1169, this roofless edifice is cruciform in layout, with a long choir and a short nave, two chapels in each transept, and a great tower over the crossing. To the right is a 92-foot **Round Tower** dating back to the 10th century when the Rock was still in the hands of the kings.

The *piece de resistence* is **Cormac's Chapel**, the 12th-century cathedral built by King Cormac McCarthy. It is regarded as the finest example of Irish Romanesque architecture, with rich decoration and solid construction. The walls reveal tracings of colorful frescoes, thought to be the only 12th-century paintings still in Ireland.

Take time outside to explore the many Celtic crosses and burial monuments erected over the centuries; and to enjoy the panoramic views from the Rock overlooking the surrounding countryside.

Tours last approximately 45 minutes and are conducted on the hour.

Depart Cashel on the local R660 and drive for 10 miles to a national monument with a totally religious focus:

**\*HOLYCROSS ABBEY** (3), Holycross, Co. Tipperary. ☎ 0504-43241. *Open daily 10–6. Admission is free. Tours. Shop. Café.*

Dating back to 1180 and nestled on the banks of the River Suir, this abbey was the fourth to be endowed by Donal Mór O'Brien, King of Thomond, the same benefactor who erected the cathedral at Cashel and the cathedrals at Limerick and Killaloe. Given to the Cistercian order, the building assumed its name because it housed a relic passed down from the cross of Christ, known as the *True Cross* or *Holy Cross*. In the Middle Ages, just as Cashel became a mecca, this abbey also became a hub of religious pilgrimages, drawing the faithful from all over Ireland who came to pay homage to the relic. It was so popular, in fact, that it was remodeled and enlarged in the 15th century to include some new Irish Gothic craftsmanship that remains to this day. Like Cashel and other Catholic foundations, Holycross was suppressed and plundered during the reign of Henry VIII and its relic was sent to a convent in Cork.

Declared a national monument in 1880, this abbey was restored in 1971–75 as a parish church by the local community and is still revered as a center for prayer and reconciliation. A new relic of the True Cross, authenticated and sent from St. Peter's in Rome in 1977, is now on display in the north transept. The original relic has also been returned and is exhibited in an adjacent reliquary. Other highlights include a medieval sedilia, 17 feet high, with richly carved leaf ornamentation; and a hunting scene mural believed to have originated in the 14th century. The grounds include Stations of the Cross, a glass-enclosed outdoor altar, and gardens dedicated to Padre Pio.

Retrace your route slightly via Cashel back to the N8 national road, heading south for 11 miles to **Cahir** (pronounced *Care*). The Irish word for Cahir is *An Chathair*, meaning "The stone fort," a term very similar to the meaning of Cashel. Here you can visit the last of the Tipperary trio of national monuments:

**\*CAHIR CASTLE** (4), Castle St., Cahir, ☎ 052-41011. *Open daily April to mid-June and mid-Sept. to mid-Oct. 10–6; mid-June to mid-Sept. 9–7:30; and mid-Oct. to March 10–1 and 2–4:30. Adults £2, seniors £1.50, students and children £1. Tours. Shop.*

Perched on a rocky inlet of the River Suir, this castle is one of Ireland's largest medieval fortresses, with a massive keep, high walls, spacious courtyards, and a great hall, all fully restored. It dates mainly from the 15th century, although the main courtyard and its buildings can be traced to the 8th century and later additions from the 13th century.

Unlike its counterparts at Cashel and Holycross, this fortress was a private castle—home of the Butlers—and did not draw hoards of pilgrims for political or religious gatherings. Instead it attracted a fair share of conquerors including the Earl of Essex who deemed it "the bulwark of Munster." The castle was eventually surrendered in 1650 to Cromwell without a shot being fired. Few conquerors wanted to damage this majestic site.

The size and grandeur of this castle are so impressive that it has been used often as a movie location, for films such as *Barry Lyndon, Tristan and Isolde,* and *Excalibur.* A visit includes a guided tour, a series of exhibits, and a 20-minute audiovisual presentation on the history of the castle and the area.

From Cahir, it is easy to retrace your route via the N24 road beside the Galtee Mountains and Tipperary town back to Limerick and the Shannon area. If time allows, follow the signposts through the **\*Glen of Aherlow** (5). Fondly called Ireland's Greenest Valley, this seven-mile-long route is one of Tipperary's most scenic drives, and well-worth a slight detour.

## Trip 34

# The Castle Corridor— From Limerick to Galway

The wide main road between the cities of Limerick and Galway (N18) is one of Ireland's busiest traffic corridors, as Shannon Airport passengers travel to and from the west and south of Ireland. Although some people pass quickly along the route, others take time to stop and enjoy its many inviting towns, villages, monuments, and especially its castles.

Yes, this is the "castle corridor"—home to more than a half-dozen genuine castles that were not only important in Ireland's past, but also play a vital role today as tourist attractions, hotels, banquet halls, and literary landmarks. One of these, Bunratty Castle, is the most popular tourist attraction in Ireland, outside of Dublin.

So, don't rush by on the Limerick–Galway road. It may be only 65 miles in length, but it is packed with all the makings of a daytrip that is truly fit for a king or queen.

## GETTING THERE:

By car, depart Limerick or Shannon Airport and simply follow signs for N18 toward Galway. **Bus Eireann** provides daily bus service from Limerick or Shannon to many of the towns along the N18 route, such as Bunratty, Newmarket-on-Fergus, Ennis, and Gort, but there is no continuous on-off service.

## PRACTICALITIES:

The best way to follow this tour is by car, although it is possible to reach some of the towns individually by bus. You can take a bus from Limerick to Bunratty and spend a half-day there, and later board another bus to Ennis or Gort, but you would not have the flexibility of visiting the off-the-road attractions.

Many of the castles and attractions along this route are set in their own grounds and require walking along stone or dirt pathways or climbing up steps for access.

For information, contact the **Ennis Tourist Office**, Arthur's Row (off O'Connell St.), Town Centre, Ennis, ☎ 065-682-8366, open all year.

The telephone numbers along this corridor belong to at least three area codes—061, 065, and 091. To avoid confusion, the area code for each telephone number is specified.

## FOOD AND DRINK:

**The Cloister** (Abbey St., Ennis) Situated in the heart of town next to the landmark 13th-century friary, this cozy pub- restaurant offers creative Irish cuisine in an Old World setting. The bar food includes seafood chowders, traditional Irish stew, beefburgers, and chicken and mushroom brioches. Full dinners are served at night. ☎ 065-682-9521. £ to ££

**Cruises** (Abbey St., Ennis) With beamed ceilings, lantern lights, flag-stone floors, open fireplaces, and local memorabilia, this homey pub-restaurant sits in the middle of town, housed in a restored 17th-century building. The menu offers seafood soups, sandwiches, Irish stew, club sandwiches, and steaks, as well as full dinners at night. ☎ 065-682-8963. £ to ££

**Durty Nelly's** (Main St., Bunratty) For over 375 years, this enchanting mustard-colored pub has been a tradition in the area. Nestled next to Bunratty Castle, it was originally a watering hole for the castle guards, but now it is a favorite with passing travelers from all over the world. Specialties include Irish beef stew in Guinness, local seafood, and steaks. ☎ 061-364861. ££

**Gallagher's** (Main St., Bunratty) Step inside the cheery red half-door entrance of this restaurant and enjoy dining in a thatched-roof cottage atmosphere—with open fireplaces, white-washed walls, lanterns, nautical trappings, and local memorabilia. Although the setting is traditional, the menu is very up-to-date—sun-dried tomato bread, farm-raised chicken, char-grilled meats; and an array of fresh seafood from lobsters, oysters, and prawns to seared salmon and baked sole on the bone. Very popular with the locals; reservations are "a must." Open for dinner only. X: Sun. ☎ 061-363363. ££ to £££

**Moran's Oyster Cottage** (Kilcolgan) Watching the sun go down on Galway Bay is part of the fun at this 220-year-old thatched-cottage pub, situated on a country road overlooking the water. A haven for seafood lovers, it specializes in fresh oysters, smoked salmon, prawns, and crab claws, all accompanied by heaping platters of home-baked brown bread. ☎ 091-796113. ££

**Paddy Burkes** (Clarenbridge) With a thatched roof, this legendary cottage-style tavern on the main road is known for its nautical decor and seafood menu. The choices include platters of fresh oysters, mussels, and seafood chowders, salads, and sandwiches. Full dinners in the evening. ☎ 091-796226. £ to ££

## SUGGESTED TOUR:

The first stop along this route is invariably Bunratty, whether the tour is started in **Limerick** (1), eight miles away, or Shannon Airport, 5 miles

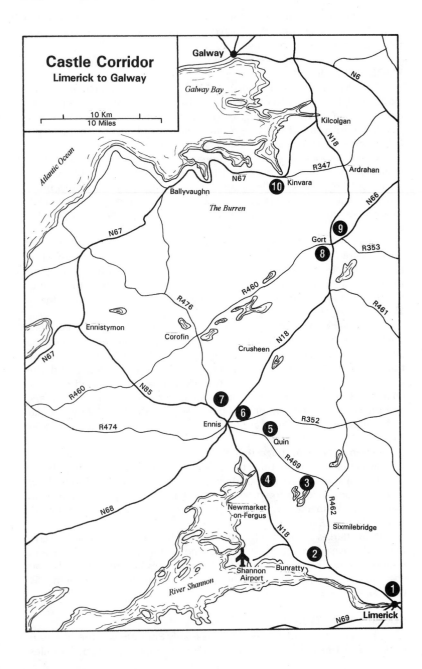

**Castle Corridor**
Limerick to Galway

10 Km
10 Miles

Galway

Galway Bay

Atlantic Ocean

N6

Kilcolgan

N18

R347    Ardrahan

N67    Kinvara

Ballyvaughn

The Burren

N66

N67

Gort

R353

R460

R461

R476

R476

Ennistymon

Corofin

N18

R461

N67

Crusheen

R460

N85

Ennis

R352

R474

Quin

R469

Newmarket
on-Fergus

R462

Sixmilebridge

N68

N18

Shannon
Airport    Bunratty

River Shannon

Limerick

N69

away. Just follow the signs for the Bunratty exit off N18.

The small village of **Bunratty** takes its name from the Irish language, *Bun Raite*, meaning "Mouth of the (river) Ratty." Although the River Ratty has always been important to the town, the focal point is the splendid castle beside the river:

**\*BUNRATTY CASTLE** (2), Bunratty Folk Park, Bunratty, Co. Clare, ☎ 061-360788. *Open Sept.–May 9:30–5:30, June–Aug. 9:30–6. Adults £5.25, seniors £3.80, children £3. Tours. Shop. Café.*

No matter from which direction you are coming, you will soon see the turrets and battlements of this mighty fortress, the most complete and authentic medieval castle in Ireland. Built in 1425 and plundered often, although long a stronghold of the powerful O'Brien clan, it was fully restored in 1954, with authentic furnishings, armorial stained glass, tapestries, and works of art reflecting the aura of the 15th century. By day, the building's inner chambers are open for public tours; at night, the castle's Great Hall becomes a candlelit setting for medieval banquets and entertainment.

In addition, the castle is flanked by a 20-acre theme park. This park is laid out to re-create a typical 19th-century Irish village. Step inside—and literally step back in time.

Experience an insider's tour of authentic thatched-roof cottages, farmhouses, watermill, and working blacksmith's forge. Stroll along a typical village street with post office, grocery store, doctor's office, print shop, school, church, drapery shop, pawn shop, and village hotel and pub. See craftspeople at work, from knitting and weaving, to candle-making, pottery, and basketry; farmers working in a traditional hay barn, and women baking fresh breads and scones in fireplace ovens.

From Bunratty, it is just about five miles off the main N18 road to yet another castle with medieval roots:

**\*KNAPPOGUE CASTLE** (3), Quin, Co. Clare, ☎ 061-360788. *Open April–Oct. 9:30–5. Adults £2.75, seniors £1.90, children £1.65. Tours. Shop.*

Built in 1467, this castle was the home of the MacNamara Clan who dominated the area for over 1,000 years. The name Knappogue comes from the Irish languagae word *An Chnapóg*, meaning "The Hillock," undoubtedly a reference to the castle's setting on an sequestered embankment. The original Norman structure has been enhanced by elaborate late-Georgian and Regency wings added in the mid-19th century. Fully restored, it is furnished with authentic 15th-century pieces, and, like Bunratty, it provides a setting for medieval banquets at night.

Returning to the main N18 road, the next stop is **Newmarket-on-Fergus**, a picturesque village that sits beside the River Fergus, and hence its descriptive but basically English placename. Three miles north of the village on the right side of the road is the entrance to the verdant and undulating estate of **\*Dromoland Castle** (4), the seat of Lord Inchiquin and the O'Briens until 1962 and then refurbished and expanded into a luxury hotel resort. Although the O'Briens moved to this walled fairytale setting in the 17th century, the present baronial-style castle was not built until 1826. With an idyllic array of turrets and towers, it sits beside the River Rine amid 400 acres of parkland and gardens and an 18-hole golf course.

After Dromoland, watch for a turn to the right off the main road to Kilmurry, to experience some of Ireland's Bronze Age history that pre-dates even the oldest castles of the area:

**CRAGGAUNOWEN** (5), Kilmurry, Quin, Co. Clare, ☎ 061-360788. *Open daily mid-March to mid-Oct. 9–6. Adults £4.20, seniors £3.30, children £2.60. Tours. Shop. Café.*

Instead of a castle, the centerpiece of this historic site is an authentically reconstructed Irish crannog. Although it looks like something "out of Africa," it is a replica of a Limerick-area Bronze Age lake dwelling, constructed of wattles, reeds, and mud. Other highlights include a ring fort from the early Christian period, a fulachta fiadha (ancient cooking place), a souterrain (early refrigerator), one of Ireland's oldest dugout canoes, and an original wooden roadway from the Celtic Iron Age. The Craggaunowen grounds also shelter the history-making hide boat, *The Brendan*. This is the vessel in which explorer/author Tim Severin sailed across the Atlantic in 1976 from County Kerry to Boston, to prove that St. Brendan could have "discovered" America in the 6th century, long before Columbus.

The next major town along the main road is **Ennis**, the capital of County Clare and a thriving market town. The placename comes from the Irish language word *Inis* which means "Island" or "Riveside land." Since it sits beside the River Fergus, the latter description seems to fit Ennis best. Close to the bridge over the river is the town's prime national monument, **Ennis Friary** (6), Abbey St., Ennis, ☎ 065-682-9100. Founded c. 1250 for the Franciscans, this friary quickly grew into one of Western Europe's major seats of learning in medieval times, making Ennis a focal point for many years. Records show that it buzzed with scholarly activity in 1375, with at least 350 friars and 600 students gathered at the site. Although it was suppressed in 1692 and fell into ruin, it still shelters many unique features such as a huge five-paneled window which held blue painted glass, a vaulted sacristy, and intricately carved figures including the apostles. *Open late-May to late-Sept., daily 9:30–6. Adults £1, seniors 70p, students and children 40p. Tours.*

From Ennis, continue in a northerly direction. For a short detour, turn left onto local road R476 for about five miles to one of the area's most intriguing castles in an off-the-beaten-track area, **Dysert O'Dea Castle** (7), Corofin, Co. Clare, ☎ 065-683-7722. Built on a rocky outcrop of land in 1480 by Diarmaid O'Dea, this tower house is now an archeology center and museum, depicting the history of the area. In addition, the castle serves as a starting point for touring a cluster of other historical and archaeological ruins, all within a two-mile radius. The sites include a round tower, church, holy well, and high cross, all estimated to date back to the period 800–1200, as well as a 14th-century battlefield and an Iron Age stone fort. *Open May–Sept., daily 10–6. Adults £2, children £1. Tours. Shop. Café.*

Return to the main N18 road which then passes through a 20-mile stretch of farmland and grazing fields, interrupted only by two small villages, Barefield and Crusheen, and crossing over from County Clare to County Galway, before reaching **Gort**, a small market town. The town takes its name from the Irish word, *An Gort*, meaning "The field." Two miles north of town, on the left, is one of the area's premier natural attractions:

**\*COOLE PARK** (8), Gort, Co. Galway, ☎ 091-631804. *Open mid-April to mid-June, Tues.–Sun. 10–5; mid-June to end-Aug., daily 9:30–6:30; Sept., daily 10–5. Adults £2; seniors and students £1.50, children £1. Tours. Shop. Café.*

This lush and rambling national forest park once sheltered the summer home of Lady Augusta Gregory (1852–1932), dramatist, folklorist, leading force in the 20th-century Irish literary revival, and co-founder of the Abbey Theatre, along with W.B. Yeats and Edward Martyn. Although her house was demolished in 1941, her spirit lives on in the beautiful gardens and ancient trees including an avenue of cedars and a huge copper beech, fondly called *The Autograph Tree*. Lady Gregory and many of her literary companions, including Yeats, Shaw, and O'Casey, carved their initials on the tree, still readable today. The restored courtyard building houses a visitor center which presents exhibits on Lady Gregory and her literary friends and an audiovisual on the flora and fauna of the park.

Continue on the main road north and watch for a sign-post to Thoor Ballylee on the right. Follow the road inland for about one mile to reach one of Ireland's most revered literary castles:

**\*THOOR BALLYLEE** (9), Gort, Co. Galway, ☎ 091-631436. *Open Easter–Sept. daily 10–6. Adults £3.30, seniors, students and children age 12–16 £2.80, children under 12 £1. Tours. Shop. Café.*

Once a part of Lady Gregory's estate at Coole and known then as Ballylee Castle, this 16th-century Norman tower was purchased in 1916 by Nobel Prize winning poet William Butler Yeats for £35. The castle, which Yeats restored for himself, his wife "George" and their two children, became his summer retreat and the inspiration for much of his poetry including *The Winding Stair* and *The Tower* collection. In 1992 he re-christened the building "Thoor Ballylee," using the word *Thoor* which is the Irish word for "tower." The castle now houses a Yeatsean museum with exhibits and an audiovisual on the poet's life and works, as well as push-button narrations in each room.

The main road continues north for 20 more miles, passing stone walls and farmlands via the hamlet of Ardrahan, a hilly area. Its placename, *Ard Raithin,* means "Height of the ferns" in the Irish language. You may wish to take a detour to the left, for five miles via R347, to Kinvara to visit yet another castle:

**\*DUN GUAIRE CASTLE** (10), Kinvara, Co. Galway, ☎ 061-360788. *Open May–Sept. 9:30–5:30. Adults £2.75, seniors £1.90, children £1.65. Tours.*

Dramatically situated overlooking Galway Bay, this castle consists of a tower house and bawn dating back to the 16th century. It sits on the site of an earlier 7th-century castle that was the royal seat of King Guaire of Connacht. In the early part of this century, it was later the country retreat of Oliver St. John Gogarty (1878–1957), Irish surgeon, author, poet, and wit. Displays in the castle now gives an insight into the lifestyle of the people who lived there over the centuries. Like Bunratty and Knappogue in County Clare, this castle is also the scene of nightly medieval banquets.

Return to the main N18 road, and continue to the next two towns, **Kilcolgan,** and **Clarenbridge**, both of which have close access to Galway Bay and are considered the heart of "oyster country." Many of the events of Galway's annual oyster festival each September are held here and the local pubs are known for serving hearty platters of the briny bivalves. Follow the main N18 road for less than 10 miles into Galway City for the completion of this tour.

# Section VII

# THE WEST

The West of Ireland is a world of its own—like nowhere else in Ireland or on Earth. With barren fields and rocky soil, the West is one of the poorest parts of Ireland, yet it is the richest in scenic beauty and natural attractions. Comprising the province of Connacht, the West takes in a large chunk of the Emerald Isle. It contains the second- and third-largest counties of Ireland—Galway and Mayo—and spills over into the neighboring counties of Roscommon and Offaly.

With Galway, a true Renaissance city as its hub, the West offers a diverse set of experiences for every visitor. From the sunsets over Galway Bay to the panoramas of Clew Bay or Lough Corrib, or from the rocky shores of the Aran Islands to the fuschia-filled route around Achill Island, or the enchanting isthmus of "Quiet Man Country," the West offers unrivaled variety.

For the pilgrim, the West holds Knock, Ireland's leading Marian shrine plus Croagh Patrick, St. Patrick's Holy Mountain, as well as Clonmacnois, the benchmark of early Christian monasteries, and Clonfert, the settlement founded by St. Brendan the Navigator.

From the museums and mansions of Roscommon to the natural wonders of Connemara National Park or Birr Castle Gardens, the West of Ireland is vibrant and thriving. No wonder the old song intones *The West's Awake!*

# *Galway City

As the unofficial capital of the West of Ireland, Galway City has a personality of its own, wholly unlike Ireland's other major cities. There are no Georgian streetscapes like Dublin, no castles like Limerick, no grand parades like Cork, and no Viking towers like Waterford.

Influenced by its remote location amid rocky lands at the head of Galway Bay and the River Corrib, Galway is small and compact, with narrow streets and a style of cut-stone architecture not usually seen in other Irish cities. Galway takes its name from the Irish language *Gaillimh*, meaning "stony," and specifically a "stony place" or "stony river."

Like the rest of Ireland, Galway has been shaped by history, but a history that is unique to its remoteness. The earliest printed references to the area date back to 1124 and describe it as a "Gaelic hinterland."

Although not conquered by the Vikings like Ireland's other major cities, Galway was invaded by the Anglo-Normans in the 13th century. The deBurgos (Burkes) founded a settlement beside a ford on the River Corrib. By 1270 strong stone walls were added and a great medieval city grew up inside the walls.

Because of its position on the Atlantic, Galway emerged as a thriving seaport for wine, spices, and fish, and developed a brisk trade with Spain and other European countries during medieval times. The Galway docks hummed with the arrival of ships from foreign lands. Even Christopher Columbus is said to have landed at the port of Galway, en route to his historic voyage across the Atlantic to "discover" a New World.

In the 14th through mid-17th centuries, Galway was a powerful city state. It became known as "The City of the Tribes," due to the influence of 14 wealthy merchant Anglo-Norman families who settled here, ruling the town as an oligarchy for many years. Each of these families (named Athy, Blake, Bodkin, Browne, Darcy, Deane, Font, French, Joyce, Kirwan, Lynch, Martin, Morris, and Skerret) had its own street and mansion or castle, with stone-faced designs. Remnants of the buildings and the stone work remain today.

Like the rest of the country, Galway's independence and prosperity was cut short in the late 17th and 18th centuries by English rule, with final blows coming during the Great Famine of the 1840's.

Two developments helped Galway to rebound—the foundation of Queens College (now the University College—Galway) in 1848, infusing into Galway all the youthful vibrance of a university town, and the establishment of a permanent rail link with Dublin in 1854, re-inventing Galway as a true hub of the West.

Growth has been the city's buzz word ever since. Happily, it has been growth controlled by an enlightened local government, allowing Galway to leap into the 21st century as Europe's fastest growing city, while still preserving its rich heritage. Although the medieval walls have almost disappeared and the city has spread out in all directions, there is still a core of 14 streets founded by the original tribes. This area, the heart of downtown, holds many landmarks that still bear the names of some of these families, such as Lynch's Memorial Window, Blake's Castle, and the Browne Doorway.

Yes, Galway has a unique personality. Well aged, yet ever youthful. Rich in tradition, yet always embracing innovation. It's a Renaissance city in the truest sense.

## GETTING THERE:

As the hub of transport in the west, Galway is easy to reach. Both **Irish Rail** and **Bus Eireann** operate daily services from Dublin and other parts of the country into Galway's Ceannt Station, in the heart of the city, within walking distance of many hotels and guesthouses.

## PRACTICALITIES:

Because the streets are narrow and distances are short, the best way to get to know the downtown area of Galway City is on foot. Wear comfortable walking shoes and watch out for uneven pavements, slender sidewalks, and some cobbled areas.

Guided sightseeing bus tours of the city via vintage double-decker bus are operated by **Old Galway Tours**, 19 Shop St., Galway, ☎ 091-562905, departing hourly from Eyre Square. For walkers, a company called **Western Heritage**, Victoria Place, Eyre Square, Galway, ☎ 091-521699, offers guided walking tours, departing from the tourist office.

**Galway City Bus Service** has a good local transport network, with regular bus service from Eyre Square to many residential areas, such as Mervue and Merlin Park, as well as the beach resort of Salthill.

For complete listings of all tours and other local information, contact the **Galway Tourist Office**, Victoria Place, off Eyre Square, Galway, ☎ 091-563081.

Galway is pronounced *Gawl-way*. Although it may seem strange, Galway citizens are fond of being called Galwegians.

The telephone area code for all numbers in the Galway City area is 091, unless indicated otherwise.

## FOOD AND DRINK:

**Bialann** (Galway Crystal Heritage Centre, Merlin Park) It's worth a visit to Galway's signature crystal-producing factory/museum just to sample the fresh salads, soups, and home-baked treats of this self-service restaurant. The decor includes Galway Crystal accessories and stemware amid a

Georgian-themed setting. ☎ 757311. £

**Bridge Mills** (O'Brien's Bridge) Sitting beside the River Corrib in a converted 18th-century mill building, this restaurant offers indoor seating beside the old mill wheel or outdoors overlooking the riverbank. The menu is international, with a good selection of seafood platters and pastas. ☎ 566231. ££

**The Cobblestone** (Kirwan's Lane) Offering indoor and outdoor seating on Galway's oldest medieval lane, this little café is one of the brightest stars on the daytime food scene. The menu offers fresh made-to-order sandwiches, salads, soups, quiches and pastas, as well as unique dishes such as "beany shepherd pie" or vegetable-and-walnut bake. Croissants, breads, muffins, and cookies are baked on the premises each day. ☎ 567227. £

**GBC—The Galway Baking Company** (7 Williamsgate St.) For a snack or a full meal, it's hard to match the value of this landmark shopfront restaurant. Freshly baked breads and pastries are featured here, as are Irish traditional dishes such as Irish stew and steaks, as well as quiches, crêpes, omelets, and salads. Downstairs is a coffee shop format and upstairs is a full-service restaurant. ☎ 563087. £ to ££

**Malt House** (High street) An "Old Galway" atmosphere prevails at this cozy white-washed restaurant, positioned on a cobblestone alley off the main street. Bar food, available all day, includes prawn salad, crab claws, lasagne, and hearty soups. Early-bird dinners offer exceptional value. X: Sun. ☎ 567866. ££ to £££

**McDonagh's** (22 Quay St) Established in 1912, this seafood market-cum-restaurant is synonymous with fresh seafood. It offers a choice of settings—an informal fish-and-chips bar or a full-service restaurant, offering the best of the local catch. Shellfish platters are a house specialty as is barbecued or grilled salmon. Arrive early, though—this place is very popular and no reservations are accepted. X: Sun. in Oct.–April. ☎ 565001. £ to £££

## SUGGESTED TOUR:

Start the tour at Galway's rail and bus center, **Ceannt Station** (1), Station Road. Turn left and walk one-half block to the front entrance of the Great Southern Hotel, a lodging landmark dating back to 1845. The hotel overlooks *Eyre Square (2), the city's focal point. Originally a market area known as Fair Green, it was given its current name in 1710 when presented to the city by then-Mayor Edward Eyre who had inherited this grassy patch of land from his father.

Now a pedestrian park, Eyre Square is the city's playground, with pathways and benches, lined by colorful flower beds and statuary. Spend a few moments to reflect at the **Pádraic Ó Conaire Statue** (1882–1923), erected in honor of a Galwayman recognized as one of Ireland's great short story writers in the Irish language, or stroll beside **The Browne Doorway**, a fine cut-stone doorway and window, now free-standing and framed in cement, but once the entrance to the mansion belonging to one

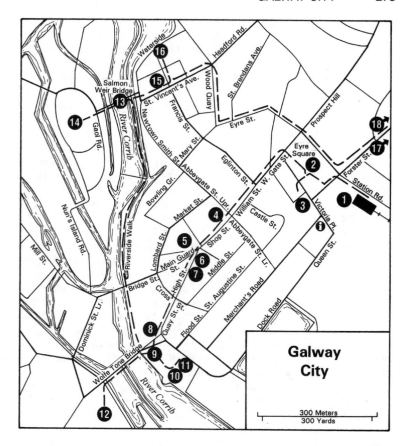

Galway
City

300 Meters
300 Yards

of Galway's 14 tribes. There are several carvings on it, including two coats of arms dated 1627 and belonging to the Brownes and the Lynches. Known locally as "marriage stones," they commemorate the union of two families. Many other city buildings hold similar sets of carved stones with family names.

The adjacent **Quincentennial Fountain**, erected in 1984 to celebrate the 500th anniversary of Galway becoming a city, consists of sheets of iron mounted to depict the Galway area's distinctive sail boat, the *Galway Hooker*.

On the west side of Eyre Square is the **Eyre Square Shopping Centre** (3), one of many such developments in this shop-happy town. This modern multi-level complex is unique because it includes a section of the recently restored medieval wall of the city.

From Eyre Square, head westward to Galway's main thoroughfare—a street that changes its name five times—from **Williamsgate** and **William**, to

**Shop**, **High**, and **Quay** Streets, before it crosses the River Corrib and changes again. By normal standards for a main city street, it is extremely narrow, with traffic moving at a crawl most of the time. Happily, plans are afoot to pedestrianize the entire route.

As William Street becomes **Shop Street**, on the right is **Lynch's Castle** (4) (now the Allied Irish Bank), one of the finest surviving town castles in Ireland, dating from the late 15th or early 16th century, and former home of one of the 14 original Galway Tribe families. On the front is a large framed roundel bearing the arms of the Lynches, plus many decoratively carved windows and projecting gargoyles peering down from the roof.

From Shop Street, turn right onto Church Lane, to visit the **\*Collegiate Church of St. Nicholas**, Lombard Street, ☎ 564648, the centerpiece of Galway's medieval heritage. Founded in 1320, it is said that Columbus prayed at this church before embarking on his transatlantic voyage. Restored and expanded over the centuries, this church has changed hands from Roman Catholic to Protestant at least four times. Currently under the aegis of the Church of Ireland/Episcopal denomination, it is a showcase of many medieval church furnishings and fixtures including the Crusader's Tomb, a 12th- or 13th-century burial vault with a rare Norman-French inscription; a beautifully caved baptismal font, dating back to the 16th or early 17th century, with different designs on each side; a lectern with "barley sugar" twist columns of 15th- or 16th-century vintage; and a free-standing benitier or holy water stoup, uncommon in Ireland and one of the most unusual features of the church, made in the late 15th or early 16th century. *Open April–Sept., Mon.–Sat. 9-5:45, Sun. 1–5:45. Donations: Adults £1, seniors and students 50p. Tours.*

Return to Shop Street and make a right onto **High Street**. Notice the occasional decorative or arched stone doorways and family crests of the 14 original Galway names, now adapted and incorporated into the shopfront facades of Galway's commercial enterprises. On the left is **\*ÓMaille's**, 16 High St. (6), ☎ 562696, a family-run tweed shop established in 1938. It became world famous by producing the clothing for the classic movie, *The Quiet Man,* and has done a brisk trade ever since. Next on the left is the Malt Arcade, a cobbled laneway from bygone years, and several doors along on the left is **\*Kenny's Book Shop** (7), High St., ☎ 562739, a family-operated book store and art gallery. A Galway fixture for over 50 years, this shop is a treasure-trove of old and new books, maps, prints, engravings, and volumes about Galway history.

Next is **Quay Street**, the heart of Galway's colorful Left Bank, lined with interesting curio shops and cafés reflecting the latest hip trends.

On the right is **Kirwan's Lane**, one of the city's surviving medieval laneways.

Just beyond is Jurys Inn, a 1990's addition to the Galway scene. It sits beside the remnants of 17th-century **Blake's Castle** (8), a fortified residence tower house that once belonged to one of Galway's 14 Tribes. Over the years, it has had many uses, ranging from a jail, distillery, and fertilizer factory. The bar of the hotel preserves two stone carvings from the building—the coats of arms of the Lynch and Browne families, dated 1645 and displayed over a door and a fireplace.

Directly opposite Jurys is the **Fishmarket** (9), an outdoor area beside the River Corrib (sometimes referred to as the Galway River by the locals) that used to attract local fishmongers to sell their wares. This is the heart of the city's medieval quarter. Behind the market area is the **Spanish Arch** (10), built in 1594 and one of Galway's most-photographed landmarks. It was the focal point of the landing dock area where Spanish ships unloaded their cargoes of wine and brandy from their galleons in the heyday of trading between Galway and Spain.

Beside the arch is the **Galway City Museum** (11), off Flood Street, ☎ 568151, displaying a collection of local memorabilia, photographs, and documents. *Open daily 10–1 and 2–5. Adults 60p, children 30p.*

On the opposite side of the River Corrib is **The Claddagh** (12), a residential area now but once a small fishing village of uncertain origin and possibly older than Galway itself. It gets its name from the Irish language *An Cladach,* meaning "The sea shore." The original settlers were native Irish who spoke the Gaelic tongue, as distinct from the Anglo-Norman families within the walled city. The Claddagh residents, who made their living by fishing, sold their wares at the Fishmarket beside the Spanish Arch. They lived in small thatched cottages of mud walls, haphazardly arranged amid cobbled streets. Although they lived in poverty, they had one treasure. Legend has it that they originated the Claddagh ring, a wedding ring cast in the form of two hands clasping a heart with a crown at the top. Over the years, the ring has become a popular piece of jewelry for Galwegians and visitors alike. Although the world of The Claddagh fishing community came to an end in 1934 with the construction of a modern housing development, the tradition of the Claddagh ring lives on and thrives.

Cross back over the Wolfe Tone Bridge. From the front of Jurys, take a right and walk along the side of the hotel. This is the beginning of *Riverside Walk, a path that rims the east side of Lough Corrib. Walk north as far as the *Salmon Weir Bridge** (13), a popular landmark that allows people to stop and watch the salmon leaping upstream. Cross over the bridge to see one of the city's newest buildings, the *Catholic Cathedral of Our Lady Assumed into Heaven and St. Nicholas** (14), University and Gaol Roads, ☎ 563577, completed in 1965. Dominating the Galway skyline with its huge dome, it is a modern Renaissance-style edifice that is made of limestone and marble from local quarries and enhanced by the work of contemporary Irish artisans who designed the statues, stained-glass windows, and mosaics. It sits on the site of the former city jail. *Open daily 8–6. Admission is free. Donations welcome.*

Cross back over the bridge and take a right to St. Vincent's Avenue. On the left is another of Galway's newest additions, **Town Hall Theatre** (15), Courthouse Square, ☎ 569777, Galway's major performing arts venue, formerly the town hall.

Straight ahead is **Wood Quay**, departure point for afternoon cruises on the River Corrib on board the 157-passenger double-deck ship, *The Corrib Princess*. Trips last 90 minutes, taking in a variety of riverside sights from castles to wildlife. It's a delightful way to see Galway from a different perspective. For information, contact the **\*Corrib Tours**, Furbo Hill, Furbo, Co. Galway, ☎ 592447. *Open May–Sept. at 2:30 and 4:30. Fare is £5 per person.*

From Wood Quay, walk southeast via Daly's Place and Eyre Street back to Eyre Square and the starting/completion point for this tour.

As luck would have it, two of Galway's top attractions are located outside of town, beyond a walking tour route. If you do not have access to a car, both are less than a five-minute taxi or local bus ride away from Eyre Square.

Head first to the **\*Galway Crystal Heritage Centre** (17), Merlin Park, Dublin Rd., ☎ 757311, aptly called a "museum of Irish crystal." Step inside and be dazzled by the huge Georgian-style Great Hall, the reception area, decorated with intricate glasswork, crystal chandeliers, and a ceremonial staircase. Tours start with an audiovisual on the craft, followed by a tour of workshops, to see craftspeople design, etch, and inscribe the delicate patterns and tracings. In addition, there are four other exhibits: The Celtic Room, housing scroll work of early artists; the Hall of Tribes, outlining the history of the great Galway families; Boatbuilders Workshop, focusing on the traditional boats of the west including the *Galway Hooker*; the Claddagh Village, a prototype of the city's famous old quarter, and birthplace of the Claddagh ring. To all of this, add a terrace balcony with sweeping views of Galway Bay. Don't leave Galway without a visit here. *Open June–Aug., Mon.–Fri. 9–7, Sat. 9–6, Sun. 10–6; Sept.–May, Mon.–Sat. 9–5:30, Sun. 10–5:30. Admission is free. Tours. Shop. Café.*

For insight into Galway's other signature craft, visit **\*Royal Tara China** (18), Tara Hall, Monivea Rd., Mervue, ☎ 751301. Housed in a 17th-century mansion that was formerly the seat of the Joyces, one of the 14 tribes of Galway, this enterprise was founded in 1953. Visitors are invited to tour the workshops to watch craftspeople producing the fine bone china plus cold cast bronzes, crystal cast cottages, and hand-painted cold cast porcelain figures. All of the items are on display in the building's library and drawing room, replete with original fireplaces, now serving as showrooms. *Open June–Aug., Mon.–Fri. 9–7, Sat. 9–6, Sun. 10–6; Sept.–May, Mon.–Sat. 9–5:30, Sun. 10–5:30. Tours Mon.-Fri. on half-hour. Admission is free. Tours. Shop. Café.*

# Galway Bay & Connemara

Galway Bay needs no introduction. Celebrated in story and song, Galway Bay automatically draws visitors to see its splendid sunsets and azure waters. While you can enjoy glimpses of the bay from downtown Galway, it is the coastline west of Galway that presents the most panoramic views. Once you have traveled a few miles west to see Galway Bay, a bonus awaits—Connemara.

*Connemara.* The very name sounds alluring. The placename is derived from the Irish language word *Cuain na Mara,* means "Harbors of the sea." And indeed there are many harbors along Connemara's richly curved coast.

Unlike most placenames, Connemara is neither a city nor a town. It is a region, the section of County Galway that sits west of Galway City. After the Ring of Kerry, it is one of the most popular "must see" drives in Ireland.

Connemara does not have any outstanding museums, landmarks, great houses, or national monuments, but it is synonymous with stunning scenery—wide and open, rugged and natural. Connemara is the picture-postcard image of Ireland that most people envision. The coast is indented with little bays, inlets, and beaches. At almost every turn, there are lakes, waterfalls, rivers, and creeks, while a dozen glorious mountains, known as "The Twelve Bens," rise at the center to overshadow a landscape dominated by bog. Acres of dreary useless rock are enlivened by gorse and heather, rhododendrons, fuschia, and wildflowers.

Like the rest of Ireland, the people of this remote region have progressed and prospered in recent years. Traditional white-washed cottages are topped by TV antennas, slate roofs have replaced much of the original thatching, and a car is in almost every driveway. Still, there are vestiges of days gone by - stone fences, piles of newly cut turf, and donkey-carts line the back roads. Sheep graze on the hillsides and Connemara ponies frolic in the meadows. The sweet aroma of turf fires permeate the countryside.

Shops are filled with the sounds of lively conversations in the Irish language and pubs ring with native music, song, and dance. Cottage industries carry on ageless crafts. Old ways are treasured. People have time to stop and chat. Tradition is indeed alive and well in Connemara.

## GETTING THERE:

This tour literally starts at Galway City's back door. Depart Galway from the west, beside the River Corrib. Follow the coast road to R336, and then continue west.

## PRACTICALITIES:

The best way to tour Connemara is by car. You can meander and wander down country roads, or stop and explore craft centers and local attractions. If you prefer not to drive, however, three companies offer full-day escorted sightseeing tours of Connemara, departing in the summer months from Galway City. For more information, call **Bus Eireann**, ☎ 091-562000; **O'Neachtain Day Tours**, ☎ 091-83188; or **Lally's Coach Tours**, ☎ 091-562905.

Connemara is at its busiest in the summer, especially in mid-August when the area hosts the annual **Connemara Pony Show**. Don't come then without reservations.

For information, contact the **Galway Tourist Office**, Victoria Place, off Eyre Square, ☎ 091-563081; or the **Clifden Tourist Office**, Market St., Clifden, ☎ 095-21163, open mid-March to early October.

There are two area codes for telephone numbers in the Galway and Connemara areas, 091 and 095. To avoid confusion, an area code will be specified with each number.

## FOOD AND DRINK:

**Boluisce** (Main St., Spiddal) With a name that means "patch of grazing by the water," this restaurant is a mainstay along the Galway Bay route. There are no water views, but the atmosphere is homey, with brick walls, fireplace, and local art. Specialties include mussels and lobsters as well as steaks, duckling, and vegetarian dishes. The house seafood chowder alone is worth the 13-mile drive out from Galway City. ☎ 091-553286. £ to ££

**High Moors** (Dooneen, Clifden) Dine in a private home at this restaurant run by John and Eileen Griffin, just one mile from town, sitting atop a hill with panoramic views of the countryside. Specialties include Connemara lamb, Carna Bay scallops, and vegetables and herbs from the family garden. Dinner only. X: Mon.–Tues. and Nov.–April. ☎ 095-21342. ££ to £££

**Kylemore Abbey** (Kylemore) With seating indoors and outside, this flower-bedecked self-service restaurant is no ordinary café. For one thing, there is a huge non-smoking section, sometimes hard to find in this corner of the world. The food, all prepared fresh daily, is set out like a banquet—salads, casseroles, quiches, sandwiches, home-baked breads, cakes, pies, and more. Much of the produce comes from the nuns' own gardens. X: Nov.–March. ☎ 095-41113. £

**Mitchell's** (Market St., Clifden) In the center of town, this shopfront restaurant has a turn-of-the-century ambiance with a cozy decor of brick and stone walls, open fireplace, and local memorabilia. House specialties range from Irish stew to mussels, oysters, salmon, and creative combination dishes such as smoked salmon quiche or seafood pastas. X: mid-Nov. to mid-March. ☎ 095-21867. £ to ££

**O'Grady's Seafood** (Lr. Market St., Clifden) For over 30 years, this shopfront restaurant has been a standout on the Connemara circuit. The menu features whatever is fresh from the sea, with lobsters a specialty. X: Sun. and Nov.–Feb. ☎ 095-21450. ££ to £££

## SUGGESTED TOUR:

Depart Galway City from the west side of town, beside the famous **Spanish Arch** (1) and the River Corrib. Cross over the Wolfe Tone Bridge and follow the signs for **Salthill**, a popular beach resort with a 2.5-mile-long promenade and easily walkable stretch of beach overlooking Galway Bay. Continue from the hustle and bustle of Salthill westward to Barna, spelled Bearna in the Irish language, a word that means "gap." This begins a rugged Gaelic-speaking area known as *Cois Fharraige* (beside the sea). From here on, for about 15 miles, there are splendid open views of Galway Bay to the left. On a clear day, you can easy see the coast of County Clare and the Aran Islands.

Many homes, wherein the women knit the traditional Aran bainin sweaters, display signs outside saying "Handknits for sale" and most shops in the area offer locally-made knitwear. You will also notice that the road signs appear in both the Irish language and in English, and sometimes only in Irish. To make identifying places easier, we'll include both spellings, when appropriate, with the English first.

**Spiddal** or **An Spidéal**, is in the heart of the Irish-speaking area. The Irish placename refers to a hospital that once stood here. Today the town is known for its views of Galway Bay and two very fine craft centers. On the left side of the road is **\*Standún's** (2), Spiddal, ☎ 091-553108, the grand-daddy of the sweater stockists. Operating for over 50 years on this site, this craft center is a hub and clearing house for handknit Aran fishermen sweaters, made by local residents in their cottages. Besides knits, there is a good selection of tweeds, pottery, glassware, books, and other souvenirs. The views of the bay from the rear of the store make shopping a scenic treat. *Open Mon.–Fri. 9:30-6:30. Admission is free. Shop. Café.*

Continue on the road for a few hundred yards and to the right is **\*Ceardlann An Spidéil—Spiddal Craft Centre** (3), Spiddal, ☎ 091-553376, a cluster of cottage shops where craftspeople ply their trades each day. The selection includes wood-turning, stone sculpture, screen printing, pottery, weaving, floral art, and Celtic-design jewelry. See your souvenir being made before you buy. The views of this site are also hard to equal. *Open Mon.–Sat. 9–6, Sun. 2–6. Admission is free. Shop. Café.*

Return to R336, with dramatic views of Galway Bay to the left. Dry stone walls, called *Claíocha*, are the most striking aspect of the landscape. These walls, which enclose individual plots of land, are a relic of a time

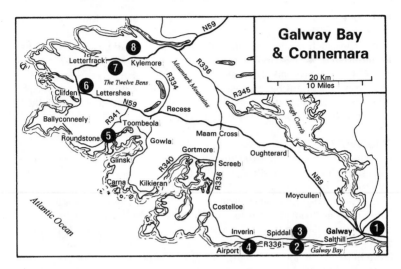

when small farmers labored doggedly to clear their tiny fields for tillage. In the waters around Galway Bay and Connemara, you will see various conventional boats, as well as two types of local craft—the *currach,* a long canoe-like vessel, originally used for fishing, and the *Huicéir,* or *Hooker,* which is a heavy timber-hulled sailboat, mainly used for carrying turf and easily recognizable by its large colorful sails.

The next town is **Inverin** or **Indreabhán,** derived from the Irish word for "estuary," is the home of **Connemara Regional Airport** (4), which is the gateway for flights to the Aran Islands via Aer Arann (See page 000). Here the road swings in a northerly direction, passing **Rossaveal** or **Ros an Míl.** This placename means "The peninsula of the whale or sea-monster." Although there may not be any monsters lurking at Rossaveal today, it is the chief fishing harbor of Connemara, with a series of new quays used by the many modern fishing trawlers that dock here. High-speed ferries, bound for the Aran Islands, also depart daily from the this busy port (See page 000).

At the end of the bay lies the crossroads at **Costelloe** or **Casla,** which means "sea inlet" in the Irish language. The *Udarás na Gaeltachta* (Gaeltacht Authority) has established an industrial estate here beside the headquarters of *Radio na Gaeltachta* and *Telefis na Gaeilge,* the Irish-language radio and television broadcasting services.

Continue north on R336 to **Screeb** or **Scríb,** which means "track" or "furrow" in the Irish language. Turn left onto R340 and follow this scenic road along the Iorras Ainteach peninsula to **Gortmore (Gort Mór),** meaning "Great field," and **Kilkieran (Cill Ciarán),** meaning "St. Ciarán's Church," a small village named after St. Ciarán of Clonmacnois (See Clonmacnois & Bog Country). It is said that he passed through this area after visiting the

Aran Islands. Seaweed processing, salmon-farming, and sea fishing are the main activities today. It is now a short journey of less than five miles to **Carna**, a placename that is the same in English and Irish, the main center of the peninsula. A prime lobster fishing center and home of the University College of Galway's marine biology station, Carna is surrounded by rocky hills, lakes, sandy beaches, and a cluster of offshore islands including **St. MacDara's Island**, revered locally and known for its 7th-century early Christian oratory.

Continue northward on R340 via **Glinsk (Glinsce)** and **Gowla (Gabhla)**, turning left on to R341 to **Cashel Bay**, a lush oasis in the midst of Connemara's barren landscape—and the return to placenames that are used commonly in English only. This is the setting for several hotels include Cashel House, a luxurious country inn known for its exotic gardens and woodlands. It has attracted many famous media stars and politicians who seek an out-of-the-way retreat, including President Charles De Gaulle of France in 1969.

Follow R341 when it wends to the left at **Toombeola**, which means "Tomb of the giant Beola," to **Roundstone** which translates as "rock of the seals." Considered by the locals to be the most picturesque of Connemara's many sea villages, Roundstone was founded and designed in the early 19th century by a Scottish engineer, Alexander Nimmo who constructed the pier and the delightful streetscape. The focal point is a local craft village that houses local artisans plying traditional crafts including **\*Roundstone Musical Instruments** (5), IDA Craft Centre, Roundstone, ☎ 095-35875. Step into this small shop, housed in the former Franciscan monastery, and watch as master craftsman Malachy Kearns hand-fashions bodhráns (traditional one-sided drums) from goatskins that have been treated with an age-old formula. Each drum is then hand-decorated with Celtic designs, initials, family crests, or names. Tin whistles, flutes, harps, and other musical instruments are also for sale. *Open daily July–Aug. 9–9; April–June and Sept.–Oct. 9–7; Nov.–March, Mon.–Sat. 9–7. Shop. Café.*

The road continues for nine miles west to **Ballyconneely**, a small hamlet on an isthmus between Ballyconneely Bay and Mannin Bay where there is a beautiful coral beach. One mile north on the left is a large stone monument commemorating the landing in 1919 of John Alcock and Arthur Whitten Brown who crash-landed here after the first-ever west-to-east transatlantic flight.

Five miles to the north is **Clifden**, derived from the Irish word *An Clochán*, meaning "Stepping stones." A busy marketing hub founded in the 19th century, Clifden is the largest town in Connemara and is considered the region's unofficial "capital." To enjoy panoramic views of the Clifden skyline with the mountains in the background, take a short detour on the **Sky Road**, a well-sign-posted seven-mile circuit leading west of town to the Atlantic, with both a high road and a low road that meet in the middle. Clifden is a good shopping town, with a handful of fine restaurants as well.

For insight into what it has been like to live in Connemara over the centuries, take a four-mile detour east of town to the **Connemara Heritage & History Centre** (6), Lettershea, Clifden, ☎ 095-21246. Surrounded by the Roundstone Bog and views of the Twelve Bens mountains, this eight-acre site blends ancient history with pre-famine days. It contains a reconstructed Bronze Age crannog (fortified lake dwelling), an authentic megalithic tomb, and a dolmen, all dating back to prehistoric times. The focal point is a pre-famine farm, worked in the 1840s by Dan O'Hara, who was eventually forced to emigrate to the US because he couldn't pay the high rents of the local landlord, a case repeated over and over among the poor tenant farmers of Connemara. Visitors can do a walk-around tour of the farm including taking part in the traditional methods of cutting turf, tilling the land, or digging the potatoes. The visitor center, which presents a short audiovisual on the area, is entered via a bridge that is also of historic interest. Moved here from Clifden, it is known as O'Connell's Bridge, because the great Irish Liberator, Daniel O'Connell entered Clifden via this bridge in 1843. *Open April–Oct., daily 10–6. Adults £3.50, seniors and students £3, children £1.75. Tours. Shop. Café.*

Retrace your route back to Clifden and follow the main N59 road north for six miles for the entrance, on the right, to the jewel in Connemara's landscape:

**\*CONNEMARA NATIONAL PARK** (7), Letterfrack, ☎ 095-41054. *Open May and Sept. 10–5:30, June 10–6:30, July–Aug. 9:30-6:30. Adults £2, seniors £1.50, students and children £1. Tours. Café.*

A kaleidoscope of Connemara's most beautiful scenery is contained at this 4,000-acre park. With very little man-made development, it is a blend of mountains, bogs, heaths, grasslands, rivers, waterfalls, and nature tails. Connemara ponies run wild, and assorted wildlife including a herd of red deer roam the gentle landscape. Some of the park's mountains, such as Benbaun, Bencullagh, Benbrack, and Muckanaght, are part of the famous Twelve Bens Mountain range. Glanmore, which means large glen in the Irish language, forms the center of the park, as the Polladirk River flows through. A visitor center offers an exhibition on the Connemara landscape and an audiovisual show, *Man and the Landscape,* on the park.

Return to the main N59 road and on the left is the majestic profile of Connemara's finest building:

**\*KYLEMORE ABBEY** (8), Kylemore, ☎ 095-41146. *Open: daily 9:30–6. Adults £3, students and seniors £2. Tours. Shop. Café.*

Overlooking Kylemore Lake, this splendid castellated mansion was originally built in 1864 as a private residence for Mitchell Henry, a wealthy merchant from Manchester, who presented it as gift to his wife who died shortly afterward. The entire estate was given in 1922 to the Benedictine nuns who operate it as a girls' school and as a visitor attraction. Although the abbey itself is not open to the public, visitors are encouraged to take pictures, picnic, or tour the grounds including a recently restored Gothic chapel, considered a mini-cathedral, that was erected in Mrs. Henry's memory between 1877 and 1881. Visitors are also welcome at a working pottery operated by the nuns. Watch as the clay is prepared, shaped, glazed, and decorated with the soft colors that reflect the local flora including a popular fuschia-studded pattern. The restaurant, which is an attraction in itself, serves produce grown on the nuns' own farm. A tour includes an audiovisual on the history of the abbey. Try to be on the grounds at noon or 6 p.m. when bells ring out calling the nuns to prayer, adding an enchanting Sound of Music aura to the entire estate.

From Kylemore, follow the main N59 road to local road R344, heading south. This route leads through the **Inagh Valley**, a sheltered area where the Maamturk Mountains rise up on the left, with Derryclare Lough and Lough Inagh are on the right beside the Beanna Beola Mountains. This road ends at **Recess**, sign-posted locally by its Irish name of **Sraith Salach**, which means "fenland of the willows," a very fitting description of the area.

From Recess, it's just over 35 miles back to Galway City, via Maam Cross, Oughterard, and Moycullen.(For information on Maam, Maam Cross, Oughterard, and Moycullen along this portion of the route, see pages 293–294).

# The Aran Islands

What was Ireland like in days long ago? One of the best ways to find out is to take a daytrip to the Aran Islands, sitting 30 miles out at sea where Galway Bay meets the Atlantic Ocean. There are three islands *Inis Mór* (Inishmore) which means Great Island, *Inis Meáin* (Inishmaan) which means Middle Island, and *Inis Oírr* (Inishere), which means Eastern Island.

Far-flung outposts of Gaelic culture, language, and lifestyle, these three storied islands are basically primitive compared with the mainland, although electricity, running water, TVs, and motorized vehicles have come ashore in recent years.

Isolation takes a toll, but also challenges the spirit. Gusty winds often blow in off the Atlantic and treat the people and the rock-strewn landscape harshly, but yet their lives are filled with enthusiasm and spunk. Graphically portrayed in John Millington Synge's play *Riders to the Sea* and Robert Flaherty's film *Man of Aran*, the Aran Islands have always had many tales to tell.

The people live a simple life. Their cottages are white-washed in the old tradition, but slate roofs have replaced the original thatching. Many of the 1,500 natives earn a living by fishing, using the traditional *currachs*, light but seaworthy little crafts made of tarred canvas stretched over a timber frame. Some of the people farm the rocky land, using seaweed and sand to augment the poor soil, while still others find new sources of income in the growing tourism industry.

Many of the women earn extra money by producing the crafts for which the islands have become famous, especially the legendary Aran handknit sweaters. Made of oatmeal-colored "bainin" wool from the native sheep, these semi-waterproof sweaters were originally knit by the women of the islands for their fishermen husbands and sons; each family would have a different stitch or pattern, such as honeycomb, diamond, trellis, cable, and the tree of life. Distinctively decorative, these intricate designs served a sombre purpose years ago—they gave a clue to the identity of men drowned in the rough waters off the coast. Today they are the most popular purchase for tourists. Visitors also seek out handknit wool socks and hats, traditional rawhide shoes, and finger-braided belts of colored wool known as crios.

Surprisingly, people have inhabited these islands for thousands of years. The landscape is dotted with remnants of early Christian monasteries and church settlements as well as Bronze Age stone forts including *Dún Aonghasa* (Dun Aengus), considered one of the finest prehistoric monuments of Western Europe. Endless stretches of stone fences wend around these islands, separating the rocky fields from picturesque pockets of small beaches, to round out the Aran tableau.

Above all, the Aran Islands beckon visitors to experience a different way of life—far from traffic and bustle, away from noise and pressure. Walk or bike along the fuschia-filled roads, stop and breathe in the sea air, step into a pub and listen to the locals as they speak among themselves in the rhythmic cadence of the Irish language. Wander where you will, take your time, don't rush, renew yourself. The Aran Islands are a different world.

## GETTING THERE:

The Aran Islands can only be reached by air or sea—there are no bridges. The fastest way to go (less than 10 minutes) is to fly via the local airline, **Aer Árann**, Connemara Regional Airport, Inverin, Co. Galway, ☎ 091-593034, about 20 miles west of Galway City. The most popular mode of sea travel is via high-speed ferry to Inishmore from Rossaveal, a 40-minute drive west of Galway and the shortest crossing point between Galway and the islands. The boat journey time is just over a half-hour. For schedules and full information, contact **Island Ferries**, Victoria Place, off Eyre Square, Galway, ☎ 091-561767. Island Ferries also operate **Sea Sprinter/Inter Island Service**, boat connections from Inishmore to Inisheer or Inishmaan, several times a day. The planes and ferries take passenger traffic only; you have to leave your car behind in Galway or Rossaveal.

## PRACTICALITIES:

The normal routing for planes and ferries is to arrive on the big island, Inishmore. Although there is a local service that will take you to the other two islands, most visitors spend the day on Inishmore. For purposes of a daytrip, we'll confine our tour to the big island. Once you arrive at the Kilronan Pier, you have to decide how you will get around. Several hundred feet from the dock, there are three groups of islanders who provide local transport. Complete or partial tours of the island are offered by drivers with minibuses or horse- or pony-drawn carts. If you'd like to get around on your own steam, bicycles are also for rent along the dock and on the main street. Prices for the minibus or cart services depend on the number of passengers and duration of tour. Bike rentals are charged according to hourly or daily rates, usually no more than £5 per day. Competition keeps the prices within the £5 to £10 range for most arrangements.

Walking is a practical way to get around, especially if you want to meander in and out of shops and explore the various sites. Inishmore is eight miles long and two miles at its widest point. The island has a well sign-posted walking route, *The Inis Mór Way,* that extends for 21 miles around the island, but it can easily be done in sections. Streets or roads are not named, but there are plenty of signposts and directional signs pointing to towns and major sites. Whether you are walking, biking, or touring in a covered vehicle, remember that the Aran Islands sit out in the middle of the ocean and can be much breezier and colder than the mainland. The weather is very changeable, with frequent and often unexpected showers blowing in off the sea. Dress in layers; bring waterproof outerwear, a head covering, and wear boots or rubbers over comfortable yet sturdy walking shoes. A change of socks is also a wise idea in case your feet get wet. When the sun does shine on the islands, it is very bright, so don't forget sunglasses and sun block or suntan lotion. On the boat trips to and from the islands, the seas are often choppy, so be prepared for possible seasickness.

Copies of the walking routes and other information can be obtained from the **Aran Islands Tourist Office**, Kilronan, ☎ 099-61263, open from the end of March to the beginning of October.

The area code for telephone numbers on the Aran Islands is 099, unless indicated otherwise.

## FOOD AND DRINK:

**Deoclann/Joe Watty** (Kilronan) With a flower-decked facade, this little white washed cottage offers a homey atmosphere on the western outskirts of town. House specialties include Irish stew, fish chowders, smoked salmon sandwiches, fresh baked scones, and Irish coffee. Seating is also available at picnic tables on the front lawn and traditional music is on tap at night. X: Nov.–March. ☎ 61155. £

**Dún Aonghasa/Dun Aengus** (Kilronan, a 10-minute walk from center of town) Set high overlooking Galway Bay with commanding seascape views, this cottage-style restaurant has timbered stone walls, open fireplace, and interesting local memorabilia. Fish dominates the menu, including lobster and other local seafood, as well as meat and poultry, all prepared using traditional island recipes. X: Nov.–Mar. ☎ 61104. £ to ££

**Lucky Star Bar** (Kilronan, opposite Heritage Centre) For straightforward drinks or a pint in a vintage Aran Island atmosphere, this bar is indeed a star. Sit back and listen to the locals conversing in Gaelic. ☎ 61218. £

**Pota Stóir Café** (Kilronan, at the Heritage Centre) For a light lunch or a warming cup of tea or coffee throughout the day, this small upstairs self-service eatery is a gem. The menu changes every day, but usually includes soups, sandwiches, chowders, quiches, scones, and delicious home-baked cakes and pies laced with fresh cream. X: Nov.–March. ☎ 61355. £

**An tSean Chéibh/The Old Pier** (Kilronan) Conveniently nestled in the center of the village, at the crossroads overlooking the harbor, this cottage-style restaurant offers seating indoors and on an outdoor covered terrace, where customers can park their bikes. The menu offers snacks such as fish-and-chips, chicken-and-chips, and burgers, as well as full entrees of seafood, beef and lamb dishes. There is a take-out counter if you want to have a picnic. X: Oct.–April. ☎ 61228. £ to ££

## SUGGESTED TOUR:

If you have engaged a minibus or pony-and-trap ride, your tour will be laid out for you by a local guide. If you have decided to walk or bike, start a tour at the **Aran Tourist Office** (1), overlooking the pier and boat dock or a short walk from the airstrip. Turn right and walk to the heart of **Kilronan** village. The placename, like many similar ones beginning with the prefix "Kil," comes from the Irish language, *Cill Rónáin*, meaning "St. Rónán's Church. All that currently remains of the saint's settlement is a holy well, Toberonan. At the crossroads, take a right and follow the road, slightly hilly at times. After a few shops and local enterprises, on the right is the:

**\*IONAD ÁRANN, ARAN'S HERITAGE CENTRE** (2), Kilronan, Inishmore, ☎ 61355. *Open April–May and Sept.–Oct., daily 11–5; June–Aug. 10–7. Adults £2.50, seniors and students £2, children £1.50. Film admission only £2. Combined museum-film admission: Adults £4, seniors and students £3.50, children £3. Shop. Café.*

For a comprehensive overview of local history, language, and lifestyle, spend some time inside this well-designed museum. Using a walk-through format, the exhibits introduce the unique traditions of the islands including the native-born writers, the monasteries, and the use of currachs as fishing boats. Other displays focus on the landscape and geological aspects such as the types of rocks, formation of the limestone, fossils trapped in stone, and the various stone forts such as Dún Aonghasa. In addition, there are exhibits on the harvesting of seaweed as a fertilizer for the potato crop, and making soil from this rocky landscape. The traditional dress of the islanders is also on display, as is a life-size *hooker*, the Connemara sailing boat which brought turf for fuel to the islands for many years. If it's rainy out, head upstairs; there is a small theater which screens the *Man of Aran* film at regular intervals (12, 2, 3:15, and 5:30). The film lasts one hour and fifteen minutes.

Exit the heritage center and take a right, continuing to follow the road which cuts through the entire island, passing cottages, pubs, and shops of varying size and age. On both sides of the road are monuments and ruins of the past; all are clearly marked on local walking maps. To the right, the views of open seas rimmed by sandy and rock-strewn beaches are panoramic. After about five miles, the next major town is **Kilmurvey**, derived from the Irish placename, *Cill Mhuirbhigh,* meaning "Church of the sandy shores." To reach this point, if you have been touring by bicycle, you should have spent about one hour to 90 minutes in duration, and walking time should be a little longer.

Look now to the left for signs to the island's major prehistoric wonder, **\*Dún Aonghasa** (3), a huge stone fort, rising to a height of almost 300 feet above the Atlantic waters. Covering over 11 acres, the fort consists of three concentric enclosures supported by strong walls of stone masonry,

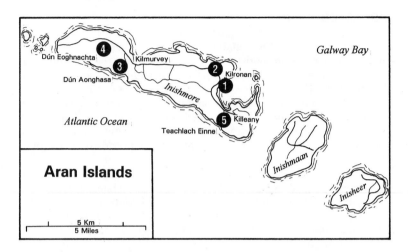

Aran Islands

5 Km
5 Miles

laid out as follows: an outer enclosure, 1,174 feet long and 650 feet wide; a middle enclosure, 400 feet long and 300 feet wide; and an inner citadel, 150 feet in diameter. It is claimed that the fort was built by the *Fir Bolg,* a prehistoric tribe, whose leader was Aengus, and hence the name of the fort. Recent excavations have revealed traces of activity on the site from the late Bronze Age (between 1000 and 700 BC) until early Christian times, around the 5th century. Evidence of habitation in the Bronze age includes remnants of huts and hearth sites. Exploring the fort requires walking in open fields and along sometimes muddy pathways.

At this point, many visitors begin to head back toward Kilronan. If you wish to continue to the westward tip of the island, however, after another two miles, you will see **Dún Eoghnachta** (4), estimated to be at least 3,000 years old. It is an inland stone fort with a circular terraced wall enclosing the remains of clochans (stone houses).

Return to Kilronan at your leisure, exploring along the way. As you travel, you can visit local businesses, churches, shops, restaurants, and pubs. You'll hear the Irish (Gaelic) language being spoken in everyday conversation and see the famous Aran sweaters for sale at their points of origin.

When you reach Kilronan, you may wish to continue on the main road, rather than turning into the village. Travel about 1.5 miles to reach **Teachlach Einne** (5) (St. Enda's Household), the most sacred spot on the island. It contains the ruins of a church built by St. Enda, a 5th-century saint who is credited with being the founder of monasticism in Ireland. Not only are the remains of St. Enda buried here, but the site is reputed to hold the remains of 120 other saints.

Return to the pier area to complete the tour and board your ferry for return to the mainland.

# Lough Corrib—
# "Quiet Man" Country

Tourists may flock to sing the praises of Galway Bay, but this storied bay is only the beginning of Galway's liquid assets. Lesser known but equally beguiling is Lough Corrib, the Republic of Ireland' s largest lake, at 42,000 acres in size. Stretching from the Corrib River in Galway City up along the eastern half of the county, this lovely lake is picturesque, unspoiled, and fish-filled, providing some of Europe's best fishing waters for salmon and brown trout. If you'd like to cast a rod, it's hard to find better waters.

Great fishing is only half of the story here. Straddling both Counties Galway and Mayo, Lough Corrib is home to Ashford Castle, one of Ireland's great resorts, and is the gateway to some of the west's most splendid scenery—the Maam Valley, Partry Mountains, and the legendary Joyce Country, a wild territory ruled from the 13th to the 19th centuries by the Joyce clan, one of Galway's 14 original tribes. It is said that exactly 365 islands, one for every day of the year, float in Lough Comb, including Inchagoill Island, site of an early Christian monastic settlement dating back to the 5th century.

Above all, Lough Corrib is celebrated as the home of Cong, the small village that served as the setting for the legendary film, *The Quiet Man*.

**GETTING THERE:**

By car, depart Galway by following the east shore of Lough Corrib via the main N84 road toward Headford and then local road R334. The remainder of the route will follow local roads, ending in the main N59 road returning to Galway. The complete circuit is about 100 miles.

**PRACTICALITIES:**

This tour requires a car; public transport would not be practical. The driving is not difficult, but it can be slow at times, particularly in remote scenic areas, over bumpy bog roads.

For information, contact the **Galway Tourist Office**, Victoria Place, Eyre Square, Galway, ☎ 091-563081, open all year; the **Cong Tourist Office**, Main St., Cong, Co. Mayo, ☎ 092-46542, open end of June through August; or the **Oughterard Tourist Office**, Main St., Oughterard, Co. Galway, ☎ 091-552808, open all year.

There are at least three area codes for telephone numbers in this region, 091,092, and 094. To avoid confusion, the area code will be specified with each number.

## FOOD AND DRINK:

**Echoes** (Main St., Cong) Housed in a shopfront location, this family-run restaurant is known far-and-wide for its local wild fresh and smoked salmon and other seafoods. For picnics or quick bites, there is a delicatessen and sandwich bar. X: Mon.–Thurs. Nov.–March. ☎ 092-46059. £ to ££

**Joseph Keane** (Maam Bridge) In the middle of nowhere, this place is Mecca. Hearty hot soups and baskets of sandwiches are served amid a homey fireside atmosphere. In typical country fashion, the proprietor also operates as a newsagent, general store, and wool dealer. ☎ 091-571110. £

**Peacocke's** (Maam Cross) Often called the Piccadilly or Celtic Bazaar of Connemara, this busy crossroads enterprise offers snacks and full meals, specializing in Connemara lamb, seafood, steaks, and soups. For diversion, there is a supermarket, souvenir shop, and a replica of *The Quiet Man* cottage on the grounds. X: Dec. 25 and Good Friday. ☎ 091-552306. £ to ££

## SUGGESTED TOUR:

Depart **Galway City** (1) and follow signs to national road N84, on the eastern shore of Lough Corrib, toward Headford, a small market village 17 miles to the north.

From Headford, bear left onto local road R334 and travel northwest 12 miles into County Mayo and **Cong**, a picturesque village nestled on the northeast corner of Lough Corrib. The placename, which comes from the Irish language *Conga*, meaning isthmus, describes Cong's position on a large four-mile isthmus of land that separates Lough Corrib and Lough Mask.

For such a small and out-of-the-way town, Cong has many claims to fame, not the least of which is the fact that it was the setting for the classic 1952 movie, *The Quiet Man*, starring John Wayne, Maureen O'Hara, and Barry Fitzgerald. Naturally, the town has not forgotten its moment of glory. Follow the main street to the river and turn right to see **The Quiet Man Heritage Cottage** (2), Circular Road, Cong, Co. Mayo, ☎ 092-46089. This authentic whitewashed cottage, complete with an emerald green half-door and thatched roof, is literally a museum built to perpetuate the memory of the film. The ground floor has been designed as a replica of the original cottage set where the interior scenes were filmed. All of the costumes, implements, and furnishings—from the four-poster bed to the tables and chairs, are authentic reproductions of those used in the film. Scenes and life-size figures add to the nostalgia. The upstairs rooms serve as an exhibit hall for local archaeological and historical displays. *Open March–Nov., 10–6. Adults £2.50, seniors and students £2, children £1.*

Long before *The Quiet Man*, Cong was making history as the site of

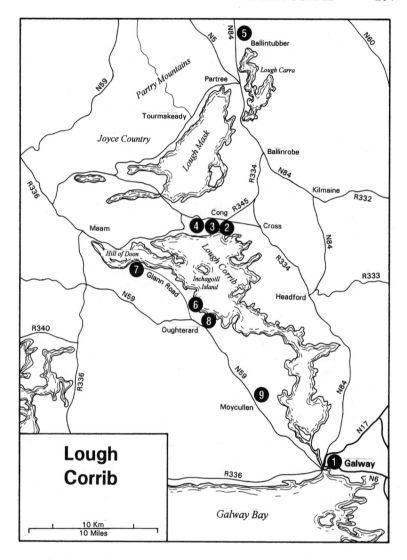

**Lough Corrib**

10 Km
10 Miles

**Cong Abbey** (3), a monastery founded by St. Féichín in the 6th century and rebuilt as an abbey of the Augustinians by King Turloch Mór O'Conor in the 12th century. Turloch's son, Rory, the last high king of Ireland, retired to the abbey in 1183 and died there in 1198; he is buried at Clonmacnois (See *Clonmacnois and Bog Country*).

From this abbey came the Cross of Cong, created in the 1120s. A masterpiece of 12th-century religious art, the cross was hidden for many years after the suppression of the monasteries in the 15th and 16th centuries and then discovered in the early 19th century in a chest in the village. Made of oak plated with copper and decorated with gold filigree in a Celtic pattern, it is considered as one of the great processional crosses of Ireland, now on display at the National Museum in Dublin.

Of the abbey church, only the chancel survives, entered from the car park through a north doorway built of stones reassembled there in the 1860s. In contrast, the doorways along the eastern side of the cloister are genuine examples of 12th-century mason work, with delicate Romanesque-Early Gothic carvings. The details of these doorways are classified among the finest products of Irish medieval stone carving.

The ruins of the abbey are beside one of the entrance gates to *Ashford Castle (4), Cong, Co. Mayo, ☎ 092-46003, dating back to the 13th century and today serving as one of Ireland's major five-star hotel resorts. Drive along the long entrance pathway, park your car, and then cross over the drawbridge on foot to enter the fairytale world of Ashford, a broad vista of turrets and towers, arches and battlements. Over the years it has served as a residence to the De Burgos (Burkes), one of the original 14 tribes of Galway, who conquered the surrounding land. In the 18th century, owned by the Oranmore and Browne families (the latter also of the original Galway tribes), it was enlarged to include a château-style section. Much of the current facade was added in the late 19th century by the Guinness family of brewing fame who lived here until 1939 when it was transformed into a hotel. The name derives from the Irish language, Áth na Fuinseoige, meaning "ford of the ash." Sitting as it does on the northern edge of Lough Corrib, that is a fitting name since this great fortress/residence is not only surrounded by ash but dozens of other ancient tress, shrubs, and flowers of all kinds. The grounds and gardens are open to the public, for a fee, and boats trips on Lough Corrib are also offered from the pier next to the hotel. Grounds open during daylight hours. Admission £3 per person.

From Cong, take a slight detour northward around the eastern shore of Lough Mask, via **Ballinrobe**, a small market town that is a hub of outdoor sports activity. The home of the only racetrack in County Mayo, it also hosts the World Wet Fly Angling Championships each year.

From here, follow the main N84 road for seven miles to *Ballintubber Abbey, (5), Ballintubber, Co. Mayo, ☎ 094-30934, known as "the abbey that refused to die." This story of determination began in 1216 when Cathal O'Conor, king of Connacht, built the abbey on the site of an earlier church attributed to St. Patrick in 441. The word Ballintubber comes from the Irish language, Baile Tobair Phadraig, meaning "the townland of St. Patrick's well." Like other abbeys in Ireland, Ballintubber was suppressed by Henry VIII. After destruction by Cromwell in 1653, the abbey was roofless, but not deserted. For 250 years, the people attended services in the wind, rain, and other elements, making Ballintubber one of the few Irish churches in continuous use for nearly 800 years. The first attempts at restoration came in 1846, but work was abandoned due to the Famine. Eventually, the abbey was completely restored in 1966. Proud of their heritage, volunteers offer a 20-minute audiovisual on the history of the abbey and guided tours of the building and garden-filled grounds. *Open Mon.–Fri. 9:30–6:30, Sat. 10:30–6, Sun. 1–6. Admission is free. Tours. Shop.*

From Ballintubber, retrace your route southward as far as Partree and then turn right onto a local road along the western shore of Lough Mask, with the Partry Mountains on your right. Follow this scenic drive via Tourmakeady, passing from County Mayo back into County Galway. This is the heart of Joyce Country, the far-flung lands inhabited in medieval times by the Joyces, one of Galway's 14 original tribes. It is said that the Joyces were of princely Welsh stock, very tall in stature. Tom Joyce, the patriarch of the Irish sept, who came from Wales to Ireland and settled in Connemara during the reign of Edward I, is reputed to have been seven feet tall, a gigantic height for the times. But don't look for any giants along the route now. The clan eventually dispersed and resettled all over Ireland including Dublin from whence came the great 20th-century scribe, James Joyce. His wife, Nora Barnacle, was from Galway City, but he claimed no Galway connections other than his surname.

The road leads to **Maam**, also known as Maam Bridge, in the heart of the Maam Valley, an isolated spot flanked by the craggy Maamturk Mountains on the fight and upper reaches of Lough Corrib on the left. The curious placename is derived from the Irish language word *An Mám*, meaning "the mountain pass." There is a small bridge here over a body of water known appropriately as the Joyces River. Follow R336 south for five miles to Maam Cross, a crossroads point, at the intersection of the main N59 road.

Turn left onto the main road and head east, driving though desolate and bare rock-strewn lands, with a lake-studded valley flecked with purple heather to the right and distant views of Lough Corrib on the left. After 10 miles, straight ahead is ***Oughterard**, a fishing town nestled between the Owenriff River and one of Lough Corrib's most picturesque points. The placename comes from the Irish language, *Uachtar Árd,* meaning "upper height." Surrounded by trees, Oughterard is a mix of substantial Georgian houses and small fishing cottages. Directly south of the town center, you can embark on two-hour guided sightseeing cruises of Lough Corrib via ***Corrib Ferries** (6), Oughterard Pier, Oughterard, ☎ 091-552644. The trips include a visit to Inchagoill Island, the most famous of Lough Corrib's 365 islands, located in the center of the lake, half-way between Oughterard and Cong. *Trips operate daily May–Sept. Fares range from £5 to £8, depending on route.*

Uninhabited since the 1940s, Inchagoill Island contains the remains of **Teampull Phádraig** (St. Patrick's Church), believed to have been built of wood or wattle and daub by St. Patrick. The present stone church was erected in the 5th century by his nephew, Lugnaed, who is buried on the island. A unique "rudder stone," so-called because of its shape, marks Lugnaed's grave, reputed to be the oldest inscribed Christian stone in Europe outside of the Catacombs of Rome.

Before you leave Oughterard, consider one of the favorite local drives—northwest of town to see the **Hill of Doon** (7). Follow the signposts from town for the Glann Road. The road winds along the Corrib's shores and moves inland before returning to the shore and a picnic spot. After this, the road narrows and climbs for another two miles, before reaching a car park overlooking Lough Corrib, and giving panoramic views of the Lough and the Hill of Doon. The drive totals about nine extra miles, each way.

From Oughterard, travel two miles south of town and make a left at the sign-post for **Aughnanure Castle** (8), Oughterard, ☎ 091-552214, a six-story tower house dating back to c. 1500. Standing on a rocky island along the shores of Lough Corrib, this well-preserved stone fortress was the home of the O'Flahertys, a ferocious Irish clan who were the masters of West Connacht—the area between Lough Corrib and the sea. The site also contains the remains of a banqueting hall, a watch tower, two bawns, and a dry harbor. *Open daily mid-June to mid-Sept. 9:30–6:30. Adults £2, seniors £1.50, children £1.*

Return to the main road and continue for 10 miles east to the village of **Moycullen**, a picturesque spot with an equally evocative placename. In the Irish language, *Maigh Cuilinn* means "plain of holly." To the right is **Connemara Marble Industries, Ltd.** (9), Moycullen, Co. Galway, ☎ 091-555102, a local enterprise that makes good use of Connemara's natural green rock, known as Connemara marble. Estimated by geologists to be about 500 million years old, the marble has twists and interlocking bands of serpentine in various shades, ranging from light green to emerald, all diverse in marking and veining. It is quarried in the Connemara mountains and brought here for cutting, shaping, and polishing. Craftsmen then fashion the marble into jewelry, paperweights, Celtic crosses, and other gifts. *Open daily May–Oct. 9:30–5:30, with reduced schedule in off-season. Admission is free. Tours. Shop. Café.*

From here, it is just eight miles back to Galway City.

# Along Clew Bay

Clew Bay is an unsung hero or heroine, as the case may be. Among the waters of the west of Ireland, Clew Bay is a stand-out for great scenic beauty, but yet it is easily overshadowed in story, song, and popularity by Galway Bay.

The stunning vistas of Clew Bay may be unsung, but they have never been unreachable. Even St. Patrick trudged his way here in the 5th century and climbed the nearest mountain overlooking Clew Bay, setting a spiritual precedent that is still followed today.

Remote as it is, Clew Bay featured in Irish history as the base for 16th-century pirate queen, Grace O'Malley. The English also found their way to Clew Bay in the 17th and 18th centuries, building two picturesque Georgian towns, Westport and Newport.

Spanning a distance of over 15 miles long and seven miles wide along the remote western shoreline between County Galway and County Mayo, Clew Bay is dotted with hundreds of small islands that form a fascinating archipelago. The focal point is Achill Island, Ireland's largest offshore island and a favorite vacation spot for the Irish people.

Above all, Clew Bay is an oasis of unspoiled and tranquil coastal waters. It won't be long before someone writes a song about Clew Bay. Maybe it will be you!

### GETTING THERE:

Clew Bay is not the easiest place to reach. It can be approached via Connemara and the main N59 road, but this can be very slow driving. It is usually best to start off with the faster, although less scenic, route along N84 from Galway to Castlebar and then west on local road R311 to Newport. This drive, about 60 miles, should take just over one hour and a half to Castlebar and then another half-hour to Newport.

### PRACTICALITIES:

Since this is primarily a driving scenic tour, the only way to follow the route is by car. If you do not have a car and want to reach just one point along Clew Bay, **Bus Eireann** provides daily bus service from Galway to Westport. Local services could then take you to Achill Island for the day.

For information, contact the **Westport Tourist Office**, James Street, Westport, Co. Mayo, ☎ 098-25711, open all year; **Newport Tourist Office**, Main St., Newport, Co. Mayo, ☎ 098-41895, open June through August; **Achill Island Tourist Office**, Keel, Achill Island, Co. Mayo, ☎ 098-45384, open from June through early September; and the **Louisburgh Tourist Office**, Bridge St., Louisburgh, Co. Mayo, ☎ 098-66400, open June through August.

The area code for telephone numbers along this route is 098, unless otherwise specified.

## FOOD AND DRINK:

**Atoka** (The Valley, Dugort) Using a bird as its symbol, this family-run restaurant is a little oasis on the northern shore of Achill Island, over-looking the Achill Sound Golf Course. The menu features home-style cooking, with breakfast all day, and as well as snacks and light meals, from omelets and mixed grills, to seafood and steaks. ☎ 47229. £ to ££

**The Beehive** (Keel, Achill Island) This informal café- craftshop is a bee-hive of activity, serving snacks and light meals in a setting of locally-made pottery, knitwear, jewelry, and art. There are four rooms to choose from inside and picnic tables outside. The self-service menu features seafood salads, soups, sandwiches, and casseroles. ☎ 43134. £

**Calvey's** (Keel, Achill Island) A favorite with the locals, this casual restaurant is known for its local seafood menu—featuring 20 varieties of Achill seafood, from crab and oysters to turbot and wild salmon. Achill Island lamb and beef, raised on the Calvey family farm, are also featured, as are award-winning vegetarian dishes. ☎ 43158. £ to ££

**Traditional Irish Kitchen** (The Quay, Newport) Furnished with memo-rabilia and family heirlooms from the local folk, this tea room is housed in a 300-year-old building that produces hand-made toys. The menu is sim-ple but perfect for quick refreshment—steaming pots of tea with huge scones freshly baked by the Sisters of St. Lucy. ☎ 41139. £

**The Towers** (Westport Harbour) Situated on the edge of the water, this pub-restaurant is housed in an old castle-like tower with a beer garden on the outside. It not only dishes up a relaxing nautical atmosphere but great food as well. The choices range from seafood chowders, fish pies, mus-sels, and seafood platters, to salads, shepherd's pie, burgers, toasted sand-wiches, pastas, and baked potatoes with various fillings. ☎ 26534. £ to ££

## SUGGESTED TOUR:

From **Galway** (1), take the main N84 road via Headford and Ballinrobe to **Castlebar**, a busy marketing and industrial town, the administrative cap-ital of Mayo. Bear left and follow the signs to R311 and Newport, a distance of just over 11 miles.

Hugging the northeast corner of Clew Bay, *Newport is a prime fish-ing center for salmon on the Newport River and other nearby waters. A focal point of the town is the unique seven-arch viaduct over the river, a blend of red sandstone and limestone. Newport's main claim to fame is that it is the ancestral home of Princess Grace of Monaco, the former Hollywood actress Grace Kelly, whose grandfather was a Newport native before he emigrated to the US. Princess Grace and Prince Rainier often

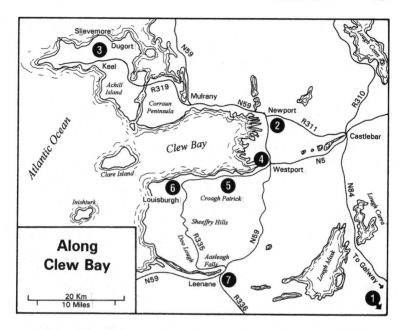

Along
Clew Bay

20 Km
10 Miles

visited Newport, although nothing remains of the original homestead today. During her visits, the late Princess usually stayed at Newport House, a lovely 18th-century Georgian-style country inn beside the river.

Adjacent to the hotel is **Green Isle Crafts** (2), The Quay, Newport, ☎ 41139, a local handcraft enterprise producing unusual soft wool toys and clothing. Housed in a 300-year-old warehouse beside the river, Green Isle was started over 30 years ago by the Sisters of St. Lucy to provide employment for the local people. The facility includes the Traditional Irish Kitchen, which displays memorabilia from homesteads of the area. Steaming pots of tea with convent-baked goods are also served. *Open daily 10–6. Admission is free. Tours. Shop. Café.*

From Newport, it's just over 17 miles to Achill Island. Just before you reach the island, you will pass through *Mulrany, a delightful seaside village located on an isthmus between Clew Bay and Blacksod Bay. Rimmed by colorful giant fuschias, rhododenrons, and exotic palms, Mulrany almost has a Mediterranean atmosphere. Its placename, which comes from the Irish language, *An Mhala Raithní*, means "The hilltop of (the) ferns."

*Achill Island** (3) is Ireland's largest offshore island, 14 miles long and 12 miles wide. Joined to the mainland by a bridge at Achill Sound, Achill is not as isolated as the Aran Islands or other offshore outposts around the Irish coast. Yet it is relatively undeveloped and unspoiled. Home to about 3,000 people, this island is gifted with an amazingly diverse assortment of scenery, from sandy Blue Flag beaches and steep seaside cliffs, to boglands and farmlands, as well as mountains, lakes, valleys, and moors, all rimmed by heather and fuschia hedges. Part of the area is a Gaeltacht, where the local people speak Irish as their everyday language. You'll know you are in the Gaeltacht when the usual "B & B" (bed and breakfast) signs are noticeably outnumbered by "B agus B" signs.

Follow the main R319 road westward for about 10 miles to **Keel**, a popular beach village. Beyond Keel is **Trawmore**, a fine two-mile-long beach, and the **Cliffs of Menawn** which rise to a height of 800 feet, taller than the highly touted Cliffs of Moher of County Clare. At the western tip of the island is **Croaghaun**, a peak rising to 2,192 feet in height.

On the return drive, you may wish to detour northward toward **Slievemore** (2,204 feet), a cone-topped mountain of quartz and mica. In the waters behind Slievemore Mountain, seals bask on hot summer days on caves and little islands that have been carved out by the erosion of the waves. At the foot of the mountain is **Dugort**, another popular vacation village.

Return to the mainland and retrace your route to Newport, and then via the main road N59 for eight miles, with Clew Bay on your right, to ***Westport**, one of the West of Ireland's few purposely planned towns. Designed by the English architect James Wyatt, c. 1780, it has a beautiful long boulevard, known as The Mall, with a colonnade of trees on both sides of the Carrowbeg River. The streets, lined with handsome Georgian buildings, converge around a central Octagon-shaped monument. At the western edge of the town is **Westport House** (4), off Quay Road, Westport, ☎ 25430, an 18th-century Georgian country mansion that is the home of Lord Altamont, a descendant of Grace O'Malley, the famous 16th-century pirate queen of the Irish seas. Conceived by the German architect Richard Castle, the house was completed in 1778 by James Wyatt. Interior highlights include an ornate staircase of white Sicilian marble, a wide selection of family portraits and other paintings, early 19th-century Waterford Glass chandeliers, 18th-century hand-painted Chinese wallpaper, and Irish silver. In an effort to appeal to a wide range of visitors, the grounds include an antique shop, children's zoo, miniature train, camping park, and pitch-and-putt and tennis facilities. *Open May–June and Sept. daily 2–5; July–Aug. Mon.–Sat. 10:30–6 and Sun. 2–6. House only: Adults £6, children £3; house with other attractions: Adults £8.50, children £4. Tours. Shop. Café.*

The front gate of Westport House faces the harbor. It is worth a stroll along the quay to see the variety of pubs, restaurants, and other local enterprises. This is also the embarkation point for cruises to Clare Island, one of Clew Bay's many islands and the only one that has a regular ferry service. With a current population of 150 people, **Clare Island** has a long and colorful history. In the 16th century, it was reputedly the base of operations for Grace O'Malley, Ireland's legendary pirate queen who is buried on the island, according to local lore. The ferry ride takes 1.5 hours each way. For information about fares and schedules, contact the **Pirate Queen**, Westport Harbour, Westport, ☎ 26307. Note: Alternatively, the **Ocean Star** ferry, ☎ 25045, operates a shorter 15-minute ferry service from Ronagh Pier at Louisburgh (see below).

Depart Westport and travel via the local road R335 (or R395, as it appears on some maps), with panoramic views of Clew Bay to the right. After six miles the glorious profile of *****Croagh Patrick** (5) rises on the left to a height of 2,510 feet. Known locally as The Reek, it is an isolated quartzite cone-shaped peak, considered one of the most striking features of the West of Ireland landscape. The name of the mountain, which literally means "St. Patrick's Hill," is derived from the fact that St. Patrick is said to have spent 40 days and nights on the summit, fasting and praying for the people of Ireland during the mid-5th century. To commemorate the event each year, Christian pilgrims gather here on the last Sunday in July, to climb the mountain, many in bare feet, in the footsteps of Patrick. On the summit of Croagh Patrick is a church, built in 1905 on the site of a small oratory that dated back to 842. The present edifice was built over a period of a year at the cost of £1,000. Materials for construction were prepared at the foot of the mountain and transported to the top by donkey.

Continue for five miles to Louisburgh, an 18th-century town on Clew Bay. Although the present name is English in origin, the original place-name was *Cluain Cearbán*, meaning "Meadow of the buttercups," and giving a clue to the surrounding landscape. The focal point of the town is the **Granuaile (Grace O'Malley) Centre** (6), off Main St., Louisburgh, ☎ 66195, a museum dedicated to the memory of Grace O'Malley (1530–1600), Ireland's legendary pirate queen. Housed in the former St. Catherine's Church of Ireland, it includes exhibits, paintings, and an audiovisual on Grace's daring exploits, seafaring travels, and achievements in the male-dominated society of the 16th century. *Open June to mid-Sept., 10–6. Adults £2.50, seniors £1.50, and children £1.25. Shop. Café.*

Continue southward for 18 miles via R335 with Clew Bay on the right and the Sheffry Hills rising to the left. About mid-way is *****Doo Lough** on the left, a long lake set among steep mountains. With panoramic vistas on all sides, there is very little that is man-made here, except for a small stone monument to the memory of 400 people who died in 1847, at the height of the Great Famine, as they walked from Louisburgh in a vain attempt to obtain help from a local authority meeting being held three miles away to the south. On the right is *****Mweelrea Mountain**, the highest peak in the province of Connacht, at 2,688 feet.

The road gradually wends its way through the Delphi Valley to the shores of *****Killary Harbour**, a natural fjord, and *****Aasleagh Falls**, on the Erriff River. This scenic area was used as the setting for the movie, *The Field*, starring Richard Harris. Here the road turns right to enter County Galway at Leenane, a lovely hamlet aptly described by its Irish placename, *An Lionan*, meaning "the shallow sea-bed."

At the edge of town overlooking the harbor is the *****Leenane Cultural

**Centre** (7), Main St., Leenane, Co. Galway, ☎ 095-42323, a museum that focuses on the 20 different kinds of sheep that are indigenous to the Mayo and Galway area. Through a series of exhibits and hands-on presentations, it tells the story of the local wool industry, including carding, spinning, weaving, and using natural dyes. Daily demonstrations of sheep-shearing are given outdoors in the summer months. There is also a 13-minute audiovisual, shown continuously, on local history and places of interest. *Open March–Oct. daily 10–7. Adults £2, seniors students, and children £1. Tours. Shop. Café.*

From Leenane, follow local road R345 to Maam and then R336 to Maam Cross, a total of 14 miles. Then turn left and join the main N59 road for the final 25 miles back to Galway City. (For information on Maam, Maam Cross, Oughterard, and Moycullen along this portion of the route, see *Lough Corrib & Quiet Man Country*).

# Clonmacnois
# & Bog Country

Ever wonder why Ireland is called "The Island of Saints and Scholars?" The answer lies east of Galway, in the heart of the boglands of County Offaly, at an awesome ruin called Clonmacnois.

Clonmacnois is the epitome of an early Irish monastery, an everlasting remnant from the days when Ireland was a hub of medieval learning and scholarly activity. Irish-trained teachers went out to all of Europe, bringing light to the Dark Ages. Even Pope John Paul II made time in his hectic two-day 1979 trip to Ireland to visit Clonmacnois. "The very stones speak," he declared after touring the site.

Happily, Clonmacnois is not alone. Sitting at a bend of the River Shannon between Lough Derg and Lough Ree, Clonmacnois is surrounded by vast open boglands, a curious feature of the Irish landscape that was formed millions of years ago. A narrow-gauge train takes visitors right through this mushy turf to learn all about an important natural resource.

Once in County Offaly, you are literally in the heart of Ireland, far from the usual tourist routes. The town of Birr, home of a revered castle and garden, is considered the exact geographic center of the country. The route to and from Offaly also takes in a diverse assortment of historic castles, battlefields, and landmarks, including Ireland's only working town moat. Indeed the lesser-traveled roads east of Galway are roads well worth taking.

## GETTING THERE:

By car, depart Galway City on the main N6 road via Loughrea, and then switch over to N65, through the east County Galway countryside and across the River Shannon to Clonmacnois via local roads R356 and R357. You may wish to take a slight detour south via N62 to Birr and then north on the same road into Athlone. Either way, the main N6 road will bring you back to Galway. Total mileage will average 90 to 110 miles.

## PRACTICALITIES:

Like many off-the-beaten-track routes, this tour requires a car. It is relatively easy driving on straight roads and distances are not great. The route is well signposted, in most cases.

Touring Clonmacnois requires walking outdoors, so good all-weather clothing and footwear are necessary. Likewise, the train tour of the bog allows passengers to get out of the train and walk around, so boots or rubber shoes are recommended, especially in rainy weather.

For information, contact the **Clonmacnois Tourist Office**, Clonmacnois, Co. Offaly, ☎ 0905-74134, open from April to September; **Birr Tourist Office**, Castle Street, Birr, Co. Offaly, ☎ 0509-20110, open from mid-May to mid-September; **Athlone Tourist Office**, Athlone Castle, Co. Westmeath, ☎ 0902-94630, open April to October; and the **Aughrim Tourist Office**, Aughrim Village, Co. Galway, ☎ 0905-73939, open from April to early October.

The area codes for telephone numbers in this region include 091, 0509, 0902, and 0905. To avoid confusion, the required area code will be specified with each number.

## FOOD AND DRINK:

Since County Offaly and other points along this route are slightly off the beaten tourist track, opportunities for casual lunches are not numerous. Your best bet for lunch is the on-premises café of major sites such as Clonmacnois, the Bog Railway Visitor Centre, Athlone Castle, and the Battle of Aughrim Interpretative Centre. A few other recommendations:

**Brosna Lodge** (Main St., Banagher) Set back from the main thoroughfare amid flower-filled gardens, this country inn is located in the middle of a busy town beside the River Shannon, directly en route from Clonfert to Clonmacnois. The cozy Old World bar, full of local memorabilia, is an ideal setting to enjoy a drink or hearty soups, sandwiches, and salads, for a quick lunch. X: Jan. ☎ 0902-51350. £ to ££

**Dooly's** (Emmet Square, Birr) Originally one of Ireland's first coaching inns, this 240-year-old hotel is a popular spot in the middle of town. Relax amid a Georgian decor and enjoy a snack, drink, or light meal in the cozy Coach House Bar or the handy all-day coffee shop. ☎ 0902-20032. £ to ££

**Riverbank Restaurant** (Riverstown, 1 mile west of Birr) Views of the Little Brosna River are surpassed only by the fine cuisine and friendly service at this family-run restaurant. The decor exudes country inn charm with brick walls, fireplace, pink linens, and local memorabilia, capped by wide picture windows beside the flower-decked riverbank. House specialties include grilled trout from local waters, roast beef, and chicken with brandy and peppercorn sauce. Lighter items, such as cheese and onion omelet, soups, and salads, are served in the bar all day. X: Tues. ☎ 0509-21528. £ to ££

**Wineport** (Glasson, 3 miles north of Athlone) Overlooking the shoreline of the Lough Ree, this rustic cottage blends an informal sailboating ambiance with a menu that features freshwater fish from the River Shannon, especially eel and pike, as well as steaks, burgers, and vegetarian treats. X: Dec. 25–26 and Jan. 1. ☎ 0902-85466. £ to ££

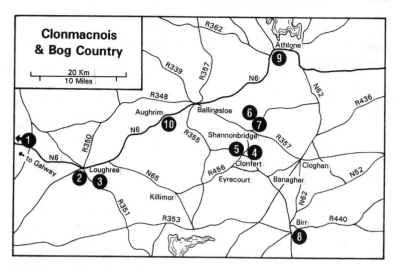

## SUGGESTED TOUR:

Head east today, inland along the River Shannon to some of Ireland's hidden treasures. From **Galway City** (1), drive along the main N6 road for 22 miles to **Loughrea**, a picturesque market town on a lake. The town, in fact, is named after its lake. The Irish language words, *Baile Locha Riach*, mean "The town of the gray lake." In the Middle Ages, Loughrea was the principal seat of the MacWilliam Uachtair Burkes, leading chieftains of the west. To see the lake and the highlights of the town, turn right at West Bridge as you enter from the main road.

Go one block south to Barrack Street which runs along the lake. Here, on the left side, is the 13th-century **Town Moat** (2), the only functioning water-filled medieval moat in Ireland. Turn left and continue, with the lake on your right, to see **\*St. Brendan's Cathedral** (3), Barrack St., Loughrea, ☎ 091-841212, built during the period 1897–1903. A treasure house of Celtic Renaissance art, it contains an unrivaled collection of stained-glass windows by leading Irish artists including Evie Hone, Sarah Purser, and Michael Healy; 30 embroidered banners made to the designs of noted Irish artist Jack Yeats; and benches with individual carvings at the ends of each seat, as well as noteworthy metal-work in the lamps. *Open daily 8–6. Admission is free. Donations welcome.*

Depart Loughrea via main road N65 for 10 miles as far as Killimor, and then make a left on to local road R356. Follow this road via Eyrecourt for about 10 miles east and make a left at the signpost that says **Clonfert**. Once you have made the turn, proceed for about two miles. The signposting can be a little neglected in this area, however, so watch the road carefully for a turn to the right. This will bring you to a isolated monastery foundation attributed to St. Brendan the Navigator in c. 558, the same intrepid saint who is revered in County Kerry as the first discoverer of America. The saint is reputed to be buried on the grounds. This is supported by the place-name of the town, *Cluain Fearta* in the Irish language, which means "Meadow of the grave."

Other than the early grave slabs, little remains of the original foundation. The site does have a small stone church (circa. 1200), known as **St. Brendan's Cathedral** (4) (Church of Ireland), noted for its Gothic chancel and Gothic windows. The *west doorway, which is considered one of the finest specimens of Hiberno-Romanesque art in existence, is replete with columns and arches and surmounted by pilasters and a throng of carved human heads. *Open during daylight hours. Admission is free. Donations welcome.*

From this secluded place, travel one mile west to **Our Lady of Clonfert Church** (5), the local Catholic edifice. This modern structure is not significant in itself, but it houses a *statue known as *Our Lady of Clonfert* which attracts people from far and wide. It is a unique painted wooden figure of local craftsmanship dating back to the 14th century. Often referred to as the "smiling Madonna of Clonfert," it portrays the Mother of Christ in very earthly terms, with her infant child playing with her hair. It is in marked contrast to the serene and serious art of earlier times which stressed her heavenly majesty instead of human qualities. For these reasons, it is considered very significant art.

Return to R356, cross over the Shannon, and follow the signposts via Banagher and Cloghan to the benchmark of early Irish monasticism:

*CLONMACNOIS (6), near Shannonbridge, Co. Offaly, ☎ 0905-74273. *Open daily Nov. to mid-March 10–5:30; mid-March to mid-May and Sept.–Oct. 10–6; mid-May to early Sept. 9–7. Adults £3.50, seniors £2.50, students and children £1.50. Tours. Shop. Café.*

Standing somberly on the east bank along a great S-bend of the River Shannon, this sequestered site is one of Ireland's most significant ancient monuments. Founded as a monastery by St. Ciarán in 545, this settlement was one of Europe's great centers of learning for nearly 1,000 years, flourishing under the patronage of many kings, including the last High King of Ireland, Rory O'Conor, who is buried here. Great scholars were trained here and then set forth to enlighten the rest of Europe during the Dark Ages. Among the famous alumni of Clonmacnois was Alcuin, tutor to Charlemagne.

In its heyday, Clonmacnois was more than a monastery or a university—it was a virtual city, with hundreds of houses and workshops. Because it was superbly situated where the main east-west roadway of early Ireland crossed the prime north–south traffic artery—the River Shannon, Clonmacnois drew abbots, mentors, and students from all over Ireland. Like other Irish monasteries, it was burned and plundered by many forces, from the Vikings to the English; finally reduced to a complete ruin in 1552, and eventually turned over to the Irish government in 1955 to be preserved as a national monument.

Start a visit at the interpretative center which presents an 18-minute audiovisual on the history and background of the site. Guided tours are then conducted outside. Allow at least an hour to see the remains of the cathedral, eight churches, round towers, high crosses, and over 200 other monuments, including the following:

**The Cathedral**, a blend of 10th- to 15th-century architecture. The remains include an early 13th-century sacristy, part of a 12th-century Romanesque doorway that was reconstructed in the 15th century; and a 15th-century Gothic chancel. Near the high altar are the graves of Turloch Mór O'Conor (who died in 1156), King of Connacht and High King of Ireland, and his son Rory (who died in 1198), the last High King of Ireland.

**Temple Ciarán**, a small chapel going back to St. Ciarán's time, but with many later additions. It is reputed to be the burial place of St. Ciarán. In the 11th century, a collection of early Irish ecclesiastical art treasures was unearthed including the Crozier of the Abbots of Clonmacnois, now in the National Museum of Dublin.

**Cross of the Scriptures** (*Cros na Screaptra*), erected in 914, takes its name from the many Biblical scenes carved on it, including The Crucifixion, The Last Judgment, Soldiers Casting Lots, and Christ Handing the Keys to Peter.

**The South Cross**, dating back to 9th/10th centuries, is significant because it is covered with panels of interlacing vine-scrolls and other ornaments as well as a depiction of *The Crucifixion* on the west face of the shaft.

**O'Rourke's Tower**, a 12th-century round tower that rises to 62 feet. Although impressive, it is imperfect because the top was struck off by lightning in 1135.

For a totally different perspective of Irish life, turn left at the exit of Clonmacnois and follow the signs to the **\*Clonmacnois and West Offaly Railway** (7), Shannonbridge, Co. Offaly, ☎ 0905-74114, to learn about the boglands, Ireland's unique natural resource formed thousands of years ago. Stretching for miles throughout County Offaly and the neighboring countryside, the bogs are comprised mainly of decayed trees and foliage, which have decomposed over the centuries to form peat or turf, a major source of fuel for the Irish. The narrated tour follows a five-mile circular route around the Blackwater Bog, providing a first-hand look at the bog landscape and its flora and fauna. The tour provides an opportunity to watch turf being cut, stacked, dried, and transported. The tours are sponsored by Bord na Móna, the Irish government agency responsible for preserving and mining the bogs. The complex includes a visitor center that presents displays and a continuous audiovisual about the various facets of the bog as a part of Irish life including art and sculptures made from bog oak. Trains depart every hour on the hour; tours last 45 minutes. *Open April–Oct. 10–5. Adults £3.95, seniors and students £2.95, children £2.50.*

*Tours. Shop. Café.*

Take a left at the exit of the bog railway, and make a detour to Birr, less than 20 miles via R357 east and 62 south.

**\*Birr**, a tree-lined Georgian-style town beside the River Camcor at the very geographic center of Ireland, comes as a pleasant and decorative surprise after traveling through the barren boglands. The placename of Birr, derived from the Irish language *Biorra,* means "watery place." The centerpiece of the town of Birr is:

**BIRR CASTLE DEMESNE** (8), Rosse Row, Birr, Co. Offaly, ☎ 0509-20336. *Open daily 9–6. Adults £5, seniors and students £3.50, children £2.50.*

Dating back to the 17th century, this castle and estate belong to the Parsons family. The present head of the family, the 7th Earl of Rosse, represents the 14th generation to live here. Since the castle is the family home, it is private, but the 100-acre garden is open to the public. Incorporating a lake, waterfalls, and two adjacent rivers, the Birr Castle Demesne is a horticultural wonderland, containing more than 1,000 species of trees and shrubs, from magnolias and cherry trees to chestnut and weeping beech. The hornbeam alleys and box hedges are featured in the *Guinness Book of Records* as the tallest in the world. The grounds also house an astronomical exhibit, bequeathed to the estate by the 3rd Earl of Rosse, who built a six-foot reflecting telescope in 1845. It was the largest in the world at the time and remained as such for over 75 years.

In addition, the 19th-century coach house on the castle grounds houses **Ireland's Historic Science Centre**—a unique museum spotlighting Ireland's great contributions to science, from astronomy and photography to the invention of the steam turbine engine. Browse through original artifacts, photographs, drawings, letters, and learn from interactive models, audiovisuals, and interpretive displays. The galleries here show a much-underrated side of Ireland. It's a fascinating place to visit on a rainy (or a sunny) day.

The fastest route back to the main road to Galway is via main road N62 north for just over 20 miles to **Athlone**, a thriving commercial hub and the largest town on the River Shannon. Athlone is best known, however, as the birthplace of the great Irish tenor, Count John McCormack (1884–1945).

The Athlone streetscape is dominated by the high profile of **\*Athlone Castle** (9), off N6, Athlone, Co. Westmeath, ☎ 0902-92912, a sprawling stone fortress with turrets, towers, and cannons, sitting on the edge of the river. If you wish to stop and visit, it is well signposted from the main road. Built in 1210 for King John of England, this huge castle played an important part in Athlone's history, first  as the seat of the Presidents of Connacht and later as the headquarters of the Governor of Athlone during both the first Siege of Athlone in 1690 and the second in 1691. Declared a national monument in 1970, the castle is noted for its original medieval walls and authentic cannons and mortars. The interior now houses a museum and visitor center with a series of exhibits including an audiovisual presentation on the Siege of Athlone, displays on the castle itself, the town of Athlone, the flora and fauna of the River Shannon region, and a review of the life of John McCormack. *Open April–Oct., daily 9:30–6. Adults £2.60, for youth aged 12–16 £2, children to age 12 £1. Tours. Shop. Café.*

From Athlone to Galway, follow the main N6 road, a distance of approximately 55 miles. It should take about one hour and a half. If you wish to make a stop en route, almost midway is **Aughrim**, a small village with a very telling history—it was the scene of the bloodiest battle of Irish history—the Battle of Aughrim on July 12, 1691. Often referred to "The Gettysburg of Ireland," the Battle of Aughrim involved a confrontation between 45,000 soldiers from eight European countries and cost 9,000 lives.

The **\*Battle of Aughrim Interpretative Centre** (10), N6, Aughrim Village, Co. Galway, ☎ 0905-73939, invites visitors to re-live the battle via a high-tech three-dimensional audiovisual presentation and "hands-on" multi-sensory displays. A tour takes about a half-hour. Afterwards, you can go outside and walk the adjacent battlefield area which is signposted for visitors. *Open Easter–Oct. daily 10–6. Adults £3, seniors, £2, children £1. Tours. Shop. Café.*

From Aughrim, it is about 37 miles to Galway City and the completion of this tour.

**Trip 41**

# Knock

The hub of religious pilgrimage in Ireland is Knock, a small one-street town in the southeastern corner of County Mayo. Just over a century ago, Knock rarely appeared on maps. It was just a poor, famine-ravaged, and obscure area in the west of Ireland, with a short one-syllable placename, *An Cnoc,* meaning "The Hill."

All this changed suddenly on the dark and rainy night of August 21, 1879. Knock was jolted into prominence as 15 local residents told of seeing a vision of the Blessed Mother, St. Joseph, and St. John the Evangelist. At first their story was given little attention, but over the years and after several commissions of inquiry met and reviewed the case, the witnesses proved to be credible. The Catholic Church put its seal of approval on the Knock apparition in 1979 when Pope John Paul II visited the site himself. Ever since then, Knock has grown to the status of an internationally recognized shrine, ranked with Lourdes or Fatima as major places of Christian pilgrimage. Knock now draws well over 1.5 million visitors per year.

As is the case with many shrines, Knock has grown from one humble site to a major enterprise, complete with a huge basilica, folk museum, caravan and camping park, international airport, and dozens of commercial shops and vending stands. Rarely does a tour bus or car arrive in the west of Ireland without making a daytrip to Knock.

**GETTING THERE:**

From Galway, Knock is just over 50 miles north via the main N17 road, a journey of about 70 minutes. **Bus Eireann** operates daily service to Knock; travel time with intermediate stops is just over one hour and 20 minutes. For long-range travelers, Knock also has its own airport, served by daily flights from Dublin, London, and other international gateways including charter flights from US cities in the summer months.

**PRACTICALITIES:**

Knock is a very well organized place, with three large car parking areas, clearly signposted for the convenience of arriving motorists. In addition, there is free parking on the main street, on a first-come basis. No matter where you park, you will have to walk a lot outdoors at Knock to take in all of the sites.

During the main pilgrimage season, from the end of April to the middle of October, Knock is at its busiest. Expect crowds. Public ceremonies and processions normally take place during the pilgrimage season each afternoon both indoors and outdoors. There are all-night public vigils on the first Friday of each month, May–October and in December.

In addition, during the pilgrimage season, guided tours of the shrine grounds are provided, each morning and afternoon, commencing at the shrine site itself. Posters on grounds give details of daily schedules.

One of the most popular practices for people who come to Knock is to get some of the holy water to take home. The water is free for the taking, from a row of faucets along a stone wall opposite the shrine. If you wish to get some, you will need a bottle or two, unless you have brought one with you. Selling plastic bottles to visitors is almost a cottage industry at Knock. Everywhere you turn, you'll see huge containers and baskets full of bottles of every size. Prices usually start at about the equivalent of 25¢ and go up to several dollars. Many other souvenirs, from religious pictures, statues, and rosaries, to Knock-imprinted shillelaghs, tee-shirts, and teapots, are also for sale. The presence of so many vendors smacks of crass commercialism and turns many people away in disillusionment. Be prepared for the marketplace atmosphere. The popularity of Knock means big business for the locals.

It does not cost anything to tour the sites at Knock or to attend any of the processions or services, except for admission to the Folk Museum. Donations are welcome. Most sites within the Knock Shrine complex are open year-round from 8 or 9 in the morning until 6 or 7 in the evening, and often longer in the summer months.

For a complete program of events, contact the **Knock Shrine Information Centre**, Knock, ☎ 094-88100. For tourist information, contact the **Knock Tourist Office**, Knock, ☎ 094-88193, open May through September. The area code for all telephone numbers in the Knock area is 094.

### FOOD AND DRINK:

The main street of Knock is lined by cafés, pubs, and food stands. They tend to be very busy at meal times, with busloads of pilgrims. Among the better restaurants, here are four suggestions, two of which are out of town.

**An Bialann** (Main St., Belmont Hotel, Knock) Convenience is the keynote of this hotel restaurant in the heart of town, opposite the shrine grounds. The menu emphasizes steaks, roasts, and other dishes in the Irish tradition of hearty fare. ☎ 88122. £ to ££

**Cill Aodáin** (Main St., Kiltimagh, five miles north of Knock) Situated in the heart of an artisan village, this little inn is known for creative country cuisine with a Continental flair. Snacks, fresh-carved meats, and homemade soups are served for lunch in the cozy paneled bar with an open fireplace. Full dinners are available at night in the candlelit restaurant. X: Dec. 25. ☎ 81761. £ to ££

**Four Seasons** (Knock House Hotel, Ballyhaunis Rd., Knock) Set on 100 acres of parkland east of the shrine grounds, this hotel/restaurant offers a serene setting overlooking the gardens and countryside, yet it is within easy walking distance of the shrine and basilica. The menu features hearty soups and traditional Irish favorites such as roast chicken-and-ham. A smaller self-service café also operates throughout the day for snacks and fast meals. ☎ 88088. £ to ££.

**Raftery Room** (Main St., Kiltimagh, five miles north of Knock) Named after the town's legendary blind poet, this friendly tavern has an "Old Mayo" atmosphere. Soups and steaks are the specialty dishes. X: Dec. 25 and Good Friday. ☎ 81116. £££

## SUGGESTED TOUR:

From Galway, travel via the main N17 road which runs right through the center of Knock and serves as the main street of the town. Park your car, preferably in the West Bus and Car Park which makes a good starting point.

Walk straight ahead to the main street. On the right are several offices and shops including the seasonal Knock Tourist Office, and on the left is a cluster of all-purpose souvenir stands and stalls.

Cross over the main street and directly to the left is the *Church of St. John the Baptist (1) (sometimes referred to as the Church of the Apparition), the original parish church of Knock. It was here, beside the gable of the west wall that the apparition was reported to have taken place in 1879. A small glass-enclosed oratory has since been built over the site and is known as the Shrine Oratory (2). Services are held both in the church and in the oratory throughout the day; schedules are posted.

To the right of the Oratory are the Holy Water Taps (3), a stone wall of faucets which dispense holy water. The water is free and there is no limit to the quantity that you may take.

Walk to the front of the church and straight ahead is the Knock Shrine & Information Office (4), which distributes leaflets and brochures about the shrine and its events. Books about the shrine and other religious topics are for sale. Mass offerings are also accepted here.

Exit the office and to the left is a large cross known as the Calvary Shrine (5). Directly behind it is the Papal Cross (6), commemorating the visit of Pope John Paul II to Knock in 1979. To the left is Mary's Garden and the Blessed Sacrament Chapel.

Straight ahead is the centerpiece of Knock, the *Basilica of Our Lady—Queen of Ireland (7), a huge circular building, the largest church in Ireland with a capacity of 20,000 people. Of relatively recent vintage, the basilica was completed in 1979 and opened in conjunction with the Papal visit.

The architecture includes materials or furnishings from every county in Ireland. Some of Ireland's leading contemporary artists and craftspeople have contributed works to the interior including a large tapestry by Ray Carroll, a tabernacle by Patrick McElroy, and two stations of the cross by Nell and Patrick Pollen. The statues include *The Sacred Heart* by Eamon

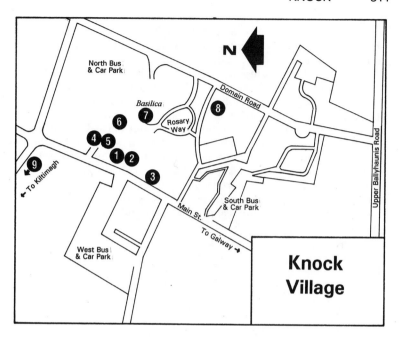

**Knock Village**

Hogan, *St. Joseph* by Imogen Stuart, *Our Lady of Knock* by Domhnall Ó Murchadha, *St. John the Evangelist* by Nuala Creagh, and *St. Columbanus* by Henry Flanagan. O.P. Services are held throughout the day; schedules are posted.

From the Basilica follow the path known as Rosary Way, cross over the small bridge, and turn left to see the **Knock Folk Museum** (8), ☎ 88100, an informative interpretative center that examines what life was like in rural Knock at the time of the 1879 apparition. It contains a wide variety of rural artifacts from the 19th and early 20th centuries, and documents relating to the apparition. The collection includes a fully furnished thatched cottage, considered a "museum within a museum," with a half-door, open fireplace, crane, and hag-bed. In addition, there is a pony and trap, currach leather boat, penny farthing bicycle, and life-size turn-of-the-century classroom, as well as an exhibit of the local crafts and trades such as shoemaker, carpenter, blacksmith, and fisherman. *Open daily May–June and Oct. 10–6, July–Aug. 10–7. Adults £2, seniors and children over age 5 £1.25.*

Depart the museum, surrounded by lovely gardens, and follow the path passing the cemeteries through the grounds back to the main street. Turn right and take some time to explore the main thoroughfare with its many shops, hostels, guesthouses, and pubs.

Return to the West Bus and Car Park to complete the tour. Before returning to Galway, take a short five-mile detour via local road R321 to

*Kiltimagh (9), a small County Mayo village in a scenic setting. The place-name comes from the Irish language, *Coillte Mach* meaning "Wood of (the) plain." It is known primarily today as an artisan village, with a collection of attractive craft shop facades rimming its central Market Square. Kiltimagh also has a literary aura as the birthplace of Anthony Raftery (1784–1835), known simply as *Rafteiri*, a blind oral poet whose works influenced William Butler Yeats, Nobel Prize winning poet, and Douglas Hyde, first president of Ireland, poet, and proponent of Irish language and traditions. The town's focal point is the **Kiltimagh Museum and Sculpture Park**, Aiden St., Kiltimagh, ☎ 81494, housed in a restored railway station and stationmaster's house, with various exhibits on the history of the area and local arts. *Open June–Sept., daily 2–6. Adults £2, children £1.*

Kiltimagh also has a restored working forge, as well as a selection of restaurants, offering a good alternative if Knock is crowded. Return on the main N17 road via Claremorris and Tuam to Galway.

# The Mansions & Museums Trail of County Roscommon

D irectly east of Galway, in the heart of the Irish midlands, lies the county of Roscommon, beside the western shores of Lough Ree and Lough Allen, the River Shannon's second- and third-largest lakes. Frequently overlooked by passing motorists heading between Ireland's east and west coasts, this area offers wooded and lakeland scenery, refreshing but not spectacular. The placename Roscommon comes from the Irish language, *Ros Comáin,* meaning "St. Comán's woods." The 8th-century saint is said to have found the area so pleasant that he build a monastery among the trees.

Unlike the rocky coastal lands of Galway and Mayo, Roscommon is adorned with relatively fertile and pastoral lands. During the 17th to 19th centuries, it proved attractive to the British aristocracy and their agents who became unpopular landlords while the Irish tenant farmers worked the land.

As a result, the Roscommon countryside is flecked with great houses and country manors, once owned by the landed gentry, the Earls and Lords of long ago. Many of the houses have been sold into private hands and a few have passed to the Irish government or local organizations to maintain as museums and testimonies of the past.

In a relatively small radius, Roscommon offers a rich legacy of Gothic, Georgian, Victorian, and Italianate architecture, as well as priceless treasures of the past—all of which help to illustrate yet another phase of Ireland's unique history.

## GETTING THERE:

By car, Roscommon town, which is the chief town of the county, is 40 miles northeast of Galway city via the main N17 and N63 roads. **Bus Eireann** provides daily service to Roscommon town, but not to the historic sites and museums throughout the county.

## PRACTICALITIES:

The only way to do this tour is by car, since some of the prime sites are not on or near public transport routes. Since each mansion or museum takes an hour or more to walk around, it is wise to pick two or three places to tour, and not try to visit all of the places along the route in one day. Each house does require walking and usually up stairs.

For information, contact the **Roscommon Tourist Office**, Harrison Hall, Main St., Roscommon, ☎ 0903-26342, open from late May to mid-September; and the **Boyle Tourist Office**, Main St., Boyle, ☎ 079-62145, open from May to early October.

There are at least four area codes for telephone numbers on this route, 078, 079, 0903, and 0907. To avoid confusion, the area code will be specified with each telephone number.

## FOOD AND DRINK:

Since County Roscommon is off the beaten tourist track, opportunities for casual lunches are not numerous. Your best bet for lunch is the on-premises café of major sites such as the Irish Famine Museum at Strokestown, King House at Boyle, and Clonalis House at Castlerea. A few other recommendations:

**Abbey** (Abbey Hotel, Galway Rd., Roscommon) The atmosphere of an 18th-century manor prevails at this restaurant on the edge of town amid private gardens. The bar menu offers soups, sandwiches and salads, while the main dining room serves full-service meals in the Irish tradition. X: Dec. 24–26. ☎ 0903-26505. £ to ££

**Lough Key Café** (Rockingham, Lough Key Forest Park, Boyle) Situated on the shores of Lough Key, this casual eatery offers snacks, sandwiches, and grilled burgers and steaks throughout the day, as well as picnic supplies. ☎ 079-62214. £

**Moylurg Inn** (The Crescent, Boyle) A favorite with the locals, this friendly pub in the heart of town offers homemade soups and sandwiches throughout the day. ☎ 079-62274. £

## SUGGESTED TOUR:

Depart **Galway** (1) on the main N17 road which leads to N63, also a main road. It should take a little over an hour to reach Roscommon, the chief town of County Roscommon and a busy market center. Follow N63 through the town, going eastward toward Ballyclare, and then make a left turn onto R371 to Strokestown.

Strokestown is an 18th- and early-19th-century village, laid out for Maurice Mahon (1738-1819), on whom the title Baron Hartland was conferred in 1800. The Mahon family had been granted these lands in the 1650s in return for their support of the English colonial campaign. To learn more about how the family lived, visit:

**STROKESTOWN PARK HOUSE** (2), Strokestown, Co. Roscommon, ☎ 078-33013. *Open Easter to Oct., daily 11–5:30. Adults £3.25, seniors and students £2.40, children £1.25. Tours. Shop. Café.*

A prime example of a gentleman farmer's country house, this huge

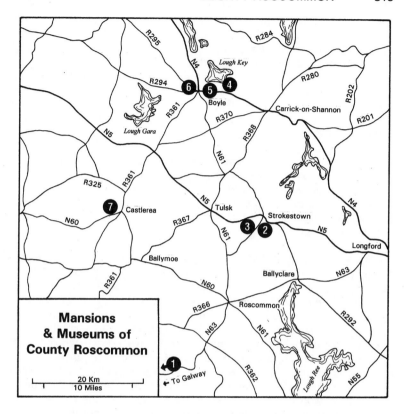

Mansions
& Museums of
County Roscommon

20 Km
10 Miles

45-room Palladian mansion was built in the 1730s for Thomas Mahon, and incorporates many parts of an earlier tower house. It is the focal point of an estate that was the seat of the Pakenham–Mahon families for over 300 years until 1979—reflecting how the landed gentry pampered themselves at the expense of the native population. The center block of the house, fully furnished as it was in earlier days, contains the private residential rooms. It is surrounded by two wings which contain the service areas, including Ireland's last galleried kitchen in the north wing, and an elaborate vaulted stable described as an "equine cathedral" in the south wing. A guided tour of the house includes all of the main reception rooms on the ground floor, the first floor bedrooms and the children's day and night nurseries and schoolroom. The galleried kitchen, now a tea room, illustrates how each day's menu was dropped to the cook from the gallery, so the lady of the house did not have to encounter the commotion of the kitchen staff.

Outside, the stable yards have been converted into one of Ireland's newest and most significant museums:

**\*IRISH FAMINE MUSEUM** (3), Strokestown, Co. Roscommon, ☎ 078-33013. *Open Easter–Oct., daily 11–5:30. Adults £3, seniors and students £2.40, children £1.25. Tours. Shop. Café.*

In contrast to the grandeur of the main house, step inside this adjacent museum to learn about one of the most far-reaching events of Irish history—the Great Potato Famine of the 1840's. Housed in the stableyards of Strokestown Park House, this museum illustrates *how* and *why* the famine started and was allowed to spread, reducing the Irish population of 8.1 million people by almost a third through death and mass emigration. The exhibits range from photographs, letters, documents, and satirical cartoons of the times to farm implements and a huge caldron that was used for soup to feed the starving people in a famine-relief program.

Leaving Strokestown, follow the main N5 road west for five miles via Tulsk, and then turn right onto N61 for 15 miles to **Boyle**, a busy market town beside the Boyle River. As you approach the town, on the right side you will see the entrance to:

**\*LOUGH KEY FOREST PARK** (4), Boyle, Co. Roscommon, ☎ 079-62363. *Open daily during daylight hours. Admission charge is £2 per car. Shop. Café.*

Spanning 840 acres along the shores of the Shannon's third-largest lake, this was originally part of an estate that belonged to the King-Stafford-Harman family, influential local landowners. In 1788, they built here a magnificent lakeside country house, known as Rockingham, which burned down in 1957. Shortly afterward, the grounds were turned over to the Irish government's Forest & Wildlife Service for public use. It has since become one of Ireland's foremost lakeside parks, comprising of mixed woodlands, with cypress groves, diverse foliage, and bog gardens with peat-loving plants. The grounds include a lake with more than a dozen islands, extensive nature walks, tree-identity trails, ancient monuments, ring forts, a central viewing tower, picnic grounds, and more.

The town of Boyle is also the setting of:

**KING HOUSE** (5), Main St., Boyle, Co. Roscommon, ☎ 079-63242. *Open April and Oct., Sat.–Sun. 10–6; May–Sept. daily 10–6. Adults £3, seniors and students £2.50, children, £2. Shop. Café.*

Built for Sir Henry King in 1730, this Palladian-style residence was considered as one of the finest town houses in rural Ireland. It is thought to have been the work of Sir Edward Lovett Pearce who also designed the Irish Parliament House on College Green, now the Bank of Ireland. Highlights include a long entrance gallery with tripartite windows and an original fireplace, plus extensive vaulted ceilings on all floors. In 1788, the family built a new and grander house, Rockingham (see above) and moved outside of town beside Lough Key, and then this building became the headquarters of the Roscommon Militia. It was occupied by the Connaught Rangers and used as a barracks until 1930. In 1989 the

Roscommon County Council began restoration work and the house was opened to the public in 1994. Displays in the various rooms reflect the house's varied history including its military usage and recent restoration. A room has been left partially restored so that visitors can see the fabric of the house. In addition, there are exhibits on the King family and families of local kings. An audiovisual, *Kings of Connaught,* uses special effects and life-size models to tell the stories.

Boyle is also the home of **Boyle Abbey** (6), Boyle, ☎ 079-62604, one of Ireland's best preserved ecclesiastical ruins. Founded in 1161 by Cistercian monks from Mellifont Abbey in Co. Louth, the abbey was a transitional creation, bridging the Romanesque and Gothic periods. This is graphically illustrated by the juxtaposition of a row of rounded arches on one side of the nave and a row of pointed arches on the other side. Although suppressed and mutilated in the 17th and 18th centuries, the Abbey still retains a remarkable framework including a church, cloisters, kitchens, sacristy, cellars, and a gatehouse which houses an interpretative center. *Open mid-June to mid-Sept. daily 9:30–6:30. Adults £1.50, seniors £1, students and children 60p.*

From Boyle, depart on local road R361 and travel southwest for 15 miles to **Castlerea**, a busy market town famous for its connections to the last high king of Ireland. Drive through the town and follow the sign-posts west on main road N60 for 2.5 miles to visit:

**\*CLONALIS HOUSE** (7), Castlerea, Co. Roscommon, ☎ 0907-20014. *Open June to mid-Sept., Tues–Sun. 11–5. Adults £3.50, seniors and students £2.50, children over age 7 £1.50. Tours. Shop. Café.*

One of Ireland's great stately houses, this is the ancestral home of the O'Conors, kings of Connacht, and home of the O'Conor Don, the direct descendant of the last high king of Ireland. Standing on land that has belonged to the O'Conors for more than 1,500 years, this house was built in 1880, a combination of Victorian, Italianate, and Queen Anne architecture, with mostly Louis XV-style furnishings. The displays include ancient portraits and documents, a rare harp said to have belonged to the legendary poet and bard Turlough O'Carolan, antique lace, horsedrawn farm machinery, and other memorabilia. The grounds, with terraced and woodland gardens, also hold the O'Conor inauguration stone, the Irish version of the Stone of Scone, the revered Scottish royal stone dating back to the 9th century.

You can now return to Roscommon town and retrace the route back to Galway. For a faster journey from Castlerea, continue west on the main N60 road, via Ballyhaunis, and then south on main road N83 via Dunmore and Tuam to the main N17 road into Galway. Allow at least an hour for the return trip.

# Galway City—
# Smart Shoppers' Tour

Galway City is the shopping capital of the west of Ireland, the prime source for quality hand-crafted Irish souvenirs, such as Galway Crystal, Royal Tara China, hand-crafted gold and silver jewelry, Connemara marble, hand-knit woolen sweaters and colorful tweeds.

In particular, the Claddagh Ring—a simple gold band shaped at the front into two hands supporting a crowned heart—is synonymous with Galway. A favorite souvenir for most visitors to the Ireland, this ring originated in Galway's Claddagh district when it was fashioned for the first time by a goldsmith named Richard Joyce in circa. 1700.

Initially, the Claddagh ring became popular as a wedding ring, a tradition that continues today although the ring is also used as a symbol of love, friendship, and loyalty. It can be obtained in silver as well as gold, and the design is also used for brooches, pendants, bracelets, earrings, charms, and even door-knockers. Although Claddagh rings are sold throughout Ireland, most visitors prefer to buy at the source from one of Galway's many jewelers or gift shops.

As Irish luck would have it, Galway is a very compact city, and some of the best shopping is virtually confined to one long narrow main thoroughfare (which changes its name five times)—known as Williamsgate Street, William Street, Shop Street, High Street, and Quay Street. And during prime shopping hours (11 a.m. to 7:30 p.m.), it is a pedestrian zone. Consequently, shopping in Galway is an easy experience, with a real "hometown" feel. Relax and stroll. It's hard to get lost. No traffic to bother you. Walking around Galway is one continuous—and very enjoyable—shopping tour.

## GETTING THERE:

Galway, the hub of Ireland's west coast, is easily reachable by car, train or bus. It is 57 miles north of Shannon Airport. Both Irish Rail and Irish Bus, which have stations in the heart of Galway City just off Eyre Square, operate daily services into and out of Galway to all parts of the west and onward to the rest of Ireland.

## GETTING AROUND:

Small and compact in layout, Galway's downtown area is best negotiated on foot. The main shopping corridor is pedestrianized during most of the day.

## PRACTICALITIES:

The best time to follow this tour is during normal shopping hours, usually 9 a.m. to 9:30 a.m. to 5:30 p.m. or 6 p.m., Monday through Saturday, except for summer when most shops stay open until 9 p.m., and also open for part of Sunday.

For visitor information at any time of year, contact the Galway Tourist Office, Victoria Place, off Eyre Square, Galway, ☎ 091-563081. The area code for all phone numbers on this tour is 091.

## FOOD AND DRINK:

**Busker Brownes** (Cross St. at Kirwan's Lane) Housed in two of Galway's oldest buildings—a slate house dating back to 1615 and a former convent, this multi-room pub offers lots of old world atmosphere in a choice of seating areas, snugs, and alcoves. Soups, sandwiches, salads, and seafood platters are served all day. Traditional Irish music is the norm but Dixieland jazz is also played as background to Sunday brunch. ☎ 569402. £ to ££

**Conlon's** (Eglinton St., just off William St.) For fresh local seafood, head to this long-established restaurant, specializing in traditional fish-and-chips or wild Corrib smoked salmon, as well as oysters, scallops, mussels, crab and lobster. ☎ 562268 £ to ££

**K.C. Blakes Brasserie** (10 Quay St.), presents a stylish setting in a 17th-century medieval stone tower house, located next to Jurys Inn opposite the Spanish Arch. The menu offers Irish dishes such as beef and Guinness stew and black pudding croquettes, as well as modern international fare (such as chicken fajitas). ☎ 561826. £ to ££

**Mocha Beans** (2 Cross St.) is one of Galway's favorite coffee houses, serving a choice of coffees and teas, from 8 a.m. to 7 p.m., plus freshly squeezed juices, open sandwiches, salads, soups, and more. ☎ 565919. £

**NetAccess Internet Café** (Olde Malte Arcade, off High Street). If you want to check your e-mail or surf the Internet amid your shopping tour, this is an ideal stop, and the coffee is "on the house." ☎ 569772. £

**Scotty's Casual Gourmet** (1 Middle St.) is a totally "No Smoking" restaurant, a rare find in Ireland. The menu, heavily influenced by the USA, offers fresh salads, deli-style sandwiches, burgers, and subs, plus heapings of accompaniments of your choice—mayo, lettuce, tomatoes, pickles, olives, peppers, onions, and more. For dessert, old fashioned ice cream sundaes are a specialty. ☎ 566400. X: Sun. £ to ££

**Seventh Heaven** (Courthouse Lane, Quay St.) is situated beside the Druid Theatre in the heart of Galway's "Left Bank"). The menu is an eclectic blend of Irish, Cajun, and Tex-Mex, offering everything from steaks, chicken, and seafood dishes, to vegetarian, pastas, and enchiladas. ☎ 563838. £ to ££

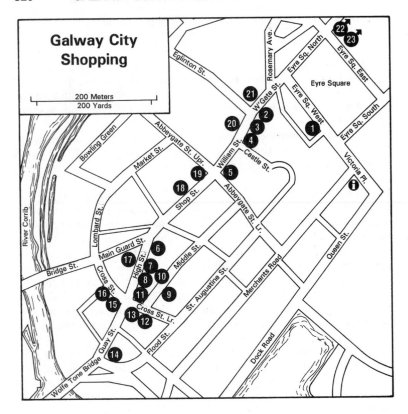

**Galway City Shopping**

200 Meters
200 Yards

## SUGGESTED TOUR:

Start this tour at the Galway Tourist Office, Victoria Place, off Eyre Square. Walk a quarter-block and you are on Eyre Square. On the left will be the entrance to the **Eyre Square Centre** (1), Eyre Square West, Galway's prime indoor shopping mall, incorporating 60 national and international shopping outlets. Part of the interior structure includes Galway's medieval town wall and several townhouses. On weekends, an antique market is held under the medieval wall. The shops, which are laid out on two levels, range from men's and women's clothing to books, candles, heraldry, jewelry, gifts, souvenirs, toys, and music. It's a great place for rainy day shopping since everything is under one skylit roof.

After exploring the shopping centre, return to Eyre Square West and walk to the corner. Make a left and you are on Williamsgate Street—formerly the main east gate into the 17th-century walled town of Galway, leading into William Street. Because it was originally only a gated area, it is a very short street and the first of the five adjoining streets that make up Galway's prime thoroughfare. The first part of our tour concentrates on the left side of this corridor, and the second half will move to the opposite side. This will save you crossing from side to side, and perhaps missing one of the highlights.

The first shop to note on the left side is just beyond Williamsgate— **Galway Camera Shop** (2), 1 William St., ☎ 565678, a good place to know if your camera is acting up. You can buy a new camera here at tax-free prices, or disposable cameras, batteries, film, or just get good advice from the knowledgeable staff. They also operate a 1-hour film processing service and a repair service.

A few doors down on left is **A. Hartmann & Son** (3), 29 William St., ☎ 562063, watchmakers and jewelers for over three generations. The Hartmann family, who began in the jewelry business in the late 1800's in Germany, brought their skills and wares to Ireland in 1895, eventually opening this Galway shop in 1942. They still enjoy a far-reaching reputation in the timepiece and goldsmithing line, and they also make Claddagh rings, and sell Celtic crosses, silverware, pens, crystal, and unusual clocks.

Next you will see the decorative blue and white Wedgewood-style façade of the **Treasure Chest** (4), 31-33 William St., ☎ 563862. For over 30 years, the Bennett family have brought a touch of class to Galway at this aptly-named store. It is a one-stop source for an amazing array of Irish products—from Waterford Crystal and Galway Crystal, to Royal Tara China and Belleek China, as well as Lladro figurines, Claddagh rings, Aran knitwear, Irish linens, and designer fashions. You also find tee-shirts, hats, stationery, leprechaun figurines, dolls, and much more on two well-stocked floors.

Continue along William Street, passing Castle Street and Arch Mews on the left, and you will come to **P. Powell & Sons** (5), 53 William St., ☎ 562295. This is a not-to-be-missed store for anyone interested in Irish traditional music. Not only will you find a wide range of CDs and cassette tapes, but you will also be able to buy your own tin whistle, flute, bodhran, accordion, or violin. Sheet music and music books are also in abundant supply.

At this point, William Street is intersected by Abbeygate Street and becomes Shop Street. Walk along the left side of Shop Street (there are several shops of interest on the right side, but we'll come to them later in the tour), passing Buttermilk Lane, one of Galway's old cobbled streets, and, as Mainguard Street intersects from the right, Shop Street changes its name to High Street.

Coming up on the left is **O'Maille** (6),16 High St., ☎ 562696. For over 60 years, the O'Maille (O'Malley) name has been synonymous with the finest Irish tweeds and fashions in the West of Ireland. The shop gained worldwide fame in the early 1950's when it outfitted the cast of the classic movie "The Quiet Man," and has done a brisk trade ever since. It is considered "the original house of style," when it comes to fashionable tweeds, knitwear, and rainwear.

The next archway is The Malt Arcade, another of Galway's charming (but hard on the shoes) old cobbled lanes. After passing the arcade, you will see **Freeney's Sports** (7), 19 High St., ☎ 568794, a good shop to know if you plan to do any fishing in the nearby Connemara lakes and rivers. This shop will supply you with fishing guide books, plus salmon and trout flies, lures, reels, and rods. There is also some lovely environmental art  and illustrations for sale.

A few paces brings you to **Kennys Bookshop and Art Galleries** (8), High St., ☎ 562739, a literary haven in the West for over 50 years. Browse for hours amid new and old books, maps, prints, engravings, and volumes about Galway history. The books are wedged on shelves and along window ledges, and piled in crates and turf baskets. The walls are lined with signed photos of more than 200 writers (including this author) whose books are stocked here and have visited the shop over the years. In addition, Kennys is famous for its antiquarian department and binding workshop. If you prefer art to books, just step toward the back and enjoy the contemporary art gallery of watercolors, oils, and sculptures by local talent. You can also enter or exit Kennys from Middle Street which runs parallel behind High Street.

As a slight detour, you may wish to visit two long-established shops on Middle Street: **Charlie Byrne** (9), Cornstore Mall, Middle St., ☎ 561766, for a large selection of used books particularly Irish literature and poetry, including review copies, discounted books, and warehouse clearance stock; and **Mulligan** (10), 5 Middle Street, ☎ 564961, offering a comprehensive selection of Irish and Scottish music, plus jazz, blues, country and folk from all over the world.

Return to High Street and continue our tour, stopping next at the **Galway Woollen Market/Mac Eocagain** (11), 21-22 High St., ☎ 562491, specializing in Aran hand-knit sweaters and designer knitwear, linen and lace, sheepskins, woollen accessories, and gifts of all types such as tee-shirts.

The next street to intersect is Cross Street, and here High Street changes its name for the last time—to Quay Street. Take a slight detour to the left and visit a unique small shop—**Galway Bead Shop** (12), 2 Lr. Cross St., ☎ 567347, displaying all types of colorful beads and buttons, plus necklaces, rings, earrings, pins, shell art, mobiles, pendants, and brooches.

Return to the corner and turn left onto Quay Street. Here you will see **Thomas Dillons** (13), Quay St., ☎ 561317, another famous Galway jeweler, associated with making and selling a wide range of Claddagh rings—Galway's legendary clasped heart ring. Founded in 1750 at another location and recently moved to Quay Street, this shop also operates a small *Claddagh Ring Museum* on its premises.

Follow Quay Street to the end and make a fast left onto Quay Lane. Here you will see **Cobwebs** (14), 7 Quay Lane, ☎ 564388, an antique shop specializing in small items, ideal as souvenirs, from estate jewelry, to nostalgic toys, from all parts of Ireland.

The remainder of this tour works its way back along the opposite side of the main pedestrian thoroughfare. Retrace your steps along Quay Street and when you come to Cross Street, turn left to see one of Galway's finest pottery artists—**Judy Greene Pottery** (15), 11 Cross St., ☎ 561753, selling handmade pottery decorated with colorful wildflowers inspired by the nearby Connemara countryside. Choose from goblets, vases, teapots, to candleholders, lamps, and jewelry. Many of the local hotels and restaurants use Judy's pottery on their tables.

Next door is another fine antique shop for small collectibles and curios—**Tempo Antiques** (16), 9 Cross St., ☎ 562282, selling jewelry, bric-a-brac, cutlery, silver and porcelain from the Victorian, Edwardian, and Art Deco periods.

Return to the corner of Cross Street and Quay Street, and turn left as Quay Street now becomes High Street. Stroll along High Street, making a stop at **Kelly's Crafts** (17), 10 High St. This shop has a fine selection of Irish craft work including hand-turned pottery, hand-woven scarves, rugs, Celtic jewelry and stationery. It's directly opposite the entrance to The Malt Arcade on the other side of the street.

Continue on High Street, passing the intersections on the left of Mainguard Street, Churchyard, Street, Churchyard Lane, and then as High Street becomes Shop Street, you will see a branch of one of Ireland's oldest leading booksellers, **Eason's** (18), 33 Shop St., ☎ 562284, established in Dublin over 110 years ago. It is a prime source of books, maps and magazines about Galway and the west of Ireland as well as foreign newspapers, postcards, and stationery, plus books on literary, historical and cultural topics.

Very shortly following is another of Galway's interesting jewelry shops—**Robert Blacoe** (19), Shop St., ☎ 568556. Unlike so many of the others jewelers which vie with each other in selling Claddagh rings, this shop has developed its own special style of ring, simply called The Galway Ring. It is a plain band with engravings showing the various phases of Galway history—these images include the City of the Tribes Crest, the Spanish Arch from whence Christopher Columbus sailed to America and the Leaping Salmon that represents the Salmon Weir Bridge. It is designed and handcrafted exclusively in the Blacoe Galway workshops, and makes a lovely souvenir of this special city.

From the left, Upr. Abbeygate Street intersects Shop Street, and our tour has now returned to William Street. The highlight on this segment of the tour is **Moons** (20), William St., ☎ 565254, Galway's long-established mid-city department store, with several floors of shopping for clothing and household items as well as an array of gifts, from Waterford and Galway crystal, to Royal Tara and Belleek china, and fine linens.

Next Eglinton Street intersects from the left, and as you cross over Eglinton, William Street now becomes Williamsgate Street. Dominating the left side of the street is **Stephen Faller Ltd.** (21), Williamsgate St., ☎ 561226, a well-known jewelry shop founded in 1879 and specializing in Claddagh rings of all sizes, shapes, and prices, most of which are made on the premises. By sure to ask for a free copy of the Faller-published booklet, *The History of the Claddagh Ring*. This large shop is run by the 4th generation of the Faller family who also offer a wide array of other types of gold and silver jewelry in Irish and Celtic designs, plus Waterford Crystal, Galway Crystal, Belleek China, Royal Tara China, and more.

Now you have come full circle, back again at Eyre Square.

Two suburban detours that you might want to consider outside the city, to be made by car, taxi, or bus, are to the leading manufacturers of Galway's most famous non-jewelry products: **Galway Irish Crystal** (22), Merlin Park, Dublin Rd., ☎ 757311, and **Royal Tara China** (23), Mervue, ☎ 751301. Both of these factories operate visitor centers (with guided tours and cafés/tearooms) and have large shops on the premises that sell seconds as well as first-quality merchandise. For full details about opening days and times for these factories, refer back to our *Galway City* chapter.

# Section VIII

# SLIGO & DONEGAL

Sligo and Donegal, Ireland's two most northwesterly counties, are off the usual geographic track for tourists. In fact, just 20% of all overseas visitors to Ireland ever get to them. To most people looking at a map, the northwest is just too far away—in mileage and time—from the usual hubs of Dublin, Killarney, Shannon, or Galway. What a pity! Without a visit to Sligo and Donegal, the Ireland experience is really not complete.

Reaching out into the North Atlantic coast, Sligo and Donegal are not only rich in scenery and natural unspoiled beauty, but they also offer heaping doses of Irish culture and tradition. Sligo, called *The Land of Heart's Desire* by the poet William Butler Yeats, is well-known as a literary beacon, while Donegal has always been at the forefront of Ireland's colorful history and traditions.

At 1,876 square miles in size, Donegal comprises the largest chunk of Ireland's northwest coast. It is not only the largest county in the province of Ulster but also the fourth-largest county in Ireland.

As big as it is, it is also a land of wide open spaces. It has a population density of only 69 people per square mile, 28th in rank among all the 32 counties. In modern parlance, it is truly the most "laid back" of all of Ireland's counties. Here you can roam the countryside and literally enjoy getting lost in the Gaelic-speaking hinterlands. Meander along dune-filled and cliff-etched seacoasts, through narrow passes and winding peninsulas, rock-strewn gaps and sheep-populated valleys, all the way to the northern-most tip of Ireland. Learn how to make Donegal tweed or parian china, step into 300-year-old thatched cottages, make a pilgrimage in the footsteps of St Patrick, discover a Picasso painting, be a surfer, or tap your feet to the sounds of Irish music.

# Sligo & Yeats Country

Alarge and lively market town wedged between Ulster and the Atlantic, Sligo is not technically a city, but it has always been the gateway to Ireland's remote northwest.

Dating back to the early Christian period, Sligo was probably founded c. 450 by Bishop Bronus, a disciple of St. Patrick. Ideally situated, Sligo sits in a valley between the two mountains of Ben Bulben and Knockarea, at the mouth of the River Garavogue, with Sligo Bay and the Atlantic on its western shores and Lough Gill to the east. The placename for Sligo is indeed fitting—from the Irish language *Sligeach,* maning "Shelly place."

Although Sligo has had its ups and downs historically like the rest of Ireland, it is literature and art that have given a distinctive character to Sligo. For many years, this town and its environs were the source of inspiration for Ireland's Nobel Prize-winning poet William Butler Yeats and his painter brother Jack. Hence Sligo's main fame has been as the hub of "Yeats Country." Visitors come from all over the world to see this little corner of Ireland that Yeats described as *The Land of Heart's Desire.*

### GETTING THERE:

A true hub of the northwest, many roads converge in Sligo. By car, you can get there via the N4 from Dublin and the east, N17 from Galway and the south, N59 from Mayo and the west, N15 from Donegal, and N16/M16 from Enniskillen and the North. **Irish Rail** operates daily service to Sligo from Dublin and other major cities, while **Bus Eireann** provides daily bus service to Sligo from Galway, Dublin, and other major cities and towns. All trains and buses arrive in downtown Sligo at the Bus/Rail Station on Lord Edward Street. Many hotels and guesthouses are within walking distance of the station.

### PRACTICALITIES:

The best way to get to know Sligo town is to walk. Park your car in one of the designated areas including two car parks within one block of the bus and rail station. Conversely, the only way to see the sights in the surrounding countryside is by car.

Sligo, which is pronounced *Sly-go,* is at its busiest each August as it hosts the **Yeats International Summer School**, a two- week gathering of students, teachers, scholars, and interested visitors from around the world. Advance reservations are needed.

For information, contact the **Sligo Tourist Office**, Temple St., Sligo, ☎ 071-61201, open all year. The area code for telephone numbers in the Sligo area is 071.

## FOOD AND DRINK:

**The Cottage** (4 Castle St.) Situated in the heart of town one block from Sligo Abbey, this homey restaurant offers breakfast all day or snacks and light meals. House specials include hot open sandwiches, quiches, chilis, pizzas, and baked potatoes with various fillings, plus Cajun entrées on weekends. Vegetarian and wholefood dishes are also featured. X: Sun. ☎ 45319. £

**Hargadon's** (4 O'Connell St.) Dating back over 130 years, this centrally located pub is a Sligo tradition, with well-preserve snugs, wooden benches, stone floors, colored glass, old barrels and bottles, and a potbelly stove. Bar food is a specialty, with emphasis on homemade soups, fresh salads, and hot meat platters, along with just-baked scones, croissants, pastries, pies, and cheese cakes. X: Sun. ☎ 70933. £

**Kate's Kitchen** (24 Market St.) If you're looking for a snack or fixings for a picnic on Lough Gill, don't miss this gourmet delicatessen. Step in and savor the aromas of fresh breads baked on the premises, plus gourmet salads, meats, cheeses, and patés. Don't pass by the Irish gourmet chocolates and preserves. X: Sun. ☎ 43022. £

**Markree Castle** (Collooney, 7 miles south of Sligo) Dating back to 1640, Sligo's only castle hotel-restaurant is nestled in a fairytale setting amid meadows, woods, and gardens reaching to the River Unsin. The formal dining room, enhanced by splendid gold-filigree plasterwork and chandeliers, offers French cuisine with fresh Irish ingredients and creative sauces. Dinner only and Sunday lunch. X: Feb. ☎ 67800. ££ to £££

**Yeats Tavern** (Drumcliffe Bridge, 4 miles north of Sligo) Named after the poet and located across the street from his grave, this pub-restaurant is a popular stop on the local circuit. The decor features Yeats memorabilia, while the menu offers snacks, sandwiches, soups, steaks, and more. ☎ 63117. £ to ££

## SUGGESTED TOUR:

A tour of Sligo comes in two parts, a walk in the town and a drive around the surrounding countryside. Start the walking phase of the tour at Sligo's **Bus and Rail Station** (1) on Lord Edward Street. Turn left and cross over to Adelaide Street. Walk one block and make a left to see Sligo's two cathedrals, both side-by-side on John Street. On the corner is the **Cathedral of the Immaculate Conception** (2), a Romanesque-style edifice dating back to 1874 and noteworthy for an interior of 69 stained-glass windows. Adjacent is the **Cathedral of St. John the Baptist** (3), a Gothic building designed in 1730 by the German architect Richard Castle. The north transept contains a brass tablet in memory of Susan Mary Yeats, mother of William Butler Yeats and Jack Yeats. She married John Butler Yeats in this church in 1863. *Hours for both cathedrals are posted outside; no admission charges.*

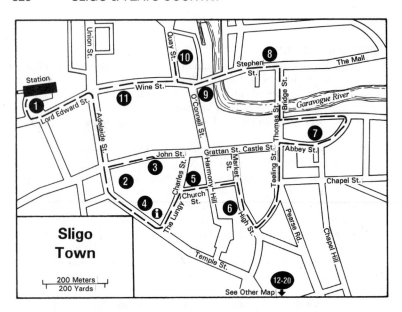

Sligo Town

200 Meters
200 Yards

    Return to Temple Street and walk one block south to the Sligo Tourist
Office, a large complex that also includes the **Hawk's Well Theatre** (4),
Temple St., ☎ 61526, a hub of theatrical activity year-round. The theater,
which derives its name from one of Yeats' one-act plays, carries on the
legacy of Sligo's great literary traditions.

    Turn left at the corner and walk one-half block to make a right onto
Church Street. Across the street is the **Sligo Presbyterian Church** (5), built
in 1828, and straight ahead is **Harmony Hill**, high ground that offers fine
views of the rest of the town. Continue for one-half block to **High Street**,
one of Sligo's oldest streets, dating from medieval times or earlier, but no
traces of its ancient buildings remain.

    Turn right here to see **The Dominican Church** (6), High Street, com-
monly known as The Friary. It is one of Sligo's most modern structures,
opened in 1973. It sits on the grounds of an early Renaissance Gothic edifice of 1845 and incorporates the apse of the older church in the rear section. *Open daily 8–6 or later. Admission is free.*

    Walk one-half block and turn left onto Old Market Street, although
nothing really remains from Sligo's old market days except the placename.
Turn left on to Teeling Street, passing the court house and post office on
the left, and then make a right turn onto Abbey Street. The focal point of
this street is \***Sligo Abbey** (7), Abbey St., ☎ 46406, Sligo's only surviving
medieval building. Built for the Dominicans in 1252, the abbey was the
burial place of the kings and princes of Sligo. It is now in ruin, but the
nave, choir, arched tower, and three-sided cloister survive. The 15th-cen-

tury altar is one of the few medieval altars still intact in Ireland. Access to the site is via a stone stairway. *Open mid-June to mid-Sept., daily 9:30–6:30. Adults £1.50, seniors £1, children, 60p. Tours.*

Turn left after the Abbey and straight ahead is the River Garavogue, which runs through the heart of the town. Turn left onto **Kennedy Parade**, named after the former US President, John F. Kennedy, who visited Ireland but not Sligo in 1963. Cross the river at Bridge Street and walk one block straight ahead.

Make a left to visit the **\*Sligo County Museum & Art Gallery** (8), Stephen Street, ☎ 42212, which displays the first editions of William Butler Yeats' complete works and his Nobel Prize for Literature (1923), as well as a collection of oils, watercolors, and drawings by Jack B. Yeats. *Open Mon.–Fri. 10:20–12:30 and 2:30–4:30. Admission is free.*

Follow Stephen Street westward, passing a statue of William Butler Yeats on the right, and then cross over the **Douglas Hyde Bridge**, named after Ireland's first president, a major figure in the Irish cultural revival at the turn of the century. Straight ahead on the left is the **\*Yeats Memorial Building** (9), Hyde Bridge at O'Connell St., ☎ 45847, to see an extensive collection of Yeats memorabilia. **Open June–Aug., Mon.–Fri. 2-5. Admission is free.**

Walk one block along **Wine Street**, named after the wine vaults that once stood here, and turn right on **Quay Street** to see the facade of **Town Hall** (10), dating from 1865 and a fine example of Italian Renaissance style. On this site in 1245, a castle was built by the Anglo-Norman leader, Maurice Fitzgerald, signaling the official birth of Sligo as a town. In 1995, the 750th anniversary of Sligo Castle was celebrated, although no trace of the building remains.

Retrace your steps to Wine Street, and on the left is **Wesley Chapel** (11), Wine Street, ☎ 42346, dating back to 1832. It replaced an earlier site begun by the Methodists in Sligo in 1775. It is said that the founder of Methodism found fertile ground in Sligo and visited 14 times between 1758 and 1789. *Opening times are posted outside. Admission is free; donations welcome.*

Straight ahead is Lord Edward Street and the completion of the walking phase of the tour. The rest of the route (map on page 000) requires a car. From the bus and train station, drive south on Adelaide and Temple Streets to the main road, also known as Pearse Road. Proceed approximately one mile south of **Sligo** (12) and make a left at the sign for the **\*Lough Gill Drive**, a 26-mile route east of town that encircles **Lough Gill**, the beautiful lake that figured prominently in Yeats' writings. Like Sligo town itself, Lough Gill is also well named. The placename comes from the Irish language, *Loch Gile*, meaning "Lake of brightness." It is a constant and unspoiled panorama of silvery blue waters, encircled by wooded hills and lush foliage.

Drive the 26-mile route in a counter-clockwise direction, with the lake always at your left. Signposted highlights include **Dooney Rock** (13),

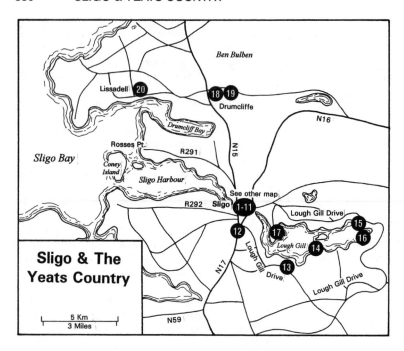

with its own nature trail and lakeside walk (inspiration for Yeats' poem *Fiddler of Dooney*); and the **Lake Isle of Innisfree** (14), one of the lake's 22 islands. The poem of the same name is one of Yeats' most famous works, almost becoming an anthem for Sligo.

As the road swings to the east and north sides of the lake, you are temporarily in County Leitrim. Stop at **Parke's Castle** (15), Fivemile Bourne, ☎ 64149, a fine example of a 17th-century fortified manor house. Named after the English family who gained possession of the land during the 1620 plantation of Leitrim, the castle was recently restored with an Irish oak interior showing great craftsmanship. Distinctive features include a diamond-shaped chimney, mullioned windows, parapets, and a courtyard that pre-dates the castle. The visitor center presents an audiovisual on the history and restoration of the building, *Stone by Stone,* plus a series of colorful exhibits. *Open April–May, Tues.–Sun. 10–5; June–Sept. daily 9:30–6:30; Oct. daily 10–5. Adults £2, seniors £1.50, children £1. Tours. Shop. Café.*

Although Parke's Castle itself has little connection to Yeats, the castle's dock is the boarding point for a one-hour narrated boat cruise on Lough Gill including close-up views of the Isle of Innisfree. Boat captain George McGoldrick will even recite the poem or sing the song that uses Yeats' words. For information on exact departure times, contact **Wild Rose**

**Waterbus** (16), ☎ 64266. *Open April–May and Oct., Sun. 12:30–5:30; mid-June–Sept. daily 12:30–6:30. Adults £5, children £2. Tours. Café.*

The next point of interest is **Hazelwood Forest** (17), signposted to the left off the road. The grounds include the Hazelwood Sculpture Trail, a forest walk along the lake with 13 sculptures carved out of local wood by Irish and international artists. Created in 1985–87, it was the first permanent sculpture trail in Ireland.

The road now wends its way back into Sligo. Turn right and continue along the main N15 in a northward direction for four miles. Soon the unmistakable loaf-like profile of *Ben Bulben mountain comes into view on the right (1,730 feet). One of Ireland's most famous mountains, Ben Bulben is featured prominently in Yeats' writings. As he requested, the poet is buried at the foot of the mountain in **Drumcliffe Churchyard** (18). A simple stone marks the grave of William Butler Yeats (1865–1939), who wrote his own dreary if poetic epitaph: *Cast a cold eye on life, on death; horseman, pass by.* He is buried with his wife, George. *Open during daylight hours. No admission charge.*

The church on the grounds, a former Church of Ireland edifice, has been turned into the **Drumcliffe Visitors Centre** (19), ☎ 44956, with a permanent exhibit that outlines the history of the church and the surrounding area before it became synonymous with Yeats. The interactive displays go back to 574 when St. Columcille founded a monastery here. An audiovisual traces the history of a battle that took place in the middle of the 6th century on the banks of the Drumcliffe River between the High King of Ireland and leaders of the O'Neill clan. *Open Mon.–Fri. 8:30–6, Sat. 10–6, Sun. 1–6. Adults £1.75, seniors £1.25, children £1. Shop. Café.*

Continue on the main road for four more miles to **Lissadell House** (20), Drumcliffe, ☎ 63150, a fine example of a large 19th-century home in the Grecian Revival style. The focal point of the house is a two-story hallway lined with Doric columns leading to a double staircase of Kilkenny marble. A favorite country retreat for Yeats, the house was owned by his friends, the Gore-Booth family. The decor and layout reflects the varied dimensions of the family interests. Eva was a distinguished poet and book collector, Sir Josslyn was a keen horticulturist who planted the grounds, and Constance was a political activist who took part in Ireland's 1916 Easter Rising. She was the first woman ever elected a member of the British Parliament, but took a seat instead in the newly formed Irish Parliament and was the Minister for Labor in the first Irish government. She married Count Markievicz, a Polish nobleman whose larger-than-life-sized portrait paintings line the walls of the Lissadell dining room. *Open June to mid-Sept., Mon.–Sat. 10:30–12:30 and 2–4:30. Adults £3, children £1. Tours.*

From Lissadell, retrace your route to the main N15 road and turn right to return to Sligo or turn left to continue on toward Donegal or the other northern parts of Ireland.

# Trip 45

# From Sligo Bay to Killala Bay

Looking for something different? And off the beaten path? Go west, as the old adage recommends. It is good advice in this corner of Ireland.

West of Sligo town, the Ox Mountains form a splendid backdrop beside Sligo Bay along a coastal route that wends its way as far as Killala Bay before it heads toward the Atlantic. It is a route that few tourists follow, undoubtedly because it is hard to define. It is partly in County Sligo and partly in County Mayo.

For most itineraries, this Sligo/Mayo combination is "out of the way." It runs against the normal flow of traffic from Sligo to Donegal or Sligo to Dublin or Sligo to Galway. Yet, with Sligo as a base, this daytrip is well worth doing.

Historically, the area has been drawing people for many centuries. Carrowmore, the largest cemetery of Megalithic remains in Ireland, is on this route, as is Céide Fields, said to be the most extensive Stone Age monument in the world. This area also came close to changing Irish history. In August of 1798 France's General Humbert landed at Killala with one thousand men in an unsuccessful attempt to lead the United Irishmen in a full-scale rebellion against the British. In recent years, American writer Thomas Flanagan used the incident as the focal point for his successful book and film set in this corner of Ireland, *The Year of the French*.

Most of all, the Sligo-Mayo tour is a beautiful drive, an ever-changing route of beaches and bays, lakes and rivers, hillsides and mountains.

## GETTING THERE:

It's very simple. From Sligo, drive west via main road N59. For variety, use N17 for the return trip to Sligo. Total mileage for this tour is just over 100 miles, depending on detours.

## PRACTICALITIES:

The only way to follow this tour is by car. The driving is relatively easy, on main roads or well-kept secondary roads. Some of the attractions, such as Céide Fields or Foxford Woollen Mills need one to two hours of time to explore fully, usually longer. Outdoor attractions, such as Carrowmore or Downpatrick Head, require strong and waterproof footwear.

This tour covers parts of two counties, Sligo and Mayo. For information, contact the **Sligo Tourist Office**, Temple St., Sligo, ☎ 071-61201, open all year; or the **Ballina Tourist Office**, Cathedral Rd., Ballina, ☎ 096-70848, open from April to early October. Three area codes are used for telephone numbers in this area, 071,094, and 096. To avoid confusion, the area code will be listed with each number.

## FOOD AND DRINK:

**Enniscoe House** (Castlehill, Crossmolina) Overlooking Lough Conn, this Georgian-style country inn offers an elegant yet relaxed setting, with antiques, family heirlooms, and open fireplaces. The menu changes daily, but usually features fresh local salmon and other fish caught from the adjacent waters of the Cloonamoyne Fishery. Organically-grown vegetables and herbs come from the garden outside. Dinner only. X: mid-Oct. to March. ☎ 096-31112. ££ to £££

**Gaughans** (O'Rahilly St., Ballina) Located in the heart of town just over a block from the River Moy, this cozy enclave has all the trappings of a traditional pub including a pipe smokers' corner. It's a popular spot for bar food lunches, offering homemade soups, sandwiches, and a selection of hot dishes. ☎ 096-21151. £

**Old Mill** (St. Joseph's Pl., Foxford) Nestled on the mezzanine level overlooking all the comings-and-goings of the Foxford Woollen Mills, this skylit self-service restaurant is an attraction in itself. The long buffet counter offers a wide array of freshly prepared items, from soups, salads, and sandwiches, to hot casseroles, sausage rolls, quiches, muffins, and scones. ☎ 094-56756. £

**The Thatch** (Dublin Rd., Ballysadare, 5 miles south of Sligo) As its name proclaims, this pub is laid out in the format of a traditional thatched cottage, dating back to 1638 and originally a coaching inn. Sit by the fireside and enjoy hearty soups or sandwiches at any time of day or stop by in the evening and hear some traditional music. ☎ 071-67288. £

## SUGGESTED TOUR:

Depart from **Sligo** (1) on the main N4 road for two miles and then take a right at the sign for Strandhill. Follow this road for about three miles to *Strandhill, a small seaside village with a dune-filled sandy beach on Sligo Bay. The placename of Strandhill comes from the Irish language *An Leathros*, meaning "the half-headland." Directly offshore to the right is **Coney Island**, a tiny island that is accessible by land at low tide. It is said to have given its name to the popular New York beach amusement area, but surprisingly, not much is known about the origin of the name.

Strandhill sits at the foot of *Knocknarea Mountain, rising to a height of 1,083 feet. If you are fit for mountain climbing, a sign-posted walk starts here. The route leads to a gigantic cairn or gravesite, known as *Miscaun Meadhbh* (Maeve's Mound), 200 feet in diameter and 34 feet high. It is traditionally considered as the resting place of an Irish queen who reigned in the first century BC. From the summit, there are panoramic views of Sligo and Sligo Bay.

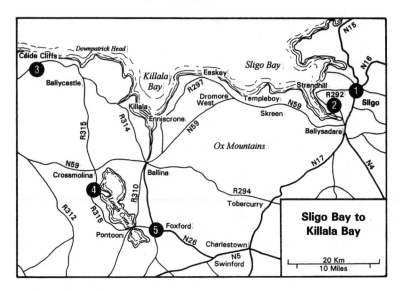

The road along the beach curves back inland. For a look at one of Sligo's oldest treasures in the area, follow the sign-posts to **Carrowmore Megalithic Cemetery** (2), Carrowmore, Sligo, ☎ 071-61534, considered the largest cemetery of its kind in Ireland and one of the largest in Europe. Spread over an area 1.5 miles long and a half-mile wide, it contains over 60 tombs, dolmens, small passage graves, and stone circles. Archaeologists claim that some of the graves are at least 700 years older than those at Newgrange. For background information, a restored cottage at the site houses a small exhibition and slide show. *Open May–Sept., daily 9:30–6:30. Adults £1.50, seniors £1, students or children 60p. Tours.*

Just off the main N4 road is **Ballysadare**, a small village at the mouth of the Owenmore River. Its lyrical-sounding name comes from the Irish language, *Baile Easa Dara,* which means "homestead of the waterfall of the oak." William Butler Yeats drew inspiration from this site to write his lovely poem and song, *Down by the Sally Gardens.*

As N4 road turns left, take a right onto the main N59 road. The next 30 miles present an ever-changing selection of views, with Sligo Bay to the right and the **Ox Mountains** to the left. Estimated to be six hundred million years old, the Ox Mountains, also known as Slieve Gamph, comprise the oldest range of mountains in Sligo.

After traveling 10 miles, you will come to **Skreen**, a small hamlet that derives its placename from the Irish language, *An Scrín,* meaning "the shrine." St. Columba founded an early monastery here, known as *Scrín Adhamhnáin* (Shrine of St. Adhamhnán), because the relics of St. Eunan (*Adhamhnán*), pronounced *Awnawn,* were deposited here. To the left is

Knockachree Mountain, rising to 1,766 feet, beside Loch Achree, referred to as Ireland's youngest lake since it was formed in 1490 as a result of an earthquake.

The route continues via Templeboy and Dromore West, two small villages. Make a right at Dromore West onto local road R297 to visit **Easkey**, a small seaside village whose name translates from the Irish language, *Iascaigh*, meaning "abounding with fish." Today it is not only a favorite spot for fishermen but for surfers as well. The next ten miles of road, hugging the coast as the waters of Sligo Bay meet Killaha Bay, are particularly rich in coastal scenery. Next is **Enniscrone** (sometimes spelled Inniscrone), a popular seaside resort with a long and sandy beach, huge dunes, and sea water baths. It is also a haven for surfers. The explanation of this placename varies but it is usually taken to mean "riverside land." Although it overlooks Killala Bay, it is also positioned at the start of the estuary of the River Moy.

Follow the road R297 for eight miles, as County Sligo meets County Mayo, until it joins the main N59 road and turns into Ballina. **Ballina**, the largest town in County Mayo, sits beside River Moy and is synonymous with salmon and trout fishing. The placename is derived from the Irish language, *Béal an Átha*, meaning "(place at the) mouth of the ford." Ballina is the birthplace of Mary Robinson, the first woman president of Ireland, elected in 1990.

From Ballina, follow local road R314 north for eight miles to **Killala**, a small town on the west shore of Killala Bay. The placename, taken from the Irish language, *Cill Ala*, meaning the "Church of St. Ala," refers to a foundation dating back to the 5th century at the time of St. Patrick. It was at this tiny port in August of 1798 that General Humbert of France landed with 1,000 men to help the United Irishmen, under patriot Wolfe Tone, in their quest for freedom from English rule. Although Humbert took Killala and Ballina, his efforts eventually met defeat as they marched farther south. Killala's moment of glory is chronicled in Thomas Flanagan's *Year of the French*, a book and movie.

As you travel along R314, notice the series of sculptures along the roadside. These are part of the North Mayo Sculpture Trail, created by Irish and international artists, to illustrate their impressions of the local landscape and folklore.

From Killala, you can stay on the main R314 road westward. Alternately, for a scenic seacoastal drive on a minor road, take a detour by following sign-posts to the right, for seven miles west of Killala, to ***Downpatrick Head**, a scenic cliff rising to 125 feet above Killala Bay, providing panoramic views in all directions. The ruins of a church and holy well attributed to St. Patrick are here, giving the area its name. Straight ahead is *Dún Briste*, a fragment of a cliff broken off during some natural cataclysm and now isolated at sea.

Return to the R314 road and continue westward to **Ballycastle**, a small resort village nine miles west of Killala. It takes its name from the Irish

*Baile an Chaisil,* meaning "homestead of the stone fort." This name is appropriate because the town is surrounded by stone forts and court-tombs dating from the Neolithic Period.

Five miles west of Ballycastle, the R314 road runs close to the edge of **\*Céide Cliffs**, offering spectacular coastal views, comparable to the Cliffs of Moher and often deemed more stunning and expansive. It is also the home of one of Ireland's oldest developments, rated as the most extensive Stone Age site in the world:

**\*CÉIDE FIELDS** (3), Ballycastle, Co. Mayo, ☎ 096-43325. *Open daily mid-March to May, 10–5; June–Sept., 9:30–6:30; Oct., 10–5; Nov., 10–4:30. Adults £2.50, seniors £1.75, children £1. Tours. Shop. Café.*

Preserved in a blanket of bog, this 5,000-year-old farm is believed to pre-date the pyramids of Egypt and Stonehenge of Britain. It consists of a 2,500-acre parcel of land that was once a thriving village in the Stone Age (3500 to 3000 BC). It has been unearthed from the bog, to show stone walls, rectangular fields, tombs, houses, hearthsides, pottery, and tools. Start a tour in the visitor center, an attraction it itself in this remote area. It is a pyramid-shaped building, made partly of limestone and partly of peat, with a glazed lantern apex. Step inside and watch a 20-minute audiovisual that presents valuable archaeological background in laymen's terms. Exhibits also provide helpful insight into the geology, botany, and wildlife of the region, as well as shedding light on the level and nature of the social organization of this ancient civilization. Walking tours outside are then conducted on the site at regular intervals by well-versed guides. Note: Céide is pronounced *Kayd-ja.*

At this point, retrace your route eastward on R314 to Ballycastle. Turn fight onto R315 for 15 miles south to **Crossmolina**, a small town on the River Deel. The placename is derived from *Crois Mhaoilíona,* meaning simply "Mhaoiltíona's cross," a reference to an early saint. Bear right on local road R315 which rims Lough Conn, one of Ireland's premier lakes for brown trout fishing.

Two miles south of the village is the **North Mayo Heritage Centre** (4), Enniscoe, Castlehill, Crossmolina, ☎ 096-31809, an ideal place to learn about the local area. Housed in a former stableyard, the center presents a collection of old household furnishings and memorabilia, pictures and artifacts, plus farm machinery and tools including a gowl-gob, a spade-like implement exclusive to this part of Mayo. Volunteers also provide regular demonstrations of traditional crafts. Adjacent is a genealogical research center, for those with County Mayo roots. *Open Jan.–May and Oct.–Dec., Mon.–Fri. 9–4; June–Sept., Mon.–Fri. 9–4, Sat.–Sun. 2–4. Admission: Adults £3, seniors, students and children £1.*

From here proceed southward on R315 for about five miles, the road is particularly scenic, with constant views of Lough Conn to the left. At Pontoon, a leading salmon and trout fishing center, take a left and travel about three miles to Foxford, to see one of Ireland's oldest craft centers:

**\*FOXFORD WOOLLEN MILLS** (5), St. Joseph's Place, Foxford, Co. Mayo, ☎ 094-56756. *Open daily April–Oct., Mon.–Sat. 10–5:30 and Sun. noon–5:30; Nov.–April, Mon.–Sat. 10–5:30, Sun. 2–5:30. Adults £3.50, seniors, students, and children £2.50. Tours. Shop. Café.*

Founded in 1892 by a local nun, Mother Agnes Morrogh-Bernard, to provide work for a community ravaged by the effects of the Irish Famine, these mills have brought prosperity to the area. At the same time, the Foxford label—on colorful blankets, rugs, and tweed clothing—has become a benchmark of fine woolen fabrics throughout the world. A visit starts with a walk-through audiovisual with life-like figures recounting the history of the town and nun's trail-blazing efforts, rare for this part of Ireland and even rarer for a woman 100 years ago. Afterwards, visitors are welcome to take a "hands-on" tour of the mills and watch the weaving process. The layout also includes an art gallery exhibit of the work of local artists. Tours depart every 20 minutes.

From Foxford, travel 10 miles south on N26 to join the main N17, driving north and east. Enroute, with the Ox Mountains on the left, you will pass through several noteworthy market towns including Swinford and Charlestown, both in County Mayo, and Tobercurry and Coolloney in County Sligo. Return to Sligo town or continue to other parts of Ireland.

# Donegal Town

Tweed is the lifeblood of Donegal Town. No one knows exactly when the industry originated, but one thing is certain—the weaving of beautiful hand-woven tweed has put Donegal Town on the map. Although beautiful tweeds are produced all over the county, the most famous name in tweed production is Magee, located in the heart of Donegal Town since 1866. And once people come here for the tweed, they find many other reasons to be glad they have made the long journey.

And it is a long journey. Sitting on a sheltered curve of land where Donegal Bay meets the River Eske, Donegal Town is the most remote of Ireland's major towns—almost 140 miles out of Dublin and nearly 180 miles from Shannon. Remote, yes, but not isolated or deserted. Donegal has always drawn people up to Ireland's northwest coast, no matter how long or difficult the journey.

Even the Vikings found their way to Donegal, establishing a fort in the 9th century. The area then was known as *Tír Conaill,* meaning "The land of Conall," an ancestor of the O'Donnells, powerful Gaelic chieftains. In time, the native Irish described the Viking fort as *Dún na nGall,* meaning "Fort of the foreigners." And hence the placename of Donegal evolved.

In the 15th century, the O'Donnells, led by Red Hugh O'Donnell, built a Norman-style castle on the site of the original Viking fort. With his wife, Nuala, Red Hugh is also credited with erecting a monastery in 1474 on the banks of the river for use by the Franciscan friars. Known as Donegal Abbey, the monastery prospered as a scholarly hub for over 150 years. One of Ireland's most important records of history, *The Annals of the Four Masters,* was conceived and written here.

Like other parts of Ireland, Donegal also felt the domination of the English. After the Battle of Kinsale in 1607, when the O'Donnells and other Irish chieftains were forced to leave Ireland during the Flight of the Earls, the O'Donnell territory of Donegal was granted to Sir Basil Brooke. He laid out the town as it exists today, with a central square or "Diamond," and expanded the castle by adding a Jacobean-style wing.

During the subsequent Famine years and other times of economic hardship, Donegal has survived, thanks to the tweed industry. Whether produced in the homes or in factories, the tweeds of Donegal are part of a great tradition. It's a tradition that melds old ways into everyday life. So, come to Donegal for the tweed—and while you are here, enjoy a rich heritage of other crafts, plus music and song as well.

## GETTING THERE:

By car, Donegal can be reached from points south or north via main road N15. **Bus Eireann** provides daily service from Sligo, Dublin, Derry, and other major cities. From Sligo, it's an easy 70-minute bus trip to Donegal Town. There is no bus station in Donegal, so buses stop on The Diamond, in front of Donegal's two main hotels, the Hyland Central or The Abbey.

## PRACTICALITIES:

Donegal is small and compact, composed of a central square, called The Diamond, and less than a half-dozen streets. There is no local transport system, but distances are not great, so the best way to see the sights is on foot. Park your car at a designated parking area along The Quay and walk.

In the summer months, a delightful way to see the environs of the town is to take a 90-minute cruise aboard the **Donegal Bay Waterbus**, The Quay, ☎ 23666. The glass-enclosed 60-passenger boat passes 20 points of interest on the route. Departure times, which vary with the tides, are posted at the dock; tickets can be purchased at the dockside office.

For information, contact the **Donegal Tourist Office**, The Quay, Donegal, ☎ 073-21148, open all year. The area code for telephone numbers in Donegal is 073.

## FOOD AND DRINK:

**The Blueberry Tea Room** (Castle St.) Overlooking The Diamond, this cozy upstairs restaurant is the perfect spot for a proper afternoon tea, as well as a cappucino or espresso. Light meals are also served throughout the day and evening. ☎ 22933. £ to ££

**The Harbour** (Quay St.) This popular restaurant offers views overlooking the water and a seafood menu, as well as steaks and pizzas. House specialty is baked potatoes filled with a choice of stuffings. ☎ 21702. £ to ££

**Just Williams** (Hyland Central Hotel, The Diamond) Fast service, combined with a cornucopia of freshly prepared foods is the secret of success for this brasserie-style restaurant. The menu offers soups, salads, sandwiches, meats carved-to-order, and all sorts of pastries, pies, and sweet treats. ☎ 21027. £ to ££

**Olde Castle** (Castle St.) Situated across from Donegal Castle, this rustic restaurant specializes in traditional Irish dishes such as bacon and cabbage, stuffed turkey and ham, as well as steaks and international fare. Bar meals are available all day in the downstairs pub and full meals upstairs in the evening. ☎ 21062. £ to ££

**Schooner Inn** (Upr. Main St.) Although noted for its evening traditional music sessions, this pub is also a good spot for a snack at any time of day. Soups, sandwiches, and hot dishes are available in a nautical setting of model ships and seafaring memorabilia. ☎ 21671. £

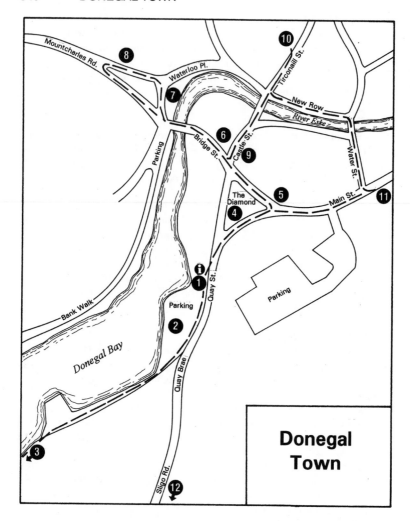

## SUGGESTED TOUR:

Since there is no train or bus depot, start a tour at the **Donegal Tourist Office** (1) on The Quay, beside the **\*River Eske**. From here, take a right turn and walk along **The Quay**. On the right is **The Anchor** (2), a 15-foot, one-ton Napoleonic anchor manufactured in France. Local lore says that it belonged to the French frigate, the *Romaine,* which was part of a squadron that came in 1798 to join the Irish in battling the English *(see From Sligo Bay to Killala Bay).* When the French-Irish forces met with defeat, the *Romaine* left behind its anchor in the waters of Donegal Bay and hastened back to France. The anchor was brought to Donegal Town in 1951 and put on display in its present position.

One-quarter mile down river are the remains of **Donegal Abbey** (3), otherwise known as the Friary of Donegal. It was founded in 1474 by one of the great Gaelic chieftains of the area, Red Hugh O'Donnell and his wife Nuala, who invited the Franciscans to take up residence. In time, great gatherings of clergy and lay leaders assembled here, at this peaceful spot beside the river. It was from this friary that four scholars—Michael and Peregrine O'Clery, Peregrine Duignan, and Fearfeasa O'Mulconry, undertook to salvage old Gaelic manuscripts and compile *The Annals of the Four Masters,* now recognized as the most comprehensive early history of Ireland. It took them four years to write the book (1632–36), a year-by-year narrative that goes back to the time of Noah's grandmother and chronicles the events until 1616. Judged of utmost importance in documenting Ireland's Celtic heritage, the *Annals* are housed today in the National Library in Dublin. Unfortunately, little remains of the abbey's great stone structure except part of a church and a cloister arcade. *The ruins are accessible at all times; no admission charge.*

From the Abbey, turn left and retrace your steps along The Quay, past the tourist office, for one-half block to **The Diamond**, the triangle-shaped centerpiece of Donegal Town. Part of the town plan laid out by Sir Basil Brooke in the early 17th century, The Diamond was originally designed as a market square for livestock and produce. No trace of the market house or market yard remain. It was redeveloped in the spring of 1993 as a pedestrian area. Around The Diamond today are three- and four-story shops, hotels, and private houses, built of local sandstone.

The most significant monument on The Diamond is the **Four Masters Memorial Obelisk** (4), a 25-foot-high red granite structure of Irish Romanesque style. It was erected in 1937 to honor the men from Donegal Abbey who wrote *The Annals of the Four Masters.* Their names are inscribed on the obelisk in the Irish language.

On the opposite side is **Magee of Donegal** (5), The Diamond, ☎ 22660. Established in 1866, the Magee name is synonymous with Donegal tweed. In the time-honored tradition, most of the tweeds are woven by hand in the homes of the weavers and are assembled at a factory two blocks away (not open to the public), but a weaver gives demonstrations of the craft in this large shop (June to September). Browse amid the racks of colorful tweeds and get a feel for the diversity of color, texture, and style of Donegal tweeds. Here's a little local trivia: the famous novelist James Joyce, while still a struggling writer living in Italy, acted as a sales agent for Magee. *Open Mon.–Sat. 9–6; extended hours in summer. Admission is free.*

Take a left to Bridge Street and straight ahead is the town's major focal point:

**\*DONEGAL CASTLE** (6), Castle Street, ☎ 22405. *Open mid-June to mid-Sept., daily 10–6:30. Adults £3, seniors £2, children £1.25. Tours.*

Once the stronghold of Irish chieftains, later the seat of an English overlord, and now a national monument, this castle is Donegal's centerpiece, recently restored and opened to the public in 1996 after a century of neglect and eight years of restoration. It was built c. 1470 in the format of a tower house by Red Hugh O'Donnell, head of a powerful Donegal clan. In the early 17th century, during the Plantation era, it came into the possession of Sir Basil Brooke, who added an extension of ten gables and mullioned windows in the Jacobean style. Most of the restoration work focused on the painstaking repair of the original stonework and windows. The castle is furnished inside with authentic period pieces—from Persian rugs and French tapestries to boars' heads and stuffed pheasants, as well as informative display panels that chronicle the history of the structure.

From the castle's front gates, take a right turn onto **Bridge Street**. Follow the street across the river to see two of Donegal's old churches. On the right is the **Methodist Church** (7), Waterloo Place, ☎ 21825, more than a century old; and also on the right one block farther west is the **Presbyterian Church** (8), Meetinghouse St., ☎ 21113, founded in 1824. *Opening hours as posted; no admission charges.*

While on the west bank of the river, you may wish to take a slight detour. Follow the sign on Mountcharles Road for *Bank Walk, a pleasant 1.5-mile walk along the River Eske as it empties into Donegal Bay. From this side of the river, you can enjoy sweeping views of the town, Donegal Abbey, and Donegal Bay.

Return to Mountcharles Road, cross back over the bridge onto Bridge Street, passing the castle and continuing in a northward direction. On the right side, opposite the castle entrance, is the **Church of Ireland** (9), Castle Street, ☎ 21075, notable for its tall spire and facade of hand-cut stone. It was built in 1828 and completed in its present form in 1890 when the chancel and vestry were added. *Open hours are posted outside; no admission charge.*

Continue as Castle Street becomes **Tirconnail Street** (sometimes spelled Tyrconnell). Straight ahead on the left is the **Donegal Railway Heritage Centre** (10), Tirconnail St., ☎ 22655. Housed in the town's Old Station House, this museum focuses on local railroad history, going back to the days when narrow-gauge railways connected Donegal Town to many other parts of the county, for transporting animals, produce, and people. Although the system closed in 1959, members of the South Donegal Railway Restoration Society are currently restoring old cars and a steam locomotive in the hope of providing a segment of narrow-gauge service as a tourist attraction. The displays include a continuous video showing, photo archive, facsimile posters, artifacts, old tickets, and more. *Open June–Sept., Mon.–Sat. 10–5, Sun. 2–5; Oct.–May, Mon.–Fri. 10–4. Adults £1.50, seniors and children aged 5–15 75p, under age 5 free. Shop.*

From Tirconnail St., turn right onto New Row, following the river, and then right again on Water Street. Water Street leads to Donegal's prime

thoroughfare, **Main Street**. To the left, on a hillside, is *St. Patrick's Church
of the Four Masters** (11), Upr. Main St., ☎ 21026. Designed to commemorate the four scholars who wrote the *Annals of the Four Masters* at
Donegal Abbey, this church was built in 1935, in an ornate Irish
Romanesque style, with a distinctive facade of local Barnesmore red granite. *Open daily 8–6 or later. Admission is free.*

From the front entrance of the church, turn left and walk the length
of Main Street, a continuous row of colorful shopfronts, restaurants, and
pubs, many of which offer traditional music at night. Main Street brings
you back to The Diamond and The Quay, to complete the walking tour.

One final segment of the tour requires a car. Drive one mile south of
town to see a wide range of crafts for which Donegal is famous:

*DONEGAL CRAFT VILLAGE** (12), Ballyshannon Rd., ☎ 23312. *Open
Mon.–Sat. 9–6, Sun.. 11–6. Admission is free. Shop. Café.*

Housed in a small cluster of cottage-style buildings surrounding a
central courtyard, this craft-producing complex reconstitutes the true
atmosphere and creative environment of Donegal's cottage industries.
Walk from cottage to cottage, and watch as an ever-changing group of
young artisans practice traditional and modern crafts—ranging from
porcelain and ceramics to hand-weaving, batik, crystal, jewelry, metal-
work, and visual art. You can browse and learn, or buy directly from the
craftspeople.

To complete the tour, return to Donegal Town or continue on to
other parts of Ireland.

**Trip 47**

# Along Donegal Bay

D onegal Bay is the surfing capital of Ireland. Did we say surfing? Yes! Surprising as it may seem, this beautiful bay is synonymous with surf, thanks to its wide sandy beaches and formidable waves roaring in off the Atlantic. Even the World Surfing Championships have been held here.

Galway Bay may have its sunsets, Bantry Bay its palm trees, Clew Bay its islands, but Donegal Bay has its churning foam-rimmed waters. Each year thousands of visitors come and suit up, to ride the waves into Rossnowlagh, Bundoran, and other Donegal Bay beaches. These waters are also among the clearest and most unpolluted in Ireland—award-winning European Blue Flag status.

The best part about Donegal Bay is that it has a lot to offer over and above the surf. Rimmed by cliffs and mountains, Donegal Bay is home to a diverse collection of resorts and fishing ports, old abbeys and pilgrim sites, craft centers and folk museum cottages. Remote and rural, Donegal Bay presents some of Ireland's most photographic coastal views—whether the surf's up or not!

**GETTING THERE:**

By car, the drive around Donegal Bay requires several routes. To cover the lower half of the drive, follow the main N15 road south of Donegal Town, with a possible detour along local road R232. To cover the upper half, drive west of Donegal Town via main road N56, in combination with several local roads including R263. There are no tours of the bay area using public transport.

**PRACTICALITIES:**

A drive along Donegal Bay comes in two parts, using Donegal Town as the hub. The first part of the drive, south of Donegal Town, covers approximately 20 miles, with an optional detour adding another 30 miles round-trip. The second part of the drive extends westward from Donegal Town to Glencolumbkille and back via Ardara, a total of 70 to 80 miles, depending on detours. Together these two drives comprise one full daytrip.

The roads, particularly on the second half of the tour, are narrow and hilly, often curving around scenic mountain passes, deep valleys, and coastal cliffs. Expect to average no more than 30 miles per hour and sometimes less.

For information, contact the **Donegal Tourist Office**, The Quay, Donegal Town, ☎ 073-21148, open all year; and the **Bundoran Tourist Office**, Main St., Bundoran, ☎ 072-41350, open June through September. There are at least three area codes for telephone numbers in the Donegal Bay region, 072, 073, and 075. To avoid confusion, the appropriate area code will be given for each number.

## FOOD AND DRINK:

**Blue Haven** (Largymore, Kilcar) For views of Donegal Bay, this is a prime spot. Set on a hill between Killybegs and Kilcar, this modern skylit restaurant offers 180-degree views of the water from a semi-circular curve of windows. Bar food, served all day, includes soups, sandwiches, and omelets with unusual fillings. Dinner items range from seafood and steaks, to cold meat buffet or savory mushroom pancakes. X: Oct.–April. ☎ 073- 38090. £ to ££

**Nancy's** (Main St., Ardara) Tradition is the keynote of this cottage-style inn, which has been in the same family for seven generations and is named after the great-grandmother of the current owner. The decor is replete with open fireplaces, antiques, and memorabilia, while the menu offers homemade soups and chowder, plus oysters, smoked salmon platters, and a range of salads. ☎ 075-41187. £ to ££

**Sand House** (Rossnowlagh) Set on a crescent of beach overlooking Donegal Bay, this local landmark has long been a focal point of the area, first as a fishing lodge in 1886, later a thatched pub by 1906, and then expanded into a stellar hotel since 1949. Enjoy a snack or light meal in the nautically-themed Surfers Bar or the antique-filled lounge by a turf fireplace. The main dining room specializes in local seafood harvested in Donegal Bay such as lobster, oysters, scallops, and mussels. X: mid-Oct.–April. ☎ 072-41204. £ to ££

**Smugglers Creek Inn** (Rossnowlagh) For a nautical decor, panoramic views of Donegal Bay, and great seafood, this is the place. The bar menu offers oysters and mussels harvested from local beds, soups, salads, and sandwiches. House dinner specials include *Smugglers Sea Casserole* (scallops, salmon, and prawns), deep-fried squid, or tiger prawns. X: mid-Nov. to mid-Dec. and Mon.–Tues. in Oct.–April. ☎ 072-52366. £ to ££

**The Tea House** (The Folk Village, Glencolumbkille) Come through the half-door and step back in time at this thatched-roof cottage, furnished with tables and chairs hand-crafted by the local people. Operated as a charitable trust, this homey self-service restaurant offers the best of local produce and freshly-baked goodies, produced by members of the community. The menu emphasizes traditional Irish recipes for Guinness cake, scones, brown bread, and apple tart, as well as homemade soups and salads. X: Nov.–March. ☎ 073-30017. £

## SUGGESTED TOUR:

Start this tour in **Bundoran** (1), equally distant from Sligo or Donegal

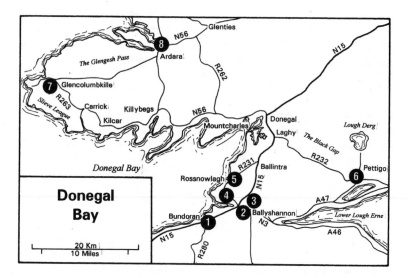

Town, about 20 miles in either direction, on the main N15 road. This tour can also be followed when en route from Sligo to Donegal.

**Bundoran** is one of Ireland's main seaside resorts, thanks to its lovely location on a crest of Donegal Bay and its wide sandy Blue Flag-winning beach, known as Tullan, which is among the cleanest in Europe. At the south end of the beach are unique rock formations, carved by the erosive motions of the sea, with descriptive names such as Puffing Hole, the Wishing Chair, and the Fairy Bridge.

Four miles north on the main N15 road is **Ballyshannon**, a busy seaport and market town, sitting on a steep bank overlooking the River Erne. It has a fitting placename, derived from the Irish language, *Béal Átha Seanaidhm* meaning "Ford-mouth of the hillside." Founded in the 17th century, the town is full of character, with well-kept Georgian-style homes, narrow and hilly streets, and a backdrop of mountains, waterfalls, and river views.

Two local enterprises are worth a visit. On the main road, to the right, is **Donegal Parian China** (2), Ballyshannon, ☎ 072-51826, producing delicate wafer-like parian china, hand-crafted from the mold to decorating stages, in patterns of Irish flowers and Celtic designs. The complex includes an exhibition room, showing off the best of the wares, plus a continuous audiovisual presentation, and an art gallery. Tours of the workshops are conducted every 20 minutes. *Open Oct.–April, Mon.–Fri. 9–6; May, Mon.–Sat. 9–6; June–Sept., Mon.–Sat. 9–6, Sun. 1–6. Free admission. Tours. Shop. Café.*

Follow the signposts to the right off the main road to **Celtic Weave** (3), Cloghore, Ballyshannon, ☎ 072-51844. This company specializes in hand-crafted and hand-painted china baskets in patterns of Irish roses. *Open*

*Mon.–Sat. 9–6. Free admission. Tours. Shop.*

Continuing north of N15, follow the sign for local road R231. On the left is a signpost for **The Abbey Mill** (4), Abbey Asaroe, Ballyshannon, ☎ 072-51580, an old monastic site beside the River Abbey. Founded by the Cistercians in the 12th century, this site was developed to provide mechanical power using water wheels, so that the monks could have more time for prayer and contemplation. Although it eventually fell into ruin and was left derelict for many years, the waterwheels and mill build-ings were recently restored, providing visitors with insight into early power generation in this area. One water wheel now powers a generator that supplies light and heat. The complex includes an audiovisual presen-tation. *Open June–Sept. daily 11–7; Oct.–May, Sun. 2:30–7. Admission £1 per person. Tours. Café.*

Return to local road R231 for approximately four miles to Rossnowlagh, as the vistas to the left reveal a two-mile-long crescent of dune-rimmed beach.

Before descending to the beach, on the left is the ***Franciscan Friary** (5), Rossnowlagh, ☎ 072-51342, home of the **Donegal History Society Museum**. This museum contains a variety of displays on the area including two volumes of the 1848 English translation of the *Annals of the Four Masters*, as well as historical artifacts, photographs, and memorabilia. In addition, the friary, founded in 1946, is an attraction in itself, with various outdoor shrines and gardens including a Christmas garden. The grounds—perched on a cliff overlooking the sea, offer sign-posted walk-ing trails, prayer paths, and a viewing point that overlooks the broad expanse of Rossnowlagh beach. *Open daily 10–6. No admission charge, but donations are welcome. Tours. Shop. Café.*

From the Friary grounds, turn left and follow signposts to ***Rossnowlagh** beach. Derived from the Irish language, *Ros Neamhlach*, this placename is interpreted variously to mean "Wood of the apple trees" or "The heavenly cove." Either way, it is a picturesque place, ideal for surfing, windsurfing, and board-sailing, and other watersports. If time allows, walk or drive along the beach. Yes, cars are encouraged to drive along the hard and wide expanse of sand. Riding horses along the beach is also a favorite sport with the locals.

Continue north as the road parallels the coast for a while. Turn right at the sign for Ballintra, leading back to the main N15 road. Make a left onto the N15 and go north. You can follow it into Donegal Town, or take a detour at Laghy to the right on local road R232 to visit one of Ireland's main sites of Christian pilgrimage, Lough Derg at Pettigo. Note: Even though the name is the same, this Lough Derg has no relationship to Lough Derg in County Clare, the largest lake in the River Shannon.

The road R232 from Laghy rises to a heather-covered bog, with tiny lakes on the right and left. In the distance, on the approach to Pettigo, is the broad expanse of Lough Erne to the right and Black Gap on the left.

**Pettigo** is an interesting village on the border, literally between the

Republic of Ireland and Northern Ireland. On the left is the:

**\*LOUGH DERG JOURNEY** (6), Main St., Pettigo, ☎ 072-61565. *Open March–April, Sat. 10–5, Sun. 2–5; May–Sept., Mon.–Sat. 10–5, Sun. noon–5. Adults £2, students and seniors £1.50. Tours. Shop.*
    Situated five miles south of Lough Derg, this heritage center enables you to learn all about the famous pilgrimage—and to experience the sights, sounds, and feelings—without having to go through all the rigors. The story of Lough Derg goes back to St. Patrick's time, in the mid-5th century, when Ireland's patron saint is said to have come here to do penance on an island in the middle of the lake. Christian pilgrims have followed in his footsteps ever since, coming to the same island, now known as St Patrick's Purgatory, for a day or more of prayer and fasting each spring and summer.
    A walk-around tour of the center includes quotes on the meaning of penance, with appropriate music, bells, voices, and poetry such as *The Pilgrim* by W.B. Yeats, and relevant poems by a range of writers from Shakespeare to Seamus Heaney, Ireland's latest Nobel Prize winner. Exhibits include a penitential bed, a cave, a desert garden, and a display of Lough Derg "wine"—salt, pepper, and hot water.

    From Pettigo, it is just a 15-minute drive to **Lough Derg** itself. Boats take visitors to the island regularly for one-day retreats in May and September, and traditional three-day pilgrimages from June through mid-August. The centerpiece of the island is an octagonal church built in 1921. It is customary to fast and walk around in bare feet on the longer pilgrimages, but not on the shorter trips. All trips require advance reservations. For more information, contact The Prior, St. Patrick's Purgatory, Lough Derg, Co. Donegal, ☎ 072-61546 or 61518. *Boat trips operate March–April, Sat. noon–3, Sun. at 4; May–Sept., Mon.–Fri. noon–3, Sat. noon–3, Sun. 3–5:30. Adults £2, seniors and students £1.50, children £1.*
    From Pettigo retrace your route back on R232 to Laghy, passing through Donegal Town and then follow the sign to the left for Mountcharles via N56. Views of Donegal Bay appear on the left as you approach the fishing village of Mountcharles. A small lake, St. Peter's Lough, can be seen on the right, as you proceed toward Iver, the next village. Continue on to Dunkineely, where the bay opens up on the left. Enjoy lovely coastal views of Donegal Bay on the left for the next five miles.
    Next is **\*Killybegs**, one of Ireland's busiest fishing ports and an important herring-fishing station. Strong salty fish aromas fill the air as you pass through the town.
    As you depart Killybegs, the main N56 road swings north, so you follow local road R263. The road swings west and there is a viewing point that offers panoramic views at Fintragh Bay, with Donegal Bay in the distance. Continuing west, enjoy wonderful seascapes to the left and the great pro-

files of Crownarad and Mulnanaff mountains looming ahead.

As you approach **Kilcar**, you enter a *Gaeltacht* or Gaelic-speaking area. This means the road signs will appear in both the Irish and English languages, with a preference for the former. Signs for **Kilcar** will also say **Cill Charthaigh**. The placename, which means "St. Carthach's church," commemorates a church built here in the 6th century by a bishop named Carthach.

Continue to follow the coast road to **Carrick** or **An Charraig,** which means "The rock," evident from the rocky land which surrounds the town including the stony peaks of **Slieve League** to the left towering over Donegal Bay. These are said to be the highest marine cliffs in Europe but only the most sure-footed hiker should attempt to explore them.

Travel seven miles west and next is **\*Glencolumbkille** or **Gleann Cholm Cille**, meaning "St. Columba's valley" or "The glen of St. Columba's Church," a reference to the fact that St. Columba established a monastery here in the 6th century. It is a very remote and peaceful valley, where sheep far outnumber the people. Up until the early 1960s local industry was almost non-existent, and young people were emigrating abroad at a rapid rate. To stem the tide of emigration and create employment in the area, a man with great foresight and business acumen came on the scene, Fr. James McDyer. Although born in the region, he had been away for many years doing priestly work in England. When he returned to Glencolumbkille, he was saddened at the lack of opportunity amid such scenic beauty and set about converting the area's natural attributes into local enterprises. He organized the people into self-reliance cooperatives for knitting, farming, fishing, fish-processing, and other small industries. Fr. McDyer saw great potential for tourism, but realized no one would make the journey out to this far-flung corner of Donegal for scenery alone, so he conceived the idea of a "living history" museum. In 30 years, it has grown to be the area's major attraction:

**\*FOLK VILLAGE MUSEUM** (7), Glencolumbkille, ☎ 073-30017. *Open Easter–May, Mon.–Sat. 10–6, Sun. noon–6; June–Oct., Mon.–Sat. 10–6:30; Sun. noon–6:30. Adults £2.50, children £1. Tours. Shop. Café.*

Designed, assembled, and maintained by the people of Glencolumbkille, this outdoor village seeks to re-create life in the town over the past 300 years. The complex includes a cluster of cottages or clachan, built and thatched in the traditional rounded Donegal style—tied down to withstand the prevailing winds off the Atlantic. Each cottage represents a different era and way of life—18th, 19th, 20th centuries, and is furnished with the tools, implements, and utensils appropriate to that period. Other buildings include a 19th-century school, a shebeen (pub), craft shop, tea house, and bakery. A walk-through tour aims to acquaint visitors with local customs and traditions while maintaining the community's rich culture. The grounds, set into a hillside overlooking the sea below, feature an herb garden and a nature walk incorporating replicas of local history including standing stones, a limekiln, mass rock, hedge school, sweat house, and round tower. The *shops in the complex offer the craftwork of the local community, and since the folk park operates as a charitable trust, all purchases are tax-free.

Take the road sign-posted to Ardara, a distance of 16 miles. It will bring you through a very scenic drive known as *The Glengesh Pass, a high gorge between the steep-sided Glengesh and Mulmosog mountains over-looking Loughros Beg Bay.

**Ardara** or **Árd an Ratha,** meaning "Height of the ring-fort," appears to be named after a nearby fort on top of a cliff, although Ardara itself is in a deep valley. Today Ardara is noted as a major center for the manufacture of hand-woven tweeds and hand-knit garments. The main street is lined with shops selling woolen goods.

The **Ardara Heritage Centre** (8), Main St., Ardara, ☎ 075-41704, a small museum, tells the story of tweed from the sheep to the wool and eventually into woven cloth. It consists of a series of walk-around exhibits, old photographs, displays, and models of equipment used in the process. In addition, a weaver is always on duty to answer questions and demonstrate how to work a loom. *Open Easter–Sept., Mon.–Sat. 10–6, Sun. 2–6. Adults £2, children £1. Shop. Café.*

From Ardara, return via N56 south. The road presents good views of Donegal Bay as it descends toward Killybegs. Retrace your route from Killybegs back to Donegal Town, a distance of 17 miles, for the completion of the tour.

# The Atlantic Highlands

The ruggedly rural highlands of Donegal hold a lot of surprises. You wouldn't expect to find an art gallery housing works by Picasso here, but you will, just as you'll encounter a national park with exotic edible plants and a castle with links to Tabasco sauce.

Most of all, this remote territory, extending beyond Donegal Town out into the hinterlands along the Atlantic, holds incredibly beautiful scenery—endless lakes and bays, peninsulas and headlands, islands and inlets, boglands and valleys, all dominated by the Blue Stack and Derryveagh Mountains.

More than half of this area is part of a *Gaeltacht* or Irish-speaking district. This not only enhances the rural character of these far-flung communities, but it preserves the native culture and crafts. It also adds music to the air. Some of Ireland's finest contemporary singers and musicians were nurtured here, from Daniel O'Donnell to Enya and the folk groups Altan and Clannad.

Because of the vast scope of this territory, it would take weeks or even years to follow every road, drive every peninsula, or explore every byway. This daytrip presents a sampling of the most interesting towns and experiences. It is a road less traveled, but indeed full of surprises.

### GETTING THERE:

By car, this tour follows the main N56 road from Donegal Town for most of the route, with a few local roads, and then proceeds along N15 for the last lap back to Donegal town. The basic route covers approximately 100 miles, but this can be extended substantially with detours.

### PRACTICALITIES:

The best way to do this tour is by car. The driving is slow and tedious in many places because of poor roads and the variety of bogland, mountain, and seacoast terrain. Mileage will average 30 miles per hour, although in some places, it will be less.

Since much of this area belongs to a *Gaeltacht*, the road signs are printed in the Irish language first, followed by the English words. In some of the more remote sections, signs are only in Irish. Often the Irish word for a place bears no resemblance to the English equivalent, i.e. *An Clochán Liath* in Irish is *Dungloe* in English. This can be daunting, but our daytrip gives the placenames in both languages. Remember that the Irish language is also used for pub and shop signs.

If you'd prefer to leave the driving to someone else, **Bus Eireann** operates guided sightseeing tours of the area during July and August, departing from Donegal Town each Wednesday. For more details or reservations, call ☎ 074-21309.

For information about the area, contact the **Donegal Tourist Office**, The Quay, Donegal Town, ☎ 073-21148, open all year; **Dungloe Tourist Office**, Main St., Dungloe, ☎ 075-21297, open June through August; and the **Letterkenny Tourist Office**, Derry Rd., Letterkenny, ☎ 074-21160, open all year.

At least three area codes apply in this area, 073, 074, and 075. To avoid confusion, the appropriate area code will be specified with each telephone number.

## FOOD AND DRINK:

In addition to the places listed below, there are excellent cafés at the Lakeside Centre in Dunlewy and at Glenveagh National Park.

**Biddy O'Barnes** (Barnesmore Gap) In the wilderness along the main N15 road between Ballybofey and Donegal Town, this is a good pub to know, with the scenic backdrop of the Blue Stack Mountains to the west. The country cottage decor includes blazing turf fires and local memorabilia, plus a picture of the original "Biddy" over the mantle. Snacks, soups, and sandwiches are served, with seating outdoors as well. ☎ 073-21402. £

**Carolina House** (Ramelton Rd., Loughnagin, Letterkenny) Views of Lough Swilly are featured at this flower-decked country cottage set on high ground north of town. The menu changes daily but specialties of the house include traditional loin of bacon with a fresh herb crust, wild Donegal salmon with sorrel sauce, and chicken ballotine with a tomato-and-basil sauce. Dinner only. X: Sun.–Mon. ☎ 074-22480. ££

**Danny Minnies** (Teach Killindarragh, Annagry, 5 miles west of Crolly) Deep in the heart of the Gaeltacht area, this restaurant has a country inn atmosphere, with seating inside and outdoors. Local seafood is the specialty, including lobster, as well as vegetarian dishes and steaks. ☎ 075-48201. ££ to £££

**Leo's Tavern** (Meenaleck, Crolly) Locals and visitors alike flock to this little pub for the music and the Gaelic hinterland atmosphere. The owner is the father of the members of the well-known Irish traditional music group Clannad. Stop in for some music, a drink, a snack, or just for a good conversation. ☎ 075-48143. £

**Lobster Pot** (Burtonport, 5 miles west of Dungloe) In this fishing port known for its big catches, this restaurant wisely specializes in lobster and other local seafood platters, as well as hearty soups and steaks. The atmosphere is cozy, with dark woods, open fireplaces, and lots of memorabilia. ☎ 075-42012. £ to ££

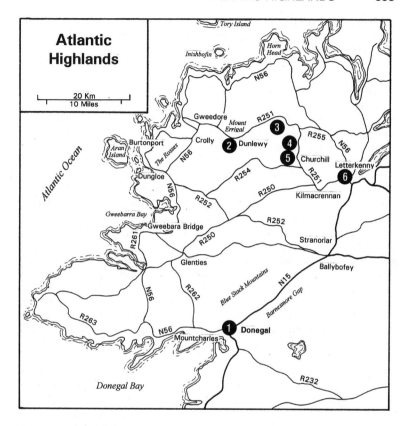

## SUGGESTED TOUR:

From **Donegal Town** (1), take the main N56 road west as far as Mountcharles and then make a right onto R262, a scenic road with the Blue Stack Mountains rising on the right. In just over 10 miles you will reach ***Glenties** or **Na Gleannta**, nestled in the hills where two glens and two rivers meet. Not surprisingly, the Irish placename for this delightful village means "The glens." The attractive layout of the village, which four times has been a national award winner in Ireland's annual Tidy Towns competition, includes an early 19th-century courthouse and a market house. Glenties is considered as the official gateway to the Donegal highlands and to the Donegal Gaeltacht. This area is home to the largest native Irish-speaking population in Ireland. From now on, the route passes shops and pubs with signs in the Irish language.

From here, you can rejoin the main N56 road as it wends its way northward. After eight miles, the road crosses the **Gweebara Bridge** or **Droichead Gaoth Barra**, over the Gweebara River, and another eight miles to **Dungloe** or **An Clochán Liath**, meaning "The gray stepping stones." This name is appropriate since the rocks around this small fishing port have a distinctive gray hue.

Dungloe is celebrated as the "capital" of **The Rosses**, an area of countless promontories, islands, and headlands of rock- strewn land tucked amid bays and inlets. The bleakness of the large and lonely stretches of uninhabited land draws many visitors who seek solitude. A detour of five miles to the left will bring you to one of Donegal's major fishing ports, **Burtonport**, otherwise known as **Ailt an Chorráin**, which means "Ravine of the curve." It is said that more salmon and lobster are landed at this port than anywhere else in Ireland.

The next town, seven miles to the north, is **Crolly** or **Croithlí**, a place-name meaning "quagmire," because of the marshy boglands nearby. This area marks the end of The Rosses and the beginning of a new Gaeltacht district or parish known as **Gweedore** or **Gaoth Dobhair**, meaning "Water inlet." Outside the towns and villages, the houses and cottages are very scarce in this territory. It is a lonely land.

Two miles north is the hamlet of Gweedore, gateway to a promontory known as the *Bloody Foreland. The term has nothing to do with ancient battles or massacres, but is used to describe the reddish hue given to the rocks by the evening sun. Take a detour on R257 to do the complete Bloody Foreland circuit (about 12 miles), for broad views of the Atlantic and the massive *Horn Head cliffs rising to the east, as well as a picturesque collection of offshore islands including Inishbofin, Inishdooey, Inishbeg, and Tory.

Although more peninsulas, such as Rosguill, Ards, and Fanad lie ahead, they must await another day. This tour now turns inland, following the R251 road to **Dunlewy** or **Dún Lúiche**, simply meaning "Lughaidh's fort." *Mount Errigal, Donegal's highest peak (2,466 feet), rising on the left, presents a scenic backdrop to this tiny village, set in a shallow peat valley and rimmed by two lovely lakes.

Take time to visit a local community development that has given new life and the hum of activity to this area:

*IONAD COIS LOCHA—THE LAKESIDE CENTRE (2), Dunlewy, ☎ 075-31699. *Open mid-March–Nov., Mon.–Sat. 11:30–6, Sun. 12:30–7. Visitor center: Adults £3, children £1.50. Boat trip: Adults £3, children £1.50. Tours. Shop. Café.*

Once the small homestead of a local weaver named Manus Ferry, this place is fast becoming "an oasis in the Gaeltacht" for visitors in search of a lovely setting to enjoy a bit of history, some fresh air on a boat ride, or a cup of tea by a fireside. The old farmhouse has been converted into a visitor center with exhibits and demonstrations on weaving from carding and dyeing to spinning. It is furnished just as it would have been in Manus Ferry's days, complete with a time-worn loom, and a kitchen with cupboard bed and a hob for grilling over the fire. The project has been spearheaded by a group of locals who emigrated abroad for work, but longed to be in Dunlewy. One by one, they returned and got together, inspired to make a place that would draw visitors to this scenic valley. After a tour of the house, step out into the farmyard to see the animals or the herb and vegetable gardens, watch sheep being sheared, or take a boat ride on the lake. Old fashioned Irish story-telling is part of the guided tour, as is traditional music and dance of the most authentic kind. There is a relaxed aura about the place, a welcome change after a long drive. Listen as the locals speak in the Irish language. You'll be encouraged to try a few Gaelic words, too.

Return to R251 and travel east along this scenic valley for eight miles to reach the area's prime natural attraction:

**\*GLENVEAGH NATIONAL PARK** (3), Churchill, Letterkenny, ☎ 074-37088. *Open daily April–May, 10–6:30; June–Sept., Mon.–Sat. 10–6:30 and Sun. 10–7:30; Oct.–Nov., Mon.–Thurs. and Sat.–Sun. 10–6:30. Adults £2, seniors and students £1.50, children £1. Tours. Shop. Café.*

It is hard to imagine that one of Ireland's finest national parks is secluded out in these Donegal hinterlands, but here it is—24,000 acres of gardens, moorlands, lakes, woods, and mountains including the two highest mountains in Donegal—Errigal and Slieve Snacht. This vast natural expanse was not always a happy place. The estate was created by Englishman John George Adair in 1857, who added a Gothic-style granite castle in 1870. He drove over 200 families from their homes on the land so he could live by himself. Although he died in 1885, his wife remained here until 1921. In the 1930s, it was purchased by Henry McIlhenny, of the Tabasco sauce family who was also a distinguished art historian and chairman of the board of the Philadelphia Museum of Art. The grandson of a Donegal emigrant, McIlhenny restored the castle and made many artistic improvements in the buildings and gardens, spending several months a year here until 1983 when he presented the castle and gardens as a gift to the Irish nation. A tour starts at the visitor center with an audiovisual that presents background on the castle and estate. Mini-buses then await to take you to the castle and gardens. If you prefer to walk, it takes about 45 minutes between the two sites. Guided tours of the castle are conducted every 20 minutes and last about a half-hour. Save time to explore the gardens which have a rich variety of exotic and rare plants from as far away as Tasmania, Madeira, and Chile. In addition, there are themed sections such as the Belgian Walk, Swiss Walk, Italian Garden, Rose Garden, View Garden, and Vegetable Garden with edible and ornamental vegetables. The grounds also provide a variety of nature trails and a lush habitat for wildlife including the largest red deer herd in Ireland.

Return to R251 and turn right. Three more surprises await four miles away on the shores of Lough Gartan. A right turn will bring you to the:

**\*GLEBE HOUSE & GALLERY** (4), Churchill, Letterkenny, ☎ 074-37071. *Open May–Sept., Sat.–Thurs. 11–6:30. Adults £2, seniors and students £1.50, children £1. Tours. Café.*

This is the art hub of Donegal, donated to the people of Ireland by English artist Derek Hill who lived and painted in this area. Glebe House, a fine Regency-style building that was formerly Hill's home, is a museum of masterpiece art including more than 300 works by leading 20th-century artists such as Picasso, Bonnard, Kokoschka, and Jack Yeats, plus Donegal folk art, Japanese and Islamic art, and papers and textiles by William Morris. Outside, the former stables have been converted into a gallery showing selections of Derek Hill's paintings, as well as a changing program of visiting exhibits.

Turn right and follow signs for **Colmcille Heritage Centre** (5), Churchill, Letterkenny, ☎ 074-37306. Situated beside Lough Gartan, this heritage center aims to tell the story of the life and times of Donegal's patron saint, St. Colmcille (521–597). Born in Gartan, he first spent time spreading Christianity in the area around Glencolumbkille and then set up at least three religious foundations in Ireland—at Derry, Durrow, and Moone, before he went on to bring Christianity to Scotland, becoming known there as St. Columba of Iona. The story is told via several media including artistically designed banners, stained glass, illustrated panels, artifacts, and wax models in authentic clothing. There is also a step-by-step explanation of how ancient manuscripts were produced by the monks. *Open May–Sept., Mon.–Sat. 10:30–6:30, Sun. 1–6:30. Adults £1.50, students £1.*

This point also marks the end of the Gaeltacht area. Turn right and the local road links up with N56 for the next seven miles to **Letterkenny**, a large and busy town at the head of Lough Swilly. The placename is taken from the Irish language, *Leitir Ceannan* which means "White-streaked hill face."

It is the home of the **Donegal County Museum** (6), High Rd., Letterkenny, ☎ 074-24613, a treasure-trove of exhibits about all facets of life in the county, from folklife to history, geology, archaeology, and local railways. *Open Tues.–Fri. 11–4:30, Sat. 1–4:30. Admission is free.*

Continue through Letterkenny, turning south onto N56 for the 30-mile trip back to Donegal town. En route, the road will merge to become N15 as you pass through the "twin towns" of **Stranorlar** and **Ballybofey**, separated by the River Finn. The road is particularly scenic south of Ballybofey as you drive through **\*Barnesmore Gap**, with the Blue Stack Mountains and Lough Eske on the right.

# Inishowen Peninsula

The largest of County Donegal's many peninsulas, Inishowen sits at the top of the county, the most northerly point of the entire island of Ireland. It is literally wedged between the Republic of Ireland and Northern Ireland.

Very few people ever get this far, but those who do make the journey are well rewarded. Bounded on three sides by water, Inishowen is almost triangular in shape, between Lough Swilly and Lough Foyle and facing the Atlantic. It is a collage of dramatic seacoasts, dune-filled beaches, challenging mountain drives, deep green valleys, and cliff-etched headlands. With such rich scenery plus a fine collection of ancient forts and monuments, traditional craft centers, and a dozen friendly towns, many people consider Inishowen to be a miniature Donegal or even a miniature Ireland.

The area takes its name from the Irish language, *Inis Eoghain*, meaning "Owen's island." Owen was an early member of the *Ui Neill* or O'Neill clan. In medieval times, Inishowen was part of the great northern kingdom of the O'Neills and was ruled from the royal palace at Grianán of Aileach.

In spite of its remote location, the Inishowen Peninsula is compact and easy to tour, making it a very good choice for a quick sampling of Irish landscape. The entire peninsula is rimmed by a well-signposted 100-mile drive, aptly named the Inishowen 100.

## GETTING THERE:

By car, it is 40 miles from Donegal Town northeast to Burt, the starting point of this tour, via N15, N56, and N13. From Derry, it is just less than five miles west via the main N13 road.

## PRACTICALITIES:

Many people do this tour as a daytrip from Donegal Town, even though Donegal is 40 miles away from the start of the Inishowen Peninsula. It is more practical to embark on this tour from Derry, just over the border in Northern Ireland and literally five miles away from the suggested tour starting point at Grianán of Aileach. However, since more people overnight in Donegal Town than in Derry, we'll assume that Donegal Town is the starting point for this tour.

The Inishowen 100, the driving route around the peninsula, is one of the best signposted routes in Ireland, with directionals clearly printed in

English as well as Irish and all distances shown in miles and kilometers. However, the roads can be steep, narrow, and hilly. The driving is tedious and slow in many spots. Expect to average no more than 20–30 miles an hour.

If you prefer to leave the driving to someone else, during June-August, **Bus Eireann** operates a weekly sightseeing tour of the Inishowen Peninsula from Donegal Town, departing on Tuesdays. For information or reservations, call ☎ 074-21309.

For information about the area, contact the **Buncrana Tourist Office**, Shore Front, Buncrana, ☎ 077-20020, open June through August; or the **Inishowen Tourism Society, Ltd.**, Chapel St., Carndonagh, Inishowen, ☎ 077-74933, open all year. The area code for all telephone numbers on the Inishowen Peninsula is 077.

## FOOD AND DRINK:

In addition to the restaurants listed below, there is an excellent all-day restaurant at the Grianán of Aileach Visitor Centre, and good cafés or coffee shops at Tullyvaran Mill, the National Knitting Center, and Fort Dunree.

**Harry's** (Bridgend) At the start or finish of an Inishowen tour, this restaurant-pub awaits, with a relaxing bi-level brasserie-style layout of polished woods and brass. House specialties are steaks and seafood. ☎ 077-68444. £ to ££

**Kealy's Seafood Bar** (Greencastle) Perched on the harborfront beside the Foyle Fishermen's Co-op, this informal restaurant is known for fresh seafood, particularly Greencastle seafood chowder, local oysters and lobsters, and smoked salmon, as well as southern fried chicken, sandwiches, and burgers. X: Mon. in Oct.–April. ☎ 077-81010. £ to £££

**Restaurant St. John's** (Fahan) Overlooking Lough Swilly, this Georgian house restaurant offers an elegant ambiance beside a cozy fireplace. The menu concentrates on fresh vegetables and local produce. Specialties include Donegal lamb, Swilly salmon, and stuffed mussels. Dinner only. X: Mon. ☎ 077-60289. ££ to £££

## SUGGESTED TOUR:

Start out early from **Donegal Town** (1), driving approximately 40 miles via N15, N56, and N13, to Grianán of Aileach, the gateway to the Inishowen Peninsula. *If you are traveling in Northern Ireland, it is a lot easier to start this tour from Derry.*

However, assuming that you have made your way to this area, your first stop is:

**\*GRIANÁN AN AILEACH CENTRE** (2), Burt, Co. Donegal, ☎ 077-68512. *Open summer, daily 10–6; winter, daily 12–6. Adults £2, seniors and students £1.10. Tours. Shop. Café.*

One of Ireland's greatest ring forts, this mighty stone structure sits

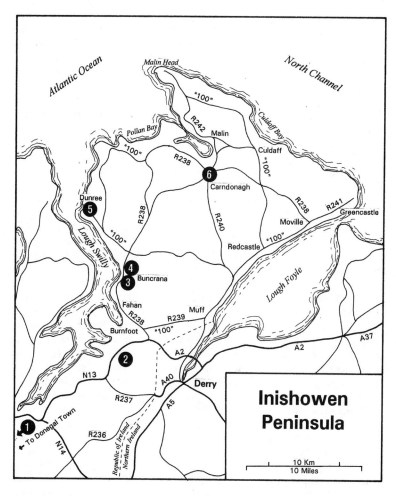

**Inishowen Peninsula**

10 Km
10 Miles

750 feet above sea level atop the Donegal countryside, at the southern tip of the Inishowen Peninsula. The placename, derived from the Irish language, *Grianán Ailigh*, is usually interpreted to mean "The stone fort of the sun." Archaeologists maintain that the fort itself dates from 500 BC or earlier, but the circular ramparts may go back as far back as 5,000 years ago. Considering its commanding position, it is thought to have originally been a pagan temple. From the 5th century to the 12th century, it was the royal residence of the Ulster chieftains, the O'Neills. Although greatly ravaged in medieval times, it was partly restored in 1870s. It is still one of the most impressive circular ring forts in Ireland, with a diameter of 77 feet and walls that are 17 feet high and 13 feet thick. A visit starts at the heritage

center, housed in a former 150-year-old stone church, situated less than a mile away at the foot of the monument. Various exhibits and interactive multimedia displays provide background on the fort ranging from its history and mythology, to the flora and fauna of the area. You can then drive to the fort itself and walk around. It is a great vantage point for taking panoramic pictures.

From the fort, return to the main road and turn left for **Burnfoot**, a small village overlooking Lough Swilly. The rather unusual placename is derived from the Irish language *Bun na hAbhann*, meaning "Mouth of the river," an apparent reference to its position by the water. This village marks the start of the circular drive around the peninsula known as the **Inishowen 100** or Inis Eoghain 100.

In just over three miles, the road leads into the picturesque marina village of **Fahan** overlooking Lough Swilly. The name comes from the Irish language *Fathain* which means "Grave." It is probably so named because the local cemetery may hold the remains of St. Mura, the first recorded abbot here in the early 7th century. A seven-foot-high stone cross is known locally at St. Mura's cross, c. 7th-century. It contains a rare Greek inscription, said to be the only one of its kind known to date from early Christian Ireland. St. Mura's crozier, which was found here, is on display in the National Museum in Dublin.

Continue north for five miles heading toward **Buncrana**, a name derived from the Irish language, *Bun Cranncha*, that simply means "Mouth of the River Crana." In addition to its proximity to the river, the town also overlooks Lough Swilly and has a three-mile-long sandy beach, making it a focal point for vacationers, particularly from the North of Ireland.

The largest town on the peninsula, Buncrana has always been a center of industry, particularly for textiles, tweeds, and knits. A recent extension of Buncrana's reputation in this field has been the opening of an Irish branch of the American company Fruit of the Loom here, but the traditional local crafts still predominate.

Just south of the town, opposite a golf course, on the right is the **Irish National Knitting Centre** (3), Lisfannon, Buncrana, ☎ 077-62355, a one-stop source for information about the local cottage industry of hand-knitting. The center offers displays tracing knitting as it developed through the ages and how it has provided a valuable source of income for this area. In addition, there is a yarn center which illustrates the old methods of spinning and dyeing. *Open May–Sept., Mon.–Fri. 9:30–7, Sat. 10–7, Sun. noon–7; Oct.–April., Mon.–Fri. 9:30–6. No admission charge. Tours. Shop. Café.*

Still another interpretation of Buncrana's prowess in the textile industry is profiled at *****Tullyarvan Mill** (4), Buncrana, ☎ 077-61613, signposted as you cross over the Cranna River a little over a half-mile north of town. Housed in a 19th-century converted corn mill, this center illustrates the town's 250-year-old involvement in the textile industry. It includes a complete textile museum, with displays of knitwear, wools, and other cloths, as well as the tools and implements used to make them. *Open Easter–Sept., Mon.–Sat. 10–6, Sun. noon–6. Adults £2, children £1. Shop. Café.*

Depart Buncrana and follow the "Inishowen 100" signs on local road R238. As the road swings right, you may wish to take a slight detour to the left to Dunree Head. This will bring you to **Fort Dunree Military Museum** (5), Dunree, Buncrana, ☎ 074-24613, Ireland's first public military museum, on the site of World War I defenses on the north Irish coast. Even if you have no interest in military history, this is a worthwhile diversion because of its location. Perched high on a cliff overlooking Lough Swilly, this old fort has one of the best *vantage points in Donegal, an ideal spot to take pictures or just to enjoy sweeping sea views on a clear day. The museum incorporates a Napoleonic martello tower that houses a wide range of exhibits, an audiovisual center, and a restored forge. *Open June–Sept., Mon.–Sat. 10–6, Sun. 1–6. Adults £2, children £1. Shop. Café.*

Retrace your path back to the R238 road and continue going north. The road swings left for the **Gap of *Mamore**, a scenic roadway that passes between two almost equal hills—Mamore Hill (1,381 feet), and Croaghcarragh (1,379 feet), part of the Urris Hills. The road rises to a height of 800 feet above sea level before following a spiraling corkscrew descent. In the process, it offers panoramic views of the entire northern coastline.

At the bottom, the road comes to a fork. Keep right to stay on the Inishowen 100 drive, and pass through Clonmany and Ballyliffin, two small villages less than two miles apart, both with fine beaches overlooking Pollan Bay.

Follow the road east for just over five miles for **Carndonagh**, a busy market village. It takes its name from the Irish words, *Carn Domhnach,* meaning "Cairn of the church." The church in question is a Church of Ireland edifice about one-third of a mile west of town. It is the site of some interesting ancient monuments, grouped together on a roadside platform on the church grounds. The focal point is **St. Patrick's Cross** (6), a primitive ringless cross decorated on one side with interlaced ornamentation and on the other with an interlaced cross and a simple crucifixion scene. The cross has frequently been estimated to date back to the 7th century, making it among the earliest High Crosses in Ireland, although it may be two or three centuries younger. The cross is flanked on either side by small pillars. The first has two carved figures—the harpist David and the warrior Goliath, while the second pillar is not as readily identifiable, showing a figure with unusual ears.

The Inishowen 100 now takes a northerly direction, following R238 and R242 for three miles to **Malin**, a lovely village with a 10-arched bridge on Trawbreaga Bay. Malin takes its name from the Irish word *Málainn,* meaning "brow," because it sits at the brow or forehead of the peninsula.

Planned and laid out in the 17th century, Malin revolves around a triangular village green, lined with lime, sycamore, and cherry trees. The local beach on Trawbreaga Bay is known as Five Fingers Strand because it is marked by five standing rocks, jutting out into the bay. The sand dunes along the bay are reputedly the highest in Europe, formed by the sea and wind over 5,000 years.

Follow R242 for 8.5 miles to *Malin Head, Ireland's most northerly point. As the road rises, a stunning panorama appears, with views of Trawbreaga Bay to the south, and Dunaff Head, Fanad Head, and Horn Head to the west, and wild sea-ravaged seascapes to the north. On a clear day the hills of Scotland are visible to the east.

As might be expected, the Irish Meteorological Service has a weather station here. There is little else, except for a 19th-century signal tower, an old cottage ruin locally referred to as the "Wee House of Malin," and a hermit's rock cell cut into a cliff.

Return to the Inishowen 100 drive, going southeasterly via R242 and R243 toward Culdaff, a resort village with a descriptive placename in the Irish language—Cúill Dabhcha, meaning "Secluded place of the sandhills."

Follow the Inishowen 100 as it switches back to R238, in descent to the shores of Lough Foyle. Turn left for Greencastle, a thriving commercial fishing port, perched at the point where the Foyle narrows and Northern Ireland is only a mile away across the water. The placename is derived from the Irish language An Caisleán Nua, meaning "The new castle," referring to a castle built in 1305 by Norman Earl Richard de Burgo. No longer new, it lies in ruins north of the town.

Continue south now on R241 for two miles to Moville, an attractive 18th-century town and resort overlooking Lough Foyle. Prior to World War II, it was a popular port of call for transatlantic liners. The placename is derived from the Irish language, Maigh Bhile, meaning "The plain of the ancient tree."

The Inishowen 100 now follows R238 for 10 miles, southward to Redcastle, a resort area popular with families because of its children's amusement and play center and challenging golf course. Continue driving south for eight miles to Muff, an unusual name derived from the Irish language, Magh, meaning "a plain." From the *shoreline, you can see Derry City in the distance. In the early part of this century, a US Naval air service station was located here.

From Muff, follow R239 back to Burnfoot, to complete the Inishowen 100 circuit. From here, head back to Donegal Town or Derry, or to other parts of Ireland.

# Section IX

# THE NORTH

The northeast quarter of Ireland, variously called The North, Ulster, The Six Counties, or more commonly Northern Ireland, is different from the rest of the island of Ireland. It is different politically, economically, philosophically, and even visually. Yet, in so many ways, it is the same—sharing the same history, geography, language, customs, traditions, cultural heritage, and, of course, weather.

Northern Ireland has been made different by circumstances. The British, who laid claim to Ireland in various ways for over 800 years—plundered, conquered, and subjugated all of Ireland, but they enforced a "Plantation policy" primarily in the northern six counties, deemed as the "most profitable" and desirable land. English and Scottish settlers were "planted" in the northeast counties, encouraged to establish villages, towns, and industries. They pushed the native Irish westward to the difficult rocky lands of Donegal, Galway, and Mayo. To complicate matters, the new settlers were predominantly Protestant and the natives were Catholic, adding a religious dimension to the friction.

In time, the newcomers felt at home in this corner of Ireland; their descendants were truly natives. They not only got the best land, they also controlled the power and the jobs. These "Scots-Irish," as they were sometimes called, had been given their property by their government and it belonged to them, just as the "colonies" in the Americas belonged to the English settlers. The only difference between the colonists in the New World and in Ireland is that the Americans had a Revolution and achieved total independence. The Irish had many rebellions, but only won 26 out of 32 counties. The settlers in the northeast of Ireland have remained tied to the crown. The rest is history, particularly in the last 30 years of The Troubles, as Nationalists (mostly Catholic), who still dream of a united Ireland, have battled Unionists (mostly Protestant), who prefer life to remain as it is.

Having said all of that, it is still difficult to understand the nemesis of Northern Ireland. Indeed volumes have been written about the North, but it can't really be explained nor fully understood, even by those who live there. There are, of course, two sides; each with some merit. Most

Northerners long for peace, but don't know how to achieve it.

In recent years, there have been significant bright spots. The cease-fire of 1994–1996 was a beginning, re-enforced and extended by the Good Friday Agreement of April 10, 1998 and the Mitchell Review of 1999. As a result, a new north-south cooperation has blossomed including a great sphere of unity in tourism. Both the Irish Tourist Board and the Northern Irish Tourist Board have pooled their resources to draw visitors to "the island of Ireland," instead of two separate destinations. "Immovable mountains are moving," according to one tourism official.

It makes sense to experience Ireland as one land, without regard to difference in borders or political divisions. If you are going to Sligo or Donegal, it's so simple to add Derry, the Antrim coast, or Enniskillen and Lough Erne, to your touring plans. A visit to Dublin can easily include a day in Belfast or Armagh.

Don't be afraid to tour the North. The vast majority of the land is peaceful and friendly. The Troubles are usually confined to small pockets, far from the usual tourist routes. The roads are excellent—wide, well-paved, and well-maintained. The system of addresses is precise—every house or business has a number and street address—it's easy to find things. The countryside is lush and rich, fields are neatly cordoned off with symmetrical wooden fences instead of uneven stone hedges.

Many of the island of Ireland's most appealing scenery and experiences are packed into the northeast—from the vibrant cities of Derry, Armagh, and Belfast, and beautiful drives along the Glens of Antrim and Mountains of Mourne to the silvery shorelines of Lough Erne, not to mention the 8th wonder of the world, the unique coastal phenomenon known as the Giant's Causeway. The North, synonymous with fine linens, is also the home of the world's oldest distillery at Bushmills and the benchmark of potteries at Belleek. Legendary castles, stately mansions, great gardens, unique museums, and enlightening heritage centers are all part of the Northern experience. Only if you venture into the North will your Ireland itinerary be truly complete.

# Belfast

Newspaper headlines and TV reports have kept Belfast in the news for over three decades, but not for happy reasons. As the "capital" of Northern Ireland, Belfast is synonymous with guns and tanks, armed patrols and civil strife. Media summaries are quick to point out the worst, but each time the city has bounced back brilliantly to be better than ever. Spunky and spirited, Belfast is a survivor.

And why not? Rimmed by mountains and hills and nestled beside the River Lagan and Belfast Lough, Belfast is an appealing city, in spite of its war-torn image. As more and more visitors who come here learn, "the Troubles" are confined to certain off-center neighborhoods, usually far out of reach to the average traveler.

To a large degree, Belfast has been kept humming due to its role as the industrial and business hub of Northern Ireland. Unlike Dublin, which thrives on tourism, Belfast can exist without it. Purpose-built "tourist attractions" are few and far between in Belfast.

Although only 100 miles north of Dublin, Belfast is a world apart, even in history and appearance. While Dublin basks in its strong Viking, Norman, and Georgian facades and traditions, Belfast is a much younger city with distinctive Victorian and Edwardian flavors.

As late as the 17th century, in fact, Belfast was still a village. In the 1800's, however, Belfast came into its own as a driving force in the industrial revolution in Ulster. With the development of industries like linen, rope-making, engineering, and shipbuilding, Belfast doubled in population every ten years. By 1888, as the census topped 300,000 people, Belfast was finally given the status of a city.

Today, Belfast has a population of over 500,000 people, one third of the citizens of Northern Ireland. It is a big and busy city, home of the world's largest dry dock and countless industries. Above all, it is an optimistic place. In recent years, a superb new convention and performing arts center, Waterfront Hall, opened as the keystone of a massive urban development project along the river. In addition, a half-dozen major new hotels have debuted in or near the city center including at least two Dublin-owned properties and international brands such as Hilton, Holiday Inn, and Choice. They are but a sampling of the latest voices of confidence in the future of Belfast.

## GETTING THERE:

From major cities in the Republic of Ireland, the best way to get to

Belfast is from Dublin. By car, Belfast is 100 miles north of Dublin via the N1/A1 highway, a journey of about three hours. By train, **Irish Rail** and **Northern Ireland Railways** operate a joint service between Dublin and Belfast; travel time is about two hours and 20 minutes. By bus, **Bus Eireann's** Expressway Services connect Dublin and Belfast in just over three hours.

## PRACTICALITIES:

Walking is the ideal way to see Belfast. **Donegall Square**, in the heart of the city, is the focal point of the downtown area. Most of the city's prime sites are within a few blocks of Donegall Square, except for the Queens University, Ulster Museum, and Botanic Gardens. These three sites are clustered together approximately one mile south of the city center.

If you prefer not to walk, you can take a taxi or a local **Citybus** to Queens University. Buses #69, #70, or #71 serve that area, all departing from Donegall Square East. For full details, call **Citybus**, ☎ 028-9024-6485, or go directly to the Citybus Kiosk, Donegall Square West.

Most local inter-city buses depart from Donegall Square, while trains from Dublin arrive at the city's Central Rail Station, East Bridge Street, about six blocks east of Donegall Square.

Another good option for tired feet is the **Belfast Citybus Tour**, a 3.5-hour tour providing a good overview of the city. It departs daily from Castle Place, 1.5 blocks north of Donegall Square. For schedules or reservations, call ☎ 028-9045-8484.

If you have come to Belfast by car, it is best to park the vehicle at your hotel and leave it there while you go out to tour. Belfast is a city of many pedestrianzed streets, no-parking zones, control zones, and cordoned-off areas, a legacy of more than 25 years of "The Troubles." There is ample parking around Queens University and Ulster Museum, however, so you may wish to use your car for transport to that area.

For information, contact the **Northern Ireland Tourist Board**, St. Anne's Court, 59 North St., Belfast, ☎ 028-9023-1221; or the **Tourism Development Office** of Belfast City Council, City Hall, Belfast, ☎ 028-9032-0202. Both are open all year.

Aa of April 22, 2000, Northern Ireland has a new uniform area code—**028**—instead of various codes for different cities and counties. All numbers have changed from six to eight digits, and all are preceded by 028.

## FOOD AND DRINK:

**Bewley's** (Donegall Arcade, off Royal Ave.) Ensconced in the heart of Belfast's shopping quarter, this dependable café is a branch of the famous Dublin landmark dating back to 1840. It's a convenient spot for coffee, tea, pastries, soups, sandwiches, or hearty hot dishes. X: Sun. ☎ 028-9023-4955. £

**Crown Liquor Saloon** (44 Great Victoria St.) Maintained by the National Trust, this "must see" pub (see Suggested Tour) is a feast of Victorian decor and a great spot for a taste of "Old Belfast." Pub lunches include traditional dishes such as steak and kidney pie, champ, and lamb stew. ☎ 028-9024-9476. £

**Nick's Warehouse** (35 Hill St.) Situated near St. Anne's Cathedral, this wine bar-cum-restaurant offers trendy and tasty cuisine, such as curly kale soup, hot-and-sour beef, lamb chops with honey and ginger, or mixed nut bake. Owner Nick Price has transformed an old warehouse into a relaxing setting with brick walls, open kitchen, and wrought-iron culinary sculptures. X: Sun., Dec. 24–25, Easter Mon. and July 13–14. ☎ 028-9043-9690. ££

**Roscoff** (7 Lesley House, Shaftsbury Square) For a big splurge, head to this Michelin-starred restaurant. The black-and-white decor is austere, but the menu is a rich blend of classic French recipes enhanced by colorful Mediterranean and Californian influences. Specialties include ballotine of salmon and lobster with sun-dried tomato sauce; pigeon and wild mushroom brushetta; char-grilled Moroccan lamb with couscous; and seared beef with celery, Parmesan and truffle oil. X: Sun. ☎ 028-9033-1532. ££ to £££

**Skandia** (50 Howard St.) In the heart of downtown just a block from Donegall Square, this homey restaurant is known for its multi-ingredient seafood salads, as well as pastas, burgers, steaks, ribs, and omelets. Cajun and Oriental dishes are also featured. X: Sun. and Dec. 25. ☎ 028-9024-0239. £ to ££

## SUGGESTED TOUR:

Start a tour at the **Central Rail Station** (1), East Bridge Street. As you depart the front (north) door of the station, straight ahead is the new Laganbank development, a burst of urban renewal along the River Lagan.

In an effort to re-focus the city around the beauty of its river, Belfast created the **Lagan Weir** in 1993. It has helped to keep the river's water level up to beautify the waterfront and to encourage wildlife to return. It has also spurred investment and building on a large scale. The centerpiece along the riverfront is now the striking round domed facade of **Waterfront Hall** (2), Oxford St., ☎ 028-9033-4400, a state-of-the-art concert hall and conference center with a 2,235-seat main auditorium and many smaller rooms. It is the first purpose-built meeting and performing arts center of its kind ever built in Northern Ireland, and already it is acting as a magnet for additional waterfront attractions including the Hilton Belfast Hotel—Northern Ireland's first 5-star international hotel.

From Oxford Street, take a left turn onto May Street, heading west. After two blocks, you may wish to take a left onto Albert Street. Here you can visit **St. Malachy's Church** (3), 24 Alfred St., ☎ 028-9032-1713, the most central of Belfast's Catholic churches. Opened in 1842, this church is one of the most original Tudor Revival churches in Ireland, with a unique facade of red brick, stone-dressed castellations, and octangular corner turrets. The interior is even more interesting, designed on a lateral plan with the carved white marble altar on one of the longer walls. The lace-like fan-vaulted ceiling is said to have been inspired by Henry VII's chapel at

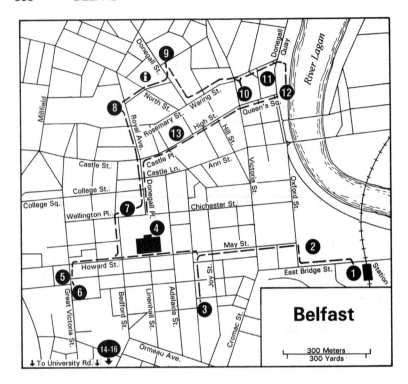

Westminster Abbey. *Hours of opening are posted at the entrance; admission is free, but donations are welcome.*

Return to May Street and walk one-half block east to Donegall Square, the focal point of the downtown area and the setting for:

**\*CITY HALL** (4), Donegall Square, ☎ 028-9032-0202. *Open only for tours, given June–Sept., Mon.–Fri. at 10:30, 11:30 and 2:30, and Sat. at 2:30; Oct.–May, Mon.–Sat. at 2:30. Free admission.*

With its great green 173-foot-high dome visible for miles, this huge edifice is a vast Renaissance-style structure of Portland stone, modeled after St. Paul's Cathedral of London. It opened in 1906, almost 20 years after Belfast had achieved the status of a city from Queen Victoria whose statue stands at the front entrance of the building. The palace-like building was erected as a symbol of the city's wealth and self-confidence. It is also impressive inside, with a decor of Edwardian-style stained glass and marble, ornate plasterwork, and a mural by Belfast artist John Luke depicting the industries such as shipbuilding and linen-making that have made the city prosperous. Tours, which last about 45 minutes, require advance reservations.

From Donegal Square S., take a short detour west along Howard Street for two blocks to Great Victoria Street and turn left. On the right is the **Grand Opera House** (5), Great Victoria St., ☎ 028-9024-1919, an ornate Victorian gem of a building dating back to 1894. The exterior is rich in fanciful turrets and curlicues, while the interior is a panorama of brass rails, gilded balconies, and exotic motifs. It is the home of Opera Northern Ireland, an ever-changing program of ballet and concerts. *Not open to the public except for performances.*

Still more Victoriana awaits directly across the street at the **\*Crown Liquor Saloon** (6), 44 Great Victoria St., ☎ 028-9024-9476, the veritable benchmark of Belfast pubs, built in 1885. Although it functions as a full-time pub, it is maintained by the National Trust and revered with a museum-like awe by its regular patrons and visitors from near and far. Step inside and sit in one of the 10 authentic carved oak snugs on the right, each with its own bell and doors topped by lions or griffons; or take a place along the long bar with inlaid colored glass and marble trim. Savor your favorite beverage amid a decor of richly colored tiles, stained and smoked glass, gas lights, beveled mirrors, wooden arches, and red-and-yellow tin ceiling. *Open Mon.–Sat. 11:30–11, Sun. 12:30–2:30 and 7–10. No admission charge.*

Retrace your steps back to Donegall Square to visit the **\*Linen Hall Library** (7), 17 Donegall Sq. N., ☎ 028-9032-1707, Belfast's oldest library, founded in 1788 as an independent charitable institution. Now housed in an old linen warehouse, the library was originally across the street at the old White Linen Hall which was demolished a century ago to make way for the coming of City Hall. This building was designed in a distinctly Edwardian style by Charles Lanyon, a Belfast architect who is credited with many of the city's finest buildings. The shelves are lined with old and rare books as well as current volumes. Standout sections include a Robert Burns collection, an Irish collection of over 20,000 volumes, and a political collection of over 80,000 documents on every aspect of political life in Northern Ireland since 1968. *Open Mon.–Wed. and Fri. 9:30–5:30, Thurs. 9:30–8:30, Sat. 9:30–4. Admission is free. Café.*

Turn left at the Library and left again onto Donegall Place. This marks the beginning of a pedestrianized area, delightful for strolling. It is lined with interesting stores featuring local crafts including linen shops. After two blocks, Donegall Place becomes Royal Avenue, the prime shopping street of Belfast. Take some time to browse. On the left is the **Castlecourt Centre** (8), the main downtown multi-story enclosed shopping mall, with a dozen boutiques, shops, and eateries.

Take a right onto the North Street Arcade and follow it to North Street. On the left is the Northern Ireland Tourist Board, a good source of information about Belfast and beyond. Continue for one-half block to Donegall Street, and turn left. Walk one-half block and straight ahead on the right is **St. Anne's Cathedral** (9), Lr. Donegall St., ☎ 028-9032-8332, Belfast's principal Anglican Cathedral. It took 86 years to build it completely—from 1899 to 1985, so it combines several architectural styles, but Irish Romanesque predominates. The interior is dominated by a long and lofty nave, and the baptistry ceiling features a striking mosaic commemorating the landing of St. Patrick at Saul in 432. *Hours of opening are posted outside. Admission is free.*

Take a left and walk one block south to Waring Street and turn left. This street displays some of Belfast's distinctive architecture. Take note of the **Ulster Bank** (1860), which looks like a Venetian palace, with sculptured rooftop figures of Britannia flanked by Justice and Commerce, and a dozen smaller classical figures.

From Waring Street, cross over to Albert Square. On the right is the **Albert Memorial Clock Tower** (10), Belfast's "Big Ben," a Gothic Revival landmark erected in 1867–1869. Continue east on Albert Square. To the right is the E-shaped **Custom House** (11), a large mellow yellow edifice built in 1857 by Charles Lanyon. The front of the building, which faces the River Lagan, features a sculptured pediment with *Britannia, Neptune,* and *Mercury* gazing out to sea. To the right, stretching over the river, is the **Lagan Weir**, erected in 1993 to improve the waterfront.

Make your way across the busy thoroughfare of swirling traffic, following traffic lights, signals, and signposts, to visit one of the city's newest purpose-built attractions, the **Lagan Lookout** (12), Donegall Quay, ☎ 028-9031-5444, a visitor center focusing on the River Lagan and its new weir. Using a series of high-tech and hands-on videos, computers, exhibits, and illustrations, visitors can explore the industrial, engineering, and folk history of the harbor. Huge wrap-around windows look out onto the river and all of its activities. *Open Mar.–Sept., Mon.–Fri. 11–5, Sat. noon–5, Sun 2–5; Oct.–Feb., Mon.–Fri. 11:30–3:30, Sat. 1–4:30, Sun. 2–4. Adults £1.50, seniors £1, children, 75p. Shop.*

Retrace your steps back to the Clock Tower and then make a left onto **High Street**, one of the city's oldest streets. After one block, you will come to a small cobblestone lane, known as Wine Cellar Entry. It is the setting for Belfast's oldest pub, **White's Tavern** (13), established in 1630 as a wine and spirit merchant shop, and rebuilt in 1790. Step in, order your favorite beverage, and enjoy the old Belfast ambiance amid the brick arches, ornate snugs, old barrels, and framed newspaper clippings dating back at least 200 years. *Open Mon.–Sat. 11:30-11, Sun. 12:30–2:30 and 7–10. No admission charge.*

Return to High Street, which becomes Castle Place as it melds into a pedestrian area. Make a left onto Donegall Place, and straight ahead is Donegall Square. Walk to the east side of the square and board bus #69, #70, or #71 (or a taxi) to complete the rest of the tour in Belfast's university quarter.

The bus will take you to **Queen's University** (14), University Road, ☎ 028-9024-5133, Belfast's hub of learning. Established in 1845, the same year as the universities in Cork and Galway as part of the national system, this school became independent in 1909. Charles Lanyon, who designed so

many of Belfast's buildings, was the architect of this red brick Tudor complex. It is said that the central college building was modeled after
Magdalen College of Oxford. The main features here are a Tudor cloister
and mullioned windows. Each November, the university hosts a leading
musical and arts event open to the public, *The Belfast Festival at Queen's*.
Although most buildings are not open to the public, the campus film theater is; phone ☎ 028-9024-4857 for schedules.

Directly south of the campus is Belfast's star attraction:

**\*THE ULSTER MUSEUM** (15), Stranmillis Rd., ☎ 028-9038-3000. *Open
Mon.–Fri. 10–5, Sat. 1–5, Sun. 2–5. Admission is free. Shop. Café.*

As the national museum for Northern Ireland, this graceful classical-
style four-story building is a treasure-trove of history, geography, science,
and culture, reflecting 9,000 years of information and discoveries.
Highlights include a section on Ulster with samples of original spinning
wheels used in linen-making, currency dating back to the 13th century,
and watercolors and oil paintings of Belfast's early days. In the antiquities
section, you'll find everything from Neolithic tools and gold pieces dating
from Ireland's Bronze Age, to an authentic Egyptian mummy named
*Takabuti*. The Botany and Zoology section not only displays specimens
Irish flora and fauna, but exotic rare butterflies and a giant bird-eating spi-
der as well. Other collections range from contemporary international and
Irish art, to Irish furniture, glass, silver, ceramics, and costume. Of special
interest is a gold and silver jewelry collection recovered by divers in 1968
from the Armada treasure ship *Girona*, wrecked off the Giant's Causeway
in 1588. Allow two to three hours at a minimum to take it all in. A free
"route map" is yours for the asking.

Directly behind the museum is Belfast's chief horticultural attraction,
the:

**\*BOTANIC GARDENS** (16), University Rd and Stranmillis Rd., ☎ 028-9032-
4902. *Gardens open daily dawn to dusk. Palm House and Tropical Ravine
open April–Sept., Mon.–Fri. 10–12 and 1–5, Sat.–Sun. 2–5; Oct.–March,
Mon.–Fri. 10–12 and 1–4, Sat.–Sun. 2–4. Admission is free to all attractions.*

Located between the grounds of the university and the River Lagan,
this 28-acre verdant setting was established in 1829 by the Belfast Botanic
and Horticultural Society as a place of natural beauty for the local people
to enjoy. It has grown ever more beautiful over the years, particularly the
rose garden and herbaceous borders sections. The grounds include two
buildings that shelter exotic and tender plants. The **Palm House**, designed
in 1839 by the ubiquitous Charles Lanyon, is the earliest surviving example
of a curvilinear cast-iron glasshouse. Lanyon created the building with the
Dublin ironfounder Richard Turner who went on to build the palm houses at Kew Gardens in London and the Botanic Gardens at Glasnevein in
Dublin. Restored in 1983, it is well stocked with exotic palms and other
delicate plants from around the world. The **Tropical Ravine**, or Fernery,

added in 1889, is designed in grand Victorian style with a sunken glen overlooked by a balcony, to provide a steamy atmosphere for exotic warm weather ferns and jungle plants such as sugar cane, coffee, cinnamon, banana, aloe, ivory nut, rubber, bamboo, and guava.

Return to Donegall Square in the city center via bus, taxi, or by strolling the one mile north via University Road to Shaftsbury Square, and then via Great Victoria Street, or via Dublin Road and Bedford Street, to complete the tour.

# The Antrim Coast

A s the home of the Giant's Causeway and Old Bushmills Distillery, the coast of County Antrim probably does not need anything else to draw visitors. But those two popular attractions are only the beginning. On the same route, you can take in all the beauties of the nine Glens of Antrim plus endless coastal vistas, and an enchanting assortment of colorful harbor towns and seaside villages, not to mention two of Ireland's most impressive castles at Carrickfergus and Dunluce.

How to do it all in one day? Start early.

## GETTING THERE:

The Antrim Coast is literally at Belfast's back door. Just follow the M1 north out of Belfast to the A2, which rims the whole coast. From Belfast to Portrush on this scenic route is just over 75 miles. On the return trip, you can save time and mileage by returning via Ballymena, a distance of about 60 miles via A26 and M2.

## PRACTICALITIES:

The best news is that the roads in County Antrim are excellent, wide and well-surfaced, even along the curving coastline. You can make good mileage, averaging 40 miles an hour at most times, although you'll probably be making a lot of stops for exploring, picture-taking, and touring. The return trip to Belfast will take only a little over an hour since part of the journey will be done on M2, one of the North's superhighways.

If you prefer to take public transport, sightseeing tours of the Antrim Coast and Giant's Causeway are operated every Tuesday, late June through September, by **Ulsterbus**, Europa Bus Centre, Glengall St., Belfast, ☎ 028-9033-3000.

Touring individual sites takes time—at least two hours at the Giant's Causeway or Carrick-a-rede, one hour at Old Bushmills, and a half-hour at the various castles. It's impossible to do everything in one day, so pick the attractions that interest you most and skip the others. The scenic drive along the Glens of Antrim coast can easily be done en route. If you wish to explore the side roads into individual glens, you'll need another day.

For information, contact the **Carrickfergus Tourist Office**, Antrim St., Carrickfergus, ☎ 028-8336-6455, open all year; **Ballycastle Tourist Office**, 7 Mary St., Ballycastle, ☎ 028-2076-2024, open all year; **Giant's Causeway Tourist Office**, Giant's Causeway, 44 Causeway Rd., Co. Antrim, ☎ 028-2073-1855, open all year; or **Portrush Tourist Office**, Dunluce Centre, 10 Sandhill

Dr., Portrush, ☎ 028-2582-3333, open April to October.

As of April 22, 2000, Northern Ireland has a new uniform area code—028—instead of various codes for different cities and counties. All numbers have changed from six to eight digits, and all are preceded by 028.

## FOOD AND DRINK:

**Bushmills Inn** (25 Main St., Bushmills) Dating back to the 17th century, this inn is a popular spot for a snack or full meal, within walking distance of the famous distillery. Relax amid an Old World decor of open fireplaces, gas lamps, and antiques. The bar food ranges from creative salads to hearty soups and sandwiches, while the main dining room uses recipes featuring Bushmills whiskies. ☎ 028-2073-2339. £ to ££

**The Coffee Shop** (Dunluce Centre, 10 Sandhill Dr., Portrush) Located in a busy and conveniently located visitor center near the beach, this bi-level self-service restaurant offers light meals all day in a Victorian setting. Specialties include North of Ireland favorites such as Ulster fry, steak and onion pie, and sausage rolls, as well as beef or chicken burgers, baked potatoes with a choice of fillings, and home-baked pastries, croissants, biscuits, and scones. X: Mon.–Fri. in mid-Sept.–March. ☎ 028- 2582-4444. £

**Harbour Lights** (11 Harbour Rd., Carnlough) For lunch or dinner or just a cup of coffee/tea and a freshly baked scone, this is a great stop along the scenic Glens of Antrim drive. Situated on the second floor of a harbourfront building overlooking both the town and the sea, this charming café offers views to match the great food. X: Mon.–Thurs. in Sept.–May. ☎ 028-2888-5950. £ to ££

**Hillcrest House** (306 Whitepark Rd., Giant's Causeway) Ideally positioned opposite the entrance to the causeway and overlooking the coast, this modern wide-windowed restaurant is especially in demand at sunset time. Bar food is served all day and full meals in the evening. The menu features local ingredients such as Antrim duck or sole Inishowen, as well as sauces laced with Bushmills whiskeys. X: Sun. ☎ 028-2073-1577. £ to ££

**Londonderry Arms** (20 Harbour Rd., Carnlough) Dating back to 1848 and once in the hands of Winston Churchill via inheritance, this historic ivy-clad inn is hard to pass by. It overlooks the harbor, at the foot of Glencloy. Bar food ranges from soups and sandwiches to a ploughman's platter of local cheeses, while full meals focus on traditional dishes such as roast chicken and bacon, or rib of beef with horseradish sauce. ☎ 028-2888-5235. £ to ££

**Ramore** (Ramore St., Portrush) Overlooking the harbor of a popular seaside resort, this modern restaurant/wine-bar offers international cuisine prepared in an open kitchen with gourmet flair. House specialties range from paella and Thai chicken to tempura prawns or tagliatelle with Roquefort cheese sauce and bacon. Dinner only, but bistro snacks are served for lunch in the wine bar. X: Mon.–Sun. and Feb. ☎ 028-2584-2313. ££ to £££

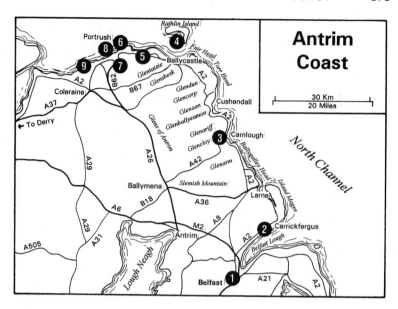

## SUGGESTED TOUR:

Depart **Belfast** (1) in a northerly direction on the main M1 roadway, accessible easily from most parts of the city including from Donegall Square via Howard Street. Continue north through pleasant residential sections, bearing right to join the A2 road, with Belfast Lough visible on the right. Follow A2 all the way to **Carrickfergus**, almost 12 miles up the coast. One of the oldest towns in Northern Ireland, it is named after a 6th-century Gaelic king called Fergus. It is said proudly by the locals that Carrickfergus was a thriving town when Belfast was a sandbank. Be that as it may, it was indeed the north's main port until Belfast began to expand in the 17th century. The principal structure of the town is built on an outcrop of basalt rock standing watch over the harbor:

**\*CARRICKFERGUS CASTLE** (2), Antrim St., Carrickfergus, ☎ 028-8335-1273. *Open April–Sept., Mon.–Sat. 10–6, Sun. 2–6; Oct.–March, Mon.–Sat. 10–4, Sun. 2–4. Adults £2.70, seniors and children £1.35. Tours. Shop. Café.*

Considered as Northern Ireland's largest and best preserved Norman castle, this massive stone fortress was started in 1180 by John de Courcy, the first Norman lord of Ulster. It has since had a long and glorious history and was garrisoned until 1928. The focal point is a much-photographed square keep that is 90-feet high (five stories), with eight-foot-thick walls. Enter through a gate flanked by two round towers. Inside, well-versed guides explain the castle's history, and show off various highlights such as an old castle well and a dungeon. Take time to explore the interior, authentically refurbished and filled with its many exhibits and a 10-minute audiovisual. In addition, there are opportunities to try your hand at medieval writing, dressing up in armor, or taking part in medieval games. In the summer months, the grounds hold medieval fairs, crafts markets, and pageants, as well as ever-changing exhibits and events on archery and military tatoos.

Continue on A2 for 8.5 miles, skirting around **Larne**, a busy manufacturing town and seaport, second only to Belfast as a port. It is the closest point to Britain, just about 12 miles west of Scotland, so there are many super-speed car ferries, huge freight ships and pleasure craft coming and going in the harbor.

Continue north along the A2. The road is particularly wide and well-surfaced. This stretch of road, the 25 miles from Larne to Cushendall, was widely recognized as a great engineering feat when it was constructed in the 1830s. The magnificent coast curves around the base of steep headlands, with the Irish Sea on the right and the Glens of Antrim rising on the left. It is one of Ireland's most spectacular drives.

As you embark north of Larne, to the left in the distance, is **Slemish Mountain** (1,437 feet), where St. Patrick, captured as a boy and brought to Ireland, is said to have been a shepherd. Next on the left, after four miles, is **Ballygalley Head**, rising to 300 feet and offering panoramic coastal views of Ballygalley Harbour.

Within five miles, on the left the road now begins to reveal the verdant panoramas of the *Glens of Antrim, nine lovely valleys, formed 20,000 years ago by retreating glaciers. Each glen has an individual name, based on the original Gaelic language or on local legends and lore. Although not all of the meanings are absolutely known for certain, the popular translations are as follows:

**Glenarm**, from the Irish language, *Gleann Arma,* meaning "glen of the army." It is thought to refer to some battle or military gathering that might have taken place here, which is highly likely since the glen was the home of the Irish MacDonnell clan for many centuries. This glen is deemed to have been the first and oldest of the glens.

**Glencloy**, from the Irish language *Gleann Claidhe,* meaning "the glen of the fences," thought to imply a stone fence, or possibly "glen of the hedges." This glen is dotted with a lattice of stone barriers, interspersed with streams and waterfalls.

**Glenariff**, from the Irish language *Gleann Aireamh,* meaning "glen of the arable land" or "ploughman's glen." It is a lovely blend or farms and waterfalls, once described by William Makepiece Thackery as "Switzerland in miniature." At the foot of Glenariff is Red Bay which takes its name from its sloping red sandstone cliffs.

**Glenballyeamon**, from the Irish language, *Gleann Bhaile Éamainn,* meaning "glen of Éamainn's homestead" or, to be more Anglicized, "glen of Edward's homestead." This glen is said to be the barest of all, with traces of ancient forts throughout the countryside.

**Glenaan,** from the Irish language *An Gleann,* meaning "the valley" or "glen of the rush lights." This glen is famed as the setting for the grave of the legendary Oisin, a poet warrior of the 3rd century, who was thought to have been the son of the mythological Irish hero Finn MacCool.

**Glencorp,** thought to mean "glen of the slaughter," but probably based on legend more than language. It is known today for its lovely hill farms and white-clad slopes.

**Glendun,** from the Irish language *Gleann Duinne,* meaning "valley of the river Dunn" or traditionally "the brown glen." The most characteristic feature today is its wealth of bridges and fords over the river.

**Glenshesk,** from the Irish language *Glean Seirc,* meaning "glen of the sedges." This glen is deemed the wildest and most unspoiled of all.

**Glentaisie,** traditionally taken to mean "Taisie's glen." The overall characteristic of this glen is that it is neat and tidy.

Many of the people who live here are descended from the ancient Irish and their Hebridean cousins, the Scots, so this area is one of the last places in Northern Ireland where Gaelic is still a spoken language.

As you drive from one glen to the other, you'll see that the geological variety of the glens provides an ever-changing pattern of scenery so that each glen has its own particular profile and personality, while the whole area has a unity seldom found in nature.

Better than any guide, the glens speak for themselves in a language of lush natural beauty and wide open vistas. There are also several towns to look out for and stop to explore. Between Glencloy and Glenariff is **Carnlough**, an old limestone quarry town with a sandy bay and picturesque harbor with an enticing ivy-clad Old World inn dating back to 1848. Known as **The Londonderry Arms** (3), it was once owned by Winston Churchill (see Food and Drink).

Near the foot of Glenballyeamon is **Cushendall**, a quiet resort village whose streets are lined with stately Georgian and Regency houses. It takes its name from the River Dall which runs through it. In the village center is a curious structure called Curfew Tower, built as a jail in 1809.

Three miles to the north is **\*Cushendun**, sitting on the shore where Glendun and Glencorp sweep together toward the sea. It is one of the most picturesque villages in all of Ireland, and certainly one of the smallest, with a population of 50. Almost everyone stops to take a picture of its lovely Cornish-style whitewashed cottages. The entire village is now maintained by the National Trust.

From Cushendun, you have a choice of taking the coast road via Torr Head and Fair Head, both looking out toward the Scottish Isle of Mull, or following the main A2 road, to Ballycastle. Either way, it is just over 12 miles, but your choice should be dictated by timing, weather visibility, and interests, since the coastal route will take longer.

**Ballycastle**, a popular beach resort village, stands at the junction of Glenshesk and Glentaisie, north of Knocklayd Hill (1,696 feet). The town revolves around The Diamond, a central area that was the original setting of the Scottish MacDonnell family castle. Today The Diamond is surrounded by shops, pubs, and other enterprises. Each August it is also the setting for the *Oul' Lammas Fair,* one of the oldest traditional festivals in all of Ireland. Six miles off the coast sits **Rathlin Island**, said to have been the first place in Ireland attacked by Vikings (in 795). Steep 200-foot-high white limestone cliffs surround most of the island, and it is a haven for sea birds, although 100 hardy human souls still continue to occupy it. Each day a boat goes out from Ballycastle at 10:30 in the morning for the 50-minute crossing and returns at 4 in the afternoon. For more information, contact **Rathlin Cruises** (4), ☎ 028-2076-2024.

Take the coastal road from Ballycastle, B15, heading toward the Giant's Causeway, about 12 miles. En route, after five miles, if you feel like a bit of exercise, follow signs for the **Carrick-a-rede Rope Bridge** (5), a swaying 63-foot wooden plank bridge with a wire handrail positioned 80 feet above the sea, spanning an open chasm between the mainland and Carrick-a-rede Island. Each spring fishermen put up the bridge to give them access to a salmon fishery on the island, but the general public is welcome to use the bridge, just for the thrill of it. Don't be surprised if the whole scene looks a little familiar. This is the bridge featured in current Irish Tourist Board/Northern Ireland Tourist Board joint print and television advertising, showing a bride hesitatingly crossing the bridge, with her veil blowing skyward in the winds, as she goes to meet her groom. Access is from Larrybane car park, where there is a visitor center operated by the National Trust, ☎ 028-2073-1159. After parking your car, you'll have to walk one mile (about 15–20 minutes) along a cliff path to get to the bridge. *Bridge open May to mid-Sept. in daylight; visitor center is open May, Sat.–Sun.1–5; June–Aug. daily noon–6. Parking costs £2.*

After passing White Park Bay on the right, all signs literally lead to:

**\*GIANT'S CAUSEWAY** (6), Causeway Head, near Bushmills, ☎ 028-2073-1159. *Open daily during daylight hours. Free access to the site at all times. Visitor Centre, ☎ 028-2073-1855. Open daily March 17–Oct. 10–7; Nov. to mid-March 10–4:30. Admission is free, but parking is £3 per car. Audiovisual: Adults £1, seniors 80p, children 50p. Minibus: 80p per person round-trip. Shop. Café.*

Extending for three miles along the coast, this unique natural rock formation is undoubtedly Northern Ireland's most photographed attraction. Often called the 8th wonder of the world, it is listed on the UNESCO World Heritage List of sites. It consists of more than 37,000 tightly packed basalt columns, almost like stone steps. The tops of the stones begin at the foot of the coastal cliffs and reach into the sea, disappearing under the water. Most of the stones are six-sided in shape and vary in size, with some as tall as 40 feet. They were formed by quick cooling and shrinking lava that burst to the Earth's surface about 70 million years ago, according to geologists, but local lore has a different view. It is believed that Finn

MacCool, a legendary Irish giant, put the stones in place as a causeway or highway across the sea to Scotland, and hence the name "Giant's Causeway." No matter what explanation you accept, it is a one-of-a-kind site, not duplicated anywhere else in Ireland. Start a tour by looking at the various exhibits and displays in the visitor center, maintained by the National Trust. The 25-minute audiovisual provides a thorough overview on the history and geology of the area. Then step outside and explore the rocks for yourself. You can walk down a graded pathway, which takes about a half-hour, but the walk back up the hill can be strenuous and take even longer. The best plan is to buy a round-trip fare on the minibus which departs every 15 minutes from the back door of the center. This ride down takes less than five minutes, and once you are at the site, you can stay as long as you wish, taking the minibus of your choice back up the hill, on a first-come basis. It is breezy and open at the site so dress warmly, and bring rain gear in case of a sudden shower. If you want to do some climbing on the rocks, wear appropriate footwear. Once you are down at the rock site, there is no place to take shelter until you return to the visitor center. In spite of these minor cautions, it is well worth making the trek down to the actual coastline site—a definite "must see" on a tour of Northern Ireland. Allow about two hours between the visitor center and the actual site itself.

From the causeway, re-join the A2 road, heading southwest, and visit **Bushmills**, a small town on the River Bush that whiskey has made famous around the world. Take time to visit the:

**\*OLD BUSHMILLS DISTILLERY & VISITOR CENTRE** (7), Main St., Bushmills, ☎ 028-2073-1521. *Open Sept.–May, Mon.–Thurs. 9–12 and 1:30–3:30, Fri. 9–12; June–Aug., Mon.–Thurs. 9–12 and 1:30–4, Fri. 9–4, Sat. 10–4. Adults £3.50, seniors £3, children £1.50 (must be accompanied by an adult). Tours. Shop. Café.*

Officially licensed in 1608, this landmark distillery is the oldest of its kind in the world. Visitors are welcome to take a walk-through tour of the plant to view the whole process, essentially unchanged over the centuries. Escorted by well-versed guides with informative and amusing commentaries, the tours begin with the barley. You'll see ripe golden Irish barley as it is examined, graded and cleaned. The chosen barley is then poured into tanks of water supplied by the River Bush which runs alongside the distillery. Next the barley is spread out to sprout and become malt. After the malt is dried in a kiln that is kept separate from any smoke or heat, it is stored in great bins to mellow for several weeks. The tour then moves on to fermenting process, followed by triple distillation, as the whiskey-to-be flows through three consecutive copper pot stills. The resulting spirits are then placed in oak casks to mature. The final step is the assembly line for bottling, labeling, and boxing. The tours, which last about 40 minutes, culminate at the Potstill Bar, a pub-style "tasting room" where guests are invited to sample the results.

Return to the A2 road, and two miles west is **Dunluce Castle** (8), Bushmills/Portrush Rd., Portrush, ☎ 028-2073-1938, another of Northern Ireland's well-photographed castles. Built by Richard de Burgh, the Earl of Ulster in c. 1300, it is a splendid structure sitting on basalt rock jutting out over the sea, reached by a wooden walkway. Like most castles, it has a storied history. It was captured by the Irish MacDonnells, chiefs of Antrim, in 1584 and remained their base of power for many years. In 1639, the kitchen fell off into the sea, along with several domestic staff. That unfortunate incident signaled the demise of the castle and it declined into ruin shortly afterward. A curtain wall and two towers are still in remarkable shape, as is a gatehouse. *Open April–Sept., Mon.–Sat. 10–7, Sun. 11–7; Oct.–March, Tues.–Sat. 10–4, Sun. 2–4. Adults £1.50, seniors and children 75p. Tours.*

It is three miles west to **Portrush**, a popular seaside resort and home of the world-class Royal Portrush Golf Club. If time allows, take a stroll on the beach or visit **Dunluce Centre** (9), 10 Sandhill Dr., Portrush, ☎ 028-2582-4444, a visitor center that is geared toward families with multimedia shows and thrill rides. For adults, it is a good comfort stop, with a Victorian-style arcade of shops and restaurants. It also has a viewing tower offering panoramic views of the whole northern coast. *Open April–June, Mon.–Fri. noon–5, Sat.–Sun. noon–7; July–Aug., daily 10–8; first two weeks Sept. daily noon–5; mid-Sept–March, Sat.–Sun. noon–5. Admission is free to restaurants and shops, but £5 per person for rides and shows.*

At this point, the day must draw to a close. Follow signs south toward Coleraine, but don't get involved in that busy city's downtown traffic. Take the ring-road around Coleraine and head for A26 toward Ballymena, and then linking up with the M2 main road into Belfast.

# Armagh &
# St. Patrick's Country

Who has not heard of St. Patrick? Each year, on March 17th, almost the whole world marks St. Patrick's Day in some way, whether it be by marching in parades, wearing little green shamrocks, singing Irish songs, or drinking green beer. No other European saint, except perhaps St. Nicholas, has such wide recognition.

Although no one knows exactly where or when Patrick was born, most people agree that he was one of Ireland's most frequent travelers between 432 and 461, the years when he went about spreading Christianity to every city and town, mountain and hillside, nook and cranny of the country.

It is certainly impossible to come to Ireland without hearing of Patrick. Although churches, shrines, monasteries, and holy wells of various sizes and types are attributed to Patrick all over the Emerald Isle, nowhere are there more Patrick-connections than in Armagh, the main city of County Armagh, about 40 miles southwest of Belfast.

Of all the high and mighty spots of Ireland, Patrick chose Armagh as his base to spread the new religion of Christianity, probably c. 445. He began his mission by asking the local chieftain Daire for permission to build a church. At first Daire gave him a site near the base of the hill, but later when the chieftain saw how well the evangelist was doing, Daire gave Patrick a hilltop, and Patrick built a great church, later to become known as St. Patrick's Cathedral. It was henceforth considered as his principal church and bishopric.

As history shows, Patrick's foundation was only the beginning. Many other churches, schools, and colleges grew up around the original site as the settlement developed into one of the greatest known centers of religion and learning during the Dark Ages. By the 8th century, Armagh was generally accepted as the ecclesiastical capital of Ireland, surpassing Cashel, Clonmacnois, and all others. In c. 807 the great *Book of Armagh* was written by Ferdomnach, a scribe at the School of Armagh. That treasured manuscript, like *The Book of Kells,* is now on display in Dublin's Trinity College (see page 39).

Unfortunately, by the middle of 9th century this "city of saints and scholars" experienced unwelcome raids and plunderings by the Vikings. With its reputation of learning and wealth, Armagh proved an irresistible target, with at least 10 attacks recorded between 831 and 1013. The power of the Vikings was finally broken at Clontarf in 1014 by the Irish high king

Brian Boru. Although he perished in that battle, Brian's dying wish was to be buried in Armagh at St. Patrick's original church site. The burial of the high king at Armagh only magnified the importance of the city even more. In 1152 the Synod of Kells bestowed on the archbishop of Armagh the title of Primate of All Ireland, a epithet that still is carried on today.

Like the rest of Ireland, Armagh eventually endured raids and conquests by the Normans and English forces from medieval times onward. It did not begin to recover until the 18th century when it was rebuilt in a largely Georgian style, thanks to a resident primate, Archbishop Robinson. He employed Thomas Cooley and Francis Johnston, two architects responsible for some of Ireland's finest Georgian buildings including those in Dublin, both of whom created a legacy of beautiful streetscapes and terraces in Armagh.

Even with Georgian enhancements, the focal point of Armagh today remains the site of the 5th-century church. Since Patrick's time, a house of God has stood on the hill for over 15 centuries, and Armagh is still the ecclesiastical capital of Ireland. Today, however, there are two St. Patrick's Cathedrals—the original site which now belongs to the Church of Ireland (Anglican) and a Catholic edifice, less than a half-mile away. The city of Armagh offers a number of attractions that help to illuminate the story of St. Patrick. But the story does not end here. From Armagh, it is an easy drive eastward to County Down and an area known as St. Patrick's Vale—a beautiful section of countryside that also embraced St. Patrick. This area is the place where he completed his ministry. St. Patrick was laid to rest in the cemetery of Downpatrick Cathedral in the shadow of the Mountains of Mourne.

## GETTING THERE:

From Belfast, it is just an hour's drive to Armagh, via the M1 Motorway and the M12. **Ulsterbus** operates a regular schedule of buses every day from Belfast to Armagh; travel time is 1 hour and 20 minutes. However, to do this complete tour requires going from Armagh through County Down, so a car is required. The complete circuit is just over 100 miles.

## PRACTICALITIES:

The best way to do this tour is in two parts. Drive to Armagh and then spend the morning touring the sights of the city, primarily on foot. Park your car at the parking area next to the tourist office and walk around the town. In the afternoon, return to your car to drive the scenic route through St. Patrick's Vale in County Down and back to Belfast.

If you prefer to take public transport, sightseeing tours of Armagh and part of County Down are operated every Thursday, late June through September, by **Ulsterbus**, Europa Bus Centre, Glengall St., Belfast, ☎ 028-9033-3000.

For information, contact the **Armagh Tourist Information Centre**, Old Bank Building, 40 English St., Armagh, Co. Armagh, ☎ 028-3752-1800, open all year; **Down Tourist Information Centre**, 74 Market St., Downpatrick, Co. Down, ☎ 028-4461-2233, open all year; and **Newcastle Tourist Information Centre**, 10–14 Central Promenade, Newcastle, Co. Down, ☎ 028-4372-2222, open all year.

As of April 23, 200, Northern Ireland has a new uniform area code— **028**—instead of various codes for different cities and counties. All numbers have changed from six to eight digits, and all are preceded by 028.

## FOOD AND DRINK:

In the heart of apple orchard country, Armagh is noted for dishes such as potato apple bread and apple pudding. County Down, on the edge of the sea, is a seafood haven, with local specialties such as Strangford oysters, and Kilkeel herring and prawns.

**Charlemont Arms** (63-65 Lr. English St., Armagh) An 18th-century atmosphere prevails at this little inn tucked in the heart of town. Bar snacks, available all day, feature local favorites such as mince steak pie, steak and kidney pie, stuffed bacon rolls and chips, and Irish stew, as well as burgers and sandwiches. ☎ 028-3752-2028. £ to ££

**Hester's Place** (12 English St.) Situated in the heart of downtown near the tourist office, this friendly daytime café serves breakfast, lunch and afternoon tea. Specialties range from home-baked scones to Irish stew, bacon and cabbage, and (a local favorite) Armagh apple tart and cream. X: Wed. & Sun. ☎ 028- 3752-2374. £

**Pavilion** (36 Downs Rd., Newcastle) Situated on the waterfront, this informal conservatory-style restaurant serves light food all day on ground level and full dinners upstairs at night. House specials include homemade soups, salads, steaks, chicken Kiev, and scampi. ☎ 028-4372-6239. £ to ££

**Percy French** (Downs Rd., Newcastle) An Old World atmosphere prevails at this cozy pub-restaurant named after the famous songwriter who composed the signature tune in praise of "the Mountains of Mourne which sweep down to the sea" outside. The menu offers snacks and full meals throughout the day, with emphasis on traditional stews and meat pies as well as refreshing salads and seafoods. ☎ 028-4372-3175. ££

**Pilgrim's Table** (40 English St, Armagh) Housed within the St. Patrick's Trian complex, this restaurant offers indoor and outdoor seating overlooking the city and its cathedrals. The self-service menu offers an ever-changing array of fresh salads, soups, casseroles, sandwiches, and tempting pastries. ☎ 028- 3752-7808. £

## SUGGESTED TOUR:

Start out from **Belfast** (1) via the main M1 Motorway and the M12, about 40 miles and a drive of one hour's duration. As you arrive in Armagh, follow the signs for the Tourist Information Office, 40 English Street, and park your car in the adjacent parking garage.

From here, make a sharp right turn to start your tour where St. Patrick started, the focal point of Armagh:

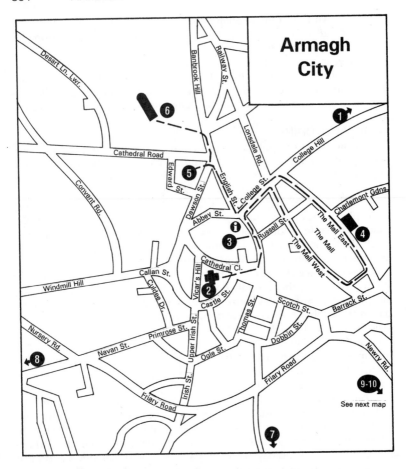

Armagh City

**\*ST. PATRICK'S CHURCH OF IRELAND CATHEDRAL** (2), Cathedral Close,
off Abbey St., Armagh, ☎ 028-3752-3142 or 028-3752-2611. *Open April–Oct.
daily 10–5; Nov.–March Mon.–Sat. 10–4. Tours during June–Aug. at 11:30 and
2:30. Admission is free, but donations are welcome.*

Set on high ground, this is the site on which St. Patrick built his principal church and headquarters in c. 445. Although little is left of the original structure, it has been a house of worship in Patrick's name for over
1,500 years. Today, rebuilt at least 17 times, it melds a mixture of architecture, with a rich variety of carved heads forming a frieze around the exterior. The predominant structure is from a 1834 restoration of a 13th-centu-
ry church. Highlights include an old medieval stairway in the south
transept; sections of an 11th-century Celtic Cross; an ancient granite figure known as the *Tandragee Idol,* an Irish warrior believed to date back to

Celtic times; and a baptismal font that is a copy of a curiously carved octagonal stone font found seven feet underground near the west door of the cathedral in 1805. Most visitors head straight to the north transept where a tablet on the west wall marks the grave of Brian Boru, Ireland's great high king of the 10th and 1lth centuries.

To get an overview on the city of Armagh and its other connections with St. Patrick, return to the tourist office and walk through for access into the city's newest attraction:

*ST. PATRICK'S TRIAN (3), 40 English St., Armagh, ☎ 028-3752-1801. *Open April–Sept., Mon.–Sat. 10–6, Sun. 1–6; Oct.–March, Mon.–Sat. 10–5, Sun. 2–5. Adults £3.75, seniors £2.75, children £2. Tours. Shop. Café.*

Who was St. Patrick? Where did he come from? What did he do? How and why did he make Armagh his headquarters? These and many other questions about the "Apostle of the Irish" are answered in this impressive three-part heritage center. Start with a walk-through tour of *The Armagh Story*, an interpretative area that relates the history of the city even before St. Patrick, in prehistoric and Celtic times. The focus then shifts to Patrick and his life and times in Armagh, followed by the Viking and Georgian eras. From here, you enter an audiovisual theater to see the 20-minute film *Belief*, which profiles the many types of beliefs held by humanity. The final segment, a particular favorite with children, is *The Land of Lilliput*, a hands-on exploration of Jonathan Swift's world as outlined in his book *Gulliver's Travels* which was partly written in Armagh. The center also includes art galleries, craft shops, and a permanent display on the *Book of Armagh*, a Biblical manuscript written in 807 by the Irish scribe Ferdomnach.

From the tourist office, take a left onto English Street and then a right on College Street. This will bring you to **The Mall**, Armagh's tree-lined Georgian centerpiece. This area, originally a race course, was also used for bull-baiting, cock-fighting and other sports, as well as a common grazing land. In 1773, these pursuits ceased and this grassy area evolved into its present format. The star feature of The Mall is the Georgian architecture of the buildings which line either side. The townhouses and terraces are ranked as the finest Georgian work in Northern Ireland. Here you can also visit the **Armagh County Museum** (4), The Mall East, Armagh, ☎ 028-3752-3070, for an in-depth look at the natural and social history of Armagh. Originally built as a national school in 1833, this museum also has an art gallery and extensive map collection. *Open Mon.–Fri. 10–5, Sat. 10–1 and 2–5. Admission is free.*

Return to English Street, and walk one block north to Cathedral Road. To the left is **The Shambles Market** (5), a local market area topped by an elegant cupola clock tower. Built in 1827, The Shambles still hosts a market for local produce every Tuesday and Friday.

Straight ahead is a steep climb up another hill to the *Roman Catholic Cathedral of St. Patrick* (6), Cathedral Rd., "the other" and much younger Patrician namesake which was built a little over a century ago (1840–73).

Perched high above the rest of the city, this Byzantine-style building with two loft spires and a carillon of 39 bells is in complete architectural contrast to the "original" cathedral. The interior is rich in lavish coloring, mosaics, and carvings. The pale blue ceiling and walls are painted and etched with the image of every Irish saint and a multitude of angels. In the summer months, visitors are welcome to tour a very comprehensive and interesting ecclesiastical museum on the premises. Sign-posts alert visitors when the museum is staffed and open. Panoramic city *views from the top of the cathedral's front steps are alone worth the trip to this site. *Open daily 8–6 or longer; admission is free.*

If you have not already retrieved your car for the trip up Cathedral Road, do so now and depart the downtown area, heading to the south end of the city. If time allows, visit:

**THE PALACE STABLES** (7), Friary Rd., Armagh, ☎ 028-3752-9629. *Open April–Sept., Mon.–Sat. 10–6, Sun. 1–6; Oct.–March, Mon.–Sat. 10–5, Sun. 2–5. Adults £3.50, seniors £2.70, children £2. Tours. Shop. Café.*

Although this site has little to do with St. Patrick, it does offer some enjoyable "hands-on" insight into Armagh as an ecclesiastical capital. This living-history museum, a former stable on the grounds of a bishop's residential palace, surrounds a cobbled courtyard, re-creating an 18th-century ambiance. Built by Archbishop Robinson when he came to Armagh in 1765, the palace itself today comprises the offices of the Armagh District Council. The interior of the stables now presents a walk-through tour of life in Armagh in 1776, using "a day in the life" format, with life-like figures in period dress, an audio commentary, and colorful murals. The tour also takes you into the Primate's Chapel, completed in 1786, one of the finest examples of Georgian neo-classicism in Ireland; the coachman's house, tack room, servants' tunnel, and ice house.

Before you leave Armagh, travel two miles west via A28 for a look at what Armagh was like long before St. Patrick:

**\*EMAIN MACHA/NAVAN FORT** (8), Killylea Rd., Armagh, ☎ 028-3752-5550. *Open April–June and Sept., Mon.–Fri. 10–6, Sat.–Sun. 11–6; July–Aug. Mon.–Sat. 10–7, Sun. 11–7; Oct.–March, Mon.–Fri. 10–5, Sat.–Sun. 11–6. Adults £3.95, children £2.25. Tours. Shop. Café.*

Although Armagh is integrally associated with St. Patrick, it was a significant place long before Christianity. The name Armagh, which comes from the Irish language *Ard Macha* means "Macha's Height," after the legendary pagan queen Macha who lived the mid-first millennium BC. The queen built a fortress on top of a hill and this great ceremonial enclosure is reputedly the spot she chose. It remained a royal site of the ancient kings of Ulster for 800 years until its destruction in AD 332. Today it is considered as Ulster's most important historical site. To re-create the illusion of an underground building, the visitor center has been built into the side of a small hill with a grassed-over roof. The exhibits and multimedia programs inside introduce the visitor to the world of pre-Christian Ireland and the wonder of the Celts, including Celtic rituals and beliefs.

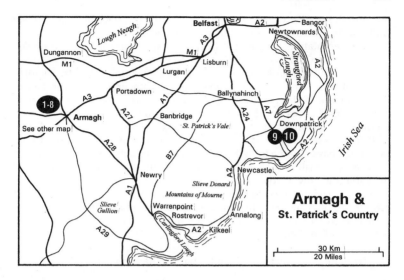

Armagh &
St. Patrick's Country

30 Km
20 Miles

Afterwards, you can walk to the fort itself and view the mound as well as a system of impressive earthworks, settlement sites, and sacred places, an area of unparalleled archaeological importance.

Depending on how much time you spend at Navan Fort, you may wish to go directly back to Belfast. If you still have a few hours to spare, then travel over to County Down via A28. It's just 18 miles to **Newry**, a busy manufacturing and mercantile town with a lovely setting in the center of a mountainous region divided in two parts by Carlingford Lough, a long arm of the Irish Sea. Mountains are visible from both sides of the town. On the west is Slieve Gullion (1,900 feet), and on the east are the legendary *Mountains of Mourne, immortalized in the Percy French song, *Where the Mountains of Mourne Sweep down to the Sea*.

From Newry, follow the A2 road for the scenic drive beside the Mourne Mountains, a 25-mile sweep along the coast of Carlingford Lough. To the left, 15 summits rise to over 2,000 feet, providing an ever-changing panorama in every mile. This is the start of the area known as **St. Patrick's Vale**.

Follow this splendid drive along A2 passing through a series of delightful seaports and fishing towns, including **Rostrevor**, the most sheltered place in Northern Ireland, known for the Mediterranean plants that grow by the seashore; **Warrenpoint**, with a lively waterfront and yacht marina; and **Kilkeel**, a fishing port specializing in prawns and herrings.

The drive culminates at Newcastle, a 19th-century Victorian seaside resort, with the Mourne Mountains on one side and the Irish Sea on the other. It is here that *Slieve Donard (2,796 feet), the highest mountain in the Mourne range and the highest peak in Northern Ireland, "sweeps down to the sea," as the song proclaims. Nearby is the **Royal County Down Golf Course,** one of the top-rated golf courses in the world.

The temptation is to linger, but the final chapter on St. Patrick still awaits. Take the A25 road 10 miles north to **Downpatrick.** The placename is derived from the Irish language *Dún Pádraig,* meaning "St. Patrick's fort." The focal point of the town is **Downpatrick Cathedral** (9) on the Hill of Down, off The Mall, a place of Christian prayer and worship since the time of St. Patrick. Successive churches have been built, replaced, and restored on this site, evolving to the present building. In the 12th century relics of St. Patrick were discovered here, giving rise to the belief that the intrepid saint must have spent a lot of time here, after Armagh. To add credence to the theory, a *slab of rock engraved simply with one word, *Pádraig,* sits in the cathedral graveyard.

The adjacent **Down County Museum** (10), The Mall, Downpatrick, ☎ 028-4461-5218, provides interesting exhibits and artifacts emphasizing St. Patrick' s strong links to this area. *Open mid-June to Sept., Mon.–Fri. 11–5, Sat.–Sun. 2–5; mid-Sept. to mid-June, Tues.–Fri. 11–5, Sat. 2–5. Free admission. Shop.*

From here it is just over 20 miles back to Belfast via the A7 road.

# Derry City

Perched on a hillside overlooking the Foyle Estuary, Derry is one of Ireland's oldest and most beautiful locations and unequivocally the finest example of a walled city. Yet life has not been easy here.

Derry, the second-largest city of Northern Ireland (population: 90,000) and the unofficial "capital" of the Northwest, has had many faces, both happy and sad. For almost 400 years, it has also had two names. Its original placename, from the Irish language *Doire*, meaning "oak grove," was given by its founder St. Columbkille (also known as Columb or Columba) in the 6th century, while the name Londonderry was conferred in 1613 by a group of wealthy English companies collectively known as The Honourable Irish Society.

The Society not only renamed the city, they built a strong mile-long wall around it and populated it with Protestant settlers from Britain. In the turbulent 16th and 17th centuries, the walled city of Londonderry resisted siege after siege, but never surrendered to a would-be conqueror, earning it the title of "Maiden City."

During the 18th and 19th centuries, Londonderry became the principal point of embarkation for emigrants leaving Ulster for the New World, giving it many lasting links with America. It also grew as a great port, shipbuilding hub, and shirt-manufacturing center. During World War II, Londonderry was one of the major naval bases used by the Allied forces.

In the past 30 years, the city has been deeply embroiled in The Troubles, almost torn apart as a geographic and political buffer between Northern Ireland and the Republic. The famous walls were closed off and sealed with barbed wire. It became a city divided, as the Unionists (mostly Protestants) gravitated to the east side of the Foyle, in an area known as Waterside, while the Nationalists (largely Catholics) remained on the west side of the water in an area known as Bogside.

In spite of age-old animosities, things have brightened in recent years. The cease-fire of 1994–1996, although short-lived, did much to restore harmony and hope to the people. Buildings were repaired, new attractions and shopping centers were added to the cityscape, and the celebrated walls were opened once again for unlimited pedestrian access. Tourism attractions in the city began to win major awards. At the edge of the walled city the Trinity Hotel debuted in late 1996—the first downtown lodging to open in a quarter-century. The Derry City Council has voted to drop the "London" from its name. Optimism and enthusiasm have begun to fill the air. And, on the world stage, Derry people have earned much-deserved plaudits, from Nobel Prize-winning poet Seamus Heaney to Tony Award-winning playwright Brian Friel.

Derry-born songwriter and musician Phil Coulter has won wide recognition for his song about Derry—*The Town I Loved So Well*. In many ways, his words have become a new anthem for Derry: "... deep inside (is) a burning pride... they carry on ... their spirit's been bruised, but never broken.... They will not forget, but their hearts are all set on tomorrow, and peace once again ...."

## GETTING THERE:

Derry is 73 miles west of Belfast, about a two-hour drive via M2 and A6. It is 43 miles from Donegal via N15 and A5, just over an hour's drive.

**Ulsterbus** provides frequent service from both Belfast and Donegal into Derry Bus Depot on Foyle Street, while **Northern Ireland Railways** operates several trains a day from Belfast into the Derry Rail Station, Waterside. Indirect rail service is also available to/from Dublin via Belfast.

In addition, sightseeing tours from Belfast to Derry are operated on certain dates, late June through September, by **Ulsterbus**, Foyle St., Derry City, ☎ 028-7126-2261.

## PRACTICALITIES:

Small and compact, the walled city of Derry, also referred to as the "Inner City," is ideal for walking, although it is built on a hill and the streets within the walls are steep. Walking on the walls requires climbing steps.

Parking within the walled city is difficult and scarce. The best plan is to park your car at one of the city's many enclosed parking areas, such as the Foyleside Shopping Complex, Foyle St. and Orchard St., or the Quayside Centre, Strand Road. Both are within easy walking distance of an entrance to the walled city. Once your car is securely parked, set out on foot for touring.

To assist visitors in getting to know Derry, **Inner City Guided Walking Tours** are conducted twice daily in the summer and at other times according to demand. Tours leave from the Tourist Information Centre at 44 Foyle St. Alternatively, **Foyle Civic Bus Tours** are operated on Tuesdays during July and August, departing from the Bus Depot on Foyle Street. For details about either type of tour, call ☎ 028-7126-7284.

For information, contact the **Derry Visitor & Convention Bureau**, 44 Foyle St., Derry, ☎ 028-7126-7284, open all year. As of April 22, 2000, Northern Ireland has a new uniform area code—**028**—instead of various codes for different cities and counties. All numbers have changed from six to eight digits, and all are preceded by 028.

## FOOD AND DRINK:

**Ardtara Country House** (8 Gorteade Rd., Upperlands, Maghera, Co. Derry, off the A6) Midway en route between Belfast and Derry, this country inn makes a relaxing stop for morning coffee, afternoon tea, or an elegant meal in the skylit Victorian dining room. Built in 1855, it is set on 8 acres of gardens and woodlands. ☎ 028-7964-4490. ££ to £££

**Austins Coffee Shop** (The Diamond) Situated on the top floor of the Victorian landmark department store of the same name, this informal café provides some of the best views of the inner city along with fresh salads, sandwiches, soups, and tempting pastries. X: Sun. ☎ 028-7126-1817. £

**Boston Tea Party** (Shipquay St.) Ensconced in the heart of the Derry Craft Village, this delightful spot offers a lot more than tea—soups, salads, sandwiches, sausage rolls, fish and chips, stews, and more. X: Sun. ☎ 028-7126-9667. £

**Schooner's** (59 Victoria Rd.) Panoramic views of Derry and the Foyle can be enjoyed at this wide-windowed restaurant on the Waterside of the city. The interior provides a nautical theme, complete with a 30-foot schooner built into the decor. Specialties include captain's seafood soup, pasta quills in rich cheese sauce, prawns "n" sauce, paupiettes of plaice, salmon and seafood bake, steaks, ribs, and burgers. ☎ 028-7131-1500. £ to ££

## SUGGESTED TOUR:

Start a tour on **Foyle Street** (1), named after the river beside it, the setting for the Ulsterbus Depot and the Foyleside Shopping Complex. Directly east, along the water, is **Foyle Quay**, originally known as Derry Quay, from whence the many emigrant ships docked and departed in the 19th century.

From Foyle Street, walk one block north to **Shipquay Place**, gateway to the walled city. Before entering through the gate, take a right to visit:

**\*THE GUILDHALL** (2), Guildhall Square, ☎ 028-7137-7335. *Open Mon.–Fri. 9–5. Admission is free. Free guided tours in July–Aug.*

One of Derry's most significant buildings outside the walls, this richly decorated Tudor Gothic sandstone structure stands out with mullioned and transomed windows, and topped by a four-faced chiming spire clock, one of the largest in Ireland or Britain. The original Guildhall, built in 1890 but badly damaged by fire in 1908, was rebuilt in 1912, only to be bombed in 1972. It was reconstructed in recent years, and now is the leading concert hall and cultural showplace for Derry. The interior offers a feast of stained-glass windows, each depicting a different segment in the long history of the city.

After visiting the Guildhall, walk straight ahead, between Shipquay Gate and Magazine Gate, to:

**\*THE TOWER MUSEUM** (3), Union Hall Place, ☎ 028-7137-2411. *Open Sept.–June, Tues.–Sat. 10–5; July–Aug., Mon.–Sat. 10–5, Sun. 10–2. Adults £3.50, seniors free, students £2, children £1.20. Tours. Shop. Café.*

This cleverly designed and award-winning heritage center depicts *The Story of Derry,* through a series of exhibits, life-size figures,

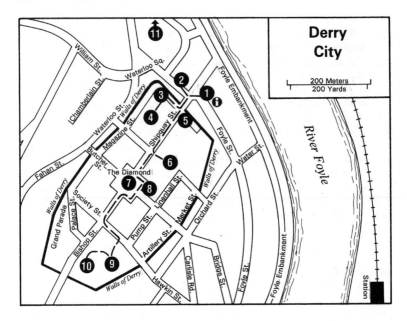

holograms, tableaux, audiovisual displays, historical artifacts, and re-enactments. Enter through a stone and brick tunnel, one of the original passageways of the city, a legacy of the 17th century. The displays bring to life the city's eras of monasticism, Irish chieftains, English Plantation, wall-building, sieges, emigration, shipbuilding, and industry, as well as current social history. The museum takes its name from the adjacent O'Doherty Tower, site of a castle built by the O'Doherty family of Ulster in the 16th century. The tour ends with the screening of *In Our Lifetime*, a well-documented film chronicling "The Troubles" of the past 30 years.

The Tower Museum also provides access into the adjacent complex known as **The Craft Village** (4), Shipquay St., ☎ 028-7126-0329, a shopping and entertainment complex that combines retail, workshop, and residential units. It is laid out in a format that portrays life in Derry from 16th to 19th centuries including an authentic thatched cottage that provides informal *Teach Ceoil* (Music House) sessions of music, song, and dance regularly throughout the summer. One of the most distinctive features of the village is the individual style of the windows—each window represents a particular period of Irish history and illustrates the various changes that have taken place in design and appearance. *Open Mon.–Sat. 9–5:30. Admission is free.*

Delay no further. It's time to "walk the walls." From Shipquay Gate, you can climb the steps up to enter:

**\*THE WALLS OF DERRY** (5). *Open dawn to dusk. Admission is free. Guided tours of the walls organized by Derry City Council* ☎ *028- 7136-5151. Tours cost: Adults £3.25, seniors, students, and children £2.*

The city's pride and joy, these 18-foot-thick walls enclose the entire inner city with a one-mile-long raised terrace walk, lined with seven arch gates, six bastions, and many canons. The walls provide a great platform to view the entire city—both inside and outside the walls, from a panoramic height. Built between 1614 and 1619, the walls were made by London stonemasons using earth, lime, and local stone, some of which came from ruined medieval monastery buildings, all skillfully constructed as thick defensive ramparts with angular artillery bastions. Despite sieges in 1641, 1649, and 1689, Derry's walls were never breached. Today Derry is widely recognized not only as Ireland's finest intact walled city, but also as one of the best in Europe.

Originally there were just four entrances (or gates) into the walled city—Bishop's Gate, Shipquay Gate, Ferryquay Gate, and Butcher's Gate, arranged in a cross pattern with the Diamond as its center. Drawbridges were used to protect some of the Gates when under attack. Later additions were New Gate (1789), Castle Gate (1803) and Magazine Gate (1865). Walk the entire circuit on your own or with a guided tour, provided by local volunteers. All tours start from the tourist information office.

After completing your walk on the walls, now there is time to explore some of the sights seen from the heights. Return to Shipquay Gate and enter the inner city, heading up Shipquay Street, passing the streetside entrance to The Craft Village on the right. On the left is the **Richmond Centre** (6), a complex of 30 shops, and the largest merchant trading center of its kind within the inner city. It's a steep walk up a big hill for two blocks and then you arrive at **The Diamond** (7), the inner city's hub. Currently occupied by a war memorial statue erected in 1927, this central parklet was originally the site of Derry's first town hall. The winged centerpiece figure represents Victory. Notice that many of the buildings surrounding the Diamond are of relatively recent vintage, dating back to 18th-century Georgian origins and some 19th-century Victorian facades including **Austins** (8), Derry's landmark department store on the left.

Walk around The Diamond to Bishop Street, then take a left onto London Street and follow the path to **\*St. Columb's Cathedral** (9), London St., ☎ 028-7126-7313, Derry's ecclesiastical focal point. Built on the highest ground within the walled city, this church is named after Derry's founder, St. Columb, also known as Columbkille and Columba (521–597), who built a monastery here in 546. Although he went on to found other monasteries in Ireland and Scotland, this place is synonymous with him. The present Anglican cathedral was the first in the British Isles to have been built after the Reformation and is a fine example of Planters Gothic. Built by the Irish Society between 1628 and 1633, this edifice has many interesting relics of Derry's early days including the locks and keys of the four original city gates and the bishop's consecration chair of 1633. Audiovisuals illustrate the sieges of Derry and the history of the cathedral. *Open March–Oct., Mon.–Sat. 9–5; Nov.–Feb., Mon.–Sat. 9–4. Adults £1, children 50p.*

In architectural contrast, just beyond the cathedral is the **Derry Court House** (10), one of Ireland's best examples of Greek Revival (1813) building.

Retrace your steps to complete the tour. On the return trip, take time to visit each of the city's gates and examine the various styles, arches, and stonework.

If you are heading back to Belfast from Derry, here's a stop that is worth a special detour especially for fans of Seamus Heaney, Ireland's master poet:

**BELLAGHY BAWN** (11), Castle Street, Bellaghy, Magherafelt, Co. Londonderry ☎ 028-7968-6812. *Open June–Sept., Mon.–Fri. 10–5, Sat. noon–5, Sun. 2–6; Oct.–May, Mon.–Sat. 10–5. Adults £2, seniors and children £1. Café. Shop. Tours.*

If you don't get to meet the Nobel Prize-winning poet Seamus Heaney in your travels, a visit to Bellaghy Bawn is the next best thing. Set deep in the countryside almost mid-way between Derry and Belfast, Bellaghy Bawn is a locally-inspired and maintained literary museum focusing on the works of Heaney who grew up in Bellaghy and wrote his earliest poetry about the surrounding countryside.

Step into the small 25-seat theatre and watch the 15-minute audiovisual, "Where Are You Now," written and narrated by Heaney. It's almost like having a chat with the poet who tells all his fondest memories of the area and then recites many of his well-known poems such "The Thatcher," "Bellaghy Graveyard," "The Strand at Lough Beg," "The Forge," and "The Old School Bag." Visitors are welcome to wander upstairs through the Heaney Archives and see mounted copies of his works, a photo gallery on his life, rare publications, and copies of his original manuscripts in his own handwriting. His "old school bag" is there, too!

Bellaghy Bawn is also a museum of local history. The building itself is a genuine English-style bawn or fort, built in the 1620's with a lookout tower and thick walls for defense. Nowadays the tower is used for poetry readings-in-the-round. Other exhibits spotlight the history of the area from 5,000 BC to the present.

# Along Lough Erne

D ominating County Fermanagh deep in the southwest corner of Northern Ireland, Lough Erne is a lakeland paradise—stretching for 50 miles with over 154 islands and countless alcoves and inlets. Silvery blue waters, lush leafy greenery, and unspoiled wooded shorelines are the trademarks of Lough Erne, offering an ever-changing pattern of scenic views and easily earning it the reputation as the "Killarney of the North." Not surprisingly, it is a favorite resort destination for Irish, British, and other European boating fans and fishing enthusiasts.

Although a little off the beaten track for most North American tourists, Lough Erne is a link between the North and the South. Many tour buses heading from Dublin often travel via Lough Erne to reach Donegal.

Unlike some resort areas, Lough Erne is a lot more than water and fish. It is the setting for some of Northern Ireland's finest stately homes and castles, as well as one of the best cave networks in Europe. Most of all, this is the home of Belleek, the benchmark of Irish pottery and a name that ranks with Waterford at the top of its craft.

## GETTING THERE:

Enniskillen, the chief town along Lough Erne, is over 80 miles southwest of Belfast via the M1 and A4 roads; 60 miles southwest of Derry via A5 and A32; just over 40 miles east of Sligo via N16 and A4; and 35 miles from Donegal Town via N15 and A46. Even though Lough Erne is in the North of Ireland, it takes about half the time and mileage to reach Enniskillen from major bases in the Republic of Ireland.

**Ulsterbus** provides daily service from Belfast or Derry to Enniskillen; while **Bus Eireann** and **Ulsterbus** provide daily service from Sligo and Donegal to Enniskillen. However, since this tour involves sightseeing in the countryside surrounding Enniskillen, it is best to do this daytrip by car.

## PRACTICALITIES:

Even though Lough Erne is in Northern Ireland, the quickest and most judicious way to reach this area is from Sligo or Donegal in the Republic. To be even more practical, the most sensible starting point for this tour is mid-way between Sligo and Donegal at Ballyshannon, which is a veritable "gateway" into Lough Erne territory.

If you prefer to tour by public transport from Belfast, sightseeing tours to the Lough Erne area are operated at least four days a week from late June through September by **Ulsterbus**, Europa Bus Centre, Glengall

St., Belfast, ☎ 028-9033-3000.

Geographically, Lough Erne is divided into two parts—Upper and Lower Lough Erne. The "upper" part is actually the bottom or southern portion of the water, while the "lower" section is on the northern end. Of the two sections, the bottom or "upper" part of the lough is loaded with tiny islands and coves, a haven for watersports. Lower Lough Erne, in contrast, has a more scenic unbroken shoreline, with a couple of easily accessible islands. Lower Lough Erne, 18 miles long, is also rimmed by a variety of attractions that are open to the public. In the interest of time and reasonable mileage, our daytrip concentrates on Lower Lough Erne.

For information, contact the **Fermanagh Tourist Information Centre**, Wellington Rd., Enniskillen, ☎ 028-6632-3110, open all year.

As of April 22, 2000, Northern Ireland has a new uniform area code—**028**—instead of various codes for different cities and counties. All numbers have changed from six to eight digits, and all are preceded by 028.

## FOOD AND DRINK:

**Belleek Café** (Belleek Pottery, Main St., Belleek) Although housed in the landmark china-producing factory, this bi-level Georgian-style self-service restaurant deserves special mention in its own right. Soups, fresh salads, sandwiches, pastries and other treats are served on delicate Belleek china overlooking the Erne River. In this part of Ireland, everything tastes better when it's served on Belleek! X: Sat.–Sun. in Nov.–Feb. ☎ 028-6665-8501. £

**Blakes of the Hollow** (6 Church St., Enniskillen) A landmark in the center of town two blocks from the castle, this pub dates back to the 1880s. It has a lovely Victorian decor with a long marble-topped bar, pinewood snugs, and lots of local memorabilia. Bar food includes soups and sandwiches. ☎ 028-6632-2143. £

**Franco's** (Queen Elizabeth Rd., Enniskillen) Ensconced in a series of restored buildings along the riverfront, this lively restaurant is decorated with colorful wall murals hand-painted by a local artist. The menu features a blend of Italian dishes, such as pizza and pasta, plus local seafood—salmon, crab, oysters, and mussels. ☎ 028-6632-4424. ££

**Hollander** (5 Main St., Irvinestown, 9 miles west of Enniskillen) As its name suggests, this restaurant adds a Dutch touch to the Lough Erne scene, with waitresses in full Netherlands-style costume and a windmill-themed decor. The menu offers Irish and European favorites, using local produce and seafood. Bar lunches feature hearty soups, stews, and sandwiches. ☎ 028-6662-1231. £ to ££

**Killyhelvin Hotel** (Dublin Rd., Enniskillen) Set on its own garden-filled grounds one mile south of town, this country inn is the best bet for wide-windowed views of Lough Erne. The bistro offers quick meals all day including bar snacks such as soups, salads, and sandwiches, or a bountiful lunchtime buffet. ☎ 028- 6632-3481. £ to ££

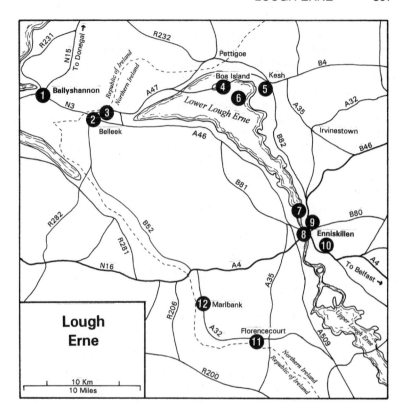

Lough
Erne

10 Km
10 Miles

## SUGGESTED TOUR:

The ideal place to start this tour is from **Ballyshannon** (1), mid-way between Donegal Town and Sligo Town. It will take about a half-hour to reach Ballyshannon from either direction.

From Ballyshannon, it's just five miles over the border into Northern Ireland and the town of **Belleek**, a small village on the River Erne whose name in the Irish language is *Béal Leice,* meaning "ford-mouth of the flag-stone." This curious name came from the fact that a flat rock in the river bed appeared as a smooth level floor when the water grew shallow in summer. The main industry of the town is also the region's premier tourist attraction:

**\*BELLEEK POTTERY** (2), Main St., Belleek, ☎ 028-6665-8501. *Open March–June, Mon.–Fri. 9–6, Sat. 10–6, Sun. 2–6; July–Aug., Mon.–Fri. 9–8, Sat. 10–6, Sun. 11–8; Sept., Mon.–Fri. 9–6, Sat. 10–6, Sun. 2–6; Oct., Mon.–Fri. 9–5, Sat. 10–5:30, Sun. 2–6; Nov.–Feb., Mon.–Fri. 9–5:30. Admission £1 per person. Tours. Shop. Café.*

Established in 1857, Belleek is one of the names identified throughout the world as a symbol of ultimate Irish craftsmanship. Tours are conducted every half-hour to show visitors how the delicate "basket weave" creamy white porcelain china is manufactured, starting with the raw materials—china clay, feldspar, ground flint glass, water, and a few other ingredients. These are ground and mixed into a thick substance called "slip." After the slip is put through giant sieves, it is poured into molds which absorb water and shape the pieces into vases, ornaments, tableware, and statues. When dry, the shaped pieces are decorated with Irish motifs. The production line also demonstrates how the intricate strands of basketware are woven together, and how tiny petals, stems, and twigs are created by hand. Firing is next, followed by rigorous inspection. No "seconds" are ever sold at Belleek. In addition to the behind-the-scenes tour, there is an audiovisual presentation and a museum that illustrates the history of Belleek, and displays some of the oldest and rarest pieces, including an earthenware collection that dates back to the pottery's earliest days almost 140 years ago. Allow at least 1.5 hours for the entire visit.

Adjacent to the pottery is the **Explore Erne Exhibition** (3), Erne Gateway Centre, Corry, Belleek, ☎ 028-6665-8866, a new heritage center that tells the story of Lough Erne, from its formation to the present day. *Open mid-March to Oct., daily 10–6. Adults £1, seniors and children 50p. Shop.*

From Belleek, commence a drive around Lower Lough Erne. Take A47 heading east on the northern side of Lower Lough Erne. The road follows a route across a bridge onto **Boa Island** (4), a five-mile-long land mass that has been incorporated into part of the roadway. To the right is a sign for Caldragh Cemetery. If time allows, follow the signposts over some uneven grounds to see one of Ireland's oldest stone figures—*Janus*, a human figure with a face on each side. It is thought to date back to pagan times, perhaps the first century.

Continue in a easterly direction for 10 miles to **Kesh**, a small town whose name is derived from the Irish language *An Cheis*, meaning "wicker causeway." It is thought to be a reference to an early bridge crossing over the town stream. From Kesh, make a right and travel for three miles to the Lough Erne shoreline to **Castle Archdale Country Park** (5), Kesh, ☎ 028-6862-1588, for some close-up views of the lough. From the marina here, you can also take a passenger ferryboat to **White Island** (6), a 74-acre island that holds the remains of a 12th-century monastery. It's an ideal spot for a picnic. *Ferries operate June through September. For advance information and schedules, call ☎ 028-6862-1333.*

Alternatively, drive another five miles along the shore to **Trory Point**, for a passenger ferry to **Devenish Island** (7), a 70-acre island that was chosen in the 6th century by St. Molaise as the site for a monastery that remained functional until the 16th century. The remains are considered today to be the most extensive early and medieval Christian settlement in Northern Ireland. The layout includes a well preserved 81-foot 12th-century round tower with four carved heads, a 15th-century High Cross, an oratory with Romanesque angle pilaster bases, and various other buildings. Ferries operate April through September. *For details and reservations, call* ☎ *028-6632-2711.*

Continue eastward via B82, with Lough Erne on the left, for three miles to **Enniskillen**, a lovely lakeside town that is actually an island, separating Lower Lough Erne from Upper Lough Erne. The placename in the Irish language, *Inis Ceithleann*, means "Cethlenn's island." According to legend, Cethlenn was a local pirate's wife who owned the island.

Because of its strategic location, Enniskillen was always a place of military importance. It was the stronghold of the Irish Maguire clan in the Middle Ages, and in the 17th century was given to Sir William Cole of England who built the town as it is today. The British Army regiment known as the *Iniskilling Fusilers* took their name from Enniskillen where they were raised in 1689 (the regiment is now part of the Irish Rangers). The centerpiece of the town is its castle:

**\*ENNISKILLEN CASTLE** (8), Castle Barracks, Enniskillen, ☎ 028-6632-5000. *Open May–June and Sept., Tues.–Fri. 10–5, Sat. and Mon. 2–5; July–Aug., Tues.–Fri. 10–5, Sat.–Sun. and Mon. 2–5; Oct.–April, Mon. 2–5, Tues.–Fri. 10–5. Adults £2, seniors and students £1.50, children £1. Shop. Café.*

Overlooking Lough Erne on the western edge of town, this mighty stone fortress has had a long and colorful history. Originally built in the 15th century by the Maguire chieftains, it remained their stronghold until passing into English hands in 1594 after an eight-day siege. In 1612 Sir William Cole, who was appointed constable, founded the town and rebuilt the castle. He added the distinctive "watergate" feature to the outer walls; it is not in fact a gate, but a twin turreted tower that is a favorite with photographers today. In the 18th century, the castle became an artillery barracks. The interior exhibitions reflect all facets of the castle's history, from the Maguires to its military importance as the onetime home of the Royal Iniskilling Fusiliers and the Fifth Dragoon Guards.

Take time to walk the town or arrange for a narrated sightseeing boat cruise on Lough Erne. Across the bridge on the right side is the base for **\*Erne Tours** (9), Round O Jetty, ☎ 028-6632-2882. This company operates 1.5 hour waterbus cruises via the M.V. *Kestrel* on Lough Erne, with a 30-minute visit to Devenish Island as part of the itinerary. *Trips operate May through September. Fares are: Adults £5, children £2.50.*

From Enniskillen, take a short one mile detour south of town via the A4 road to a building that has been rated by some experts as the finest classical mansion in Ireland:

**\*CASTLE COOLE** (10), Enniskillen. ☎ 028-6632-2690. *Open April and Sept., Sat.–Sun. 1–6; May–Aug., Mon.–Wed. and Fri–Sun. 1–6. House: Adults £2.80, children £1.40. Grounds only: £2 per car. Tours. Shop. Café.*

Built in 1789–98 for the 1st Earl of Belmore, this stately mansion was designed by James Wyatt in a tranquil setting overlooking the east bank of Lough Erne. White Portland stone transported from England was used on the exterior including the magnificent Palladian front. Now in the care of the National Trust, the home is marked by elaborate plasterwork, stucco, and carvings. A tour takes in the ground-floor reception and dining rooms furnished with many original Regency pieces, plus an ornate silk-paneled state bedroom, servants' tunnel, five of the original stables in the grand yard, and an elaborate private coach in its original coach house. The grounds, which encompass mature oak woodlands, provide a habitat for a rare flock of grey geese, introduced c. 1700.

Return to Enniskillen and begin the second lap of the scenic route around Lower Lough Erne via A46. Before you start out, depending on time, you may wish to make another detour eight miles southwest via A4 and A32 to visit another great house in the care of the National Trust, *Florence Court (11), Florencecourt, ☎ 028-6634-8249. Built by the Earls of Enniskillen in the 18th century, this Georgian building is noted for its fine rococo plasterwork and walled garden. *Open April and Sept., Sat.–Sun. 1–6; May–Aug., Mon.–Wed. and Fri.–Sun. 1–6. Adults £2.80, children £1.40. Tours. Shop. Café.*

The adjacent **Florencecourt Forest Park**, Florencecourt, ☎ 028-6634-8497, features Irish yew and oak trees planted about 200 years ago. *Open daily 10 to an hour before dusk. Admission per car £2.*

Four miles further west via A32 is *Marble Arch Caves (12), Marlbank, ☎ 028-6634-8963, an extensive cave system that is recognized as one of the best in Europe. Access is via underground boat tours that allow visitors to explore a natural underworld of stalactites, stalagmites, rivers, waterfalls, winding passages, and lofty chambers. Tours last about 1.5 hours and also include geology exhibitions and an audiovisual. *Open mid-March–Sept., (weather permitting) 10:30–4:30. Adults £5, seniors £3, children £2. Shop. Café.*

If you have taken both options, it will require a 12-mile drive via A32 and A4 to bring you back to the Lough Erne shoreline. At Enniskillen, join the A46 road heading west for the 24-mile drive back to Belleek. This route is the most scenic stretch of Lower Lough Erne, with a constant panorama of lakeside *views on the right. There are very few man-made attractions on this road, so sit back and relax as some of Northern Ireland's most memorable scenery unfolds before you.

From Belleek, it's just five miles back to Ballyshannon and the starting point for this daytrip. Continue on to Sligo or Donegal, or back to Derry or Belfast, or other parts of Ireland.

# Belfast City—
# Smart Shoppers' Tour

The North of Ireland is known for its high quality crafts—from pure Irish linen tablecloths, napkins, and handkerchiefs; to Tyrone hand-cut glassware, and Belleek pottery. And no better place to find all of these items in one spot than in Belfast.

Belfast is a shopper's city, with a network of pedestrianized streets. Not only can you find uniquely Northern Ireland products, but you also have easy access to an array of British-owned and international shopping chains, from London's Marks & Spencer to California's Disney Store.

## GETTING THERE:

Belfast, in the northeast quarter of the island of Ireland, is easily reached by car, train or bus, from Dublin and all major Irish cities. By car, it is 100 miles north of Dublin via the main M1/N1 road. By train, Irish Rail and Northern Ireland Railways operate a joint service between Dublin and Belfast; travel time is about 2 hours and 20 minutes. By bus, Bus Eireann's Expressway Services connect the two cities in just over 3 hours.

## GETTING AROUND:

Because so much of Belfast's shopping area is pedestrianized, the only way to do this tour is on foot.

## PRACTICALITIES:

The best time to follow this tour is during normal shopping hours, usually from 9 a.m. to 5:30 p.m., Monday through Saturday, with extended hours on Thursday evening until 8 or 9 p.m.

For visitor information at any time of year, contact the **Northern Ireland Tourist Board**, St. Anne's Court, 59 North St., Belfast , ☎ 028-9032-0202.

As of April 22, 2000, Northern Ireland has a new uniform area code—028—instead of various codes for different cities and counties. All numbers have changed from six to eight digits, and all are preceded by 028.

## FOOD AND DRINK:

**Café Equinox** (32 Howard Street) is a small but stylish eatery within a household gift shop, located behind City Hall. The menu offers creative sandwiches, pastas, and salads, as well as pastries, milkshakes, fresh baked scones and six different kinds of farmhouse apple juice from local sources. ☎ 028-9023-0089. X: Sun. £

**Copperfields** (9 Fountain St.), is a bi-level bar and restaurant in the heart of the pedestrianized shopping corridor. It offers an eclectic mix of international cuisine from Irish stew to Mexican dishes. ☎ 028-9024-7367. X: Sun. £ to ££

**Deane's** (38 Howard Street), located behind City Hall, is two restaurants in one—a clubby 40-seat dining room upstairs and a more affordable brasserie on ground level. Both are the domain of the same chef, Michael Deane, a Michelin-star award winner. The décor is ornate in Baroque style but the food is simply delicious—a fusion of Irish and international cooking, with dishes such as Thai spiced salmon, ravioli of lobster, roast cod with ratatouille, or lamb with roast fennel and roquefort dressing. ☎ 028-9056-0000. X: Sun.–Mon. ££ to £££

**Feasts** (39 Dublin Rd.), is an aptly-named little gem south of City Hall. It is gourmet deli café, offering the usual sandwiches, soups, and salads, as well as specialty dishes using freshly-made pasta and farmhouse cheeses. ☎ 028-9033-2887. X:Sun. £ to ££

**Kelly's Cellars** (30 Bank St.) provides a vintage pub atmopshere, just a half-block from Royal Avenue. Dating back to 1720, this pub claims to be Belfast's oldest tavern in continuous use, and the décor proves it—vaulted ceilings, paned windows, arches and alcoves, and walls full of memorabilia. The pub grub includes fresh oysters, steaks, and burgers. ☎ 028-9032-4835. £ to ££

**Roscoff Café** (21 Fountain St.) sits in the heart of the shopping area. As an off-shoot of the award-winning gourmet Roscoff restaurant on Shaftsbury Square, this continental-style café carries on the family tradition, but with simpler fare and much lower prices. The menu offers soups, pastas, croissants, pastries and a specialty of focaccia pizzas (pizzas made from focaccia bread and coated with fresh tomato sauce, freshly grated mozzarella cheese,  and a choice of unique combinations of toppings, from leek and black pudding, to chicken and rosemary potato, or chorizo with red and yellow peppers). ☎ 028-9031-5090. X: Sun. £ to ££

## SUGGESTED TOUR:

Start this tour at the Northern Ireland Tourist Office, on North Street, a good place to get the latest maps and literature on Belfast. From North Street, walk straight ahead one block and you will be on Royal Avenue, the main shopping thoroughfare of Belfast and a pedestrian area. What Grafton Street is to Dublin, so Royal Avenue is to Belfast.

On the opposite side of the street is the gigantic **Castle Court Centre** (1), Royal Avenue, ☎ 028-9023-4591, a skylit and glass-roofed mega-shopping centre housing over 70 different shops and drawing more than 20 million visitors a year. The shops include branches of well-known British merchants such as Debenhams Department Store and Laura Ashley, Irish

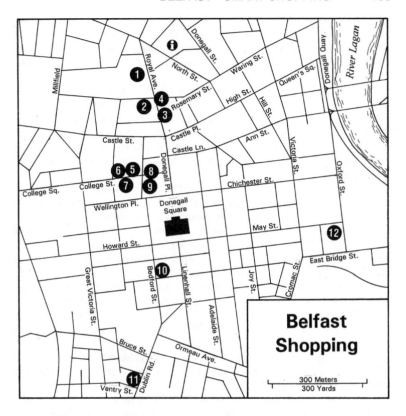

**Belfast Shopping**

300 Meters
300 Yards

favorites such as Eason & Son, and familiar American names like Benetton and The Gap.

Adjacent is **Waterstone's** (2), 8 Royal Avenue, ☎ 028-9024-7355, a popular British-owned chain, with other branches in Dublin and Cork. This large shop is known for a wide selection of books about Ireland and especially Belfast and The North. It also stocks a variety of other topics—from art and antiques, to biography, the classics, crime, gay literature, health, new age, religion, sport, travel, women's studies, and wine.

After the flurry of more international names and chains, cast your eyes left across to the other side of the street, walking south, and you will see a Belfast original that is a mainstay along this famous shopping corridor—**Smyth's Irish Linens** (3), 65 Royal Avenue, ☎ 028-9024-2232. As its name aptly implies, this shop is a landmark shop for fine linens, dating back to 1860. It is run by the 4th generation of the Smyth family who still make linens at their factory at Peter's Hill in Belfast. In addition to linens and damask, they stock hand-knits, china, and jewelry, as well as other souvenirs and traditional gifts.

The small shop adjacent to Smyth's is also worth a visit, especially if you are fond of antiques—**E. Lauro—Antiquarian** (4), 67 Royal Avenue, ☎ 028-9032-7301. It sells all types of small antiques, watches, jewelry, and clocks as well as rare stamps, coins, medals, books, and military memorabilia.

Follow Royal Avenue south as it ends and becomes Donegall Place, also a pedestrian street. Make a right here, at Castle Street, and walk a half block, making a left onto Fountain Street, also a pedestrian area. Like Royal Avenue, Fountain Street is a major shopping street for Belfast. The difference is that while Royal Avenue features many international names, Fountain Street is known for its smaller local shops, which usually offer more allure for visitors.

Walk south on Fountain Street until you reach the intersection of College Street and take a right. Here is the Fountain Centre, a bi-level complex of small and interesting shops. Take the escalator to the upper level to reach the **Irish Linen Shop** (5), 46 Fountain Centre, College St. ☎ 028-9032-2727. It is a one-stop source for a fine collection of Northern Ireland-made table linens, as well as other traditional hand-crafts such as crochet lace, tea towels, ceramics, and clothing.

The Fountain Centre is also the setting for **Utopia** (6), College Street, ☎ 028-9024-1342, a contemporary shop filled with useful and unusual gifts from all part of Northern Ireland, such as chess sets, paper mobiles, puppets, and stuffed animals, as well as hand-made candles, glassware, and decorative greeting cards.

On the opposite side of the street is **The Pen Shop** (7), 8 College St., ☎ 028-9024-3910, a specialist in all types of fine writing instruments, nibs, and other stationery gifts.

Return to Fountain Street and on the opposite side of the street are **Dillons** (8), 44 Fountain St., ☎ 028-9024-0159, a well-stocked local bookstore; and **Past Times** (9), 48-50 Fountain St., ☎ 028-9031-2311, a unique shop featuring gifts and home accessories with Victorian, medieval, and Celtic themes. The assortment ranges from jewelry and clothing, to frames, posters, tableware, games, mugs, books, paper goods, baby gifts, stained glass, statuary, and music CDs.

Stroll back up Fountain Street and return to Donegall Place (the continuation of Royal Avenue) in a southward direction. This broad street, like Royal Avenue, is pedestrianized and lined with British-based shops, such as Marks & Spencer, Boots, and Habitat, and international chains, such as Levis and the Disney Store.

Straight ahead is City Hall on Donegall Square, the central hub of Belfast. Take a right and walk along Donegall Square West which leads into Bedford Street. Walk two short blocks on the left side of Bedford Street to visit **Craftworks** (10), Bedford House, Bedford St., ☎ 028-9024-4465, between James Street and Franklin Street. It is more than a shop—it is an All-Ireland showcase that espouses the theme, "The best of Irish crafts." It offers the work of individual craftspeople from Ulster and all over

Ireland—from natural linens, ceramics, and contemporary Celtic-inspired jewelry to woodwork, baskets, books, toys, leather products, glassware, wrought-iron candlesticks, scarves, ties, wall hangings, and clothing for all ages.

For some local Northern Ireland art, follow Bedford Street for two blocks and then it becomes Dublin Road. Continue for two more blocks on the right side of Dublin Road to Ventry Lane. Here you can visit **Local Artists** (11), 73 Dublin Rd., ☎ 028-9031-9589, a small gallery selling a variety of oil paintings, watercolors and more.

Retrace your steps back to Donegall Square and your tour is complete. If it is a Tuesday or Friday, however, here is a special addendum.

Turn right onto Donegall Square S. and walk along May Street to Oxford Street. Here you will find a vintage Belfast shopping experience— **St. George's Market** (12), May St. at Oxford St., ☎ 028-9032-0202. This is Belfast's original "Variety Market," dating back to the 19th century. Situated opposite the new Waterfront Hall, the market was completely restored in 1999, and is open on Tuesdays and Fridays (from 8 a.m.). It's a genuine traditional outlet for fresh fruit, home-baked goods and pastries, preserves, spices, flowers, fish, vegetables, bargain clothing, crafts, CDs, and lots more. Even if you are not buying, it's fun to savor the aromas, listen to the lilting accents, and see the colorful commodities. Stroll from stall to stall and take it all in, perhaps snap a few pictures. The market is Belfast shopping at its best!

# Index

Special interest attractions are also listed under their category headings.

# *Daytrips*
## • OTHER EUROPEAN TITLES •

## *Daytrips* LONDON

By Earl Steinbicker. Explores the metropolis on 10 one-day walking tours, then describes 45 daytrips to destinations throughout southern England, with excursions to the Midlands, West Country, and Wales — all by either rail or car. Expanded 6th edition, 352 pages, 62 maps. ISBN: 0-8038-9443-0.

## *Daytrips* FRANCE

By Earl Steinbicker. Describes 48 daytrips — including 5 walking tours of Paris, 24 excursions from the city, 5 in Provence, and 14 along the Riviera. Expanded 5th edition, 304 pages, 60 maps, and a menu translator. ISBN: 0-8038-2006-2.

## *Daytrips* GERMANY

By Earl Steinbicker. 60 of Germany's most enticing destinations can be savored on daytrips from Munich, Frankfurt, Hamburg, and Berlin. Walking tours of the big cities are included. Expanded 5th edition, 352 pages, 67 maps, and a menu translator. ISBN: 0-8038-9428-7.

## *Daytrips* SWITZERLAND

By Norman P.T. Renouf. 45 one-day adventures in and from convenient bases including Zurich and Geneva, with forays into nearby Germany, Austria, and Italy. 320 pages, 38 maps. ISBN: 0-8038-9417-7.

## *Daytrips* SPAIN & PORTUGAL

By Norman P.T. Renouf. Fifty one-day adventures by rail, bus, or car — including many walking tours, as well as side trips to Gibraltar and Morocco. All the major tourist sights are covered, plus several excursions to little-known, off-the-beaten-track destinations. 368 pages, 18 full-color photos, 28 B&W photos, 51 maps. ISBN: 0-8038-9389-2.

## *Daytrips* ITALY

By Earl Steinbicker. Features 40 one-day adventures in and around Rome, Florence, Milan, Venice, and Naples. 3rd edition, 304 pages, 45 maps, 69 B&W photos. ISBN: 0-8038-9372-8.

## *Daytrips* HOLLAND, BELGIUM & LUXEMBOURG

By Earl Steinbicker. Many unusual places are covered on these 40 daytrips, along with all the favorites plus the 3 major cities. 2nd edition, 288 pages, 45 maps, 69 B&W photos. ISBN: 0-8038-9368-X.

## *Daytrips* ISRAEL

By Earl Steinbicker. 25 one-day adventures by bus or car to the Holy Land's most interesting sites. Includes Jerusalem walking tours. 2nd edition, 206 pages, 40 maps, 40 B&W photos. ISBN: 0-8038-9374-4.

# *Daytrips*
## • AMERICAN TITLES •

## *Daytrips* WASHINGTON, D.C.

By Earl Steinbicker. Fifty one-day adventures in the Nation's Capital, and to nearby Virginia, Maryland, Delaware, and Pennsylvania. Both walking and driving tours are featured. 368 pages, 60 maps. Revised 2nd edition. ISBN: 0-8038-9429-5.

## *Daytrips* PENNSYLVANIA DUTCH COUNTRY & PHILADELPHIA

By Earl Steinbicker. Completely covers the City of Brotherly Love, then goes on to probe southeastern Pennsylvania, southern New Jersey, and Delaware before moving west to Lancaster, the "Dutch" country, and Gettysburg. There are 50 daytrips in all. 288 pages, 54 maps. ISBN: 0-8038-9394-9.

## *Daytrips* SAN FRANCISCO & NORTHERN CALIFORNIA

By David Cheever. Fifty enjoyable one-day adventures from the sea to the mountains; from north of the wine country to south of Monterey. Includes 16 self-guided discovery tours of San Francisco itself. 336 pages, 64 maps. ISBN: 0-8038-9441-4.

## *Daytrips* HAWAII

By David Cheever. Thoroughly explores all the major islands — by car, by bus, on foot, and by bicycle, boat, and air. Includes many off-beat discoveries you won't find elsewhere, plus all the big attractions in detail. 288 pages, 55 maps. ISBN: 0-8038-9401-5.

## *Daytrips* NEW ENGLAND

By Earl Steinbicker. Discover the 50 most delightful excursions within a day's drive of Boston or Central New England, from Maine to Connecticut. Includes Boston walking tours. 336 pages, 60 maps, 48 B&W photos. ISBN: 0-8038-9379-5.

### *Daytrips* NEW YORK

Edited by Earl Steinbicker. 107 easy excursions by car throughout southern New York State, New Jersey, eastern Pennsylvania, Connecticut, and southern Massachusetts. 7th edition, 336 pages, 44 maps, 46 B&W photos. ISBN: 0-8038-9371-X.

### *Daytrips* FLORIDA

By Blair Howard. Fifty one-day adventures from bases in Miami, Orlando, St. Petersburg, Jacksonville, and Pensacola. From little-known discoveries to bustling theme parks; from America's oldest city to isolated getaways — this guide covers it all. 320 pages, 47 maps, 28 B&W photos. ISBN: 0-8038-9380-9.

### HASTINGS HOUSE Book Publishers

9 Mott St., Norwalk, CT 06850 • ☎ (203) 838-4083, Fax (203) 838-4084.
☎ orders toll-free (800) 206-7822 • Internet: www.daytripsbooks.com

# ABOUT THE AUTHOR:

Being named after St. Patrick has undoubtedly influenced the life of author Patricia Tunison Preston. Although born in New York, she has spent most of her working years promoting or writing about Ireland. A third-generation Irish American, she visited the land of her ancestors for the first time in 1966 and felt right at home. In fact, she was so completely enthralled by Ireland that she returned to New York and took a job with the Irish Tourist Board. For almost 20 years, she publicized the Emerald Isle and traveled there regularly in the course of her work.

In 1985, Patricia branched off in a different direction as a freelance writer, fulfilling assignments on Ireland and the US. She has written 16 travel guides and books and contributed to over 25 others. Daytrips Ireland is her sixth book about the Emerald Isle.

Pat's "partner" in her travels and writings is her husband John J. Preston, son of Mayo-born parents. Together they have collaborated on many articles and books about destinations near and far. In 1996, the state of Delaware honored the Prestons jointly as the first-ever recipients of the "Governor's Travel Writer of the Year Award."

In 1998, Pat launched the "Ireland Expert" web site — providing the latest information about Ireland including the interactive "Ask Pat Q & A." Ask Pat a question and she will give you a personalized answer within 24 hours — it's the only Irish travel web site to provide such a service — and it's free. Visit www.irelandexpert.com

The Prestons reside in the Hudson River Valley in an area reminiscent of the Emerald Isle. When not writing, they organize and accompany group trips to Ireland.